SPEECH

A TEXT WITH ADAPTED READINGS

Under the Advisory Editorship of J. Jeffery Auer

SPEECH

A TEXT WITH ADAPTED READINGS

SECOND EDITION

ROBERT C. JEFFREY
University of Texas

OWEN PETERSON
Louisiana State University

Harper & Row, Publishers
New York, Evanston, San Francisco, London

Sponsoring Editor: Walter H. Lippincott, Jr.
Project Editor: Holly Detgen
Designer: Michel Craig
Production Supervisor: Will C. Jomarrón

Speech: A Text with Adapted Readings, Second Edition

Library of Congress Cataloging in Publication Data
Jeffrey, Robert Campbell, 1927–
  Speech: a text with adapted readings.

  Includes bibliographies.
  1. Public speaking.   I. Peterson, Owen, 1924–
joint author.   II. Title.
PN4121.J34 1975   808.5'1   74–12471
ISBN 0–06–043277–2

CONTENTS

PREFACE

The purpose of this book is to introduce the student to the principles and basic skills of effective oral communication and to provide him with an appreciation of the nature and uses of speech. In the first edition of this book, the authors noted the growing use of "body rhetoric" and formless discourse as substitutes for the democratic ideal of decision-reaching by reasoned discussion and debate. Since then, the bitterness engendered by a divisive war, apprehension over the environment, and a decline of public faith in our institutions and leadership have created a sense of alienation among the people which make it even more essential that the values of effective communication be reaffirmed and promoted. Believing that the use of reason within the structure of our democratic institutions offers the best hope for the future, we have attempted to produce a text that superimposes modern forms, theories, and developments in speech communication upon the best of traditional rhetoric.

A significant feature of the book is the inclusion of relevant adapted readings designed to augment the textual materials. Some of the adapted readings elaborate upon the theoretical principles discussed in the text; others exemplify those principles; and still others present contrasting points of view. We have tried to select readings that are contemporary and relate to contemporary problems confronting the student in today's colleges and universities. The adapted readings are as important as the regular text for acquiring an understanding of speech and for developing skill as a speaker. These materials should make the use of a supplementary textbook unnecessary.

This edition contains two entirely new chapters: "Interpersonal Speech Communication" and "Persuasion." In addition, fifteen new adapted readings are included and a significant portion of the examples and illustrations used throughout the text have been replaced with more timely material.

Attention is devoted to both interpersonal communication and public speaking. The ideas and techniques discussed in the text apply to most forms of spoken discourse, including conversation, discussion, debate, and oral reading. The principles of human communication do not vary from one situation to another; only the form changes.

If the student wishes to pursue further any of the concepts introduced in the book, additional sources are listed at the ends of the chapters. To aid the student, each chapter begins with an outline of its contents and ends with study questions and exercises.

The authors are grateful to the publishers and authors of materials adapted for use in the book, with special appreciation to Patricia Jefferson Bammer; Barnet Baskerville; Senator Birch Bayh; Haig Bosmajian; William Honan; Wes Gallagher; Paul C. Harper, Jr.; Gilbert Highet; Alfred McClung Lee; O. Hobart Mowrer; James G. Powell; and Walter W. Stevens. A number of persons have assisted in reading, proofreading, and typing the manuscript. To them we are indebted.

R.C.J.
O.P.

S P E E C H

A TEXT WITH ADAPTED READINGS

1

SPEECH IN A DEMOCRATIC SOCIETY

Twentieth-century man lives in an age when communication is probably more important than at any other time in history. With the development of weaponry capable of destroying mankind, the expansion of population, the emergence of new nations, the exploration of space, and the ever-accelerating advances in science and technology, the world is beset with a welter of political, social, and economic problems. The advent of television has made it possible for men to view instantaneously events occurring halfway around the earth, with the result that what happens in one place is known by and affects the entire world. Most of the problems attendant upon the twentieth century can be solved only through the development of mutual understanding based on effective communication. See J. Martin Klotsche (Adapted Reading 1.1).

The development of skill in communication through speech demands an awareness of the environment in which speaking functions. Speech never occurs in a vacuum. Every speech is shaped by the situation in which it is given; by the distinctive nature of the speech act; by the restrictions of the society in which it is delivered; and by the speaker's own recognition of his ethical responsibilities as a communicator. This chapter discusses the legal and ethical framework within which speech occurs in a democratic society.

LEGAL RESPONSIBILITIES OF THE SPEAKER

Speech achieves its greatest importance in the conduct of human affairs in those societies placing fewest restraints on what the speaker may say. Politically, states encouraging the widest expression of opinion on all issues and relying on the judgment of an informed electorate for their policies produce the most effective public discussion. Where freedom of expression is restricted, speech tends to become little more than the mouthing of government-approved doctrine and dogma. In the totalitarian state, speech deteriorates into mere propaganda. Under a one-party system, no real exchange of ideas occurs and the lack of competition among conflicting ideologies often prevents the people from discovering and instituting needed reforms.

> The most important tenet of our democratic elective process is the obligation of each candidate to speak out on basic issues in order to present the electorate with a suitable basis for judgment.
>
> JAMES MADISON

Even in a democratic state, public fear and intolerance of certain beliefs can restrict the exchange of ideas. The United States experienced this during and after World War I when more than two thousand prosecutions were brought against persons under the Espionage Act of 1917 and the Sedition Act of 1918. These laws permitted persons to be prosecuted for urging taxes rather than bond issues for financing the war, for defending the legality of the sinking of merchant vessels, for advocating a referendum on participation in the war, and for calling the war un-Christian. Again, during the McCarthy era of the 1950s, a wave of hysteria resulting from fear of communism silenced many speakers who feared investigation by congressional committees and possible loss of jobs if they spoke out. The politics of confrontation of the 1960s illustrate the importance of freedom of speech in a democratic society. The attempts of minorities to force their views on the majority by demonstrations and the seizure of buildings almost invariably led to rioting, bloodshed, and public reaction against what may have been legitimate grievances.

In areas other than politics, freedom of expression is equally important. Whether communication occurs in the form of a speech, debate, discussion, or conversation, whether it takes place in the classroom, church, at a business conference, committee session, organization meeting, or during social intercourse, the most stimulating and productive discourse results when the participants express themselves freely. Through the open exchange of ideas and information, better understanding and acceptable solutions to group problems are more likely to occur. Worthwhile communication seldom takes place when the participants are inhibited or restrained by fear of retribution or reprisal and whenever speakers believe that their ideas will have no influence on the actions of others.

Perhaps never in history has speech been so important as it is today. With the advent of radio, television, and communication satellites, speakers now are able to be heard around the world instantaneously. More than 80 million Americans viewed at least part of the famous Kennedy–Nixon debates in 1960. Millions of people in all parts of the world watched telecasts of the United Nations debate on the Arab–Israeli crisis in 1967. Almost half of the world's population heard astronaut Neil Armstrong's first words as he set foot on the moon. Telecasts of the Watergate hearings in 1973 provided millions of Americans with an intimate glimpse of their government in operation. As the communication industry reaches even more remote countries, ever larger numbers of people — many of whom are unable to read or write — are brought into direct contact with the ideas and events of the rest of the world. Because of these developments, the influence of the spoken word on peoples all over the globe is destined to become ever more important.

> If all my talents and powers were to be taken from me by some inscrutable Providence, and I had my choice of keeping but one, I would unhesitatingly ask to be allowed to keep the Power of Speaking, for through it, I would quickly recover all the rest.
>
> DANIEL WEBSTER

It is reassuring in this age of mass communications that the individual can still be heard and can affect the course of events, as André Maurois explains (see Adapted Reading 1.2). At a time when many feel alienated by the growing complexity of the world, individual speakers still demonstrate the power of the spoken word in producing marked changes in the conduct of human affairs. One need only recall Newton Minow, who in 1961 instituted a critical reexamination of the fare on American television with his speech, "A Vast Wasteland," delivered to the National Association of Broadcasters. In 1964, J. William Fulbright, in his address, "Foreign Policy — Old Myths and New Realities," stimulated a reappraisal of American foreign policy that continues today. During the 1963 march on Washington, Martin Luther King, Jr., revitalized a flagging civil rights movement and inspired millions of people with his "I Have a Dream" speech. Eugene J. McCarthy's quiet attacks on American involvement in Vietnam (delivered to small audiences in New Hampshire villages but relayed to the entire country by the mass media of communication) toppled an incumbent administration almost single-handedly. Battling one of the largest corporations in America, Ralph Nader, through testimony at congressional hearings and lecture appearances, forced manufacturers to produce safer automobiles. A speaker need not have a national reputation to influence opinion. The speaking activities of a countless number of women, most unknown beyond their local communities, have focused attention on the status of women in our society. The ecology movement has been largely the work of relatively unknown individuals interested in improving the environment of their area or community.

These examples substantiate the view that the spoken word of the individual remains a powerful force for social change.

LEGAL RESTRICTIONS ON THE SPEAKER

Although it is desirable to have the widest possible scope in the discussion and debate of ideas, some restrictions are necessary even in the most democratic society. When freedom of expression begins to conflict with other rights guaranteed to the citizen, some resolution must occur. Accordingly, over the years legislation and court decisions have established various legal limitations on the speaker. In the United States, the principal restrictions concern advocacy of the forcible overthrow of the government; speech that provokes a breach of the peace; obscenity; the regulation of the time, location, and manner of speaking; defamation of character; and the use of radio and television.

Advocacy of Forcible Overthrow of the Government

Because the governmental system of the United States provides for peaceful change through free elections and amendment of the constitution, laws prohibiting the forcible overthrow of the government have consistently been upheld by the courts. The constitutionality of acts banning the *advocacy* of forcible overthrow of the government, however, is not so clear. At one time, the Supreme Court was of the opinion that:

> One may not counsel or advise others to violate the law as it stands. Words are not only the keys of persuasion, but the triggers of action, and those which have no purport but to counsel the violation of law cannot by any latitude of interpretation be a part of that public opinion which is the final source of government in a democratic state.

However, the Court later modified its position, applying a criterion that has come to be known as the "clear and present danger test." It has indicated that the test does not prohibit mere abstract discussion of violent overthrow of the government, but only such speech as actually urges the listeners to take overt action toward the overthrow of the government. In a 1969 decision, the Court ruled that advocating the violent overthrow of the government was punishable only if the speaker intended to produce imminent lawless action and that violence was likely to occur as a result of the speech. The speaker must have both the intention and capacity to accomplish the violent overthrow of the government before he can be punished.

Furthermore, the Court has specified that the danger must be both clear and present—in other words neither a vague or ambiguous statement that might be construed by some as urging violent action nor a statement that proposed action at some unspecified future date could be considered actionable. Mere membership in a political party dedicated to changing the form of government of the United States (the Communist party, American Nazi party, or some other group) cannot be deemed an attempt to overthrow the government forcibly, and members of such parties are allowed the same freedom of speech as members of other political organizations. Participation in a *conspiracy* to overthrow the government by force can be prosecuted if the conspirators take steps to implement their plan. However, they must act; mere plotting of such action by the conspirators is not unconstitutional.

> . . . The ultimate good desired is better reached by free trade in ideas. The best test of truth is the power of the thought to get itself accepted in the competition of the market. . . . We should be eternally vigilant against attempts to check the expression of opinions that we loathe and believe to be fraught with death, unless they so immediately threaten immediate interference with the lawful and pressing purposes of the law that an immediate check is required to save the country.
>
> OLIVER WENDELL HOLMES

Breach of the Peace

Restrictions are also placed on speech that provokes a breach of the peace or other types of disturbance. Cases involving a breach of the peace usually result from some speaker arousing his audience to the point at which they violate the law by destroying public property, attacking others, or assaulting the speaker himself. Since the Constitution does not deprive a speaker of the right to be intolerant, offensive, ill informed, or bigoted, some speakers evoke intense hostility. The problem facing public officials is to protect the right of free speech of such speakers while preventing them from inciting their listeners to the point where physical violence or violation of the law occurs.

> A believer in democratic rights who denies a hearing to speakers whom he regards as opposed to democratic rights is acting on their alleged principles, not on his.
>
> EDITORIAL COMMENT
> *The Observer* (London)

Decisions of the courts have repeatedly held that the police cannot be used as an instrument for the suppression of unpopular views; yet they have also recognized that when the speaker passes the bounds of argument and undertakes incitement to riot, the police should not be powerless to prevent a breach of the peace.

In the case of a speaker whose audience is hostile and threatens his safety, the courts have ruled that the police must make all reasonable efforts to protect him.

> If all mankind minus one, were of one opinion, and only one person were of the contrary opinion, mankind would be no more justified in silencing that one person, than he, if he had the power, would be justified in silencing mankind.
>
> JOHN STUART MILL

Although the courts have never set forth a clear formula for determining when a speaker can be restrained, the factors that have been important in their decisions in such cases have been the place where the speech is given, the character and temper of the audience, and the exact nature of the danger at the critical moment when a breach of the peace is likely to occur. Even when the entire speaking situation presents an immediate danger of violence, the police face the question of whether to try to restrain the audience or to stop the speaker. Obviously, every effort must be made to permit the speaker to continue, for to do otherwise would be an open invitation to opponents to silence the speaker simply by threatening disorder. A vivid example of the necessity for restraining the audience rather than stopping the speaker was provided by the 1968 presidential campaign when all three major candidates were repeatedly harassed by demonstrators hoping to disrupt their rallies. Failure to restrain the demonstrators would have effectively silenced the candidates, thereby depriving them of the right of free speech.

Obscenity

Another area in which government restricts the freedom of the speaker is that of obscenity. Obscenity is not governed by the "clear and present danger" test. Instead, the courts have held that obscenity simply is not constitutionally protected under the First Amendment and that both the state and federal governments have the right to enact legislation to suppress obscenity. During the late 1960s, the courts became increasingly reluctant to ban anything as being obscene. Arguing that "any material having any social importance" is permissible — regardless of how crude or offensive it may be to some members of the community — the courts frequently reversed state and local laws governing obscenity in stage presentations, motion pictures, television, and night club performances. As the courts relaxed their attitude toward obscenity, so did several voluntary regulatory agencies such as the Motion Picture Association with the result that nudity and sexual acts not permitted a short time before were openly shown on the stage and screen.

However, in June 1973, the Supreme Court handed down a new set of guidelines on obscenity giving states greater scope in banning books, magazines, plays, and motion pictures that are offensive to local standards. Among the more important guidelines set forth in its decision, the Court ruled that in judging whether a work appeals to prurient interests, a jury should apply the views of "the average person, applying contemporary community standards," rather than any hypothetical national definition. The Court further ruled that it will no longer be a defense to prosecution for obscenity that the work has some "redeeming social value," as it had been since a 1966 decision.

Time, Place, and Manner of Speaking

Because the right of free speech often conflicts with other rights and may interfere with the orderly functioning of a community, the courts have held that certain regulations on the time, place, and manner of speaking may be justified. However, the courts have clearly ruled that the government, under the guise of preserving law and order, has absolutely no power to prevent a speaker from presenting his message to a particular audience; at the same time, the courts have also made it clear that the speaker's constitutional right does not mean that he can convey his message at any time or any place under any circumstances he wishes.

Among the situations in which public officials may intervene to regulate the use of speaking facilities are the following: when the speech obstructs traffic or the passage of pedestrians; when more than one speaker seeks to use a particular podium, park, or public hall at the same time; when the presentation of a speech interferes with another speaker; when extensive police protection is required to preserve order; and when the speaker disturbs the tranquility or the health of individuals through excessive noise (for example, a public meeting outside a hospital, extreme amplification, or the use of sound trucks at particular times and locations).

> You have not converted a man when you have silenced him.
>
> JOHN, VISCOUNT MORLEY

In regulating situations of the kind just described, the courts have repeatedly emphasized that none of the restrictions may have anything to do with the content of the speech and that all groups must be treated equally. While the government may insist that speakers secure a permit or register on a "sign-up" sheet, it cannot show any preference in the granting of permits. At times, government bodies may even charge fees to cover expenses such as providing police protection, cleaning up after the meeting, or simply for processing the applications for rallies or meetings; but when fees are charged, they cannot be so large as to discourage small groups or unpopular speakers and they must be equal for all seeking permits.

Furthermore, while the courts have ruled that state and local governments are under no obligation to make public halls available to any speaker whatsoever, if they do permit the hall to be used for a public meeting, they thereafter have no right to determine which groups may or may not utilize the building, nor can the government establish conditions censoring what may and may not be said before granting the use of the facility.

With regard to the problem of regulating excessive noise, the courts have approved restrictions ranging from an absolute ban in certain zones (such as hospitals and schools), to limitations on the volume of the amplification and the length of time a sound truck may remain in one spot, to regulations on the hours when such broadcasting may be done. However, in applying these regulations, the governmental body or official must act without discrimination and with no regard for the popularity of the speaker or his message.

> When men can freely communicate their thoughts and their sufferings, real or imaginary, their passions spend themselves in air, like gunpowder scattered upon the surface; but pent up by terrors, they work unseen, burst forth in a moment, and destroy everything in their course.
>
> THOMAS ERSKINE

Defamation

The right of free speech is further limited when the speaker's remarks injure the reputation of another person. Injurious statements of this kind are known as defamation of character. For many years, a distinction was made between oral defamation, known as slander, and written defamation, or libel. Because of the permanency of the written word, libel was generally considered a more serious offense. However, with the advent of radio and television the distinction between libel and slander has become extremely hazy. One of the reasons for this is the fact that the spoken word on a broadcast can now reach many more people than a written defamation can; another reason is that writers, as well as speakers, are usually involved in the preparation of broadcast statements that may be defamatory.

Several conditions must exist before one can claim defamation of character. First, the allegedly defamatory statement must have been communicated to a third party; it is impossible to claim defamation of character if only the speaker and the individual claiming to have been slandered participate in the exchange. Second, the speaker's intent clearly must have been defamatory—that is, his words were not simply stated as a joke. Third, the person claiming to have been defamed must be clearly identifiable. Statements such as "Some of the members of the Student Council are Communist agents," or "Many of the legislators are in the pay of gangsters," or "One of the ministers in town is having an affair with a high school girl" are not actionable because the subject has not been specifically identified. On the other hand, statements such as "The president of the Student Council is a

Communist agent," "All four of the state's representatives are in the pay of gangsters," and "The pastor of the First Presbyterian Church is having an affair with a high school girl" might be slanderous because, even though the individuals are not actually named, they can be clearly identified.

In a case of defamation, if the defendant can prove that what he said was true, he usually will be acquitted. If, on the other hand, the plaintiff can prove the statement to be false, the defendant usually will be held guilty of defamation.

There are exceptions to both of these generalizations. It is possible for a speaker to be guilty of defamation even though what he said was completely true. Such a verdict would probably result only if it could be proved that the speaker had spoken maliciously with the sole intent of creating trouble and his remarks could not in any way be construed to contribute to the general welfare of the community. For example, let us suppose that Mr. Jones becomes irritated because Mr. Smith, his next-door neighbor, has erected a fence ten feet high between their lots. Smith has lived in the community for many years and has a good reputation as a parent, citizen, and church member. Jones, however, discovers that twenty years earlier Smith had served a short prison term for a minor theft. Angry because his neighbor has erected the fence, Jones goes about the neighborhood telling everyone that Smith is an ex-convict. If Smith were to sue for defamation of character, he probably would win the case (even though it was true that he had served a prison term) because Jones's intent was purely malicious; in other words, the dissemination of this information served no useful social purpose.

On the other hand, had Smith been a candidate for city treasurer and were Jones to reveal the same information, it is almost certain that no case of slander would exist.

A second exception would be the case of a speaker who makes a defamatory statement that is wholly untrue. If he can prove that he made the allegation in good faith and was innocent of malice in his intent, he *may* be acquitted of the charge. This occurred when a priest who had been attacked repeatedly in the press and in speeches by a former parishioner was told by a physician that the man had been under psychiatric care and had spent several years in a mental hospital. In a sermon, the priest told his congregation to ignore the attacks of the critic because of his history of mental illness. The man brought suit for slander and at the trial proved that he had never been in a mental hospital and had never received psychiatric treatment. The priest, whose defense was that he had had every reason to believe the physician and that he had not spoken maliciously, was acquitted.

Certain groups are immune to prosecution for defamation under particular conditions. The statements of legislators during a legislative session, the pronouncements of governors and other executive officials on certain subjects, and the testimony of judges, jurors, witnesses, and lawyers during a trial are regarded as privileged and not subject to defamation proceedings. Critics of plays, motion pictures, books, sports events, concerts, and similar public presentations are generally immune from suits for defamation so long as they do not misrepresent the facts and comment in a manner that seeks to enlighten and serve the public interest.

Radio and Television

In the early days of radio, broadcasters simply set up their equipment and began transmitting whatever they wanted at any frequency they chose. However, as the number of stations increased and their signals began to interfere with each other, it became apparent that some kind of control was needed. Accordingly, Congress in 1912 enacted legislation providing for regulation of the broadcasting industry. Succeeding acts extended the regulatory powers of the government and created the Federal Communications Commission to enforce these controls.

The basis of the Federal Communications Commission's authority rests on its right to grant and renew licenses to broadcasters. Since the number of applicants for licenses exceeds the number of frequencies available, from the outset the F.C.C. has insisted that the airwaves belong to the people and that a license will be granted only if the public convenience, interest, or necessity is served. The commission has no authority to censor any broadcast. However, because it is empowered to review how well a broadcaster has served the public when his license comes up for renewal, in a sense it *does* exercise a form of censorship after the fact.

Four of the most important provisions of the code regulating broadcasters concern (1) the presentation of public affairs programs, (2) fairness in dealing with controversial issues, (3) granting of equal time to political candidates, and (4) avoidance of offensive material.

Because programs that are purely entertainment attract larger audiences than public affairs presentations and, therefore, are more easily sold to sponsors, broadcasters tend to shy away from programs dealing with public affairs. However, the F.C.C. has insisted that broadcasters are obligated to devote time to public affairs — even if they are unpopular — because such programs clearly serve the public interest.

Closely related to the broadcaster's obligation to air public affairs programs is the requirement that he deal fairly with controversial issues. Thus, if a licensee presents a program favoring a particular policy, proposal, or group, he is obligated to see that the other side has an opportunity to air its views. Or, if a station broadcasts an editorial, it must make time available for opposing points of view. Broadcasters have long contended that the requirement that they make time available for the presentation of conflicting points of view violates their freedom of speech. However, as recently as June 1969, the Supreme Court reaffirmed the "fairness" rules, contending that they "enhance rather than abridge the freedoms of speech and press protected by the First Amendment."

In political campaigns, broadcasters are governed by Section 315 of the Federal Communications Act, which provides that if the licensee makes air time available — either free or for a price — to one candidate, he must afford equal opportunities to all other candidates for that office in the use of his facilities. The law applies to candidates at all levels — national, state, and local. While this regulation seems fair in that it provides every candidate with equal access to the airwaves, it does tend to discourage stations from setting aside free air time for worthwhile political programs since they would have to grant equal amounts of time to all aspirants for the office. As a result, most political programs are paid for by the candidate or his supporters, which means that the less affluent candidates, although legally entitled to equal time, often are deprived of it for financial reasons. It should be noted that the famous "great debates" between John F. Kennedy and Richard M. Nixon in the 1960 presidential campaign were possible only because Congress suspended the "equal time" provision that year to permit them. Had Congress not suspended the provision, every obscure minority party candidate could have demanded equal national network time to present his views.

Finally, another important restriction on radio and television broadcasting is that the stations have a responsibility to resist presenting material that is vulgar, in bad taste, indecent, obscene, or profane.

While the Federal Communications Commission has additional regulatory powers, and other federal agencies also exercise some control over broadcasting, the four provisions discussed are probably the most important government restrictions on what can be said or done on the air. In addition to these federal controls, however, the networks and individual stations often voluntarily regulate themselves with regard to the presentation of certain kinds of material.

FREEDOM OF SPEECH ON THE CAMPUS

Because of the university's importance as an institution where the most searching and critical examination of ideas can take place, freedom of speech is extremely vital on the college campus. Here, if anywhere, is a place where the widest possible latitude in the discussion of ideas, values, and concepts should be encouraged. However, it is also here that controversy over what can or should be said seems most often to erupt.

Speech on the campus is not exempt from any of the restrictions that society places on speakers in general. However, the very nature of an institution of higher learning seems to lead to disagreement over the limits of free speech on the campus. Parents, trustees, and state legislators, on the one hand, are concerned about what their children and students hear and are being taught; students and faculty, on the other hand, usually want the greatest possible freedom to discuss and examine all ideas. Most campus disputes concerning freedom of speech revolve around the rights of (1) the faculty, (2) the students, and (3) the outside speaker.

Rights of the Faculty

Attempts to limit the freedom of speech of faculty members at institutions of higher learning are commonplace and have been so throughout America's history. Groups have tried to silence or even discharge college teachers for their political views and activities, their religious beliefs, and even for their

FREE SPEECH
Progress by dissent . . . is characteristic of human societies. It has been responsible for the growth and success of democracy in the last four hundred years,
and the decline and failure of absolute forms of government: For the crucial
feature of democracy is not simply that the majority rules, but that *the minority is free to persuade people* to come over to its side and make a new majority.
Of course, the minority is abused at first—Socrates was, and so was Charles
Darwin. But the strength of democracy is that the dissident minority is not
silenced; on the contrary, it is the business of the minority to convert the majority; and this is how a democratic society invigorates and renews itself in
change as no totalitarian society can.

J. BRONOWSKI
"Protest—Past and Present." San Diego, Calif., June 2, 1969.
(Representative American Speeches, 1969–1970, p. 121.)

classroom discussion of unpopular philosophies within their professional
disciplines. Unless the professor is a tenured faculty member with his rights
clearly detailed in his contract or in the regulations of the institution, he
often has little legal recourse in cases in which he is attacked for advocating
an unpopular idea. The American Association of University Professors has
long championed academic freedom, but the organization has little power
beyond that of censuring a university and urging teachers to refuse employment at the school. Because it cannot be said that a faculty member has a
constitutional right to teach at a particular institution, often the courts will
not intervene, or they will uphold the validity of a professor's discharge.
However, by publicizing violations of academic freedom and applying pressure on the universities and their governing bodies, organizations such as
the American Association of University Professors and the American Civil
Liberties Union frequently are able to persuade the offending party to change
its policies voluntarily.

Rights of the Student

Until the 1960s students seemed to show little concern over their rights of
free speech. Colleges and universities often exercised tight control over what
kinds of student meetings could be held, what speakers could be invited,
and even what subjects students might discuss without any serious protest
by the students themselves. Only a few years ago, it was not uncommon for a
school committee to ban debates on certain topics, for speech departments to
prohibit student speeches on particular subjects, and for administrative officials to refuse to permit certain kinds of student meetings to be held on
campus. However, the widespread student revolt against such restrictions
which began at the University of California at Berkeley in 1964, and spread
throughout most of the nation in subsequent years, has largely brought to an
end most of these restrictions. A large number of schools, either under pressure from dissenting students or faced with the possibility of future disorder
if they did not liberalize their policies, have eliminated many of the most re-

strictive regulations on free speech. Most disputes between colleges and students over free speech never reach the courts. However, one important court decision in 1961 held that students may not be expelled from state colleges or universities for disciplinary reasons without some form of hearing that meets the tests of due process of law.

The Outside Speaker

Most disputes over whether a speaker should be permitted to come to the campus to address a student audience involve political, religious, or racial extremists (for example, Communists, atheists, Ku Klux Klansmen, American Nazis, etc.). Students and faculty members tend to support a nondiscriminatory policy that would not prohibit any speaker from appearing on campus. They contend that students come to college to learn and that they should be exposed to as many different points of view as possible. Furthermore, they argue that no one is required to attend such lectures and so students who do not wish to hear the speaker may simply stay away. Parents and the general public, however, often oppose the appearance of certain speakers on campus. They maintain that the ideas of some speakers are so thoroughly discredited, subversive, or repugnant to society that there is no value in listening to them. They further contend that since they support the school financially, either through taxes or tuition, they have a right to be heard on the question of what speakers should be permitted on campus. The college administrator usually is caught in the middle, trying to satisfy the demands of the faculty and the student groups and attempting to please the parents and the public.

It should be understood that no speaker has the constitutional right to demand that he be permitted to use college facilities for a speech. Every school has the privilege of refusing its facilities to any or all outside speakers. While a significant number of colleges and universities permit campus groups to invite *any* speaker to come to the campus, most schools exercise some type of control over the appearance of outside speakers. Regulations may range from a simple rule that the speakers be invited by a recognized campus group and that the school be notified, to provisions requiring approval of a speaker by some committee or administrative official, to an outright ban on speakers belonging to certain groups. In an effort to resolve the question of who may speak on campus, many schools have worked out detailed codes and some state legislatures have even enacted laws prohibiting the appearance of speakers belonging to unpopular or allegedly subversive organizations.

There are many arguments on both sides of the issue, but basically the objection to any form of restriction on outside speakers is this: When the college or university officials prohibit the appearance of one speaker because they regard his message as intellectually worthless, dangerous, or incompatible with the aims of the school, they automatically endorse the educational value and academic respectability of the ideas of any speaker they permit on campus. Almost no college or university would condone such censorship in its library; yet speakers are banned where books are not.

> We can never be sure that the opinion we are endeavoring to stifle is a false opinion; and if we were sure, stifling it would be an evil still.
>
> JOHN STUART MILL

ETHICS OF THE SPEAKER

While a democratic society places legal restraints on the exercise of free speech in order to protect itself, to guarantee the rights of others, to maintain order, and to provide equal opportunity of expression to all, these safeguards alone will not ensure either responsible communication or the penetrating examination of ideas necessary for the most effective exercise of democratic government. In addition, the speaker himself has certain ethical responsibilities he must fulfill if citizens are to understand and resolve the issues confronting them.

The first and most important of the speaker's ethical responsibilities is to be well informed about his subject. While the Constitution does not deny the right of free speech to anyone, no matter how ignorant or ill informed, there is no excuse for a speaker misleading the public simply because he was too lazy or too irresponsible to learn the facts. If the democratic process is to flourish and the people are to make intelligent decisions, it is imperative that their decisions be based on the best information and the most searching analysis. To mislead the public through ignorance is no less reprehensible than to operate an automobile without knowing how to drive or to practice surgery without a medical background.

To be well informed a speaker must examine all sides of a question as honestly and impartially as he can. He must utilize all of the information available to him. He must weigh the reliability of his sources of knowledge and test the validity of his own reasoning. He must look into the future and attempt to foresee the consequences of any action he might propose. Only when the speaker has completed the most rigorous and extensive preparation can he ethically go before an audience.

Second, the speaker has an ethical obligation to present the facts upon which his conclusions are based. If public confidence in the spoken word is to be maintained, audiences must believe that the speaker is telling the truth, that he is not distorting the facts, and that he is not suppressing vital information. Confusion and unrest result when the public feels that it is being misled. Much of the dissatisfaction and dissent of the 1960s and 1970s can be attributed to the "credibility gap," the feeling on the part of many Americans that they were not being told the truth by their leaders. Conflicting reports on the aims and progress of the war in Vietnam, uncertainty concerning what really happened at Tonkin Gulf, the disclosure that student organizations were being financed secretly by the Central Intelligence Agency, the suppression of information and false denials of information concerning the bombing of Cambodia, the attempted cover-up and conflicting testimony of persons allegedly involved in the Watergate scandal, as well as other efforts by prominent leaders to suppress or distort the truth, all combined to create a growing distrust of the spoken word and subsequent discontent.

Unquestionably, certain information essential to national security cannot be widely circulated. However, except for a few items of this kind, the public has the right to know the facts. The example of Winston Churchill during World War II suggests that when the citizenry believes that it is being told the truth, however unpleasant, the populace can be trusted to act in the best interests of the country. Never mincing words about the hardship of the war, Britain's setbacks and defeats, and the grimness of the struggle ahead, Churchill nevertheless so inspired the British with his words that the beleaguered island stood alone against the Nazis for more than a year before the United States entered the war.

Third, the speaker has an ethical obligation to accept full responsibility for all that he says. This applies equally to prominent public figures and to student speakers. At a time when busy politicians, executives, educators, labor leaders, and others make extensive use of ghostwriters in the preparation of speeches, the speaker has an obligation to take an active part in the formulation of the speech and to make certain that the finished address represents his personal attitude and position on the subject. The speaker who turns over to a public relations agency or professional speech writer full responsibility for the preparation of his speeches has totally abdicated his duty as a citizen in a democratic society and is not deserving of the public ear.

At the student level, speakers are expected to prepare their own speeches. The whole purpose of presenting a classroom speech is to gain knowledge and skill in the speechmaking process. If the student has not prepared his speech, he cannot possibly have learned anything about speechmaking. While the speaker should consult as many sources as he thinks necessary in order to obtain ideas and information, the final speech should be the result of his own thinking on and understanding of the subject. If he uses material from other sources, he should always give proper credit to the author or publication. To simply lift an entire speech or article from a file, newspaper, book, or magazine and to pass it off as one's own is not only unethical, but also constitutes plagiarism — an offense which at most schools is subject to the severest penalties.

> **Seldom or never will a man be eloquent, but when he is in earnest and uttering his own sentiments.**
>
> HUGH BLAIR

A fourth ethical responsibility of the speaker is to present his message in such a way that the listeners are able to react rationally and intelligently. Man is not governed by intellect alone; in fact, instinct and emotion are important factors in most of his decisions. Nevertheless, most persons regard decisions based on knowledge and understanding as being superior to those resulting from pure feeling. Indeed, this is the assumption underlying all education. Thus, if man in a democratic society is to make the wisest choices, he must be supplied with sufficient knowledge to permit him to judge intelligently.

Having said this, it is important to acknowledge that facts and pure reason often are not enough to motivate a person to make a rational decision or to take action. Examples to illustrate this point are plentiful: In spite of all the statistics showing a high correlation between smoking and lung cancer, millions of Americans continue to smoke cigarettes; in spite of almost incontrovertible evidence that operating an automobile while intoxicated is dangerous, people continue to drive while drunk; in spite of evidence pointing to the perils of overpopulation in the near future, many nations show no real interest in effective birth control measures. These examples indicate that mere factual evidence does not always evoke the desired response. Thus, the speaker is often faced with the necessity of trying to motivate his audience by appealing to their emotions.

> Slogans are both exciting and comforting, but they are also powerful opiates for the conscience. . . . Some of mankind's most terrible misdeeds have been committed under the spell of certain magic words or phrases.
>
> JAMES B. CONANT

However, the fact that a speaker may attempt to stimulate his listeners by associating his cause with feelings of love, patriotism, security, self-preservation, or some other emotion does not give him license to substitute sentiment for thought or to attempt to influence his listeners primarily through appeals to their feelings. Ethically, he is still obligated to provide his audience with enough information to make an informed decision. No matter how virtuous, right, or important he feels his cause to be, the end never justifies the means.

If people do not base their decisions on information and understanding, the democratic process fails. Thus, the substitution of slogans for rational argument, the oversimplification of issues, appeals to hysteria, intolerance, mob action, and other tricks of the propagandist—although they may succeed—can never be condoned as ethically responsible, as Thomas Nilsen stresses (see Adapted Reading 1.3).

A fifth ethical responsibility of the speaker is to let the other side be heard. Some individuals and groups employ a variety of stratagems to silence any opposition. Their techniques include heckling, shouting down speakers, disrupting meetings, physical attacks, threats, and intimidation. More subtly, these same individuals may try to prevent access to a public hall, church, theater, park, or other forum. Private groups such as civic, educational, and professional organizations sometimes simply refuse to schedule speakers whose ideas they oppose. While it cannot be claimed that such

> Many have fallen by the edge of the sword: but not so many as have fallen by the tongue.
>
> ECCLESIASTICUS 28:18

groups have a legal obligation to hear both sides of a question, nor can it be argued that the speaker has a constitutional right to address any group he wishes, if people are to make intelligent choices, it is imperative that they avail themselves of the opportunity to hear as many diverse views as possible. Furthermore, the group that is afraid to let the other side be heard might well question the soundness of its own position; for if what they believe cannot withstand attack, it probably is not a very strong cause. Thomas Nilsen discusses this in Adapted Reading 1.3.

While no group has an ethical responsibility to solicit a contradictory point of view for every speech it hears, individuals and organizations that try to suppress speakers of opposing viewpoints are not acting in the best interests of freedom of inquiry and democratic government.

SUMMARY

To understand the process of speechmaking and to acquire proficiency in the art of public address, the student of speech must be aware of the political environment in which speech operates.

Public address is most important in those societies that permit the widest scope in the discussion of issues. However, even in a democratic society, certain restrictions further shape the nature of a speech. In the United States these limitations include regulations on time, place, and manner of speaking; defamation of character; advocacy of the forcible overthrow of the government; and speech that breaches the peace. Because of the nature of broadcasting, speakers on radio and television are further restricted by specific federal regulations. The college community is governed by the same legal restrictions as those affecting the populace in general. However, because of the educational function of the university, the question of who should be allowed to address students and exactly what speakers should be permitted to say is a constant controversy.

In addition to the legal restrictions placed upon speakers, if speech is to function as it should in a democracy, the speaker must adhere to certain ethical standards. He has the duty to be well informed, to present factually accurate material, to accept responsibility for what he says, to present his message in such a manner that his listeners are able to react intelligently and rationally, and to permit opposing viewpoints to be heard. Without these self-imposed standards, speech cannot fulfill its vital role in giving the public the insight and understanding necessary for the efficient functioning of democratic government.

ADAPTED READING 1.1

THE IMPORTANCE OF COMMUNICATION IN TODAY'S WORLD

J. Martin Klotsche

The basic proposition that underlies this article is the very simple one that we are living at a time when ideas are vital to our survival. They are decisive in the world . . . which confronts us. . . . Ideas have become weapons more vital to us than the armies we mobilize, the bombs we mount, or the physical strength we harness to protect ourselves. Let there be no misunderstanding. We must be strong and use our physical power wherever it is required to preserve the integrity of the free world. But to the gun in our hand we must also add ideas in our head. For our survival over the long pull will depend upon the skill we employ in making known our ideas to others and in convincing them that they are infinitely better than those that are being advanced by our adversaries. . . .

This may seem so obvious that it scarcely bears repeating. Yet we have demonstrated some real shortcomings. . . . This is a great tragedy for we do have something of great importance to say to others. Yet our failure to communicate in a manner that others can understand represents one of our greatest shortcomings.

The revolution in science and technology which has taken place in the last generation makes the communication of ideas all the more important. Changes have been so rapid that in our lifetime the world has been converted into a neighborhood, with instantaneous communication and the rapid transmission of ideas important by-products. Aristotle is said to have stated that the size of the state should be determined by the range of a man's voice. Applying this concept to today's world then, science and technology have transformed the world into a single community with people everywhere having something to say to others and wanting to be heard.

A few years ago, Norman Cousins, editor of the *Saturday Review,* made an extensive trip to a number of Far Eastern countries. In the course of his visit he stopped in a small village not far from Calcutta. There he met the finest conversationalist he had ever encountered. This man was a leading citizen of the village, renowned for his knowledge of religion and philosophy. He spoke through an interpreter. At the end of the dialogue, Mr. Cousins expressed the hope that the two men could continue their discussion by correspondence. The interpreter stammered the following reply: "Our friend is deeply honored at the suggestion that you and he correspond, but regrets that he is unable to do so as he has never been taught how to read or write. He would be glad to correspond through a translator but there is no one in this village or the next who is qualified for such work. But he is grateful indeed for your kind thought." Mr. Cousins reported that incidents such as this were

From *The Speech Teacher*, November 1962, pp. 322–326.

repeated many times during the course of his trip. After some feeling of momentary shock, he concluded that the art of oral communication did make it possible for people who are illiterate in the commonly accepted sense of the word to transmit to others knowledge, insight, and understanding about many profound questions.

Speech can be used in many different ways. It can, for instance, become an instrument of *tyranny*. This is the manner in which the Nazis employed it in Germany in the 1930's. Here was a crude example of a small group of willful men, who, possessing a monopoly of communication, accomplished a devastating conformity designed to deprive the individual of his freedom and his right to differ with constituted authority. In the Soviet Union we have seen a repetition of this process in an even more systematic form, with the coercive methods of the police state being used to deprive citizens of their freedom to communicate other than in the framework of a controlled society. So all-embracing is this system of mind control that criticism is prohibited, idiosyncracy penalized, and all creativeness discouraged. Thus, communication, instead of being an art, has become an instrument of tyrannical power. Nor is this device limited to these two examples, for in every area of the world there is fertile ground for the tyrannical use of power. Even in a free society such as ours, it requires eternal vigilance and a constantly alert citizenry to prevent speech, thought, and the written word from being used as a weapon of deceit and deception. For the demagogue in any society finds the spoken word a useful tool to pursue his objectives. . . .

Speech can also be used as an instrument of *deception*. The Soviets provide a dramatic example of this method. Through lies, half-truths, exaggerations, and upside-down language they have succeeded in making ignorance seem a virtue, and falsehood appear as truth. . . . Milton once asked: "Whoever heard truth put to the worse, in a free and open encounter?" To which John Stuart Mill replied: "The dictum that the truth always triumphs over persecution is one of those pleasant falsehoods which men repeat after one another till they pass into commonplace, but which all experience refutes. History teems with instances of truth put down by persecution. If not suppressed forever, it may be thrown back for centuries." Actually, one would not need to go too far afield for examples of the written and spoken word being used to deceive. There is, for example, the gobbledegook of the office memorandum, the luscious overtones in advertising copy, or the reassuring manner in which a military defeat was recently reported: "The return of American forces to previously prepared positions in the rear was accomplished briskly and efficiently." Words have often been used to distort and to deceive.

Speech can also be used as an instrument of *self-congratulation*. The most barren kind of existence is one in which an individual converses only with those who agree and share his views. There is a strong inclination for us to seek out only those who acquiesce with our position. Yet we lose one of the great opportunities for self-education if we close our minds and refuse to listen to and absorb other people's ideas. The late Professor Robert Redfield of the University of Chicago, once asked, "Does America need a hearing aid?" and then answered his own question by pointing out that our talking is not always balanced by our listening. Conversation, he reminded us, is more than just two people talking loudly to each other. Rather it is one person talking, the other listening, and then reversing the process. He concluded that Americans do need a hearing aid to improve their listening.

But speech can also be used as an instrument of *enlightenment.* To do so it must serve at least three purposes. First, it must advance the cause of truth. What is truth? . . .

Too frequently we marshall facts either to rearrange our prejudices or to bring them up to date. Mr. Julian Huxley, upon his retirement as Director General of UNESCO in 1948, discussed truth in relation to power. He identified the power of the soldier as based upon fear and naked force; that of the policeman as combining force with a sense of justice; that of the witch doctor as using supernatural sanctions and resorting to irrational deeds; and that of the propagandist as employing skill to arrange and manipulate people's passions. But he concluded that the greatest power was that of wisdom and truth which holds that the way to lead men is to know where they should go and to tell them, explaining to them as if they were rational beings, why it is the right way.

In addition to serving the interests of truth, speech must also be meaningful. We must do more than unleash an avalanche of words, for what we say may be significantly related to the world around us. Slogans can easily be clothed with a magical quality. Even righteous ones can be used to enslave as well as liberate. There is danger in using words without meaning, for when so employed they can easily become pernicious abstractions. In a recent six-minute campaign speech delivered by a candidate for office, the speaker used the word "freedom" forty times. Obviously this word had little meaning or significance either to him or to his audience.

One of the main difficulties that we encounter in this regard is that we have not yet determined what it is that we want to communicate to others. There was a time in our history when we knew what we wanted to say and we expressed it in some of the most contagious writing of all time. But then we became pragmatists, impatient with theory and reflection, and unable to communicate ideas in a meaningful and relevant manner. Thus, because of our failure to express our ideas in an idiom that could be understood by others, we found ourselves ideologically isolated in many areas of the world. This is a great pity, for we do have in our possession a constellation of ideas that can be made appealing to peoples all over the world. There are countless examples, for instance, of the Declaration of Independence being used to shore up the hopes and aspirations of peoples all over the world.

Actually there are many themes in American history that can be . . . made meaningful if we will but identify them, relate them to other people's needs, and express them in a manner that they can understand.

Finally, what we say must also be related to what we do. There is a great discrepancy between our profession and our practice, between our beliefs and our actions, between our commitment and its fulfillment. . . .

There must . . . be a greater correlation between speech and performance. We subscribe, for example, to the belief in the dignity of man. We state that all men should be brothers unto each other and that what is granted to one should not be denied to others. These are long recognized truths. But while they are self-evident, they are not self-explanatory, nor are they self-operating. . . .

In summary, then, these comments can be made, *First,* what we say must be honest. It must be founded on the truth. It must contain the highest degree of integrity. Our speech should be used to speak out against prejudice, half-truths, and distortions. *Second,* what we say must be meaningful. It must be significant. It must be related to the world around us. Our ideas must be relevant not only to our own situation here at home, but to the requirements of people everywhere. In fact, those who have been great in our history have been the men who have spoken out in behalf of universal concepts of freedom, equality, and social justice which can be embraced by people everywhere. *Third,* what we say must be socially significant. Speech must be used as a means to some social end. It must throw light on, or provide some answers to the problems that perplex us. Our ideas must be honestly conceived, meaningfully and frequently stated, and practiced so that they become self-operating. Speech can be used as an instrument of tyranny, of deception, and of self-congratulation, but it can also be used as an instrument of enlightenment. Let us use it in this latter sense as we seek the truth, as we attach meaning to life, and as we see ourselves as socially responsible individuals.

ADAPTED READING 1.2

MASTERS OF ELOQUENCE— AND OF MEN
André Maurois

It has been said that one speech may be worth three divisions. And history seems to confirm this. Throughout man's past there have been decisive moments when a certain kind of eloquence succeeded in releasing an immense force, setting people in motion and inspiring them with the will to action.

Is such eloquence a thing of the past; are present-day statesmen incapable of it? The applause spreading out from the General Assembly floor to government officials, commentators and ordinary men and women all over the world after President Kennedy's recent speech to the U.N. indicates that contemporary leaders still have the power to voice the fears and hopes and to stir the hearts of men.

"Together," he said, "we shall save our planet or together we shall perish in its flames. Save it we can and save it we must, and then shall we earn the eternal thanks of mankind and, as peacemakers, the eternal blessing of God." In this, as in many other parts of the thirty-minute address ("Mankind must put an end to war or war will put an end to mankind. . . ."), he echoed the solemn, impassioned tone of his own inaugural speech, already a kind of classic, which has recalled to many Lincoln's Gettysburg Address.

Mr. Kennedy's inaugural address included such fine turns of phrase as, "that uncertain balance of terror." It was full of rhythmic and perfectly constructed periods; for example, "We dare not tempt them with weakness. For only when our arms are sufficient beyond doubt can we be certain beyond doubt that they will never be employed"; or, "Ask not what your country can do for you—ask what you can do for your country," and the memorable apothegm, which he restated in the U.N. address: "Let us never negotiate out of fear. But let us never fear to negotiate. . . ."

Schoolday memories of famous speeches by famous men notwithstanding, there was never an age when all statesmen wrote well. Demosthenes and Cicero stood out from a group of colleagues who offered them little competition. The French Revolution produced innumerable orators, but posterity remembers only Mirabeau, Danton, Vergniaud, Robespierre, and Saint-Just. Our time, too, has its masters of language.

The world has never heard more sublime words than Winston Churchill's: "We shall not flag or fail. We shall go on to the end, we shall fight in France, we shall fight on the seas and oceans, we shall fight with growing confidence and growing strength in the air; we shall defend our island, whatever the cost may be; we shall fight on the beaches, we shall fight in the fields and in the streets, we shall fight in the hills"; and so on until the final promise that, if need be, the Empire "would carry on the struggle until, in God's good time, the New World, with all its power and might, steps forth to the rescue and liberation of the Old. . . ."

Spoken by someone else in less stirring circumstances, the same words might produce less of an effect. But when the time is right and, through the words, the vigor and resolution of a great man are discernible, a stirring speech can have great influence. Style is the child of opportunity.

Winston Churchill's power has been matched, in France, by General de Gaulle's. Here again tragic events brought forth a man capable of dominating them and enlisting popular support through his words. Like Churchill, de Gaulle writes admirable prose.

Despite the classic ring of their prose, both these statesmen and masters of style often delight in using more popular expressions. The reader may remember the words of welcome spoken by the President of the French Republic to Mr. Krushchev at the time of his first (the good) trip to Paris: "Well, here you are!" Or Churchill's retort when, in 1940, men of little faith had said that in three weeks' time England would have her neck wrung like a chicken. After quoting the remark, he added: "Some chicken; some neck. . . ."

The art of being familiar is particularly necessary in these days of radio and TV, where the problem is not to rouse a crowd to enthusiasm but to convince each citizen in his own home. Franklin Delano Roosevelt was the great master of the fireside chat; General de Gaulle proved in the course of two referendums that he knows the way to the hearts and minds of the great mass of citizens without descending to demagogy. He is sensitive to the pattern of common speech and uses colloquial expressions ("Well, then? So what! Come on!").

In the past speeches were almost always addressed to assemblies of professional politicians. This kind of audience relished the subtlety of political reference and the nicety of classical allusion that would leave an average contemporary listener unmoved, if not uncomprehending. . . . Then, too, people took pleasure in a well-developed metaphor, like Disraeli's "The Right Honorable Gentleman caught the Whigs bathing and walked away with their clothes. He has left them in full enjoyment of their liberal position and he is himself a strict conservative of their garments. . . ."

In America today, the humor of Adlai Stevenson is probably the nearest approach to Benjamin Disraeli's. . . . I remember hearing Stevenson, during an election speech, remark that his opponent, General Eisenhower, seemed to be taking credit for measures that were in reality those of the New Deal. "I've been tempted," he went on, "to say that I was proud to stand on that record, if only the General would move over and make room for me." It was amusing and felicitous, but few of the people around me got the joke. The general public is on the whole sentimental and serious-minded. For example, it gave Nixon an ovation when, as candidate for the Vice-Presidency, he defended his family life, his modest home, his wife and children, in homely, touching terms. . . .

Arthur Schlesinger, Jr., recalls that at the time Governor Landon stood as Presidential candidate against F. D. R., "he was convinced that his very flatness as a political performer might constitute a campaign virtue." Landon noted, "The American people have always been fearful in the end of a great man." He wanted to be "the everyday American whose very lack of polish attested his sincerity." And a supporter sent this message, "Do urge Governor Landon not to try to improve his delivery."

We have heard remarks of the same kind in England. The Duke of Devonshire was so boring a speaker that he yawned during his own speeches. . . . He would have readily agreed with the remark which another British statesman made to the writer after a very uninspiring speech: "It's safe to be dull!"

It may be safe, but it is not always effective; for the upshot was that it was not Governor Landon who was elected President of the United States but Franklin Roosevelt, who could find such striking formulas as, "The only thing we have to fear is fear itself"; "Governments can err; Presidents do make mistakes, but the immortal Dante tells us that divine justice weighs the sins of the cold-blooded and the sins of the warm-hearted in different scales"; "We now know that government by organized money is just as dangerous as government by organized mobs."

In fact, it is not the tedious Ribot, Premier and insipid writer, who saved France during World War I, but the brilliant Clemenceau, a great journalist and great orator. It was not Neville Chamberlain, an honest man with no command of language, who saved Britain in World War II, but the stylist Winston Churchill. And who but Lincoln, an admirable writer, saved the United States from the secession which would have meant the collapse of the nation? . . .

There are brief moments in the life of nations when it gives the people pleasure to hear: "The chief business of the American people is business"; or again, "What is good for our country is good for General Motors and vice versa." There are other times when "the old unctuousness, the old pulpit vagueness, the hackneyed phrases" are tolerated. But such moments are fleeting. Very soon the time comes when everyone thinks and says: "Now he is crossing the thirty-eighth Platitude again!" It is then that the whole nation awaits a chief who has some distinction of style, for it seems to feel that the worth of a statesman's character is often equivalent to the excellence of his prose.

ADAPTED READING **1.3**
FREE SPEECH, PERSUASION, AND THE DEMOCRATIC PROCESS
Thomas R. Nilsen

Since the advent of mass advertising, professional public relations, and motivation research, persuasion has been used on a scale of such magnitude with techniques of such refinement as to raise with renewed urgency the problem of its relationship to traditional democratic principles. . . .

To those of us who have lived our lives in a democratic society the democratic process may seem to be a pattern of simple and natural ways of organizing the political relationships of men. We may readily take for granted its methods, its values, its opportunities. Yet that this process is complex and difficult is attested to by the slow and laborious way societies learn to live by such means, and by the ways in which . . . democracy can undermine itself in the name of democracy. . . .

If democracy is to function, ideas need to be expressed, the ideas need to be critically examined, the best ideas need to be found, and these ideas need to be accepted by the people if they are to be effectively translated into policies. For the expression of ideas we have freedom of speech and assembly, and freedom of the press. That ideas may be examined, understood, and tested, we have discussion and debate, and tests of evidence upon which all can agree. To gain acceptance of ideas we have persuasion. Since issues are complex, interests widely disparate, and apathy only too common, persuasion plays an important part. And herein lies our problem. Persuasion can take many forms, and it can have varied effects. . . .

Persuasion, the inducement in others of belief or action, is an essential part of any society, for ultimately government . . . rests upon some form of support in public opinion. In a democratic society regular procedures exist to make that public opinion instrumental in affecting government. The influencing and shaping of this public opinion then becomes of extreme importance. . . . The use of professional PR and ad men in campaigns during the past decade

From *The Quarterly Journal of Speech*, October 1958, pp. 235–243.

has intensified some of the old and introduced some new problems for democratic society. . . .

Historically, the PR man's role has been primarily to create and foster favorable attitudes toward a business or a product. Higher sales and increased profits have been the immediate and the ultimate objectives, but there have been by-products of various kinds. . . . It has also given rise to many skills and techniques in influencing public opinion . . . in as short a time as possible and as inexpensively as practicable. All possible short-cuts are taken, the most telling appeals are used, the critical faculties are bypassed as much as possible. There is in commercial selling, it would appear, a built-in bias toward simplicity and emotional appeal, and against complexity and critical appraisal. It is the past decade that has seen a dramatic introduction of these methods of merchandising on a mass scale into the area of political campaigning.

The editor of *Tide*, an ad and sales publication, remarked during the 1952 campaign that "advertising demonstrated beyond question that it can sell a good idea as successfully as it can sell a good product." Among the many techniques used in the selling of ideas and candidates I shall briefly point up seven: the concentration on "issues," the emphasis on attack, the use of timing, the use of the "appeal beyond politics" and the "negative appeal," the elimination of debate, and the mass distribution of ideas. These methods, of course, frequently overlap, and are often used in combination.

The concentration on issues is sometimes explained by the PR professional as education. For instance, Leone Baxter of the Whitaker and Baxter team says:

> It's because the public relations profession, and its allied professions, know something about presenting abstract ideas in attractive form to masses of people who are too occupied with their daily lives to think analytically on their own account, that the average man of today is in a position to know more about the trends of human affairs than ever before in history. . . .

But the issues on which the campaign concentrates are usually, if not always, the issues chosen by, or at least shaped by, the propaganda specialist for their impact value, and by no means necessarily because they are the real or significant issues in the campaign.

Closely related to the emphasis on "issues" is the emphasis in the campaign on attack. "To attack is to press on the public," says Mr. Whitaker, "the issues that are to one's advantage. To attack is not just to give one's side of the question but to *define* the political situation." A powerful attack forces the opposition to reply and to explain, and, further, the attacked group is not able to get to the issues it considers important, or is able to get to them only after wasteful expenditure of time and resources.

In campaigns careful use is also frequently made of timing. Campaigns are given a sense of movement or build-up which has nothing in particular to do with the importance of the issues. The mass media of communication permit such a steady build-up of intensity and enable the arousing of maximum interest and excitement just before the elections. One firm reserves about 75% of its expenditures in a campaign for the final three weeks before the voters go to the polls. . . .

Through the mass media a great many people are reached, but they are not likely to be giving close or continuous attention to what they read or hear. As a consequence, for maximum effect issues are condensed into themes or slogans to catch the attention of the indifferent voter and to make the issues able to compete with the other mass media content such as sports, soap operas, and murder mysteries. . . . Mr. Whitaker . . . sums up his basic philosophy:

> The average American, when you catch him after hours, as we must, doesn't want to be educated; he doesn't want to improve his mind; he doesn't want to work, consciously, at being a good citizen. But there are two ways you can interest him in a campaign, and only two that we have ever found successful.
>
> Most every American loves a *contest*. He likes a good hot battle, with no punches pulled. He likes the clash of arms. *So you can interest him if you put on a fight! No matter what you fight for, fight for something.* . . .
>
> Then, too, most every American likes to be entertained. He likes the movies; he likes mysteries; he likes fireworks and parades. He likes Jack Benny and Bob Hope and Joe E. Brown! So if you can't fight, PUT ON A SHOW! And if you put on a good show, Mr. and Mrs. America will turn out to see it.

In order to compete with entertainment on the mass media, Campaigns Incorporated, the Whitaker and Baxter firm, makes politics entertainment. . . .

Fundamental to the public relations man's approach is the elimination of debate and of competing propaganda. In 1949 the *Dallas Medical Journal* carried some advice from Whitaker and Baxter. . . .

> We do not believe it is sound campaign procedure to sponsor too many debates. They would make a forum for the opposition which would be difficult for them to secure otherwise, and they are too easily stacked. This is particularly true of broadcasts to the public. . . .

Closely related to the elimination of debate . . . is the method of mass distribution of "ideas." This method is simply that of providing almost endless repetition of the so-called issue and virtually crowding out competing ideas. Some indication of how this method is used is provided by Whitaker's description of media used for a ballot proposition in 1948. In that year, to publicize one issue to California's 4½ million voters Whitaker's firm put out 10 million pamphlets and leaflets, 4½ million postcards, 500,000 letters, 70,000 inches of newspaper display advertising in 700 daily and weekly newspapers, theatre slides and trailers in 160 theatres playing to nearly 2 million people each week, 3,000 radio spot announcements on 109 radio stations, plus radio programs, billboards, posters, speeches, etc., reaching millions of people.

What are the implications for the democratic process of the persuasive techniques used in this growing business of merchandizing government?

THOMAS R. NILSEN

It might be argued that the philosophy and methods . . . described here have long been the stock in trade of politicians in a democratic society. And this is true, with some significant differences. The politician has not previously had available to him the mass media to the degree that a well-financed public relations firm now has, nor has the politician had the professional skills and contacts necessary to use the mass media to capacity. A modern public relations firm has the accumulated experience of many professional propagandists. . . .

A difference too can be noted in the place of the press in modern society. Political issues traditionally have been given publicity through a free press and not by professional propagandists. Now, however, as Mr. Kelley points out, "For the public relations man the press and the other media are not only distributors of information but instruments of social control, and the media have for various reasons been forced to accept this estimate of themselves. . . ."

The scope or extent of the social control function of the press is indicated by a *Fortune* magazine statement that now "nearly half the content of the nation's better newspapers comes from publicity releases." Publicity releases, we may remind ourselves, are not random revelations of information but statements carefully chosen for the effect they will have.

There is a difference too in the relationships of the present-day professional persuader to the issues and to the people he persuades. The politician by himself at least had some direct contact with his constituents. He was or might become their official representative, and out of this relationship there grew at least some sense of direct responsibility. The ad man brought in to sell a candidate sees the candidate and the voters with much greater impartiality. He has a product to sell, and the voters are buyers. As one ad man put it, "I think of a man in a voting booth who hesitates between two levers as if he were pausing between competing tubes of toothpaste in a drugstore. . . . The brand that has made the highest penetration on his brain will win his choice. . . ."

So much for the differences between modern public relations technique and traditional political persuasion. Now what of the processes of persuasion as seen in professional public relations and their relationships to the democratic process? Certainly a basic principle in the larger democratic process is that of majority rule. This principle implies that large numbers of citizens must make definite choices, often on gravely complex issues. If freedom of choice is to have meaning there must be adequate information upon which to base the choice. . . . Most of the persuasive methods of professional public relations and ad men have the net effect of reducing the opportunities for free and rational choice based on adequate information. . . . Perhaps the most serious violation of the basic principle comes in the implication that the truth is being told, that the issues are simple. . . .

Coupled with the lack of significant information, the oversimplification of issues, and the selection of issues for their propaganda value is the deliberate attempt to avoid competing ideas. This is done by deliberately avoiding public discussion and debate, by forcing the opposition to answer attacks, and by overpowering opposing views by sheer massiveness of material and by continuous presentation of views. Such techniques, of course, directly violate the basic principles of constructive debate so important to the democratic process. As Walter Lippmann has put it in *The Public Philosophy:*

> Freedom of speech has become a central concern of the Western society because of the discovery among the Greeks that dialectic, as demonstrated in the Socratic dialogues, is a principal method of attaining truth, and particularly a method of attaining moral and political truth. . . . The method of dialectic is to confront ideas with opposing ideas in order that the pro and con of the dispute will lead to true ideas. . . .

and elsewhere:

> Thus the essence of freedom of opinion is not mere toleration as such, but in the debate which toleration provides. . . . We must insist that free oratory is only the beginning of free speech; it is not the end, but a means to an end. The end is to find the truth. The practical justification of civil liberty is not that self-expression is one of the rights of man. It is that the examination of opinions is one of the necessities of man.

The need for the opposition of ideas is one of the basic tenets of the democratic faith. . . . With the use of modern PR methods employing the media of the press, radio, and television, the process of debate is circumscribed . . . to a degree never before seen in our democratic society. . . . To the side with the most money to buy the most favorable time goes the opportunity for the maximum saturation with its ideas with the least possibility of competition. . . .

The reply might be made that this is simply another manifestation of the democratic process. Suppose the views are partisan; in the competition of the market the best views will prevail. The citizen still has a choice. If it were true that opposing sides were nearly equally represented by PR firms this might be partially true. But then we would have the interesting spectacle of a political struggle being waged not between candidates and issues but between public relations professionals, which would make success very much dependent upon financial backing and propaganda skills. It would be highly doubtful whether the significant issues in the campaign would ever be presented. . . .

. . . There is also the problem of individual responsibility for what is said. . . . There are rules of evidence and of parliamentary procedure, and codes of fair dealing and fair comment, by which the loyal man will consider himself bound when he exercises the right to publish opinions. There has been a strong tendency in our society to escape personal responsibility for what is said by retreat to the traditional position that it is the competition of the market place that will determine which ideas have merit. . . .

The persuasive techniques in question are also inconsistent with the democratic process in that they tend to eliminate checks and balances. . . . Prior to the day of publicity releases in volume, prior to press, radio, and TV chains, there were more checks and balances in the form of more independent and diversified press coverage, more direct contact with constituents, more confrontation in debate. With millions of listeners and viewers reached at once, with money to buy the time of favorite shows, with money to print fabulous amounts of literature, with a predetermined point of view on the part of major PR agencies, the checks and balances have been drastically reduced . . . .

Further, the persuasive techniques we have discussed are inconsistent with the fundamental democratic view that the human being is inviolable, that he is not to be treated as a thing, as a means, but as a person, as an end. . . . The more the reader or listener can be made to respond in fear or anger, the more readily he responds to suggestion, the less he makes use of his critical faculties, the less he is induced to inform himself, the more successful the PR and ad men are. In other words, the fewer the distinctly human qualities of reason, self-determination, individuality which men develop, the better for the political advertising profession. And the worse for democracy, which is based on the assumption that citizens can and will make informed and rational choices.

Fundamental to the whole problem of persuasion in a democratic society is the problem of ends and means. . . . Persuasive techniques are usually classed as means, means to some end which may be good or bad. . . . When being persuaded a man is not only influenced directly or indirectly in his choice of a course of action, he is influenced in his *method of making the choice.* . . .

In a democratic society — I do not think it can be denied — the method of decision is vital; *how* we go about making up our minds is vital. Whether we vote for a particular candidate in a particular election may not be momentous for democracy, but how we make up our minds about candidates is indeed momentous. By constantly limiting the critical faculties in making a decision we are limiting the basis upon which it is possible to have a responsible citizenry, and thus we weaken the very foundations of democracy.

There is, of course, no intention here of implying that all human behavior should or can be completely "rational." Today we are aware that our behavior results from a large variety of motivations; our needs, desires, anxieties, conscious and unconscious, play an important part in what we do. We also know, however, that much careful, reflective, critical thought is needed on the part of all citizens, leaders and followers alike, if we are to deal with our myriad domestic and foreign problems within the democratic framework. . . .

Most of the average citizen's political actions consist of making choices between alternatives presented to him. When we determine how he makes his choices, we determine to a large extent the kind of person he is and the kind of citizen he is, whether he is a person who grows in his ability to make rational choices and develops the capacities that make him truly a man, or whether he tends toward the robot whose control buttons substitute for independent choice. And we determine whether as a citizen he strengthens the democratic community or weakens it.

Freedom of speech, which includes the freedom to persuade, imposes on everyone who exercises that right an obligation to use speech so that it becomes a carrier of freedom. "Free speech is promoted by the kind of speech that makes men free."

ADDITIONAL READINGS

Fortas, Abe, *Concerning Dissent and Civil Disobedience* (New York: Signet Special Broadside, 1968).

Haiman, Franklyn S., *Freedom of Speech, Issues and Cases* (New York: Random House, 1965).

Johannesen, Richard L., *Ethics and Persuasion, Selected Readings* (New York: Random House, 1967), Part I, "Overview," and Part II, "The Democratic Premise."

Langer, Susanne K., "The Origins of Speech and Its Communicative Function," *Quarterly Journal of Speech*, XLVI (April 1960), 121–134.

McCroskey, James C., *An Introduction to Rhetorical Communication* (Englewood Cliffs, N.J.: Prentice-Hall, 1972), chap. 2, "The Nature of Rhetorical Communication."

Nilsen, Thomas R., *Ethics of Speech Communication* (Indianapolis: Bobbs-Merrill, 1966).

O'Neil, Robert M., *Free Speech: Responsible Communication Under Law* (Indianapolis: Bobbs-Merrill, 1972).

Rice, George P., *Law for the Public Speaker* (Boston: Christopher Publishing House, 1958).

STUDY QUESTIONS AND EXERCISES

1. What is the "clear and present danger" test?
2. What is meant by *breach of the peace*?
3. What is obscenity? Is it constitutionally protected?
4. How do time, place, and manner of speaking affect the individual's right to free speech?
5. What is defamation? libel? slander?
6. Is truth always a defense against libel and slander?
7. In the United States, who owns the broadcasting airwaves?
8. Why is Section 315 of the Federal Communications Act important?
9. Do noncampus speakers have a constitutional right to speak at colleges and universities if they wish?
10. What ethical responsibilities must speakers assume if the democratic process is to flourish?
11. What is your opinion on each of the following questions:
    a. Should a democratic government allow complete freedom of expression to persons espousing unpopular causes? dangerous causes? antidemocratic viewpoints?
    b. Should there be any legal restraints on public speakers who advocate atheism? communism? fascism?
    c. Can society be trusted to see through the claims of demagogues and subversive speakers?
    d. Should Communists be allowed to address college students?
    e. Should our laws against libel and slander be strengthened?
    f. Do we need federal legislation to prevent profanity and obscenity on the airwaves?
    g. Should college students refrain from publicly criticizing their schools?

h. Is a speaker justified in promoting discontent, dissension, and demonstrations?

i. Does a speaker have an ethical responsibility to avoid highly controversial subjects?

j. Do most college students believe strongly in freedom of speech?

12. Project: Prepare a short questionnaire designed to discover the attitudes of students at your school toward (1) free speech, (2) academic freedom, (3) restrictions on outside speakers appearing on campus, or some other related topic. Administer the questionnaire to 20 students.

INTERPERSONAL
SPEECH
COMMUNICATION

Considering how much talking a person does and the variety of ways he uses speech in his daily life, it is surprising how little attention most people give to the way in which they speak. Even people in jobs or professions where success depends on their ability to communicate with others often have little understanding of the speech process. Perhaps this is because, like walking, most people have spoken so much and so often since first learning to talk that they simply accept the fact that they can speak and only rarely stop to think about how, why, and when they do it. Sometimes this unconcern can prevent a person from recognizing and eliminating the causes of some of his difficulties with speech. If things go wrong, the individual tends to blame others when, in fact, it may be his own communication inadequacies that have caused or contributed to the problem. To improve communication and reduce the likelihood of communication breakdowns, speakers need to understand the speech process.

IMPORTANCE OF EFFECTIVE SPEECH COMMUNICATION

A first step toward better communication is to develop an appreciation for the importance of speech in one's daily activity. The student should recognize that speech communication does not refer only to public addresses such as lectures, sermons, and political talks. While such speaking is important, the average person spends much more of his time communicating in less formal speech situations.

During a typical week, the average person is likely to engage in spoken communication with members of his family, friends, co-workers, supervisors or employees, servicemen, repairmen, waiters, waitresses, receptionists, cashiers, professional consultants such as doctors, lawyers, dentists, and educators, as well as many others. The communication may consist of making a telephone call, ordering lunch, arranging a business transaction, making a purchase, visiting a doctor, giving directions or advice, asking for information or help, explaining a problem to a mechanic or repairman, participating in a class discussion, or conversing at a party or meeting, to mention only a few examples.

> In the United States there are more than twenty thousand different ways of earning a living and effective speech is essential to every one.
>
> ANDREW WEAVER

To regard these situations as mundane, everyday events of little significance is a mistake. A breakdown in communication can easily result in a bitter argument, confusion in carrying out an assignment, incorrect servicing of an automobile or appliance, the loss of a sale, the irritation of a friend, or some other frustrating or disappointing development.

Saul Alinsky, who spent most of his life teaching people how to organize and influence others, emphasizes the importance of communication in person-to-person encounters. Although he is referring specifically to organizers, his words are applicable to other communication situations:

> One can lack any of the qualities of an organizer—with one exception—and still be effective and successful. That exception is the art of communication. It does not matter what you know about anything if you cannot communicate to your people. In that event you are not even a failure. You're just not there.
>
> Communication with others takes place when they understand what you're trying to get across to them. If they don't understand, then you are not communicating regardless of words, pictures, or anything else.

FUNCTIONS OF SPEECH COMMUNICATION

Speech communication fulfills many functions and purposes. Probably the most important use of speech is to influence others. In almost all spoken discourse, the speaker—consciously or unconsciously—seeks to affect the listener in some way: to provide him with information; to modify or change his attitudes, beliefs, or conduct; to entertain, amuse, or attract him; to strengthen his resolve or conviction; to conciliate or antagonize him; or to win his respect, friendship, or support. Except for those infrequent occasions when the individual expresses his feelings in a totally spontaneous manner — such as "Ouch!" or something stronger when he hits his thumb with a hammer — virtually all speech communication is purposive. Because speech is purposive, it is important to the individual in fulfilling his needs and wants and in understanding and responding to the needs and wants of others.

From a psychological point of view, speech communication is important to the individual in the self-realization of his goals, in his acceptance and expression of his own personality, and in his adjustment to society. It is easy to imagine the frustration and sense of futility a person would feel if he were unable to communicate to others, if he were forever condemned to be a silent observer whose existence was hardly acknowledged and whose opinion was never sought or heard. Speech communication contributes to social growth and psychological stability by enabling the individual to make known his ideas and feelings, to proclaim his existence, and to learn to adjust and adapt to his environment and society.

From a broader perspective, speech communication serves an important function in the preservation of one's heritage, the transmission of cultural values and ideals, and the maintenance of social cohesion. To a large extent, it is through the spoken word that beliefs, traditions, customs, mores, and sense of social identity are reinforced and passed from one generation to the next in any culture.

ESSENTIAL ELEMENTS OF SPEECH COMMUNICATION

Scholars in a variety of fields have advanced definitions and descriptions to explain the process of oral communication. Their approaches differ and their terminology is not the same. The purpose of this textbook is not to provide an exhaustive review of all the different theories of communication nor to advance the merits of one approach over another, but rather to provide the student with basic information concerning the nature of oral communication and those elements which most scholars agree are involved in the speech process.

Regardless of their terminology, most scholars would agree that speech communication involves at least four essential elements: the source, the message, the channel, and the receiver.

The Source

In spoken communication, the source is a speaker. Communication is possible without a speaker, but *speech communication* is not. Clocks, speedometers, calendars, traffic signals, fog horns, thermometers, sirens, and class bells communicate, but these are not forms of speech communication and, of course, do not require a speaker. Newspapers, magazines, books, letters, billboards, signs, blueprints, labels, shorthand, sign language, braille, semiphore, and Morse code are also forms of communication, but none of them requires a speaker for transmission of their messages.

Distinguishing between forms of communication in which a speaker is the source of information and other types of communication is important in understanding the speech process.

The Message
In addition to a source, another element essential to speech communication is a message. The message is the expression by the speaker of his ideas through the use of symbols. A distinction should be made between the source's ideas and the message. So long as the source merely *thinks* his ideas without actually uttering them, no message exists.

Only when the speaker takes deliberate action to communicate his ideas audibly does a message come into being. The message can be said to consist of those disturbances, alterations, or disruptions of the physical environment set in motion by the speaker for the purpose of conveying his ideas to someone else.

The Channel
The third essential element of speech communication, the channel, may be defined as the means, medium, or instruments used to convey the message. Conceivably, the source might elect to convey his message through smoke signals, sign language, Morse code, semiphore, or any of several other channels, all capable of carrying a message. However, in spoken communication the source depends upon the audible and visible symbols of human speech. The audible symbols are the sounds the speaker makes by vibrating the vocal cords and manipulating the tongue, lips, teeth, palate, and breath supply. The visible symbols include the speaker's facial expressions, gestures, eye contact, movements, and other physical characteristics which reinforce or modify the meaning of the words and sentences.

The Receiver
The final element essential to spoken communication is a receiver of the message. The receiver is more commonly called the listener, hearer, or auditor, but receiver is probably a more accurate term because the person to whom a message is directed does more than passively listen to or hear the message. He also perceives the physical attributes and activities of the source and influences the speaker by his own reactions and responses.

CHARACTERISTICS OF SPEECH COMMUNICATION
Speech communication is unlike any other form of communication. Although it shares common characteristics with other modes of communication, several factors make it unique. To clarify its unusual nature, the principal characteristics of speech communication are discussed below.

Speech Is Purposive
Almost every word that man utters is said with a definite purpose in mind. From a simple request such as "Please pass the salt" to a classroom discussion, a conversation, a committee meeting, a sermon, a campaign speech, or

a ceremonial oration, most speaking springs from a desire to obtain a specific response from the listener or listeners. Except for language whose purpose is purely self-expression ("What a beautiful morning!"), all oral communication aims to achieve one of five goals — to inform, to convince, to persuade, to inspire, or to entertain.

If the speaker's aim is to inform, he wants the listener to understand and remember what he says. In trying to convince, the speaker's goal is to alter the beliefs or attitudes of the auditor. Persuasive speaking goes a step further and seeks to influence the conduct or future actions of the hearer. Inspirational speeches aim to enhance and strengthen beliefs and attitudes already held by the listener. If the speaker's aim is to entertain, he seeks simply to provide enjoyment and relaxation for the auditor.

Speech Involves Interaction

Except for a few situations, speech communication is characterized by an interaction between two or more individuals: the source and the receiver or receivers. The exceptions to this general statement consist of situations such as a talk that is broadcast from a studio where no listeners are present, a closed-circuit television lecture, an announcement over a public address system in an office, school, or business, or the dictating of a message into a recording machine. Even in these situations, it is possible that technicians or aides present might provide some form of response or feedback which could influence the speaker.

But the above exceptions are not representative of most interpersonal discourse. Speech communication usually occurs in face-to-face situations where the speaker can observe his auditors and vice versa. It is important to recognize that when both the speaker and the listener face each other directly, the source-message-receiver relationship differs significantly from that of written communication. Written communication is largely a one-way process, while speech involves an interaction between the source and the receiver. In writing, the source (writer) expresses his message with no indication of how the receiver (reader) will respond to it. If he is a capable and perceptive writer, he will probably try to anticipate possible reader reactions and to present the message in such a way that it will obtain the response he desires. But he has no way of *knowing* anything about his prospective readers' reactions and, once the message is committed to paper, no way of adjusting or adapting to their responses.

The speaker, however, has the distinct advantage of having the receiver present and directly in front of him. As he speaks he is constantly receiving cues from the auditor. The cue may be in the form of a yawn, a smile, a laugh, a look of confusion, an expression of boredom, nervous fidgeting, an appearance of interest, a shaking of the head, inattention, alertness, note-taking, interruptions, questions, or any other indication of the receiver's feelings. With large groups, the cues may include such overt responses as applause, booing, heckling, hisses, and cheers.

These reactions, known as *feedback*, provide the source with information on how well he is communicating. The capable speaker will take these cues into consideration and modify or adapt his message in an effort to improve the effectiveness of his communication or to maintain the interest and enthusiasm he has generated.

Even the most inept and inexperienced speaker probably cannot entirely escape the influence of these cues from the listener. Although he may not be skillful enough to make the adjustments necessary to obtain the response he desires, he probably is at least partially aware of how well he is getting his message across to the auditor.

This interaction, this flow of information back and forth between the source and the receiver in speech communication is an important aid to the speaker in achieving effective communication.

Speech Is Transitory

Unlike a book, newspaper, magazine, or other printed document, speech is fleeting. Once a spoken message has been uttered, it is not likely to be repeated and cannot be reread or picked up at leisure for review or study. Only the smallest fraction of all the oral communication that takes place in one day is recorded or reproduced in print. This means that if the auditor is to grasp the speaker's meaning and to respond in the manner desired, the stimulus for his response must be provided at the time the speech is given. Unlike written communication, the listener exercises little control over the conditions that may affect his reception of the speaker's message: He cannot choose a time when he is more alert; he cannot change the temperature if he is uncomfortable; he is unable to look up the meaning of unfamiliar words or to ponder complex concepts; he possesses no control over the rate at which the speaker speaks; he cannot review difficult passages; and he often can do nothing to eliminate distracting elements.

The listener's lack of control over the speaking situation forces the speaker to anticipate any problems that may detract from the effectiveness of his communication. He must devise and present his message in such a manner that the auditor is able to understand and respond to his ideas at the time, for if the listener is not influenced in the desired manner at that time, it is virtually certain that later he will not react as the speaker wishes.

Speech Occurs in Specific Settings

Few people probably know where, when, and under what circumstances Ernest Hemingway wrote *A Farewell to Arms*, Mozart composed *The Marriage of Figaro*, Rembrandt painted *The Night Watch*, Samuel Goldwyn filmed *Gone with the Wind*, or George Schultz draws his "Peanuts" cartoons. Yet all of these communicate messages and have provided countless persons with pleasure, inspiration, and ideas. As is true of much communication, an individual's responses to these works are not dependent upon the circumstances surrounding their creation.

A distinctive feature of speech communication, however, is that its effectiveness may be greatly influenced by the place, time, and conditions of its expression. As discussed earlier, speech is both purposive and transitory. It is designed for a specific purpose and a specific receiver or receivers at a specific time. Because of this, the result of any oral communication venture is often greatly affected by the specific setting in which it occurs.

Certain times, places, and occasions restrict a speaker's choice of messages and manner of presentation. A religious service, bridal shower, funeral, birthday party, retirement banquet, pep rally, inauguration ceremony, or wedding are all occasions in which the mood of the participants may render certain subjects and kinds of communication inappropriate. The place where the communication occurs—a courtroom, office, church, fraternity house, home, auditorium, street corner, dormitory room, legislative chamber, classroom, or restaurant—may also influence the type and manner of communication of a speaker. The size of the room, seating arrangements, acoustics, lighting, heating, and the number of people present may affect the listeners' receptiveness to a speaker's message. Even the décor may contribute to a speaker's success or failure: a flag and red, white, and blue bunting; stained glass windows and religious symbols; a dim, dark, run-down hall; or a brightly lit, colorful, and plushly furnished setting can create an atmosphere either conducive or detrimental to a speaker's purpose.

Time—time of day, time of year—can be important. Many people are not fully awake early in the morning, many are tired and drowsy late at night, and most people tend to be somewhat lethargic immediately following a meal. All of these factors affect a listener's receptiveness to messages and must be taken into account by the speaker. In addition, people's interests tend to vary according to the time of year. In the winter, people are more likely to be interested in skiing, Christmas, football bowl games, and snowmobiles than at other times of the year. Camping trips, air conditioning, vacations, baseball, picnics, yard care, and swimming are topics of more immediate interest to most persons in the summer than at any other season. In the spring, thoughts turn to planting, Easter, outdoor activities, and plans for the summer. Fall for many people is the season for the reopening of school, raking leaves, football, and elections.

Particular events may affect the listener's attitude and interest at various times. Holidays such as Halloween, Thanksgiving, St. Patrick's Day, the Fourth of July, Mardi Gras, and Labor Day may create interest in a subject. Events such as the World Series, the Kentucky Derby, the Super Bowl, the Indianapolis 500, and a championship boxing match may serve to focus attention on a sport. A crisis, scandal, or sensational trial; a hurricane, flood, or other natural disaster; the death or assassination of a prominent figure may lead to a greater interest and concern about these topics on the part of most people than they would otherwise feel.

Speech communication does not occur in a vacuum. Effective speech communication takes into account and adapts to the time, place, and circumstances of the speech setting.

Speech Is Influenced by the Fields of Experience of the Participants

Edgar Dale, in Adapted Reading 16.1, reports a conversation between a rabid baseball fan and an Englishman seeing a baseball game for the first time.

The Englishman asked, "What is a pitcher?"

"He's the man down there pitching the ball to the catcher."

"But," said the Englishman, "all of the players pitch the ball and all of them catch the ball. There aren't just two persons who pitch and catch."

Later the Englishman asked, "How many strikes do you get before you are out?"

The baseball fan said, "Three."

"But," replied the Englishman, "that man struck at the ball five times before he was out."

This conversation is an example of communication that ran into difficulty because the participants lacked a common field of experience. Neither one was actually wrong. Both agreed generally on what the words "pitch," "catch," and "strike" meant, but because of differences in their background and experience the terms did not have precisely the same meaning for the two of them.

Because words are symbols, language can produce common understanding only if the words mean the same to both the source and the receiver of the message. When the source and the receiver attach different meanings to a word or words, the result is a misunderstanding—even though the two parties may not realize it.

Words mean different things to different people because of differences in their experience or field of experience. In spite of the tremendous advances in mass communications in recent years, the civilian whose field of experience with war consists of what he has seen on television and read in the press cannot have the same understanding of war as the veteran who was an active participant in it.

In the same way, can a person who has never been in jail fully share an ex-convict's knowledge and feelings about prison? How well can a successful executive understand the problems and attitudes of a migrant worker? Does an increase in the cost of food mean the same thing to a well-to-do suburban housewife as it does to a black mother living in a ghetto on welfare? Differences in experience not only determine each person's knowledge, understanding, and values, they also influence his priorities and values. What is important to each individual is the result of his past experience.

Because every person's understanding of the meaning of words is determined by his experiences, a speaker, in order to achieve the response he desires, must be cognizant of the background of the receiver and adapt to his field of experience. Age, sex, education, religion, nationality, cultural and ethnic background, occupation, financial status, and social acceptance will influence the receiver's understanding of a speaker's language and message.

Speech Lacks the Visual Cues of Writing

A reader can open this textbook or most other books to almost any page and he will find before him a variety of visible cues to aid him in understanding the writer's message. He will find capitalization and punctuation marks to assist him in comprehending the meanings of individual sentences. He will see indentations to show new divisions or paragraphs. Italics and boldface type may be used to emphasize important ideas. Headings and subheadings distributed throughout the text will assist him in determining the writer's pattern of organization. Although most readers are so familiar with these common writing devices that they are hardly aware of them, they are of inestimable value to the writer. Lacking visual cues, the speaker must employ other means of indicating his meaning and organization. These include inflection of the voice; pauses; changes in rate and loudness; emphasis of important words and sentences; gestures; facial expression; previews of points; transitional statements; internal summaries; and visual aids.

Speech Has a Distinctive Vocabulary

Most people have a reading vocabulary that is considerably larger than their listening vocabulary. It is not uncommon for a reader to understand printed words whose pronunciation he does not know and would not recognize if he heard them spoken. Because of the more limited vocabulary of the listener, a speaker usually has to use somewhat simpler language than does the writer.

Furthermore, today people are accustomed to speech that is more conversational and informal than written discourse. Consequently, contractions the writer might avoid may actually prove helpful to the speaker. Thus, the speaker will probably use *can't, shouldn't, aren't, I'm, we'll,* and *they're* while the writer would employ *cannot, should not, are not, I am, we will,* and *they are.* Colloquial and regional words and expressions that might detract from a written work are usually readily accepted when appropriately used in speech.

Speech and writing not only differ in the words used, but they are also often unlike in the way these words are put together into sentences. As most experienced speakers who have prepared manuscript speeches know, some passages that read well simply do not sound well when spoken aloud. They may be too involved, too complex, too lengthy, or they may be tongue-twisters—almost impossible to utter smoothly and meaningfully. To achieve a natural, conversational quality, most speakers find that short, simple sentences with few subordinate clauses are more effective than longer and more complex sentences.

Because of its distinctive vocabulary, speech cannot be viewed as the same kind of communication activity as writing. In order to achieve a natural oral quality the speaker must take care in his choice of words and construction of sentences.

THE SPEECH COMMUNICATION PROCESS

Everything discussed so far in this chapter has been included for the purpose of preparing the student to understand the elements and characteristics of speech communication. It is now time to examine the process itself.

Formulation of the Message

Speech communication begins when someone decides to express his ideas in order to influence another person. Any of many factors may motivate the speaker in reaching this decision. A desire to help, a sense of duty, a need for assistance, feelings of outrage or anger, a sense of justice, respect for truth, a wish to impress, a desire to be accepted, a challenge to one's reputation, or a need for acceptance are only a few of the possible motives that may prompt a person to wish to say something.

A variety of intrapersonal stimuli contribute to an individual's motivation to communicate with others. These intrapersonal stimuli include all those factors which contribute to the originization and formulation of the speaker's idea or message. Intrapersonal communication is the recognition, creation, reflection upon, and evaluation of a thought within the speaker's mind. In the development of his thought or message, the potential speaker is influenced by both internal and external stimuli.

Internal Stimuli. Internal stimuli are those impulses received by the brain as a result of the individual's physiological or psychological state. For example, fatigue, illness, hunger, thirst, good health, a full stomach, and physical relaxation will affect a person's perception of a situation or problem and his desire to do something about it. Psychologically, depression, shock, anxiety, happiness, enthusiasm, acceptance, frustration, and a sense of security may influence an individual's understanding and reaction to a given idea or condition.

External Stimuli. In addition to these general states of physical and mental well-being or distress, the speaker receives other specific stimuli from various sources outside his own body. These are known as external stimuli. External stimuli come to the individual through his senses — sight, hearing, smell, touch, and taste. The stimulus may be a single experience which has a profound effect upon the individual or, more commonly, a series of stimuli which in combination lead to a particular response. For example, personal observation of a fatal automobile accident might prompt one to express concern for safe driving; or, on the other hand, this same impulse might be the result of reading newspaper stories about the increase in traffic fatalities, seeing television reports of automobile accidents, and listening to a lecture on the causes of automobile accidents.

External factors shaping one's intrapersonal communication often are even less obvious than the above. The unpleasant smell of cigarette smoke in a classroom, the disagreeable taste of cafeteria food, or the boring drone of a dull teacher might subtly influence one's attitudes toward smoking regulations, the university food service, or the quality of education. Some stimuli affect people only at the unconscious level. For example, a student's attitude toward a particular course may be influenced by the poor lighting, the inadequate ventilation, the drab color of the classroom, the seating arrangement, the distracting hum of outside traffic, and other covert stimuli of which he is not consciously aware and which, in reality, have little or nothing to do with the value of the course.

External stimuli affecting one's attitudes and drive to communicate may be immediate or remote. A specific, immediate act, event, or statement may serve to motivate a person's wish to communicate his reaction or opinion. More often, the speaker's urge to express himself is the product of his entire background. While a specific event may trigger a response, the way a person reacts to any situation is usually determined by his past training and experiences.

Because everyone is the product of his environment, a single stimulus may evoke a variety of communication responses. What is accepted without a second thought by one person may arouse the indignation of another. Not only do individuals differ in the way in which they react to a stimulus; they also differ in the kinds of stimuli that they consciously perceive. For example, ask a group of people to glance out a window for a few moments and then to list what they recall having seen. Some will list items that others have overlooked. It is almost certain that no two lists will be identical. This can be explained by what is known as *selectivity* or *discrimination* in perceiving stimuli. At any given moment, everyone is bombarded by a variety of stimuli and each individual will select or consciously perceive only a limited number of the stimuli. Thus, until someone says, "I hear a faucet dripping," you may not notice it. In the same manner, each individual will perceive different stimuli which may affect his desire to communicate and influence the formulation of the ideas he wishes to express.

The stimuli of which a person is consciously aware are constantly changing. These changes are based on the immediacy or importance of the stimuli to the individual. While he perceives many stimuli—at least unconsciously—at any given moment, he allows only the more important ones to enter his consciousness.

Encoding the Message

Encoding is the process of translating thought into the audible symbols (spoken language) and visible symbols (facial expression, gestures, movement, etc.) of speech. It is highly unlikely that any two persons will select exactly the same symbols to express the same idea. The words that a speaker chooses to present his message and the physical manner in which he expresses it will differ according to the individual's perceptions, experiences, values, vocabulary, and facility with language. In addition, the context in which the communication takes place may alter the speaker's choice of language and physical expression.

A speaker who is aware of the importance of adapting his message to his listener and the occasion will encode his ideas into language suited to the attitudes and understanding of his auditor as well as to the site of the communication act. Some situations may prompt a speaker to encode his message in calm, dispassionate symbols; other circumstances may lead him to employ more emotive words and physical expressions.

Transmission of the Message

The third step in the speech communication process is the transmission of signals destined for the listener. This is the stage of the process when the speaker actually utters his ideas. In some speaking situations, the formulation and encoding of an idea may occur almost instantaneously — as when a person replies to a question or is prompted to respond immediately to something that someone has said. In prepared speeches, however, the speaker may have carefully thought through his ideas and decided how to present them well in advance of their actual transmission. Regardless of the amount of time and thought the speaker has given to the formulation and presentation of his message, communication begins only when he actually expresses his thoughts.

The transmission of the message consists of disturbing the airwaves with audible sounds (spoken language) and the light waves with physical movements (gestures, eye contact, facial expressions). These disturbances are then perceived by the receiver or listener.

Decoding of the Message

Once the message reaches the receiver, the process of decoding begins. At this point, the listener begins to play a role in the speech communication process. Depending upon what he has seen and heard (he may have missed an important word or misunderstood a key sentence because of distracting noises, poor acoustics, inattention, or any of several other reasons) and how he interprets what he has seen and heard (which will be determined by his past experiences, knowledge, and attitudes), the listener will then proceed to decode the speaker's message.

It is when the listener decodes the speaker's message that breakdowns in communication most often occur. The speaker may be at fault because he misjudged the listener's field of experience, knowledge of the subject, vocabulary, or attitudes. The listener may be at fault due to his own inattention, prejudice, or whatever. But, regardless of who is to blame, when the receiver understands a message differently from the way in which the speaker intended it to be understood, effective communication has broken down.

At the decoding stage, communication may break down for any of several reasons. One reason may be that the listener is unfamiliar with the symbols employed by the speaker. For example, if the message is communicated in a foreign language unfamiliar to the receiver, the symbols will mean nothing to him. Even when the source and the receiver speak a common language, the listener may be unable to decode the signals correctly because of the abstract nature of the language, technical terminology, or jargon. At times, the receiver may understand every word used by the speaker but interpret the message differently from the way in which the speaker intended him to because of the structure of the speaker's sentences; because of ambiguous words, phrases, and sentences having more than one meaning; or because of confusion caused by an inappropriate gesture, facial expression, or inflection used by the speaker. A communication breakdown may occur simply because the receiver thought he heard one word when, in fact, the speaker had used another. Or, finally, the listener may have difficulty decoding because he could not hear part of what the speaker said.

Interpreting the Message

As he decodes the signals transmited to him by the source, the auditor determines what he thinks the speaker's symbols mean and sends this understanding to its final destination, his own mind. If for any reason the auditor decodes the speaker's signals inaccurately, he will interpret the message incorrectly. The hearer may also transmit to his brain a message different from that intended by the source because of differences in their fields of experience. For example, a listener may understand exactly what the speaker has said but fail to respond in the way the speaker desires because he does not share with the speaker a common understanding or attitude toward the subject of the message. If, for example, a speaker urges the hearer to "take a Christian attitude," the receiver may comprehend what the speaker means but, if he is not a Christian, may fail to respond in the manner expected by the speaker. People who have never personally experienced famine, unemployment, discrimination, physical incapacity, serious illness, drought, floods, wealth, fame, success, or luxury will have a different understanding of these conditions and will respond in a different manner. Thus, although the receiver may think that he understands the speaker's ideas, he may transmit to his brain a message quite different from that intended by the source.

Interference in the Speech Communication Process

While the success of an oral communication is to a large extent dependent upon the knowledge, experiences, and values of the participants, its success may also be significantly affected by factors beyond the control of either the source or the receiver. Extraneous factors, for which neither party in the communication process has responsibility, may materially alter the speaker's effectiveness in getting his message across to the receiver.

These extraneous factors are known as *interference*, or *noise*. Most people are probably familiar with the interference caused by static during a radio broadcast, "snow" and floating pictures on the television screen, and the buzzing, clicking, and hum of a poor telephone connection, but interference is not restricted to mechanical or technical difficulties of this kind.

Interference may take many forms. One of the most common types of interference is noise: the noise of people talking, whispering, clearing their throats, coughing, shuffling their feet, or shifting position; the noise of equipment such as radiators, air conditioners, fluorescent lighting, piped-in music, or the sound of nearby typewriters or office machines; and the noise of outside traffic, honking horns, airplanes passing overhead, an ambulance siren, or a sound truck. Even the weather may provide interference in the form of rain, thunder, lightning, and gusts of wind.

At other times the interference may be visual: a light shining in one's eyes, reflections of the sun, or poor lighting in a room. The décor of a room may prove distracting if it includes signs, pictures, posters, unusual furnishings, or a view of outside activities. Even the dress or appearance of the communicator could distract the listener and thereby interfere with effective communication.

The conditions under which the communication act occurs may interfere. Cold, heat, poor ventilation, the smell of smoke or gas, or an unpleasant odor may be the cause of interference. Disrupting activities such as people coming and going, the delivery of a message, the interruption caused by a telephone call, and the seating of late-comers are other sources of interference.

Interference may even result from the presence of some particularly pleasing or fascinating distraction. The presence of a celebrity, important personage, or unusually attractive individual; the splendor or historic significance of the setting; or the tempting aroma of food emanating from a nearby room could easily distract the listener and intefere with the communication process.

In addition to these distractions which could occur in any place, interference in the public situation may result from a faulty microphone or amplifier; difficulty in seeing the speaker because of the person in front; the seating arrangement; a pillar or some other obstruction; poor acoustics; heckling, cheering, booing, hissing, and applause; or the activity of reporters, photographers, and television cameramen.

Occasionally, a momentous or tragic event preoccupies the listeners' minds to such a degree that it interferes with normal communication. The writer recalls having to suspend classes on the day of President John F. Kennedy's assassination because students were in such a state of shock and confusion that they were unable to concentrate. The end of World War II on V-J Day produced such a feeling of joy and relief that most Americans were incapable of paying attention to anything else.

Whatever the cause, interference may prevent the auditor from hearing the speaker's message or from interpreting it in the way desired by the source.

Interaction in the Speech Communication Process

In addition to those problems caused by interference in the transmission of a message from a source to a receiver, the effectiveness of speech communication is dependent upon the interaction between the speaker and the hearer. Unlike the source in most other communication situations, the speaker usually enjoys the advantage of receiving immediate, on-the-spot indications of his success or failure in transmitting his message. Except in situations such as prerecorded speeches and radio or television addresses broadcast without a studio audience, the speech communicator is in the fortunate position of being able to observe face-to-face the receivers' reactions to his message. This is an inestimable advantage to the speaker. If he is perceptive, he does not have to guess the response of the auditor; he can see it and can therefore adapt and adjust to his reaction. If the auditor seems confused, the speaker can clarify; if bored, can arouse interest; if hostile, can mollify or placate; if uncertain, can reaffirm.

Unlike most forms of communication, speech involves give and take, action and reaction. It is never static, but always moving, changing, and dynamic.

SPEECH COMMUNICATION MODELS

Now that the elements, characteristics, and process of speech communication have been described, some models may prove helpful in pulling together and clarifying these concepts and relationships. The models are attempts to represent graphically the nature and theory of communication.

The first model, Figure 1, depicts one-way communication. This model shows the kind of communication that occurs in motion pictures, prerecorded broadcasts, and all forms of writing, including books, magazine stories, newspaper articles and editorials. It also applies to such communications as posters, billboards, signs, and radio and television commercials. One-way communication provides the source with no indication of the reactions of the receiver and no opportunity to adjust or adapt to his receiver's responses.

This model does not accurately depict speech communication because in most spoken discourse the source is influenced by feedback—the responses of the receiver—and will modify his remarks as a result of these re-

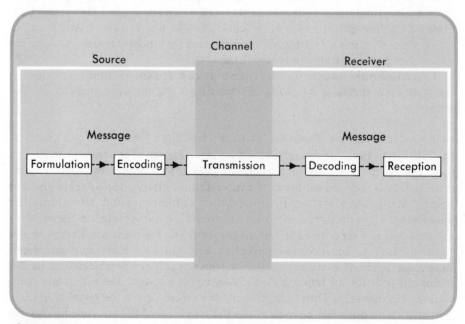

Figure 1

actions. Only in situations where the speaker has recorded his message in advance, speaks to an unseen radio or television audience from an empty studio, or misguidedly adheres to a prepared manuscript without any regard for feedback from his auditors would this model be a satisfactory representation of the speech communication process.

Figure 2 is a much better representation of what occurs in most speech situations.

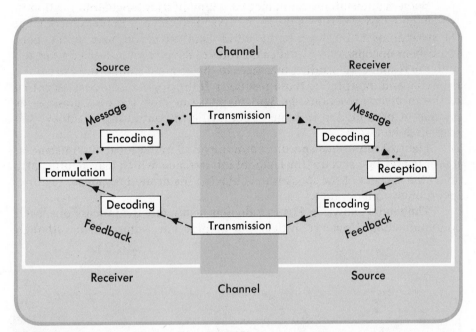

Figure 2

The communication process, as shown in Figure 2, begins with the source formulating his ideas. He is influenced by external and internal, immediate and remote, conscious and unconscious stimuli. The stimuli that exert the greatest influence upon him at the time will determine his selection of language (encoding) and the expression of his ideas (message). Should the source decide to say nothing, the process ends there. But if he elects to speak to another person, he embarks upon an interpersonal speech communication act. His channel of communication in transmitting the message to the receiver consists of the audible and visible symbols of speech—language, sounds, inflections, volume, rate, appearance, facial expression, body movement, and gestures. These audible and visible symbols produce sound and light disturbances which are perceived by the receiver who, influenced both by what he thinks the source has said and the way he has said it, will then decode the speaker's message to the best of his ability. After decoding the message, the receiver interprets it in his own mind.

As the receiver's understanding of the message "sinks into" his mind, he probably will react with shock, dismay, agreement, boredom, awe, enthusiasm, irritation, confusion, enjoyment, or some other feeling.

Most people manifest their feelings in some overt way. The manifestation may be visual; a smile, frown, shake or nod of the head, yawn, blank stare, sneer, appearance or shock, rapt attention, raised eyebrows, sarcastic grin, or look of utter contempt. Or the receiver may express his feelings audibly through laughter, questions, sarcastic remarks, contradictions, snickers, jeers, name-calling, applause, insults, booing, hissing, heckling, or cheering.

Such manifestations set in motion a kind of counter-communication in which the receiver becomes the source. As the receiver's impression of what the speaker meant impinges on his mind, he, the receiver, may—either consciously or unconsciously—cause the roles of the participants to be reversed, with the respondent sending messages to the original source and the source receiving and interpreting these reactions. If the original source is receptive to the receiver's reactions, he will maintain or alter his own message or method of presentation in hope of achieving or continuing to achieve the responses he desires.

Figure 2 represents speech communication under ideal circumstances. It fails to take into account the factor of interference, which may significantly affect the success of the speaker in achieving his desired response. Figure 3 incorporates interference.

The model shown in Figure 3 depicts accurately the process of speech communication. However, it does not include one factor which, although

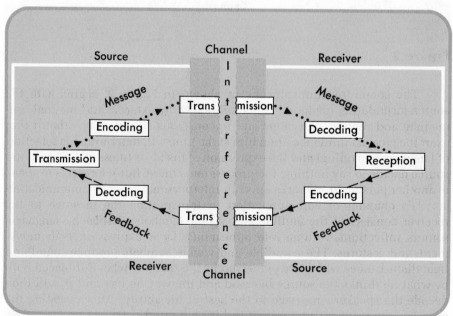

Figure 3

not a part of the speech communication process, nevertheless exerts a profound influence upon the effectiveness of a speaker's communication effort. This important factor is the fields of experience of the participants. If the source and receiver do not share common fields of experience regarding the subject matter of the speaker's message, the hearer may misconstrue or entirely fail to understand the message. Figure 4 illustrates the influence of the fields of experience of the participants upon the speech process.

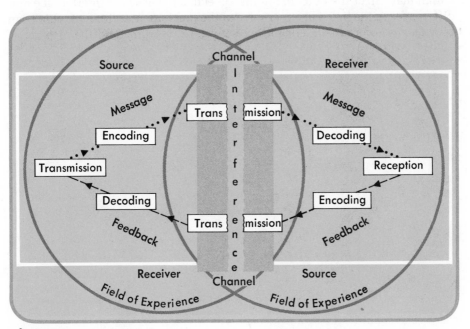

Figure 4

SUMMARY

Understanding speech communication is vital to everyone. Effective communication is no less important to people whose lives and work require little or no formal speaking than it is to others who must frequently speak to the public. Speech is essential to everyone in the conduct of day-to-day, routine activity. Speech is the medium by which people seek to influence others—to inform, to convince, to persuade, to inspire, and to entertain.

Speech communication requires a speaker or source, a message, a channel, and a receiver. The principal characteristics that distinguish speech from other forms of communication are (1) that it is purposive, (2) that it involves interaction, (3) that it is transitory, (4) that it occurs in specific settings, (5) that it is influenced by the fields of experience of the participants, (6) that it lacks the visual cues of writing, and (7) that it has a distinctive vocabulary.

The speech communication process begins with the formulation of an idea or message by the would-be communicator, the source. He then encodes his ideas into language which he transmits by audible and visible symbols to the receiver. As these light and sound waves reach the receiver, the receiver decodes them to the best of his ability and sends his interpretation of the message to its destination, his mind. He may then either physically or verbally respond to the speaker, who, if he is perceptive, will modify his message or manner of delivery to accommodate the hearer's reactions.

The speech communication process involves two additional factors which may affect the outcome of the speech act. These are interference and differences in the fields of experience of the participants, either of which can be the cause of a misunderstanding between the source and the receiver.

ADAPTED READING 2.1

COMMUNICATION
AS PARTICIPATION

Edgar Dale

A typical communication model includes the sender, the message, and the receiver. Political scientist Harold Lasswell's formula asks: "Who says what in which channel to whom with what effect?" Many models suggest that communication moves one way—from speaker to listener, writer to reader, and visualizer to observer. Communication is seen as linear rather than circular. There is limited feedback.

When communication fails we say that the message didn't get *across*, meaning that the sender's message didn't reach and influence the intended receiver. Herein lies a fallacy in much thinking about communication. Effective communication is not a one-way process aimed chiefly to change the receiver. Rather it is a two-way dialogue which changes both sender and receiver. Communication at its best is the *sharing* of ideas and feelings in a mood of mutuality. There is continuing dialogue.

In one-way communication, however, the sender assumes that the receiver is a target to be aimed at but with little or no provision for the "target" to shoot back. There is no creative interaction. One-way communication assumes the rightness of the message and is judged by whether it reaches and changes the "target audience." But who wants to be a target? There is no real communication between manipulator and manipulated.

If students do not typically accept or understand the message of the teacher or the textbook, we then discuss ways to motivate the learner. But we might better assume that a failure to communicate should be followed by motivating the teacher or the textbook writer to do better.

We need to redefine communication as a two-way process and I offer a definition which the dictionary calls archaic. It describes communication as "to share in common, to participate in." An example is given in Ben Jonson's phrase "to thousands that communicate our loss."

To communicate is to take part, hence to partake in a joint effort which transforms those so engaged, reconstructs their lives a little and sometimes a lot. Our richest memories are often those of doing important things together or just enjoying being a unitary part of something larger than ourselves. The rewards of communication include a sense of augmented power, the feeling that we are both giving and receiving. Ineffective communication makes us feel smaller, causes us to think less well of ourselves.

The root idea of the word *communication* is to make "common." This is what our schools and colleges are for—to share the intellectual and spiritual wealth of our society, to see that it becomes a common possession. I like the emphasis on *participation* which John Dewey considers fundamental in communication. He says:

From *The News Letter* (School of Education, Ohio State University, Columbus), XXXVI, no. 3, December 1970.

The keynote of democracy as a way of life may be expressed, it seems to me, as the necessity for the *participation* (my emphasis) of every mature human being in formation of the values that regulate the living of men together; which is necessary from the standpoint of both the general welfare and the full development of human beings as individuals.

Participation is a necessary condition for effective communication. Indeed, the success of communication between men and women, black and white, the young and old, the rich and the poor relates directly to the extent of their participation in the development of common values, their sharing of ideas as they deal with problems of joint concern.

We should exclude no one from participating in communication since we are trying to build an "inclusive" society, not an "exclusive" one. Communication is often thwarted in an atmosphere of authoritarianism, of compulsion, of segregation. It is promoted when students and faculty *feel* that they should face problems together and *act* on this belief. We communicate best when we participate as equals. As equals we are talking *with* others, not *at* them.

Sometimes, of course, we incorrectly think that communication is carried on only by speech or by use of some overt symbol. Communication is sometimes verbal, sometimes nonverbal, and often both. In Thomas Hardy's *The Return of the Native,* two men were walking down a road. They were a little distance apart and neither one said anything to the other. But they were in communication because, as Hardy points out, if either one of them wished to walk slower or faster, he could put himself out of communication with his companion.

The root failure in communication, I believe, is the lack of a democratic atmosphere, an unwillingness or an inability to share. In an authoritarian atmosphere certain barriers are set up and ideas do not pass freely from person to person. Thus people do not have enough common experiences to communicate with each other.

What are some of the circumstances which cause these differences in experience? Just getting older may make a difference in one's experience. The father wishes he could better understand his sixteen-year-old son and the sixteen-year-old son wishes he could understand his father. The father, of course, has been a sixteen-year-old but his son has never really stood in his father's shoes.

There is an experience barrier between boys and girls, men and women. It is both biological and cultural. It was only fifty years ago, in 1920, that women were "given" the right to vote in state and federal elections, to participate in making political decisions, to take part in the responsibility for governing. Even today, women do not get their just proportion of political, professional, and business positions. Effective communication requires participation.

Another barrier to communication as participation, as sharing, is the stratification of classes. We may not have a caste system, as in India, but there are "castes" and classes in all societies. Indeed, in 1940 President James Conant of Harvard commented as follows:

I have ventured on other occasions to speak of the American ideal as that of a free and classless society—a society made classless through the maximum of social mobility. . . . Such is the American ideal. But I gravely fear that social and economic changes during the last forty years have whittled away much of the reality on which the ideal is founded.

Stratification also occurs because of race, sex, and color. In the United States millions of Negroes have suffered for many years an inferior status, not because of something they have done or failed to do but because the white majority—by legislation, by custom, and by habit—has prevented them from participating as full citizens in jobs, in choice of housing, in opportunities for education. Progress is being made in equalizing these opportunities for all persons, but there is still a long way to go.

An ever-present barrier to communication lies in the fact that people who live differently think differently. People who live and work on farms do not think the same way as people who live and work in the cities. They do not think the same way about rain or sun or soil or churches or labor unions. Since they lack certain common experiences, communication through sharing is reduced.

Similarly, the geographic region in which one lives in the United States may raise barriers to communication. There is a difference between growing up in Texas and in New York City, in Massachusetts or in California. Regionalism or sectionalism are often present in barriers to understanding. Is it good for meat prices to go down? It is if you are a consumer, but not if you raise beef cattle in Montana.

Another constant barrier to communication lies in one's economic condition. This partially fixes one's class status, prevents a wide and deep exposure to new experience through jobs, travel, books, lectures, concerts, plays. It influences the amount of education an individual gets, prevents people from working together—a basic need for effective communication.

In his studies of motivation, Jack Frymier has pointed out that "the data in our studies clearly support the notion that youngsters who come from disadvantaged backgrounds have less positive motivation to learn in school than youngsters who come from advantaged backgrounds. . . . Motivation is inextricably intertwined with socioeconomic situations, and somehow, someway, we must get hold of that problem more effectively than we have to date."

Another barrier to communication lies in the apparent and real differences in native ability. People are not born equally able to profit by experience, equally able to abstract and to generalize. Most persons do not develop their full potential; many reach no more than fifty per cent of possible capacity. We must become aware of this ability barrier but on the other hand we should not exaggerate it. Clearly we do not adequately develop the potential of all children to learn, do not provide them optimally favorable environing influences. Contrast, for example, the life and opportunities of a child on the North Shore of Chicago with that of a child in a Chicago slum.

Our communication problem is not only an intellectual one, that of conveying information, it is also a problem of attitude, of emotion. And just as we have the language of information and intellect, so too, we have hidden, often nonverbal communication. It is a language which says to a person: "Come closer," "Stay where you are," or "Go away."

Our words and actions tell others whether we want to work with them, be participating partners. Our actions may communicate the idea that I will do something *for* you (and satisfy my conscience that I am a wonderful, unselfish person) or it may convey the idea that I will work *with* you, be willing to get into your shoes and let you step into mine.

Communication by participation is our way of acting upon our environment. We often speak of the effect of environment on the individual, what the environment does to a person. But the real story is what the individual does to his environment — his ability to use it in his own self-renewal. Is the individual mastered by his environment, or does he master it? "Life," Dewey says, "is a self-renewing process through action upon the environment."

Do we want to be partners in a cooperative enterprise, enjoy achieving a sense of our common humanity? Do we want to be me-centered, or do we prefer to be we-centered? Do we really want to communicate with our fellow man, share ideas and feelings in a mood of mutuality? If we do, we might as well make up our minds that it won't be easy. When parents do not understand their own children, we can hardly expect that they will understand and communicate freely with people who do not think, feel, or act as they do.

To understand others (as we must, to communicate with them), we must first understand ourselves. We must not only understand our hopes but our fears, our deep-seated envies and resentments as well as our friendliness. A pleasant, good-natured skepticism about our superior ability to communicate with others would also seem to be in order.

ADDITIONAL READINGS

Andersch, Elizabeth G., Lorin C. Staats, and Robert N. Bostrom, *Communication in Everyday Use* (New York: Holt, Rinehart & Winston, 3rd ed., 1969).

Nadeau, Ray E., *A Modern Rhetoric of Speech Communication* (Reading, Mass.: Addison-Wesley, 2nd ed., 1972).

Ross, Raymond S., *Speech Communication: Fundamentals and Practice* (Englewood Cliffs, N.J.: Prentice-Hall, 2nd ed., 1970).

Scheidel, Thomas M., *Speech Communication and Human Interaction* (Glenview, Ill.: Scott, Foresman, 1972).

Wiseman, Gordon, and Larry Barker, *Speech — Interpersonal Communication* (San Francisco: Chandler, 1967).

EXERCISES

1. Make a list of everyone you have spoken or listened to over the last three days. Indicate with the following numbers which were important to you: **1** for important; **2** for somewhat important; and **3** for unimportant.
2. Cite an example of a breakdown in communication (a disagreement or misunderstanding) that you have observed recently. Analyze the situation and, to the best of your ability, explain why it occurred.
3. Make a list of speech topics (other than those listed in the text) which would be inappropriate or difficult to discuss in (1) winter, (2) spring, (3) summer, and (4) fall.
4. Cite an occurrence which you either observed or participated in where interfer-

ence made communication difficult. Explain how the speaker and listener attempted to cope with this interference.

5. Observe a speaker (a classroom lecturer, clergyman, salesman, or a participant in a conversation) and analyze how the receiver reacted to the message and how well the speaker recognized and adapted to this feedback.

STUDY QUESTIONS

1. How does speech communication differ from written communication?
2. What are some kinds of nonverbal communication?
3. What are the four essential elements of the speech communication situation?
4. What are the audible and visible symbols of speech?
5. Is speech the only form of communication that is purposive? Explain your answer.
6. What is feedback? Give several examples. Why is it important in interpersonal speech communications?
7. How is the speaker influenced by internal stimuli in the formulation of his message? How is he influenced by external stimuli?
8. What is meant by selectivity or discrimination in perceiving stimuli?
9. What is interference? What are some examples of interference that may lead to a breakdown in communication?
10. How do differences in the fields of experience of the source and the receiver influence the effectiveness of speech communication?

CHAPTER
3

THE SPEAKER'S ATTITUDE AND PURPOSE

The centipede was happy quite
   Until a toad in fun
Said, "Pray, which leg goes after which?"
That worked her mind to such a pitch,
She lay distracted in a ditch,
   Considering how to run.

MRS. EDWARD CRASTER

The perplexed state of mind of the centipede resembles the mental condition of many people when they are faced with giving a speech. Although they talk every day without hesitation or fear, the thought of having to address an audience raises all kinds of doubts and questions in their minds. "What can I talk about?" "How should I begin?" and "What do I do next?" they ponder until, almost like the centipede, they begin to wonder, "Am I capable of doing this?"

This chapter seeks to quell some of these misgivings by considering the speaker's attitude, the nature and causes of nervous tension, and the purposes or goals of public speaking.

THE SPEAKER'S ATTITUDE

One of the most important factors in determining the success or failure of a speech is the attitude of the speaker. If he is to perform competently and effectively, the speaker should approach the speech situation with confidence, with a desire to communicate with his listeners, and with the expectation of success. He should regard the occasion as a challenge, as an opportunity to accomplish an important and worthwhile objective.

Unfortunately, many beginning speakers are unable to generate any real desire to communicate or to develop confidence in their ability to command the interest and respect of their listeners because of excessive nervous tension or stage fright. Some speakers become so nervous that they are able to complete their speeches only with the greatest effort. Others worry incessantly for hours or even days before the speech. In the most severe cases of stage fright, the speaker may actually feel nauseous, experience a loss of appetite, or be unable to sleep. This inordinate fear of public speaking leads some people to avoid opportunities to speak, to reject invitations to address groups that might benefit from their knowledge and ideas, and even to jeopardize their own chances for professional advancement.

While excessive nervousness is most common among beginning speakers, it is by no means confined to them. A 1973 survey of over 2500 adults who were asked to pick items from a list representing situations in which they had some degree of fear revealed that 40.6 percent of these adults feared speaking before a group. Even experienced public speakers sometimes become tense when confronted by a new, unusual, or particularly challenging speech situation, as Keir Hardie shows in Adapted Reading 3.1.

Distressing as this phenomenon may be to the speaker, a degree of nervous tension probably serves a useful function in delivering a speech. It seems doubtful that a speaker totally free from anxiety would be very interesting. If he simply did not care what the outcome might be, it is unlikely that he would produce an effective talk. But when the speaker's apprehension and nervousness become so great that they begin to interfere with his ability to communicate, the problem of stage fright becomes a matter of concern. Thus, the speaker's aim should be to learn to control nervous tension, rather than to eliminate it entirely.

In his effort to overcome the harmful effects of stage fright, the speaker must be familiar with its symptoms and causes, as well as its possible remedies.

Symptoms of Stage Fright

Persons who suffer from stage fright usually react both physiologically and psychologically. The physiological symptoms may include trembling of the hands or legs; increased perspiration, especially in the palms of the hands and under the arms; shortage of breath; accelerated heartbeat; a parched or dry mouth; voice tremors; and a tenseness throughout the body.

Psychologically, the speaker may experience a desire to withdraw; he may fear that the listeners will notice his nervousness or his embarrassing difficulties in controlling his own voice. These symptoms, in turn, may lead him to avoid looking at the audience, to hide behind the lectern, or to speak more rapidly. Some speakers become so distressed over their nervousness that they can think of nothing else, with the result that they may suddenly discover that they cannot remember the point they were making or what they planned to say next. This sudden lapse of memory adds to the speaker's consternation, and so he becomes increasingly desperate.

Causes of Stage Fright

Interestingly, most of the physiological symptoms of stage fright are almost identical to the body's reaction to a sudden threat or danger. For example, if unexpectedly confronted by an attacker, one's body responds automatically. In preparation for warding off the attack or threat, the heart beats more rapidly, more oxygen is required to supply the heart, the mouth becomes parched, the muscles of the body tense, and the individual begins to perspire. In the case of actual danger, the excess energy summoned to meet the emergency would soon be released through some physical exertion such as fighting off one's attacker, fleeing, or in some other way coping with the threat. If, however, one were to discover that no real danger existed, the tension and additional energy automatically provided by the body would not be released and the individual would discover that he had all the physiological symptoms of stage fright—trembling hands and knees, moist palms, a pounding heart, shortness of breath, and muscular tension.

The similarity between an individual's reaction to the threat of physical danger and to giving a speech suggests that one of the main causes of stage fright may be that the speaker regards the speech situation as a threat to his welfare. This attitude could stem from several factors. One cause could be the speaker's knowledge that the outcome of the speech is important to him; he would therefore regard it as a threat to his security. Shakespeare warned, "Mend your speech a little, lest you may mar your fortunes." Some speakers are afraid that this is exactly what may happen to them.

Another reason for a speaker's fear may be his awareness that he is being judged, that many auditors will get to know him only through his speaking, and that they will form opinions regarding his personality, character, and intelligence solely on the basis of his skill as a speaker. The possibility of being judged inadequate on the basis of his speaking ability alone haunts him.

Stage fright may also be an expression of chronic personal insecurity. In other words, the speaker feels insecure in many situations, not only when speaking. Giving a speech merely brings this general insecurity to a peak. O. Hobart Mowrer (see Adapted Reading 3.3) points out that if a person is generally afraid of being "seen through," there is no more threatening situation for him than being before an audience, the object of all eyes.

Other possible causes of stage fright may result from the speaker's lack of knowledge concerning public speaking. His fear may stem in part from lack of experience. He may have spoken to audiences so seldom that he does not know how he will fare. He may also suffer from lack of knowledge of what an audience expects and what constitutes a good speech. Thus, he may believe that his listeners will be disappointed with anything but a polished oration and, with his lack of training, he doubts that he can produce a speech that will meet their standards.

His nervousness may also be the result, in part, of inadequate preparation; he is unfamiliar with his material, uncertain of whether he really understands his subject, and questions whether he can remember what he had planned to say.

Even an experienced speaker with considerable confidence may at times suffer from stage fright. This could happen if he encounters a new and totally unfamiliar audience or occasion, if he has not had time to prepare carefully, or if the consequences of the speech are more important than usual. However, the experienced speaker probably would be able to exercise enough control over his nervousness that it would not interfere with his ability to communicate effectively.

Developing Confidence: General Principles

No simple formula has been found for overcoming stage fright. However, several general principles can be recommended for reducing nervous tension and bringing it under control. These suggestions can be divided into a long-range program for reducing stage fright and specific techniques that may prove helpful in the immediate situation.

The first principle in developing confidence as a speaker is to gain experience before a variety of audiences. In almost any endeavor, the first attempt will be accompanied by tension and anxiety. The youngster making his first dive from the high board at the swimming pool, the learner driving an automobile for the first time, the beginning teacher meeting his first class, the student pilot making his first solo flight, and the athlete preparing for his first competition, all experience nervous strain and uncertainty. But with repeated exposure to these situations or activities, all gain experience and self-assurance. In a like manner, beginning speakers can increase their self-confidence by speaking often and, since no two audiences are identical, by speaking before many different groups. As a young man, George Bernard Shaw, the playwright and lecturer, embarked on such a program to overcome his anxiety about speaking. Joining a variety of organizations ranging from the Browning and Shakespeare societies to socialist political groups, Shaw took advantage of every opportunity to address their members, eventually gaining such wide experience that he could face almost any audience with poise and assurance.

In order to develop poise and skill as a speaker, Senator Everett Dirksen spoke before many different audiences as a young man, trying out various approaches and observing the listeners' reactions. See Milton Viorst's study of Dirksen's speech patterns in Adapted Reading 3.4.

A second suggestion for overcoming stage fright is to put the speaking situation into its proper perspective. While speeches are important, some speakers overemphasize their significance. Very seldom will a single speech determine future policy, settle a controversy, or greatly alter an individual's professional future. A poor speech is a disappointment to an audience, but it is not a disaster. Even the greatest speakers fail from time to time. If a speaker keeps in mind that the consequences of an unsatisfactory speech are likely to be no more than temporary embarrassment to the speaker—that a poor speech will not result in shame, imprisonment, harm to one's family, social ostracism, or some other outrageous effect—he probably can approach the speaking situation with less strain and nervous anxiety.

Third, the speaker should rid himself of misconceptions about the audience's expectations. When a speaker addresses a group, most listeners do not expect the talk to be the most moving experience of their lives or to herald the dawn of a new era. If the speaker is interesting and provides them with useful information, stimulating insights, or fresh ideas, most listeners are satisfied. The speaker who overestimates the expectations of the audience is bound to fail.

Fourth, the speaker should develop a desire to communicate. The speaker who is talking about something that interests him and who feels that he is fulfilling a useful function by sharing his ideas with the audience will have little time or attention to devote to worrying about his nervousness. The speaker who approaches the speech situation with the attitude that he is there to aid or help the listeners, rather than to be judged by them, is likely to speak with calm assurance.

A fifth recommendation for controlling stage fright is to learn about speechmaking by studying the theories and principles of effective speech, by reading about the techniques of great speakers of the past and present, and by thinking about speech problems and possible solutions to them. A course in speech, books about speaking and speakers, and participation in voluntary speech improvement groups such as Toastmasters clubs can all contribute to a better knowledge of what constitutes a good speech and how to prepare and deliver an effective address.

Sixth, if a speaker wishes to reduce nervous tension, he should be well prepared for every speech he gives. He should speak on subjects with which he is familiar; he should have planned his talk carefully and have practiced it frequently so that he knows what he wants to say and how he plans to say it. It would be the utmost folly for any speaker who is afraid of becoming extremely nervous when he faces the audience to compound those fears with worries about what he is going to say and how he is going to say it.

By gaining experience in speaking, putting the speech situation into proper perspective, ridding one's self of misconceptions about the audience's expectations, developing a desire to communicate, learning about speech, and being well prepared for each speech, the beginning speaker can eliminate some of the common causes of stage fright. These steps will not reduce nervousness overnight, but in time they should lead to a positive and more confident attitude on the part of most speakers.

Controlling Nervousness: Specific Techniques

In addition to the long-range program described, some speakers find that various specific techniques are helpful in combating nervous tension. While these approaches do not attack the underlying causes of stage fright, they may prove helpful in immediately reducing tension on a particular speaking occasion.

One technique used by some speakers is to pause briefly before beginning a speech to make sure that their notes are properly arranged, to review mentally the first few sentences of the introduction, and to calm themselves. This device gets the speaker off to a good start. Since fear of failure is one cause of stage fright, the speaker who starts hastily and therefore becomes confused at the very outset will probably find his anxieties compounded. Taking time to make sure that everything is in order and to review quickly the opening lines of the speech often can prevent a bad beginning.

Another practice that some speakers believe helpful is to breathe deeply several times just before beginning the speech. Since shortness of breath is one symptom of stage fright, pausing to fill the lungs with air may alleviate this problem.

A third technique favored by some for reducing tension is the speaker's mental "pep talk." If, just before beginning, the speaker reminds himself that talking is an everyday activity, that the audience consists of people much like himself, and that no dire repercussions are likely to follow should he fail in his effort, he may be reassured.

Some speakers employ a fourth technique to allay nervousness. This consists of seeking a favorable response of some kind from the listeners at the very start of the speech. The speaker may tell a joke to get his audience to laugh, or he may ask for a show of hands on some question about their experiences or knowledge of his topic. Such overt responses may reassure him that the audience is good natured and cooperative and thereby reduce his fear of them.

Still another method used by some to overcome anxiety is to pick out seemingly friendly or interested people in the audience and address the early part of the speech to them, ignoring those who appear bored or hostile. Eventually, the speaker's eye contact should encompass his entire audience, but speaking mainly to individuals who appear sympathetic at the outset may reassure the speaker.

A sixth technique employed to get rid of excessive nervousness is that of movement. Since the speaker has an excessive amount of unreleased nervous energy, he simply uses up some of the energy by moving about on the platform, writing on the blackboard, displaying a model or visual aid, or demonstrating how to do something. While all speeches and situations do not lend themselves to this kind of physical activity, at times it may be an effective way to release nervous energy.

A few suggestions should also be made about things a speaker should avoid.

First, the speaker should not talk about his nervousness with the listeners. Remarks such as "I'm so nervous I don't know if I can go on" or "I hope you can't see my knees shaking" serve no useful function. They merely distract the audience from the speaker's subject and call attention to something that may not have been noticed. Many speakers suffering from intense nervous anxiety appear completely calm, cool, and poised to their listeners. To call attention to one's stage fright not only interjects an irrelevant thought in the listener's mind, but may also diminish his confidence in the speaker.

A second cautionary suggestion is that the speaker should not plunge ahead heedlessly if he has become badly confused due to stage fright. It is much better for him to pause, even for a rather long time if necessary, to try to get control of himself, to go over his notes or mentally review his speech, to find his place, to call to mind what he wants to say next, and then to resume speaking.

Third, a speaker should not indirectly advertise his nervousness. The speaker whose notes or visual aids are on flimsy, thin sheets of paper that clearly and sometimes noisily shake when he holds them embarrasses himself by calling the audience's attention to his trembling. Demonstrations requiring a calm or steady hand (threading a needle, loading certain types of cameras, or other acts demanding precision) should be avoided by the tense speaker, for in all probability not only will he experience difficulty in carrying out the demonstration, but he will also focus the audience's attention on his nervousness.

Finally, a speaker who experiences severe stage fright should not stop abruptly in the middle of his speech. If a pause to review notes and regain self-control fails, the speaker who is hopelessly lost should attempt some kind of summary, review, or conclusion before giving up. The reason for this recommendation is that at times one finds that speakers who feel that their speech has been a total failure have actually performed fairly well and have made progress toward achieving their goal. To quit abruptly or to say, "I can't go on," and then just sit down not only stuns the audience but also tells them that the speaker regards his effort as a failure, with the result that they think less of what he has said so far.

While some of these "dos" and "don'ts" for coping with stage fright may prove helpful on particular occasions, nervous tension can in the long run be more effectively reduced by gaining experience in speaking, by learning about speech, and by approaching the speech situation in the right frame of mind.

THE SPEAKER'S PURPOSE

One of the distinctive characteristics of speech is that it is purposive. Unlike the poet, artist, or composer who at times may create a work for no purpose other than self-expression, the speaker almost always seeks to evoke a specific response from his listeners. Whether he is addressing a large assembly, participating in a small discussion group, or only engaging in conversation, the speaker probably hopes to influence the understanding, feelings, convictions, or actions of his audience in some predetermined way.

> In speaking there is always some end proposed, or some effect which the speaker intends to produce in the hearer. The word *eloquence,* in its greatest latitude, denotes "that art or talent by which the discourse is adapted to its end."
> GEORGE CAMPBELL

The speaker who regards speech in this practical, utilitarian way—as an activity designed to accomplish a specific purpose, rather than as a performance or adherence to a set of rules—will probably approach the speech situation with confidence and direction. The practical uses to which speech is put are many. For example, a lawyer may speak to obtain information from clients; to present information to the client, to another lawyer, or to the court; to confer; to give advice; to negotiate; to reach agreements; and to persuade. In Adapted Reading 3.5, Charles Bunn cites ways in which lawyers use speech. In each of these activities, the lawyer's success is measured not in terms of the impact of his words upon history or how he compares to Clarence Darrow, but how well he accomplished his purpose. The same is true of speaking in other professions and situations.

Because speech is purposive in nature, the speaker's general goal in any speech is to create in the audience the response he desires. The key word in this principle is *desires*. The speaker does not seek just *any* response. For example, the speaker who sets out to inform an audience fails in his purpose if his listeners merely enjoy the speech but do not understand his subject or recall anything he has told them. The speaker who hopes to persuade also is unsuccessful if the auditors only understand his remarks, but fail to act upon them in the way he wishes. In both of these instances, the speaker has obtained *a* response, but has not accomplished his primary objective. Although a speaker may have one goal in mind, this does not mean that he may not at times utilize materials usually employed to elicit other responses. For example, a speech intended to persuade often includes humor, information, and inspirational passages. But the speaker's ultimate objective is to persuade, and his inclusion of materials to entertain, inform, or inspire is justified only so long as they contribute to the realization of his main goal. If the speaker is to succeed in obtaining the desired response, he must always keep his central purpose foremost in his mind.

General Purposes

Speech purposes may be classified in various ways, but traditionally they have been divided into five general types: to inform, to entertain, to convince, to persuade, and to inspire.

To Inform. The speech to inform might also be called a speech to teach, to enlighten, or to educate. In the speech to inform, the speaker aims to present his material so that the audience will understand and remember what he has to say. Once informed, the listener may elect to act upon the information and to put it to use in a certain way; however, in an informative speech the speaker does not seek to initiate action or influence the listener's behavior, but aims only at the audience's comprehension and retention of his ideas.

Informative speaking occurs in any teaching situation, whether in a classroom, office, plant, conference room, or at a club meeting. It consists of explanations, analyses, descriptions, demonstrations, definitions, and narratives. It may utilize specific instances or examples, statistics, comparisons and contrasts, and the opinions of experts.

Topics that lend themselves to informative speaking might include: "How the federal reserve banking system operates," "The causes of the Seven Years War," "How to wrap a gift," "The difference between empathy and sympathy," "Crop rotation," and "How to play soccer."

To Entertain. The speech to entertain aims at nothing more than providing momentary enjoyment for the listeners. The speaker wants his audience to sit back, relax, forget their problems, and have a good time. He does not care whether they remember what he says, and he has no desire to influence their beliefs or actions.

The speech to entertain is most often heard at banquets, dinner meetings, and functions primarily social in nature. It is not necessarily a humorous speech, although many are. In addition to the possible use of humor, the entertaining speaker may choose to utilize the quaint, the exotic, or the unusual. He may employ material that is startling, exciting, surprising, suspenseful, bizarre, little known, or incredible. He may describe, explain, narrate, analyze, or demonstrate.

It is difficult to cite examples of topics well suited to entertaining speeches because so much depends on how the material is handled. However, some topics that might be developed into entertaining talks include: "Blind dates," "History rewritten: What if?" "New Orleans' voodoo queens," "My feud with computers," or "The antiwhistling campaign in Britain."

To Convince. The difference between a speech to convince and a speech to persuade is largely an academic one. The distinction between them grows out of the belief once held by faculty psychologists that the mind can be divided into segments, with one part controlling the will and another regulating the feelings. This belief has long since been discarded, but the separation of speeches into those aimed to alter a listener's convictions and those designed to influence his actions is perhaps useful for our purposes.

The speech to convince is defined as one that seeks to alter the listeners' beliefs on subjects where action is not requested or, in most cases, even possible. For example, a speaker might try to convince his listeners that Jesse Owens was the greatest athlete in American history; that abstract art does not communicate; that Verdi was a greater composer than Wagner; or that Earl Warren was a great Chief Justice. In these examples, no action on the part of the listener is urged. In fact, the listener could do little about any of these matters even if he were impelled to do so.

Convincing speeches, as defined, are usually given by individuals who are interested in evaluating people or events, in establishing values, in fitting everything into its proper slot, in resolving factual disputes, and in "keeping the record straight." This kind of speaking may frequently be heard in any educational, cultural, or historical group and, as the debate over the authorship of Shakespeare's works indicates, some of the most heated controversies revolve around such issues.

The speaker's materials are the same as those used by the persuasive speaker: specific instances and examples, statistics, comparisons and contrasts, and expert testimony.

To Persuade. The speech to persuade, like the speech to convince, aims at changing the listener's convictions; but it goes a step beyond simply seeking agreement and, explicitly or implicitly, urges the listener to pursue a course of action in accord with the speaker's beliefs. If the persuasive speaker fails to motivate his listeners to act in the way he wishes, he cannot regard his speech as wholly successsful. For example, if a speaker urges his audience to have regular medical examinations, he will not be satisfied if the members of the audience merely nod their heads in agreement and say, "That's a good idea," but continue to see their doctors only irregularly. To be completely successful in realizing his goal, the speaker must somehow motivate the listeners to perform the action he desires.

> A speaker who exhausts the whole philosophy of a question, who displays every grace of style, yet produces no effect on his audience, may be a great essayist, a great statesman, a great master of composition; but he is not an orator.
>
> THOMAS BABINGTON MACAULAY

At times, the persuasive speaker identifies very specifically the exact steps he wishes the audience to take. He may, for example, urge the listeners to vote for a certain candidate, to mail their contributions to a particular charity, to sign a petition, or to write to their congressman. At other times, he may be less explicit in outlining the steps he wishes the audience to take. He may, for example, ask his audience to exercise tolerance, to support foreign aid, or to drive safely, without giving detailed instructions on exactly how he expects them to carry out his recommendation. But, regardless of whether the course of action is explicitly stated or merely implied, any speech that urges listeners to behave in a certain manner may be classified as a speech to persuade. Whenever a speaker's thesis or main idea contains the words *should* or *need to*, it is fairly certain that his purpose is persuasive.

Persuasive speeches utilize the same materials (specific instances, statistics, analogies, and testimony) as do other kinds of speeches. However, the persuasive speaker selects and arranges these materials in such a way that they support a course of action. In addition, in an effort to influence his auditors' feelings and thereby impel them to take the steps he urges, the persuasive speaker often makes extensive use of materials designed to arouse the listener's emotions.

Persuasive speeches are heard in almost any situation in which audience members have a voice in determining policy. Some of the most obvious places are political rallies, legislative bodies, club and organizational business meetings, radio and television commercials, and sales talks.

Some examples of persuasive speech topics are: "The president of the United States should be elected by a direct vote of the people," "College students should have a voice in the hiring and firing of teachers," "The United States should abolish all censorship," "Communists should not be allowed to speak on college campuses," and "The sale and use of marijuana should be legalized."

To Inspire. In a speech to inspire, the speaker seeks to increase the audience's appreciation or respect for an individual, group, cause, or event toward which they are already favorably disposed. This type of speech also is referred to as a speech to impress or a speech to stimulate. In everyday conversation, the word "inspirational" is frequently used to describe anything that moves the feelings of the listener. Thus, members of a congregation may refer to a particularly moving sermon as being "inspiring." Actually, many speeches that are called "inspiring" urge a course of action and are, in fact, persuasive rather than inspirational.

The speech to inspire, as here defined, requires an audience that is either neutral or already sympathetic to the speaker's point of view. His task then is to create favorable attitudes toward his subject among the neutral members of the audience and to enhance the favorable attitudes of those who already agree with him. If, on the other hand, the hearers disagree with the point of view of the speaker, he will of necessity be engaged in convincing or persuading them.

Speeches to inspire are appropriate when an audience has gathered to honor or to pay tribute or homage to some individual, group, organization, or event toward which they feel deep devotion, affection, or respect. For example, a ceremony honoring a fellow employee upon his retirement, the end-of-the-season athletic awards banquet, and a Fourth of July observance are occasions that demand a speech to inspire. The unsympathetic, the cynical, and the hostile will either not be in attendance or will be in the minority. Most of those present will already admire, respect, or appreciate the person, body, or achievement being honored. Obviously, then, the speaker's task is simply to heighten or stimulate the audience's feelings.

Inspirational speeches include eulogies, speeches of commendation, speeches of commemoration, presentation and acceptance speeches, and welcoming and farewell speeches.

Specific Purposes

Once the speaker has decided what is to be his general goal, he comes to the task of determining his specific purpose. He cannot hope to prepare a successful speech with only a topic and general purpose in mind. Suppose that his purpose is to inform his audience about tape recording. In order to proceed meaningfully, he must at once ask himself the question, "Inform them of *what* about tape recording?'' He has several choices. He could limit his speech to the uses of a tape recorder, how to operate a tape recorder, how to edit tapes, how sound is recorded on tape, or several other aspects of this subject; he could discuss any combination of these; or he could attempt to cover all of them.

The importance of determining a specific purpose early in the preparation of a speech was emphasized by Harry Emerson Fosdick. This famous preacher pointed out that "an essayist may be content with the discussion of a subject, but a preacher can be content only with the attainment of an object. I mean not simply some over-all aim — such as the presentation of Christian truth and the persuasion of men to accept it," he continued, ". . . but for each sermon a specific intent. It may be the help of individuals in facing some personal problem, or the answering of a puzzling question in theology, or the persuasion of tempted souls to abandon some popular sin, or the confrontation of some public evil with the Christian ethic, or the winning of wavering minds and consciences to a definite decision for Christ." He concluded, "I, for one, cannot start a sermon until I clearly see what I propose to get *done* on Sunday morning."

The speaker should consider several factors in determining his specific purpose. These include the amount of time available to him, the audience's knowledge of the topic, the interests of the listeners in different aspects of the subject, his own understanding of the topic, the relative importance of the possible alternatives, and the nature of the occasion. After considering all of these factors, the speaker is ready to determine his specific purpose.

The specific purpose should be put in the form of an explicit statement of exactly what the speaker hopes to accomplish. For example, if a speaker decides to give an informative speech on the use of the library, his general purpose would be *to inform*. His specific purpose might be *to inform the audience on the use of selected aids and facilities of the library*. In formulating his specific purpose, the speaker should decide exactly what it is that he wishes to cover in the speech. For example, a specific purpose of informing the audience on "how to use the library" probably is too general, unless the speaker actually intends to cover every aspect of library usage. If not, he might decide that his specific purpose is more accurately stated when worded in one of the following ways:

> To inform the audience how to check out a book at the library.
> To inform the audience how to use the card catalog and *Reader's Guide to Periodical Literature.*
> To inform the audience of the special collections of the library.

The speaker who attempts to proceed with the preparation of his speech without knowing exactly what he wishes to accomplish is likely to be plagued with false starts, wasted time, and confusion.

Some examples of statements of specific purpose for different types of speeches are:

To inform the audience of the three main causes of forest fires.

To persuade the listeners to use automobile seatbelts.

To inspire the audience to greater respect for Thomas Edison.

To convince the audience that Leif Ericson discovered America.

To entertain the listeners with an account of a summer vacation.

Immediate and Long-Range Goals

In determining his specific purpose, the speaker must consider the audience's prior knowledge of his subject, their attitudes toward his ideas, and the time available for his speech.

When the audience has little knowledge of his subject, the speaker often finds it necessary to present considerable background information and, if the time available to the speaker is limited, he may be unable to present enough material for the listeners to understand his topic. For example, if the speaker wishes to explain the use made of the twelve-tone scale by different composers to an audience with little knowledge of music, he may find it impossible in the amount of time allotted to present enough information to enable the listeners to comprehend his topic. The speaker then has two choices — he can either abandon his subject entirely or settle for a lesser objective. Using the same example, he might decide to limit his speech to an explanation of the difference between the regular eight-tone scale and the twelve-tone scale. This would be his immediate goal. His long-range goal, however, might be to help the audience to understand how various contemporary composers have used the twelve-tone scale. This goal, of course, could be reached only if the speaker or an associate had the opportunity to address the audience on the same general topic at some future date.

In determining what his immediate goal should be, the speaker must also take cognizance of the attitudes, opinions, and biases of his audience. In a single speech, a speaker can rarely hope to convert an audience from deep-seated opposition to whole-hearted support of his point of view. This is especially true if the audience is influenced by a personal or selfish interest in the outcome or if the speaker's position contradicts social customs, mores, or firmly established beliefs.

In such a situation, the speaker may wish temporarily to abandon his hope for acceptance of his entire program, platform, or point of view, and focus instead on reducing hostility to his position or on gaining support for a limited portion of his proposal.

For example, a speaker who strongly favors the abolition of intercollegiate athletics may — through some strange circumstance — have an opportunity to address the university athletic boosters' club. Aware of the preconceived attitudes and hostility of the members to his point of view, he knows that he cannot expect, with one speech, to get them to support his long-range goal — the abolition of intercollegiate football and basketball. However, the speaker might well hope to persuade his listeners of any of several short-range or immediate goals that would curtail some of the abuses to which he objects. He might choose to try to persuade his listeners that:

1. The faculty should exercise greater control over the school's athletic programs.
2. Athletes and fans should always remember that the student's education is more important than his athletic prowess.
3. Greater attention needs to be paid to good sportsmanship and less to winning games.
4. Intercollegiate athletics can do the participants harm as well as good.
5. The number of athletic scholarships offered by the school is excessive in comparison to the number of grants for academic achievement.

If the speaker's talk is carefully prepared and well presented, he might reasonably hope to persuade his listeners to accept one of these points.

Hidden Goals

At times a speaker may not wish to reveal his true goal or purpose. He may prefer to hide or withold his actual goals because he believes he can better accomplish his purpose by refraining from an open statement, because he feels the time is not right to indicate his objective, or because such a statement might be personally embarrassing or seem immodest.

The unstated or withheld objective may be called a hidden goal. Examples of speakers with hidden goals are plentiful. The active community leader who takes every opportunity offered to speak in support of the local symphony, charity drives, and philanthropic endeavors may covertly be trying to convince the audience of his interest in civic affairs in anticipation of a later candidacy for political office. The speaker who announces that he "just wants to present the facts in an objective manner and let the audience decide for itself" may actually be seeking to disarm the audience before presenting a partisan approach. The politician who urges support of a low-income housing project as a general welfare measure may be hiding the fact that he stands to profit personally from such a proposal.

Hidden motives are not necessarily evil or unethical. In the examples cited, it is possible that the future candidate might make an excellent political leader, that the cause being espoused by the deceptively impartial speaker might be virtuous and noble, and that a low-income housing project might greatly benefit the public. Listeners, however, will wish to locate any hidden motives that a speaker may have in order to avoid being deceived or misled.

The Central Thought

In addition to determining his specific purpose, the speaker should also know his central thought before attempting to proceed further in his speech preparation. The central thought is sometimes also referred to as the main idea, the theme, or the thesis. It is a refinement of the speaker's specific purpose—a concise statement of exactly what he plans to say. The central thought, like the specific purpose, indicates what the speaker hopes to accomplish. Both consist of a single declarative sentence. Some examples of typical statements of specific purpose and central thought are:

Specific purpose   My purpose is to inform the audience of three principal causes of forest fires.

Central thought   The principal causes of forest fires are lack of rainfall, public carelessness, and acts of nature.

Specific purpose   The purpose of this speech is to persuade the audience to support a bond issue to build a city auditorium.

Central thought   You should support a bond issue to build a city auditorium because our community has no satisfactory place to hold conventions, concerts, and large public meetings.

Specific purpose   My purpose is to inspire respect and admiration for Professor Morse.

Central thought   Professor Morse deserves our respect and admiration for his scholarly research into the history of our state and for his long and able leadership of the state historical society.

The formulation of a central thought is an important step in speech preparation because it requires the speaker to crystalize his thinking on his subject. Of the many possible approaches and the several aspects of his topic that could be discussed, he must settle on those he feels are most important or most conducive to achieving the response he desires. Until the speaker formulates his central thought, he cannot proceed with the organization and development of his materials, for he does not know exactly what he wants to say. Once he has determined his central thought, the speaker knows where he is going and will find his subsequent speech preparation easier and more systematic.

Stating the Purpose and Central Thought

The speaker will often find that an actual statement of his specific purpose or his central thought early in the speech will promote clarity and understanding. In announcing his purpose or main idea, letting his audience know in advance what he is going to discuss, the speaker encourages his auditors to listen more intelligently. For example, he may indicate, "Today, I would like to explain how sugar cane is harvested." The audience then knows the speaker's exact topic. They know he is not going to discuss planting sugar cane, its cultivation, sugar refining, or marketing the finished product. They also know that he is not going to attempt to persuade them of the nutritional value of sugar, the need for greater sugar imports, the superiority of cane sugar to beet sugar, or some other point of view. Having been told what to expect, they are better prepared to understand the speech.

When the specific purpose or central thought is stated in a speech, the speaker usually presents this information in the introduction. In most speeches, the speaker begins by seeking to create interest in his topic. Once this is accomplished, he is ready to state his specific purpose or central thought.

Occasionally speakers withhold any statement of their purpose or central thought until late in the speech. This occurs most often in talks on controversial subjects. If a speaker is trying to convince or persuade a hostile audience, he may alienate his listeners with an early statement of his thesis. Knowing the speaker supports a proposal with which they disagree, an antagonistic audience often will close their minds and seek to detect flaws and shortcomings in the speaker's arguments.

To obtain a fair and impartial hearing in such instances, the speaker may wish to develop the less controversial aspects of his subject before revealing his central thought. For example, early in the speech he might emphasize arguments and attitudes that he shares with his listeners. He might demonstrate his fairness, honesty, and objectivity and display good will toward the audience. Then, having prepared the audience by winning their respect, by laying the foundation for his proposals, and by obtaining agreement on several basic ideas, the speaker is ready to move on to the more controversial aspects of his topic. Such an approach by no means guarantees success, but it usually improves the speaker's chances of winning hostile listeners to his point of view.

SUMMARY

The speaker's attitude is important in determining the success or failure of his speech. While the speaker should be concerned with how well he does, inordinate fear and tension can interfere with effective communication. Among the causes of stage fright are insecurity, inexperience, lack of knowledge of the audience and of what constitutes a good speech, and inadequate preparation. To develop confidence, the speaker should gain experience before many different kinds of audiences. He should put the speaking situation into its proper perspective, rid himself of misconceptions about the audience's expectations, and develop a desire to communicate. The study of speeches and speakers and careful preparation can increase his knowledge of speechmaking and contribute to the development of his confidence.

People give speeches not because of some idle whim, but because they have a specific purpose which they hope to accomplish. Thus, speaking is a very practical activity. The speaker's general purpose may be to inform, to entertain, to convince, to persuade, or to inspire an audience. The effectiveness of a speech is determined by how well the speaker succeeds in obtaining the response he desires from his listeners. The speech to inform seeks audience understanding and retention. The entertaining speech aims only to provide relaxation and enjoyment. The speaker whose goal is to convince hopes to alter the beliefs or attitudes of the listener. The persuader goes one step further, attempting to influence the conduct of his audience as well as their beliefs. The speech to inspire aims at heightening the auditors' admiration for an already respected person, group, cause, institution, or event.

If the speaker is to obtain the response he wishes, it is essential that he know specifically what he hopes to accomplish. At times, because of the nature of his audience or the occasion, the speaker may elect to work for a short-range, immediate goal, with a view toward ultimately accomplishing a broader and more long-range objective. At other times, a speaker may find it inexpedient to reveal his true goal and so will conceal it from the audience.

The speaker's central thought consists of a single, declarative sentence summarizing the speech in its entirety. The formulation of the central thought—whether actually stated in the speech or not—is important because it forces the speaker to determine exactly what he hopes to communicate to his listeners. In most speeches, stating the central thought or purpose early in the speech helps the audience to understand the speaker's ideas. However, at times the speaker may elect to withhold any statement of his main purpose or idea until later in the speech, so as to improve his chances of obtaining the response he desires from his audience.

ADAPTED READING 3.1
ONE MAN'S STAGE FRIGHT
Keir Hardie

Keir Hardie, one of the founders of the British Labor Party, a member of Parliament, and a man who delivered speeches almost daily for years, described his own stage fright in the pages of his newspaper, The Labor Leader. Although a popular and capable speaker, Hardie experienced nervous reactions not too different from those of many beginning speech students.

I almost envy those public speakers, but not always their audiences, who can mount a platform or face a meeting without a qualm or a doubt. It must be pleasant to have such unlimited confidence in their own power. . . . For myself, I usually begin a speech, literally, in fear and trembling. Not only so, but when it happens that I approach a meeting in a spirit of cold indifference, as is sometimes the case, my speech is certain to be a failure. Further, I never get in touch with my subject until I am thoroughly in touch with my audience. Stepping on to the platform, especially if there is little show of enthusiasm, a wave of cold feeling works its way down from the brain to my toe nails, often producing a shiver as if I had struck a chill. At the same time, away somewhere in the inner recesses of my subconscious being, I am not a man, but a little tiny speck of green protoplasm floating on the surface of a stagnant pool, a leaf tossing in the whirls and eddies of a mountain brook, a shell half embedded in the sand and washed by the lapping waves of a troubled sea under a grey sky, or, and I hate this worst of any, I shrink within myself until I am a mere pygmy surrounded by a circle of big brawny giants, each armed with a club. But whatever form the feeling takes it always produces a sense of my own insignificance.

When rising to speak the feeling subsides. But I am still an isolated unit. When the hall is good, and the audience indulgent, a genial thaw soon sets in, and as it makes its way through me I cease to be a separate person. I absorb and am absorbed by my audience. In spirit we seem to melt and fuse into one, and I am not speaking to them, but through them, and my thoughts are not my thoughts but their thoughts, and we are on the most comfortable and confidential terms, one with the other. But all the time wicked little Elfins and Goblins and Sprites are working their hardest to detach me and usually at the end of the time I have allotted to myself they succeed, and the flow of ideas and words cease, and I begin to flounder. Happy, thrice happy, the speaker who has learned to perorate. I don't perorate, worse luck.

From *The Labor Leader*, London, February 28, 1903, pp. 114–115.

NOT ONLY SPEAKERS
HAVE STAGE FRIGHT

Musicians in a prestigious orchestra suffer as much stress as pilots of trans-Atlantic airliners and industrial managers, a team of Viennese scientists has found. Severe anxiety setting in as early as two weeks before a challenging concert, extreme tension during the performance and fatigue after it, sleeplessness and an almost permanent mood of frustration were named as symptoms.

The researchers investigated a sample of 24 members of the Vienna Symphony during the last 10 months. The 24 musicians, chosen from all instrument sectors, were examined before, during, and after concerts. A clear profile of what may be called the symphony syndrome emerged.

The project was headed by Maximilian Piperek, a psychologist. Dr. Piperek noted in an interview that a concert performance demanded extreme mental concentration from all the musicians involved for a much longer period than most persons are used to sustain. He said that the average span of concentrated attention was 20 to 30 minutes, and that after an hour of such attention fatigue was frequent.

"The normal two-hour length of a concert therefore places a heavy strain on musicians," Dr. Piperek remarked. "In addition, they are forced to perform teamwork requiring precise timing with no more toleration than the hundredth part of a second. The individual musician can fulfill his task only with closest attention to the signals of the conductor and the playing of his colleagues."

Die Presse of Vienna quoted several of the examined musicians as admitting that during concerts they suffered from fits of perspiration, trembling, and giddiness for fear of missing their cues. Only three of the 24 musicians under observation were found to be reasonably free of emotional disturbances after concerts. The others declared that they could not sleep for at least three hours after a performance, and they showed many signs of fatigue.

Soloists were, not surprisingly, found to be exposed to the highest levels of stress. "The greater the importance of an individual musician's contribution for the success of the entire performance," Dr. Piperek said, "the more severe is physical and mental tension."

The study projected a "specific malaise" in the musical profession: The contribution of an individual orchestra member, though it may be superlative, often is lost in the over-all impression of a concert, whereas the slightest fault or wrong reaction is immediately noticed and often sharply criticized. Constant fear of such failures creates stress.

ADAPTED READING 3.3

STAGE FRIGHT AND SELF-REGARD

O. Hobart Mowrer

The subject of stage fright is often approached in terms of rather superficial fears which, it is assumed, will wear off or disappear as the person becomes more experienced in the role of public speaker. I am sure that this view of the matter has some validity, that it is applicable in some cases and perhaps has a limited applicability in all cases. But I would invite your attention to a more fundamental aspect of the problem, one which, we may say, has to do with the whole person, his self-concept, and his general strategy in relating to others.

For many years I have been interested in the subject of psychopathology; and it seems to me that stage fright is in many instances merely a concentrated, "localized" version of the anxiety, the fear, the panic which we see in more chronic form in so-called neurosis and the functional psychoses. It was Shakespeare, was it not, who likened the whole world to a stage, on which we are actors — and on which, we may add, "stage fright" is the "loss of nerve," the fearful apprehension which we think of as the essence of personality disorder in general. Patients in mental hospitals will often tell you that they are pervasively "afraid of people," i.e., that they are fearful not just when they face a formal audience but also when they meet or interact with others in even the most commonplace circumstances; and "retreat" and "withdrawal," in one form or another, is the way in which they manifest their uneasiness. The most plausible interpretation of this kind of fear that I know is to the effect that such persons are suffering from guilt, i.e., a knowledge that they have behaved in socially inappropriate ways, have concealed the fact of their misbehavior from others, and are now fearful lest they be found out, "seen through," and called to account.

There is, of course, nothing new in the assumption that the central problem in personality disturbance is guilt. Freud assumed, quite correctly it seems, that the neurotic is suffering from a discrepancy between the standards he holds for himself and his actual conduct. But Freud's supposition was that this painful discrepancy arises, not because a person's performance has been too low, but because his standards are too high and ought, with the aid of psychoanalytic treatment, to be lowered. However, many investigators are now coming to see that this is a misleading "diagnosis" and that the problem is one of *real* guilt rather than mere guilt *feelings*. If one were dealing with guilt feelings, feelings which are unrealistic and false, then one might indeed think of them as subject to extinction, habituation, "wearing off" with the passage of time and continued experience. But real guilt does not behave in this manner. Here the sense of "danger" is realistic and durable. The mere fact that one has not been found out or caught to date is no guarantee that he will not be tomorrow, or the next day — and the possibility of punishment is, so to say, "always there."

From *Western Speech*, Fall, 1965, pp. 197–200.

Now if the foregoing is a reasonably accurate and sound way of view-ing the chronic personal insecurity which we see in neurosis (Erikson's term "identity crisis" is, it seems, a far more apt one), and if stage fright is simply an acute, "peak" expression of this state, it will perhaps be illuminating to look at this phenomenon explicitly in terms of the hypothesis that real, current, unresolved personal guilt is the basic problem. If a somewhat insecure person is afraid of being "seen through," what more vulnerable or threatening situa-tion than that of being before an audience with all eyes upon him? He is being watched, scrutinized, "examined," in a way that otherwise rarely occurs; and if there are guilty secrets in a person's life, such a situation is obviously pre-carious. Eyes (with their implications of watchfulness, inquiry, attention) are a proverbial symbol of *conscience;* and if one is on bad terms with this part of his personality and is trying not to "think about" what it is that conscience has "against" him, an audience, with its concentrated gaze, is a powerful reminder of his moral vulnerability.

Too often, I suspect, public speaking is taught as an act or performance which one "puts on." And there are, to be sure, times when one must play a role, not only in frankly dramatic presentations and entertainments, but also in teaching and lecturing on many other occasions. But I suggest that in the preparation of students for public appearances of all kinds, it would be a wonderful thing if they could be led through a "graded series" of self-disclosures and self-authentications which would help resolve real guilt in their lives and thus lay the basis for a genuine security and confidence in the presence of an audience, whatever the occasion.

Let me give an illustration of what I have in mind. As is well known, Alco-holics Anonymous is today proving far more effective in dealing with the problem of alcoholism than any other approach. And AA is producing "public speakers" by the score. How, precisely, does this program operate and why was it evolved? The philosophy of alcoholism which AA accepts holds that this addiction comes about because of chronic deception and un-truthfulness in the life of the afflicted individual. All alcoholics are assumed to be "phony," and a large part of the AA program is devoted to helping its members "get honest." This is done, in the first place, by means of *encour-agement.* That is, newcomers hear the testimony of older members concern-ing their own past deviant actions and deceptions and how they got rid of the compulsion to drink when they became more responsible, reliable, and "open."

And how does the program of honesty begin for the new member him-self? In addition to being admonished to "attend meetings," he is given a sponsor, who works particularly closely with him by way of providing encour-agement and guidance. And eventually the new member is urged to take the "Fifth Step," either with the sponsor or someone else, which is in effect an act of personal confession. This takes the form of "admitting the exact nature of our wrongs to God, to ourselves, and to another person." At this point the "audience" is, from one point of view, still not very large, but it is larger than it has previously been — and this is a real therapeutic gain.

Then, in the Twelfth Step of the program, the member is urged to "carry the message" to other alcoholics. And what is "the message"? It is the notion that covertness, secrecy, phoniness will drive a man to drink (as well as crazy) and that AA has a program which helps one move from secrecy to openness, from destructive privacy to "public speaking." For not only does the AA member "tell his story" in connection with the Fifth Step and in his "Twelfth-Stepping" with other alcoholics, he is also schooled in speaking about his experience with his own AA group; and little by little he begins to be invited to speak to other local groups, and then perhaps at regional or even national conferences.

By and large, AA speakers, although not always particularly literate or brilliant, make very moving and effective presentations. They do not use manuscripts and rarely even have recourse to notes. They don't need to. They are speaking directly out of their own experiences, which they can never forget, and they are speaking truthfully. I have often heard AA speakers admit to being scared. But they keep going, and I have never seen one of them break down or have to leave the platform disorganized.

If I were teaching public speaking, I think I would do it in the context of "group therapy," as AA does. I would start with interviews with individual students, sharing deeply out of my own life with them and inviting them to do the same with me. Then I would begin to enlarge the "audience," from one to three or four. And then, with perhaps some safeguards taken out of consideration for others, each person would be encouraged to "tell his story" before the class as a whole. This, in my judgment, would be a highly efficient and reliable method for producing secure and effective public speakers. I have sometimes remarked that AA is turning out better "evangelists" than any theological seminary I know. It is also, I suspect, producing more effective public speakers than most formal classes in the subject.

This approach to the problem may seem so unconventional as not to be feasible. But in composition courses, students are not infrequently asked to write frank autobiographies. And I see no reason why, in other courses, they could not learn to speak autobiographically, in an authentic and liberating way. An attack of uncontrollable stage fright is, itself, a kind of involuntary, inexplicit "confession." A part of the personality is thus trying to make an "admission" of some sort which another part is trying to block. How much better, then, to go right to the heart of the matter and deal with the guilt and fear-engendering secrets directly, voluntarily, instead of having them dumbly "acted out" in incapacitating stage fright. The best way I know to deal with the problem of impaired identity, i.e., an "identity crisis," is to become able to say who one genuinely is — to speak publicly, rather than privately or not at all.

On another occasion, I have suggested that stuttering may have much the same "dynamics" as is here posited for stage fright: namely, that the individual is trying to stifle and at the same time make an admission of some sort. The result is that he says neither what he consciously intends nor what another part of him is trying to reveal. Although I myself have never been a stutterer, I have repeatedly had the experience of getting up to talk before an audience, feeling nervous, making a slip or "goof," and then feeling embarrassed, yet strangely relieved. I can only infer that I had come to the situation with some pretention which I thus involuntarily "corrected." By my slip or blunder, I "admitted" that I perhaps "wasn't so much" after all. When I eventually came to see this as a pattern and began to practice a little self-conscious humility, I found that the involuntary self-revelations did not occur nearly so often.

In thus stressing the concealment of one's true identity and its involuntary disclosure in stage fright, I do not wish to deny or neglect other variables. Lack of adequate preparation, legitimate fear of failure, and stress caused by extraneous circumstances may certainly interfere with smooth performance in a public speaking situation. I remember, a few years ago, having to go directly from a situation in which I had become very angry to make a public presentation. At one point my train of thought was interrupted, and I just had to admit that I had "blocked." One interpretation could be that in an effort not to show the anger which had been generated in the other situation, I was "over-controlling" in the lecture. But one could also view the blocking as a kind of automatic admission of the not-too-dignified hassle I had just been involved in and as a form of self-punishment for not having conducted myself with greater dignity and restraint.

I hope that these reflections will sufficiently interest speech teachers and researchers that they will put them to empirical test. On the basis of evidence drawn from other fields, I believe this approach to the problem of stage fright will be found to have considerable validity and power.

ADAPTED READING 3.4

EVERETT DIRKSEN: THE DEVELOPMENT OF AN INDIVIDUAL SPEECH PHILOSOPHY
Milton Viorst

One of the most colorful speakers in the United States Senate in recent years was Everett M. Dirksen. "Oleaginous Ev's" unique manner of speaking was no accident. The senator carefully trained himself as a speaker, deliberately cultivating several eccentricities that became his trademark as an orator. Nevertheless, Dirksen never lost sight of his ultimate purpose in speaking: to move his listeners.

Everett Dirksen's secret is that he, alone among major American politicians, has mastered the technique of translating style into power. What is power? In politics, as in other forms of human endeavor, power is nothing more than the capacity to make one's will prevail. In the United States, its most obvious instrument is public office, which conveys power by consent. The higher the office, of course, the greater the power. But rare is the politician who attains a public office of substantial inherent power without first obtaining the coercive power of money and organization, instruments of independent force. Everett Dirksen, however, makes his will prevail through neither high office nor money nor organization, but through the persuasive power of his style. Such power has an elusive quality, hard to fix in the conventional terms that Washington understands. It is exercised through entertainment and ingratiation. Its symbols are the mask and the oil can. Dirksen has placed himself on the public market place as a comic and won himself a top rating. He has thrust himself, unarmed but for his charm, among the political gladiators and has proved himself a champion. Dirksen's inherent power is negligible and his coercive power is practically nonexistent. It is astonishing that through the persuasive power of an ingenious style Everett Dirksen has become a major force in American politics.

Yet, despite his rejection of the trodden paths to power, Everett Dirksen is a force to be reckoned with in the White House, on Capitol Hill and in those stuffy chambers where Republican Party decisions are made. It is Dirksen whose approval the President seeks first in his pursuit of consensus. It is Dirksen to whom Congressional Democrats turn for the word on whether a controversial piece of legislation will pass. It is Dirksen to whom the Republican Party looks—from left, right, and center—to heal its self-inflicted wounds. Dirksen's influence is an established fact, even if it is hard to reduce to conventional terms. It is influence that is enveloped in melody, like the Pied Piper's. Dirksen's pipes render words into action, form into substance, style into power. . . .

Young Dirksen interrupted college to sign up for World War I, then returned to his shabby hometown of Pekin to prepare himself for a political career. He was only a baker's helper then but he was an enthusiastic Legionnaire, in those postwar days when the American Legion was the most potent force in Illinois politics. Dirksen's specialty was arranging parties and entertaining at them. Later he cultivated a reputation as a toastmaster and afterdinner speaker. Soon he was volunteering his services to towns nearby, ultimately to groups throughout downstate Illinois. Dirksen would talk to anyone on any subject. One still hears in Pekin how Everett Dirksen dazzled a hardware dealers' convention by a tour de force on the history of tools. "It started out that nobody heard of him," said "Peach" Preston, an old Legion buddy who perpetuates Dirksen lore in Pekin, "and ended up that everybody wanted him." A whole crowd of Pekin septuagenarians, including some Democrats, will testify that even forty years ago Everett Dirksen was known for his ability to delight and amuse.

"Those were the trial years," said Dirksen. "I went around studying my techniques. I'd make a sally and see what kind of response it received. Then I'd try another. I particularly watched the audiences. I learned how to appraise an audience—whether it was hostile, friendly or indifferent. The indifferent ones, they're the worst. I learned to make contact with an audience —because if you don't make contact, only a little will be remembered and even less understood. I made a study of people, their attributes and their foibles, what registered with them and what didn't.

"Those were the years when I learned to tell a story. There are very few good storytellers, you know. Most storytellers are too verbose. They're dabblers. They lose their audiences. A good story has a genuine biological effect. If you can get a good sound belly laugh, it starts a blood surge. Your audience might have tired, its attention was wandering. You come up with a good story and they're back with you. You have to keep stimulating the audience. If it becomes ill at ease, you lose your effectiveness. Many people remember nothing about a speech but the story. I get letters from people asking me to repeat a story they heard me tell years before. It's a great asset to be a storyteller.

"But if I acquired nothing else during those years, it was poise, and let me tell you, poise is transcendent in dealing with an audience. It will dictate the mannerisms, the gestures, the style, the dedication you bring to a speech. The kind of poise I bring to the platform is one of total informality. The stilted and brittle style of another age simply won't do. I'll bet you don't know who Edward Everett was. He's the fellow who delivered the other speech at Gettysburg. It was a long speech written out in great detail. When we think of Gettysburg, we think of Lincoln's few simple but immortal words. Who thinks of Everett? It's the informality that establishes a bond with the audience and allows you to keep it. That, for me, is the real meaning of poise."

Dirksen today is the undisputed master of the informal speech. He disdains a prepared text. He often begins with the ageless trick of holding up the back of an envelope or a laundry ticket and announcing, "I scribbled a few notes on this and out of it will come thousands of words. I wonder what they'll be." From it he draws a guffaw that sets the tone for the rest of the talk. But because he carries only a laundry ticket does not mean that Dirksen goes into a speech unprepared. "Webster said," he notes, "that it took him only a few minutes to prepare a speech but fifty years to get ready for it. The incubation process is always going on. You never know when a happy thought will strike you." Over the years, of course, Dirksen has acquired more and more material to draw on. "The great handicap of a newcomer," he said, "is that he doesn't have a reservoir of recollection and data committed to memory. I've been dealing with housing bills, for example, since 1934. I don't have to do research on that kind of speech." Dirksen's standard oratory is not characterized by research. On his staff are neither researchers nor speech writers. Dirksen's addresses are a personal thing. They are characterized by reminiscence, literary allusions, Biblical reference. He makes his points by deducing from history rather than from fresh evidence. A Dirksen speech is not elegant when it is read; it is rambling and often repetitious. It has none of the beauty and polish of, say, a Stevenson speech. "My speeches have an immediate purpose." Dirksen maintains, "They are not intended as timeless documents. I have never confronted myself with questions on posterity." Dirksen's objective is to move his audience, whether for votes, for money or just for pleasure. His goal is to generate a reaction on a human-to-human level. Such is the quality of his manner that both friend and foe find themselves reacting with thoroughly uninhibited delight.

ADAPTED READING 3.5

HOW LAWYERS USE SPEECH
Charles Bunn

Most laws consist of words. Words—spoken, written, studied, and listened to—are among the fundamental tools of the lawyer's trade. The lawyer in active practice uses speech and speech's sister, listening, for many purposes: to get information and to give it, to confer, to advise, to negotiate, to record agreements, and to persuade.

TO GET INFORMATION

I think no one who is not a lawyer can imagine how much time a lawyer must put in getting information. I do not mean information about the law. Of course he must get that, but he will get it out of books. I mean information about the client's problems and the facts connected with them. A lawyer's work is very seldom *about* law. Once in a blue moon he may serve on some committee to improve some statute or the like. Most of his work, though, starts with his client's problem, which may concern anything. Whatever it is, his first job is to learn about it; not only the specific thing his client is concerned about, but the whole factual background. And by *factual* I mean everything bearing on the problem except law.

When my grandfather was practicing in up-state New York more than 100 years ago, the situation, as he reported it much later, was that almost all litigation was about horse trades. The lawyer needed, therefore, principally one book, "The Points of the Horse." He needed to know everything there was to know about horses, but he needed to know very little else. (I am quite sure my grandfather's report was biased, but it makes the point.)

To get information about a subject not his own, the lawyer will do what any other sensible person would do—he will read the best books, et cetera, that he can find about it. But generally this will not solve his problem. Clients' problems have a way of being not something that happened 50 years ago which is reported in the books with its solution, but something new that you have to learn about by asking questions. So—simply asking questions becomes a continuous, important, and fundamental part of almost every lawyer's practice. Asking questions and, of course, listening to the answers.

TO GIVE INFORMATION

Not so continuous but nevertheless frequent is the lawyer's need to give information to his client, to another lawyer, and to a court. Many judges of appellate courts have said that the most important part of a lawyer's argument is his statement of the facts which make up the case he is presenting. The judges

From *Speech Teacher*, January 1964, pp. 6–9.

say that they know something themselves about the law, but that they have no way of learning what the facts of the case are until counsel tells them. Therefore, a well organized, orderly, and truthful statement of what happened and what the lawsuit is about is the most important part of every argument in an appellate court. And the same is true, only a little less so, in speaking to a trial judge or to the jury.

TO CONFER

A great deal of the lawyer's work is done quietly in the lawyer's office or his client's office, *talking the problem over.* I don't know how to describe this process further. The lawyer is learning what is in his client's mind. The client is learning what his lawyer thinks. They together are planning what to do about the matter that concerns them.

Another kind of conference, likely to be more formal, is with the trial judge and the lawyer on the other side before the trial begins, trying to find out what facts can be agreed on and what are really in dispute. Still another, common especially in practice before some administrative agencies, is with an officer of the agency, to find out what is going to be required or what the disputed questions are.

TO ADVISE

In the end, the client wants to know what the lawyer has to recommend. Advice, of course, is often given in a letter. But a great deal of it is given in quiet talk which is a part of conferring last referred to. This differs not at all from the process of advising as it might occur with anyone whom another person consulted for advice.

TO NEGOTIATE

This is an important function which the lawyer shares with many other people: diplomats, salesmen, businessmen of all varieties, and so on. There is, I think, nothing special about the lawyer as a negotiator as distinguished from anybody else. I am not at all sure that legal training adds to negotiating skill. Some lawyers are good at it, others are not. The same is true of laymen. It is one of the most used skills of the lawyers who have it and it is, of course, done mainly with spoken words.

TO RECORD AGREEMENTS

Most of this is naturally done in writing. The important contract, which the lawyer helped to draw, is written out and signed. But there are many occasions, especially in the trial of cases when agreements of one sort or another are made between counsel for opposite parties in the presence of the Court, orally, though often dictated to the clerk for record.

Again this is by no means unique. Many businessmen make more oral agreements than lawyers ever do. But it is one part of the lawyer's job.

While we are talking about trials, I leave out, because everybody knows it, the second most conspicuous use of speech by lawyers, the interrogation of the witness.

Again, everybody knows about this, but I think most laymen regard it as the most important function of speech as used by lawyers. It is, of course, important, and it is a great art to do it well, but I have tried to show that it occupies only a small part of most lawyers' working time.

Is there any single quality or virtue that all of these varied uses of the spoken word require? I think there is and that its name is "clearness." And I don't mean just clearness to the speaker or to some third person but clearness to the actual audience in the sense intended by the speaker. *This will take some doing.*

There is no use asking questions of even the friendliest source of information unless you tell him what you want. It is a waste of time or worse to report facts to others unless they understand you. A conference fails, whether two people or ten, unless they understand each other. Advice, mistaken, is dangerous. (There are tragic stories of orders, especially of military orders, misunderstood and executed in the wrong sense.)

To negotiate, I suppose, requires greater clarity than anything else. We have some bad examples of misunderstanding in the negotiations by great men. When Winston Churchill and Franklin Roosevelt talked with Stalin at Yalta, the records make it clear that they spoke of a "friendly government" as desirable for Poland. The Western statesmen took a friendly government to mean what you or I would understand. Stalin understood it differently. In his book, capitalist and communist governments were necessarily, in the long run, enemies. Therefore, a friendly government in Poland meant to him a communist government. At least he said so later and it is plain that this *could* indeed have been what happened. And notice that it could happen whether "friendly" was spoken in English or in Russian. The confusion is *not* in the words used but in the different backgrounds of two people, which give the same words different meanings.

There used to be a story about a traveler abroad who, when his requests were not understood, repeated them, slowly and twice as loud, in his own language. None of us, I hope, are quite that silly when the barrier to understanding is a difference of language. But most of us do the same thing all the time when the trouble is a difference of background or of training. In serious matters, and perhaps most of all in negotiation, the results can be destructive. For there is likely to emerge a purely verbal agreement, understood quite honestly in different senses, and acted on accordingly. How often have American Indians sold hunting rights, and white negotiators purchased title in fee simple? When things like that happen, watch out for fireworks! For nothing gets most people madder than bad faith after agreement, unless it is unfounded charges of the same.

Whatever the lawyer's professional use of speech, the essential thing is that it reach, in the sense intended by the speaker, not only the eardrums of the hearer, but his mind. This can best be done by talking about concrete things and actions whenever that is possible, and avoiding the abstractions. How many kinds of "democracy" exist in people's minds? Beyond that, the best device I know is to make it a discussion, not a monologue. Then, it is often possible, by careful listening, to detect where the other person has misunderstood what you have said. This is one of the reasons why, in teaching, a discussion is so often more fruitful than a lecture.

However attained, to be understood as you intend is the main thing any lawyer ought to seek in speech. . . .

To be clearly understood is not inconsistent, either, with eloquent expression of a deeply felt conviction. Hear Justice Brandeis, dissenting, on a case of, in his view, free speech denied:

> Those who won our independence believed that the final end of the state was to make men free to develop their faculties; and that in its government the deliberative forces should prevail over the arbitrary. They valued liberty both as an end and as a means. They believed liberty to be the secret of happiness and courage to be the secret of liberty. They believed that freedom to think as you will and to speak as you think are means indispensable to the discovery and spread of political truth; that without free speech and assembly discussion would be futile; that with them, discussion affords ordinarily adequate protection against the dissemination of noxious doctrine; that the greatest menace to freedom is an inert people; that public discussion is a political duty; and that this should be a fundamental principle of the American government. They recognized the risks to which all human institutions are subject. But they knew that order cannot be secured merely through fear of punishment for its infraction; that it is hazardous to discourage thought, hope, and imagination; that fear breeds repression; that repression breeds hate; that hate menaces stable government; that the path of safety lies in the opportunity to discuss freely supposed grievances and proposed remedies; and that the fitting remedy for evil counsels is good ones. Believing in the power of reason as applied through public discussion, they eschewed silence coerced by law—the argument of force in its worst form. Recognizing the occasional tyrannies of governing majorities, they amended the Constitution so that free speech and assembly should be guaranteed.

To make oneself clear is quite compatible with anger and strong language. Hear Oliver Cromwell, to the Kirk: "Brethren, I beseech thee, in the bowels of Christ, consider that ye may be wrong!"

But I suppose the best illustration I can give is in two sentences, both by great masters of the language, saying the same thing.

The first is in Act I of Shakespeare's *Julius Caesar*, Cassius speaking privately to Brutus, to recruit him for the attack on Caesar:

> I cannot tell what you and other men
> Think of this life, but, for my single self,
> I had as lief not be as live to be
> In awe of such a thing as I, myself.

The other is Patrick Henry, at a meeting in a Richmond church, 1775: "I know not what course others may take, but as for me, give me liberty or give me death."

Did you fully understand Cassius's sentence the first time you heard it? Could any English speaking person doubt the meaning of Henry's?

ADDITIONAL READINGS

Clevenger, Jr., Theodore, "A Synthesis of Experimental Research in Stage Fright," *Quarterly Journal of Speech*, 45 (April 1959), 134–145.

Lillywhite, Harold, "Symposium on a Broader Concept of Communication Disorders," *Journal of Communication*, 14 (March 1964), 3–18.

McBurney, James and Ernest Wrage, *Guide to Good Speech* (Englewood Cliffs, N.J.: Prentice-Hall, 1965), chap. 5, "Speaking with a Purpose."

Mills, Glen E., *Message Preparation* (Indianapolis: Bobbs-Merrill, 1966), chap. 2, "Selecting a Subject: Purposes and Types of Speeches."

Monroe, Alan and Douglas Ehninger, *Principles and Types of Speech* (Glenview, Ill.: Scott, Foresman, 1967), chap. 7, "Determining the Subject and the Purpose of a Speech."

Oliver, Robert T. and Rupert L. Cortright, *Effective Speech* (New York: Holt, Rinehart & Winston, 1970), chap. 3, "The Personality of the Speaker."

STUDY QUESTIONS

1. What are some reasons why speakers experience stage fright? In what ways does giving a speech differ from "just talking" in a small group? Are these differences great enough to explain why speakers who converse easily often are frightened at the prospect of giving a speech?
2. Do you think that giving speeches of "personal revelation," as suggested by O. Hobart Mowrer, would prove helpful in reducing stage fright? Could they increase nervousness?
3. To what degree should the speaker feel at ease while delivering a speech? Justify your answer.
4. Of the six steps recommended for controlling nervous tension, which ones do you think are most essential? Why?
5. Could a speech that does not obtain the response desired by the speaker ever be called successful? Why or why not?
6. Is it always essential for a speaker to have formulated a specific purpose and central thought before preparing the rest of his speech? Explain your answer.
7. Under what circumstances might hidden motives or goals be considered unethical? When would they be ethical?
8. When should a speaker usually state his purpose or central thought? Why? Under what circumstances might he wish to withold a statement of purpose or his central thought?
9. In what ways does the tension which musicians feel when giving a concert (see Adapted Reading 3.2) resemble a speaker's stage fright? In what ways are they different?

EXERCISES

1. Read a speech in *Vital Speeches* or *Representative American Speeches*. Indicate (1) the speaker's general purpose, (2) his specific purpose, and (3), if stated, his central thought. If the central thought is not specifically stated, frame a statement of his central thought.
2. Taking the general subject of *education*, frame a specific purpose for (1) a speech to inform, (2) a speech to convince, (3) a speech to persuade, (4) a speech to inspire, and (5) a speech to entertain.

3. Using the topic *television*, frame a central thought for a speech (1) to inform, (2) to convince, (3) to persuade, (4) to inspire, and (5) to entertain.

4. Find three subjects on which a speaker might not wish to reveal his specific purpose or central thought to an audience early in the speech. In a paragraph discussing each topic, explain the reasons why it might be advisable for the speaker to withhold his statement of purpose or central thought until later.

5. What usually is the general purpose of each of the following kinds of speeches? After writing down the most frequent general purpose for each, list exceptions (occasions when the speaker might have a different general purpose).

   a. sermons
   b. campaign speeches
   c. classroom lectures
   d. funeral orations
   e. television commercials
   f. talks at pep rallies
   g. debate speeches
   h. announcements at club meetings

ANALYZING THE AUDIENCE AND THE OCCASION

THE PREPARATION OF A SPEECH

Abraham Lincoln reputedly wrote his most memorable address by jotting notes on the back of an envelope while en route to Gettysburg. A recent President, on the other hand, employed twenty-four speech writers over a period of six weeks in the preparation of a forty-minute State of the Union address. (See Adapted Reading 6.2.) These two extremes demonstrate that there is no single correct method for preparing a speech.

Nevertheless, as in most activities, a systematic approach to planning and presenting a speech is preferable to a random, haphazard preparation. While under some circumstances the speaker might wish to alter the order of preparation, for most occasions he will find that he can develop the speech most efficiently if he follows the plan outlined below:

1. *Analysis of the audience and the occasion* to determine the background, interests, and attitudes of the listeners and the nature of the speaking occasion.
2. *Selection of a subject* suitable to the audience and occasion, and narrowing of the topic so that it can be covered in the time available.
3. *Determination of the speaker's purpose,* including his general purpose, specific purpose, and central thought.
4. *Gathering materials for the speech* from the speaker's own knowledge and understanding of the topic and from other sources.
5. *Evaluation and selection of materials* for inclusion in the speech.
6. *Organization of the materials of the speech* and the preparation of an outline and speaker's notes.

7. *Wording the speech* through the preparation of a written text for manuscript and memorized speeches or through oral practice for extemporaneous addresses.
8. *Practice in delivery* of the speech, giving attention to both the audible and visible aspects of presentation.

The chapters in this book examine each of these steps. This chapter deals with the first step, analyzing the audience and the occasion.

THE AUDIENCE

Not long ago, an experienced speaker was asked to deliver his first high school commencement address. He was determined to be more original than most speakers he had heard at such events and break with the traditional patterns of commencement speeches. Consequently, he prepared his speech exclusively for the graduating seniors, without regard for the families and friends who would attend the exercises. It was a good idea, and a good speech.

Upon arriving at the auditorium he discovered, to his amazement, that the audience was separated; the graduating seniors were on the stage of the auditorium, the families and friends in the seats out front. The speaker's rostrum stood between the groups, facing the guests. What a predicament! He had a speech for the graduates, but he was to face the guests. What should he do?

Alternatives ran through his mind. "I can change the speech a bit and adapt it to the general public," he thought to himself. But that was contrary to his intention when he accepted the assignment. "I can speak to the graduates even though they are behind me." But then he would be facing one group and addressing another. "I can turn the rostrum around and ignore the parents and friends." But that might be considered rude. The speaker had to solve the dilemma. With proper explanations and an apology, he turned the rostrum to face the graduates, leaving the larger part of the audience to gape at his back.

This whole situation could have been avoided had the speaker analyzed his audience in advance; by doing so he would have discovered the seating arrangement and planned accordingly. A speaker should consider several questions concerning the audience and occasion before he begins the preparation of his speech.

Determining the specific audience for a speech is sometimes difficult. For example, when the president of the United States makes a policy speech on television, he knows in advance that his audience is not confined to persons in the studio, or even to the groups of people gathered around television sets to listen to the live presentation. His audience extends to the members of the press who will print his remarks for millions of other people to read the following day; to the radio and television news agencies that will later rebroadcast portions of his speech for still others to hear; to the millions of people around the world who will hear the same speech live via satellite or from tape recordings; and to others around the world who will read his speech translated into their native languages. His audience is composed of the whole civilized world.

Other political and social leaders may have similar broad exposure. However, for the great majority of speeches the audiences are more easily defined. The student speaker in the classroom knows that his audience is composed of eighteen to twenty-five other students. The minister is aware that his audience on Sunday morning will probably consist of the same people who heard him the previous Sunday, and perhaps for years of Sundays before. The commencement speaker should know that his audience will be composed of the graduates, their families, and friends. Within all of these situations the two psychological concepts of polarization and social facilitation operate to create unity and cohesiveness among the members of the audience. Walter Stevens discusses this in Adapted Reading 4.1. To capitalize on these concepts, a speaker should determine the audience's *knowledge, interest,* and *attitudes* toward the *subject,* the *speaker,* and the *occasion* early in the preparation of his speech. To discover these, the speaker must examine the composition of the audience and its reason for assembling.

> **To study persuasion intensively is to study human nature minutely.**
> CHARLES WOOLBERT

Audience Composition

The speaker should be aware of many aspects of audience composition before he develops his speech. The twelve dimensions of audience composition discussed here are at once elusive, self-evident, and immutable.

Age. The speaker must know the age level of his audience, for he will need to adapt his explanations, examples, language, and other speech components to the age of his listeners. It is rather obvious that some subjects and illustrative materials that might be readily perceived by an adult audience would not be intelligible to a teen-age audience. Historical allusion to a period through which an adult lived, for example, might make sense to the older person who recalls this era, but may be meaningless to a younger person. On the other hand, language and materials appropriate to a youthful audience might be unclear to an adult audience.

When audiences are composed of people in the same general age group, adaptation is relatively easy. Of course, when the audience consists of people of various ages, adaptation taxes the speaker's ability. He may prefer to select subject matter, materials, and language that will be generally interesting and meaningful.

Sex. Often speakers are called upon to address all-male audiences such as the Rotary Club, Lions Club, and the Junior Chamber of Commerce; or they are called upon to address all-female gatherings, such as meetings of the League of Women Voters, Business and Professional Women's Club, and ladies' church groups. It is important to realize that members of the two sexes are often motivated by different types of appeals. For example, if a speaker were to talk on the advantages of life insurance, he might attempt to persuade an audience of men by appealing to them as guardians of the family welfare and, particularly, of their loved ones for whom they would want to provide financial security in the event of accidental death. But when speaking to a group of ladies, the speaker might appeal to their maternal instinct to protect their children's future through life insurance.

Topics for sexually segregated audiences should be carefully selected. If the speaker has a special knowledge and interest in auto racing, for example, a talk about the thrills of racing might be particularly interesting to a male audience, but not necessarily to a female one since auto racing is still a predominantly male-oriented occupation. A speech on the attitudes and fears of the wives of the drivers or the special problems that surround their lives would probably be better suited to a feminine audience.

A speaker should select his topic, supporting materials, and language with an awareness of the different interests and motivations of male and female listeners.

Religion. Because persons of different religious beliefs react differently to some appeals, it is essential that the speaker analyze his audience with this in mind. Some religious convictions are so personal and so deeply felt that the individuals are unable to tolerate or even discuss contrary beliefs.

Because religious groups differ on matters such as war, birth control, observance of the Sabbath, gambling, and the sale of intoxicating beverages, it is foolish to approach a group without first knowing its predisposition. For example, a speaker advocating birth control to curb over-population would use different approaches when speaking to a Catholic group than he would when speaking to a Unitarian audience. The speaker should feel no obligation to change his basic ideas to suit the two audiences, but he certainly should adapt his arguments to the values and doctrinal differences of his audiences. The religious affiliations of the listeners should be ascertained by the speaker, especially if his subject has religious implications or includes religious appeals.

The speaker who fails to adapt to his audience's religious beliefs and attitudes might well find himself in the predicament of the Baptist minister who, when his church burned down, received a call from the Jewish rabbi. The rabbi, in the best ecumenical tradition, offered the use of his synagogue to the Baptists until the church could be rebuilt. Accepting the invitation, the minister expressed his appreciation by saying, "That is very Christian of you." Teaching the minister a lesson in audience adaptation the rabbi responded, "It is very Jewish, too." Good taste and a personal sensitivity to the religious attitudes and beliefs of the audience are essential to the effectiveness of a speech.

Politics. How often have you heard the statement, "There is no sense in arguing about religion and politics"? Although it is inherently false, for both subjects are so vital that they should be discussed often, the statement does serve as a warning to speakers.

Political affiliation takes on a religious fervor for some people. For them it is difficult to argue rationally, or even to discuss intelligently, problems within these two realms. Political belief, like religious conviction, is, to a large degree, based on faith, and often permits little intellectual examination. To abuse the political sensibilities of an audience could be disastrous for a speaker. The good speaker will adapt his materials to the political attitudes of his audience, not by becoming fraudulent or dishonest in the development of his arguments, but by avoiding useless antagonism and by capitalizing on those arguments that relate positively to his auditors' political convictions.

Although political differences are often deeply ingrained and may sharply divide groups on many questions, the speaker should not overlook the common bonds that unite most people regardless of political affiliation. Men of all political faiths tend to agree in their love of country; in their belief in liberty, justice, and freedom; in their desire for a satisfactory standard of living; in helping others; and in the general welfare of the community. Their means of attaining these goals may differ; but regardless of party loyalty, most persons share many common aspirations and values.

Race. It is important for a speaker to know in advance both the racial characteristics of the audience he plans to address and to be appraised of their attitudes toward racial differences. To avoid injuring his cause, the speaker should eschew any reference that might cause racial antagonism. If might be harmless to tell a "colored" joke to a black audience, but it could also prove disastrous. The attitude of the audience toward the speaker and his subject and the atmosphere of the occasion will determine the propriety of racial references. The ability to adapt to racially different audiences was demonstrated by Stokely Carmichael in 1967. Pat Jefferson's analysis of Carmichael's adaptation is reproduced in Adapted Reading 11.3.

Information about the racial characteristics of the audience provides the speaker with insight into the cultural orientation of the members of the audience and reveals something of their attitudes toward various programs, policies, and institutions. For example, white Americans often assume that all black Americans share the same goals. We now know that this belief is often unfounded. White Americans may look to Patrick Henry, George Washington, and Thomas Jefferson for inspiration, but many black Americans look to W. E. B. Du Bois, Malcolm X, and Martin Luther King. White Americans aspire to success; black Americans aspire to freedom. White Americans are concerned about taxes and pollution; black Americans are concerned about prejudice and limited opportunities. The speaker who understands and adapts to these differences stands a better chance of winning audience approval than the speaker who ignores them.

On the other hand, the speaker should not make the mistake of stereotyping racial groups and assuming that all Negroes are black militants, all whites are repressive segregationists, or all Orientals run laundries. In any country there are within each racial group many shades of opinion, conflicting attitudes, and differing aspirations. Furthermore, within each racial or ethnic group there is usually a large segment whose goals and values are the same as those of the general population. Much misunderstanding could be avoided by resisting the tendency to classify all members of a group as psychologically and philosophically identical simply because of the color of their skin.

Nationality. The considerations that apply to the racial sensitivities of an audience also apply to nationality groups. No one may appreciate a "Polack" story more than a Pole, but the particular group, occasion, topic of the speech, and personality of the speaker will determine the appropriateness of such a story. Ethnic references need not be avoided, but they should be selected with care, for if members of an audience feel that their race or nationality is being derided, the speaker will probably lose the respect of his listeners and jeopardize the cause for which he speaks. Former Vice President Agnew, for example, referred to a reporter of Japanese descent as a "fat Jap" in the 1968 political campaign, thereby offending Japanese–Americans.

Ethnic groups often differ in their attitudes, beliefs, customs, and interests. In areas of nationality concentration—Germans in Pennsylvania, Scandinavians in Minnesota, Mexican–Americans along the southwestern border, Japanese–Americans in California, and Italians, Puerto Ricans, and Irish in New York—holidays and customs of native countries are frequently observed. The speaker should know the degree of ethnic identification felt by the members of his audience in order to avoid offending them or to win their approval. Perhaps no one is more aware of the significance of such sensitivities than the mayor of New York City. In New York City, the acceptability of any policy depends on its appeal to various ethnic groups.

The presence of international students on college campuses offers excellent opportunities for the student speaker to test his ability to adapt to listeners of different nationalities. Persuading Israelis and Jordanians to accept a common point of view toward Middle-East problems would indeed be challenging. Or imagine the obstacles in convincing students from Formosa of the need to recognize Communist China. Yet the public speaker is often faced with just such challenges.

Occupation. Vocations of audience members often serve as an index to the listeners' economic status and attitudes. Physicians, for example, are financially better off than nurses; college administrators are better paid than elementary school teachers. Physicians and cab drivers probably differ in their attitudes toward Medicare; plumbers and corporation executives rarely agree on unionization; farmers and businessmen have contrasting views on agricultural subsidies. Not only do various occupational groups hold different attitudes toward many topics, but because of their vocations, they may have special knowledge about certain subjects. The speaker should be aware of the occupations represented in his audience.

If the audience is composed of people from a single occupation or profession (machinists, professors, secretaries, dentists, nurses, etc.), adaptation of language and topic may be less difficult for the speaker. The language of such groups is often specialized, and the speaker can use their jargon freely. In addition, interests are likely to be similar, which makes the task of selecting topic and supporting materials easier. If, however, the audience is composed of persons from diverse occupations or professions, the speaker has a more difficult problem. He must select a topic of universal appeal, use supporting materials appropriate to the various occupations represented, and avoid professional jargon.

Economic Status. Economic status, of course, is closely related to occupation or profession, although the relationship is becoming less rigid as members of traditionally "lower income" occupations begin to share more equitably in the national wealth. It is important for the speaker to know the economic status of his audience, however, since people's interests and attitudes are often governed by their pocketbooks. The poor, for example, are rarely interested in such topics as investing in the stock market, international travel, yachting, and debutante balls. The rich, on the other hand, are generally not interested in shopping bargains, job hunting, buying on the installment plan, or retirement savings policies.

Social legislation and civic improvement, the building of roads, and the clearing of slums all demand the expenditure of money. If a speaker chooses to advocate such programs and to win support for them from his audience, he must know and adapt to their attitudes toward higher taxes. His approach to an audience of businessmen should differ considerably from that he would employ with an audience of migrant laborers. Since most social and political issues have economic implications, the wise speaker will avoid abrasive appeals by knowing the economic status attitudes of his audience prior to delivering the speech.

Social Status. Social status is more important to many people than income or wealth. Some professional groups, such as educators, have social prestige unrelated to their incomes. The authority and prestige that accompany social position is sometimes sufficient cause for persons to abandon high-income positions and accept low-paying jobs with greater social prestige. An example of this is Dean Rusk, Secretary of State under President Johnson, who reportedly gave up a lucrative law business in order to accept the cabinet post.

Social status differs greatly from one group to another. Royalty or members of prestigious old families probably enjoy little social prestige among radical students, black militants, and socialists. Motion picture and television performers may command a great deal of respect in some circles, but may be regarded as socially unacceptable in others. The college athlete is rated high on the social ladder by some and rated low by others. If the speaker knows in advance the social status of the listeners and their attitudes toward other social groups, he will have a better understanding of their values, interests, and opinion of him and his subject.

Education. The knowledge a person possesses is not directly related to the number of years of formal education or the number of degrees he has earned. Eric Hoffer, for example, author of several books that have brought him national and international fame for his incisive examination of contemporary society, failed to finish high school and has spent most of his adult life as a common laborer. Although Hoffer is an exceptional case, no speaker should make the mistake of inferring that people lacking a formal education are uneducated.

There is a difference, of course, between the *type* or *kind* of education and the *amount* of education. The Ph.D. may be totally ignorant in some areas that are well understood by high school dropouts. Thus a person who has a Ph.D. in biology or music may know nothing about repairing an automobile, baking bread, or playing football. The person with a Ph.D. in biology and one with a Ph.D. in music may be unable to talk to each other about anything technical in their respective fields. Therefore, the speaker should not make unwarranted assumptions, based entirely upon the degree of formal education attained by the audience members, about their knowledge of a specific topic. He should discover the amount of formal education attained by the majority of his audience, but should also include in his evaluation the extent of their nonformal learning. His responsibility then is to adapt his language and illustrative materials to their particular kind and range of knowledge.

Size. The size of the audience will help the speaker determine the manner in which he should approach his listeners. A general rule of thumb can be used: the larger the audience, the more formal the presentation. Although not always true, experienced speakers testify that it is difficult to be informal with a large group and often awkward to be formal with a small one.

The size of the audience may also influence the degree of difficulty a speaker has in stimulating the emotions of his listeners, in employing visual aids, and in obtaining audience participation. Individuals in small groups, for example, tend to be less subject to emotional appeals than persons in large crowds, for persons in small groups establish an intimacy with the speaker and with other members of the audience that produces inhibitions not found in large gatherings. Thus, the fewer present the more inhibited the audience and the more rational the response. Also, a large assemblage may preclude the use of some types of visual aids or, at least, will place different demands on the speaker who wishes to employ them. The size of the audience also influences the amount and type of audience participation during a speech. Small groups may become involved in active discussion with the speaker, whereas the audience participation by members of large audiences is usually restricted to asking questions at the end of the speech.

Homogeneity. Polarization or "one-mindedness" of an audience is partially achieved when the members are of the same profession or occupation, have the same interests, or share similar social, political, or religious attitudes. Since the speaker seeks to polarize the thinking of the audience, it is obvious that the greater the similarity of characteristics shared by the listeners, the easier it is to accomplish this goal. For example, the speaker's task is greatly simplified if he has an audience composed entirely of elementary school teachers, members of the Young Democrats, accountants, or liberal arts majors.

Audience homogeneity may consist of similarity in any of a number of characteristics such as sex, religion, politics, race, occupation, nationality, or combinations of these. Usually, the greater the number of shared interests and attitudes, the greater the polarization and the simpler the task for the speaker who can select materials aimed at stimulating those shared interests.

Many audiences, however, are not highly homogeneous; the members may come from a variety of occupations, professions, social levels, and income groups. Often the members may have different values. Saul Alinsky describes the fundamentals of a hierarchy of values in Adapted Reading 4.3. Such groups test the imagination of the speaker. He must attempt to find general areas of common belief (political *values* rather than political party, economic *values* rather than income, religious *values* rather than sect, etc.) and interests that tend to unify the group. The community needs shared by all, or the shared goals and aspirations of the members, might offer the speaker a cue to the selection of appropriate materials. For instance, suppose a speaker wanted to address a group in support of a program to solve the problem of pollution created by local industry. His audience is to include not only proponents of the program but also members of a political party opposed to the program. Under these conditions, it would be wise for the speaker to appeal to such general community interests as greater urban beauty, better health conditions, and improved opportunities for attracting *new,* "clean" industry. A speaker can always find shared interests among the members of a heterogeneous audience, although sometimes they are obscure and the speaker must search hard to find them.

Audience Expectations

When a person takes the time and effort to hear someone else speak, he does so with guarded predispositions to listen; he has certain expectations that the speaker must fulfill if the speech is to be effective. Consequently, the speaker must discover those expectations and attempt to satisfy them.

Not long ago, a director of a debate tournament made a series of announcements to the assembled participants. Although not planned to be so, his remarks were humorous. The next day, at a dinner meeting of the same group, the director was again called upon to make some announcements. He knew that the audience anticipated an amusing effort similar to that of the previous day, so he deliberately employed humor to satisfy those expectations. So it is with the political or the occasional speaker. The audience forms an image of a speaker that must be satisfied in his future speaking performances. Audience expectancy is not limited to the manner of presentation, but extends to the ideas the speaker will talk about, arguments he will use, language he will employ, and attitudes he will exhibit toward his audience.

These audience requirements present not only a guide for the speaker to follow in planning what he *must* do, but they also dictate, to an extent, what he must *not* do. For example, if a speaker publicly supports the United Nations, he is limited by those public commitments in future statements about the U.N. The audience not only assumes that he will speak favorably of the United Nations, but that he will not speak unfavorably of it. What does this mean? It means that the relationship between expectations and performance will be thrown out of balance if the speaker takes a position that is contrary to his previous position on an issue. Incongruity will make his goals more difficult to achieve.

This concept can be illustrated by the political fortunes of Hubert Humphrey. As a United States senator, Humphrey championed liberal causes and, consequently, enjoyed the support of liberals. During his tenure as vice-president in the Johnson Administration, Humphrey endorsed the Vietnam war policy of the United States—a policy held to be untenable by many liberals. Hence, many former liberal supporters became detractors when he ran for president in 1968. Humphrey, the man, did not change; Humphrey, the advocate, did change. His rhetoric of post-1964 was inconsistent with his rhetoric of pre-1964. He failed to retain his liberal image among many of those who had contributed time and money to his earlier political campaigns. Although not necessarily politically ruinous, it is dangerous for a politician to shift positions on controversial issues, especially if he has been a major spokesman on the issue. It is relatively easy, however, for a private citizen to shift positions, not having evoked any public expectations.

> You persuade a man only in as far as you can talk his language, by speech, gesture, tonality, order, image, attitude, idea, identifying your ways with him.
>
> KENNETH BURKE

The speaker is limited by the nature of the occasion and the audience's expectations for that particular occasion. For example, a sports banquet demands a speech on athletics, a testimonial dinner calls for a speech on the honoree or his accomplishments, and a religious meeting requires discussion of some moral or theological question. The speaker who delivers a partisan political address to a Parent–Teachers Association group expecting to hear a talk on education risks rejection and failure, as does the speaker who addresses the Tuesday Afternoon Garden Club on race relations or crime.

To be effective, the speaker must determine the expectations of the audience and atttempt to satisfy them by selecting appropriate subject matter.

Reason for Assembling

An audience does not just happen; people usually gather for a reason. Occasionally, the group may be simply a collection of passersby who congregate out of curiosity to hear someone on a soap box in Central Park. But most audiences are formed of people who planned to be present at a particular event or to hear a person speak. Such audiences may be divided into three major categories: (1) coerced or captive, (2) voluntary, and (3) organizational.

Coerced. Perhaps the best example of a coerced audience is that of college students in a classroom. Once a student is assigned to a course, he is often required to attend all of the lecture sessions. This is one type of coerced audience, but not the only one.

Coercion also exists when a group of salesmen are called together for a meeting with the district manager, when a group of junior executives are ordered to a session with the president of the company, or when an athletic team is assembled for a meeting with their coach or manager. In these instances, a common interest is shared by those being coerced; a desire for self-improvement or advancement in the organization provides interest and incentive for them to be attentive.

A third type of captive audience is the one that has gathered voluntarily to hear one speaker and then finds itself the victim of another, unexpected speaker. Often people attend a meeting to hear a United States senator or a Hollywood actor and find themselves forced to sit through the harangues of a battery of other speakers they may not care to hear. Chairmen of meetings sometimes use these occasions to make speeches of their own, taking advantage of an audience gathered for another reason. This is seldom advantageous to the speaker.

Arousing the interest of a coerced audience is often difficult. A particularly challenging assignment is to lecture to a college class. Many students exhibit the attitude: "O.K. I've paid my fee; I dare you to teach me." Some members of the audience may be openly belligerent if the course is a required one. Others are often apathetic. Even the eager student feels coerced when on a particular day he thinks that his time might be better spent elsewhere but is forced to attend the lecture for fear of forfeiting a grade advantage. The lecturer has a built-in hostility to overcome. The same is true of the speaker who intrudes on the time of the audience when he is not scheduled on the program. In such situations, the speaker must convince the auditors of the value or significance of his subject, and he must constantly strive to maintain interest through the use of vivid, striking, and memorable material.

Voluntary. A voluntary audience is one that gathers of free will in order to hear a speaker. Its voluntary nature makes preparation no less important, for often these "volunteers" may be hostile to the topic, the speaker, or the organization the speaker represents.

Examples of speakers who faced voluntary but hostile audiences are not difficult to find. When former Vice-President Humphrey toured colleges and universities in an attempt to explain United States policy in Vietnam during the years 1965 through 1968, he met opposition from portions of his audiences who attended for the specific purpose of openly opposing his position and presence. At times, they interrupted the vice-president with heckling and, at other times, walked out during his speech. They always displayed signs of protest.

A second example is Governor George C. Wallace of Alabama who, in his bid for the presidency in 1964 and again in 1968, faced student audiences similar to Humphrey's. Governor Wallace was frequently shouted down and forced to leave the platform. The speakers in both instances usually handled themselves with skill, anticipating and planning for opposition.

Having a voluntary audience, however, whether favorable or hostile, has advantages, for the members are not apathetic or indifferent; they approach the speech with an interest in either the speaker, his subject, or both. The speaker is thus spared the necessity of overcoming apathy and can concentrate on sustaining interest and influencing audience attitudes.

Organizational Membership. Some speakers are often called upon to talk to local business and service clubs. The interests of the members of these audiences are rather well defined. Although the membership is often heterogenous in profession, income, and political and social background, the speaker knows that they all share the interests of the group to which they belong. He can direct his remarks to those interests. For example, the national project for the Lions International is the procurement of seeing-eye dogs for the blind. The speaker knows, then, that all members of the Lions Club share an interest in that project. The speaker should discover the national and local goals and projects of the group he is to address and, if possible, use that information to strengthen his personal appeal and his audience's support for the ideas he presents.

Obtaining Information About the Audience

Little is gained from knowing *what* information to find out about an audience if the speaker does not know *where* to obtain it. Many times the speaker is aware, from prior experience, of the interests of his audience. But if he is going into a new situation with an audience he does not know, he should do some investigating.

The person who arranged the speaking assignment normally will be happy to provide whatever information he can. Usually it is not difficult to discover from him the more mechanical aspects of the audience such as the size, sex composition, race, and age. If the program chairman cannot provide answers to questions concerning the religious, social, political, and other characteristics of the audience, the speaker has several alternatives. He may seek out other officers of the organization or talk to individual members in advance of the program. He may consult someone who has previously appeared before the group. From these sources he should try to obtain information concerning the predisposition of the audience to the speaker who addressed them previously and to his topic, as well as their interests and attitudes toward the issues the current speaker plans to talk about.

Another source of information is printed material. If a speaker has accepted an invitation to address the B'nai B'rith Society and knows nothing about the organization, he might turn to an encyclopedia or a book about the society for general information regarding its history, membership, and aims or goals. Newspaper accounts of recent activities of the group and publications of the association may be helpful. Labor unions, religious groups, businesses or corporations, civic and service clubs, fraternities and sororities, all publish magazines or "house organs" containing information on issues vital to the group and can provide a general understanding of the group's activities.

The speaker should investigate all of the suggested sources of information before preparing his speech. The more he knows about the audience before he begins his preparation the more effective his effort will be.

THE OCCASION

The setting for a speech is just as important to the speaker's preparation as his knowledge of the audience. To realize the significance of the occasion, consider the speaker who prepares a forty-five minute speech as requested by the program planner. Upon arriving at the designated place, he finds that he is the sixth speaker on a program that begins at 9 P.M. He quickly figures that if all five speakers preceding him have prepared speeches of the same length, he will begin his speech at 12:45 A.M., by which time the audience either will have disappeared completely or dwindled to those who lack the strength to leave. All of his preparation was for naught. What is he to do? The more significant question is: Why did he not discover this situation in advance? To avoid the embarrassment and wasted effort suffered by this speaker, five aspects of a speaking situation should be investigated early in the preparation stage: (1) the length of the meeting, (2) the time of day, (3) the size of the room and the anticipated number of listeners, (4) facilities available to the speaker, and (5) the nature of the meeting.

The Length of the Meeting

It is important for the speaker to know the length of the meeting, for even if he is told by the program chairman that he has 30 to 40 minutes for his speech, the speaker may want to pare down the time if he discovers that the meeting begins late or that a business session precedes his speech. The good audience analyst takes into consideration the audience fatigue factor. Although his listeners might tolerate a longer time limit for a given speech, their receptivity diminishes rapidly with time. Sometimes it is necessary for a speaker to adjust the length of his speech to adapt to the situation. John F.

Kennedy did just that when, in 1959, he followed a rather long and tedious speech delivered by Nelson Rockefeller. Kennedy put aside his prepared text and delivered a short speech that contrasted with Rockefeller's. James Golden shows Kennedy's ability to do this in "John F. Kennedy's Audience Adaptation," Adapted Reading 4.5. Often the audience will respect him more and listen with greater interest and retention if the speaker limits himself to less time than that allotted to him.

> General Alexander Smith, a tedious speaker in Congress, observed: "You, sir, speak for the present generation; but I speak for posterity." "Yes," replied Henry Clay, "and you seem resolved to speak until the arrival of your audience."

The Time of Day

As all college students know, and as the low enrollments reveal, it is more difficult to listen attentively to a 7:30 A.M. lecture than to a 9:30 A.M. lecture, regardless of the speaker. The professor knows (or should know) that it is more challenging to deliver the earlier lecture than the later one. One of the authors recalls that he registered for a course in music appreciation when in college, and was assigned to a 1:30 P.M. class. Three times a week he attended the class for two weeks. Three times a week for two weeks he went to sleep listening to Beethoven, Brahms, and Bach. A full stomach combined with soothing music defeated his will to stay awake. He dropped the course and took it in a subsequent semester at a more appropriate time.

A speaker should adjust to the time of day and when planning his speech take into consideration such universally shared physical states as early morning sleepiness, early afternoon listlessness, late afternoon fatigue, and late evening grogginess. The speaker should discover his own periods of high and low alertness and adjust to them. It may be necessary for him to make an extra effort during particular parts of the day.

The Size of the Room and Audience

The degree of formality of a speech is dictated in part by the size and shape of the room and the number of people present. The comfort of both the speaker and the members of the audience is also affected by these two aspects of the situation.

Few things are more disconcerting to a speaker than to address an audience of 25 persons in a room that seats 300. The audience, too, is embarrassed. The program chairman should anticipate the number of listeners and select a room that seats approximately that number. If there is little information upon which to base an estimate of attendance, it is better to schedule a room that is too small for the audience than one that is too large. The optimum ratio of seats to people is one to one, but it is better for the speaker's morale to have people standing or turned away than to have a few listeners surrounded by a sea of empty chairs. Jerry Bruno describes some of the practical considerations of room selection as it affects political campaign speeches in Adapted Reading 4.2.

If a speaker plans to use visual aids, the size and type of aids will vary with the distance from the platform or projection screen to the farthest person. He may want to use more personalized illustrative materials with a small audience than he would normally use with a large one. His manner of delivery certainly will be modified according to the size of the room and the number of people present; he will normally speak more softly and use less expansive gestures in a small room than in a large auditorium.

The Facilities

It is always a good idea for a speaker to visit the room in which he is going to speak to determine for himself not only the dimensions, but to inspect the facilities so that he may request any additional items he needs. If a speaker is to use notes or a manuscript, he may want a lectern. If it is a large room, he may desire a public address system to avoid shouting to be heard. On the other hand, if the auditorium has poor acoustics, the speaker may request that an existing public address system be removed. Electronic amplification is sometimes used when not actually required, and often a speaker will feel restricted by the presence of a public address system if there is no need for it.

If a speaker plans to use photographic slides to illustrate his speech, he should make sure that the room can be darkened (some cannot), and he should be certain that a screen and projector will be provided. He should know where the light switches are located and plan to have the lights dimmed or turned off at the appropriate time in the course of his speech. And if the lighting in the room is not adequate for exhibiting prepared visual aids, he should request additional lighting or modify his talk to exclude the visual aids.

The speaker should also learn in advance whether he will perform on a stage, raised dais, or other kind of platform, for special challenges confront the speaker if he is raised physically above his audience. The situation of the commencement speaker described earlier in this chapter would not have occurred had the speaker discovered in advance that he was to speak from a stage where part of his audience would be seated. For the best rapport with his listeners, the speaker should be on the same level as the audience and as close to them as possible. The higher and farther removed in distance a speaker is from his audience, the greater is the psychological distance between him and them. It is important, then, that the speaker be familiar with the facilities and total environment of the speaking situation.

The Nature of the Meeting

As stressed earlier, people gather to hear a speech for some particular reason. It may be a regularly scheduled meeting of a group or a special occasion. It may be a special gathering of a group that meets regularly. The speaker should ask three basic questions concerning the nature of the meeting: (1) Is it a regular meeting? (2) Is it a special occasion? and (3) What is the nature of the program?

Is It a Regular Meeting? Groups that meet on a regular basis are usually starved for programs and often invite guests to speak with little or no long-range planning. It is the responsibility of the speaker to determine the interests of the members, discover what previous speakers have talked about in order to avoid repetition, and to adapt to those speeches. Normally such situations require a relatively short speech and, if the speech follows a meal, it should probably entertain as well as enlighten or persuade.

Is It a Special Occasion? Often groups hold meetings to commemorate special events in the history of the country or their own organizations. Universities celebrate Founders Day and schedule service award meetings for selected employees; social organizations recognize anniversaries and holidays such as the Fourth of July, Lincoln's birthday, and Labor Day. Civic groups commemorate events that gave rise to their formation, such as United Nations Day by local United Nations Leagues and Registration Day by the League of Women Voters. A myriad of special banquets are held for a variety of reasons, such as political fund-raising, charitable campaigns, and the presentation of awards. If one is asked to speak to a group gathered to celebrate a special event, he should be familiar with the event and the relationship of the event to the organization. He should then, of course, adapt his speech to that special occasion.

What Is the Nature of the Program? Is there other entertainment? Are there to be other speakers? If so, what are their topics? Am I to be the main speaker or a supplementary one? All of these questions should be answered by the speaker before he begins his preparation.

It is disconcerting to a speaker to appear at an occasion thinking he is the principal speaker only to discover that three other people share the same belief. Distress turns into panic when he further learns that he is to be the second speaker and that the first speaker is talking on the same topic he has selected. What to do now? Perhaps the better part of wisdom would be to feign illness and make a strategic exit. But not many persons exhibit that kind of wisdom and it is certainly the coward's way out. The average speaker would stumble through his prepared text with a nervous preface to the effect that he "didn't have much to add to the remarks of the previous speaker." He may then proceed to prove his preface remarkably accurate. How embarrassing for the speaker! Worse, how cruel to the audience! Yet the situation has occurred a multitude of times and always because of poor planning.

A good program planner will avoid this embarrassment by fully informing the participating speakers of the entire program and their role in it. But many programs are planned by inexperienced chairmen. (One program chairman telephoned a speech department and asked them to present a debate, but to be sure it wasn't controversial.) The alert speaker will avoid embarrassment by requesting this information should it not be supplied by the chairman. If necessary, he can then adapt his remarks to those of the other speakers. It is helpful, although frequently impossible, to obtain outlines or even manuscripts of the other speeches in advance of the occasion so that the adaptation can be better developed.

Finally, the speaker should ascertain his role in the program. If he is to be the featured speaker, all other portions of the program should be subordinate to his talk. If he is to be one of several speakers of equal significance, he should adapt his speech accordingly.

SUMMARY

Preparing a speech is a complicated task that requires a systematic method. The first step a speaker should take in preparing for a speech is analyzing the audience and occasion. When analyzing the audience, the speaker should investigate its composition—age, sex, religion, politics, race, nationality, occupation, economic status, social status, education, size and homogeneity—in order to aid him in selecting a topic and supporting materials that will be of interest. He should also discover the audience's expectations and their reason for assembling. The speaker should select a topic and supporting materials consistent with the occasion as well. He should know something about the length of the meeting, the time of day, the size of the group, the facilities, and whether the audience is captive or voluntary. With this kind of information about the audience and occasion, the speaker is prepared to select a topic and to begin gathering materials for the speech.

ADAPTED READING 4.1

POLARIZATION, SOCIAL FACILITATION, AND LISTENING

Walter W. Stevens

The increasing volume of research which has been completed during the last decade in the area of listening is encouraging. Compared to the other communication skills, progress in the sophistication of listening theory has been remarkable, undoubtedly in part because the auditor has been so thoroughly ignored in the past. However, two psychological concepts which are vitally linked with listening have not as yet been sufficiently explored by those in speech. These concepts are polarization and social facilitation. . . .

Polarization is strong group cohesiveness, unity, "we feeling," human homogenization so that everyone present in an audience situation becomes an integral member of the group. There is a sympathetic relationship between speaker and listener because the physical and mental processes of the auditor are in tune with those of the speaker and extreme sensitivity exists between the two. Bryant and Wallace affirmed that "the greater the feeling of solidarity and oneness an audience has, the stronger and surer its favorable response is likely to be." Polarization, an old technique, is unfamiliar to many people, although it is a perfectly ethical but powerful psychological device used to advantage by both the principled orator and the demagogue. Every citizen should recognize and understand its implications. The speaker who wishes to polarize an audience will maneuver it into taking joint action. He may use humor to get his listeners to laugh together; he may ask for a show of hands; he may get them to sing or chant together; he may ask them to stand together, kneel together, pray together, rise together, sit together, or read together. These procedures are repeated again and again for it takes time to polarize a group; but, as most skillful orators know, it is well worth the effort.

What happens to a listener when he becomes polarized? He tends to relinquish his own set of values and to adopt the values of the audience. Instead of many diverse, individual reflective responses to a speech, we observe a unified group response. As the group reacts, so does each person conform. Independent critical appraisal of what is being said is reduced to a minimum because nonconformity in a polarized group is socially unacceptable, even if it is only silent mental disagreement. The auditor is reduced to a private in a military drill platoon. When the speaker says, "Right face," he does so along with everybody else without asking himself, "Why should I do a right face?" He has become a victim of a type of group hypnosis. The critical listener resists polarization. He identifies polarizing devices for what they are—emotional and psychological straitjackets that rob him of his individualism. He is aware that his critical judgment is impaired when he is under their spell. In a

From *Western Speech*, Summer 1961, pp. 168–170.

polarized audience, said Woolbert, "it takes energy to oppose. Men have to be schooled to hesitate and to doubt. . . . The fixed tendency is to receive willingly and without opposition."

A phenomenon similar to polarization is social facilitation, the effect of the members of a group upon each other because of their physical proximity. Obviously, stimuli move from speaker to auditor and from auditor to speaker; but in addition, each listener tends to be stimulated more than he realizes by the reactions of other persons near him. As a member of an audience one has heard at some time a very poor speech or has attended a poor play or recital. Perhaps the only reason that one did not get up and walk out of the hall was that such an action would have been embarrassing. At the conclusion of the performance one felt as if he wanted to throw a tomato, but instead he applauded. Why? It was clapping time; everybody was clapping. To take another example, we have all laughed heartily with a group as we turned to the person next to us and asked, "What did he say?" Why were we laughing? It was social facilitation. Allport defined social facilitation as "an increase of response merely from the sight or sound of others making the same movements." It is radiation of social influence which can be obvious but more often occurs subliminally. The larger the group and the more emotional the stimulation presented by the speaker the greater the effect of social facilitation.

Clark said that "some emotions, especially fear and sorrow, are produced or intensified by witnessing in others the expressions of like emotions. . . . It is evident that we tend to interpret objects as our fellows interpret them, to consider as real what others, by their behavior, seem to recognize as real, and to accept as true the ideas which our companions appear to accept." Woolbert corroborated: "The sound of other persons laughing, the sight of men who look angry, the perception of handkerchiefs dabbing at red eyes, snuffling and sobbing muttered ejaculations, sounds that represent protest—all these add to the response which the individual gives to the speaker. . . ."

Gurnee discovered that in a *viva voce* vote "uncertain members tended to be influenced to vote in the direction of the most vigorous response. . . ." and Burnham emphasized that "the individual alone and the individual in a group are two different psychological beings. . . ."

There is no lack of interest and documentation as to the conforming nature of man's behavior. Lasswell said that "there are counties where no white man has ever voted a Republican ticket, and there are counties where a respectable Democrat is a contradiction in terms." Campbell, Gurin, and Miller corroborate that "if the group has high positive significance to the individual, he will tend to conform to what he perceives to be its standards." Berelson *et al.* reported from a case study that "a worker's voting behavior is influenced by the pressures of the environment in which he works; the extent to which he is influenced by such stimuli depends on the amount of his exposure to that environment, and the amount of such exposure depends upon his interaction with others in the environment. In this way an individual comes to learn what is considered 'appropriate' by the participants in that environment. Rather than direct communications from leaders to followers, this is an indirect process that might be called 'social absorption.' "

According to some of the best information we can get, man's herd behavior is not only common, it is a sign of health and stability. Bonner stated that "every normal individual wants acceptance, and he will strive to please others — that is, play the role of a friendly and accepting individual — because of the anticipated belongingness that will accrue from it." Johnson said that "what most clinical psychologists call social adjustment lies in part in the fundamentally negative skill of not making oneself too conspicuous. Good adjustment for any individual, therefore, is generally assumed by these clinical workers to depend more or less on his feeling, thinking, acting pretty much as other people do, of liking what they like, hating what they hate, believing what they believe — and not knowing why. . . ."

Asch conducted an experiment which investigated the effect of group pressure upon the individual member of a group. There were nine subjects employed, eight of whom were in league with the experimenter and one of whom was completely unaware of the structure of the experiment. The subjects were requested to match a straight line with three other straight lines of various lengths, one of which was exactly the same length as the given line. The eight cooperating subjects at specified times were previously instructed to agree on an erroneous decision. The purpose of the experiment was to see if group pressure would force the single test subject to lie in order to conform with the group. The correct answer was obvious and unavoidable if one trusted his own sense of sight. Yet, in spite of what he perceived, one out of three of the test subjects, of fifty tested, conformed with the majority when the latter made an incorrect choice. This experiment is an excellent illustration of the effects of social facilitation and of the type of study which can be made in this area.

The critical listener tries to maintain his intellectual free will. No matter what the audience thinks of the speaker, no matter how it reacts to his skill and charm, the reflective auditor attempts to make an individual judgment independent of others in terms of his own criteria, to make his response truly his and not one subliminally forced upon him by the group. But so often the reaction of the audience in part determines the individual listener's reaction to the speaker; that is, his response tends to be a compromise between his impressions and those of the group. And social facilitation operates most irresistibly when the audience is polarized. We like to think that we possess a high degree of rationality, but the psychological consequences of polarization and social facilitation are so subtle that usually we are unable to recognize and oppose them when they occur. After the occasion, we may still be at a loss to explain why we responded as we did. This certainly suggests a powerful reason for further experimental research into polarization and social facilitation as they relate to platform speaking. Their true influence upon the responses of the listener ought to be empirically validated under carefully controlled conditions and this powerful and hidden force in the communication process more thoroughly understood.

MY BUSINESS IS CROWDS
Jerry Bruno and Jeff Greenfield

Jerry Bruno worked at various times as advance man for William Proxmire, John Kennedy, Robert Kennedy, and Lyndon Johnson. The duties of an advance man are to make all prior arrangements for a rally or speech by a candidate or political office-holder including the selection of the site of the speech, arrangements for publicity and transportation, contacts with local committees, and other details.

There's nothing really rewarding about being denounced in front of five thousand people by a congressman. . . . It's just one of those things — or two or five of those things — that I ran into in politics. It just seemed that, working for Robert Kennedy, I happened to run into them all the time. . . .

This particular denunciation was the result of a fight with Congresswoman Edith Green of Oregon. . . . Edith Green is a very tough politician — one of the toughest anywhere — and as a lot of badly scarred people in Washington will tell you, when she wants something, she knows how to fight for it. She's also somebody Robert Kennedy felt a debt to, because of her help to John Kennedy in 1960.

Now my business is crowds: how to get them in, how to get them out, even how to count them. . . . Edith Green had her ideas about what Bob Kennedy should do — namely, speak at this new auditorium in Portland that seated 14,000. Remember the first rule of crowds: 25,000 people in a 50,000-seat stadium is a half-empty turnout. But 4,000 people in a hall that seats 3,000 is an overflow crowd. And it works that way on a crowd. People want the sense of being somewhere special, somewhere a lot of people are trying to get to. It depresses people to see empty seats all around them, makes them feel they've been conned into turning out for an event that wasn't all that special.

In this case I took a look around and realized that you couldn't fill those fourteen thousand seats if Raquel Welch and Paul Newman put on a stag show as a warm-up.

So I called the Washington office.

"Joe," I said to Dolan, "you just can't fill this hall Edith wants us to go to. It'll be just terrible."

"Well," Dolan said, "don't do it."

So I looked around and found a Labor Temple that was perfect. It held maybe four thousand people and I knew we could get an overflow crowd out to that auditorium. It was just right. At least, that's what I thought until I spoke to Edith Green.

"That Temple can't hold the crowd that's going to turn out for Kennedy," she said.

"How many do you think will come out?" I asked.

"Maybe six thousand people," she said.

"Yeah, but that won't even half fill the new hall," I said. "It'll be terrible."

"Why can't we hang a curtain over the empty seats?" she said.

This is a common trick in political advance, and it really works great in places like the old Madison Square Garden where you can barely see the balcony from the floor. The press never notices those things. But when we went out to look at this new hall, it was one of those well-lit modern places, with no posts and no hidden corners. There was just no way to hide eight thousand empty seats, not from newsmen, and God knows not from Robert Kennedy.

The argument showed no signs of settlement, so I settled it myself. I had thousands of flyers printed up announcing that Robert Kennedy and Edith Green would appear at the Labor Temple. Edith Green just about hit the ceiling and threatened to cancel the whole affair.

"I don't think you can do that," I said. "You've got fifty thousand flyers saying you and Kennedy will be there. That could mean a lot of disappointed voters."

So Bob Kennedy came to Portland, and at the Labor Temple they were hanging from the rafters, and I mean literally up there in the rafters. There were two thousand people or so outside, the hall was packed, the press was impressed by the turnout, and it was the kind of evening Kennedy loved. And then Edith Green stood up to introduce Kennedy.

"I want all you people to know," she said, turning in my direction, "that had I had my way, we would all have been comfortable and been able to hear Bob Kennedy. But because of that man there" — and she points to me — "we're in this crowded, sweaty room. And I want you to know, Senator Kennedy, that it was that man who caused this problem."

There I am — my first public recognition in all my years in politics! And there's Bob Kennedy, his head down as though in deep thought, trying to keep from bursting out laughing on the stage. . . .

In a funny kind of way, elections give candidates the chance to break up myths which separate them from people. . . . Look at John Kennedy in 1960. He was a Catholic. And hard as it is to remember, there were a lot of places in America where a Catholic was considered a subversive, who would smuggle the Pope into Washington the day after he was inaugurated. So he went into West Virginia, and just the idea of going to people, talking with them informally, helped dispel that myth; because when you talk with a guy, laugh at his jokes, listen to his ideas, even if you don't agree with everything he says, he stops being a villain. You forget to hate him. And that's what John Kennedy did in West Virginia, and at a meeting of Houston ministers, which was run as a half-hour TV commercial in Bible Belt states because it showed Kennedy as he *was*, talking right out at the issue which was in the back of everybody's minds.

Or think about Bob Kennedy in 1968. What was his myth? Ruthless — a cold, cynical, calculating street fighter. You can't knock that out of people with commercials, because people *really* don't believe what they see on TV. . . . It's something they turn on and that comes at them, from out there somewhere.

So for Bob Kennedy, the street route was critical. And the whistle-stop—that was a perfect thing for RFK to use, in half a dozen ways. First, it brought you into the real Middle America, the places left behind by jet planes and the death of railroads and new industrial plants. Many of these towns had never seen a Presidential candidate for fifty or sixty years, much less a Kennedy. Here was that guy who was a New Yorker, a jet-setter, an alien, with all those crazy ideas about blacks and blood for the Viet Cong, and here he was, in Wabash or whatever. And Kennedy would always say, "Has McCarthy been here? Did Hubert come here?" There'd be all these people—different from Bob Kennedy in every way, farmers with red faces and rough hands, guys who worked in factories—who'd be at the back of the train, and there was Bob Kennedy teasing them, joshing them, talking about why he wanted to be President, and no matter what else they thought, the "ruthless" tag dropped right away. Kennedy was a warm, affectionate man who really loved his country, and that came across in those stops.

ADAPTED READING 4.3

THE LISTENER'S PERSONAL PRIORITIES
Saul Alinsky

In analyzing his listeners, the speaker must recognize that each person or bloc has a hierarchy of values. For instance, let us assume that we are in a ghetto community where everyone is for civil rights.

A black man there had bought a small house when the neighborhood was first changing, and he wound up paying a highly inflated price—more than four times the value of the property. Everything he owns is tied into that house. Urban renewal, now, is threatening to come in and take it on the basis of a value appraisal according to their criteria, which would be less than a fourth of his financial commitment. He is desperately trying to save his own small economic world. Civil rights would get him to a meeting once a month, maybe he'd sign some petitions and maybe he'd give a dollar here and there, but on a fight against urban renewal's threat to wipe out his property, he would come to meetings every night.

Next door to him is a woman who is renting. She is not concerned about urban renewal. She has three small girls, and her major worry is the drug pushers and pimps that infest the neighborhood and threaten the future of her children. She is for civil rights too, but she is more concerned about a community free of pimps and pushers, and she wants better schools for her children. Those are her No. 1 priorities.

Next door to her is a family on welfare; their No. 1 priority is more money. Across the street there is a family who can be described as the working poor, struggling to get along on their drastically limited budget—to them, consumer prices and local merchants gouging are the No. 1 priorities. Any tenant of a slum landlord, living among rats and cockroaches, will quickly tell you what his No. 1 priority is — and so it goes.

ADAPTED READING 4.4

THE PROFESSOR
AND THE GHOSTS

Eric Sevareid

If we sound a bit low tonight, it isn't just this cold in the head; it's because we've seen new evidence that our personal campaign against synthetics and substitutes, both human and material, is going nowhere except backward. We have just learned that one of the most ominous false fronts of all is going to be institutionalized. Men are actually going to be trained in the production of synthetic personality.

American University, here in the capital city, is beginning a course of study for ghost writers. Impressed by the fact that there are already about 150 ghost writers writing speeches for government leaders, the university has leaped to the conclusion that here is a new career, a "felt need," as ghost writers say on their worst days, that requires filling.

Professor Bowman of the University says: "Most of the great speeches we hear are written in whole or in part by someone backstage."

Listen, Professor; we know of people who see ghosts where there is nothing, but you are seeing ghosts where there are people. Any great speeches you've heard around here in recent years, and they are pitifully few, were written by the men who delivered them. Speech — that is thoughts, words, voice — is personality itself, and as soon as you dilute it from the outside you have something else, and it's never great because it's never real.

President Truman stumbled along over ghost writers' stuff, sounding phony as a six-dollar bill, until one night about four years ago at an editors' meeting he threw away the ghosted stuff and just talked. It was a pretty great speech — it electrified that audience — simply because it was the real, honest Harry Truman. Why were Franklin Roosevelt's speeches in the early days greater speeches than in the later days? Chiefly because they came straight from his own heart and pen. Why are Dean Acheson's formal speeches less effective than Dean Acheson pacing up and down his office and just talking? Because his formal speeches are full of ghosts — grammatic, erudite ghosts, but ghosts just the same.

We scarcely recall any great speeches in the U.S. Senate since Vandenberg's days, and Vandenberg painfully pecked out those speeches, word by word, on his own typewriter. A bit hammy, yes — but pure Vandenberg, therefore effective.

A few years ago in a Senate hearing, David Lilienthal couldn't stand

McKellar's needling about his loyalty any longer, and in a tense voice let go, beginning with the words: "This I do believe," a speech that is now part of current American literature. It lives. A ghost writer would have killed it dead as — a ghost.

The three most effective American orators today are probably John L. Lewis, General MacArthur, and General Eisenhower. Imagine a ghost writer tinkering with those thundering Shakespearean sentences of Lewis's. Imagine MacArthur on that returning plane saying to an aide: "Fix me up a speech for Congress, something about old soldiers never dying, something along that general line." Nonsense, Professor.

As for Ike, he takes incredible pains with his public words. He worked three weeks on his great Guildhall speech, testing, polishing, savoring the words. Ike is where he is today because of his pen, not his sword. General Marshall first sent him to Europe because he was so deeply impressed with a thirty-page document written by Ike. Eisenhower *wrote* his way to power; and if the professor at American can prove to us that a ghost writer really did all this, then we demand he be produced so we can vote for *him* for President.

We admit there are a lot of ghost writers in Washington. And we claim that is one reason government has become less articulate, its leaders less able to move and excite the American people. We don't understand government leaders who are too busy to write their own speeches, for a man's own words are the man's own self. He wouldn't dare use a false face or a false name: it is equally fraudulent to use false words.

Abraham Lincoln is dead, but we do wish the professors would talk this whole thing over with Winston Churchill before they make another move.

ADAPTED READING 4.5

JOHN F. KENNEDY'S AUDIENCE ADAPTATION
James L. Golden

Kennedy followed carefully cleared texts closely in most of the addresses delivered from the White House and in those speeches presented at other dignified special occasions such as a university commencement, a dedication ceremony, or a joint session of Congress. Quite a different procedure was used, on the other hand, when he spoke at a political rally or when he was engaged in face-to-face confrontation with a large and enthusiastic group of people.

The Alfred E. Smith Foundation banquet at the Waldorf Astoria in October, 1959, reveals his practice of making sudden and significant changes in his speaking plans so that he could adapt his remarks to the prevailing mood of the audience and to the lateness of the hour. For two reasons Kennedy viewed this setting as crucial to the success of his future political goals. First, he recognized the possibility that he might become a candidate for the Demo-

From "John F. Kennedy and the 'Ghosts'," *Quarterly Journal of Speech*, December 1966, p. 355.

cratic nomination in 1960. Second, he regarded Governor Nelson Rockefeller, who also was scheduled to speak, as a potential Republican nominee.

During the dinner hour, therefore, Kennedy nervously played with his manuscript while noting his opponent's animated conversation and carefree manner. Later, at the close of the governor's manuscript speech, Kennedy decided to put aside his own text to change the atmosphere of comfortable indifference which, according to the *New York Times*, had settled over the 2500 people in the audience. After making humorous references both to himself and to Rockefeller, he alluded to General Winfield Scott, Alf Landon, and Richard Nixon, who he suggested was perhaps standing on the steps of the Nation's Capitol with the spyglass turned toward Albany. His witty and spontaneous presentation evoked laughter and applause ten times in nine minutes. More important, in his first encounter with Rockefeller, Kennedy had made a stronger impact on the audience.

ADDITIONAL READINGS

Clevenger, Theodore, *Audience Analysis* (Indianapolis: Bobbs-Merrill, 1966).
Eisenson, Jon, J. Jeffery Auer, and John V. Irwin, *The Psychology of Communication* (New York: Appleton, 1963), chap. 16, "Psychology of Public Address."
Hance, Kenneth, David Ralph, and Milton Wiksell, *Principles of Speaking* (Belmont: Wadsworth, 1969), chap. 3, "Understanding and Adapting to the Occasion"; chap. 4, "Understanding and Adapting to the Audience."
McCroskey, James, *An Introduction to Rhetorical Communication* (Englewood Cliffs, N.J.: Prentice-Hall, 1972), chap. 3, "The Nature of the Audience: Attitude Formation and Change."
Monroe, Alan and Douglas Ehninger, *Principles and Types of Speech* (Glenview, Ill.: Scott, Foresman, 1967), chap. 8, "Analyzing the Audience and Occasion."
Mudd, Charles and Malcolm Sillars, *Speech Content and Communication* (San Francisco: Chandler, 1969), chap. 5, "Analyzing the *Audience*."
Oliver, Robert and Rupert Cortright, *Effective Speech* (New York: Holt, Rinehart & Winston, 1970), chap. 10, "Adapting to the Audience."

STUDY QUESTIONS

1. What is the difference between polarization and social facilitation? Why is knowledge of both of these concepts important to a speaker?
2. In what ways did Stokely Carmichael attempt to adapt to his audiences in the speeches discussed in Adapted Reading 11.3?
3. Do you agree with Eric Sevareid that ghostwritten speeches cannot be memorable speeches? (Adapted Reading 4.4) Why or why not?
4. In what ways does the size of the audience affect the speaker's delivery, rapport with his listeners, and audience participation?
5. How do audience expectations influence the speaker's choice of subject and selection of supporting materials?
6. In what ways can a speaker adapt to a coerced audience, a voluntary audience, and an organizational audience?
7. If you were asked to give a speech to each of the following organizations, where might you obtain information about your prospective audiences: (1) the Junior League, (2) the Speech Communication Association, (3) the local chapter of the American Civil Liberties Union, (4) your state historical society?
8. What is meant by the "occasion" for a speech? Do all speeches have occasions? What kinds of information does a speaker need to obtain about the speech occasion?

EXERCISES

1. Prepare an outline for a speech for a classroom audience on some subject on which you are well informed. Then prepare a second outline adapting the materials for a speech to a businessmen's noon luncheon meeting.

2. Attend a speech and analyze the speaker's use of materials to interest or adapt to his audience. Did he use any special appeals or techniques to account for (a) the composition of the audience, (b) the expectations of his listeners, and (c) the nature of the occasion? Write a paper summarizing your analysis.

3. In outline form, prepare an analysis of the class as an audience. In what ways are they much alike? In what ways do they differ?

4. Prepare a list of five topics that most of your classroom audience would be interested in. Prepare another list of five topics on which most of the class members would be in agreement. Prepare a third list of subjects on which there probably would be differing attitudes among the class members.

5. Read a speech in *Vital Speeches* or *Representative American Speeches*. In a paper, indicate the ways that the speaker seemed to be trying to adapt to the interests, attitudes, or characteristics of his audience. How necessary, in your opinion, was audience adaptation in this situation? Indicate your opinion of the speaker's effectiveness in adapting to his listeners.

6. Select a teacher and analyze his effectiveness in adapting to his audience of students. Prepare a three- to four-minute report in which you analyze both the strong and weak points of the audience adaptation of this teacher. You need not name the teacher in your report. Deliver the report to the class.

ANALYZING
SUBJECTS

George Bernard Shaw, the British lecturer and playwright, claimed that the most popular speech he ever delivered was at the invitation of "the superior persons at Toynbee Hall who step condescendingly down from the universiies to improve the poor." Informed that his audience would consist entirely of poor people, he chose as his topic, "That the poor are useless, dangerous, and ought to be abolished." Shaw relates, "I had my poor audience, and they were delighted. They cheered me to the echo: that was what they wanted to have said."

While Shaw's selection of topic at first seems preposterous, upon reflection it becomes apparent that it was a shrewd choice. Extensive reading in economics and years of study of the social conditions in Britain had given Shaw an understanding of poverty and its causes; he appreciated that to the members of his audience nothing was more vital than their day-to-day struggle for existence and that the nature of the meeting was ideal for a discussion of their problems. The subject was right for the speaker, the audience, and the occasion.

In situations other than public speaking, the speaker often will find that his subject is predetermined. For example, when two businessmen get together to conclude a deal, when a committee meets to resolve a problem, when a personnel manager interviews a job applicant, when a supervisor explains a new method or program to employees, when a client consults his lawyer, and in similar person-to-person speaking situations, the purpose of the meeting dictates the general topic.

In much interpersonal communication, such as conversations, a student–teacher consultation, and social discourse, the participants may touch upon a wide range of subjects which grow out of the interactions of the persons involved in the communication.

In public-speaking situations, however, the speaker often must determine what his subject will be, and not all speakers will find the choice as easy as did George Bernard Shaw. For many, this first step in the preparation of a speech may be an arduous and soul-searching endeavor. The choice of a subject, of course, presents no problem if the speaker is asked to speak on a specific topic that he is qualified to discuss. More commonly, however, speakers are invited to address groups without a particular topic being specified. The speaker may be asked to deliver a talk on some general subject with which he is familiar; for example, a college president might be invited to discuss education, or a public official might be asked to speak on some aspect of government. At other times, not even a general topic is suggested. In either circumstance, the speaker has a wide range of possible subjects that he can discuss; so he must compile a list of potential topics, examine each, and select one he believes is well suited to the requirements of the situation.

The student speaker often faces a uniquely difficult task in that he must address the same audience of classmates regularly and at short intervals of time. He may choose the first two or three subjects with little difficulty, but thereafter he will probably find it increasingly difficult to choose topics for speaking assignments.

FINDING TOPICS

For a variety of reasons, speakers often find it difficult to select subjects. Often, the prime reason is the speaker's feeling of inadequacy which results in his inability to make up his mind. He may select one topic and begin preparation of the speech only to decide that another topic will be more interesting. So he starts to work on a second subject. After a while he begins to doubt his competency to discuss that topic and chooses still another. And on and on. Aside from the time wasted in these false starts, the speaker is also plagued by doubts, fears, and general insecurity. He feels that his ideas and experiences are not important enough to interest others.

Another reason why a speaker may experience difficulty in selecting speech topics is that he may not know himself. He may not have taken the time to compile an inventory of those subjects about which he is well informed and, consequently, does not know his true interests. So when the time comes to select a speech topic, he must begin the painstaking task of trying to sort out from the hundreds of things currently occupying his mind a topic suitable for the requested speech.

A third reason why speakers have trouble choosing topics is that they do not know other people. They are unable to place themselves in the position of their listeners and to understand the listeners' attitudes, interests, knowledge, and experiences. A topic that seems commonplace to the speaker may be one in which the audience would be highly interested. For example, upon being questioned by his instructor, one student who was having trouble locating speech topics revealed that he had been raised on a remote island in the Gulf of Mexico off the Louisiana coast, that he had been tutored at home by his mother until he reached high school age, and that upon entering high school he could speak only French. From such an unusual childhood the speaker probably could have chosen several potentially interesting speech topics, but he had overlooked those possibilities because to him his experiences seemed commonplace.

Upon questioning another student who claimed he could find nothing of interest to discuss with his classmates it was discovered that he had been a student in Havana at the time of Fidel Castro's overthrow of the Battista government. Yet it had never occurred to him that this was a potential speech topic of interest to others who had not been there.

To overcome these difficulties in selecting speech subjects, the speaker should recognize that everyone is an "expert" on some subject. He should take inventory of his own interests, and he should study and know his audience and the nature of the speaking occasion. The speaker who has nothing worthwhile to talk about probably does not exist. Aside from specialized information acquired on the job, in the classroom, and through reading, travel, and various other pursuits, almost everyone has a store of general knowledge, opinions, and observations based on personal experiences. Each individual is the best possible expert — actually the only expert — on his personal reactions to the people, places, and activities with which he has come into contact. Who knows better the thrill and excitement of landing a five-pound bass than the fisherman who has caught one? Who understands better the horror and fright of an automobile accident than the victim of one? Who can better appreciate the kind gesture or helping hand of a friend than the recipient? In all such personal experiences, the participants qualify as highly competent authorities.

Admittedly, some people have led more exciting lives than others; their experiences are more varied, and their knowledge more extensive. But there is nothing to prevent the speaker who feels that his life has been unduly sheltered or prosaic from broadening the scope of his knowledge and experiences through reading, conversation, hobbies, sports, television, and other activities. Indeed, he should be encouraged to do so. In today's world there is no excuse for an individual having nothing worthwhile to talk about.

> **Blessed is the man who, having nothing to say, abstains from giving in words evidence of the fact.**
>
> GEORGE ELIOT

Rather than having nothing to discuss, a speaker who has difficulty finding speech topics has, more likely, simply failed to take careful inventory of his interests. He needs to examine both the present and the past. As sources for possible topics he should consider his personal experiences and observations; his reading and study; his listening to radio, television, lectures, and conversations; his jobs; the organizations to which he belongs;

special research and investigations that he has conducted; his leisure activities; his travels; and other related items. Specifically, he might consider:

1. sports
2. hobbies
3. skills
4. pastimes
5. jobs
6. travel
7. school
8. food
9. habits
10. social life
11. clubs, organizations
12. religion, philosophy
13. music
14. health
15. personal conduct and beliefs
16. customs, traditions
17. holidays
18. art
19. home and family
20. people
21. childhood
22. home town
23. growth
24. goals and ambitions
25. unusual experiences
26. nature
27. animals and pets
28. clothing
29. grooming
30. etiquette
31. processes
32. procedures
33. equipment, tools, and apparatus
34. words, language
35. sound
36. daily chores
37. politics
38. reading
39. personality traits
40. safety
41. books, literature
42. subject matter areas:
    a. mathematics
    b. science

c. architecture
d. history
e. geography
f. anthropology
g. government
h. law
i. medicine
j. agriculture
k. forestry
l. geology
m. economics
n. sociology
o. psychology
p. speech
q. home economics
r. others

As the above list suggests, the number of areas that the speaker should examine in searching for speech topics is large. However, it is possible to extend even further the number of potential topics. Specific aspects or subtopics of various areas might serve as subjects for speeches, as shown below:

Music

1. How to play the guitar.
2. How to buy a good guitar.
3. The guitar in country and western music.
4. How to listen to country and western music.
5. Why country and western music has become popular.
6. The country and western recording industry in Nashville.
7. The Grand Old Opry.
8. Great country and western performers.
9. Care and storing of records.
10. A basic country and western record library.
11. How to save money buying records.

Tennis

1. Tennis terminology and scoring.
2. Rules in tennis.
3. How to serve.
4. How to develop a good backhand.
5. Care of a tennis court.
6. Great tennis players of the past and present.
7. The Davis Cup competition.
8. The status of amateur and professional players.
9. How to buy the right racquet.
10. The great tennis tournaments.

London

1. The Houses of Parliament.
2. Westminster Abbey.
3. London's parks.
4. British currency.
5. Free entertainment in London.
6. The Tower of London.
7. Pomp and circumstance: ceremony and the royal family.
8. Eating in Britain.
9. Differences between American and British speech.
10. London's pubs.
11. London as a theater center.
12. Transportation in London.

After the speaker has completed his self-inventory of potential speech topics, he will probably wish to file it for future consultation. In addition, he may want to start the kind of speaker's scrapbook or file of clippings discussed in Chapter 6.

SELECTING THE SUBJECT

After taking inventory of possible topics for discussion, the speaker is now ready to begin the process of finally selecting a subject. To assure a wise choice, he should apply four tests to the subjects he is considering: (1) Is the topic suitable to the speaker? (2) Is the subject suitable to the audience? (3) Is it appropriate to the occasion? and (4) Is the subject suited to the time available?

> There never was in any man so great eloquence as would not begin to stumble and hesitate so soon as his words ran counter to his inmost thoughts.
>
> QUINTILIAN

Is the Topic Suitable for the Speaker?

The most important test of a speech topic is whether it is appropriate for the speaker himself. To determine this, the speaker should consider the following questions.

1. Am I Truly Interested in this Subject? Any speaker will find it difficult to interest an audience in his topic if he cares little about it. If he is to speak with enthusiasm and conviction, he needs a subject in which he has a lively and continuing interest. He should be especially cautious about choosing to talk on something that may have caught his fancy or aroused his curiosity momentarily, but in which he has never before felt any interest. Magazine

and newspaper articles about exotic places, odd occurrences, bizarre customs, and strange coincidences often pique one's curiosity, but they are risky choices as possible speech subjects. The danger is that the speaker's interest may wane so rapidly that by the time he delivers the speech he no longer cares about his subject. The speaker would be much better advised to choose a topic in which he has been interested for some time. A reliable guide to his true interests usually can be found in the regularity or frequency with which he turns his attention to certain subjects. The parts of a newspaper he usually reads first, the kinds of books he chooses, the sports that he follows or in which he participates, hobbies he pursues, occasions that he anticipates with pleasure, and subjects he likes to discuss in conversation, all are indications of a person's true interests. The speaker who chooses a subject in which he has long been interested runs fewer risks than the speaker who chooses to discuss something that only recently caught his attention.

> To know when one's self is interested is the first condition of interesting other people.
>
> WALTER PATER

2. Is the Subject Important to Me? In choosing his topic, the speaker not only needs to feel a deep interest in it, but he should also regard the topic as significant. Most people have some interests that they know are not very important. They may enjoy reading the comics, doing crossword puzzles, soaking in the tub, reading their horoscopes, feeding the sparrows, or drinking beer. While these may be enjoyable pastimes, they probably would not make good subjects for speeches. Most speakers recognize these activities for what they are—mere diversions—and probably would find it difficult to sustain any real desire to communicate on such topics.

Norman Thomas, who spoke to an almost endless number of audiences under a wide variety of circumstances in his many years as leader of the Socialist party, emphasized that interest is contagious. He reflects on this in Adapted Reading 5.1. He believed that "to arouse interest in his speech, a speaker must be interested in it himself. His interest, moreover, must be in what he is saying and its importance, not in his own sufferings while he is speaking."

3. Do I Know Enough About the Subject? In addition to being interested in his subject and feeling that it is worthwhile, the speaker should be well informed on the topic he chooses. A controversial piece of legislation, a sensational trial, a scandal, or a remarkable discovery may arouse the speaker's interest and create a desire to communicate, but unless he thoroughly understands the subject, the speaker should avoid such topics. How much should the speaker know? Certainly he should be better informed than most of his listeners. If he is not as knowledgeable as his audience, the speaker not only will find it difficult to hold their attention, but will also run the risk of losing their confidence should they get the impression that he really does not know what he is talking about. An inaccurate piece of information, a confusing explanation, uncertainty about details, or omission of a key point or step can trigger suspicion that the speaker does not really understand his subject. Still another reason why he should be better informed than his listeners is that in many speaking situations questioning by the audience is permitted. The speaker who cannot handle listeners' queries will command little respect. However, while he should be well informed, a speaker should not hesitate to speak on a particular topic simply because a few listeners may be true experts on that subject. Ideally, the speaker will be as well informed on his subject as time and the information available permit.

4. Can I Secure Additional Information on the Subject? Most speakers, no matter how well informed, supplement their own general knowledge on a subject with information and ideas from others. They do so to refresh their understanding of the subject, to verify facts, to obtain the most recent data, to get other viewpoints, and to reevaluate their thinking. For these reasons, in selecting a topic the speaker should determine whether any additional information he may require is available. Books, magazines, newspapers, encyclopedias, interviews, broadcasts, pamphlets, government documents, atlases, indexes, yearbooks, and bibliographies are sources of supplementary information the availability of which he should determine before final selection of his topic.

Is the Subject Suitable for the Audience?
A recent presidential candidate made the mistake of failing to analyze his audiences' interests and attitudes in his selection of subjects for several major campaign speeches. In a region that had prospered because of the Tennessee Valley Authority, he spoke disparagingly of government power programs; facing an audience of elderly persons concerned about his position on social security, he totally avoided this topic and discussed law and order instead; addressing audiences in poverty-stricken Appalachia, which had one of the highest unemployment rates in the country, he attacked the war on poverty; and in a large city badly underrepresented in its state legislature, he opposed reapportionment. Unquestionably, his poor judgment in the choice of issues to discuss with each of these groups did not help his political campaign.

The errors of judgment just described suggest the second consideration in selecting a speech topic: the subject should be appropriate to the audience. In determining the suitability of his topic to his listeners, the speaker should consider whether he can develop his subject in such a way that the audience will be interested and will understand what he has to say. Specifically, he should ask himself:

1. Can I Interest This Audience in This Subject? If a speaker has been asked to address a group on a particular subject, he most likely was invited because the audience is interested in that topic. In this instance, the speaker's task consists simply of determining which aspects of the subject he should discuss. In situations in which the choice of topic is left to his discretion, the speaker's task is more complicated. However, in either case, the speaker should give careful attention to the interests of his listeners. He may wish to select a topic in which the audience has already expressed interest or he may decide to discuss a subject that is unfamiliar but of potential interest to them.

To discover the listeners' immediate and potential interests, the speaker should consider their age, sex, education, occupation, religion, politics, geographic location, race, nationality, economic status, reason for assembling, social position, and other related factors. On the basis of this study, he will attempt to determine which topics are most likely to interest them. The speaker should remember that on many subjects the interest of young and old, male and female, Democrat and Republican, Protestant and Catholic, rich and poor, rural and urban, employer and employee differ sharply.

The speaker should also consider the timeliness of his subject. He will want to examine the ways in which his topic is related to the listeners' needs and desires. He will also wish to determine whether his topic is fresh and original. Keeping these differences in mind, the speaker should ask, "Is the audience interested in this subject and, if not, can I arouse their interest in it?" The listeners need not be interested at the outset, but they must become interested early in the presentation.

2. Can My Listeners Understand This Subject? In addition to gauging his listeners' potential interest in his subject, the speaker should also give attention to their background and education. Some audiences may not have the general knowledge or specialized training necessary to understand the topic on which he would like to speak. To determine whether he is likely to be able to develop his subject in a meaningful and comprehensible manner for his auditors, the speaker should consider their formal education, personal experiences, and specialized knowledge. He must be discriminating in trying to determine exactly what kinds of knowledge the auditors possess; whether it is general or specific, practical or theoretical, out-dated or recent. He should not make the mistake of assuming that the degree of expertise and type of knowledge are the same for generals and war veterans, for executives and business school graduates, for architects and carpenters, for dieticians and cooks.

If an audience lacks the knowledge necessary to understand his topic, the speaker has three choices. First, he might try to provide the audience with the requisite background information in the course of his speech through definitions, explanations, examples, and comparisons to other more familiar matters. If, however, the audience's ignorance on this topic is so great that the speaker cannot hope in the time available to provide the necessary background, he may decide to aim at a lesser goal. Instead of seeking to develop the subject as planned, he may find that by focusing on one part of it, on a few basic principles, or on another aspect of the same general topic, he can present a speech that the audience will understand. Or, finally, he may be forced to abandon the subject and seek another.

Is the Topic Appropriate to the Occasion?

In Adapted Reading 13.5, Emily Kimbrough reports having been disconcerted to learn that she was scheduled to deliver a humorous lecture on Hollywood and motion pictures in a church. To her, the topic seemed inappropriate for an audience assembled in a place of worship.

Another speaker, invited to deliver the main address at a banquet commemorating the founding of a college, was dismayed as the master of ceremonies introduced alumnus after alumnus, most of whom embarked on reminiscences about their undergraduate days at the school. By the time the speaker was introduced, just before 11 P.M., the audience was worn out and too tired to pay attention to the speech he had prepared.

A prominent educator was asked to speak at an awards dinner held annually by a university's department of speech and theater. Unaware of the unusual nature of the event, the speaker prepared a serious talk on communication. After skits satirizing the faculty, the presentation of several facetious awards, and some clever musical numbers, he realized that the occasion called for a humorous talk and that the audience was in no mood for his serious discourse.

In each of the above instances, the speaker had chosen a topic supposedly well suited both to himself and to his auditors, but had overlooked some important element of the speaking occasion. The occasion can be defined as the situation and sorrounding circumstances in which the speech is given. The occasion includes the physical surroundings, the nature of the meeting, and the pertinent events occurring both before and during the speech. While some addresses are given on special occasions such as anniversaries, testimonial meetings, holidays, and other similar events, *every* speech is delivered under a unique set of circumstances. These circumstances constitute the occasion and include such factors as:

1. The place where the speech is given:
   a. Is it indoors or outdoors?
   b. Is the hall large or small?
   c. What is its shape, arrangement, and seating capacity?
   d. If indoors, what kind of room is it: classroom, auditorium, theatre, church, gymnasium, living room, club room, banquet room?
   e. What facilities are provided for the speaker? Does the room have a lectern, a stage, a public address system, a blackboard, projector, record player? Can it be darkened if necessary?
   f. Is it properly cooled, heated, and ventilated?

g. What are its acoustical properties?
2. The time when the speech is to be given:
    a. What time of year?
    b. What time of day?
    c. At what time or place on the program?
3. The reason for assembling:
    a. Did the audience come voluntarily?
    b. Were the listeners required to attend?
    c. Is this a regular meeting?
    d. Has the audience come for a special reason?
4. Events transpiring before the speech:
    a. Has some event that occurred outside the meeting place altered the nature of the occasion?
    b. How has the length of the program, a change in procedure, or the tone or audience reaction to an earlier speaker's remarks altered the situation?

In choosing a subject, the speaker must give attention to all these elements of the speech occasion. The place is important. Certain subjects may be inappropriate if the speech is to be given in a church or synagogue. Inadequate equipment or an outdoor setting might prevent the use of visual aids essential to the development of a particular topic. The ability of the audience to see and hear might also influence the speaker's choice of subject. Whether the surroundings are intimate and cozy or large and uncomfortable may also have some bearing on what the speaker chooses to discuss.

The time is important. The interests and activities of most people vary from season to season. Most people are more interested in vacations, baseball, travel, picnicking, camping, fishing, and swimming in the summer than during other times of the year. Other sports, activities, and holidays are associated with certain other seasons. The speaker should keep this in mind in selecting his topic. The hour of the day and his place on the program may also influence the speaker's choice of subject. To prevent duplication, repetition, and possible embarrassment, the speaker will also want to consider the personality, speech topic, and point of view of anyone else scheduled to address the group either before or after his appearance.

The speaker's choice of topic may also be influenced by the audience's reason for assembling. Has the meeting been called to observe an anniversary, commemorate an event, learn about a certain subject, or resolve a particular issue? If so, the speaker would wish to select a topic appropriate to the particular purpose of that occasion. Is the speech to be given at a regular meeting of the group? If this is the case, the speaker will want to know what type of topic the audience expects him to discuss. Is the audience — perhaps a group of students or military personnel — required to attend the meeting? All of these factors assist the speaker in finding a suitable topic.

The speaker should also take cognizance of events which may have transpired before his speech. It is possible that they might necessitate a last-minute change in subject or a radical modification of his approach. A tragic disaster, shocking occurrence, or unexpected development might so affect the mood of the audience that it would be disastrous for the speaker to continue with his original topic. For example, following the death of President John F. Kennedy, several Louisiana gubernatorial candidates cancelled prerecorded speeches in which they attacked his administration; for these speeches they substituted addresses on local topics. To have permitted the broadcasting of the original speeches would have shown shocking disrespect for the late president. Another speaker, planning to speak to a student political organization on the European Economic Community in October 1962, found his audience so distressed by the Cuban crisis that he chose instead to discuss Cuba and Soviet–American relations. Many speakers have found a last-minute change in subject necessary because an earlier speaker had presented virtually the same information. While a speaker ordinarily should be wary of substituting an impromptu talk for a carefully prepared speech, it is, in some instances, necessary.

Is the Subject Suited to the Time Available?

Whether deserved or not, Edmund Burke, the British political philosopher, earned a reputation as a "dinner bell" because of his lengthy speeches to the House of Commons. For many members, Burke's rising to speak became the signal to retire for a meal. It was said, "he went on refining and thought of convincing while they thought of dining."

It is doubtful if there is a human being on the face of the earth who has not been forced to sit through a too lengthy speech. Many an otherwise impressive speaker has failed simply because he didn't know when to stop. Some speakers, in situations in which time limits are strictly enforced, find that they literally are unable to complete their talks. In both such circumstances, the speaker has failed to consider the fourth test of a good speech topic: Is it suitable to the time available to him?

In most speech situations a time limit is suggested. The speaker may be asked to talk for "about twenty minutes" or "half an hour." In some situations, however, such as a radio or television broadcast, a debate, or a professional meeting or convention, time limits are set and rigidly enforced. One civic club had a rule that any member who felt it necessary to return to his business after the regular luncheon meeting was free to do so at 1:30 P.M. Guest speakers who ignored this warning and exceeded their allotted time were frequently embarrassed by a mass exodus at the specified time. Radio and television are merciless in their enforcement of time limits. Even as prominent a public figure as Adlai Stevenson was cut off the air when he exceeded his time limit for a speech during the 1956 presidential campaign.

If time limitations are strictly enforced, the speaker owes it to himself to choose a topic that can be covered in the time available. If time limits have only been suggested, he owes it to his audience, as a matter of courtesy, to adhere closely to that request. Even when no limitations on time have been indicated, good judgment will tell the speaker that the interest span of the audience is not limitless and he will try to complete his speech in a reasonable length of time.

NARROWING THE SUBJECT

Contrary to the beliefs of many students, a short speech is usually more demanding on a speaker than a long address. In a long talk, a speaker may approach his subject in several different ways, he may digress a bit now and then, and he may occasionally repeat himself without serious damage to the speech. However, in a short talk he must select from a wide range of available information and ideas only those facts that are most essential and vital. His approach must be direct, and his language clear and concise.

In choosing his speech topic, the speaker should recognize that some topics are so limited that they cannot possibly be expanded into a speech of the length requested. A more common problem, however, is the topic that is too broad to be covered in the specified speaking time. Faced with a subject that seems too broad for the time available, the speaker has three choices: He may abandon the topic and seek another; he may attempt to condense the subject; or he may limit his speech to just one part, aspect, or facet of the more general topic. The principal danger in trying to compress a broad subject into a limited amount of time is that the speaker may be forced to omit details and explanations essential to the audience's understanding or acceptance of his speech. Another risk in this approach is that the speech may become so general — so lacking in examples, illustrations, and concrete facts — that the auditors will lose interest. At times, the speaker may find that he can condense his subject without any serious loss; in fact, by making it more concise and direct he may actually improve it. But, in general, he is probably better advised to restrict his topic to one part of the broader subject, to eliminate some of his arguments, or to focus on the most important aspect of the topic.

In narrowing subjects that are too broad, a helpful procedure is for the speaker to select a general area suited to his knowledge and interests, as well as to the audience and occasion, and then systematically divide the subject into increasingly limited subtopics. The process is graphically illustrated in Figure 5. This procedure guides the speaker to several specific topics that might be appropriate for the situation he faces. It narrows the subject so that it can be covered in the time available for the speech.

Taking the general subject of "sports" as an example, a speaker might, by successive steps, limit it in the manner shown in Figure 5.

Specific subjects might be:

"The prospects of the Iowa football team for the coming season."
"Iowa's use of the Q formation."
"Iowa fans should support the football team."
"Great moments in Iowa football history."
"Football is over-emphasized at Iowa."

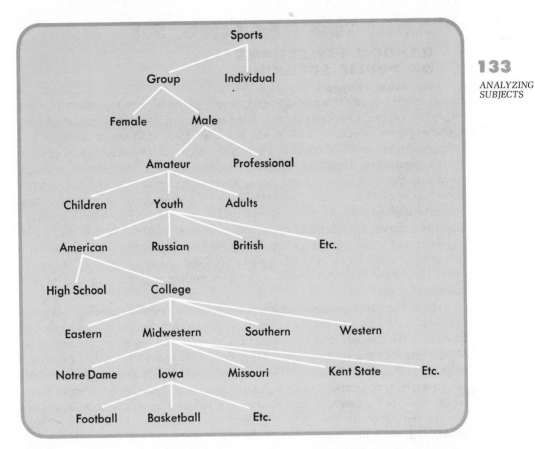

Figure 5

SUMMARY

The beginning speaker's first step in selecting subjects is largely psychological: He must recognize that he has knowledge and experiences that others will find interesting and worthwhile. In order to discover his own areas of interest that may yield speech topics, he should undertake an exhaustive self-examination of his personal skills, hobbies, experiences, and knowledge, searching for subjects he can discuss with authority and that others will find stimulating and useful.

Having compiled an inventory of potential topics, the speaker is ready to choose a specific subject for a particular speech occasion. In his final selection of a topic, the speaker should apply four tests: (1) Is the topic suitable for me, the speaker? (2) Is it appropriate to this audience? (3) Does it fit the occasion? and (4) Can I develop it in the available speaking time? When the speaker is convinced that his subject passes all four of these tests, he is ready to begin actual preparation of the speech.

RANDOM REFLECTIONS
ON PUBLIC SPEAKING
Norman Thomas

I have lost six presidential campaigns, and I forget how many others for less important offices. Obviously I have been no shining success in the art of persuasion. Nevertheless, my failure has not been total, and my experience has been extensive, much of it under circumstances which required me to gain at least a temporary attention of audiences in which the majority of listeners were suspicious of, or hostile to, my particular message. I have spoken from soap boxes, platforms, radio and television studios; in churches; at noisy street corners; at strike and protest meetings; and to educational societies and associations. I have addressed clubs of all sorts and political rallies and mass meetings and small groups and conferences. I have held forth in every American state (except Nevada) and in some foreign countries. Most of my audiences have been free, but I have addressed captive audiences in prisons and college chapels. . . .

Effective communication of ideas by means of public speech . . . can be acquired by study and practice. The first essential is that the speaker should have something to say and be reasonably sure himself what that something is. Most speakers have an emotion, a prejudice, a slogan, some facts, or even an idea which they want to impart. But many of them do not develop their theme, whatever it is, logically, critically, or persuasively. They never listen to themselves and ask the essential questions: Is that so? and So what? Some speakers assume that because they have The Truth on their side, facts don't matter; others act as if the text, "Out of the abundance of the heart, the mouth speaketh," absolved them from any use of their heads. More than once I have heard good men come out second best to demagogues in argument because they have depended on their righteous indignation and neglected their homework. (This has happened notably in some of the radio and television discussions in which Senator [Joseph] McCarthy has appeared.)

If a speech is to be of any importance at all, the speaker should live with his theme or message, turning it over and over in his mind. He will be surprised at how many useful illustrations or ways of putting his case will come to him as he walks the street, or reads a newspaper, or gets ready for bed, or wakes up in the morning. Mediocre speaking very often is merely the inevitable and the appropriate reflection of mediocre thinking, or the consequence of imperfect acquaintance with the subject in hand.

But it sometimes happens that speakers who obviously know their subject are too dull to hold attention. Unconsciously they act as if what they were saying hurt or bored them worse than it bored the audience. Interest is contagious, and to arouse interest in his speech a speaker must be interested in it himself. His interest, morever, must be in what he is saying and its importance, not in his own sufferings while he is speaking.

From *Quarterly Journal of Speech*, April 1954, pp. 145–151.

I am, of course, arguing at this point for the necessity of sincerity on the speaker's part; but also for something more. One must not only believe in what one is saying but also that it matters, especially that it matters to the people to whom one is speaking. If not, why bother?

In everyday conversation, we ordinary folk with no particular genius manage pretty well to convey our own attitudes toward a subject by tone of voice, choice of words, unconscious gestures. Surely there need be no psychological compulsion laid upon us by a platform and an audience to repress any outward manifestations of interest in what presumably we have spent time and trouble preparing for presentation to an audience. . . .

So far, my reflections on public speaking have had to do primarily with the attitude of the speaker to his subject, his material, the information, idea, or message which he wishes to convey. He should seek to be a master of his subject and honestly interested in it. He should first challenge his own statements in his own mind before presenting them to his audience.

And then he should consider his prospective audience. It is a long accepted commonplace that successful speech requires a speaker to come to proper terms with his audience as well as his subject. . . . The speaker must always be aware of his audience — that is, of his particular audience — all the more so if he is repeating a much used lecture or speech. He must come to each audience with some anticipatory notion of its probable makeup, attitude, and interest. He should look at his audience; only so can he judge the effect of his speech. He should be prepared to change pace; to indulge in humor — even the wisecrack; to introduce the unexpected, but not the irrelevant. It is not only legitimate but sometimes necessary for a speaker to rephrase and repeat an important fact or opinion until he feels that the audience understands.

It cannot be too strongly insisted that the written and spoken word, while they have much in common, are by no means the same. The speaker is concerned with the particular group before him; he is not speaking to a scattered group of readers or to posterity. Sometimes he can communicate more effectively by repetition, intonation, gesture, unfinished sentence. I have often winced at stenographic reports of speeches which had gone over well enough to receive much applause. But I am convinced that I would have made a mistake to have read a smoother speech.

ADDITIONAL READINGS

Kruger, Arthur, *Effective Speaking* (New York: Van Nostrand Reinhold, 1970), 173–186.

McBurney, James and Ernest Wrage, *Guide to Good Speech* (Englewood Cliffs, N.J.: Prentice-Hall, 1965), chap. 6, "Choosing Subjects."

Mills, Glen E., *Message Preparation* (Indianapolis: Bobbs-Merrill, 1966), chap. 1, "Selecting a Subject: General Considerations."

STUDY QUESTIONS

1. What are some reasons why speakers experience difficulty in locating speech topics?
2. What are four tests of a good speech subject?
3. How does the speaker determine whether he has chosen a topic well suited to himself?

4. In deciding whether his speech subject is appropriate for his audience, what should the speaker consider?
5. Should a speaker reject a possible subject because his audience has shown no interest in the topic *before* the speech? Why or why not?
6. If a speaker decides that his topic is too broad to be covered in the time available, what alternatives are available to him?

EXERCISES

1. Prepare an inventory of your interests and experiences that may serve as future speech topics.
2. From your speech-subjects inventory (above exercise) select the general topic that you feel best qualified to discuss. List four or five specific aspects of that subject which might serve as speech topics.
3. From your speech-subjects inventory, find topics for a speech to inform, a speech to entertain, a speech to convince, a speech to persuade, and a speech to inspire. For each, write out a specific purpose and a central thought.
4. Select one of the following subjects and graphically narrow it by steps as illustrated in Figure 5: books, school, clothing, occupations.
5. For each of the following situations select a subject that you could discuss with enthusiasm and knowledge. Justify the appropriateness of your selection for each audience.
   a. A speech to this year's senior class at your high school.
   b. A ten-minute speech to a group of German businessmen touring your state.
   c. A twenty-minute speech to a social club of retired persons.
   d. A twenty-minute speech to a class of police officers studying law enforcement.
6. Choose a subject that is suited to your interests and background, to the members of the class, and to the occasion. Prepare a four-minute informative speech to present to the class. After each speech, the class members and instructor will evaluate the speaker's choice of topic.

CHAPTER 6

GATHERING MATERIALS

Winston Churchill, upon leaving the chamber of the House of Commons one day after delivering a classic rebuttal to an opponent's arguments, was asked by a reporter, "Mr. Prime Minister, how long did you prepare for that speech?" "For forty years," Churchill responded. In a sense, a speaker spends his entire life preparing for a speech. Everything that he has learned, the experiences he has had, and the attitudes he has developed all shape and influence the speech.

A responsible speaker will not, however, rely solely on his general background in developing his subject. He will want to know what others have said; he will be interested in the most recent information; and he will seek material which will be particularly effective in obtaining the response he seeks from the group he will address. By obtaining a broad understanding of his subject and a wide range of information, the speaker can be selective in choosing those facts, reasons, and illustrations best suited to his particular audience on the specific speech occasion. The speaker who can exhaust his knowledge of a subject in the time given him to speak has done an inadequate job of preparation. The speaker is obligated to offer the best fare available. This means knowing considerably more about his topic than can be related in the speech.

When searching for quality materials, the speaker sometimes wonders whether analysis precedes investigation or investigation precedes analysis. The answer is not always clear, but, in most cases, analysis is not possible without a thorough understanding, and this requires information. Where does one locate such information?

As suggested in the preceding chapter, in this hurried and harassed world people too seldom sit down to meditate or reflect. Yet this is the first step in finding material for a speech. One should review one's present knowledge of the subject and then, for supplementary materials, turn to other sources—books, interviews, lectures, speeches, personal surveys, and experiments.

REVIEW ONE'S OWN KNOWLEDGE OF THE SUBJECT

Reflection

Every speech should be distinct and creative. The creative element is not to be found in books or interviews, but in the imagination of the speaker. Creativity is the result of the artistic responses of the author to the materials of his speech and of his personalization of those materials. Many people have written and spoken on such subjects as the United Nations, the responsibility of the United States for world leadership, traveling in Africa, readjustment to civilian life after military service, coeds' hours, political parties, and other similar topics. But each speech has been an individual creation. Each speaker has had something personal to contribute, whether it was an experience, his discriminating choice of materials, the arrangement of his ideas, or his emphasis of the materials selected. This kind of creativity is attained only by reflection.

Reflection is difficult when distractions are present. A roommate playing the guitar or loud recordings, conversation by others, people walking by in a library reading room, or a television set blaring in the corner, all contribute to muscular tension that inhibits reflection. The speaker should isolate himself from distractions to gain the most from reflection.

For the preparation of his speech for November 3, 1969, President Nixon found solitude in his Camp David retreat, as Robert Semple, Jr. relates in Adapted Reading 6.1. Most speakers do not enjoy such luxury, but many persons whose profession it is to speak—ministers, teachers, and lawyers—have studies or small cubicles into which they escape to prepare their speeches.

One clergyman of the authors' acquaintance has had a small closet in his main office fitted with a desk and bookshelves. He secludes himself in that room, even though his main office is well removed from traffic and outside sounds. He reports that he must feel confined physically in order to open his mind to conscious thought. Each speaker, indeed each person, should discover the means by which he can feel sufficiently alone to examine his thoughts.

> The mind of the orator grows and expands with his subject. Without ample materials no splendid oration was ever yet produced.
>
> TACITUS

The accumulation of ideas and knowledge is a life-long process. Learning begins at birth. The human mind serves as a catalogue in which experience is recorded. Too seldom, however, is the catalogue opened. Sears, Roebuck and Co. does a better job of making the contents of its catalogue readily available than do most people. They index it. And that is the purpose of reflection—to find the index to experience. Almost every person has been in a situation seemingly new but which appears to mirror an earlier experience; he sees a landscape so familiar that he feels he has observed it before, even though he has not previously passed that way; he hears a newly composed piece of music that he recognizes as something old; he meets a person for the first time but senses that they have met previously. For a fleeting moment, experiences are in the present. But rather than reach into his mind for the source of the experience, he dismisses it as some kind of supernatural phenomenon. The human brain is a mysterious and marvelous mechanism; it should be used more often. The good speaker is conscious of its use.

Once the subject is selected, the speaker should reflect on what he knows about the topic and then write down his thoughts as they occur to him. After he has extracted from his own memory all he knows about the subject, he should organize his reflections; he should create order from the free flow of thought. Reflection, when systematized, may provide the speaker with an outline for his speech and certainly will suggest those areas of the topic that need further research.

> He looked upon a subject like a man standing on an eminence taking a large and rounded view of it on every side, contemplating each of its parts under a vast variety of relations, and these relations often extremely complex and remote.
>
> *Description of Edmund Burke*
> by CHAUNCEY A. GOODRICH

Personal Files

Either before reflection (in order to jog his memory) or after (in order to supplement his existing knowledge of the subject), the speaker should turn to his files of materials. A good speaker maintains a collection of notes, for even though he reads widely and experiences much in life, he cannot remember everything, and no one should rely on memory alone to record events that might be helpful in the future. Consequently, the speaker should keep notes on his experiences, collect clippings, and record bibliographical listings on subjects of interest to him.

Notes. A good speaker should have a broad understanding of the times and the people, for it is people who make up the audiences and who the speaker

> **From contemplation one may become wise, but knowledge comes only from study.**
>
> A. EDWARD NEWTON

attempts to motivate. The more a speaker knows about people, the better equipped he is to influence them. Perhaps the best way to learn about people is to observe them consciously, to analyze them and their actions. The speaker should make notes concerning individual physical and intellectual responses to certain stimuli. He should observe how people react to action situations — automobile accidents, football games, weddings, funerals, barking dogs, and so forth. The notes made by an observer at such times may serve to illustrate an idea he will use in the future. He should record observations about events, statements overheard, thoughts expressed in conversations over coffee, or ideas dimly perceived in the twilight period between consciousness and slumber. Many sound ideas born in the middle of the night are forgotten by morning. If such an idea strikes, get out of bed and make a record of it before it fades.

Clippings. How often a speaker thinks to himself, "I wish I could remember where I read that." If he kept a collection of clippings, he could go to his file and pull out the exact reference. Speakers should collect a file of materials on subjects that interest them. Into that file should go clippings from newspapers (everyone should read at least one responsible newspaper daily), magazines, special publications, pamphlets, and brochures. The file should be organized in a meaningful way, classified according to general subjects. Folders containing topics of special interest can be color coded by using different colored identification tabs. An example of such a file has the following designations:

Africa
Agriculture
American Government
American Society and People
Arts
Asia
Automation and Technological Change
Business
China
Civil Rights
Cold War
Communications
Conservation
Defense Program

Eastern Europe
Education and Youth
Famous People
Foreign Aid
Foreign Policy — Department of State
France
Germany
Great Britain
Greece
History and Historical Perspective
India
Italy
Labor
Latin America
Law and Crime
Law and Freedom
Legislative Branch
Malaysia — Indonesia
Middle East
NATO
Pacific
Parties and Politics
Population Explosion
Poverty
Quotations
Religion
Science
Soviet Union
Space
Spain
United Nations
United States Economy
Urban Affairs
Western Europe

Although this is not an exhaustive list of possible folder classifications, it is an example of a workable file. General areas are easily identified and special interest areas are represented by the inclusion of folders labeled "History and Historical Perspective," "Law and Freedom," "Law and Crime," "Parties and Politics," "Population Explosion," "Poverty," and "Urban Affairs." The latter three are examples of subdivisions of the more general folder labeled "American Society and People." Two seemingly intrusive and unrelated folders are designated "Famous People" and "Quotations." Both of these categories provide examples and witticisms useful to the speaker.

The subjects on which a person collects clippings and the categories within his file will, of course, vary from individual to individual. Unquestionably, a football coach who speaks frequently will have many categories related to sports, but probably he will also have sections devoted to such topics as competition, youth, personality and character, success, cooperation, and physical fitness. Each person's file will reflect his own interests and concerns.

A speaker with a personalized file has a collection of indexed material to assist him in recalling information he may have forgotten.

Bibliographic Listings. A more detailed discussion of bibliographies appears later in this chapter, but it should be mentioned here that bibliographic clippings are valuable references. When one is reading the *Saturday Review/World*, for example, and discovers a review of several books on poverty, drug abuse, or education, he should clip that item and file it for later use.

SUPPLEMENTING KNOWLEDGE

After reflecting upon and organizing his experiential knowledge, the speaker can begin to supplement that information. He can locate the gaps that need to be filled with the assistance of information from outside sources. Many business executives and government administrators employ outside sources in the form of ghostwriters. The ideal arrangement would demand that the prospective speaker and his "ghost" sit down together to discuss the ideas the speaker wishes to include. In practice, there is rarely time even for this brief meeting. Responsible speakers, however, will contribute both to the content and the style of the speech. A great deal of time is devoted to especially significant speeches, as is shown by Nan Robertson in Adapted Reading 6.2. For more routine speeches, a pattern is usually established.

> **Genius lights its own fire, but it is constantly collecting materials to keep alive the flame.**
>
> WILMOTT

Available to all speakers are four major sources for collecting supplementary materials: (1) reading; (2) interviewing; (3) lectures, radio and television programs, and films; and (4) personal surveys and experiments.

Reading

Preparing a Bibliography. Frequently, so much has been written on a selected topic that the sheer volume of it becomes intimidating. At other times, little appears to be in print, striking fear of insufficient material. In either instance, the speaker's first step should be to prepare a bibliography. The next best thing to having the information is knowing where to find it. That is the key to research for speaking or writing. Although prepared bibliographies can be found on a variety of subjects, they constitute only a part of the speaker's bibliographical material. Existing bibliographies are often broad and speeches are usually narrow in scope. The speaker should prepare a bibliography of material specifically related to his topic; he should read extensively, but also investigate intensively, areas of the problem he has selected in order to reinforce his existing knowledge and gain new insights. Although most students are familiar with the card catalogues of libraries, some are not aware that numerous special indexes are published to help the investigator. The following is a list of sources to which a speaker might turn to prepare a bibliography. Although the list is not exhaustive, the sources are available in most libraries and are representative of other materials.

For General Information

Encyclopedia Americana
Encyclopedia Britannica
Political Handbook of the World: Parliaments, Parties and Press
Statesman's Yearbook: Statistical and Historical Annual of the States of the World
Statistical Abstract of the United States
United Nations Yearbook
World Almanac

For Specialized Information on People and Disciplines

Alexander, Carter and Arvid J. Burke, *How to Locate Educational Information and Data*
Black, Henry Campbell, *Black's Law Dictionary, Containing Definitions of the Terms and Phrases of American English Jurisprudence, Ancient and Modern*
Cambridge History of American Literature (15 Volumes)
Contemporary Authors
Current Biography: Who's New and Why
Dictionary of American Biography (22 Volumes)
Dictionary of American History (5 Volumes)
Dictionary of Education
Dictionary of National Biography (British) (66 Volumes)
Dictionary of American Scholars
Encyclopedia of Educational Research
Encyclopedia of the Social Sciences (15 Volumes)
Harriman, Philip Lawrence, *New Dictionary of Psychology*
Literary History of the United States (3 Volumes)
Oxford Classical Dictionary
Who's Who: An Annual Biographical Dictionary (British)
Who's Who in America: A Biographical Dictionary of Notable Living Men and Women of the United States

For Information on Available Books
    Art Index
    Bibliographies and Summaries in Education to July 1935
    Biography Index
    Education Index
    International Index to Periodicals
    Poole's Index to Periodical Literature
    Psychological Index
    Readers' Guide to Periodical Literature
    Vertical File Index (of current pamphlets and booklets)

For Information in Newspapers
    Directory of Newspapers and Periodicals
    New York Times Index
    Times (London) Official Index
    Palmer's Index to the Times (London)

For Information in Public Documents
    Monthly Catalogue of United States Public Documents

Not included in this list are such commonly used publications as the *Congressional Record* and *Public Affairs Pamphlets*. Bibliographies of bibliographies, such as Besterman's *World Bibliography of Bibliographies*, are not included. But the list does provide a workable base from which to gather materials. A speaker studying a specific topic might well locate a more specialized list of sources in that subject area.

When investigating potential materials to read, it is wise for the speaker to prepare two lists, one for general background and one for specific information on the subject.

How does a speaker use the bibliographical sources once located? Let's cite an example. Suppose a speaker has elected to prepare an informative speech on poverty in the cities of the United States and has limited his subject to "Some Aspects of Poverty in Chicago's Inner City." After significant investigation, further narrowing will be possible. First, the speaker reflects on all he knows about the topic. He makes notes of his recollections. He then arranges his thoughts in some meaningful way, thereby defining the extent of his understanding and his limitations and, hence, his need for further discovery.

Next, the speaker might turn to the *Book Review Digest* to locate recent books on the subject of poverty and to the *Reader's Guide to Periodical Literature* and *Poole's Index* for articles appearing in periodicals. He can refer to the *Vertical File Index* for a list of pamphlets and booklets on the subject and to the *New York Times Index* for recent newspaper articles of relevance. If he wants to know what the federal government has published concerning the poverty problem, he can consult the *Monthly Catalogue of United States Public Documents* and, of course, write his congressman for government publications. After collecting a bibliography of books and articles, the speaker should investigate the credentials of the authors. If he is unfamiliar with some of them, he can discover their backgrounds by referring to *Who's Who in America* or *Dictionary of American Scholars*. The credibility of an author will help the speaker select significant and authoritative reading material.

Should the speaker desire statistical data, he can find that information in the *Statistical Abstract of the United States*.

Securing Literature from Interested Parties. Still other sources of reading materials are available. Special interest groups representing various positions on almost every issue imaginable abound in the United States. These groups will usually provide printed material to any interested person upon request. For literature on poverty, for instance, the speaker might request materials from the Urban League; for data on the conservation of natural resources, the Audubon Society or the Sierra Club can be contacted; for information on freedom of speech, the American Civil Liberties Union or the Speech Communication Association should be solicited. The number of interest groups grows almost daily. For a list of special interest associations and societies and their mailing addresses, the speaker should consult the *Encyclopedia of Associations* in the reference room of most libraries. Should the speaker not have access to the *Encyclopedia of Associations*, he can locate many of the addresses in the *World Almanac*.

The speaker, however, runs a risk in using materials supplied by special interest groups. These organizations are, by nature, propaganda agencies whose purpose is to persuade the readers, sometimes with exaggerated claims and manipulated statistics, to accept their position on an issue. The use of slogans is also popular with such groups. The National Rifle Association, for example, attempts to persuade the public with, "When guns are outlawed, only outlaws will have guns." The absurd logic of this appeal is apparent, but a listener might be influenced by it if he does not weigh the message carefully. If the speaker is aware of the biases and limitations of information supplied by special interests, these groups can provide valuable assistance in gathering materials for a speech.

Government bureaus are another source of materials. The United States Office of Economic Opportunity, for instance, can supply information about the VISTA program, the Job Corps, the Neighborhood Youth Corps, the Community Action Program, and the College Work–Study Program. The Bureau of Labor Statistics might prove helpful in providing specialized statistical information on employment, population, food production, and so forth. Perhaps the best way for the speaker to obtain this information is to request his congressman to supply pertinent government documents. If the congressman's district address is unknown, the speaker can contact him by writing in care of the House Office Building, Washington, D.C.

Armed with a substantial bibliography of books and articles written by responsible authorities, materials supplied by interested groups and government agencies, and statistical information, the speaker is well prepared for meaningful reading.

Note-Taking. Obviously, a speaker cannot read everything published about his area of concern, unless, of course, he is an established authority himself and only needs to keep abreast of the new literature in his field. Most speakers must be selective in what they read. The larger the bibliography, the greater the need for discriminating among the materials. Some general materials should be read for background purposes. But in order to conserve time and effort, the speaker should select those books and articles that appear to be most directly related to his specific subject and purpose. He should also read vigorously. He should call on all of his powers of concentration to assimilate what he reads and to relate it to what he has already read or knows about the topic. He should read with a purpose, discriminating between items vaguely relevant and those directly related to his topic. He should constantly be aware of his purpose in reading and not waste time on interesting but relatively useless materials. For example, while searching for historical data in an old newspaper, it is so easy to become absorbed in advertisements for beef at 6 cents a pound and for hoop skirts that the speaker may find himself locked out of the library at closing time without having accomplished his purpose. Read purposively; use leisure time for reading for pleasure.

All speakers, being human, suffer the agonies of lost memory at some time or other in their speaking careers. Most people too often depend on their memory. When something significant is discovered while reading, do not say, "I'll have to remember that," but jot it down on a note card.

Two basic kinds of notes can be taken: *direct quotations* and *summaries*. If the speaker finds a statement he wishes to quote directly, he should copy the statement accurately and in full, being certain to note the source, date, and under what circumstances the authority made the statement (i.e., an answer to a question asked in an interview with Sam Smith). Related to the direct quotation is the paraphrase. If a direct statement is too lengthy or contains irrelevant material, a paraphrase of the statement may suffice. It is vital, however, that the speaker rephrase the quotation with integrity, making certain that he has not altered the sense of the original.

A second kind of note is the summary. After reading an article or book, the speaker might wish to record the general nature of the work and list the main ideas and forms of support. Again, the note-taker must summarize the gist of the article honestly and with integrity, avoiding any alteration of the author's arguments or purposes. Should the speaker wish to evaluate the article or book, he may do so on the note card. Such commentary may be helpful later when selecting ideas for the speech.

If the notes are to be used effectively, the speaker should organize them. Although no standard form is required, a few simple but important rules can be suggested. First, use note cards. Cards can be filed much more effectively than papers and they can be reused without damage. Second, keep only one piece of information on each card. If the speaker tries to save space by putting several quotations or summaries on one card, the job of organizing his references becomes almost impossible. Third, identify each card with a heading indicating its subject matter, such as "Ghostwriting," "Peace," "Campus Unrest," or "Income Tax." Fourth, the source of each piece of information should be placed on the card. This includes (1) the author's name, (2) the title of the article, (3) the name of the newspaper, periodical, or book from which the information was taken, (4) the publication date, and (5) the page number. If this information is clearly placed on the card, it will be easy for the speaker to locate the entire article for future use. Fifth, when copying a direct quotation, always set it off with quotation marks for, after a lapse of time, it is not always possible to determine what is quoted directly and what indirectly if the marks are omitted. Additionally, pains should be taken to in-

GHOSTWRITING

Bormann, Ernest G., "Ethics of Ghostwritten Speeches," *Quarterly Journal of Speech,* October 1961, pp. 262–267.

Bormann, Ernest G., "Ethics of Ghostwritten Speeches,"
<u>Quarterly Journal of Speech,</u> October 1961, pp. 262–267.

Prof. Bormann considers the ghostwritten speech to be a deception and argues that double standards are applied when students are not allowed to have speeches written for them, but presidents are. He concludes, "If we impose an ethical standard on our students and on ourselves . . . we must impose ethical standards upon . . . the president of the United States, upon the president of our college or university, upon our governor . . . upon everyone who presents himself and his ideas to an audience for its acceptance."

sure accuracy of content and meaning when extractions of materials are noted. The sense of the quotations should not differ from its original meaning within the context of the entire article. When parts of a longer quotation are copied, an ellipsis (. . .) should be used to remind the speaker that some words or thoughts have been omitted.

Interviews

A second way for the speaker to implement his understanding of a subject is by interviewing persons who have special knowledge of his topic. The type of interview that probably is most familiar is the one used by the employees of George Gallup, Louis Harris, and Elmo Roper during political campaigns. Advertising firms also frequently use interviews to test the market for new products. These market analyses provide information that helps the companies determine the desired image for the product and the best methods for creating that image. These two forms of interviews are not unlike the type a speaker might use to collect information. The same general principles of good interviewing apply.

Although no hard-and-fast rules for interviewing can be set down, some general practices should be considered in planning the interview:

1. Make arrangements in advance with the person to be interviewed. Prior arrangements not only express respect for the person to be interviewed, but may save time for the interviewer. Along with determining a time for a meeting, a proper setting should be selected. Too often an interviewer attempts to obtain information from a significant person who is pressed for time. Many television viewers have observed newsmen trying to extract information from prominent officials on their way from an automobile to the entrance of a building. Comments made by the official under such circumstances are not usually of great value to the interviewer.

2. A question outline should be prepared in advance so the interviewer will not waste the time of the interviewee. Sending an outline of the interview questions to the interviewee prior to the meeting is often wise. The interviewee should be informed that the outline will serve only as a guide. Although the outline should be flexible, it should be used to give direction to the interview. An advantage of interviewing is that full information can be obtained about a subject through additional questions based upon the interviewee's responses.

The following is an outline of a series of questions asked of Matt Koehl, commander of the American White People's Party, in Arlington, Virginia. This outline was prepared by a student for the purpose of gathering information for a speech on George Lincoln Rockwell, then deceased. A great deal of thought went into the selection and sequence of questions. The questions in the outline were not considered to be exhaustive or limiting. The interviewer hoped that responses to these questions would lead to additional questions resulting in more in-depth information.

Interview Questions for Commander Koehl

1. What is your background?
   a. Education?
   b. When did you enter the Party?
   c. Why?
   d. What is your present position and what are your responsibilities?
2. Who is the head of the Party now?
3. What plans does the Party have for future action?
4. What is the membership of the Party? How many of these are professional people? How many are in the labor movement?
5. What is the size of your staff? Can you reveal your budget of operation?
6. Is the Party strictly national or is it a part of a world organization?
7. Are there branch offices in other cities? Where?
8. Why does the title not have the word "Nazi" in it? (or) What is the significance of the name of the Party?
9. Do you feel that the press and other mass media are unfair to you and your cause?
10. Is there any symbolism in the design of the present uniform?
11. Who originated the taped telephone message your organization sponsors in Washington? Where do you get materials for these?

Questions About Commander Rockwell

1. Did public speaking come easily to Commander Rockwell or did he have to work at it?
2. Did he have any formal training? If so, what and where?
3. Did he have any private coaching in preparing and delivering his speeches?
4. What was the high point in his speaking career?
5. How did Commander Rockwell define the effective speaker?

6. What personal characteristics did he feel were important for the speaker?
7. What did the typical audience expect of Commander Rockwell?
8. How did he handle adverse audience reaction?
9. Did Commander Rockwell feel any speaker was worthy of emulation? (or) Did Commander Rockwell emulate any speaker? Who?
10. To what extent did Commander Rockwell personally prepare his speeches?
11. Who were his advisers?
12. What steps did he follow in his formal speech preparation?
13. Was he conscious of organization? What type of pattern did he follow?
14. What did he attempt to accomplish in the introduction?
15. Did he deliberately select certain types of supporting materials?
16. What type of supporting materials did he find to be most effective?
17. What did he read? What type of books and magazines was he interested in?
18. Did he link his arguments to audience motivations? (or) Did he try to show how his arguments vitally affected his listeners?
19. What did he attempt to accomplish in his conclusions?
20. Did he rehearse his speeches? What method did he use?
21. How would you describe his physical delivery (gestures and voice)?
22. How would you characterize his delivery?
23. Did he deliver extemporaneously or did he read from a manuscript?
24. If he used a manuscript, did he use any techniques to make manuscript reading easier or more effective?
25. Could you summarize his ideas on speechmaking for me?
26. Why did he tape all his interviews and speeches?
27. Was Commander Rockwell conscious of his place in history?
28. Why didn't he publish his autobiography?
29. Did he want to organize a majority party? What were his aims? Was he serious about the presidency?
30. What kind of security measures did he take?
31. Do you consider Commander Rockwell or the movement extremist?

3. Although some questions in an interview may be of the kind that can be answered with a "yes" or "no," most queries should be of an "open-ended" variety, allowing the respondent to react in his own words with as much information as he cares to provide. In this way, an interviewer achieves the greatest advantage from the interview. If all questions can be answered "yes" or "no," an interview is unnecessary since the same responses could be obtained with a written questionnaire.

4. The interviewer should be diplomatic. The questions asked should be fair and should not embarrass the interviewee. Questions that place the interviewee on the defensive simply create tension. The interviewer should be objective during the interview and avoid taking positions on issues suggested by the questions. The questions, likewise, should be asked impar-

tially with no suggestion of what the interviewer considers appropriate responses.

Anyone who interviews should be aware that people often are wary of answering questions and may alter the truth in their responses. If the person being interviewed feels that the questions he is asked are too personal, he may become uncooperative and make a conscious effort to mislead the interviewer. For example, in 1966, one political party attempted to poll all the citizens of a midwestern state. The survey was to provide information to assist the party in designing campaign materials for 1968. The poll failed because the questionnaire was lengthy and the people believed it to be too personal. People are often reluctant to answer questions relating to their religion, income, age, and marital status. In the 1966 poll they were also reluctant to inform the interviewer how they had voted in the last election. Reluctant responses to an interviewer are not at all uncommon. To avoid such difficulties, the interviewer should study his subject and questions carefully before the meeting.

Lectures, Television, Film

Along with reading and interviewing, the speaker may find supporting materials for his topic by attending lectures, watching television, and viewing films. A university is a unique community where literally hundreds of lectures are given annually on a wide variety of topics. All the student need do is examine the calendar of events for the day in the student newspaper in order to obtain times and places for lectures of special interest to him. Often the student will be able to find a lecture on a topic directly related to his speech subject.

Many scheduled television programs provide information for the speaker. The special topical programs and documentaries, and also the interview shows, may help the speaker develop a background of materials for future speeches. The growing popularity of national educational television (NET) is significant, for the programs on that "Fourth Network" are particularly designed to enlighten its viewers.

Movies often deal with complex social problems—race, poverty, drug addiction, sexual mores, and the computerized society. Even science fiction films may offer insight into the complexities of an increasingly scientific civilization.

Occasionally, purely entertaining programs on television and in films may provide materials for elaboration in the form of illustrations, examples, topical references, and humor.

Again, the speaker should not trust his memory, but should jot down notes and file them for future reference.

Personal Surveys and Experiments

Although most speakers have neither the training nor the resources to conduct a scientific poll, the student speaker may find it helpful in dealing with some topics to conduct a personal poll on his campus or among members of his church group or organization. This type of survey should be identified for what it is and, in most instances, great reliance should not be placed upon it. The results of such informal polls, however, may provide the speaker with personal insights and could add to his ethical appeal, as well as to the substance of his argument. Student newspapers frequently poll students on campus topics and report the results.

When seeking support for a proposition, a speaker might also conduct an experiment that can be done without extensive statistical analysis. Recently, a student teacher designed an experiment to collect information on the effects of social pressure upon individuals in a group. On the first day of class, the student teacher went into his beginning speech class and, using a German accent throughout, gave a lecture appropriate for a class in nineteenth-century German history. Even though the students knew that this was supposed to be a speech class, not one raised a hand to question the student teacher about the course. Each apparently felt pressured into remaining silent rather than expressing what he felt the others might interpret as irresponsible questions. Some students even took notes! Without having to quantify a mass of information and produce a statistical analysis, this student teacher had conducted an experiment that could be used as supportive material in a speech he was preparing on group social pressure. With some imagination and a desire to obtain supporting information, any speaker can conduct such experiments.

A final admonition should be made. After the speaker has collected information from reading, interviews, lectures, television, films, personal surveys, and experiments, he should contribute some originality in fitting the supporting materials together. He should synthesize the materials and summarize them when full disclosure of the information would be excessively time-consuming. He should compare and contrast the various materials he collects and then interpret the information accurately, drawing only those conclusions that are justified by the available information.

SUMMARY

The success of a speech depends largely upon the selection of the materials for a particular audience and occasion. The gathering of materials for a speech begins with a review of one's own knowledge of the subject and can be supplemented by reading, obtaining literature from special interest groups, note-taking, interviewing, attending lectures, viewing television and films, and by taking personal surveys and conducting experiments. Probably the greatest aid to the speaker in collecting materials for a speech is an effective note-taking and filing method. In addition to books and periodicals, the speaker can often obtain reading materials from special interest groups and governmental agencies. He should be aware, however, of the prejudices and purposes of special interest groups, for it is likely that the materials supplied by such organizations will be characterized by a bias, sometimes to the extent of exaggerated claims and inaccurate information. In general, the speaker should use all available sources for materials, taking care to weigh the relevance of the material and the objectivity and accuracy of the sources.

ADAPTED READING 6.1

NIXON'S NOVEMBER 3 SPEECH
Robert B. Semple, Jr.

ROBERT B.
SEMPLE, JR.

President Nixon's State of the Union Message Thursday is eagerly awaited in Washington, but it is not likely to be as revealing or profoundly important to him, to his staff, perhaps even to the country, as his speech to the nation on Vietnam last November 3. The Vietnam address has been largely passed over in the assessments of Mr. Nixon's first year in office, but his aides say that few episodes tell more about the President's style of operations and his instincts about the country, or about how he is likely to conduct himself at critical moments in the future.

They say that the Vietnam address represented his greatest gamble and greatest triumph of the year: in a substantive sense, he bought time and public patience for his Vietnam strategy with a direct appeal to the "silent majority" to trust him to withdraw American troops from Vietnam at a pace he would not disclose. In psychological terms, he gave himself and his staff a welcome boost by putting his own capacity for leadership to what he considered to be a deliberate test.

Mr. Nixon's image in some quarters is said to be that of a man who is easily corseted by an overprotective staff, seeking a consensus, rationing his energies and avoiding major gambles. This may well be the prevailing Nixon style, but the November 3 speech suggests that, on major occasions, he is likely to discard the entire apparatus in favor of his own instincts and judgments.

Against the advice of his chief foreign policy advisers, he offered a full justification for American intervention in the war; against the pleadings of his allies on Capitol Hill—notably Senator Hugh Scott of Pennsylvania, the minority leader—he proposed no further diplomatic initiatives. According to his associates, Mr. Nixon relied little on his staff, and almost entirely on his own perceptions of what the country would accept. Sources say that rather than depend on his stable of six full-time speech writers, the President wrote the address almost entirely himself in the solitude of his Camp David retreat. The evidence suggests that his first thoughts about the speech survived a two-week personal drafting process with only minor changes.

"I must tell you in all candor," his chief foreign policy adviser, Henry A. Kissinger, told him during the drafting process, "that I have no way of knowing whether this speech has any chance of being listened to." "What this speech will tell," the President reportedly replied, "is whether the American people can be led in the direction we have to go."

The decision to give the country an accounting of the Vietnam strategy was made during the President's August vacation in San Clemente, California. . . . Mr. Nixon had told visitors all along that he wanted to key such an accounting of his war policy to the first anniversary of the bombing halt in early November. . . . Accordingly, on October 13, the White House press secretary, Ronald L. Ziegler, announced that the President would deliver a "major address" November 3. Critics immediately charged that the announcement itself was timed to defuse the antiwar moratorium scheduled for October 15, and that the speech was timed to achieve maximum impact in the scattered state and municipal elections on November 4. Mr. Nixon's associates insist otherwise. . . .

In addition, the President was said to have overridden the advice of his public relations specialists, who reasoned — correctly, as it turned out — that an early announcement would give the critics three weeks in which to mount an attack and press for faster disengagement, and thus build expectations that the speech would contain precisely the sort of bold initiative that Mr. Nixon wished to avoid.

Although he wrote the speech himself, Mr. Nixon turned for preliminary data to his policy-making machinery. Mr. Kissinger asked for memorandums from the Secretaries of State and Defense and from Ellsworth Bunker in Saigon and Henry Cabot Lodge in Paris. He also asked members of the National Security Council staff to propose a set of "talking points" for the President. The following Sunday, October 18, Mr. Kissinger went to Cambridge, Massachusetts to solicit the advice of old friends in the Harvard community. What he heard apparently did not relieve his earlier nervousness about the speech. He reported that nearly all of his friends wanted the President to announce some concrete initiative or, at the very least, disclose a definite timetable for withdrawal.

This was also the substance of much of the advice Mr. Nixon was reportedly getting from his allies on Capitol Hill, in the press, and from the middle levels of the bureaucracy. . . . The President received little contrary pressure from his Cabinet, it is said, but on one point there was a fundamental disagreement. Most of the memorandums from the bureaucracy urged him to address himself to existing policies for disengagement and spend little time defending the original American commitment. Even Mr. Kissinger, it is said, argued that the American presence in Vietnam created a logic of its own and that the President should give heaviest emphasis to what the Administration had done to turn a war it had not made into a peace with which both sides could live.

The President, however, reportedly argued that to dismiss the past would be a disservice to the mothers of 40,000 men who had died in conflict; and that to imply that America should never have entered the war in the first place would have involved criticizing the judgment of not only President Johnson but also Presidents Eisenhower and Kennedy, and might well have shaken public confidence in the institution of the Presidency itself. . . .

According to White House sources, Mr. Nixon began making notes October 21. The first jottings covered four pages of plain White House stationery and were dated "October 21, 1 A.M." They began, "I speak on a problem that concerns every American. . . ." He used roughly the same phrase to begin the actual speech. Near the end, he jotted down two significant phrases. "If you want defeat, let me know. If you want peace, now is the time to speak up." This phraseology was later abandoned, in part because the President did not wish to issue so blatant an invitation to demonstrators of any kind, friendly or critical. But they suggest that, from the beginning, he intended to draw more boldly than ever before the line between the Administration and its critics.

His aides say that Mr. Nixon required extensive research material only on the middle portion of the speech, which set forth his efforts to achieve a negotiated settlement—including previously undisclosed private contacts—and a description of the parallel effort to transfer the bulk of the fighting to the Vietnamese. Memorandums flew back and forth as the President tried to buttress his case with concrete details. . . .

On October 29, for the first time, the President read Mr. Kissinger an outline of what he had written. The next day he gave three other close advisers—Attorney General John N. Mitchell, Secretary of State William P. Rogers, and Secretary of Defense Melvin R. Laird—essentially the same presentation. . . . That afternoon, in his auxiliary office in the Executive Office Building, next door to the White House, Mr. Nixon read Kissinger the entire text, and the following day, the 31st, he read aloud the ending. Associates recall that he was having trouble with the ending, and had collected scraps of yellow paper covered with phrases he wanted to use but could find no place for. "I don't want demonstrations," read one, "I want your quiet support."

That evening . . . the President flew to Camp David. Arriving by helicopter the next day, Mr. Kissinger said he discovered that the President had been up until 4 A.M. reworking the ending. It incorporated some of the thoughts from the first jottings of October 21 and the scraps he had not found room for. From these emerged perhaps the decisive paragraph: "And so, tonight, to you, the great silent majority of Americans, I ask for your support."

Mr. Kissinger and the President reviewed the speech page by page on Saturday, November 1. The President spent most of Sunday and Monday polishing it.

On Monday night, an hour before the President was to deliver the speech to the nation, copies were delivered to members of the press who had assembled for a briefing in the East Room of the White House. . . . Still nervous, Mr. Kissinger entered the East Room to brief the press. He says now that he fully expected to be overwhelmed with angry questions because the speech contained none of the initiatives the press had forecast.

Mr. Nixon himself was not certain after the Vietnam speech whether he had accomplished anything. He called an aide, Patrick J. Buchanan, to ask: "How'd I do?" But on November 4, telegrams of support began arriving in large numbers. The President said they came from the "silent majority," on whose existence he had risked the entire enterprise.

ADAPTED READING 6.2

24 WRITERS TOOK 6 WEEKS TO DRAFT 40-MINUTE SPEECH
Nan Robertson

The State of the Union Message that President Johnson delivered in 40 minutes today took six weeks to write. At least two dozen persons, including the President's wife, put pen to the test through many drafts. As for Mr. Johnson, he could not seem to let it alone.

The message was in extra-large type and well spaced for easy reading, and portions were underscored for emphasis. It was heavily crossed out in places with insertions typed above. The President made these changes just before going to Capitol Hill.

Yesterday, at breakfast, lunch and dinner, Mr. Johnson discussed the "last" draft with 123 persons, but did not necessarily take their advice. They were, in order of meals, the six leaders of the House and Senate; men on the Executive Council of the American Federation of Labor and Congress of Industrial Organizations; and members of the Business Council, who are presidents and board chairmen of the country's biggest corporations.

The two men who set the tone of the message were the President and Theodore Sorensen, White House special counsel, who was President Kennedy's principal speech writer. Mr. Sorensen wrote it all out by hand in Washington and, after Christmas, in a small isolated ranch house seven miles from the LBJ Ranch in Texas. He consulted constantly with the President at the Ranch and then returned to his hideout to revise, correct and cut.

"The President wanted it to be very short and to the point," said a trusted friend who was often present at the discussions. "After every draft he'd do he said, 'Let's cut, let's cut. . . .' "

It is believed that the President determined from the beginning that the message should be no longer than 3000 words. As delivered, it ran 3059. Mr. Kennedy's three messages on the State of the Union ran between 4600 and 6500 words. President Truman's message in 1948, the longest in history, ran more than 25,000 words. This was sent to Capitol Hill; President Truman, involved in a nationwide steel strike and other problems, did not deliver it in person.

Mr. Sorensen's draft was finished on Monday, December 30. A White House secretary typed it, finding his handwriting hard to read. Late that night it went to the President. Mr. Johnson discarded some ideas and phrases and inserted others while discussing the message with his advisers. Every Cabinet officer was consulted. . . .

White House aides estimated that in the last week the message went through 10 to 16 revisions. Mr. Sorensen's "final draft" was ready on Sunday. The President continued to go over it, adding last touches. The text was on his bedside table at the White House every night in case new ideas should come to him.

During the revisions he went over the message with Mrs. Johnson, who can turn a fine phrase herself. Throughout her husband's career she has often advised him on speeches and at political rallies has not hesitated to hand him a note saying "That's enough."

ADDITIONAL READINGS

Auer, J. Jeffery, *An Introduction to Research in Speech* (New York: Harper & Row, 1959), chap. 4, "Bibliographical Resources," especially pp. 79–99.

Ehninger, Douglas and Wayne Brockriede, *Decision by Debate* (New York: Dodd, Mead, 1963), chap. 4, "Obtaining Information: Personal Knowledge, Contacts with Experts"; chap. 5, "Obtaining Information: Printed Sources"; chap. 6, "Recording and Filing Information."

Monroe, Alan and Douglas Ehninger, *Principles and Types of Speech* (Glenview, Ill.: Scott, Foresman, 1967), chap. 9, "Speech Materials: Sources, Records, and Classification."

Terris, Walter, *Content and Organization of Speeches* (Dubuque, Iowa: William C. Brown, 1968), chap. 5, "Research: The Sources."

STUDY QUESTIONS

1. What are the advantages of beginning the process of gathering materials for a speech by reflection?
2. Why is it important to keep an organized file of materials for speeches? What kinds of materials should be filed?
3. In what ways can a speaker supplement his existing knowledge about a speech topic?
4. What is the difference between a direct quotation and a summary note?
5. What basic information should be included on a note card for inclusion in the speaker's file?
6. What are the five basic rules for filling out note cards for a speech? Why is each necessary?
7. Why is it important to make special arrangements with an interviewee in advance of the interview? Why is it important to prepare an outline of questions before the interview?

EXERCISES

1. To become familiar with the reference materials in the library and to gain practice in the correct ways of recording bibliographical material, prepare a bibliography of one piece of information from each of the special indexes listed in this chapter.
2. For your next speech, take an informal poll of students on campus or in your town to test general attitudes toward your topic. Use the survey results in the speech as introductory material or to substantiate your position on the subject.
3. Prepare and conduct an informal experiment to use in your next speech.
4. Interview an established authority who might reside in your community or teach at the university on the subject of your next speech. Follow the suggestions for interviewing found in this chapter.
5. Take any three topics listed below and locate at least two sources each for an informative speech on the subject:
   a. Why we bury the dead.
   b. How a spectrograph is made.
   c. How a warm frost develops.
   d. Esperanto.
   e. How records are pressed.
   f. Why the tower of Pisa leans.

g. The author of the letters of Junius.
h. Origins of Mardi Gras.
i. How the British observe Guy Fawkes Day.
j. How chewing gum is made.
k. How fish see.
l. The Davis Cup tennis competition.
m. The sculpting of Mt. Rushmore.
n. Paul Bunyan.
o. How to play the bagpipe.
p. Setting stones in rings.
q. Dutch cheeses.
r. How an igloo is built.
s. How boots are made.
t. The Fabian Society.

CHAPTER

7

THE PARTS OF A SPEECH

The universe exists as an organized mass of elements. Order is maintained within societies by a system of organized rules, regulations, and codes of ethical conduct. Without a proper balance between the many facets of the universe and between persons, chaos would exist. Governmental bodies— city councils, legislatures, and school boards—are formed to evaluate and implement the proposals and policies of the citizens they represent. Such bodies are necessary to operate schools, build streets, provide essential services, enforce laws, and conduct elections. Without them, anarchy would prevail.

> **Order is the first law of heaven.**
>
> JOSIAH ROYCE

Just as groups of people cannot exist without community organization, neither can people think clearly without mental organization. To be sure, people sometimes act irrationally, thoughtlessly, or on an emotional impulse. But when a person's conduct is based on rational thought, his actions are the result of a systematic pattern of analysis and reasoning. For instance, when he reads a book or newspaper, he reads from left to right and from top to bottom. If publishers printed books or other reading material at will, to be read from right to left and from bottom to top, no standard reading habits could be formed. The same is true in oral communication. A speaker must follow certain patterns of expression if he is to be understood. This process is called organization. Organization refers to the way a speaker divides his speech and its subject, arranges his ideas, and orders them for presentation. The process is also often referred to as the speech's *structure* or *arrangement*.

IMPORTANCE OF ORGANIZATION

Although well-structured communication is important in both writing and speaking, it takes on special significance for the speaker. If a reader of a book completes a page of information and realizes that he has missed the central thought, he can go back and reread the page. This is not so with the listener. Once the words are spoken and the sound waves have passed the listening sensors of the auditor, the message is gone. The listener must perceive the message upon first hearing it or be forever ignorant of its content. Consequently, the speaker must take special pains to make his purpose clear, to arrange his material logically, and to relate one idea to another in such a way that the hearer perceives the relationship between the speaker's ideas and his central purpose.

A clear pattern of organization is probably more important in speaking than in writing because in written communication the reader has many visual clues to aid him in determining how the subject has been divided. These include paragraph indentations, main headings, subheadings, and different sizes and kinds of type. The reader has an additional advantage in that he is able to pace the communication act. He can proceed as rapidly or slowly as he wishes, pausing to study difficult passages until he fully comprehends them and sees how they are related to the writer's goal or thesis. In the speech situation, however, the listener exercises almost no control over the rate of delivery and has no visual clues to assist him in understanding the arrangement of the material. For these reasons, it is usually necessary for a speaker to be somewhat more obvious and explicit in his organization than a writer need be.

The purposes of speaking are discussed at some length in Chapter 3. Before discussing specific forms of organization, let us look at the general organizational structure of speeches.

A wit once said that a speaker should first tell the audience what he is going to say, then say it, then tell them what he has said. Although often desirable, this is not always necessary. Some of today's public speaking is relatively formless. Just as the structure of sonnets has given way to soul poems, as the traditional mass has been replaced by the folk mass in some

> Every speech ought to be put together like a living creature, with a body of its own, so as to be neither without head nor without feet, but to have both a middle and extremities, described proportionately to each other and to the whole.
>
> PLATO

religious services, as Beethoven has been preempted by Schoenberg and Wyeth by Klee in the minds of some, the highly structured speeches of Daniel Webster, Franklin Roosevelt, or Adlai Stevenson have been supplanted by the more formless performances of the Eldridge Cleavers, the Saul Alinskys, and other contemporary speakers. The aim, however, of those who speak without form usually is to stimulate only feeling or emotion. Their appeal is not to the intellect, but to the passions. While emotion has its place in oral discourse, as Lionel Ruby states in Adapted Reading 12.1, when people act on feelings and impulse without regard to facts and rational thought, they are courting disaster. And it is as true today as it was a century ago that if logical decision-making is to prevail, it will do so only in the form of a structured message with rational objectives. Consequently, the student of public speaking must be aware of the importance of ordered discourse and the various methods for achieving a clear and purposeful arrangement of his materials.

Generally, a speaker should introduce the speech by telling the audience what he is going to talk about, then develop his ideas, and finally end the speech with a conclusion. We shall now turn our attention to the ingredients of these major divisions.

THE INTRODUCTION

Norman Thomas confesses that he worries most about the beginning of a speech (Adapted Reading 5.1). And with good cause, for it is in the opening remarks that a speaker often wins or loses a favorable response. The introduction serves three main purposes. It should prepare the listener (1) to be interested in the speech topic, (2) to listen intelligently, and (3) to receive the speech with an amicable, or at least objective, attitude.

Arousing Interest

The degree of the speaker's need to create interest in his topic will depend on the subject and the reasons which motivated the listeners to assemble for the speech. If the audience has come to the speaking site voluntarily, the speaker probably will not be required to stimulate enthusiasm for his topic.

However, not many speakers find themselves facing audiences that are so receptive. In most situations, the speaker's first concern is to create enthusiasm for or to intensify the audience's interest in his topic. Indeed, his first sentence should be directed toward that end.

The speaker's method of attracting attention and arousing interest will depend on his subject and the composition of the audience. An effective technique for awakening interest is to present the subject as relevant to the

> **What holds attention determines action.**
>
> WILLIAM JAMES

hearers' personal welfare. Similarly, a speaker might stress the national, state, or local significance of the topic or emphasize the urgency of his proposal.

Another approach is to arouse the curiosity of the auditors by asking questions, posing a problem, setting forth a dilemma, or referring to the bizarre, unusual, strange, or puzzling aspects of the subject. At times, a speaker can appeal to his listeners by recounting a personal experience or an historical incident. He might also make effective use of examples or illustrations. A striking, apt, or familiar quotation is yet another method of stimulating the audience. Humor in the form of jokes, anecdotes, and puns is a common attention-getting method and can often be effective. Visual aids—photographs, charts, and diagrams—are also effective devices. A speaker might even approach the audience negatively by irritating or challenging them, but he should be very careful with this technique lest he seriously offend his hearers and defeat his cause.

Whatever device the speaker decides to utilize to arouse interest, he should make certain that it is clearly related to his subject—that it will not simply focus attention on himself or some irrelevant aspect of the speaking situation. Second, his attention-gaining device must be striking. A series of ordinary questions, a dull personal experience, or an uninspiring illustration will not arouse interest. Third, the speaker's approach should be in good taste. Anything vulgar, obscene, or even risqué may prove offensive to some in the audience. Fourth, he should avoid startling or frightening his listeners. A speaker who fires a gun to animate his audience will so stun them that they may remain distracted throughout the speech. And the speaker who removes a live snake from a box is apt to frighten so many listeners that their receptivity to the speaker's message will be minimal. If the speaker *must* use a frightening action, statement, or object he should reassure his audience of its harmlessness.

A speaker has, then a variety of techniques available to him for creating interest in his subject.

Humor. "A funny thing happened to me on the way to the White House." With these words Adlai Stevenson introduced his concession speech on election night, 1952. Many people share the misconception that it is essential to begin a speech with a humorous story. This is an acceptable and sound practice so long as certain requisites are maintained. First, the anecdote should relate to the audience, the speaker, the speech, or the occasion. If the humor is unrelated to any of the four elements of the speaking situation, it fails to achieve the purpose of an introductory statement—to focus attention on the speaker's topic. In fact, if the story is totally unrelated, the speaker may actually transfer interest to another subject.

The quotation from Adlai Stevenson's concession speech reflects humor aimed at himself and the occasion. In the following introduction, the speaker relates his humor to his subject and audience. He used this introduction for a speech entitled, "How to Compose an Ancient, Undiscovered Folk Song":

One of the more baffling phenomena on the music scene today is the folk song. It was only a few years ago that folk singing became popular. Today there is a serious shortage of new ones for the old ones have been gobbled up. There are no more genuine, authentic folk songs, but only artificial, authentic folk songs. To meet the demand, everyone is now writing them, and there is no reason why you shouldn't too.

Quotation. A second popular method of creating interest is by use of quotations. Again, the quotation should refer to the speech topic or to some other element of the speaking situation. It should direct attention to the speaker's subject and evoke an immediate response. It might also be used to paraphrase the speaker's theme. If the source is unknown to the audience it should be identified for them.

In the following example, a student speaker combined humor with a quotation to arouse interest in his speech on "The Bangkok Taxicab":

"About the most hazardous thing in Thailand is a ride in a Bangkok taxi. The driver will invariably take his hands from the steering wheel each time he passes a major Buddhist shrine, clasp them before his face in the traditional *Yai*, lower his eyes and hold this ritual attitude of prayer until the taxi has hurdled—unguided by man —past the object of his devotion." A recent issue of *Reader's Digest* included this description of the hazards of riding in a Bangkok taxi. As a survivor of countless safaris in a Siamese taxi of Bangkok, I speak with a measure of authority when I say that an intra-city trip in one of these kamikaze cabs is an experience one will never forget.

Question. The rhetorical question is one that requires no answer, and is frequently used by speakers in their opening remarks. The purpose of this device is to *suggest* a response to the audience. If one were to speak on how the United States should establish priorities in using its vast resources, the audience's objective consideration of the subject might be achieved by asking the question: "Should the United States spend more money on a trip to Mars than on overcoming our domestic problems of poverty, housing, and hunger?" Or, to evoke a subjective response from the audience the speaker might ask: "Do you think there is a need for a change in American values if the United States spends 5 billion dollars in space exploration and only 697 million dollars to solve the urban problems of this country?" In the first example, the general problem is suggested to the audience, but not the speaker's point of view. In the latter, the audience is led to a conclusion suggested by the speaker's question.

Reference to the Audience or Occasion. By referring to either the audience or the occasion in his opening remarks, the speaker can readily identify with his listeners and enhance the significance of his subject. Although politicians frequently use this device, at times they seem less than sincere. References to the audience or to the occasion should be simple, direct, and sincere. Such was the case when Dr. Grayson Kirk used this technique in a convocation address celebrating the centennial of the University of Denver on April 9, 1964:

> It is a pleasure to be in Denver once more, to visit again this university where I taught one happy summer, and to have the opportunity to renew so many long standing and precious friendships. Actually, I can, in retrospect, associate this institution with one of the major changes in the direction of my life. It is here that I enjoyed my last full-time teaching — though I did not know it at the time — because immediately after my return from the pleasant summer here I was invited to become the Provost of Columbia, a decision that once made, brought my teaching days to a close. Now that I am here again, who knows but that when I go back to New York there might be a strong campus opinion developed in my absence in favor of my return to teaching. If this should be the case, then, I think I ought to come back here and start where I left off in 1949.

In a 1967 speech, historian Daniel Boorstin attempted to win the good will of his audience by associating himself with his listeners and his listeners with historians (see Adapted Reading 7.1).

Personal Reference. Opening remarks utilizing personal reference as a method of attracting attention must be handled so that the speaker appears modest, humble, and sincere. Mention of one's experience, triumphs, or personal success in the field one plans to discuss may establish the speaker's qualifications as an authority, as well as enhance interest in his topic by reminding the audience of his expertise or broad background. However, the speaker must not appear to be boasting. During the 1952 and 1956 election campaigns, Adlai Stevenson frequently employed such references as a means of audience adaptation. Often, as shown in Adapted Reading 7.2, he combined a personal reference with humor.

Reference to the Subject. If, at the outset, the audience is predisposed to the topic, even greater interest can be provoked by stressing the significance or timeliness of the subject.

President Lyndon Johnson emphasized the timeliness and significance of his subject when speaking before a televised joint session of the Congress on March 16, 1965. Titled "The Right to Vote," the speech was delivered to urge passage of the voting rights bill of that year:

> Mr. Speaker, Mr. President, members of the Congress, I speak tonight for the dignity of man and the destiny of democracy. I urge every member of both parties, Americans of all religions and of all colors, from every section of this country, to join me in that cause.
> At times, history and fate meet at a single time in a single place

to shape a turning point in man's search for freedom. So it was at Lexington and Concord. So it was a century ago at Appomattox. So it was last week in Selma, Alabama. There, long suffering men and women peacefully protested the denial of their rights as Americans. Many were brutally assaulted. One good man—a man of God—was killed.

There is no cause for pride in what happened in Selma. There is no cause for self-satisfaction in the long denial of equal rights of millions of Americans. But there is cause for hope and for faith in our democracy in what is happening here tonight. For the cries of pain and the hymns and protests of oppressed people have summoned into convocation all the majesty of this great government—the government of the greatest nation on earth.

Winston Churchill, addressing a joint session of the United States Congress during World War II, exhibited skill in employing several of the techniques for arousing interest (see Adapted Reading 7.3).

Creating a Favorable Impression for the Speaker and His Topic
While most audiences tend to regard the speaker objectively, under some circumstances the speaker may feel it necessary to improve his image with the audience before proceeding to the body of the speech: (1) If he represents a cause or group unacceptable to the audience; (2) if he has been associated with any questionable or controversial program, organization, or act; or (3) if the listeners have reason to question his motives in addressing them, they are likely to regard the speaker with hostility or, at best, skepticism. The audience may even consider him suspect simply because they regard him as an "outsider"—someone of a different race, religion, nationality, class, age, vocation, or sex—or someone from another part of the country.

Since an audience that is skeptical of or lacks confidence in a speaker is unlikely to listen impartially, it is incumbent upon the speaker, early in the speech, to eliminate or minimize any misgivings his hearers may have. Several devices are available to the speaker for removing audience reservation:

1. He may openly acknowledge that he disagrees with the audience or differs from them in several ways, but he should also stress goals, premises, and attitudes that he shares with them.
2. He may point out experiences in his past which are similar to theirs.
3. He may express his understanding of their problems and sympathize with their goals.
4. He may correct misconceptions that they have about his character or actions by directly refuting attacks that have been made on him.
5. He may associate his detractors with parties or causes generally disliked by the audience.
6. He may disclaim any selfish or personal motives for what he says and believes.
7. He may compliment the audience on its achievements, aims, or conduct.

8. He may praise leaders, individual members of the group, or the community for their activities or accomplishments.
9. He may deprecate his own achievements in order to demonstrate his humility or modesty.
10. He may poke fun at himself, thereby destroying any impression of pomposity or conceit.
11. He may relate a humorous story or joke to indicate that he has a sense of humor.
12. He may appeal to the audience's sense of fair play and implore them to listen with an open mind.

While the above by no means exhausts the possible approaches a speaker may take to achieve a favorable audience attitude toward him, it does suggest some of the methods he might pursue. Even if a speaker is highly respected and well liked, he may wish to employ some of these techniques.

Preparing the Audience to Listen Intelligently

After securing audience interest and establishing his credibility, the speaker should concern himself with the third function of the introduction: preparing the audience to listen intelligently to the subject matter. If the auditors are to follow the speaker without difficulty, it is essential that, by the time he reaches the body of his address, they know his topic. If, by this time, the listener is not provided with the specific purpose or central thought, the exact nature of the discussion within the body of the speech may elude him.

At times, however, the speaker may decide to withhold the specific purpose if he feels that revealing it will jeopardize his chances of obtaining the desired response. For example, in a speech to persuade on a highly controversial issue, revealing the main idea in the introduction may immediately alienate those in disagreement with the speaker. Instead, he might first seek to win the good will of his listeners, provide them with essential background material, and in other ways lay a foundation of fact and accepted premises, so that when he does present his main idea, the audience will be more disposed to agree with him. In these instances, the speaker would probably still reveal his general subject in the introduction, but would not introduce his central thought until an appropriate time later in the speech.

In addition to revealing the subject and purpose, the introduction may also include materials designed to assist the audience in understanding the remainder of the speech. Frequently, a preview of the main points of the speech or an outline of how the speaker plans to approach his topic will prove helpful. For example, in an informative speech analyzing the election returns of a political contest, the speaker might follow his statement of purpose ("Today, I would like to analyze the results of last month's election and try to explain why the Reform Party was defeated") with a preview of his points ("To understand why the Reform Party lost, I think we need, first, to compare the vote of the cities with that of the rural areas; second, to examine the sources of the Reformers' strength when they won four years ago; and then to look at how their record while in office affected voters who had supported the party in the past"). Previews effectively prepare the audience for what is to follow. With an outline of the main steps or parts, they know what to expect as the speech progresses.

Other information, including definitions of key words or phrases and pertinent historical data, may assist the audience in understanding. For example, a speaker might say:

> Before getting into my discussion of the weaknesses and harmful effects of this piece of legislation, I think it is important to emphasize that we cannot change it now. The courts have ruled that the law is constitutional, the governor refuses to call a special session of the legislature to repeal it, and the legislature does not meet again for two years. My purpose in addressing you tonight is to outline the defects of the law so that you can begin working to gain support in your various communities so that we can get this law repealed two years from now.

Or, the speaker might define a term in his introduction:

> When I talk about the need for a "liberal education," I am not so much talking about a wide choice of subjects with few requirements and many electives as I am about the way in which these subjects are taught. By "liberal education" I mean the kind of learning that prepares one to examine every subject with an open mind, a breadth of knowledge, and a compassion for his fellow men.

Or, the speaker might develop some necessary background material in the introduction to his speech:

> To understand why I propose consolidating Speech courses 1, 51, and 65 into a single course, it is necessary for you to know how these courses were introduced into the curriculum and why they overlap. Speech 1 was originally created to be a fundamentals course required for Speech majors and open to any interested freshman. Speech 51 was later added when the College of Liberal Arts wanted a required fundamentals course at the sophomore level with emphasis on public speaking. Speech 65 was developed to serve the College of Business Administration as a required course with emphasis on business and group speaking for their majors.

Whether information exemplified in the above excerpts is included in the introduction or presented later will, of course, depend on the audience, the subject, and the judgment of the speaker. At times, such material is essential in the introduction if the audience is to listen to the rest of the speech intelligently. The speaker should remember that his major aim in preparing the audience for the speech is to make the content in the body of his speech easy to comprehend. An excellent example of preparing an audience for the subject was exhibited by Dr. Carl Rogers, Professor of Psychology and Psychiatry at the University of Wisconsin, in a speech delivered to a faculty and staff forum at the California Institute of Technology. He spoke on a technical subject, "What We Know About Psychotherapy—Objectively and Subjectively":

> In the field of psychotherapy considerable progress has been made in the last decade in measuring the outcomes of therapy in the personality and behavior of the client. In the last two or three years additional progress has been made in identifying the basic conditions in the therapeutic relationship which bring about therapy, which facilitate personal development in the direction of psychological maturity. Another way of saying this is that we have made progress in determining those ingredients in a relationship which promote personal growth.
>
> Psychotherapy does not supply the motivation for such development of growth. This seems to be inherent in the organism, just as we find a similar tendency in the human animal to develop and mature physically, provided minimally satisfactory conditions are provided. But therapy does play an extremely important part in releasing and facilitating the tendency of the organism towards psychological development or maturity, when this tendency has been blocked.
>
> I would like, in the first part of this talk, to summarize what we know of the conditions which facilitate psychological growth, and something of what we know of the process and characteristics of that psychological growth. Let me explain what I mean when I say that I am going to summarize what we "know." I mean that I will limit my statements to those for which we have objective empirical evidence. For example, I will talk about the conditions of psychological growth. For each statement one or more studies could be cited in which it was found that changes occurred in the individual when these conditions were present which did not occur in situations where these conditions were absent, or were present to a much lesser degree. . . .
>
> I would like to give this knowledge which we have gained in the very briefest fashion, and in everyday language.

THE BODY OF THE SPEECH

The most important part of any speech is the body, or discussion, for it is here that the speaker develops his propositions and arguments. In fact, one might say that the body *is* the speech, with the introduction and conclusion serving as appendages, albeit important ones.

Since methods for dividing the body of the speech are developed in Chapter 8 and outlining is discussed in Chapter 9, this chapter will treat only four general aspects of organization as related to the body of the speech: (1)

the number of main parts or divisions within the body of the speech, (2) maintaining order, (3) maintaining balance, and (4) maintaining cohesion.

The Number of Parts

When dividing his subject, the speaker should restrict himself to a limited number of main parts (or steps, arguments, contentions, divisions, points, or issues). The major divisions of the body should be few enough that the audience can easily remember them upon conclusion of the speech. If the speech is to have a lasting effect, the audience must also be able to recall the supporting materials.

The number of divisions a speech contains varies. In most instances, the speaker should develop probably no more than four major points, although, on occasion, he might conceivably stretch this to as many as five or even six points. Beyond that number, however, most listeners will have difficulty recalling all of the principal ideas.

If a subject demands eight, nine, or more logical divisions or steps, the speaker should devise a new approach, combining several of the original points or developing an altogether different pattern of division. Reducing the number of main divisions may require some ingenuity, but it can usually be accomplished without much difficulty and almost always results in an improved speech. For example, let us suppose that a speaker plans to give an informative speech explaining how to build a bird house. After analyzing his subject, he decides that there are nine main steps involved in building a bird house. But since his audience probably would not be able to remember that many points, he might regroup the nine steps into four larger units: (1) planning the bird house, (2) assembling the necessary materials, (3) the actual construction, and (4) the finishing touches. Or let us suppose that a speaker has decided to discuss the prospect of eight conference schools for winning the football championship in the forthcoming season. Instead of assessing each school individually, thereby requiring the audience to remember eight distinct points, he might combine the schools into groups such as: (1) the leading contenders, (2) the above average teams, and (3) the also-rans.

The speaker should remember that he is restricting the number of main points to aid the audience in recalling them and not because of any limits on his speaking time; for whether a speaker has five minutes or fifty minutes, most listeners experience difficulty in remembering a lengthy list of points, steps, or contentions.

The Order of the Points

If the audience is to grasp the main parts easily, they should be arranged systematically within the body of the speech. Of the several methods available for arranging the material (see Chapter 8), the speaker should be consistent in using whatever method he chooses. For example, if the speaker decides that a chronological method of arrangement best suits his subject matter, he should retain the chronological approach throughout. Or, if he decides to divide his subject topically, every major point should be another topical division.

Within the main divisions of the speech, the speaker should also adhere to a single method of subdividing. Thus, if he decides to subdivide his first major point spatially, all of the subpoints *under that first main heading* should be part of the spatial pattern. He may wish to subdivide his second point in another way — let us say, according to cause-and-effect — but if he does, he should adhere to the cause-and-effect method throughout the development of that point. The following outlines show divisions of a subject. In one instance the pattern of arrangement is consistent throughout and in the other it is inconsistent and confusing.

Inconsistent Outline

Central thought: Student dissent today focuses on three main areas:

I. On education
   A. Berkeley demonstrations of 1965
   B. Columbia riots of 1967
   C. San Francisco State demonstrations of 1968
   D. Causes of unrest
II. On race relations
   A. In the North
   B. In the cities
III. On the war in Vietnam
   A. History of the war
   B. Causes of the war
   C. Unrest at Harvard
   D. The Chicago demonstrations

Consistent Outline

Central thought: Student dissent today focuses on three main areas:

I. On education
   A. Berkeley demonstrations of 1965
   B. Columbia riots of 1967
   C. San Francisco State demonstrations of 1968
   D. Harvard and Cornell disruptions of 1969
II. On race relations
   A. In the North
   B. In the South
III. On the war in Vietnam
   A. Causes of unrest over Vietnam
   B. Effects of this unrest on student conduct

Although the second outline is consistent in its entirety with an overall topical method of division, each point is developed differently: the first, on education, by the chronological method; the second, on race relations, by a geographical division; and the third, on the war in Vietnam, according to a cause-and-effect arrangement. In the first outline only the overall topical division of the three main points is consistent. The arrangement of the subpoints under each of the three main headings inconsistently combines two or more different methods in a confusing and meaningless manner.

Not only should the speaker adhere to a consistent method of division, but in speeches to convince and to persuade he will probably also want to give some thought to the strength or persuasiveness of the various arguments in developing his plan of organization. Should the strongest argument be presented first, second, or last? If one argument is noticeably weaker than the others, where should it be introduced? Although experimental studies of these questions have produced conflicting conclusions, the speaker should not wholly ignore such considerations. By carefully analyzing the mood and background of the audience, their knowledge of the topic, and their attitudes toward his position, the speaker may gain some insights to assist him in determining the most effective order for presenting his contentions.

A Balanced Division

Another factor the speaker should consider while organizing the body of his address is whether his overall pattern of organization is well balanced. The term *balance* refers to the amount of development or time accorded each main division. The parts of a speech may be said to be well balanced if the amount of time devoted to each is roughly equal or at least not highly disproportionate.

For example, if a speaker has 3 main divisions and he devotes 35 percent of his discussion to the first point, 30 percent to the second, and 35 percent to the third, the overall division could be regarded as unusually well balanced. Or, if he spends 40 percent of his time on the first point, 35 percent on the second, and 25 percent on the third, the speech would still be nicely balanced. However, a division in which he devoted 45 percent of his discussion to the first point, 45 percent to the second, and only 10 percent to the third would lack balance, as would an arrangement in which 70 percent of the discussion dealt with the first point and 15 percent with each of the other two divisions. In the latter two examples, so little time is devoted to the third point in one and to both the second and third points in the other that the audience would probably leave with the impression that these were of minor importance. If they are truly unimportant, the speaker should probably omit them. If, on the other hand, he regards them as significant, he needs to devote more attention to them.

While it is not necessary or even desirable for a speaker to try to balance the amount of time devoted to each part with absolute equality, the speaker should always give some attention to this aspect of organization.

A Cohesive Division

After having broken his subject down into various divisions and subdivisions and having arranged these in an orderly pattern for development, the speaker should fit the parts together in such a way that the relationship of the various divisions and subdivisions to each other and to the speaker's central thought will be clear to the audience. To achieve a cohesive organization, the speaker can draw upon six organizational techniques: (1) transitions, (2) signposts, (3) internal previews, (4) internal summaries, (5) interjections, and (6) special devices.

Transitions. Transitions are words, phrases, and sentences that serve as bridges between two ideas or thoughts to indicate to the listener that the speaker has completed his discussion of one point and is proceeding to another part of the speech. Transitions are also important to the speaker in the development of his organizational pattern, for they serve as a means of testing the relationship of one idea to the next. Ideas should flow logically, and if it is impossible to construct a logical transition between one idea and the next, the speaker should realize that the relationship between the two ideas is not correct. Some examples of transitional words and phrases are: *next, in addition to, another aspect is, we must also consider, still another reason is, also, let us now examine another,* and *I will now turn to.*

Just as bridges come to rest on both sides of the body of water they span, the best transitions also clearly indicate the place they are leaving and the area they are approaching. A few examples of transitions of this kind are listed below:

> *In addition to* inflation, we *also* have unemployment.
> *Not only* is inflation a problem, *but* we must *also* consider unemployment.
> *Having looked at* inflation, let us *now turn to* unemployment.
> *After* examining inflation, *next* we should look at unemployment.
> *Leaving* the subject of inflation, let us *move ahead to* the topic of unemployment.

In connecting two ideas, a transition may establish either a horizontal or a subordinate relationship between them. For example, if the speaker has decided that he will develop three major points in his talk, to show that the second idea is as important as the first, he might decide upon a simple transitional statement: "Not only should we seek disarmament because . . . , but another reason for adopting a policy of disarmament is. . . ." This effectively ties the second idea to the first on a horizontal or equal status. If, on the other hand, the speaker wanted to show the subordinate status of an idea, he might say, "To support this idea I offer the example of. . . ." Thus, he indicates that the example to follow is in support of, or subordinate to, the idea just presented.

Transitions can take many forms. They may be as simple as the phrase, "Let's take for example," or they may be sufficiently detailed so as to constitute an internal summary. Rhetorical questions can also act as effective transitions, as in this usage: "What are the benefits of such a policy?"

Since oral communication lacks the visual clues such as the paragraph indentations, main headings, and subheadings found in written messages to indicate a new topic, idea, or subdivision, the speaker should generously employ clear and explicit transitions to connect his ideas.

Signposts. Signposts are similar to transitions and serve the same function of identifying for the listener the introduction of a new idea or point. Usually, they are simply numbers—*first,* my *second* argument is, *third,* the *fourth* step is—although words such as *finally, the last point,* and *last* may also be regarded as signposts. Signposts have one advantage over transitions as organizational devices in that they, unlike the transition, indicate exactly where the speaker is at that moment in his speech. In other words, when a signpost is used the listener knows that the speaker is now on his *third* point or has just introduced his *second* argument. While the numbering of one's ideas with signposts may seem overly explicit and mechanical to some, this technique effectively reinforces understanding and is rarely obvious to the audience.

Internal Previews. In discussing introductions earlier in this chapter, the preview or outline of one's main ideas was recommended as a method the speaker might use to prepare the audience to listen intelligently to the remainder of the speech. The preview may also be employed effectively within the body of the speech to prepare the audience for a particularly complex, difficult, or lengthy discussion of some aspect of one's subject. Thus, after introducing a new point or subdivision, the speaker might indicate exactly how he intends to divide his discussion of this particular part of the speech.

Internal Summaries. Just as internal previews may be necessary to prepare an audience for an understanding of the development of a difficult point, so internal summaries or reviews may be required to clarify the speaker's remarks when he concludes his discussion of a highly important, complex, technical, or abstract idea. Instead of merely moving to the next subtopic, the speaker stops to repeat or emphasize the key parts of this aspect of his present topic, hoping thereby to ensure audience comprehension.

In addition to being an effective device for restating in simple form the idea just discussed, the internal summary may also serve a transitional function in permitting the speaker to complete one idea and advance to the next. An internal summary might take the following form:

> We have just examined four examples in history to prove that armament leads to greater armament and eventually to war; now let us consider some of the problems in past attempts at disarmament.

Interjections. Used as a device to emphasize key points or important ideas, the interjection can be a valuable organizational tool for the speaker. An interjection is simply a declarative statement that draws attention to an idea, such as, "Now this is important," "Now this is central to understanding the remainder of the speech," or simply, "Get this." These statements focus attention on key ideas the speaker does not want his listeners to miss.

Special Devices. Special devices to assist the memory of the audience should be considered by the speaker. It is often possible for persons to remember what they hear longer if a visual image is associated with the ideas. For instance, to explain the three major ingredients of the speaking situation—speaker, speech, and audience—a speaker may say, "If one views the speaking situation as a triangle and locates at each of the points of the triangle one of the major ingredients, speaker, speech, and audience, he can perhaps comprehend better the interrelationships of the three and the concept that without any one of these, the triangle is incomplete."

Another special organizational device is to present the major ideas of a speech by using the same first word to identify the ideas. For instance, a speaker might prepare a speech entitled "The Six *Be*'s of Public Speaking," incorporating the following major ideas: (1) *be* prepared, (2) *be* organized, (3) *be* clear, (4) *be* animated, (5) *be* enthusiastic, (6) *be* sincere. The listeners may better retain the content by associating the *be*'s with the ideas than they would if each of the major ideas was phrased in a different manner.

THE CONCLUSION

The conclusion of a speech has two major functions. The first is to reinforce the purpose of the speech and the second is to bring the speech psychologically to a conclusion for the speaker and his audience. If, for instance, the general purpose has been to instruct or inform, the speaker may want to conclude simply with a summary of the ideas presented in the body of the speech. If, on the other hand, his general purpose was to evoke a change of attitude or precipitate action, the speaker may wish to suggest a course of action for implementing the ideas. It is important to remember that audiences do not retain all the ideas the speaker presents in the course of a speech. Consequently, he should summarize the most important and compelling ones.

The second function of the conclusion, that of psychologically ending the speech, is vital to a favorable final impression. Most people have experienced a long-winded speaker who seems to conclude his speech and then begin another. This is frustrating and distracting for those in the audience, and the speaker loses respect and attention. On the other hand, the speaker who talks without hint of concluding and then suddenly stops gives his listeners an abrupt and jolting experience, again evoking a negative audience attitude. The concluding statements in the speech should be selected carefully to achieve a cathartic effect.

Summary. Many speakers believe that a summary is essential to the conclusion of a speech. If, however, the speech is a very short one—a one-idea speech—it may not be necessary to summarize. If the speech is complex, containing several important ideas, a summary conclusion is not only appropriate but probably necessary. In summarizing, the speaker may review his points in the order that they were presented or he may follow an inverse arrangement. The latter practice assumes that people will forget the ideas presented early in the speech and better retain those presented later. By reversing the order in the summary, the speaker reinforces the ideas discussed early in the body of the speech.

Whether the speaker summarizes in natural or inverse order will depend upon his analysis of the audience attitudes toward his subject and the approach he thinks is best suited to achieve his objectives. If he has presented his strongest idea early in the speech, it might be wise for him to leave the platform with the strongest idea last in the minds of the audience. On the other hand, if the speaker has selected a climactic ordering of ideas in the body of the speech, he may wish to summarize his ideas in the same order. One should admonish the speaker to avoid the trite phrases, "in conclusion" and "in summary," when preparing the concluding portion of his speech. Not only are they stylistically barren, but they also cue the audience to stop listening. Most members of an audience will interpret those words as meaning that the speaker has said all that he is going to say and is now merely repeating himself.

Referring to Introductory Material. Frequently a speaker will conclude by referring to the ideas he introduced in the opening portion of his speech. He may want to restate the purpose of his speech as a concluding technique. If he opened his introduction with a quotation, he might wish to conclude his speech with the same quotation. This was the case of one speaker who began, "'The time has come to choose between the quick and the dead.' These were the words of Bernard Baruch speaking at the opening session of the United Nations." After developing an argument for tighter arms control, the speaker concluded his speech with the following words: "Indeed, 'the time has come to choose between the quick and the dead.'" If the speaker began his speech with a narrative or an anecdote, he might wish to remind the audience of it in the conclusion.

Rhetorical Question. An effective method of concluding a speech, particularly if the speaker is suggesting action that is to be taken by the audience, is the rhetorical question. Jenkin Lloyd Jones concluded his speech titled "Who Is Tampering with the Soul of America?" with this technique. Speaking to a group of newspaper editors in 1961, he argued that the press had a responsibility to interpret and elevate the morals of America through their newspapers. He concluded with these words: "And there, gentlemen, is where you come in. You have typewriters, presses and a huge audience. How about raising hell?"

Plea for Belief or Action. In a speech to convince or persuade, the speaker may wish to leave his audience with an appeal for belief or action. Daniel Boorstin concluded a speech on "Dissent, Dissension, and the News" with this type of appeal. After pleading for greater responsibility in the press at a meeting of the Associated Press Managing Editors Association in Chicago, Dr. Boorstin implored:

> Finally, it is possible for our newspapers — without becoming Polyannas or chauvinists or super patriots or Good Humor salesmen — to find new ways of expressing and affirming, dramatizing and illuminating, what people agree upon. This is your challenge. The future of American society in no small measure depends on whether and how you answer it.

In a more direct appeal for action, Adlai Stevenson, arguing in the United Nations during the Cuban missile crisis, concluded his speech opposing the construction of missile sites in Cuba with the following words directed to Mr. Zorin, ambassador to the United Nations from the USSR.

> And now I hope that we can get down to business, that we can stop this sparring. We know the facts and so do you, sir, and we are ready to talk about them. Our job here is not to score debating points. Our job, Mr. Zorin, is to save the peace. And if you are ready to try, we are.

Personal Reference. If the occasion and subject warrant, the speaker may end with a personal reference. Such a situation occurred during the "Farewell to the Cadets" speech of General Douglas MacArthur, delivered to the United States Military Academy at West Point in 1962. In concluding this ceremonial speech, General MacArthur spoke the following words:

> The shadows are lengthening for me. The twilight is here. My days of old have vanished — tone and tints. They have gone glimmering through the dreams of things that were. Their memory is one of wondrous beauty watered by tears and coaxed and caressed by the smiles of yesterday. I listen vainly, but with thirsty ear, for the witching melody of faint bugles blowing reveille, of far drums beating the long roll.
>
> In my dreams I hear again the crash of guns, the rattle of musketry, the strange, mournful mutter of the battlefield. But in the evening of my memory always I come back to West Point. Always there echoes and reechoes: Duty, honor, country.
>
> Today marks my final roll call with you. But I want you to know that when I cross the river, my last conscious thoughts will be of the corps, and the corps, and the corps.

Some Final Words on the Conclusion. The speaker should not introduce new material in the conclusion of a speech, for the purpose of the conclusion is to close or to summarize. The introduction of new material in the conclusion can only prove distracting to the listeners.

A final, minor admonition is to avoid the use of the phrases "Thank you," or "Thank you for your attention," in closing a speech. In most instances, it is not necessary to thank the audience for listening and in some cases it may be detrimental. If a speaker has provided the listeners with useful information, with a clearer understanding of a question, or with valuable insight into how to solve a complex problem, logically, the audience should thank *him*. The phrases imply that the speaker has imposed on the audience. The speech should end on a positive rather than an apologetic note. Another reason for avoiding these phrases is that they may become crutches for a speaker; instead of ending with an effective closing statement, he uses "thank you" as a way of telling the listeners that he has finished. "Thank you" can never substitute for an effective conclusion.

Occasionally, however, it may be appropriate to thank the audience at the end of the speech. If the speaker actually has imposed on his listeners, if he has been given time normally reserved for other business, or if he has asked for and been granted permission to interfere with a regularly scheduled activity, then he probably should thank the audience for having listened to him.

SUMMARY

Organizing his material is one of the speaker's more important tasks. In arranging his subject matter, the speaker should keep in mind the fleeting nature of oral communication. To a great extent his organization will be determined by his purpose and the audience's attitudes and understanding of his topic. Most speeches have three main parts; the introduction, the body of the speech, and the conclusion. The function of the introduction is to prepare the audience to listen with interest, understanding, and a favorable disposition. The body of the speech is best organized around a limited number of main ideas or divisions. Within the body, the speaker should order his points in a consistent and psychologically meaningful manner. The divisions should be well balanced and the various parts bridged with frequent transitions, signposts, previews, and summaries. The conclusion serves to summarize or review the speaker's main ideas. In addition, it may include an exhortation to belief or action.

ADAPTED READING 7.1

AN HISTORIAN ADAPTS HIS INTRODUCTION TO AN AUDIENCE OF JOURNALISTS

Daniel J. Boorstin

In the following excerpt from his speech, "Dissent, Dissension, and the News," note how historian Daniel J. Boorstin seeks to associate himself with his listeners, members of the Associated Press Managing Editors Association, and to win their good will. Observe also how Professor Boorstin's introduction states his subject and his central thought and includes a definition of the terms dissent *and* disagreement *as he plans to use them in his speech.*

Gentlemen, it's a great pleasure and privilege to be allowed to take part in your meeting. It is especially a pleasure to come and have such a flattering introduction, the most flattering part of which was to be called a person who wrote like a newspaperman.

> The speaker demonstrates friendliness and modesty.
> The speaker compliments his listeners.

The historians, you know, sometimes try to return that compliment by saying that the best newspapermen write like historians, but I'm not sure how many of the people present would consider that a compliment.

> The speaker associates historians with journalists.
> Humorous reference implies that speaker does not regard his vocation as superior to journalism.

This afternoon I would like to talk briefly about the problems we share, we historians and newspapermen, and that we all share as Americans.

> Speaker again associates historians—and himself—with journalists.

About sixty years ago Mark Twain, who was an expert on such matters, said there are only two forces that carry light to all corners of the globe, the sun in the heaven and the Associated Press. This is, of course, not the only view of your role. Another newspaperman once said it's the duty of a newspaper to comfort the afflicted and afflict the comfortable.

> Twain statement praises Associated Press. Also increases interest.
> Newspaperman's statement adds humor, but also compliments listeners indirectly.

If there ever was a time when the light and the comfort which you can give us was needed, it's today. And I would like to focus on one problem. It seems to me that dissent is the great problem of America today. It overshadows all others. It's a symptom, an expression, a consequence and a cause of all others.

> Transition links Twain and newspaperman's comments to speaker's statement of his subject.
> Speaker states his subject.
> Speaker stresses importance of his topic.

I say *dissent* and not *disagreement*. And it is the distinction between dissent and disagreement which I really want to make. Disagreement produces debate but dissent produces dissension. Dissent, which comes from the Latin, means originally to feel apart from others. People who dis-

> The speaker inserts an extended definition of two key terms to make certain that the audience understands exactly what he plans to discuss.

agree have an argument, but people who dissent have a quarrel. People may disagree but may both count themselves in the majority, but a person who dissents is by definition in a minority. A liberal society thrives on disagreement but is killed by dissension. Disagreement is the life blood of democracy, dissension is its cancer.

A debate is an orderly exploration of a common problem that presupposes that the debaters are worried by the same question. It brings to life new facts and new arguments which make possible a better solution. But dissension means discord. As the dictionary tells us, dissension is marked by a break in friendly relations. It is an expression not of common concern but of hostile feelings. And this distinction is crucial. Disagreement is specific and programmatic, dissent is formless and unfocused. Disagreement is concerned with policy, dissenters are concerned with identity, which usually means themselves. Disagreers ask, What about the war in Vietnam? Dissenters ask, What about me? Disagreers seek solutions to common problems, dissenters seek power for themselves.

The spirit of dissent stalks our land. It seeks the dignity and privilege of disagreement, but it is entitled to neither. All over the country on more and more subjects we hear more and more people quarreling and fewer and fewer people debating. How has this happened? What can and should we do about it? This is my question this afternoon.

The speaker emphasizes the seriousness of his subject.

Rhetorical questions are used to indicate the speaker's specific topic.

ADAPTED READING 7.2

THE SPEAKER SEEKS A FAVORABLE HEARING
Adlai E. Stevenson

In his 1955 campaign for the Presidency, Adlai E. Stevenson addressed an audience of students and faculty at Yale University. Upon his arrival in New Haven, Stevenson had been greeted with "I Like Ike" and other pro-Eisenhower posters. The incumbent President, Dwight D. Eisenhower, clearly had wide support at Yale. In the introduction of his speech, Stevenson sought to win a favorable hearing from his listeners and to deal with the "egghead" issue—the question of whether he was too intellectual in his campaign addresses.

I feel that your reception has done altogether too much honor to a man whose previous undergraduate association was with a university which has often caused you acute embarrassment and me great joy on crisp autumn afternoons—namely, Princeton! I have also had some considerable association, personal and parental, with Harvard. So it is natural that I have always wanted to attend Yale, too, in one guise or another, but I never quite expected that it would be as an itinerant politician.

But your president is not only a man of warm hospitality and boundless tolerance, he is also an eminent historian, who knows that American life is made up of many strange things, and that even college students ought to be exposed to some of them. And one of the strangest is a man who runs for President; and a still stranger one is a man who runs for President twice.

Still, if I managed to circumnavigate only the wrong two of what used to be called the Big Three, I am relieved to say that I have a Yale man on the ticket with me, and I want to take this occasion to tell you how proud and happy I am about my running mate, an alumnus of your law school—Estes Kefauver.

I am particularly glad to be here at Woolsey Hall tonight because I always enjoy speaking at colleges. Now, whenever I say this I can see most of my entourage wince—particularly those eggheads who surround me, all of whom are hardboiled now. You know that word "egghead" is interesting. Some people think it means that you have a lot in your head and some think it means that you have nothing on your head. In the latter respect, I qualify as an egghead for obvious reasons.

But it is when I am deemed to qualify in the former that I am happiest. And curiously enough that is usually around universities, and especially university faculties, which I suppose proves something about the gullibility, credulity, and innocence of the learned and superior perceptions of their charges. I said something like this about enjoying my occasional visits to universities in a speech at the University of Minnesota last March, and those eggheads on my staff acted as if this were the reason why I lost the primary. But I would say to these great thinkers, the eggheads, that I really don't believe that they are as unique as they suppose; nor do I think that many Americans regard association with them as a criminal offense.

Now the fact that I enjoy talking at, to and with university audiences doesn't mean that I don't enjoy speaking at party rallies, too. What I like best perhaps is an evening that combines the best features of both—and I think we are going to have an evening like that tonight. It has been an interesting campaign, and I welcome the opportunity Woolsey Hall provides to reflect for a moment about it. . . .

ADAPTED READING 7.3

A BRITISH PRIME MINISTER ADDRESSES CONGRESS

Winston S. Churchill

In December 1941, British Prime Minister Winston S. Churchill addressed a joint session of the United States Senate and House of Representatives. The introduction of the address effectively illustrates the use of humor, praise, and references to shared beliefs and attitudes in an apparent effort to create good will.

I feel greatly honored that you should have thus invited me to enter the United States Senate chamber and address the representatives of both branches of Congress. The fact that my American forebears have for so many generations played their part in the life of the United States and that here I am, an Englishman, welcomed in your midst, makes this experience one of the most moving and thrilling in my life, which is already long and has not been entirely uneventful. I wish indeed that my mother, whose memory I cherish across the vale of years, could have been here to see. By the way, I cannot help reflecting that if my father had been American and my mother British, instead of the other way around, I might have got here on my own. In that case, this would not have been the first time you would have heard my voice. In that case, I should not have needed any invitation, but if I had it is hardly likely that it would have been unanimous. So perhaps things are better as they are.

I may confess, however, that I do not feel quite like a fish out of water in a legislative assembly where English is spoken. I am a child of the House of Commons. I was brought up in my father's house to believe in democracy; trust the people, that was his message. I used to see him cheered at meetings and in the streets by crowds of workingmen way back in those aristocratic, Victorian days, when as Disraeli said, the world was for the few and for the very few. Therefore, I have been in full harmony all my life with the tides which have flowed on both sides of the Atlantic against privilege and monopoly, and I have steered confidently towards the Gettysburg ideal of government of the people, by the people, and for the people.

I owe my advancement entirely to the House of Commons, whose servant I am. In my country as in yours public men are proud to be the servants of the state, and would be ashamed to be its masters. On any day, if they thought the people wanted it, the House of Commons could by a simple vote remove me from my office, but I am not worrying about it at all. As a matter of fact, I am sure they will approve very highly of my journey here, for which I obtained the King's permission, in order to meet the President of the United States, and to arrange with him for all that mapping out of our military plans and for all those intimate meetings of the high officers of the armed services of both countries which are indispensable to the successful prosecution of the war.

ADAPTED READING 7.4

IMPROMPTU AUDIENCE ADAPTATION IN A SPEECH TO A UNIVERSITY AUDIENCE
Hubert H. Humphrey

On April 9, 1965, Vice-President Hubert H. Humphrey addressed a convocation at Louisiana State University. Humphrey's prepared text released in advance to the press reveals that the Vice-President planned little specific audience adaptation. A recording of the speech as actually delivered, however, shows extensive last-minute additions. The purpose of these off-the-cuff remarks undoubtedly was to create good will and to establish rapport with the audience.

FROM THE PREPARED TEXT

One hundred years ago today at Appomattox Courthouse in Virginia, General Robert E. Lee donned a spotless uniform and presented his sheathed sword to General U. S. Grant. Earlier that day Lee told one of his embittered generals: "We have fought this fight as long as, and as well as, we know how. . . . For us . . . there is but one course to pursue. We must accept the situation . . . and proceed to build up our country on a new basis. . . ."

FROM THE AUDIO TAPE RECORDING

Thank you, Mr. President. Thank you, President Hunter, Governor McKeithen, Chancellor Taylor, Reverend Witcher, and the Dean of the Graduate School, Dr. Goodrich, members of the faculty of this great university, students, friends, and fellow R.O.T.C.ers. I, too, was one once, and I want to say how pleased I am to see the men and officers of these fine military training units here at this Grand Old School of Louisiana State University.

It's good to be back home. And it's particularly good to come on a day when you have such warm climate and warm hospitality. It's particularly good for a Minnesotan. (It's been a little chilly up our way, I might add.) As I said to some of your fellow citizens a little earlier today, the snowbanks were standing on the level of five feet deep; and there we had a little breeze coming in from Canada, fifteen feet deep. We're now melting that snow, and we'll inundate you with a substantial amount of Minnesota dew down the valley of the Mississippi. Let us hope that it isn't too much.

I'm glad to be back on the campus that means so much to me; I'm happy to be back in this old hippodrome and happy to be here at L.S.U., looking forward to seeing Mike the Tiger. I understand they've had two or three of these beasts since I left here. I hope that your present-day Mike can growl as good as the Mike of my day. And I know that the boys on the gridiron who are inspired by Mike the Tiger have been doing mighty well. I haven't gotten down here recently, and it hasn't been my privilege to congratulate you; so I want to say that nothing made me happier in this past year than to know that L.S.U. was in the Sugar Bowl and doing a mighty fine job, and I want to compliment you.

This is a school that has many honors. I, of course, mentioned football. I watched Y. A. Tittle play this year before he hung up the cleats. He used to do a good job down here. When I was a student at L.S.U., it was Ken Cavanaugh, All-American; and then, of course, Gus Tinsley, and many others. So the name and fame of this wonderful institution has been acclaimed throughout America, not only for its prowess in athletics, but more significantly for its high standards of academic achievement.

Today I want to visit with you as a friend and as a neighbor and as a graduate of this great institution. I came to Louisiana State University because I wanted to — because of choice, not because of order or dictation. I had the opportunity after my graduation from the University of Minnesota to attend several of our great Midwestern universities and universities to the east. But I did want the privilege of getting to know this part of America, and I wanted the opportunity to become acquainted with the new leadership that was rising in the South. And I arrived on this campus with high hopes and a low bank account. And my hopes have been sustained and my bank account did not improve for some considerable period of time. But I'm indebted to this university. I don't know, Dr. Hunter, whether you realize it, but you gave me a fellowship of four hundred and fifty dollars. I spent every dime of it right here in Baton Rouge. And, in fact, I borrowed a little elsewhere. And Mrs. Humphrey worked alongside of me, adding to the family fortune through such important tasks as typing and making sandwiches. So we worked our way through this university, and we came away with a love of it and a respect for it that lives to this day in our hearts. I cherish at home on our reading table a copy of my yearbook, the *Gumbo,* and I look back there and see some rather important personages in American life. I recall my visits here on this campus not only with faculty, but with a gentleman who serves with me now in the United States Senate, who today occupies exactly the same position that I occupied a year ago. One year ago, I was privileged to be the Majority Whip of the United States Senate; today Senator Russell Long of Louisiana is the Majority Whip of the United States Senate. So the spirit of L.S.U. marches on.

An occasion such as this is one not only for fellowship and informal visit, but I hope for thoughtful consideration of the time in which we live. One hundred years ago today at Appomattox Courthouse in Virginia, General Robert E. Lee donned a spotless uniform and presented his sheathed sword to General Ulysses S. Grant. Earlier that day General Lee told one of his embittered generals the following. Said Lee, "We have fought this fight as long and as well as we know how. . . . For us . . . there is but one course to pursue. We must accept the situation . . . and proceed to build our country on a new basis. . . ."

ADDITIONAL READINGS

Braden, Waldo and Mary Louise Gehring, *Speech Practices* (New York: Harper & Row, 1958), chap. 3, "How Speakers Organize Their Speeches."

Dickens, Milton, *Speech: Dynamic Communication* (New York: Harcourt Brace Jovanovich, 1963), chap. 8, "Conclusions, Introductions, and Transitions."

McCroskey, James, *An Introduction to Rhetorical Communication* (Englewood

Cliffs, N.J.: Prentice-Hall, 1972), chap. 12, "Introducing and Concluding Messages in Rhetorical Communication."

Mills, Glen, *Message Preparation* (Indianapolis: Bobbs-Merrill, 1966), chap, 6, "Introductions, Conclusions, and Transitions."

Terris, Walter, *Content and Organization of Speeches* (Dubuque, Iowa: Brown, 1968), chap. 3, "The Fundamental Organizational Patterns."

White, Eugene E., *Practical Public Speaking* (New York: Macmillan, 1964), chap. 8, "Developing the Introduction of the Speech"; chap. 9, "Developing the Conclusion of the Speech."

STUDY QUESTIONS

1. What are the purposes or functions of the introduction? the body? the conclusion?
2. In what ways can a speaker arouse interest among the members of his audience? Are there reasons for choosing one method over another for a particular speech or occasion?
3. Under what circumstances does it become particularly important for a speaker to create a favorable impression in the introduction of his speech? How might he go about accomplishing this?
4. What were some of the techniques used by Adlai Stevenson to create a favorable hearing for his speech at Yale? (See Adapted Reading 7.2.) How effective do you think these were?
5. What methods did Winston Churchill employ in his speech to Congress in 1941 in order to reduce any tendency on the part of the listeners to regard him as an outsider? In your opinion, were these techniques effective? In what other ways might he have associated himself with his auditors?
6. Evaluate Hubert Humphrey's impromptu effort at audience adaptation in Adapted Reading 7.4. Compile a list of the different ways in which Humphrey associated himself with Louisiana and L.S.U. Do you think Humphrey was wise to depart from his original text to include these remarks? In your opinion, was his effort at audience adaptation too obvious to be effective?
7. Why is it important for an audience to know a speaker's topic before he reaches the body of the speech? Under what conditions should a speaker not reveal his purpose or central thought early in the speech?
8. What methods are available to a speaker for concluding his speech? What are the values of each?

EXERCISES

1. Prepare three conclusions for a speech. Explain the values of each one and discuss the possible responses of the audience to each conclusion.
2. Listen to a speech, or read one in *Vital Speeches, Representative American Speeches,* or an anthology, and write a criticism of the effectiveness of the organizational techniques used by the speaker in the introduction, body, and conclusion. When writing your criticism, remain aware of the speaker's relationship to his audience and the occasion.
3. Prepare an outline for a four- to five-minute speech to inform. Then plan an introduction for the speech. Practice the introductory portion and deliver it to the class, stopping just before reaching the body of the speech. The class and instructor will then evaluate the introduction and make suggestions for improvement.
4. Incorporating the suggestions of the class and instructor, revise the introduction presented in exercise 3. Present the improved introduction again in class, this time continuing with the remainder of the speech.
5. Write out three separate introductions for a speech to inform, using a different attention-gaining device or method in each. Choose the best introduction and in 100 words indicate the reasons for your choice.
6. Write a five-hundred-word analysis of the introduction to Adlai Stevenson's speech at Yale. (See Adapted Reading 7.2.)

METHODS OF DIVIDING SPEECH MATERIALS

After the National and American football leagues agreed to merge in 1968, one of the most difficult problems they faced was deciding how to organize the new conference. Since it would be impossible for each of the 26 teams to play every other club in one season, the owners had to decide how to divide the league into smaller units and to assign teams to each subdivision.

On the question of how to divide the league, the owners had several alternatives: to keep intact the old conference alignments of 16 teams in one division and 10 in the other; to create 2 new divisions of 13 teams each; or to establish 4 to 6 subdivisions of unequal size. Once this was settled, officials faced the delicate task of deciding which clubs would be assigned to each division. Proposals for realignment were almost as numerous as fourth-down punts. Some owners favored a strictly geographical division. Others suggested an arrangement along the lines of the old leagues' memberships. Some advocated plans that would keep together traditional rivals. An important feature of several proposals was the drawing power of various teams. The prestige of playing against well-established clubs, the strength of the competition within each division, and perennial financial considerations were other factors motivating owners to choose one plan over another. After much controversy, the league finally worked out a satisfactory method of division.

The purpose in detailing here the league's reorganization difficulties is not to create sympathy for professional football, but to illustrate the variety of methods available and the many factors involved in dividing a subject — in this case, a conference of 26 football teams. The public speaker faces a similar task in dividing his topic. He not only must decide how many subdivisions he will have, but also how best to subdivide the subject matter. Like the team owners, several methods of division will be available to him and many factors will influence his decision on which approach is best suited to achieve his goal.

INFLUENCE OF SUBJECT MATTER UPON THE DIVISION OF MATERIALS

Available to the speaker is an almost infinite variety of methods for arranging materials in a speech. Selecting the proper method is important because after the subject has been analyzed and the specific purpose determined, the speaker must decide how best to arrange his material in order to obtain the desired response from his audience. This is the function of organization. With a large number of available methods for dividing the material, the speaker's selection should be based upon the time allotted to him for the speech; the knowledge, interest, and attitudes of the audience; the proportion or balance of the ideas he hopes to develop in the speech; and a logical progression of ideas leading to his conclusion.

The problems of developing the introduction and conclusion of the speech have already been discussed. Consequently, this chapter concentrates on the division, sometimes referred to as the *partition* or *pattern of arrangement*, of the body of the speech. Since the body contains the ideas the speaker hopes to communicate to his listeners, the most effective way of dividing or arranging that material should be of prime concern to him. In discussing the major methods of division, it should be stressed that more than one method might well be used within a single speech structure.

Two major influences, the subject matter of the speech and the audience's attitudes toward the subject, affect the speaking situation and help the speaker to select the best method for dividing his material. In most speeches, the subject matter lends itself to division by one of six methods: chronological, geographical, topical, causal, problem–solution, or pro and con arrangement.

Chronological or Time Sequence

The time method of arrangement of materials, as the name implies, is simply a division based on *when* events occurred. Materials or events may be arranged in their chronological order from beginning to end, from end to beginning, or by some other plan (such as past, present, and future). A speaker who wishes to talk about man's desire to explore the moon might decide that his most effective method of division would be chronological, beginning with early attempts to reach the moon, proceeding to the team effort to achieve that goal in the 1960s, and, finally, describing the first moon landing. Travelogues are frequently divided into time sequences from the beginning of the trip to the end. Mark Twain's "Recipe for New England Pie," Adapted Reading 8.1, is an example of a chronological arrangement.

One should not assume, however, that a simple chronological enumeration of events is sufficient to produce a stimulating speech. Each step of the process should be amplified and developed with interesting and descriptive material. Nothing is quite so boring as to spend an evening in a friend's home watching slides of a vacation with no elaboration on the events that took place at each location. Therefore, the speaker who decides to use the chronological method in describing man's attempts to reach the moon will have to do more than simply list the flights taken in the Mercury, Gemini, and Apollo missions. He probably would want to identify the types of information gleaned from various flights, describe the specific missions, and discuss the significance of each mission.

The chronological or time-sequence pattern is generally used for presenting historical materials, describing a process or procedure, or relating a personal experience. The following outline illustrates a time-sequence method of division. Note the development of elaborational material within each of the major time segments.

A Visit to the British House of Commons

I. The speaker's procession at 2:00 P.M.
II. Preliminary business
    A. Prayers
    B. Acceptance of petitions
    C. Announcement of bills to be considered
III. Question period from 2:15 to 2:45 P.M.
IV. Regular business
V. Adjournment debate from 10:00 to 10:30 P.M.
VI. Adjournment at 10:30 P.M.

Spatial Division

A spatial or geographical relationship is the positioning of an object in relation to the location of another object. A spatial development can create a visual appreciation for the subject matter of a speech as well as providing a logical and orderly process of division. During World War II, Winston Churchill frequently employed spatial division in his reports to the people on the progress of the war, discussing the African campaign, the Russian front, the European theater, and the conflict in the Pacific. Weather reports on radio and television often are arranged spatially, giving first the local and then the state forecast, and finally the national weather conditions. In Adapted Reading 8.2, Victor Hugo uses the letter "A" as the basis for a geographical division to describe the Battle of Waterloo.

To illustrate the various approaches available to the speaker when he divides a subject spatially, let us consider the description of the décor of a room. The speaker would begin at some logical point and then explain the location and arrangement of the various objects in the room and on the walls relative to the position of that central or original point. Normally, spatial relationships could be described in terms of north–south, east–west, up–down, inside–outside, and around. Or, if a speaker were to discuss the "domino theory" of communist infiltration, his subject matter would almost require him to arrange his material according to the geographical locations of the various nations and the effects of communist infiltration upon each geographical unit.

In a spatially divided speech, as in the case of the chronologically divided speech, the subject matter should include elaboration and clarification of the relationships of one spatial item to another. A simple listing of the relationship of various objects or places without elaboration will result in a sterile presentation.

The following is an example of a spatially divided speech in outline form:

Landscaping the Home Ground

I. Planning the landscaping of your home should begin with a study of the grounds, the placement of the house, the location of pleasure gardens, service areas, parking area, and walkways.
   A. Proportion of space to be given each.
   B. Relationship of materials to be used must be determined.
   C. The front of the house is the most important part in creating the total impression of the house.
      1. It should be considered as an outdoor room with floor (lawn), walls (shrubbery), and ceiling (trees).
      2. Some designs make the front of the house the focal point with plantings leading the eye to it.
      3. Some designs make the front of the house an enclosed "room" with "walls" on all sides hiding the house from public view.
   D. Foundation plantings that end at the house corners often lead the eye around the corners into the side yard, thus losing focus.
   E. Trees planted in front of the house can be used to frame the house.
      1. Use large trees for high house and large front yard.
      2. Use medium size trees for low house and small front yard.
   F. Special attention to landscaping will greatly improve the appearance of our cities.

Other topics that might lend themselves to a spatial arrangement include a description of a college campus; discussion of the geological formations underlying a particular area; an analysis of election results in various regions or sections of the country; a guide to a museum, library, or art gallery; and an explanation of the physical layout of a ship, park, or airport.

Topical Division

Topical division of speech materials involves the selection and development of categories of a subject. For instance, if one were to describe his recent trip around the world, rather than approach the subject chronologically, one might divide it by topics as follows:

I. Modes of transportation during the trip
II. Religious ceremonies observed

III. Architecture of different places

IV. Costs of living in various locations

By using a topical division of his materials, the speaker easily avoids the common fault of simply narrating, in order, the nations or cities visited without elaboration on the subject. Topical arrangement also provides for an extensive number of subtopics and makes selection of materials for a particular audience relatively simple.

Political speakers often arrange their ideas by topics, considering such factors as the political, economic, social, and psychological effects of various issues upon their constituents. The topical arrangement is excellent for logical consideration of controversial subjects. Paul Harper, Jr., in Adapted Reading 8.3, uses this method effectively in analyzing the problems of teenagers.

The topic, "A Visit to the British House of Commons," divided chronologically in an earlier example, might have been arranged topically. For example, it could have been outlined this way:

A Visit to the British House of Commons
  I. Officials
 II. Ceremonies
III. Regular business
IV. Special debates
    A. Adjournment debate
    B. Question period

Often, a subject may be treated topically in several different ways. For example, if a speaker were to divide a college population into topical subdivisions, he might choose from any of the following categories:

Class
  I. Freshmen
 II. Sophomores
III. Juniors
IV. Seniors

Sex
  I. Male
 II. Female

Major
  I. History
 II. Art
III. English
IV. Chemistry
 V. Engineering
VI. Etc.

Scholarship
  I. Superior students
 II. Average students
III. Below-average students

Residence
  I. In-state students
 II. Out-of-state students
III. Foreign students

Housing
  I. Dormitory students
 II. Members living in fraternities and sororities
III. Off-campus students

Religion
  I. Catholic students
 II. Protestant students
III. Jewish students
 IV. Others

Type
  I. Rah rah boys
 II. Hippies
III. Grinds
 IV. Potential drop-outs
  V. Jocks

Causal Division

The cause–effect division of materials is most frequently used in the development of a speech of advocacy or persuasion. It is, however, also useful in describing events with an instructional purpose. In a causal division, the speaker's material may be arranged either from cause to effect or from effect to cause. For example, a speaker may decide that present conditions provide a clear understanding of a particular problem, and so may wish to begin with a description of those conditions and move from there to the causes of them. On the other hand, if he desires to show the possible outcome of certain acts or proposals, he may decide to move from the act as the cause to the potential effects.

A speaker might decide to use the causal method of dividing his speech if he wishes to show the potential dangers or advantages of a particular piece of legislation being considered by a state or national legislature. In this case, he would be moving from cause to possible effect. On the other hand, a person speaking on conservation might begin by describing the unhappy litter conditions existing in our national parks or the pollution of our streams and air and, after illuminating the problem, examine the causes, possibly concluding with a plea for action to eliminate those causes.

An advocate of a program to fight urban decay might argue causally from the following outline:

I. The principal causes of urban decay are three:
  A. Poor planning by city officials.
  B. The movement of middle- and upper-class families to the suburbs.
  C. The lack of state and federal concern and financial assistance.
II. The effects of the present state of urban decay create additional problems:
  A. Poor housing, slums, and ghettos contribute to crime and delinquency.
  B. As more middle- and upper-class families move to the suburbs, needed taxes for urban renewal are lost.
  C. The lack of urban renewal, slums, and crime further accelerate the movement to the suburbs.

Problem–Solution Division

One of the most frequently used methods of speech division is the problem–solution pattern. This method is a logical way for individuals and groups to solve problems and, consequently, it is also a logical pattern to follow in a speech presenting problem–solution arguments. Based on John Dewey's method of reflective thought, this approach systematically leads the audience through a definition and analysis of the problem, a consideration of the suggested solutions, the determination of the best solution, and, finally, a suggested course of action. The pattern of collegiate debates follows the problem–solution order in that the affirmative presents a need, representing the problem, and a plan, representing the solution.

A problem–solution order is used in the following example:

I. There is a need to reduce air pollution.
  A. Automobile exhaust from combustion engines produces tons of pollution daily.
  B. Unclean smokestacks in industrial areas contribute additional tons of pollution daily.
  C. Pesticides and fungicides contribute to air pollution, as well as to pollution of edibles.
II. To solve this problem, we must:
  A. Outlaw the combustion engine as a source of automobile power.
  B. Require, under heavy penalty, all industrial users of pollution-causing processes to "burn up" the pollutants.
  C. Legislate against the uncontrolled use of pesticides and fungicides.

Or a speaker might wish to follow each step of John Dewey's formula for problem solving in the following manner:

Election Campaign Financing
I. What is meant by "election campaign financing"?

A. The funds used by candidates and their election committees to promote election campaigns.
B. Excluded from consideration are funds necessary to conduct the election.

II. In approaching this problem, what goals or guidelines should be considered?
   A. The solution should provide equal access to communication channels.
   B. The solution should encourage all those who wish to seek public office regardless of their personal wealth.
   C. The solution should resolve the problems inherent in the present system of financing elections.
III. How serious is the problem?
   A. How does the problem manifest itself?
      1. Persons of wealth use the present system to their advantage.
      2. Persons in positions of power in government and industry use the present system for personal gain.
   B. What are the causes of the problem?
      1. Unlimited financing.
      2. Unenforced legislative restrictions on spending.
      3. Loopholes in the legislation governing spending.
      4. A desire by some persons for power.
   C. What are the effects of the present system of financing elections?
      1. Access to public office is often denied to persons with little financial means.
      2. It has bred contempt for the voter.
      3. It has led to personal accumulations of wealth at the expense of the taxpayer.
IV. What possible solutions might be considered?
   A. Retain the present system.
   B. Legislate more severe penalties for violators of the law on election financing.
   C. More rigid enforcement of the laws on election financing.
   D. Reduce the limits of spending on campaigns.
   E. Finance campaigns equally for all candidates by initiating a special tax to pay campaign and election expenses.
   F. Permit free and equal access to radio and television networks.
   G. A combination of these suggested solutions is a possible remedy.
V. In view of the goals set earlier, the best solution is _____.
VI. The solution could be implemented and would work as follows:
(Here the speaker would present the details of the plan.)

In Adapted Reading 8.4, Hubert Humphrey employs the problem–solution division to urge the United States to adopt an open-door trade policy between the United States and the countries of both Western and Eastern Europe.

Pro and Con Division

In the pro and con method of division, the speaker presents both sides of a question or examines all possible solutions to a problem before he identifies the position or remedy he thinks best. For example, a speaker might discuss the arguments for and against a piece of legislation before taking a position on it, or he might elaborate upon three or four suggested remedies to a problem before indicating his own solution. The wisdom of presenting opposing points of view before outlining one's own conclusions has been questioned, for the speaker may inadvertently raise objections or create doubts in the auditors' minds that were not there before. But, if the speaker presents the opposing points of view and then convincingly minimizes their value, desirability, or benefits by showing their weaknesses, shortcomings, or inconsistencies, he can lead the audience to accept his point of view as the best or only answer to the question.

Such an approach is often effective in removing objections to the speaker's position and in pointing out weaknesses of other positions perhaps overlooked by the listener. The repudiation of other proposals is almost essential when the speaker is advocating a proposition about which many of his auditors have serious reservations or objections. To ignore alternative contentions and proposals that are well known or widely held will leave his listeners with unresolved questions and doubts. Refutation of alternative approaches may lead them to abandon their original position and agree with the speaker. The speaker, of course, must avoid antagonizing members of the audience who hold the opposing points of view while attempting to lead them to accept his position.

An outline of this type of division might look something like this:

Federally Subsidized Medical Care

I. One solution to caring for the medical needs of U.S. citizens is to extend social security benefits to include complete medical care.
   A. Advantages.
   B. Disadvantages.
   C. The disadvantages are greater than the advantages.
II. Another possible solution is to federally subsidize private health insurance companies.
   A. Advantages.
   B. Disadvantages.
   C. The disadvantages are greater than the advantages.
III. A third possibility is a federal program of compulsory health insurance.
   A. Advantages.
   B. Disadvantages.
   C. Advantages are greater than disadvantages and, therefore, should be promoted.

The speaker should be aware of the methods of division available to him and then select those best suited to the subject matter of the speech and to the audience.

OTHER INFLUENCES UPON
THE DIVISION OF MATERIALS

For most speeches, the speaker will probably find one of the methods of division already discussed to be the most satisfactory plan for developing his topic. However, at times he may feel that a special approach is needed or would prove beneficial. Two such methods are discussed below.

Adaptation to Another Speaker

In one of the great debates in the British House of Commons during the eighteenth century, Charles James Fox arose and announced that he would like to speak at that time because the issues discussed by the previous speaker had been raised in the manner he wanted to discuss them. He then took his opponent's arguments, starting with the last contention, and, in reverse order, developed his position on each major issue raised by his opponent. His plan was determined in part by his analysis of the subject as the prior speaker had divided it, but was also related to the emotional and mental condition of the listeners at that point in the debate. By taking the last argument first, he began with something still fresh in the members' minds. Then, by working through the remainder of the issues in reverse order, he systematically discredited the views of his adversary.

At times, a speaker may be moved by such considerations to adopt a method of division that he might not otherwise have chosen for his topic. He need not take the issues in reverse order as Fox did. However, there may be something about the arguments raised by another speaker, by his inclusion or exclusion of a particular contention, or by the order in which he discussed each idea that will lead a speaker to adapt the arrangement of his materials to what the speaker has said or to the frame of mind of the auditors at that moment. In adapting to such outside influences, the speaker may actually employ a topical, chronological, or other standard method of arrangement. However, the determining factor in the division of his materials is not the subject itself, but some other factor, such as the way a debate has progressed or the manner in which other speakers have dealt with the topic.

Applying a Formula

Most persons rely on at least one or two formulas or gimmicks to recall information they might not otherwise readily remember. "Never eat oysters in months with an r" and "Thirty days hath September, April, June, and November . . ." are two examples of such aids to memory. A similar type of formula to assist recall is the "Survey Q3R" method for studying. If a person can recall the name of the method, he can remember the method itself, which consists of survey, (Q) question, (3R) reread, review, and recall. At times a speaker may decide that his listener will more readily remember what he has to say or that his ideas will be more vivid and memorable if he provides the audience with some type of formula.

Thus, a speaker who hopes to impress upon his listeners the varied duties performed by law enforcement officers might develop a plan of arrangement similar to the following one.

Policemen Perform a Variety of Important and Useful Services

P   Protection. The police protect the citizen and his property.

O   Order. The police maintain order in the community.

L   Law enforcement. The police enforce the laws enacted by the people through their representatives.

I   Investigation. The police perform an important function by investigating complaints, accidents, and alleged violations of the law.

C   Crime control. The police act to apprehend violators of the law.

E   Emergency aid. Policemen provide aid in emergencies such as floods, hurricanes, blizzards, fires, and similar disasters.

Slogans lend themselves easily to this type of formula. For example, a speaker might organize his recommendations for maintaining international law and order around the letters P-E-A-C-E as follows:

P   We must take a Practical approach.

E   We must consider the Emotions of the parties involved.

A   We must Act promptly in international disputes.

C   We must secure the Cooperation of all nations.

E   We must Enforce international law.

While many topics do not lend themselves to division according to some formula, a speaker may at times find this approach particularly appropriate to his topic and helpful to the audience in recalling his ideas.

SUMMARY

Speakers may divide the materials of the body of the speech in a number of ways. The main methods available are chronological or time sequence, spatial, topical, causal, problem–solution, and pro and con. The method selected by the speaker for a specific occasion is influenced primarily by the subject matter of the speech. Some subjects, such as accounts of travels and explanations of the operation of mechanical devices, logically lend themselves to a chronological division; other topics, such as descriptions of objects or places, may be developed more effectively by a spatial or geographical arrangement. Topical division involves the arrangement of materials according to the categories, parts, or facets of a subject and the development of each subtopic. Causal, problem–solution, and pro and con methods of division are often well suited to speeches to convince or to persuade.

While not common, occasionally a speaker's method of division may be influenced by factors other than the audience and the subject matter. For example, he might wish to divide his speech in a manner used by a previous speaker. Or, he might elect to devise a formula for the arrangement of his materials in order to aid the audience in remembering his ideas.

ADAPTED READING 8.1

TIME ARRANGEMENT:
A RECIPE FOR NEW ENGLAND PIE
Mark Twain

The following passage from Mark Twain's A Tramp Abroad *is a simple example of time or chronological arrangement.*

To make this excellent breakfast dish, proceed as follows: Take a sufficiency of water and a sufficiency of flour, and construct a bullet-proof dough. Work this into the form of a disk, with the edges turned up some three-fourths of an inch. Toughen and kiln-dry it a couple of days in a mild but unvarying temperature. Construct a cover for this redoubt in the same way and of the same material. Fill with stewed dried apples; aggravate with cloves, lemon-peel, and slabs of citron, and two portions of New Orleans sugar, then solder on the lid and set in a safe place till it petrifies. Serve cold at breakfast and invite your enemy.

From *A Tramp Abroad* (New York: Harper & Row, 1907), vol. 2, p. 241.

ADAPTED READING 8.2

SPATIAL DIVISION:
THE BATTLE OF WATERLOO
Victor Hugo

The following description of the battlefield of Waterloo by Victor Hugo provides an unusual illustration of spatial division or development.

Those who would get a clear idea of the battle of Waterloo have only to lay down upon the ground in their mind a capital A. The left stroke of the A is the road from Nivelles, the right stroke is the road from Genappe, the cross of the A is the sunken road from Chain to Braine-l'Alleud. The top of the A is Mont St. Jean, Wellington is there; the left-hand lower point is Hougomont, Reille is there with Jerome Bonaparte; the right-hand lower point is La Belle Alliance, Napoleon is there. A little below the point where the cross of the A meets, and cuts the right stroke, is La Haie Sainte. At the middle of this cross is the precise point where the final battle word was spoken. There the lion is placed, the involuntary symbol of the supreme heroism of the imperial guard.

The triangle contained at the top of the A, between the two strokes and the cross, is the plateau of Mont St. Jean. The struggle for this plateau was the whole of the battle.

The wings of the two armies extended to the right and left of the two roads from Genappe and from Nivelles; D'Erlon being opposite Picton, Reille opposite Hill.

From *Les Misérables* (New York: Dodd, Mead, 1925), pp. 114–115.

Behind the point of the A, behind the plateau of Mont St. Jean is the forest of the Soignes.

As to the plain itself, we must imagine a vast, undulating country; each wave commands the next and these undulations, rising toward Mont St. Jean, are there bounded by the forest. . . .

ADAPTED READING 8.3

TOPICAL DIVISION:
WHAT'S HAPPENING, BABY?

Paul C. Harper, Jr.

The following is from a speech delivered at a meeting of the Off-the-Street Club in Chicago on June 21, 1966. The adaptation illustrates an effective use of the topical method of division.

A short time ago I was standing in a pub in London with one of my colleagues enjoying a beer. The name of the pub was "The King's Head and Eight Bells" and it is headquarters for the local pack of Mods. Four Mods were standing near us, two boy Mods in the new bellbottom trousers and bee-waist coats and two girl Mods with hair in their eyes. Then a fifth Mod with both bellbottom trousers and hair in his eyes walked up and asked casually, "What's happening, Baby?"

As nearly as I can reconstruct it, the reply from one of the girls was, "Pip's topkick just gummed his mini. We all think that's fish."

After eavesdropping a little more, it became clear that what she was reporting was that Pip's father had removed his driving privileges, which they all thought was very stuffy. The meeting at the pub was a protest rally.

The language and problems of teens are universal. Dinner table conversations at our house are not orderly discussions. The talk will be frequently interrupted by cries of rage from the victim of a furtive pinch or by the tinkle of breaking glassware. But the conversations do have a pattern. Sooner or later at the teenage end of the table one of [four] subjects almost always comes up:

1. Money
2. Sex
3. Automobiles (ours)
4. Education

    . . .

Preview of points to be treated.

From *Vital Speeches of the Day*, November 1, 1966, pp. 57–61.

These [four] subjects are actually an inventory of the problems—the big deals—facing teenagers today, and for many reasons they're worth taking a look at. It's worth asking the question, "What's happening, Baby?"

My proposition is very simple and it has three points:

1. It is just as dangerous to lump teenagers as teenagers as it is to lump adults as adults. Each teenager is different and each is following his own unwritten calendar towards maturity. No two teenagers mature at the same second in time.

2. Teenagers are the most colorful and persistent fadists in our society, but a fad is a symptom, not a disease. They wear funny clothes, funny haircuts, say and do strange things. But the fads they adopt are not to be confused with the immutable law which rules every generation of teenagers. This law says, "Thou shalt be different, but for pretty much the same old reason." No matter how odd their behavior, they are responding to the same age-old urge for independence.

3. In spite of all this, we have to face the fact that teenagers today do face a world that has changed far more between generations than at any time in history. And this has produced an unprecedented lack of understanding and sympathy between generations. These changes get back to the rather basic things discussed at our dinner table. They are:

> Money: Teenagers today have enough to make them a real economic force.
> Sex: Teenagers are reaching physical maturity at a somewhat earlier age—and there are more sexual stimuli around than ever before.
> Mobility: Teenagers today have a new dimension of independence, the automobile. They can get around. They can get away.
> School: Teenagers today are under more pressure from the educational establishment than ever before.

· · ·

Let's talk first about money. A great majority of teenagers are certainly a reflection of the affluent society they live in. As pollster Louis Harris points out: "High school Americans have never known drastic economic depression or wartime shortages—they're happy now and believe the future can only get better." Generally, youth has no worry about the basic necessities—food, clothing,

General propositions to be supported in the body of the speech.

Signpost of changes in society to be developed as topics in the body of the speech.

Signpost introduces Topic 1.

housing. Since teenagers make up the decisive market for many products—guitars, motorbikes, sports equipment and movies, for example—and a very lucrative secondary market for countless other categories, they are bombarded with commercial messages. But even without this commercial assault, teenagers would probably be big spenders. Money to teenagers is a liberating force. Spending it is an expression of adulthood. And in spending it in vast quantities they have institutionalized their tastes. We now have a teenage market.

Sex is, of course, a subject in itself. It must be if those scientists out in Kansas City could spend five years behind a one-way mirror without getting bored. But I really prefer the remark of the mayor of a little New England town as he addressed a group of aldermen worried about town morals. "Now, gentlemen," he said, "there's always been sex in this town—there's just a new crowd takin' over." Nevertheless some of the data show real changes in this area too.

Signpost introduces Topic 2.

There is no doubt that there is an earlier and more intense focusing on sex. Dates in fifth and sixth grades are commonplace. The Connecticut Health Department estimates that one of six teenage girls in the state was illegitimately pregnant last year. Since there has been no large-scale study of premarital sex among teenagers, some say that the public is confusing the known increases in premarital sex among college students with increased sex in high schools. Mervin P. Freedman in *The Young Americans* states his opinion that young men and women need to find security in marriage and a family and that this need far outweighs tendencies toward promiscuous sexual behavior. He believes that this is a reaction against the depersonalization of modern life and sees in the trend to early marriage an indication that family ties will be strengthened rather than weakened in the next several decades. The key fact is that the other pressures he is under force him to seek the security of an intense companionship—the ultimate expression of which is sex.

This brings us to my third point, mobility. It's no news that teenagers live in cars. Cars have become the standard projection of ego and virility for the boy and give him a dimension of independence he never had before.

Signpost introduces Topic 3.

According to *Newsweek's* penetrating essay, "It is a car, not truth, that sets them free, gives them a sense of romance. The automobile is this century's riverboat." Teenagers own 9 percent of all new cars and an estimated

20 percent of all cars. And, of course, a good many family cars are driven, if not owned, by teens.

The title of Wolfe's collection of essays, *The Kandy-Kolored Tangerine-Flake Streamline Baby,* refers to the postwar teen passion for customizing cars and/or hopping them up for more speed. He says that thousands of kids before they get married put all their money into this. "It is true to say that among teenagers the automobile has become the symbol and in part the physical means of triumph over family and community restrictions."

The fourth big change in the teenage environment is education—how you get it, how long you go to school, what you do when you get there, what happens to you if you don't get there. With every year that goes by, the long-term penalties for dropping out increase. And the pressures to get into college and stay there, therefore, increase too.

Signpost introduces Topic 4.

College is no longer the sanctuary of the privileged, however. The democratization of college through scholarships, the increased ability of more Americans to pay their way, and the general recognition that you need college to get ahead holds out a mighty inducement.

But the pressure and the increase in the academic pace have made millions of young Americans more thoughtful than they have ever been before. Issues are discussed at our dinner table that two generations ago were reserved for lecture halls and coffee houses. . . .

The young are increasingly questioning grownup goals and purposes. Edgar Z. Friedenberg, professor of sociology at the University of California, says: "they have learned that they cannot trust us, because we have never had any respect for them and very little for the principles by which we pretend to govern our lives and theirs." Teenagers know that many parents who are shocked at car swiping, exam cheating, and teen vandalism are themselves engaging in higher orders of immoral behavior such as tax cheating, price fixing, expense padding, and worse. They wonder why parents don't invest the time to discuss the meaningful things of life, to counsel them on their education and their future.

General proposition 1

Professor Friedenberg says: "Regulations governing dress and grooming may be trivial. What is not trivial is that submission to such regulation teaches students that they have no rights or dignity. The very triviality of the regulations makes them more effectively humiliating. Most adolescents would accept and even welcome adult direction in

General proposition 2

matters of grave consequence. But I would maintain that the real function of these regulations is to humiliate, to show any adolescents with too much autonomy what happens to wise guys and trouble makers." The fad which starts out as a symbol of identity with the group soon becomes a full-fledged, healthy symbol of rebellion against adult authority. The extent to which this rebellion can go is seen in the current fad for German helmets and iron crosses, the principal function of which seems to be to bug adults. Teenagers hold a jealous possession of their folkways. When adults took over the twist, young people dropped it like a hot pizza and moved on to dances that were exclusively their own — at least for a while. The surest way for an advertiser to assure being turned off or tuned out is for him to portray an obsolete fad, dance, or mode of dress.

The same is true of language. We may not understand the language and we certainly shouldn't try to make ourselves understood in it. The language is designed for the exclusive use of teenagers in communicating with one another; it is similar to the dialects and language variants that such species as lawyers and advertising men create to keep it in the family.

Those of us who are required to establish some form of communication with teenagers had better stick to our own particular idiom of American English, or risk making damn fools of ourselves.

It won't work for parents — and it might be disastrous for advertisers — to try to get chummy with teenagers by telling them that their products are "boss, tough, out of sight, fab or dyno." Even though "bad" means "good" in teen, it could prove confusing and downright embarrassing for a client to have to say his product is bad.

Another trap into which advertisers, or anyone else   General proposition 3
who tries to generalize about teenagers, can easily fall is to lump teenagers as a group. Teenagers resent being classified as a group. To their everlasting credit and despite their instinct for groupness, teenagers want to be accepted as individuals. Their desire to have a greater say about how their world is run, their questioning of their society, and their rebellion against parents, are all indications that they think for themselves. They are, according to Harvard Professor Jerome Bruner, "the most competent generation we have ever reared in this country — and the most maligned."

So, what's happening, Baby? Well, it's a tragedy or a   Conclusion
comedy, depending upon how you look at it, but in spite of

all the new pressures and in spite of all the new outlets, the teenager remains fundamentally the same.

None of these influences—money, sex, mobility, [or] education . . .—can mature him faster as a whole person. Nature must take its course. You can't buy emotional maturity; you can't teach it; and you certainly can't bottle it.

Summary

207

*PROBLEM-
SOLUTION
DIVISION: A
SPEECH ON THE
OPEN-DOOR POLICY*

ADAPTED READING 8.4

PROBLEM–SOLUTION DIVISION: A SPEECH ON THE OPEN-DOOR POLICY
Hubert H. Humphrey

On March 5, 1967, Hubert H. Humphrey, then Vice-President of the United States, delivered the Green Foundation Lecture at Westminster College in Fulton, Missouri. It was a foreign policy speech in which he argued for an open door policy in United States relations with Europe. This adaptation illustrates a problem–solution division of the speech materials.

Exactly 21 years ago today, Winston Churchill spoke these well-remembered words: "From Stettin in the Baltic to Trieste in the Adriatic, an Iron Curtain has descended across the continent."

When Churchill spoke here, a new phase in history had begun—that post-war conflict, centered in Europe, which was to become known as the cold war. It is my belief that we stand today upon the threshold of a new era in our relations with the peoples of Europe—a period of new engagement. And I believe that this new period, if we do not lose our wits or our nerve, or our patience, can see the replacement of the Iron Curtain by the Open Door. When Churchill spoke here on March 5, 1946, there were many in this country—and elsewhere—who would not accept his stark characterization of the state of affairs in Europe. But Churchill was right. And he was right to speak out. The beginning of wisdom, the foundation of sound policy and action, is to face the facts. What are the facts of March of 1967?

Western Europe stands today second only to the United States as a free and powerful center of economic and social well-being. Because of their brave initiatives—and with our help—the nations of Western Europe stand able once again to assert their own role in the world. In Eastern Europe the captive states of 21 years ago are once again reaching toward their own identities. The

Background material and adaptation to occasion

The problem

monolithic control which smothered and held them in the grip of terror is today diminishing. The Iron Curtain itself —although firm and impenetrable in many places, as in Berlin—has become increasingly permeable in others. Goods, ideas, and people have begun to crisscross the European continent. There is reason to believe that the new leadership of the Soviet Union finds the Iron Curtain not only a crude barrier to the West, but also a costly impediment to their own well-being and progress. Science and technology have pierced the eroding Iron Curtain. It is being replaced by a web of communication—the transistor, the computer, the space satellite—these are the building blocks of modern communications. Scientists, engineers, and technicians flew back and forth—overleaping the old barrier with the jets of contemporary air travel. The arteries of East–West trade flow ever stronger and faster. All of these physical changes, all of these profound economic changes, may well be the precursors of political change.

The essence of the situation today is this: The European family—long separated . . . long set against each other, yet still a family—is becoming reacquainted and is moving toward normal relationships. All these things have happened. Yet they did not happen by accident.

Transition

They have happened because we followed the course Winston Churchill counseled 21 years ago at Westminster College. They have happened in large part because, in the face of Stalinist tyranny, we in America brought our power and protection to rebuilding the European continent. They have happened because we helped and encouraged our European partners in their unceasing efforts toward self-renewal. They have happened because—in Berlin, in Greece and Turkey, yes, and in Cuba—the Soviet Union was brought to recognize that brute force—or its threat—could no longer be an acceptable means of attaining political goals. During this time, too, a constructive force has been at work in Western Europe—releasing the constraining bonds of old hostilities and closed institutions to the fresh stimulation of competition and cooperation across national boundaries. That constructive force has been the will of the peoples of Western Europe that they should unite.

The causes

There are a small few who conclude that the "realistic" next step toward a settlement of European problems can only be by bilateral agreement between the Soviet Union and the United States—over the heads of our Western partners. I do not believe this is "realism." Neither do I believe a realistic settlement of European problems can be

Transition

achieved by European nations without our participation, and that of the Soviet Union.

It is precisely now — at the time when new opportunities lie ahead — that we must retain cohesion with our Western partners — and they with us. If the cold war is to end, . . . if the Iron Curtain is to be lifted, we shall need them and they shall need us. The task now, in light of a new situation, is not to throw away what has been successful, but to build constructively upon it. I believe that the people of Western Europe will reject concepts of narrow nationalism and of national adventure, and will continue to move forward toward unity — toward a unified Western Europe open to expansion and conscious of its need to strengthen its ties with the nations of Eastern Europe. I believe, too, that they will reject any severing of their ties across the Atlantic — ties built firmly on common cultural heritage, on common experience, on common interest.

For our part, we do not mean either to abandon our friends or to dominate them. We know that American power continues to be necessary to stability in Central Europe.

The goals of Western European unity and of Atlantic partnership are not in opposition to the goal of the Open Door. They are a first necessity in reaching it. They are the key to that door.

As we strive toward these former goals, how shall we proceed toward the latter?

First, we must work together with our Western European partners in encouraging a further development of trade, technological and cultural contacts with Eastern Europe. We look, for example, toward the time when the nations of Eastern Europe may become members of the GATT (General Agreement on Tariffs and Trade) and full participants in the work of the U.N. Economic Commission for Europe.

Second, we must encourage the continued evolution of Soviet policy beyond the ambiguities of "peaceful coexistence" toward more substantial forms of cooperation. We have negotiated a treaty banning nuclear weapons from outer space. We are working with others to bring about a treaty banning the proliferation of nuclear weapons — a treaty acceptable and beneficial to the nuclear and non-nuclear powers alike. We have concluded an air agreement with the Soviet Union and have just signed a new U.S.–Soviet cultural agreement.

Through liberalization of credit, and easing of travel restrictions, we hope to accelerate the exchange of goods

---

Margin notes:

Solution
A. Continue to pursue former goals

B. Strive for goal of "Open Door"

Step 1: further contacts with Eastern Europe

Step 2: encourage evolution of Soviet policy

and people. We shall actively work toward closer cooperation between the Soviet Union and the nations of the West in space, in medicine, in peaceful technology.

Third, we must work toward a settlement of those European problems which have been left unresolved in the aftermath of the war. At the heart of this is the reunification of Germany. As I said earlier, this is a matter which concerns not only Europeans, but America and the Soviet Union as well. It is a matter, too—and this sometimes seems nearly forgotten—important for the people of Germany.

Fourth, no nation can hope to be an island of security in a turbulent world. We must therefore consider how the resources of the industrialized parts of the world can usefully assist the peoples of Asia, Africa and Latin America so that progress and stability and hope may overcome despair and violence. It does not require much foresight to realize that the widening gap between growing populations and diminishing food supplies is approaching a time of explosion. It is Europe's problem—and the Soviet Union's—as much as it is ours, and we must consult together, plan together, and combine our wisdom and resources to help work toward security and peaceful development in the poverty-stricken parts of the world. For poverty breeds disorder, and hunger breeds violence. And it has been the lesson of these past few years that it is precisely in the poverty-stricken and hungry parts of the world where a conflict might arise which would draw the super-powers into disastrous confrontation.

Fifth, we must continue to develop and strengthen international institutions which will provide a framework of law and order in the world, in which nations of all ideologies may find common and peaceful grounds for settlement of disputes. Most important of such institutions is the United Nations.

The United Nations, among other things, is an unmatched buffer zone between conflicting interests and ideologies. It is a place where reason and compromise may interpose themselves before major nations reach the point of no return.

Let us examine these things:

Greater exchange on all levels with the nations of Eastern Europe.
Active pursuit and encouragement of "peaceful coexistence" with the Soviet Union.

Step 3: settlement of problems

Step 4: assist underdeveloped peoples

Step 5: develop international institutions

A European settlement including the reunification of
   Germany.
Joint efforts with our former adversaries in helping
   the developing countries.
Building a system of international order in which
   these same former adversaries are our partners.

Would any of these things have been at all imaginable
when Winston Churchill stood here 21 years ago? When
the final realization sank in on the last doubter that an Iron
Curtain indeed was being erected across the heart of
Europe, how many of us had reason for hope that in 1967
—so short a time later—it might be possible to begin
replacing it with an Open Door? In the center of free Berlin
there stands today a stark ruin—the skeleton of a church,
preserved to symbolize eternally the depravity of war. It is
our hope that the Iron Curtain may one day, too, lie in
ruins—its remnants a symbol of a time that mercifully
ended.

   Therefore, I leave you with this: Who is to say, if we in   Conclusion
the West stand together and in unity, where the next two
decades may lead? Who is to say, if our rich and powerful
nation exerts the enlightened leadership of which it is
capable, what bright new fulfillment may lie ahead for the
human family? Our guide could be no better than that set
forth here 21 years ago by Churchill:

   If we adhere faithfully to the charter of the United
   Nations and walk forward in sedate and sober
   strength, seeking no one's land or treasure, seeking
   to lay no arbitrary control upon the thoughts of
   man . . . the high roads of the future will be clear,
   not only for us but for all, not only for our time,
   but for the century to come.

   So, today we honor the memory of this great statesman, and as we commemorate the twenty-first anniversary
of his historically significant address, let us lift our voices to
this spirit, to Sir Winston, and to the world, and let us say
that we in America are ready to play our role.

ADDITIONAL READINGS

Buehler, E. C. and Wil Linkugel, *Speech Communication* (New York: Harper &
   Row, 1969), part 2, chap. 3, "Organization."
Monroe, Alan and Douglas Ehninger, *Principles and Types of Speech* (Glenview,
   Ill.: Scott, Foresman, 1967), chap. 14, "Selecting, Phrasing, and Arranging
   the Ideas Within the Speech."

Terris, Walter, *Content and Organization of Speeches* (Dubuque, Iowa: Brown, 1968), chap. 6, "The Subsidiary Patterns of Organization."

White, Eugene E., *Practical Public Speaking* (New York: Macmillan, 1964), chap. 12, "Organizing the Body."

STUDY QUESTIONS

1. What are the major influences on the selection of a method of dividing the body of a speech? In what ways do they influence the selection?
2. What types of subjects are most adaptable to chronological division? to spatial division? to topical division?
3. What is the difference between the problem–solution division and the pro and con division? Under what conditions might a speaker select one of these over the other?
4. It is possible to arrange materials from cause to effect or from effect to cause. Is it possible to arrange the same materials by either method? Under what conditions might the speaker select one method over the other?
5. What is the relationship between John Dewey's reflective thought process and the problem–solution method of dividing speech materials?
6. What is the danger in using the pro and con division in a speech of advocacy? How can a speaker overcome it? What is the value of this method of division?
7. How does the attitude of the audience affect the division of materials?

EXERCISES

1. Prepare two outlines for an informative speech using a different method of dividing the materials for each. Explain the advantages of each method.
2. Read a speech in *Vital Speeches, Representative American Speeches,* or another anthology and determine the method of division used by the speaker for his main ideas. Did he use other patterns for developing each idea? Was the method chosen the best for presenting his subject in your opinion? Could he have employed an alternate method advantageously? Write a short paper summarizing your evaluation.
3. Select a speech topic that would lend itself to chronological division and prepare a short outline of the three or four main points for the body of a speech. Do the same for spatial division and causal division.
4. Select a topic for a persuasive speech which lends itself to the problem–solution division. Prepare a short outline indicating the main points of the body of the speech.
5. Select a topic that might be developed by a pro and con division. Briefly outline the main points of the body of the speech. What would be the advantages of using a pro and con division for this subject? What would be the dangers?
6. Prepare a four-minute informative speech. Choose the most appropriate method for dividing your subject. Prepare an outline of the speech to be presented to the instructor just before giving the speech. Deliver the speech in class.

CHAPTER

9

OUTLINING

IMPORTANCE AND VALUES

"Order and simplification are the first steps toward the mastery of a subject." Applied to the composition of a speech, this observation by Thomas Mann provides a compelling reason for the speaker to prepare an outline of his ideas. An outline contributes both to simplification and order: It simplifies because it reduces the content of the speech to its essentials; it provides order because it necessitates arranging materials logically and systematically. Just as an architect prepares a blueprint, a lawyer constructs a brief, a professor devises a syllabus, and a traveler makes an itinerary, so too should a speaker evolve a plan to provide an overview of what he seeks to accomplish and to give direction in achieving that goal.

Outlining permits the speaker to examine the speech visually and to test it for balance and thoroughness. The outline helps the speaker to discover whether he has included everything necessary to achieve his purpose, to determine whether the ideas are adequately supported, and to decide whether all of his material contributes to the attainment of his goal. It shows the logical relationships between his ideas and reveals flaws of imbalance or inconsistency, lack of order, and potential weaknesses in adapting the speech to the audience. The outline further serves as a memory aid for the speaker, for he can visualize and thereby better remember the major ideas and supporting materials.

When preparing his speech, it is much easier for a speaker to rearrange ideas in outline form than in a written manuscript, just as it is simpler to study the bone structure of an animal by examining the skeleton rather than the fleshed-out form. For that reason, the speaker's preparation of an outline is usually done *after* he has chosen his topic, determined his purpose, analyzed the audience and subject, and gathered and selected his supporting materials, but *before* the preparation of a manuscript or speaker's notes.

PRINCIPLES OF OUTLINING

Order in Preparation of a Speech

Since a speech follows the sequence of introduction, body, and conclusion, it may seem natural to prepare the outline of a speech in that order. Such is not the case. Since the speaker does not know exactly what he is to introduce until the main part of the speech has been planned, it is more reasonable to prepare an introduction after the body of the speech has been outlined. Otherwise, the speaker might develop an introduction that—after he has rearranged, revised, and altered his supporting materials in the body—introduces the wrong speech. It is profitable to prepare the conclusion last so that the speaker may incorporate and summarize materials from the introduction, as well as from the body of the speech, in his closing remarks.

Use of Symbols

If the speaker has been perceptive in the study of this book, he will have noticed that its organization is outlined by means of main heads, second-level heads, and third-level heads. These headings in the chapters identify major ideas, their coordinate ideas, and subordinate ideas. Major ideas or points in the speech situation are steps, events, parts, aspects, reasons, or arguments the speaker wishes the audience to understand or accept. Ideas or points that have equal value in the mind of the speaker are called coordinate, while those materials that serve to amplify, explain, or support the main ideas are considered to be subordinate. In an outline of a speech, the major ideas, coordinates, and subordinates are identified by using a symbolic system. Normally, the Roman numeral (I) is used first, followed by the capital letter (A), then the Arabic numeral (1), and then the lowercase letter (a) to identify an order of subordination. In outline form, it would look like this:

```
I.
   A.
      1.
         a.
            (1)
            (2)
         b.
      2.
   B.
      1.
      2.
II.
   A.
      1.
```

```
                  2.
                     a.
                     b.
         B.
            1.
            2.
         C.
            1.
            2.
                  a.
                  b.
         D.
            1.
            2.
      III.
         A.
            1.
            2.
         B.
```

In this example, A and B are coordinates or equals and Arabic numerals (1 and 2) are subordinate to A and B. In this typical outline form the Roman numerals might indicate the introduction, body, and conclusion.

To better understand the concept of coordination and subordination, consider the cluster of statements that follows. Among the statements are two major ideas and two subordinate ideas for each main idea. These assertions support the central idea that labor unions have promoted the general welfare of the United States.

1. Strikes have become less destructive.
2. Collective bargaining has become more widespread.
3. Strikes have become less disruptive.
4. Strikes have become less frequent.
5. The method of collective bargaining has become stronger.
6. Collective bargaining has become more efficient.

After analyzing each of the statements for levels of importance, it should be apparent that statements 3 and 5 reflect the two main points; that statements 1 and 4 are subordinate to statement 3; and that statements 2 and 6 are subordinate to statement 5. They are subordinate because they help to support more specifically the generally stated main points. Consequently, in proper outline form, the statements should be organized and set down in this way:

I. Strikes have become less disruptive. (main idea)
  A. Strikes have become less destructive. (subordinate idea)
  B. Strikes have become less frequent. (subordinate idea to I but coordinate with A)

II. The method of collective bargaining has become stronger. (main idea and coordinate with I)
   A. Collective bargaining has become more widespread. (subordinate idea)
   B. Collective bargaining has become more efficient. (subordinate to II but coordinate with A)

It is important that each of the symbols in the outline represent only one idea. If more than one idea is included, the basic advantage to outlining is lost, for the symbolic system in outlining is used to establish relationships between ideas. Also, the speaker should observe that if an idea is subdivided, it is subdivided into at least two subordinate ideas. If there seems to be just one idea subordinate to another, think again—it is probably either coordinate with the main idea or identical with it.

Indentation

In the preceding examples, each of the symbols has been indented, reflecting its proper relationship of subordination to other symbols. The indentation is essential to show, visually, proper coordination and subordination of ideas. Note the loss of visual usefulness in the following outline.

The President Should Be Elected by a Direct Vote of the People

I. Electoral votes are unrealistically apportioned according to the decennial census.
   A. Based on the census, each state receives the same number of votes as it has congressional representatives, plus two.
   B. Because of shifting population many people are not fairly represented.
1. In 1964 several hundred thousand new California residents were not reflected in the electoral vote.
2. States that have lost population will be overrepresented in the electoral vote.
3. This imbalance is inherent in the electoral college.
II. The electoral college does not reflect the popular vote.
   A. The "unit rule" gives all the electoral votes of a state to the winner regardless of his plurality.
   B. Thus, the electoral college can declare the candidate with the fewest popular votes the winner.
   C. Electors are not bound to vote for their state's winner.
III. Direct election of the President is in the best interests of America.
   A. Direct election would be consistent with the Court's "One-man–one-vote" ruling.
   B. The vote of every American should carry equal weight.

In contrast to this outline, visual identification of equal and subsidiary ideas is found much more easily in the following outline of the same material.

The President Should Be Elected by a Direct Vote of the People

I. Electoral votes are unrealistically apportioned according to the decennial census.
   A. Based on the census, each state receives the same number of votes as it has congressional representatives, plus two.
   B. Because of shifting population many people are not fairly represented.
      1. In 1964 several hundred thousand new California residents were not reflected in the electoral vote.
      2. States that have lost population will be overrepresented in the electoral vote.
      3. This imbalance is inherent in the electoral college.
II. The electoral college does not reflect the popular vote.
   A. The "unit rule" gives all the electoral votes of a state to the winner regardless of his plurality.
   B. Thus, the electoral college can declare the candidate with the fewest popular votes the winner.
   C. Electors are not bound to vote for their state's winner.
III. Direct election of the President is in the best interests of America.
   A. Direct election would be consistent with the Court's "one-man–one-vote" ruling.
   B. The vote of every American should carry equal weight.

It is important to note that in the proper visual form of subordination and indentation, if the statement of an idea takes more than one line, the second line should not begin any farther toward the left-hand margin than the beginning of the first line. To extend the second line farther left would destroy the basic principle of the outline—that is, to show proper relationships of ideas.

TYPES OF OUTLINES

The two major types of outlining are the *complete-sentence* outline and the *topic* or *key-word* and *key-phrase* outline.

Complete Sentence Outline

The complete sentence outline is used for the purpose of writing out in outline form the full content of the speech to be delivered. This type of outlining takes a great deal of discipline and time, but is essential for complex speeches or for speeches designed to meet difficult audience situations. Many people write speeches in their entirety without ever preparing an outline. However, outlining the speech is preferable to writing it out because the sentence outline is almost as complete as a written text and yet provides a much clearer guide to the relationships and order of the speech materials. In an outline, the arrangement of ideas and the need for transtions is more easily recognizable to the speaker.

However, one danger of preparing a complete sentence outline is that the speaker may follow it too closely in actually delivering the speech, resulting in a reading of a written manuscript. This is not desirable, nor is it the purpose of the outline. The specific wording of the speech rises out of the speaker's understanding of the topic. The sentence outline should be used only in the planning stages for the purpose of determining the order, balance, and completeness of the analysis of the topic.

Topic Outline

The topic outline is simply a "mini" of the complete sentence outline. All the rules of outlining are followed as in the complete sentence outline, but the language is reduced to key words or key phrases. With a simple subject and a speaking situation posing no particular problems of audience adaptation, a speaker may, at times, dispense with the preparation of a complete sentence outline and substitute a topic outline. However, in most argumentative speeches and informative addresses of any complexity or degree of technicality, the speaker probably should prepare both a complete sentence and a topic outline.

The topic outline is particularly useful as a memory device when the speaker is practicing the speech to develop familiarity and an extemporaneous method of presentation. Once the logic and the arrangement of the speech materials have been tested in the complete sentence outline, the speaker can then reduce the outline to one of key words and phrases for practice and rehearsal.

The following outline is a condensation of the complete sentence outline given earlier:

   I. Electoral votes unrealistically apportioned.
      A. Each state same number of votes.
      B. Not fairly representative.
         1. 1964 new California residents not represented.
         2. Some states overrepresented.
         3. Imbalance is inherent.
  II. Popular vote not reflected.
      A. Unit rule.
      B. Candidate with fewest votes can be elected.
      C. Electors not bound.
 III. Direct election is in best interest.
      A. "One-man–one-vote" ruling.
      B. Equal weight.

Speaker's Notes

Once the topic outline has been used for rehearsal, the speaker can further reduce his outline to a "micro-mini" of the original complete sentence outline. These are the notes he probably will wish to use during the actual presentation of the speech, and they will contain even fewer cues than the key word or phrase outline. The value of speaking from notes rather than from a manuscript or detailed outline is recognized by many speakers, including Senator John Sherman Cooper. William Honan discusses this in

Secret Session.   House of Commons.

My reliance on it as an instrument for waging
                                              war.

More active and direct part for its Members
    L.D.V.

All this in accordance with past history.

This S.S. a model of discretion.

My view always Govt. strengthened by S.S.

~~Quite ready to have others.~~

Agree with idea S.S. shd be quite a normal par
        of our procedure,
            not associated with any crisis.

Relief to be able to talk without enemy readin

Quite ready to have other S.Ss.,
        especially on precise subjects.

But I hope not press Ministers engaged in
    conduct of war too hard.
                                    t is wan!

    — efreshed b
    Mood of the House.
            Cool and robust.

Speeches most informative.   *confidence f aa*
    Difficult to betray any secrets disclosed
                                        today

Figure 6 Speech Notes by Winston Churchill.

Adapted Reading 9.1. Speakers who rely only on notes usually feel that this
permits them greater flexibility in adapting to the audience's reactions and
that it also contributes to spontaneity of expression.

Speakers vary in their type and use of notes, as described by William
Norwood Brigance in Adapted Reading 9.2. However, many speakers find it
helpful to record them on 3-by-5-inch cards so that they can be held in the

Moore-Brab (Wallesey)   Praise.

He was sorry I mentioned expert advisers
    favoured fighting on.

Politicians and Generals, -

In last war and this.

Not put too much on the politicians:
    even they may err.

Goering.   How do you class him?
    He was an airman turned politician.

I like him better as an airman.
    Not very much anyway.

Moore-Brab tells us of his wonderful brain,
    and the vast dictatorial powers and plans.

Anyhow he did not produce the best pilots
    or the best machines,
        or perhaps, as we may see presently,
            the best Science.

M.B. said 250 nights in the year
    when no defence against night bombing.

~~I hope it is not so~~

This is one of those things you can only tell
                by finding out.

Figure 6 (Continued)

hand in the event that no speaker's stand is available. This also permits greater freedom of movement and more animated physical delivery during the speech. By the time the speaker has rehearsed the speech several times using the topic outline, he can determine what notes are needed to remind him of his ideas. Figure 6, photographs of Winston Churchill's speaking notes, illustrates one type.

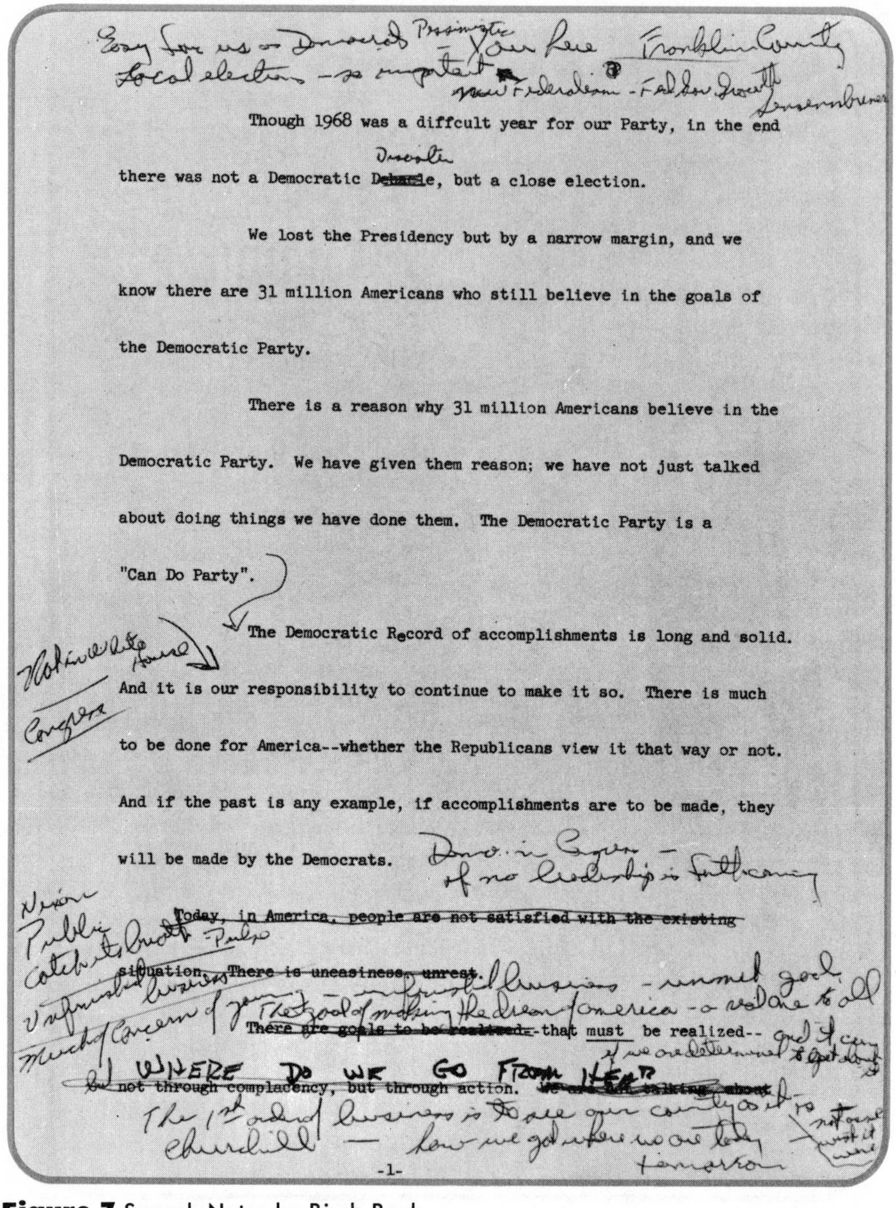

Though 1968 was a diffcult year for our Party, in the end there was not a Democratic Debacle, but a close election.

We lost the Presidency but by a narrow margin, and we know there are 31 million Americans who still believe in the goals of the Democratic Party.

There is a reason why 31 million Americans believe in the Democratic Party. We have given them reason; we have not just talked about doing things we have done them. The Democratic Party is a "Can Do Party".

The Democratic Record of accomplishments is long and solid. And it is our responsibility to continue to make it so. There is much to be done for America--whether the Republicans view it that way or not. And if the past is any example, if accomplishments are to be made, they will be made by the Democrats.

Today, in America, people are not satisfied with the existing situation. There is uneasiness, unrest.

There are goals to be realized--that must be realized--not through complacency, but through action.

WHERE DO WE GO FROM HERE

-1-

Figure 7 Speech Notes by Birch Bayh.

If the speaker uses direct quotations, he may wish to write or type these on separate cards and actually read them when the time comes. The speaker who is well prepared, however, may use no notes at all; if he does, they will be as brief as possible, providing only the barest guide to the information he needs to lead him through the speech.

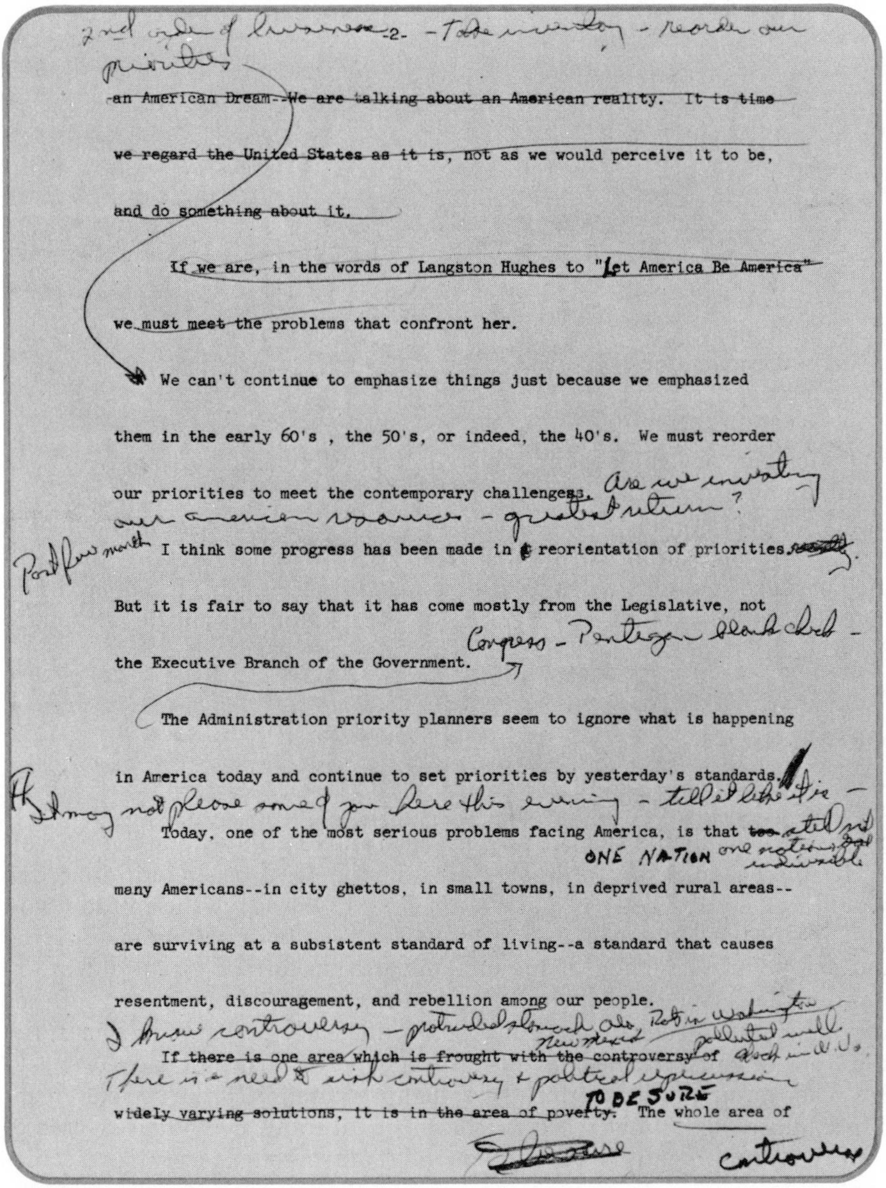

[handwritten top: 2nd order of business —2 — Take inventory — reorder our priorities]

~~an American Dream.~~ We are ~~talking about an American~~ reality. It is time

we ~~regard the United States as it is,~~ not as we would perceive it to be,

and do ~~something about it.~~

If we are, in the words of Langston Hughes to "Let America Be America"

we must meet the problems that confront her.

We can't continue to emphasize things just because we emphasized

them in the early 60's , the 50's, or indeed, the 40's. We must reorder

our priorities to meet the contemporary challenges. _[handwritten: Are we investing our american resources — greatest return?]_

[handwritten left: Point flow north] I think some progress has been made in the reorientation of priorities. _[handwritten]_

But it is fair to say that it has come mostly from the Legislative, not

the Executive Branch of the Government. _[handwritten: Congress — Pentagon blank check —]_

The Administration priority planners seem to ignore what is happening

in America today and continue to set priorities by yesterday's standards.

[handwritten: It may not please some of you here this evening — tell it like it is —]

Today, one of the most serious problems facing America, is that ~~too~~ _[handwritten: ONE NATION one nation indivisible]_

many Americans--in city ghettos, in small towns, in deprived rural areas--

are surviving at a subsistent standard of living--a standard that causes

resentment, discouragement, and rebellion among our people.

[handwritten: I know controversy — protracted struggle also. Riot in Washington — New Mexico. Rock in N.J. polluted well.]

~~If there is one area which is frought with the~~ controversy of

[handwritten: There is a need to wish controversy & political expression]

widely ~~varying solutions, it is in the area of poverty.~~ _[handwritten: TO BE SURE]_ The whole area of

[handwritten: controversy]

Figure 7 (Continued)

The following is an example of a speaker's notes outline of the same speech outlined earlier:

I. Unrealistically apportioned
   A. Same number

     B. Not fair
       1. 1964
       2. Overrepresented
       3. Imbalance
 II. Popular vote
     A. Unit rule
     B. Fewest votes
       1. 1824
       2. 1876
     C. Electors
III. Best interest
     A. One-man–one-vote
     B. Equal

Members of Congress and others in high public office frequently speak from a manuscript in order to preserve their words for publication and to be certain of stating their position on significant issues in carefully selected phrases. However, in an attempt to adapt to the speaking situation, some politicians make speaker's notes on the manuscript pages. This use of auxiliary notes is illustrated by the photographs of manuscript notes made by Senator Birch Bayh (Figure 7).

SUMMARY

In preparing a speech, an outline helps the speaker to determine whether he has used all of the ideas necessary to achieve his purpose. It permits him to determine visually the balance of the speech and to decide upon the most effective arrangement of coordinate and subordinate ideas. In outlining, one should prepare the body of the speech first, followed by the introduction and, finally, the conclusion. Using a consistent symbolic system in outlining and employing a method of indentation provide further visual aid in examining the balance and subordination of ideas. The three types of outlines are the complete sentence outline used in the early preparation stages, the key word or key phrase outline used in the rehearsal stages, and the speaker's notes outline to be used in the actual presentation. If the speaker disciplines himself to follow these procedures in outlining, he will be assured of a much better prepared and, consequently, much better received presentation.

ADAPTED READING 9.1
THIS METHOD IS QUICK
William H. Honan

William Honan tells how Senator John Sherman Cooper uses notes to deliver his Senate speeches.

Senator Cooper is so convinced an exponent of speaking from notes that at one time he introduced a resolution to prohibit the reading of speeches from manuscript by all Senators except those serving as floor managers for bills. . . . Cooper's suggestion was not nearly so radical as some of its opponents may have guessed, for Jefferson had conceived the same idea back in the 1790s, stating in his manual of Senate procedure, "A member has not a right even to read his own speech, committed to writing, without leave. This is . . . to prevent abuse of time."

When Cooper is sitting at his desk in the Senate, or at work in his office, or riding a train or an airplane, he frequently scribbles notes to himself — facts and dates, usually, rather than bons mots or felicitous phrases — on odd, sometimes different-colored scraps of paper and occasionally on the back of a bill or the corner of a restaurant doily. These he tucks into a pocket where they may be checked, added to and cross-referenced. Some of the memos get sent to the cleaner by mistake, and some wind up entombed in the large mahogany filing cabinets that line his Senate office. A fair share, however, become notes in an outline on a yellow sheet from a legal-sized tablet where they will serve as stepping stones for one of Cooper's oratorical excursions. Cooper may go so far as to write out long portions of a speech, as he did, for instance, in May, 1967, with his proposal to limit the bombing of North Vietnam to the Demilitarized Zone and the infiltration routes south, which provided the lead President Johnson followed a year later when announcing his retirement and unilateral de-escalation of the war. More typically, however, Cooper writes on the yellow tablet only the first sentence of each of the four or five paragraphs he plans to develop, noting in shorthand a fact or two after each sentence.

"This method is quick," Cooper says. "I think I was the first one or maybe the only one in the Senate to speak about Birmingham on the day of the trouble down there. And so the newspapers picked it up. I think I got some editorials. While the thing is still fresh in people's minds, you see, the press is looking for reaction stories. If I'd taken much longer, dotted all the *i*'s and all that, it wouldn't have had the same effect."

From "The Art of Oratory in the Senate of the United States," first published in *Esquire Magazine*, May 1969. © by Esquire, Inc.

GREAT SPEAKERS
OUTLINE THEIR SPEECHES
William Norwood Brigance

*William Norwood Brigance, teacher, author, and critic, investigated the
outlining methods used by notable speakers. He reports on some here.*

Perhaps no speaker ever prepared his speeches with greater ease than
William Jennings Bryan. His memory was almost as phenomenal as Macau-
lay's, and his rare gift of utterance enabled him to compose effectively before
an audience. Again and again I have heard that Bryan never outlined a
speech. Being in Lincoln, Nebraska, at the time of his death, I undertook to
find out from his closest friends the real truth. To a man they assured me that it
was so. Even his former private secretary, while discreetly refusing to state it
as a positive fact, was of the opinion that he never put an outline on paper but
carried it, clear and sharp, in his head—a practice which would serve the
same purpose. A sister of Bryan was of the same opinion.

The evidence was overwhelming, yet, when I wrote to Mrs. Bryan about
the matter, she stated that her husband, when speaking on a new subject, did
organize his thoughts, even on paper, and she was kind enough to send me a
specimen of one of his outlines.

That charming and compelling speaker, John Sharp Williams, said:
"Outlines are useful, not to follow slavishly, but first, to order one's discourse
logically, and second, to prevent one from being prolix, 'getting out on a
limb,' away from the subject." Bishop Francis J. McConnel says that in both
writing and speaking he "lays great stress upon a careful outline . . . and
gives greatest attention to the proportion to be assigned the different parts of
the subject." Harry Emerson Fosdick uses a wide variety of methods in preparing his speeches, but the methods have one element in common. He states the
common element in these words: "I would never think of speaking, without, in
some way, ordering my thoughts." We might multiply this testimony endlessly,
but it will be sufficient to point out that great speakers not only of this generation but of all generations have followed the same practice—Daniel Webster,
Wendell Phillips, John C. Calhoun, Henry W. Grady, and even the versatile
Henry Ward Beecher—have all found it necessary to order their thoughts. It
is not becoming, therefore, that a young speaker should consider himself
above a law which these men had to obey.

From *Speech Composition*, 2nd ed. (New York: Appleton-Century-Crofts, 1953), pp.
39–40.

ADDITIONAL READINGS

Dickens, Milton, *Speech: Dynamic Communication* (New York: Harcourt Brace Jovanovich, 1963), chap. 7, "Speech Outlining."

Hance, Kenneth, David Ralph, and Milton Wiksell, *Principles of Speaking* (Belmont: Wadsworth, 1969), chap. 10, "Outlining for Speaking."

McBurney, James and Glen Mills, *Argumentation and Debate* (New York: Macmillan, 1964), chap. 13, "Briefing and Outlining."

Mills, Glen E., *Message Preparation* (Indianapolis: Bobbs-Merrill, 1966), 47–55.

Monroe, Alan and Douglas Ehninger, *Principles and Types of Speech* (Glenview, Ill.: Scott, Foresman, 1967), chap. 17, "Making an Outline."

Mudd, Charles and Malcolm Sillars, *Speech: Content and Communication* (San Francisco: Chandler, 1969), chap. 8, "Outlining."

Ross, Raymond, *Speech Communication* (Englewood Cliffs, N.J.: Prentice-Hall, 1970), 125–131.

STUDY QUESTIONS

1. Why is outlining important in the preparation of a speech?
2. What principles of outlining should the speaker follow? Why is each important?
3. What is meant by coordinate and subordinate ideas in outlining?
4. What is the difference between a complete sentence outline and a key word or key phrase outline? What practical functions do each serve? How do they differ from the speaker's notes?

EXERCISES

1. Arrange the following subtopics in a topical outline with the central thought that *H-Bar-C Ranch offers vacationing guests a wide range of activities and accommodations.*
   Air-conditioned rooms
   Square dancing
   Activities
   Swimming
   At Lake Tippecanoe
   Outdoor activities
   Accommodations
   Fishing
   Trail rides
   Hiking
   On Beaucatcher Mountain
   Sailing
   Souvenirs
   Snack bar
   Bridge and other card games
   Water skiing
   Restaurant
   Indoor activities
   Weekly talent shows
2. Select a speech from *Vital Speeches, Representative American Speeches,* or another anthology and reduce it to a complete sentence outline using the principles of proper outlining. Identify the coordinate and subordinate ideas.
3. Prepare a complete sentence outline for your next speech. Reduce it to a key word or key phrase outline. Further reduce it to speaker's notes. Submit all three to your instructor after you have given the speech.

SUPPORTING MATERIALS: EXPOSITION

In the classroom, the shop, the business firm, the laboratory, the office, the consulting room, and elsewhere, the communication of information is a daily activity. Even in specialized fields such as medicine and law, communicating information in simple, understandable language is an important part of the practitioner's job. For example, a study conducted not long ago showed that a main reason why patients often fail to follow their doctor's advice is because they simply don't understand it. In the field of law, according to Charles Bunn, most of a lawyer's work consists of obtaining and conveying information. "I do not mean information about the law," Professor Bunn emphasizes, "I mean information about the client's problems and the facts connected with them. A lawyer's work is seldom *about* law," Bunn explains in Adapted Reading 3.5.

Regardless of his vocation or level of education, almost every person needs to be able to present simple, everyday information clearly and understandably. Journalist James Reston explains the importance of this ability, saying:

> I think that I could convince any group of children that there are two things that are absolutely fundamental when they leave school — no matter what work they're going into — whether they're going into a garage to fix a car or going into medicine, or law, or to higher education — and that is simply to learn the arts of accurate observation and accurate speech . . . because he ought to be able to explain himself so that a man can understand. The higher up the ladder he goes and the educational scale, of course, the more important that is.

While man's main use of speech probably always has been to communicate information to others, in recent years "the information explosion" has made this function even more important. With the scientific-technological breakthrough in this century, the expansion of knowledge has been so rapid that experts find it difficult to keep abreast of their own fields. Even if the specialist manages to keep reasonably well informed, he has the task of communicating often complex material to the general public in terms it can understand; for many scientific discoveries directly affect all of us, as is emphasized in Adapted Readings 10.1, 10.2, and 16.4.

When presenting information, the speaker's choice of supporting materials is vital in determining his success or failure. Supporting materials may be divided into two classes according to their use. Materials used for informing the listener are called expository. Materials selected to alter the listener's opinions, to reinforce his beliefs, or to influence his actions are known as evidence. Speeches to inform and to entertain consist almost entirely of expository materials. Argumentative speeches—discourse designed to convince or to persuade—rely mainly on evidence, although they may also include expository material. Inspirational talks usually contain both expository and argumentative supporting material.

The process of selecting the materials he will use to develop his topic takes place after the speaker has chosen a subject, determined his purpose, studied his topic, and decided how he wishes to approach the subject. In informative speaking, his supporting material may be used to explain or clarify a concept. At other times, he may use expository materials to amplify or develop an idea more fully. Still another use of expository supporting materials may be to make an idea or explanation more vivid, interesting, and easy to remember.

The principal types of supporting material used in exposition are details, examples, description, narration, definition, comparison, contrast, and statistics.

TYPES OF EXPOSITORY SUPPORTING MATERIALS
Details

Details are specific characteristics, features, or parts of an object, event, or concept. By presenting specific details, a speaker usually seeks to clarify the listeners' understanding with specific information about the subject. The statement, "Automobile for sale," for example, permits only a very general understanding of what is being offered for sale. However, if specific details are added, giving the brand, make, model, color, design, size, horsepower, interior, optional equipment, special features, and price of the automobile, a more thorough understanding of the subject is possible.

A speaker usually employs details in order to clarify an idea, to make it more concrete or specific in the minds of the auditors. Just as a map without boundaries or labels, a recipe omitting the amount of each ingredient, or a newspaper with only headlines would be relatively meaningless, so too are details essential to the understanding of many concepts speakers discuss.

Details, however, may serve another function. Frequently, they are employed to amplify, embellish, or more fully develop a concept, making the idea more vivid and thereby easier to recall.

Former Federal Communications Commission Chairman Newton Minow used details in his famous "A Vast Wasteland" speech to depict a typical day of television broadcasting. He said:

> I invite you to sit down in front of your television set when your station goes on the air . . . and keep your eyes glued to that set until the station signs off. . . . You will see a procession of game shows, violence, audience participation shows, formula comedies about totally unbelievable families, blood and thunder, mayhem, violence, sadism, murder, western bad men, western good men, private eyes, gangsters, more violence, and cartoons. And, endlessly, commercials — many screaming, cajoling, and offending. . . .

For an interesting comparison of methods of developing an idea — and for a more favorable view of the television industry — note the use of examples by Frank Stanton on p. 233.

In a speech at Williams College in 1962, architect Walter Gropius utilized details to re-create conditions during his boyhood. He stated:

> I remember when I was a boy my family lived in a city apartment with open gas-jets and coal-heated stoves in each room. There was no electric streetcar, no automobile, no airplane; radio, film, gramophone, x-ray, telephone were non-existent. The mental climate at that time was still of a more or less static character, rotating around a seemingly unshakable conception of the eternal truths.

In a speech to freshmen in 1964, Robert F. Goheen, president of Princeton University, employed details to describe the intellectual life of his university in the following passage.

> It involves an encounter with facts, ideas, arguments, and even teachers who will puzzle, irritate, and upset you. Many things you have taken for granted will be challenged. Much that you have assumed to be certain you will discover to be highly uncertain, as is so much of life. Learning to respect data, learning to explore concepts in depth, learning to take on to yourself the hard ways of dispassionate, disciplined thought: all this will not be a soothing experience.

Examples

Examples consist of instances and illustrations — real or hypothetical — of some action, condition, or experience. An example is a citation of one instance out of many. One might cite "streaking" as an example of a fad; Samuel Taylor Coleridge's "Kubla Khan" as an example of romantic poetry;

the Hudson River as an example of growing water pollution in the United States; or the American–Soviet cooperation as an example of *detente*.

To illustrate differing tastes among television viewers, Robert W. Sarnoff, in a speech in 1963, used examples, saying: "Most people have strong and subjective programming likes and dislikes. They might love the Beverly Hillbillies and be bored by the NBC Opera, or vice versa. They might become irritated by a commercial or by a newscaster's comments about a subject on which they have a preconceived judgment."

Also discussing television, Frank Stanton of the Columbia Broadcasting System used examples to illustrate the diversity of program offerings by taking a single month and citing some subjects and material presented:

> There were biographical studies of such diverse men as U.S. Grant and Vincent van Gogh, Al Amith and Sinclair Lewis. There were several special half-hour biographies of Speaker Sam Rayburn. There were long reports on such countries as Germany, Spain, Yugoslavia, and France. There were interviews with men representing a provocative cross section of the world today: Prime Minister Nehru, Igor Stravinsky, Hugh Gaitskill, John Kenneth Galbraith, Bertrand Russell. Full-length dramatic productions included Hans Conried and Jane Wyatt in "Little Lost Sheep," Julie Harris in "Victoria Regina," and Fred Astaire in "Moment of Decision." (Benjamin Franklin Lecture at the University of Pennsylvania, December 7, 1961)

Note the extended use of examples by Adlai E. Stevenson in one of the Godkin Lectures at Harvard in 1954. Such examples amplified his statement that "Americans have always assumed, subconsciously, that all problems can be solved; that every story has a happy ending; that the application of enough energy and good will can make everything come out right." He said:

> In view of our history, this assumption is natural enough. As a people we have never encountered any obstacle that we could not overcome. The Pilgrims had a rough first winter, but after that the colony flourished. Valley Forge was followed naturally by Yorktown. Daniel Boone always found his way through the forest. We crossed the Alleghenies and the Mississippi and the Rockies with an impetus that nothing could stop. The wagon trains got through; the Pony Express delivered the mail; in spite of Bull Run and Copperheads, the Union was somehow preserved. We never came across a river we couldn't bridge, a depression we couldn't overcome, a war we couldn't win.

At times, a speaker may use a single example to illustrate a point, as Chief Justice Warren E. Burger did in his "State of the Judiciary" address to the American Bar Association in 1970:

> In this twentieth century, wars, social upheaval, and the inventiveness of man have altered individual lives and society. The au-

tomobile, for example, did more than change the courting habits of American youth—it paved the continent with concrete and black top; it created the most mobile society on earth with all its dislocations; it led people from rural areas to crowd the unprepared cities.

Description

Another way that a speaker might develop his subject is through description. Description is the process of depicting the appearance, nature, or atmosphere of a scene, place, object, or experience, based on one's observations, impressions, and feelings. Accounts of what the Grand Canyon, the Parthenon, or Rembrandt's "Night Watch" look like are examples of description. A news story detailing the wreckage following a hurricane also would contain much descriptive material. Society page reports of weddings often describe the bride's costume in considerable detail. Accounts of the feelings, sensations, and reactions of a passenger on a hijacked airplane, of an observer at a rock festival, or of a witness to a fire, flood, or hurricane are other examples of description.

The principal value of descriptive materials in developing a subject is that they assist the auditor in visualizing clearly and vividly a situation, scene, or event.

In a speech to the Senate in 1963, Senator George McGovern employed description to depict the effects of the explosion of an atomic bomb as follows:

> A single warhead from the American or Russian stockpile if exploded over a great city would instantly transform it into a raging fireball three miles in diameter with a direct heat and blast capable of burning human flesh and collapsing buildings twenty-five miles from its center. Above a smoking crater a mile wide and several blocks deep, a gigantic, poisonous radioactive cloud would rise twenty or twenty-five miles to rain down torturous death on millions of human beings not fortunate enough to be incinerated quickly in the initial firestorm.

A vivid example of description is found in Mark Twain's lecture, "The Sandwich Islands," first delivered in 1866:

> Each island is a mountain—or two or three mountains. They begin at the seashore—in a torrid climate where the cocoa palm grows, and the coffee tree, the mango, orange, banana, and the delicious chirimoya; they begin down there in a sweltering atmosphere, rise with a grand and gradual sweep till they hide their beautiful regalia of living green in the folds of the drooping clouds, and higher and higher yet they rise among the mists till their emerald forests change to dull and stunted shrubbery, then to scattering constellations of the brilliant silver sword, then higher yet to dreary, barren desolation—no

trees, no shrubs, nothing but tern and scorched and blackened piles of lava; higher yet and then, towering toward heaven, above the dim and distant land, above the waveless sea, and high above the rolling plains of clouds themselves, stands the awful summit, wrapped in a mantle of everlasting ice and snow and burnished with a tropical sunshine that fires it with dazzling splendor! Here one may stand and shiver in the midst of eternal winter and look down upon a land reposing in the loveliest hues of a summer that hath no end. Such is Mauna Loa — 16,000 feet high by recent and accurate measurement, and such is Mauna Kea, 14,000 feet high. . . .

Narration

Narration is similar to description except that it depicts or re-creates an event or act. A narrative relates what happened, usually in a chronological order. Most accounts of personal experience are narratives. Reports of trips, sporting events, programs, and meetings are often given in narrative form.

Congressman Morris Udall of Arizona used narration to relate a personal experience in the following passage:

> Some years ago, when I was practicing law here, a troubled business-man of modest means came to me as an old friend. His closest friend during a terminal illness had asked him to help the sick man's son, who was just starting in business. He readily agreed; in other words, he made a solemn commitment. Subsequently he loaned the boy $5,000 after his friend's death. It soon became apparent the boy didn't have any business sense, but the agreement was a solemn one. Soon he had $25,000 of his own money and half his working hours invested in a clearly losing venture, and he was neglecting his own business affairs. When he came to see me, he had just talked with his banker about mortgaging his home. It was apparent to me he was on a course that would eventually lead to bankruptcy. . . . I told my Tucson friend that he had kept the spirit and word of any commitment he had made to his dead friend and that now he should tell the boy frankly that he could go no further.

Definitions

In developing his topic, a speaker often finds it necessary to employ a definition to explain what an unfamiliar word or concept means. A definition may be brief, such as: *Gauche* means awkward, tactless, or lacking grace, especially social graces; or, a *French leave* is a secret, hasty, unnoticed, or unceremonious departure. At other times, a speaker may go into greater detail in defining a concept.

Two examples of short definitions by speakers are (1) Dean Acheson's definition of *ethical* in which he said, "We are told what is ethical is characterized by what is excellent in conduct and that excellence may be judged by what is right and proper, as against what is wrong, by existing standards," and (2) George Bernard Shaw's cryptic definition of an agnostic as "only an atheist without the courage of his opinions." Examples of more detailed definitions are:

Nike-Zeus was subject, as I believe all the later systems are, to something called *blackout*; that is, if a nuclear explosion were set off to destroy an incoming missile, it also upset the gas in the air, "ionized" it—electrons strip off from the molecules and for a while the gas acts like a metal rather than a gas so that radar waves cannot go through it and you cannot see what is behind it. (Jerome B. Wiesner, "An Argument Against the ABM," November 19, 1968)

It would be well to clarify the hyphenated term *Mexican-American*. . . . *Mexican* does not properly describe those whose residence north of the Rio Grande predates the existence of both Mexico and the United States as nations. But it is less the geographical inaccuracy of the term *Mexican* that invites comment than the meaning with which the term is invested. As used and understood in the Southwest, *Mexican* is a descriptive term and carries with it an entire complex of moral and physical attributes. It excludes such commonplace notions of Americanism as godliness, cleanliness, a sense of justice and fair play, Yankee know-how. This may be denied, but proof that *Mexican* is used as a disparaging term lies in the fact of its careful avoidance on the part of those who do not at the moment wish to offend. (Armando M. Rodriguez, "This Is Our Quest: To Fight for the Right," May 8, 1969)

Research is an omnibus word that covers anything from counting fingers and toes to asking $1/100$ to 1 percent of housewives how often they brush their teeth and extrapolating the resultant mendacity into authoritative statistics on the dental care exercised by American women. (Henry Wristen, address to a national education conference in New York, October 17, 1961)

For a detailed discussion of how to define terms, the reader should consult Chapter 16.

Comparison

Comparison is a process by which the speaker seeks to clarify a subject or concept by showing how it is similar to another. Comparisons or analogies may be literal or figurative. A literal comparison develops actual existing similarities. Comparisons between American agriculture and Australian agriculture, between economic conditions in 1950 and 1970, or between Fords and Chevrolets would be literal analogies. In a figurative comparison, the two items being compared possess no real or physical resemblances. Thus, comparisons of poverty to cancer, of raising a child to writing a book, or of politics to a game of chess would be figurative.

In exposition the main function of a literal comparison is to clarify the speaker's idea, while a figurative comparison serves more to dramatize or vivify what the speaker wishes to convey.

Comparison can be particularly useful in explaining an unfamiliar concept by showing its resemblance to something better known. In Adapted Reading 10.3, Lawrence Rosenfield effectively uses an extended comparison to explain the role and functions of a critic. Comparing a critic to a sports fan, he clarifies the duties and attitudes of the critic—the unfamiliar—by showing how he resembles and differs from the sports enthusiast—the familiar.

In the example below, Columbia University President William J. McGill also uses a literal comparison to clarify a point. He says:

> A department or faculty is in many ways a family, living in intimate contact with one another. They have the capacity to protect one another, or to irritate one another unbearably. ("The Public Challenge and the Campus Response," delivered at the University of California, Berkeley, July 15, 1971)

The following passage by speech critic Lester Thonssen contains a figurative comparison that seems to have been more to enliven or vitalize the speaker's thought than to inform.

> Several years ago, an uncommonly snide trick was played on some unsuspecting members of the animal kingdom. A day-long festival was held commemorating the one hundredth anniversary of the development of the Rhode Island Red chicken. There were speeches memorializing the hen; a plaque to the hapless creature was dedicated; and the Rhode Island Red was signaled out for its contribution to the multibillion dollar poultry industry.
>
> After the kind words were spoken, do you know what the audience did? You are quite right. It ate one hundred Rhode Island Reds at a festive barbecue. A cynical attitude, it would seem, with a bit of reverse English.
>
> Yet it is not unlike the practice of some anthologists and critics who, with academic fanfare, select so-called great speeches or other creative expressions for special remembrance, and then promptly tear them to pieces with such cavalier delight as to make the readers wonder why they were chosen to begin with. (From *Representative American Speeches, 1967–1968*, Lester Thonssen, ed. [New York: Wilson], 1969, p. 3)

Shorter figurative comparisons taken from recent speeches include Arnold Toynbee's statement that "civilization is a movement and not a condition, a voyage and not a harbor," and Walter B. Wriston's, "The very speed with which the news is communicated by printed media and especially television, within countries and around the world by satellite, produce nothing more definite to the untrained eye than a Jackson Pollock painting." Another speaker quoted de Tocqueville's comparison, "The world is a strange theater. There are moments in it when the worst plays are those which succeed best."

Contrast

Contrast is similar to comparison except that it stresses differences rather than likenesses. For example, one might clarify the British educational system by showing how it differs from American schooling; or one might illustrate how technological developments have changed our way of living by contrasting transportation in 1800 with transportation today.

Robert S. Browne employed contrast in a speech in 1968 as follows:

A black child in a predominantly black school may realize that she doesn't look like the pictures in the books, magazines, and TV advertisements, but at least she looks like her schoolmates and neighbors. The black child in a predominantly white school and neighborhood lacks even this basis for identification. (Speech to National Jewish Community Relations Advisors Council Plenary Session, New York, June 30–July 3, 1968)

In an address to an honors convocation at California State College in Los Angeles in 1965, Vice-Provost Robert J. Wert of Stanford University employed contrast to explain student unrest. He said:

In former years, undergraduate students could envelop themselves in an association with their college. Having but one life to give for good old Yale was once an understandable sentiment. The college student of yesteryear knew most of his fellow students and knew his instructors. A genuine sense of community existed and what was important to one was, in a sense, important to all. Going to college was a highly personal experience and the choice of college had lasting effects. The graduate of a college was "molded" by his experience. The difference between a Harvard graduate and a Yale graduate was easily perceptible to the trained eye. A graduate of Smith and a graduate of Vassar were noticeably different. By contrast, the undergraduate in a university of 20,000 or 30,000 students can be hopelessly and tragically lost. When he enters college at about 18, he is neither quite an adolescent nor quite an adult. He is searching for an identity of his own, to find out what kind of person he is, to see how he compares with others, and to establish his own philosophy of life. He wants desperately to be a participant in a community which cares about him. He believes that faculty members should worry at least as much about him as about the research projects they are pursuing with the aid of money from the Federal Government. He scorns the rules and regulations of the IBM machine-type university, but at the same time is torturously looking for help in forming his own moral code.

Reporter Robert B. Semple, Jr., also used contrast to illuminate the 1968 campaign styles of Richard Nixon and Hubert Humphrey in the following passage:

> In pace, mood, and tone—all the things that make up a campaign style—Mr. Humphrey and Mr. Nixon are worlds apart. Where Mr. Nixon is cool sculpture, Mr. Humphrey is warm paint. Where Mr. Nixon's operation is orderly, Mr. Humphrey's is chaotic. Where Mr. Nixon is terse and usually restrained, Mr. Humphrey is full voiced and occasionally reckless. It is Mozart vs. Tchaikovsky, Boros vs. Palmer.

Statistics

Statistics are simply numbers. They may be totals, fractions, percentages, proportions, or ratios. *Two million, doubled, three to one, 65 percent, one third, eleven,* and *643,981* are all statistics. The following are some examples of the use of statistics by speakers to amplify or clarify their ideas.

In showing how the monarch was able to manipulate the British House of Commons in the eighteenth century, historian Bernard Bailyn pointed out:

> Some boroughs—twenty-five or thirty—were owned outright by the government in the sense that a majority of their electorates were office holders who could be dismissed if they opposed the government; in others the election of members favorable to the government could be assured by the proper application of electioneering funds. Beyond this, control of the House was assured by the distribution of the crown patronage available to any administration and by the management of the corps of placemen that resulted. In the middle of the eighteenth century about 200 of the 558 members of the House of Commons held crown places of one sort or another, and another 30 or 40 were more loosely tied to government by awards of profitable contracts. Of those who held places, 40 at least held offices intimately involved in the government and were absolutely reliable. The other 160 held a variety of sinecures, household offices, pensions, and military posts which brought them well within the grasp of the administration but yet required constant solicitation and management. (Charles K. Colver Lectures, Brown University, November 1965)

Additional examples of the use of statistics are:

> From 1850, when machines did 35 percent of the work, to the present time, when machines do 99 percent of the work, the American population grew more than $7\frac{1}{2}$ times. But jobs grew more than $8\frac{1}{2}$ times, and goods and services 34 times. In this period of improving machines and methods, jobs multiplied faster than the popula-

tion, and goods and services faster than people. (R. Conrad Cooper, "Let's Look at the Doughnut,"Address at Evansville College, October 10, 1961)

Nearly four million American teenagers will celebrate their eighteenth birthday this year. College enrollment, which has been nearly five million this year, is expected to approach six million next year. (Robert J. Wert, Address at California State College, Los Angeles, April 26, 1965)

TESTING EXPOSITORY SUPPORTING MATERIALS

In expository speaking, the speaker should ask the following five questions about the supporting materials he is thinking of using to amplify or clarify his ideas.

Is the Supporting Material Correct?

The speaker has three main reasons for investigating the accuracy of his supporting materials. First, he has an ethical responsibility to his listeners not to mislead them by presenting inaccurate information. The audience expects him to know his material and he, therefore, has an obligation not to misinform them. In addition, since the purpose of exposition is primarily informative, the speaker cannot expect his listeners to gain a proper understanding of his subject if his supporting material is incorrect. Third, should the auditors discover that some of his information is inaccurate, the speaker runs the risk of losing their confidence. Sometimes a single incorrect detail, inaccurate example, or erroneous statistic may be enough to disillusion an audience. For example, the student speaker whose purpose was to teach the class how to play better tennis instantly lost the confidence of many listeners when he made a mistake in illustrating how a tennis court is laid out. In a similar manner, another speaker failed in a speech on the Battle of New Orleans when she revealed her ignorance of the fact that the battle was fought after, not before, the end of the War of 1812. Even though the error in each of these instances was minor, it was enough to make the audience question the speaker's total knowledge of his topic and the reliability of his other supporting material.

Is the Supporting Material Relevant?

The speaker's supporting materials should always be necessary, pertinent, and should contribute to the achievement of his goal. Common mistakes that speakers make in selecting supporting materials include the introduction of interesting but irrelevant information, the inclusion of related but unnecessary subject matter, the overdevelopment of a point the audience has already grasped, and the presentation of material whose relationship to the main idea of the speech is unclear.

It is not unusual, for example, for a speaker to stray from his topic as he remembers a humorous or interesting anecdote; to be so enthusiastic that he goes into unnecessary depth and detail on a minor point; or to spend valuable time developing material that is totally unnecessary to the audience's understanding of his subject. The speaker should test carefully each piece of supporting material, deciding which is and which is not necessary to the achievement of his purpose, before deciding what to include in his talk. Only those materials that contribute to the achievement of his purpose should then be used.

Is the Supporting Material Specific?

All expository supporting material has the function of making the speech more meaningful by making it less abstract or less general. In expository speaking, the supporting materials are primarily illustrative and serve to elaborate or amplify the speaker's general statements so that the audience grasps their meaning.

If the speaker's supporting materials are vague, unclear, or difficult to follow, they contribute little to the audience's comprehension. Futhermore, specific supporting data is usually more interesting than other more abstract concepts. For these reasons, the speaker should strive to keep his supporting materials specific and concrete.

Is the Supporting Material Clear?

At times, supporting material can be correct, relevant, and specific without being clear. Some audiences lack the educational background needed to comprehend highly technical or specialized material. Yet the speaker may find it virtually mandatory that he include such material. For example, the average person probably has only the most elementary understanding of such concepts as inflation, balance of payments, and deficit spending; but if the speaker's purpose is to explain the government's fiscal policy, he probably will be compelled to utilize supporting material related to these concepts. In this type of situation, the speaker must be sure to recognize and define or explain unfamiliar and technical materials.

The speaker should also be careful to present statistics in such a way that they do not confuse the listeners. Unless a precise number is required, statistics often should be simplified by rounding off, thereby enabling the auditor to grasp them more easily. For example, instead of 9,883,412 the speaker might say *approximately ten million*; for 26.2 percent he could state *a little more than a fourth*; rather than 51.6 percent he could use *about one half*; and a 98.73 percent increase could be called *nearly double*.

In the passage below, quoted from a speech by Robert C. Weaver in 1963, note how the speaker has simplified his statistics:

> Median family income among nonwhites was *slightly less than 55 percent* of that for whites in 1959; for individual incomes, the figure was *50 percent. Only a third* of the Negro families in 1959 earned sufficient income to sustain an acceptable American standard of living. Yet this involved *well over a million* Negro families, of whom 6,000 earned $25,000 or more. . . . Negroes have made striking gains

in historical terms; yet their current rate of unemployment is *well over double* that among whites. *Over two-thirds* of our colored workers are still concentrated in *five* major unskilled and semiskilled occupations, as contrasted to *slightly over a third* of the white labor force. [Italics added]

Visual presentations in the form of charts, diagrams, and graphs are also helpful as a supplement to the oral citation of statistics.

Because a speaker can communicate only within the areas of experience of his auditors, materials difficult to comprehend often should be clarified by relating the unfamiliar to the known. Thus, in explaining communism to an audience in a capitalistic country or socialized medicine to a group familiar only with the private practice of medicine, rather than discussing these concepts in the abstract, the speaker might describe a day in the life of a communist farmer or tell how a patient goes about seeing a doctor, entering a hospital, and obtaining treatment under a program of socialized medicine.

Audiences sometimes have difficulty grasping the extent of huge sums of money or great distances. To make these statistics more meaningful, a speaker might compare them to something more readily understood, as Notre Dame University President Theodore Hesburgh did in his 1962 speech on foreign aid:

> "But we are spending billions on foreign aid." Yes, about 4 billion annually to be exact. But again, about half of this is military aid, and the 2 billion that are left seem hardly sacrificial when you compare it to the 6 billion we spend annually for tobacco, the 12 billion for alcohol, the 20 billion for that ancient pastime called gambling. I shall spare you the bill for entertainment.

Another example of clarifying large figures by relating them to something more readily understood is the statement from a television commercial, "Automotive travel in the United States totals more than one trillion miles a year, the equivalent of two thousand round trips to the moon." Radical agitator Saul Alinsky stresses the importance of using specific materials within the realm of the listener's experience in Adapted Reading 10.4.

Is the Supporting Material Interesting?

In choosing his materials, the speaker should select those of greatest interest to his listeners. If the supporting material is interesting, the auditor not only will grasp it more quickly, but he will also be more likely to remember it, which is one of the speaker's objectives in informative speaking.

As mentioned earlier, specific material usually is more interesting than abstract support. Materials related to the listeners' background and experience also are more likely to be of interest. If the material is up-to-date, it seems more immediate, relevant, and pertinent and, therefore, also more interesting.

Interest can be enhanced through the use of vivid language. Descriptive adjectives, forceful verbs, alliteration, parallelism, rhetorical questions, antithesis, repetition, and other stylistic devices can make an example or a narrative more striking and memorable.

Materials that contain a touch of wit or humor also add interest. For example, President Malcolm Moos of the University of Minnesota, in relating how he somewhat reluctantly concluded that he must play a more active role in the future of his institution, illustrated how he reached this decision, saying, "You will recall the bullock who, being pursued by a ferocious tiger in India, shouted to a monkey: 'Do you think I can climb this tree?' 'Brother, it's no longer a matter of opinion. You've got to climb this tree.' "

SUMMARY

Supporting materials are of two kinds: those used for exposition and those used for argumentation.

Expository supporting materials are employed mainly to clarify, amplify, elaborate, and embellish. Common types of expository supporting materials are details, examples, description, narration, definition, comparison, contrast, and statistics.

Details are the specific characteristics or features of an object, event, or concept.

Examples consist of instances and illustrations, actual or hypothetical, of some action, condition, or experience. An example is a citation of one instance out of many.

Description is the process of depicting the appearance, nature, or atmosphere of a scene, place, object, or experience. Description is the result of one's personal observations, impressions, and reactions.

Narration resembles description except that it depicts or re-creates an event or act. Narration is concerned with what happened and usually is presented chronologically.

Definitions are explanations of what a word or concept means. The purpose of a definition is to make sure that the listener understands what a word means or how the speaker is using a particular word.

Comparison is the process by which a speaker seeks to clarify his subject, showing how it is similar to another situation, event, process, or development. Comparisons may be literal or figurative.

Contrast resembles comparison except that it stresses differences rather than similarities.

Statistics are numbers: totals, fractions, percentages, proportions, or ratios.

In his selection and use of supporting materials for the purpose of exposition, the speaker should apply five tests:

1. Is the material correct?
2. Is the material relevant, pertinent, and necessary?
3. Is the material specific?

4. Is the material clear? If not, the speaker should take pains to simplify or clarify his supporting materials.
5. Is the material interesting?

If the speaker's supporting material meets these five tests, he will probably be successful in holding the interest of the listener, in presenting his message in such a way that the hearer will have no difficulty understanding his ideas, and in accomplishing his purpose.

THE INFORMATION EXPLOSION

If an average reader tried to catch up with one year's output of learned publications in the sciences, it would take him about 50 years of reading 24 hours a day, seven days a week. This gives some idea of the problem facing scholars and librarians today as the number and size of academic journals in all fields of study expand at a prodigious rate.

"The barriers of research have just fallen,"says Louis Martin, associate director of the Association of Research Libraries in Washington. "The amount of new information is staggering." Many scholars and medical men say the proliferation is the necessary by-product of a burgeoning academic establishment and the creation of many new disciplines.

There are so many scholarly journals that no one has been able to count them. Authoritative estimates vary from 200,000 to 600,000 worldwide. Sam Laserow, head of the Serial Record Division of the Library of Congress, estimates that about 15,000 new periodicals, or serials as librarians call them, appear every year—of which perhaps 1,000 can be considered scholarly.

Specialized journals, which report original research, are essential tools of inquiry—particularly in the hard sciences, where the pace of research is such that a man can spend months duplicating work already done elsewhere if he does not keep on top of the literature. (*The New York Times*, June 6, 1970)

Slowly but surely, the American physicist is being swamped by an amorphous deluge of published findings and speculations. The accumulation of journals published in 1969 by the American Institute of Physics forms a stack 20 feet high, and the world output is estimated at 60 feet. Production is doubling every eight years. Buried in this mass of reports are some of interest to any specialist, but to find them is an almost hopeless task. (*The New York Times*, December 25, 1969)

Dr. Seymour M. Farber of the University of California Medical School in San Francisco pointed out that in 1964 the National Library of Medicine received more than 18,000 different journals and the Index Medicus that year contained more than 145,000 entries, an increase of almost nine percent over the previous year. Dr. Farber estimated that the major portion of this information would become significantly obsolete in five years.

Not only is a greater volume of clinical and scientific information becoming available daily, but also such material is ever increasing in its complexity. The primary problem is both to keep the clinician up to date scientifically and to translate such information to him in usable, understandable form. (*The New York Times*, April 10, 1966)

Our greatest problem today in medicine is continuing education. You all know the surveys that show how even the most progressive-minded and best-educated doctor, practicing in an isolated community, is soon overtaxed by such a huge work load that after five years time the quality of his care falls to about the level of his less-educated and progressive colleagues. (Howard A. Rusk, Institute of Rehabilitation Medicine, New York University Medical Center, in *Annals of New York Academy of Science*)

Within the field of science, there has recently been an explosion of knowledge comparable in significance to Mendel's discoveries about inheritance in the nineteenth century. What has been learned is of great import to the whole of society. . . . The experts can't (or at least *shouldn't*) make decisions for all of us on the control of radioactive fallout or the right of people with inherited diseases to reproduce as freely as people without such diseases. Whether one race has an inherited superiority to another race is no longer a purely academic question. In our kind of society, the formation of intelligent opinion about such matters isn't going to occur until ordinary citizens understand the new genetics much better than they do now. (Muriel Beadle, *Saturday Review*, April 3, 1965)

Science can no longer hope to exist "through some mystique, without constraints or scrutiny in terms of national goals, and isolated from the competition for allocation of resources which are finite." Researchers must abandon the notion that it is either impossible or unseemly to explain their goals to the public. (Dr. Ivan L. Bennett, Jr., Director of the Department of Pathology, Johns Hopkins University, *The New York Times*, October 23, 1965)

ADAPTED READING 10.2

LAYMAN'S PEACE OF MIND
Howard A. Rusk

There is an old saying that when doctors disagree and the patient is caught in the middle, the results can be not only confusing but disastrous to the patient's peace of mind. The same is often true of highly controversial public scientific discussions.

It's the same phenomenon that occurs when the physician makes rounds in the hospital with his residents and interns—stops by the bedside of an ill and anxious patient and examines the patient and discusses with his staff the diagnostic and therapeutic possibilities in scientific terms. Unless the physician explains to the patient in words of one syllable and with understanding and sensitivity the facts in simple lay language, the consequences are anxiety and often real fear. The patient does not know whether the prognosis is good or bad, whether he will be going home next week or is suffering from a fatal and incurable disease. Once anxiety is seeded it grows like a snowball.

The recent Congressional hearings on "the pill" are a perfect example. They have precipitated the "pebble dropped in the water" reaction across the whole country. Following the testimony by scientists and clinicians, both pro and con, and the questions and comments by the committee members, there has been an epidemic of anxiety that has spread like wildfire.

One distinguished gynecologist told me recently that he was averaging a dozen telephone calls a day, not only from young women who had been taking the pill, but older women who had been taking moderate doses of needed estrogenic hormones for replacement therapy, who were frantic with fright. Therapy was given because of basic medical needs. It is well known that such replacement therapy is invaluable in treating the symptoms of menopause and a number of studies have indicated that such therapy has a deterrent effect on the development of arteriosclerosis. Many patients in both age groups precipitately stopped the prescribed medicine purely from fear.

This physician worked out a formula to graphically give his anxious patients the facts. The No. 1 fear of the younger women taking the pill was the report that in certain instances fatal thrombotic conditions (blood clot) could occur. He said, "I told my patients, if you would fill every seat in Shea Stadium and every woman goes on the pill every day for a year, when the seats are filled the next year there will be only one empty seat, for the incidence of thrombotic disease of women taking the pill is only three per 100,000 per year."

He also pointed out that in the normal pregnant population the average of thrombotic disease was 12 per 100,000 per year—four times as great as the pill group. He said, "I also point out to them that fatalities from abortions in first-class hospitals occur at the rate of 200–300 per 100,000 per year. . . ."

The point is that when scientific debate occurs in the public forum and the debate is before a forum of nonscientists, interpretation by the public is often one of general confusion. . . . Medical advice and interpretation must come from the physician in an atmosphere of true patient–doctor relationship and understanding. A frank discussion of the pros and cons, the risks and disadvantages, is the only answer to the problem of perspective.

CRITICS AND SPORTS FANS: DEVELOPMENT BY COMPARISON

Lawrence W. Rosenfield

In the following passage, Lawrence W. Rosenfield uses an extended compar-
ison to define a critic. Note also his use of definition by negation in the final
paragraph.

Whenever the word "critic" comes up in conversation, a variety of images is
liable to come to mind. Some think of the book reviewer or the drama critic
for a newspaper. Others, who equate "critic" with "carper," are reminded of
a sour, negative individual who cannot be pleased. Still others (particularly if
they are conversant with too many Master's theses in public address) may
imagine that "the speech critic" is a kind of reporter of public address in history. Clearly, common usage has made the term so vague as to be practically
meaningless. Is it possible to restrict the meaning of "critic" by adopting
semantic boundaries which enable us to distinguish the legitimate critics from
those for whom the label represents simply encomium (or invective)? To do so
we would need to ascertain what actions we may ordinarily expect of one
who is fulfilling the office of critic. If we investigate what I have chosen to call
the "critical posture," or the stance habitually assumed by one who is fulfilling
the logical requirements of critic, we can reach some consensus as to the behavior of the critic; we will then be in a better position to understand "criticism" itself. In order to clarify what is meant here, it may be helpful to draw a
rough comparison between events discussed by critics and those events we
commonly call "athletic." We shall discover that in the main the critical posture resembles the "spectator" half of an agent-spectator dichotomy.

First of all, it is easy enough to understand that some sporting events are
not only played but are observed as well — by individuals we call "spectators." And it is common that these spectators, if they are genuine fans, do
more than simply purchase a ticket of admission so that they may sit in proximity to the athletic activity. They will also devote a certain time and effort to
contemplating and discussing the events they observe. That is to say, the role
of the spectator often entails reflection and communication about the athletic
events. For instance, the baseball fan may attend winter Hot Stove meetings
where particular plays will be recalled and mulled over; likewise, the Monday
Morning Quarterbacks derive a certain satisfaction from assembling to
debunk the maneuvers executed in recent football games.

This same quality of spectatorship seems to be common among those
whom we might call fans of aesthetic events, whether their particular "sport"
be painting or public communication. One characteristic of the rhetorical
critic, then, is his interest in observing and discussing instances of rhetorical
discourse, be they speeches, essays, or advertisements, from the vantage of
the spectator.

From *Speech Monographs*, March 1968, pp. 51–52.

Another characteristic which critics share with at least some sports fans is that both show an appreciation for the execution of the event or object. The involvement of some fans is limited to being loyal followers of a favorite team; they are mainly concerned to share in the exaltation of the home team's victories. For such "part-time" fans, the outcome of a contest is of paramount interest. True enthusiasts, however, seldom gather merely to report the results of games; they do not confine their comments to the immediate, utilitarian aspects of athletic events. Such fans derive satisfaction from watching a film replay of a game whose final score they already know, a satisfaction we may label as appreciation. This appreciation, whether in the fan or the critic, is not inherently related to enthusiasm or suspense over outcome.

A third similarity between the posture of the critic and that of the athletic fan is that heightened appreciation (and hence increased satisfaction or pleasure) accompanies increased knowledge of the events or objects observed. The football fan who knows more than the formal rules of the game (e.g., understands the tactics of blocking assignments and the relative merits of the T-formation and the single wing) derives a satisfaction from second-guessing the coach which the less informed "rooter for the home team" misses. In other words, consciousness of artistic principle contributes to appreciation.

A final commonality follows from the notion of heightened appreciation. Some spectators, because of especially fine training or acute sensitivity, attain the status of "experts." In the athletic sphere such persons are often hired to act as sports-casters and sports-writers, and in the aesthetic realm they may be called upon to act as "critics" in giving reviews of books, plays, and the like. However, their titles do not derive from the fact that they are appointed or paid to perform these tasks. Rather, it is because of their competence that they are asked to assume the critic's office. An expert can be an amateur and still be a fine sports analyst or critic. What matters is exceptional understanding. Accordingly, "critical posture" refers to *the capacity a person has to act as an expert commentator,* and the critic, if he is nothing else, must be one who is capable of fulfilling this role.

Simple *capacity* to render commentary is not yet criticism. The expert-spectator who relishes the events he observes but does not relate his appreciation to others is not a critic, for "criticism" normally refers to the critic's verbal commentary on the event. Criticism is therefore the special variety of discourse which results when a person who has adopted a critical posture makes assertions, i.e., statements by an expert about "the way things are."

ADAPTED READING 10.4
MAKING THE GENERAL SPECIFIC
Saul D. Alinsky

Saul Alinsky spent most of his life organizing and teaching others how to organize groups in order to exert pressure on government and win support for their causes.

Since people understand only in terms of their own experience, an organizer must have at least a cursory familiarity with their experience. It not only serves communication but it strengthens the personal identification of the organizer with the others and facilitates further communication.

A classic example of the failure to communicate because the organizer has gone completely outside the experience of the people is the attempt by campus activists to indicate to the poor the bankruptcy of their prevailing values. "Take my word for it—if you get a good job and a split-level ranch house out in the suburbs, a color TV, two cars, and money in the bank, that just won't bring you happiness." The response without exception is always, "Yeah. Let me be the judge of that one—I'll let you know after I get it."

Communication on a general basis without being fractured into the specifics of experience becomes rhetoric and it carries a very limited meaning. It is the difference between being informed of the death of a quarter of a million people—which becomes a statistic—or the death of one or two close friends or loved ones or members of one's family. In the latter it becomes the full emotional impact of the finality of tragedy. In trying to explain what the personal relationship means, I have told various audiences, "If the chairman of this meeting had opened up by saying, 'I am shocked and sorry to have to report to you that we have just been notified that Mr. Alinsky has just been killed in a plane crash and therefore this lecture is canceled,' the only reaction you would have would be, 'Well, gee, that's too bad. I wonder what he was like, but oh, well, let's see, what are we going to do this evening. We've got the evening free now. We could go to a movie.' And that is all that one would expect, except of those who have known me in the past, regardless of what the relationship was.

"Now suppose after finishing this lecture, let us assume that all of you have disagreed with everything I have said, you don't like my face, the sound of my voice, my manner, my clothes, you just don't like me, period. Let us further assume that I am to lecture you again next week, and at that time you are informed of my sudden death. Your reaction will be very different, regardless of your dislike. You will react with shock: you will say, 'Why, just yesterday he was alive, breathing, talking, and laughing. It just seems incredible to believe that suddenly like that he's gone.' This is the human reaction to a personal relationship.

"What is of particular importance here however is the fact that you were dealing with one specific person and not a general mass."

This is the problem in trying to communicate on the issue of the H bomb. It is too big. It involves too many casualties. It is beyond the experience of people and they just react with, "Yeah, it is a terrible thing," but it really does not grip them. It is the same with figures. The moment one gets into the area of $25 million and above, let alone a billion, the listener is completely out of touch, no longer really interested, because the figures have gone above his experience and almost are meaningless. Millions of Americans do not know how many million dollars make up a billion.

This element of the specific that must be small enough to be grasped by the hands of experiences ties very definitely into the whole scene of issues. Issues must be able to be communicated. It is essential that they can be communicated. It is essential that they be simple enough to be grasped as rallying or battle cries. They cannot be generalities like sin or immorality or the good life or morals. They must be *this* immorality of *this* slum landlord with *this* slum tenement where *these* people suffer.

It should be obvious by now that communication occurs concretely, by means of one's specific experience. General theories become meaningful only when one has absorbed and understood the specific constituents and then related them back to a general concept. Unless this is done, the specifics become nothing more than a string of interesting anecdotes. That is the world as it is in communication.

ADDITIONAL READINGS

Baird, A. Craig and Franklin Knower, *Essentials of General Speech* (New York: McGraw-Hill, 1968), chap. 8, "Facts, Thought, and Details of Development."

Braden, Waldo and Mary Louise Gehring, *Speech Practices* (New York: Harper & Row, 1958), Chap. 5, "The Speaker Supports His Propositions."

Culp, Ralph, *Basic Types of Speech* (Dubuque, Iowa: Brown, 1968), chap. 2, "Speeches of Inquiry and Explanation."

Hance, Kenneth, David Ralph and Milton Wiksell, *Principles of Speaking* (Belmont: Wadsworth, 1969), chap. 6, "Materials of Speaking: Materials of Development" and chap. 7, "Materials of Development: Materials of Experience."

McBurney, James and Ernest Wrage, *Guide to Good Speech* (Englewood Cliffs, N.J.: Prentice-Hall, 1965), chap. 10, "Developing Your Ideas."

Olbricht, Thomas, *Informative Speaking* (Glenview, Ill.: Scott, Foresman, 1968), 71–89.

STUDY QUESTIONS

1. What is the difference between exposition and argumentation?
2. How does development by comparison differ from development by contrast?
3. What are five tests of good expository supporting material?
4. Why do speakers sometimes introduce irrelevant or unimportant expository materials? Is this practice desirable?
5. Why should the speaker seek to employ materials that are specific?
6. What are some ways of clarifying or simplifying statistics? When should this practice be avoided?
7. What are some methods that the speaker can use to make his supporting material interesting?

8. Indicate why the ability to present information clearly would be important to each of the following.
   a. the foreman of a construction crew
   b. a nurse
   c. a police officer
   d. a librarian
   e. a football coach
   f. an air-conditioner salesman
   g. a travel agent

EXERCISES

1. In a newspaper or magazine, find an example of each of the eight types of expository materials discussed in this chapter.
2. List three topics that would lend themselves to expository development by details, by examples, by description, by narration, by definition.
3. Select one of the topics below and write three 75- to 100-word paragraphs, each developing the subject with a different kind of expository material: (1) basketball, (2) Sunday afternoon, (3) the library, (4) procrastination, (5) roommates, (6) the Fourth of July, (7) a pep rally, (8) blind dates.
4. Prepare and deliver a four-minute expository speech in which you utilize one kind of supporting material throughout.
5. Read a speech in *Vital Speeches* or *Representative American Speeches* that is primarily expository or informative and identify the kinds of supporting materials used by the speaker. Applying the tests of good expository supporting material, evaluate his use of supporting materials.
6. Listen to a newscast on radio or television and list the different types of expository materials used by the speaker. What kind was used most frequently? Was the newscast strictly informative? Write a paper summarizing your findings.
7. Analyze a lecture by one of your teachers in order to determine what kinds of supporting materials he employs. Evaluate his use of supporting material. Were there places where you felt additional supporting material was needed to aid your understanding of the lecture? Did his supporting materials clarify and add interest to his speech?

CHAPTER
11

PERSUASION

Since Aristotle's proclamation that rhetoric is "the faculty of discovering in the particular case what are the available means of persuasion," scholars have been interested in speech as a major form of social influence and control. As citizens in a free society and in a competitive economy, we are constantly designing communication strategies to garner others' support, favor, and aid. These persuasive ploys begin as early as the child's attempts to gain an extra hour before going to bed or to coax an extra serving of dessert. Early persuasive attempts involve relatively simple strategies—a smile, a kiss, a promise to be good. As the individual matures, the strategies become more complex and the planning of them often consumes a great deal of time. The arguments that a teenager develops to prove his need for the family car on Saturday night or for an increase in allowance are often elaborate conundrums. The salesman who attempts to persuade a business manager of a company to use a particular brand of paper or electronic duplicator in his office constructs even more sophisticated strategies of persuasion.

The fact that individuals and groups design persuasive strategies strongly suggests that there is someone to be persuaded. We are, perhaps, better defined as consumers than as designers of persuasion. For example, from the time we wake up in the morning until the time we retire at night, we are constantly bombarded by radio and television with commercials for automobiles, hair dressings, life insurance, sporting goods, laxatives, energy-giving compounds, and headache-relief pills. While driving along the highway we see billboards displaying persuasive messages such as, "Join the Sociables," "Be in the Swing," "Shop at Macy's—A Family Store." All Americans are mass consumers of persuasive campaigns.

As both architects and consumers of persuasive messages, we should recognize that the roles are complementary rather than antithetical. For example, the man who is persuaded to play golf on Saturday must, in turn, persuade his wife that the lawn doesn't really need mowing this weekend. The executive who agrees to adopt an advertising campaign proposal must, in turn, present it to his superior or to the board of directors to win their support.

Several aspects of persuasion are evident from these examples. First, every person is at once a persuader and one persuaded. Second, persuasion takes place incessantly and in various settings—at home, at work, while driving, while eating. Third, persuasion is transmitted via numerous media—radio, television, billboards—and in face-to-face contact with colleagues, friends, and members of the family. Fourth, persuasion can be aimed at different types of audiences—mass (radio, television), small group (rotary club), or individual (student-to-teacher or teacher-to-chairman).

PERSUASION DEFINED

Generally, persuasion may be defined as an attempt by one person to influence the behavior of another. More specifically, persuasion is a strategy consciously designed to shape perceptions, modify attitudes, or influence responses of one or more persons to concur with those of an initiating agent. Since all communication in a very real sense influences our behavior, the consciousness of our effort to persuade takes on significance. To design a strategy of persuasion in order to win the support of another, the persuader must make a deliberate effort to discover the goals of the communicative act and the means by which those goals can be accomplished.

A manager of a business recently related an experience that served for him as a valuable lesson in using persuasion to influence behavior. The manager realized that the shifting of responsibilities among his employees had produced a negative reaction culminating in unspoken hostilities between him and the employees. It became apparent that his authoritarian control was the source of these hostilities, and he decided to investigate alternatives. After discussing the matter with other managers who had not had similar reactions from their employees, he altered his approach to employee/managerial relationships. Instead of dictatorially announcing his plans by memo, he discussed matters with the employees, seeking their

> When the conduct of men is designed to be influenced, *persuasion*, kind, unassuming persuasion should ever be adopted. It is an old and true maxim, that a "drop of honey catches more flies than a gallon of gall." So with men. If you would win a man over to your cause, first convince him that you are his sincere friend. Therein is a drop of honey that catches his heart, which, say what he will, is the great high road to his reason.
>
> ABRAHAM LINCOLN

advice and opinions on his ideas. By involving his employees in decisions and infusing his own recommendations into their discussions of the problem, he not only obtained his goal but also won the respect and cooperation of his staff. To persuade the employees, the manager systematically cited historical evidence, listing the companies which successfully utilized the new procedures he advocated; he used the prestige, but not authoritativeness, of his own position, a factor sometimes called ethical appeal; and he used logic, showing the reasons for the probable success of his proposed innovations. The manager learned to influence responses by consciously designing a communication strategy.

CONSTITUENTS OF PERSUASIVE COMMUNICATION

The four major constituents of persuasive communication are (1) a persuader, (2) a purpose or agency, (3) a persuasive message, and (4) an audience to be persuaded. Each of these constituents influence the persuasive act.

The Persuader

The persuader, or sender of the persuasive message, has several rhetorical tools with which to execute a persuasive act. He may use the power of his office and the appeal of his ethos (source credibility); he may employ rational or logical appeals; and he may employ appeals that aim at emotional response from those he wishes to persuade. The principal appeal used by the speaker is variously referred to in communication literature as ethos, ethical appeal, personal appeal, or source credibility. We shall use the last of these terms, source credibility.

Source Credibility. It is impossible to separate the speaker's effect on his audience from the content of his message. If his listeners regard him highly, they will adopt a more favorable attitude toward his proposition than if they had a negative impression of him. Consequently, it is important that the speaker bring to the platform a strong, positive, personal appeal. The importance of source credibility cannot be minimized and can be reinforced in seven principal ways.

Position. Why do millions of people listen with respect to the words of the president of the United States when he speaks on a matter of policy? Not necessarily because he represents the political views of the listeners, nor because he is more brilliant than they are, but because the nature of his position commands deference. The president of the United States brings to the speaking situation a respect he derives from the prestige and powers of his office. In a similar manner, employees will listen with great interest when the president of the company speaks, even though their contact with him may be minimal or purely formal. The very fact that he is the president of the company and represents the firm to the outside world creates respect for him that he might not otherwise enjoy. Similarly, most students are attentive and deferential to their teacher because of the teacher's position or status.

Reputation. The persuader's reputation accounts for a second source of credibility. A good reputation based on the speaker's past performances, accomplishments, publicity, and honors will contribute to the audience's acceptance of him as a credible source. In addition, the chairman of a meeting can, in his introduction, elevate the speaker's reputation and prestige by listing his qualifications as an expert on the topic. Favorable publicity preceding the speech also adds to the speaker's credibility. Most important, however, are those methods employed by the speaker in the speech to reinforce his reputation.

Goodwill. A speaker may create goodwill by associating himself with persons, institutions, and goals respected by the audience. Hubert Humphrey applied the technique of association in a speech delivered at Louisiana State University in 1965, by departing from the prepared text for an impromptu introduction (see Adapted Reading 7.4).

Not infrequently, politicians invoke mother, God, and country as means of improving their image with voters. Although this triumvirate is a bit obvious, it clarifies the point. If the speaker can identify himself with the heroes, ideals, and causes admired by the audience, he will improve his chances for acceptance.

Intellectual Integrity. Intellectual integrity, a fourth source of credibility, is imperative for the persuader. A person who is both self-assertive and self-effacing, honest and yet obviously wary of bravado, exaggeration, and deception, will elicit the approval of his audience. On the other hand, the employer, the student, and the colleague are not easily fooled. We can all spot those who display less than complete intellectual honesty, and that speaker will be an ineffective persuader. Honesty is essential to trust, and trust is essential to acceptance (see Adapted Reading 11.1). The "credibility gap" so widely discussed in the press in recent years results directly from our loss of faith in the honesty and integrity of our public officials. When persons in positions of leadership advocate contradictory policies or provide the public with false information, the listener begins to question their integrity. Listeners also believe that a speaker's words should express his own ideas and that the words should be his own. Although it may be necessary at times for some persons to employ ghostwriters, knowledge that a speaker has prepared his own speech increases his ethical appeal. Such was the case with Adlai Stevenson, who was admired almost as much for the fact that he wrote his own material as for the ideas that material conveyed. Listeners value honesty; they respect rhetorical effort. Eric Sevareid comments on this in "The Professor and the Ghosts" (Adapted Reading 4.4).

Knowledge. A fifth ingredient of source credibility is knowledge, learning, or wisdom. The pretender to wisdom, the pseudo-intellectual, will soon be discovered, while the caretaker of legitimate knowledge will earn the respect due him. Whether presenting an idea to his superior manager or to a colleague, a speaker must know his subject. The accumulation of evidence to support a position or proposition is an important aspect of persuasion. Supportive evidence not only enables the speaker to present logical reasons for accepting his position, but it creates a favorable impression with the audience.

If the speaker presents his ideas and supporting materials with thoroughness and confidence, the audience will be impressed by his grasp of the subject. However, if the speaker belabors the obvious or talks at a level beyond their comprehension, his acceptability to the audience is likely to suffer. As still another method of advancing his reputation as a knowledgeable man, the speaker may tactfully and unobtrusively remind the audience of his qualifications as an expert. For example, he might mention that he has served on a commission studying the problem, that he has long worked for reform in the area, that he has traveled widely or conferred with recognized authorities, thereby strengthening the audience's impression of his wisdom.

Sincerity. Sincerity is a sixth ingredient of credibility. There is probably no greater example of the power of sincerity than that represented by the election of President Harry Truman in 1948. While all of the polls predicted overwhelming defeat, President Truman embarked on a whistle-stop campaign talking to thousands of voters from the back of a train. A frequent comment by those who heard Truman was, "He sounds so sincere." Truman's sincerity proved a significant factor in his winning the election.

After gathering his facts, statistics, and other supporting materials, the speaker should digest them thoroughly and present them with conviction. He should beware, however, of the "persuasive fallacy," the pretense of unparalleled intelligence and unquestionable knowledge. A speaker should "never make his audience appear ignorant or stupid; nor should he belittle nor embarrass them." As a persuader, he must approach the listener in a spirit of goodwill. The speaker must make it clear that he is arguing in the interests of his listeners. If he identifies himself with the listeners as a member of their group or supporter of a common cause, he may dispel any predisposition on the part of the audience to question his motives. An audience is likely to reject the arguments of one who appears to be soliciting support for a selfish cause or for self-aggrandizement.

Delivery. The speaker's delivery is a seventh source of credibility. If he exhibits timidity, nervousness, indirectness, or lethargy, his audience may well reject him immediately. If, on the other hand, the speaker approaches his audience with confidence, firmness, and self-assurance, he will probably earn the respect of his listeners. For this reason, the speaker should, from the outset, establish direct eye contact with his audience and adopt a sure and enthusiastic manner of delivery—attributes attained by vigorous vocal and physical presentation. He should keep his speech lively, for most audiences are unimpressed by sobriety, no matter how erudite.

The Purpose of Persuasion

We defined persuasion as discourse consciously designed to influence others, to make them agree with us. Thus, the second constituent of a persuasive speech is the speaker's purpose or the specific response he desires from the audience. The persuasive speaker's purpose may be to actuate, to obtain some definite observable performance from the audience, such as asking the listeners to vote for a particular person or issue in a referendum. In the case of an evangelist, the desired observable performance may be in the form of raised hands or verbal testimonies expressing belief in the message proposed by the evangelist.

A second possible response desired by the speaker may be to change attitudes or beliefs of the members of the audience. In the case of a court trial, the ultimate goal for a defense attorney is to persuade the jury to hand down a verdict of "not guilty"; but in the process of the trial, the attorney will attempt to shape the jury's attitude favorably toward his client.

A third purpose of the speaker may be to inspire the audience, to arouse their enthusiasm, or to strengthen their existing feelings of respect or devotion. The function of a keynote speaker at a national political convention, for example, is to heighten the delegates' respect and loyalty to the party. The football coach at a pregame rally usually seeks to stimulate the loyalty and enthusiasm of the student body.

The specific purpose of the speech to persuade may be to influence beliefs, to arouse emotions, or to actuate audiences.

The Message

The third constituent of a persuasive speech, the message, may take many forms. Aristotle defined three types of messages: deliberative, forensic, and epideictic or demonstrative. He further clarified these types by describing the deliberative speech as appropriate to matters of probability and future action, the forensic speech to events, and demonstrative speeches to concerns of praise or blame. Contemporary rhetoricians define these three types of speeches as those that affirm propositions of policy (deliberative), those that affirm propositions of fact (forensic), and those that affirm propositions of value (demonstrative).

Deliberative speeches, or those affirming propositions of policy, concern themselves with the wisdom or expediency of courses of action affecting the future welfare of the audience. Members of Congress, when devising and debating laws to guide the country, utilize the deliberative form. For instance, when a bill is debated for final passage, supporters of the legislation usually argue that the new legislation will improve society. Opponents often argue that passage of the bill will create more problems than already exist. Whether the issue is tax reform, conservation, or population control, debates in Congress are usually concerned with legislation affecting future events.

The forensic form of speeches to persuade is best illustrated by courtroom speaking. The questions answered in the courtroom involve the determination of the facts surrounding past events and are all forms of the basic question, "Is the defendant guilty?" The propositions presented are basically propositions of fact. Who actually pulled the trigger during an armed robbery? Was the defendant's gun the murder weapon? But speeches that affirm propositions of fact extend beyond the courtroom and include such questions as "What is the major cause of air pollution?" "Are grades a reliable index of how much a student knows?" "Is the 'energy crisis' real or contrived?" "Is water fluoridation more effective than fluoridated toothpaste in preventing tooth decay?"

The demonstrative speech was defined by Aristotle as a speech to praise or blame. Eulogies delivered at memorial services are good examples of this type of speaking. Fourth of July orations and Labor Day speeches also fall into this category. We might think of this type of speech, however, as being more inclusive than just praising or blaming, and also include speeches that affirm propositions of value. A speech of this nature attempts to determine the value of an object or policy by comparing it with values of similar acts or policies. Examples of propositions of value would include the value of requiring study of a foreign language, the value of owning a subcompact car, and the values of a college education.

Appeals. Whatever the form of the message, it must contain information that appeals to the intellect and the emotions of the audience and creates for them a belief in the speaker. When developing the message, the speaker should consider three types of appeals that he can use to make his speech attractive and compelling to his audience. To make his argument intellectually acceptable, the speaker should employ logical appeals. To compel the audience to believe in him, the speaker should employ ethical appeals. And to motivate the listeners to act according to his wishes, the speaker should employ emotional appeals. Each of these types of appeals or proofs is discussed separately below, although often a single statement may contain all three types of appeal.

Logical Appeals. People like to think of themselves as rational beings. Consequently, if a persuasive message is to be effective, reasons for accepting the ideas and actions called for by the speaker must be provided. The reasoning process and the supporting materials used to give credence to the proposition comprise the elements of logical proof. An academic advisor, for instance, might recommend to a student majoring in English that he take a course in logic. The student might well ask "Why?" The advisor is then required to furnish support for the recommendation. That support might consist of the testimony of other English majors who said that logic

> **In order to persuade a man of sense, you must first convince him, which is only done by satisfying his understanding of the reasonableness of what you propose to him.**
>
> HUGH BLAIR

had assisted them in understanding the subject matter of English, or the testimony of a well-known and respected educator, or some examples of benefits to be gained from taking the course. The forms of evidence available to the persuader and the tests of that evidence are discussed in Chapter 12.

Ethical Appeals. Ethical proof concerns the attitude of the audience toward the speaker. We discussed earlier in this chapter the elements of source credibility which comprise ethical proof. The speaker, however, may strengthen his credibility by inserting in the speech specific references concerning his relationship to the topic or the audience. For example, it is not unusual for politicians to reinforce their identity with the local region in which they are speaking by relating a story about the community or its citizens. This type of positive identification with the audience is well illustrated by Winston Churchill in Adapted Reading 7.3 and by Hubert Humphrey in Adapted Reading 7.4. Not only does it provide an effective introductory technique for a speech, but it also contributes to the identification of the speaker with the members of the audience, thereby increasing his credibility.

> **The passions are the only orators who always convince. They have a kind of natural art with infallible rules; and the most untutored man with passion is more persuasive than the most eloquent without.**
>
> LA ROCHEFOUCAULD

Emotional Appeals. The use of emotional appeals by a speaker is thought by some scholars to be antithetical to the use of rational or logical appeals because emotional excitement often impairs rational judgment. The speaker who appeals only to the emotions abrogates his responsibilities to the audience. But emotional appeals can be used to reinforce logical appeals, and if used well, can be the major factor in exciting human motives (see Adapted Reading 11.2).

Emotional excitement tends to express itself in action. It is not surprising that in the heat of competition, an athlete occasionally will attack an opponent or that teams sometime "clear the benches" in a general mêlée. Emotions run high during close contests and those emotions result in action. We are all subject to that kind of behavior. Because emotion provokes action, persuasive speakers often seek to arouse the feelings of their listeners.

Fear is an emotion frequently appealed to by persuasive speakers. The statement on every cigarette package, "Warning: The Surgeon General Has Determined That Cigarette Smoking Is Dangerous to Your Health," is an example of this fear appeal. Antismoking films and photographs comparing sections of lungs of smokers and nonsmokers represent a more intense fear appeal. Vivid depictions of automobile accidents in television broadcasts are other examples of appeals to fear. Some other emotions to which persuasive speakers frequently appeal are self-preservation, self-respect, approval by others, patriotism, freedom, love, hate, and personal gain, to mention only a few. See Adapted Reading 11.2 for a more detailed discussion of these appeals.

Because people hold on with varying intensity to different goals and attitudes, the effective persuader will analyze his audience to determine the goals and attitudes to which his listeners are most intensely committed. He should also be aware, however, that attempts to arouse excessive fear can lead to a rejection of his argument by the audience. The emotions should not be aroused beyond believable or common-sense levels.

A proper blending of logical, ethical, and emotional appeals is needed to produce a desired response from an audience. This blending requires a thorough knowledge of the topic and of the audience.

Language. An important ingredient of the persuasive message is language. Although language is discussed in Chapters 15 and 16, certain characteristics of language important to the persuasive speaker should be mentioned here.

The persuader should be conscious of the need for vividness and energy in the language he selects. Important in creating a vivid and forceful persuasive appeal is the *intensity* of the speaker's language. Intensity can be varied by the use of qualifiers and metaphors. For example, the statement, "the elimination of emission-control systems will increase air pollution," is more intense than the statement, "the elimination of emission-control systems will *probably* increase air pollution." The introduction of different modifiers would increase intensity even more, as in the statement, "the elimination of emission-control systems will *dramatically* increase air pollution."

The same statement can be made more intense by introducing metaphors. The following statement is more emotionally charged than the previous three: "the elimination of emission-control systems in automobiles will strangle the population with polluted air."

The positiveness with which something is claimed can also contribute to the intensity and immediacy of the persuasive message. The statement used in World War II, "We can, we will, we must," exemplifies three levels of certainty and urgency. To claim that *we can* do something is less immediate or urgent than the claim that *we will*, and, in turn, the term *we must* is even more urgent.

The loaded nature of language is exemplified by the controversy surrounding implementation of national health insurance policies. When the

> He who wants to persuade should put his trust not in the right argument, but in the right word.
>
> JOSEPH CONRAD

concept of national health insurance was introduced in the 1940s, the opponents referred to it as "socialized medicine." The term is no longer used but was effective as a prejudicial and emotionally charged word that contributed to the long delay in initiating a form of government-supported health care for the American public. In other words, what you call something can affect the listener's reaction to it. The persuasive speaker should seek to find language that is acceptable to his audience but also capable of arousing their passions and feelings.

The Audience

The fourth constituent of persuasive communication is the audience. Analyzing the audience and occasion is discussed in Chapter 4, but the persuader has unique reasons to be conscious of audience composition. Based on their attitude toward a topic, audiences may be classified as friendly, hostile, or neutral. The hostile and friendly audiences have special characteristics important to the persuasive speaker because they may influence the speaker's division of his materials.

The Hostile Audience. In most speeches to persuade, the speaker faces an audience that is at least partially hostile, doubtful, or apathetic toward his ideas. Indeed, if no one in the audience disagreed with him, he would have no need to try to convince or persuade.

An extreme example of a speaker facing a hostile audience situation is the president confronting a group of reform militants on the White House lawn. Under these circumstances, the emotions of the audience may be so great that communication is almost impossible. And to greet hostility with defiance certainly will not create an atmosphere conducive to mutual understanding. Assuming, however, that the speaker is determined to be heard and that the audience is willing to give him a chance, an adroit speaker can at times arrange his materials in such a way that his listeners' antagonism can be overcome. Basic to this approach is the speaker's emphasis on areas of agreement and common interest with the audience. By locating and developing areas of common ground, the speaker not only builds a bridge permitting communication with his audience, but may also win the respect of his hearers. Gaining the listener's respect is important because, normally, the audience will transfer its hostility toward the speaker's ideas to the speaker himself. Therefore, arranging his materials so that they build confidence and respect for him is often important to the speaker in persuading hostile groups. Pat Jefferson describes how Stokely Carmichael adapted to a predominantly white and hostile audience in Adapted Reading 11.3.

Having introduced material to gain personal acceptance and to establish common ground with his auditors, the speaker is then ready to begin developing his theme. With audiences that are opposed to his central thought, the speaker probably should adopt an inductive approach. In the inductive approach, the speaker refrains from stating his main idea or conclusion at the outset. This approach permits the speaker to introduce ideas and factual information acceptable to the audience, to lay a foundation for agreement, and to lead his unsuspecting listeners toward the conclusion favored by the speaker. Use of this method of organization prevents immediate rejection of the speaker's proposal by his listeners.

To illustrate the inductive method of organization, one might take an imaginary speaker who believes that local taxes should be increased to improve the public schools. No one favors higher taxes, so the speaker knows that he has an unpopular position. However, rather than announcing his position early in the speech, thereby creating a negative attitude toward his proposal, the speaker might, instead, first develop several arguments on which he and his audience could agree. For example, he might first suggest that one of the most important duties of the community is to educate its youth — something all of his listeners would probably accept. He might then stress the advantages of a good education to the community and to the young people. From there, the speaker might proceed to his second main contention, that the local school system is not, at present, providing its students with the best possible education. While the audience may be hesitant to accept this argument, if the speaker can demonstrate that the local school is inferior — perhaps by comparisons to other schools, with statistics revealing substandard teacher salaries, with data from educational tests, and with specific information on the lack of equipment and facilities — he can probably convince his auditors that something needs to be done.

He is then ready to move to his third point, that improving the school system will cost money. Although the audience may not like the idea of having to spend more on its schools, they would undoubtedly understand that the improvements outlined by the speaker could not be made without additional funds. But, in the backs of their minds, the listeners probably entertain the hope that they will not have to provide the money. So, the speaker's next step would be to show that alternative sources are not available. Admitting that the state and federal governments might provide some financial assistance, the speaker must demonstrate that outside funds alone would not be sufficient to effect the needed improvements.

He is now ready to develop his central thought: that only a tax increase can provide the funds necessary to improve the schools. Having prepared the audience logically and psychologically by developing the importance of the problem, by removing doubts and objections, and by eliminating consideration of possible alternatives, the speaker has a better chance of winning acceptance of his proposal than he would had he opened with a direct statement saying that he favored higher taxes to aid the schools.

The speaker who organizes his materials so that areas of common interest and concern to himself and the audience are developed first, followed by an inductive method leading to his conclusion, may still fail to win the desired response from an extremely hostile audience. However, this approach usually guarantees at least a fair hearing and may reduce or even eliminate the hostility of his auditors.

The Friendly Audience. Friendly audiences are characterized by individuals who are already interested in and favorably disposed toward the speaker's subject. A speaker at a national political convention, for example, invariably faces a friendly audience, as does the minister from his pulpit, or the student who argues that every member of the class should be awarded an "A." Because the friendly audience is already inclined to agree with him, the speaker need not concentrate on argumentative development of his theme in the body of the speech. Instead, his main objective is either to intensify already existing feelings or to ensure action.

In choosing a method of division for this type of audience, the speaker will be influenced more by the attitudes of his listeners than by the nature of his subject matter. Thus, although his topic might lend itself to chronological, spatial, or some other method of development, the speaker may arrange his material in another way that will better motivate his listeners. For example, he might elect to concentrate on the direct benefits to the audience, the urgency of the problem, or the more popular arguments in favor of his proposal.

Unlike the speech delivered to a hostile group, in an address to a friendly audience the speaker probably will find it unnecessary to employ the inductive approach. Instead, he will develop his topic deductively, stating his main idea or conclusions at the outset and then providing whatever supporting material he feels is needed. Since his audience is favorably predisposed, stating his position clearly at the beginning establishes a kind of immediate rapport with the auditors.

SUMMARY

The persuasive speaker consciously designs communication strategies that will shape perceptions, modify attitudes, or influence actions of other people. It is important, therefore, that he employ all of the means available to him to make his message compelling to the audience. An element that plays a vital role in the audience's acceptance is source credibility, derived from a variety of influences including the position of the speaker, his reputation, goodwill, intellectual integrity, knowledge, sincerity, and delivery.

The message of a persuasive speech can be deliberative (affirming propositions of policy), forensic (affirming propositions of fact), or demonstrative (affirming propositions of value). Whatever the form of the persuasive message, it should include logical, ethical, and emotional appeals—all phrased in compelling language characterized by energy and vividness. Intensity of language can be achieved by using well-chosen qualifiers and metaphors.

Audience attitudes in a persuasive setting are important to the speaker and may influence the speaker's division of his materials. For a hostile audience, he may wish to adopt an inductive approach, delaying the statement of his proposition until late in the speech or until he has established common ground and areas of agreement with his auditors. In organizing a speech for a friendly audience, the inductive approach usually is not necessary and the speaker can state his position in a clear and straightforward manner at the outset.

TELL IT LIKE IT IS
Saul D. Alinsky

SAUL D. ALINSKY

The area of experience and communication is fundamental to the organizer. An organizer can communicate only within the areas of experience of his audience; otherwise there is no communication. The organizer, in his constant hunt for patterns, universalities, and meaning, is always building up a body of experience.

Through his imagination he is constantly moving in on the happenings of others, identifying with them and extracting their happenings into his own mental digestive system and thereby accumulating more experience. It is essential for communication that he know of their experiences. Since one can communicate only through the experiences of the other, it becomes clear that the organizer begins to develop an abnormally large body of experience.

He learns the local legends, anecdotes, values, idioms. He listens to small talk. He refrains from rhetoric foreign to the local culture: he knows that worn-out words like "white racist" and "fascist pig" have been so spewed about that using them is now within the negative experiences of the local people, serving only to identify the speaker as "one of those nuts" and to turn off any further communication.

And yet the organizer must not try to fake it. He must be himself. I remember a first meeting with Mexican-American leaders in a California barrio where they served me a special Mexican dinner. When we were halfway through I put down my knife and fork saying, "My God! Do you eat this stuff because you like it or because you have to? I think it's as lousy as the Jewish kosher crap I had to eat as a kid!" Suddenly barriers began to come down as they all began talking and laughing. They were so accustomed to the Anglo who would rave about the beauty of Mexican food even though they knew it was killing him, the Anglo who had memorized a few Spanish phrases with the inevitable *hasta la vista,* that it was a refreshingly honest experience to them. The incident became a legend to many and you would hear them say, for instance, "He has as much use for that guy as Alinsky has for Mexican food." A number of the Mexican-Americans present confessed that they only ate some of those dishes when they entertained an Anglo. The same faking goes on with whites on certain items of blacks' "soul food."

There is a difference between honesty and rude disrespect of another's tradition. The organizer will err far less by being himself than by engaging in "professional techniques" when the people really know better. It shows respect for people to be honest, as in the Mexican dinner episode; they are being treated as people and not guinea pigs being techniqued. It is most important that this action be understood in context. Prior to my remark there had been a warm personal discussion of the problems of the people. They knew not only of my concern about their plight but that I liked them as people. I felt their response in friendship, and we were together. It is in this totality of the situation that I did what, otherwise, would have been offensive.

ADAPTED READING 11.2

MOTIVATIONAL SITUATIONS AND RHETORICAL STRATEGIES

Otis M. Walter

For over two thousand years, rhetoricians have attempted to develop an understanding of the forces that impel the human being to act. Various concepts of "emotion," "drive," "need," "desire," and "motive" have been evolved. A recent textbook in psychology states what seems to be the most common contemporary division of these springs of action when it classifies them into primary forces and those forces derived from the primary ones:

> Since man is an organism before he becomes a person, and since physiological homeostasis must be maintained if he is to live at all, it is common usage to speak of his physiological needs as primary, his social, ethical, and religious needs as secondary, as derived. . . .

Brembeck and Howell have adapted this kind of analysis to rhetoric and list such physiological drives as hunger, thirst, sex, and security from bodily injury. The same authors include such socially derived impulses as subsistence motives, social approval motives, conformity motives, and mastery motives. A similar treatment is found in Monroe's more elementary book when he says:

> Fundamentally, there are four primary motives which influence human beings. Behind every act, belief, or emotion will be found one or more of these basic desires:
>
> 1. Self-preservation and the desire for physical well-being.
> 2. Freedom from external restraint.
> 3. Preservation and increase of self-esteem (ego expansion).
> 4. Preservation of the human race. . . .

Monroe lists eighteen motives derived from these primary ones, such as acquisition and saving, adventure, companionship, creating, curiosity, and destruction.

It is my aim here to show that motivation may be analyzed in a somewhat more detailed and perhaps more useful way.

A major reason for developing a more thorough analysis of motivation

From "Toward an Analysis of Motivation," *Quarterly Journal of Speech*, October 1955, pp. 271–278.

in rhetoric is that lists of motives together with discussions of the nature of motives furnish the student of rhetoric with only an incomplete analysis of the process of motivation. Such motives as the desire for security may be looked upon as "generalized goals" toward which the organism moves. The generalized goal of security may be gratified by securing a specific goal such as a better job. Thus it is that motivation, as treated in rhetoric, hardly involves more than a consideration of certain kinds of general and specific goals. Yet the process of motivation is more complex than a movement toward goals. For example, what is the effect on motivation of a goal from which the individual is restrained by a barrier? It will be shown later that such a situation significantly conditions the problem of persuasion. What implications are there for persuasion when one attempts to appeal to a motive and the process of gratifying that motive will subject one to danger or the possible loss of other goals? What are the implications for persuasion when goals, motives, or desires are in conflict? Most treatments of motivation ignore these significant and complicating variations. Furthermore, attitudes, sentiments, stereotypes, opinions, and the like, though related to motivation, are commonly treated as separate entities. It is possible, however, to integrate them into a theory of motivation. If motive situations involve barriers, threats, conflicting attitudes, sentiments, stereotypes, opinions, etc., how do these matters affect what Aristotle calls "the available means of persuasion?" Certainly no mere list of motives, however long, can make clear all the possibilities and implications of these problems to the student of rhetoric. The simple situation in which the individual is motivated toward a goal is by no means the only situation in which motivation operates. We must develop a theory that will include and utilize these complicating features of motivation. The purpose of this paper is to explain a coherent system by which these variations of motivational behavior may be utilized by the speaker.

It may be possible that the study of motivation would be advanced if we, temporarily at least, abandoned the search for motives. To begin with, we could describe motivational behavior by studying motivation *situations* in which the human being behaves.

Let us examine some basic motivational situations and explore their rhetorical implications. It seems to me that there are five basic situations.

The *Difficulty Situation* is the most fundamental of all. The prerequisite for it is that an individual or group of individuals perceives a difficulty.

> Before he moved his arm, the baby was subjected to . . . an annoying pressure, or he was attracted by a stimulus—object not readily within his grasp; the troubled children were restrained from . . . a high school grade . . . ; the would-be solver was challenged by the puzzle. Something was wrong in every case, some thwarting of the normal processes of the individual. . . .

Let us explore some of the rhetorical implications of this motivational situation. By "rhetorical implications" I mean the possible lines of argument a speaker may take with an audience. The implications given here will be only suggestive of the vast number of possibilities that might occur. But among other things, here are a few of the rhetorical possibilities:

A. To deny that there is a difficulty, to belittle the importance of the difficulty, to point out that yielding to the difficulty is unworthy, or to point out that others in similar situations paid no heed to the difficulty.

B. To cause the audience to realize the importance and pressing nature of the difficulty as something deserving or requiring their attention.

C. To locate and define the difficulty, to urge the audience to define the difficulty and locate the causes of the problem, or to set up procedures by which such definitions could be evolved and such causes located.

D. To attack any particular formulation of the difficulty as irrational, unjust, unworthy.

E. To direct attention to other difficulties on the grounds that they are more significant, more pressing, more possible of solution.

The *Goal-Oriented Situation* arises when individuals are considering the possibilities of certain rather well-defined goals as solutions to the difficulty. The rhetorical possibilities of this kind of situation are significantly different from those in the previous motivational situation. Here are a few suggestions of these possibilities:

A. To urge the audience to achieve a certain goal, the speaker argues that:
1. The goal is one that can produce benefits for the audience: pleasure, wealth, security, prestige.
2. The goal is one that is deserved by the members of the audience.
3. The goal is easily obtainable.
4. The goal will bring benefits for those with whom the audience is identified: family, friends, socio-economic class, occupational group.
5. The goal will be taken by those less in need or less deserving unless the audience responds quickly.
6. The goal is necessary for survival or well-being, or it will, at least, remove the difficulty that began the problem.
B. To urge that the audience give up a certain goal, the speaker argues that:
1. The reverse of the above in "A" is true, namely, that the goal is in no way necessary or that it could not remove the original difficulty.
2. An entirely different approach to the problem is needed, or other goals than those desired at the moment are superior in several ways in removing the difficulty.
3. There is no Difficulty Situation, and hence no need for any concern about goals.
4. The goal is not what the individual or group wants as a solution to their

difficulty; or it would be injurious if they possessed it; or it produces benefits of a questionable nature; or it cannot be obtained as easily as other goals; or there are more worthwhile goals.

The *Barrier Situation* arises when goals become complicated by the interposition of a barrier between the individual and a desired object. To a small child, for example, the goal may be a piece of candy and the barrier the glass case. Or the goal to the college student may be a good grade and the barrier the amount of work required to obtain the grade. In such cases, the individual is *restrained* from a goal. Such situations are extremely common. No student becomes a lawyer without years of study, no runner a champion without patience and effort, no wife a good cook without long trial and error. It could be said, in fact, that we are always separated from unachieved goals, even if the separation be one of time alone. Let us consider the rhetorical possibilities in this kind of situation:

A. To urge the audience to achieve the goal, despite the barrier, the speaker argues that:
   1. The goal is worth achieving. (See "A" under Goal-Oriented Situation.)
   2. The barrier is contemptible, unintelligent, unnecessary, or unjust.
   3. The barrier works to the advantage of our enemies.
   4. The agent that raised the barrier is contemptuous, unintelligent, or unjust.
   5. The agent that has raised the barrier has harmed us or treated us with indifference or with disparagement.
   6. The agent that raised the barrier acts as if he were doing us a favor.
   7. The agent that raised the barrier has given to others that which we deserve.
   8. The agent that raised the barrier has tried to make us feel shameful when we do not deserve to feel so.
   9. The agent that raised the barrier has injured or treated with indifference or disparagement those with whom we identify ourselves (family, friends, home, country, occupation, class).
   10. The agent that raised the barrier has slighted us, or those with whom we are identified, in regard to our strongest virtues.
   11. The agent that raised the barrier has received good treatment at our hands but has not returned it, or has returned less than he received, and has done so deliberately.
B. To urge the audience to give up the goal, the speaker argues that:
   1. There is no basic difficulty that requires the goal or the goal is not worth obtaining. (See "A" under Difficulty Situation.)
   2. The opposite of the factors in "A" above are true.
   3. There are extenuating circumstances such as these: The barrier is a necessary one, or was placed there because of our own desires, or was raised inadvertently by some act of our own, or those who raised it did so for our own good, or did not mean to cause us harm.

C. To urge the audience to detour to a substitute goal, the speaker attempts to do one of the following:
   1. Weaken the desire for the goal and the desirability of surmounting the barrier by the material suggested in "B" above.
   2. Emphasize the value of a substitute goal as being superior, or easier to obtain, as in "A" under Goal-Oriented Situation.
D. To urge the audience to a further study of the barrier and goal-oriented situation, the speaker attempts to do one of the following:
   1. Point out that the barrier is not understood properly and does not have the nature, strength, and characteristics usually attributed to it.
   2. Urge the audience to study further, or set up a procedure for studying the means of eradication, reducing, outflanking this goal, or finding ways of changing to other goals.

The *Threat Situation* appears when we find that we are moved to action because of a threat that may harm us. Thus, the young man may wish a goodnight kiss, but may fear that the young lady may slap him too hard to make the attempt worth while. Entire nations may be motivated by a threat and give up the pursuits of certain goals in favor of protecting themselves.

Notice the difference in the rhetorical possibilities of the Threat Situation from other situations. The following possibilities are suggested:

A. To urge the audience that the threat is strong enough to merit their attention, the speaker argues that:
   1. The threat has the power to harm or destroy the audience.
   2. The threat has the power to harm or destroy those identified with the audience: family, friends, institutions, occupational group, class, country.
   3. The threat is unscrupulous, immoral, merciless.
   4. Others who have been in a similar position have considered the force formidable, or if not, they were harmed or destroyed by it when they did not expect it.
B. To urge the audience to give up the goal, inhibit its desire for the goal, or expend its energies toward a different goal, the speaker argues that:
   1. The threat is too strong:
      a. The threat has the power to destroy or harm the audience, or is superior to the audience's power to resist, and is close at hand.
      b. The threat will harm or destroy those with which the audience is identified: home, family, friends, institutions, country, occupational group, class.
      c. Others who are like the audience consider the force formidable, or have been defeated by it although they did not expect to be.
      d. The threat is unscrupulous, immoral, merciless, unjust.
      e. The weaknesses rather than the strength of the audience have been attacked.
      f. Help is far away, we have no allies and no one to share our fate.
   2. The goal is not worth seeking (or keeping):

a. The goal is not worth effort or pain required to get it; it would be injurious if we possessed it; it could not be enjoyed if we had it; it produces benefits of questionable nature, or benefits that would be outweighed by the threat.

b. Other goals that can be obtained more easily are more worth while or are as good, or are satisfactory substitutes.

c. Others of as great nobility as the audience have accepted other goals in similar circumstances, or have given up the ones that threaten.

C. To urge the audience to resist or combat the threat, the speaker seeks to do the following:

1. Minimize the power of the threat by refuting any of the ideas in "B" above. (In certain cases, however, the opposite procedure should be used. When the audience fails to comprehend the magnitude of the threat, it is often sound to build up the perception of the ideas mentioned in "A" above by dramatizing some of them.)

2. Support some of the following ideas that are most appropriate:

a. Great effort can reduce the threat, has done so in similar circumstances.

b. Justice and morality are on the side of those combating the threat; the audience must join them, or must resist alone.

c. There is a plan by which the threat may be successfully combated or circumvented.

d. The audience is characterized by courage and greater power than is commonly believed or than can be defeated or harmed by the force.

e. Others less able than the audience have combated a similar force successfully and have done so courageously.

The last of the five basic motivational situations is the *Identification Situation*. It arises when human beings act for the sake of other groups. Charity drives, heroism, and much self-sacrifice come about in situations of this kind, where the individual who is acting is often concerned primarily with the welfare of another person. The hero did not jump into the water in order to pull out the drowning boy to increase his prestige, but because he felt identified with the boy and felt the boy's welfare to be his own. Let us examine the rhetorical implications of this kind of situation:

A. To urge that one group extend help or otherwise identify itself with another group, the speaker argues thus:

1. The individual or group of individuals who are to feel this identification must feel that those on behalf of whom help will be given are similar to those who will help. Similarity may be in aims, background attitudes, methods of facing life, education, status, hope, plight, foibles.

2. The group to be aided is in need, or is facing difficulties not its own fault, or has been strong in the face of a threat.

B. To urge that sympathy or sympathetic acts awarded a given individual or group should not be given, the speaker argues thus:
1. The individuals in the group to be given help are different in basic ways from those in the audience.
2. Their problem is not a great one, has been exaggerated by them, is their own fault; or they are able to solve it alone.
3. The granting of aid at this time would expose the audience to danger or would weaken them; or the granting of aid is unnecessary.

The attempt here has been to point out that the most basic tendencies in human motivation resolve into a question that has not yielded enough knowledge about the process of motivation. It is my hope that an examination of situations may lead to more productive data on the nature of motivation. Five basic motivational situations have been described. The premises of many arguments that may be used in these situations have been outlined in order to bring us closer to the possibility of analyzing the available means of persuasion. Matters involving the audience's attitudes, stereotypes, sentiments, and opinions have been included in this development of rhetorical implications. This kind of analysis will, perhaps, provide the rhetorician with a useful approach to the analysis of motivation.

ADAPTED READING 11.3
AUDIENCE ADAPTATION OF A BLACK MILITANT
Pat Jefferson

One of the most controversial figures in the 1960s was Stokely Carmichael of the Student Nonviolent Coordinating Committee. In this analysis, Pat Jefferson contrasts Carmichael's audience adaptation to a predominantly white audience in Nashville, Tennessee, with that of his talks to black groups. Carmichael spoke in Nashville on April 8, 1967.

The Nashville citizenry associated Carmichael's name with riots, and as early as March 25, announced its displeasure with Vanderbilt University for inviting him to speak at Impact '67, a symposium examining the individual and his future in American society. The front page editorial of the *Nashville Banner* succinctly stated this position in the headline: "Hate Speeling Carmichael Unwelcome in the City." In the interim — between the appearance of the headline and the symposium — the Tennessee State Legislature, the American Legion Post 5, Nashville's largest radio station, WLAC, and the *Nashville Banner* denounced Carmichael, requested Chancellor Alexander Heard to

From "The Magnificent Barbarian: The Rhetoric of Stokely Carmichael," Indiana University (unpublished M.A. thesis), pp. 46–55.

withdraw Vanderbilt's invitation, and warned him that Carmichael's speech would incite a riot. Vanderbilt officials, however, met the challenge. Chancellor Heard reaffirmed the right of free speech and complimented Impact for organizing a "stimulating program of diverse speakers." Over four thousand people, predominantly white, filled the Memorial Gymnasium at Vanderbilt University. Students crowded the aisles and lined the walls anticipating the arrival of the controversial speaker. Police patrolled the area, plainclothesmen scattered throughout the audience to discourage anticipated riots, and national television networks stood by for immediate news coverage if disturbances occurred. Carmichael, however, adapted well to the situation and delivered a scholarly talk on black power. Impressed, most auditors concluded that he "appeared in sharp contrast to what [they] expected." A listening banker "didn't realize Carmichael could conduct himself in such a manner," and Frank A. Rose, President of the University of Alabama and the following speaker, deleted the portion of his prepared address attacking Carmichael for his "passionate intensity," because the speech was not as militant as he had anticipated. Carmichael, thus, left a favorable impression on the Impact audience. The American public, however, associated the Negro celebrity with black power, incitement to riot, and violence. . . .

A hero to poor blacks and a controversial celebrity to others, Carmichael's reputation had an unusual effect on his ethical appeal. . . .

While the name Stokely Carmichael sparked fear and hatred in the white community, it injected courage and pride in oppressed blacks. His reputation illustrated the polarities of ethos, hindering his persuasibility to whites, but enhancing his effectiveness to Negroes. When he spoke before a white group, he spent the first portion of his address minimizing the unfavorable impressions held by his auditors. At Vanderbilt University, for example, he achieved his goal largely through humor. Carmichael seized upon the audience's respect for the concept of free speech and complimented them on their courage to fight for this principle. Then he launched a humorous attack on Nashville's anti-Carmichael newspaper. Announcing that he would read from the "modern day theatre of the absurd—the *Nashville Banner*," he urged the "honkies of the *Banner*" to write "comic strip" on the front cover and suggested they leave the gymnasium, because his lecture was on an "in-tel-lec-tual lev-el." The white audience then rose for the first of three standing ovations. Consequently, before he began reading his prepared manuscript, he succeeded in strengthening his ethos. By the time he completed the speech, his auditors moved from a position of tolerance and curiosity to a favorable inclination towards the man. If his concept of black power did not gain acceptance, Carmichael did. His outstanding personality and personal magnetism contributed greatly to his effectiveness as a speaker. Thus while his prior reputation was an initial disadvantage, he skillfully enhanced his ethos as he spoke —developing it into his greatest single source of persuasion.

Carmichael adapted to audiences by relating his remarks to their sets of values. At Nashville, he realized Vanderbilt students supported the right of free speech and made reference to the concept immediately. Before a white audience, however, alignment with their value system for the most part ended with his opening remarks. Carmichael, believing that his role in the white community was to relate the mood of the black, bluntly told his auditors his conception of the Negro's innermost thoughts. Since Carmichael blamed the white man for the Negro's degradation, few whites accepted his black power philosophy *in toto,* because to support it meant finding themselves guilty. Some facets of the program gained at least a sympathetic ear, however. On certain subpoints, Carmichael appealed to the white man's sense of fair play and justice. When he questioned the validity of nonviolent schools in the racist South, for example, he asked, "Can they conduct it [a nonviolent school] among the white people in Granada where six-foot-tall men kick little black children?" Such pathos would naturally evoke a compassionate response from the audience.

When he spoke to a black audience, he appealed to their basic needs. Black power became the answer to better living conditions, economic security, and an improved psychology. Carmichael gave the black man a new sense of dignity. Dispelling the stereotype of the lazy Negro, he repetitively insisted, "We are the hardest working people in this country. . . . It is we who dig the ditches. It is we who are the maids. It is we who pick the cotton. It is we who pick the fruit, and they let the Mexicans come in with us." Interrupted by zealous applause, Carmichael concluded, "That's right. Yes, sir. It is we who are the porters. It is we who are the elevator boys. It is we who are the garbage collectors, and it is we who are unemployed." He upgraded the status of their menial jobs even further when he maintained that if hard work led to success, as this country promised, the black man would own the United States "lock, stock, and barrel."

Black power was also a call for the Negro intellectual to come home. Carmichael appealed to the intellectual's sense of duty and reminded his auditors that individualism was a luxury they could no longer afford. Group standards had to be raised before equality would be reached. "You have a duty and a responsibility to come back to the black ghettoes and help your people," insisted Carmichael.

He employed the device of common ground when he attempted to minimize the strife in Negro communities. He spoke of gang shootings, killings, and other forms of violence that existed in the black ghettoes and emphasized, "We ought to teach each other to love each other." An intelligent and educated man, Carmichael used the plain clothes device when talking to black audiences. At Tennessee State University in Nashville, for example, he shed his suit coat shortly after he began speaking and remarked, "I try to keep it on but it never works. I guess I'm just a field nigger." Perhaps the most effective emotional device used was a form of exact repetition or slogan. Carmichael told his auditors that the war in Vietnam would end only when young men who were made to fight said, "Hell no. We ain't going." Crowds modified this phrase and often chanted "Hell no. Won't go" in thunderous unison while waiting for him to begin his address. During the speech, cries of "black power" rang through the air. Such uniformity of response created a polarized audience and thus led to greater uniformity of response.

ADDITIONAL READINGS

Baird, A. Craig, Franklin H. Knower and Samuel L. Becker, *General Speech Communication* (New York: McGraw-Hill, 1971), chap. 21, "Persuasion: Cognitive Domain" and chap. 22, "Persuasion: Affective Domain."

Burgoon, Michael, *Approaching Speech Communication* (New York: Holt, Rinehart & Winston, 1974), chap. 1, "Source Variables" and chap. 10, "Persuasion."

McBurney, James and Ernest Wrage, *Guide to Good Speech* (Englewood Cliffs, N.J.: Prentice-Hall, 1965), chap. 18, "Advocacy" and chap. 19, "Evocation."

Mudd, Charles S. and Malcolm Sillars, *Speech: Content and Communication* (San Francisco: Chandler, 1969), chap. 18, "Speaking to Persuade."

Ross, Raymond, *Speech Communication: Fundamentals and Practice* (Englewood Cliffs, N.J.: Prentice-Hall, 1970), chap. 2, "Emotion and Confidence" and chap. 9, "The Psychology of Persuasion."

STUDY QUESTIONS

1. Under what conditions should a speaker not reveal his purpose or central thought early in his speech?
2. How might a speaker overcome hostility among members of his audience?
3. Under what circumstances would a speaker elect to give a deliberative speech? forensic? demonstrative?
4. How might a speaker achieve highly charged language? To what end?
5. What are the advantages of using an inductive method of organizing a speech? When is a deductive method more effective?
6. What is meant by the phrase, "Excitement tends to express itself in action"?
7. What is meant by the term "intensity of language"? What is its application to persuasion?
8. How does Saul Alinsky demonstrate the destruction of communication "barriers" in an "alien" environment?
9. In what ways did Stokely Carmichael attempt to adapt to his audience in the speeches discussed in Adapted Reading 11.3?
10. How do "motivational situations" as discussed by Otis Walter (Adapted Reading 11.2) differ from "motives"? How many are there? What are the rhetorical strategies available to the persuader for each situation?

EXERCISES

1. After selecting a topic for a persuasive speech, prepare two introductions, one for a friendly audience and one for an unsympathetic audience.
2. Prepare an outline for a speech to persuade to be presented to a friendly audience. Show how it might be revised for presentation to a hostile audience.
3. Write a 500-word essay analyzing the logical, emotional, and ethical appeals in Pat Jefferson's essay (Adapted Reading 11.3) about Stokely Carmichael's audience adaptation.
4. Read a persuasive speech in *Vital Speeches* or *Representative American Speeches*. Find examples of how the speaker attempted to win support for his cause. Identify specific use of logical, emotional, and ethical appeals. Make special note of unusual or striking phrases, metaphors, qualifiers, and other motive appeals.
5. Using the phrase "excitement tends to express itself in action," observe several speech events and (1) locate the appeals that excite, and (2) describe the action that followed the appeal.
6. Select a persuasive speech from *Vital Speeches* or *Representative American Speeches*. Revise the speech to make it more persuasive by intensifying the language.

CHAPTER 12

SUPPORTING MATERIALS: PERSUASION

Effective supporting material is particularly important when a speaker seeks to convince or persuade. Audiences tend to listen to informing, entertaining, and inspiring speeches with an open mind or even a favorable attitude; so the speaker, in these cases, need be concerned only with maintaining interest as he clarifies his topic. However, in argumentative speeches he faces the difficulty of dealing with an audience which, at least in part, is apathetic, skeptical, or opposed to his ideas. Indeed, if some members of his audience were not unconvinced or opposed, the speech would be unnecessary, for he would have no need to attempt to alter their beliefs. The critical or questioning attitude of an audience toward persuasive speeches demands that the speaker apply rigorous standards in his choice of supporting material.

Effective argumentation is based on sound supporting material, or evidence, and valid reasoning. Although a speaker's message may be made more attractive by appeals to the feelings of his listeners (emotional proof) or enhanced by his good reputation (ethical proof), it is rare that an antagonistic audience can be won over by these factors alone. Essential to any argument that will withstand critical scrutiny, both at the time of delivery and upon later reflection, is a solid foundation of logical proof or factual evidence.

Our judgments when we are pleased and friendly are not the same as when we are pained and hostile.

ARISTOTLE

In supporting his beliefs, the speaker has an obligation to present evidence that is relevant to his arguments. Barnet Baskerville elaborates on this in Adapted Reading 12.2, condemning a common practice among speakers of substituting what appears to be pertinent evidence for the facts really needed to prove a contention. This sham evidence, according to Baskerville, creates an "illusion of proof" where actual proof is nonexistent. Additional ways in which speakers sometimes attempt to evade rational argument include emotional and humorous appeals, the *argumentum ad hominem*, and the *tu quoque* (Adapted Readings 12.1 and 12.3).

The responsible speaker's main appeal will be to the minds of his listeners, with emotional and ethical appeals used sparingly and appropriately.

> Let our discourses be founded upon reason, and let us establish everything we advance with solid and convincing arguments.
>
> THOMAS GIBBONS

FACTS

What Are Facts?

Although everyone talks a great deal about facts, most people probably could not explain just what a fact is. To the scientist, a fact is empirically verifiable data. More generally defined, facts are the materials from which we attempt to draw conclusions or between which we seek to establish relationships. Facts, in contrast to theories or opinions which are merely speculative, have to do with the existence and nature of things.

Facts are regarded as true only because those best fitted to judge proclaim them so. Most of what is considered fact can be determined by the judgment of the general population and is based on simple observation. For example, the reader undoubtedly feels competent to decide whether this is a sheet of paper, whether the sun rises in the east, and whether it is raining at any given moment. Most people, however, probably do not feel qualified to determine many other matters, such as the genetic effects of atomic radiation, the acoustical properties of an auditorium, or how leukemia affects the blood. In these instances, the layman defers to the judgment of accepted authorities in the field. The practical test, then, of facts is whether they are sanctioned by common knowledge and by the judgment of experts. But we must remember that both the rank and file of people and the experts continually demonstrate that they are not infallible in assessing facts.

Are Facts Provable?

It is not uncommon to hear references to "proven facts" and statements such as "I know that is true. It has been proven to be a fact." Such comments raise the question: Can facts always be proven? The answer is no. And, because facts cannot always be proven, it follows that some things that are regarded as fact have never been proven.

While much of the body of knowledge considered to be fact can be demonstrated through some kind of systematic "proof," if proof is regarded as a scientific, mathematical, or experimental testing, then a great many facts can be said to be unproven or unprovable. Much of what is fact is the result of observation rather than methodological testing. For example, "John was absent from class Wednesday," "That is a desk," "The Declaration of Independence was written in 1776," "The Mississippi River flows through Louisiana," and "I have a pear tree growing in my back yard" are statements which, if correct, are factual. But they are facts not because they have been scientifically proven to be so, but because persons qualified to judge such matters agree that each statement is a fact. Their status as facts rests not on their being proven, but on personal observation. Even facts that are derived through scientific research and carefully controlled experimentation, in the final analysis, are based on the observations of the scientist or researcher who must interpret what he has discovered or proven.

Are Facts Always True?

Surprisingly, no. To the best of our knowledge, everything we accept as fact is true; we regard it as truth and, accordingly, base our reasoning and decisions on it. However, at any moment, materials accepted as factual may be demonstrated to be false or untrue. For example, experts at one time regarded it as a fact that the earth was not round. All charting, map-making, and scientific thought rested on the fact that the earth was flat. It would have been unthinkable then to suggest that the earth was round, just as today it is unthinkable to suggest that the earth is not spheroid. Later, when it was demonstrated that the earth is not flat, it was necessary for man to correct and readjust all calculations and thought based on the formerly accepted fact. With our advanced technology, it seems inconceivable that what we *know* to be facts today could be in error, but time and progress will probably demonstrate that many presently accepted facts are untrue. So, while one may say that all facts are true today or at least presently regarded as being true, it cannot be said that all that is now considered as factual will always be true.

If facts deal with what is certain or true, what is the opposite of a fact? A falsehood or untruth could hardly be regarded as its opposite, for if something is accepted as being false or untrue, it has much the same status of certainty as a fact. Thus, if certainty and acceptability are criteria for calling something a fact, words indicating uncertainty would be appropriate opposites. So, one might say that the opposite of a fact is an *uncertainty*, a *theory*, an *opinion*, a *controversy*, a *belief*, or an *hypothesis*.

If a division of opinion is the mark of a nonfact, how widely must something be accepted before it may be regarded as fact? If the majority of those capable of deciding believe something to be true, is it then a fact? Certainly not, for if that were the case, it would be necessary to classify as fact a great many things that clearly are opinions. Popularity does not guarantee that one political candidate is better qualified than another, that a particular product is best, or that one philosophy is correct, whether the judges be laymen or experts.

So long as a difference of opinion exists among competent observers, the matter remains in the realm of belief, opinion, or theory. Unanimity of opinion is necessary before the label *fact* can correctly be applied to a condition, circumstance, or relationship. By this formula, anything universally acclaimed as fact becomes theory, opinion, or belief when qualified judges begin to doubt its accuracy. This is not meant to suggest that a fact becomes an opinion whenever human error or misunderstanding temporarily leads an otherwise competent judge to dissent. Everyone misjudges from time to time. Therefore, it is quite possible that well-qualified judges might momentarily question the validity of an otherwise accepted fact. If after further investigation they perceive their error and unanimity of opinion is restored, the fact remains a fact. If, on the other hand, the critics continue to question the accuracy of an alleged fact, then clearly the matter has fallen into the realm of controversy or conjecture and can no longer be regarded as fact.

That a concept is not a fact should not lead one to dismiss it as having no worth. A large part of every person's life is based on theories, opinions, and attitudes. Most religious, political, philosophical, and moral beliefs and codes rest largely on theory rather than fact. In their daily lives, people behave as they do, not because it is a fact that their conduct is right but simply because the individuals believe it to be best.

In speech, both theoretical and factual materials are useful in influencing others. However, it is important that the speaker recognize the difference between the two: that he know what is accepted as fact and therefore needs no proof, and what is not factual and requires supporting documentation before it will be accepted by some listeners.

In order to test your knowledge of the difference between facts and theories or opinions, read the 15 statements listed below and classify each as either factual or theoretical.

1. Democracy is the best form of government.
2. A good personality is important to success.
3. A college education is beneficial.
4. George Washington was a great president.
5. The United States is a peace-loving country.
6. Training in speech is valuable.
7. Dwight D. Eisenhower was a great general.
8. Colleges and universities should grant students a greater voice in their education.
9. Intercollegiate athletics make a worthwhile contribution to education.
10. Riots and violence will not solve America's problems.
11. The U.S. Congress consists of two houses: the Senate and the House of Representatives.
12. The New York Mets won the World Series in 1969.
13. The population trend in the United States during the last 20 years has been from rural areas to urban areas.

14. Bismarck is the capital of North Dakota.
15. The United States was the first nation to explode an atomic bomb.

The first ten of these statements are opinions or theories. In other words, any one of these ten statements might evoke both agreement and disagreement among competent, intelligent people. The last five statements are factual. No informed person would be likely to disagree with any of the final five statements — except perhaps if he were temporarily misinformed. If any of the first ten statements were to be used in a speech, the speaker would have to present supporting material to "prove" his point. Note, however, a difference between the first five statements and the second five. The first five are so widely accepted by most Americans that with many audiences little evidence would be required to support these points. Numbers six through ten, however, being more controversial, probably would demand substantial support to make them convincing to the audience.

TESTING SOURCES OF EVIDENCE

The sources of supporting material for an argumentative speech may include books, magazines, encyclopedias, government documents, newspapers, specialized reference works, professional journals, pamphlets, broadcasts, bulletins, surveys, speeches, and personal interviews.

In studying his topic, the speaker should critically evaluate all of his sources, for if the source itself is unreliable, he has little reason to place any faith in what it says. Among the questions he should ask about the source are: (1) Is it clearly identified? (2) Is it reliable? (3) Is it unbiased? (4) Is it honest? (5) Is it recent? (6) Is it corroborated by other sources?

Is the Source Clearly Identified?

In identifying sources, the speaker should ask: Who is responsible for this publication or broadcast? If the author, publisher, or sponsor is not indicated, the speaker should waste no time on it. Until he knows who prepared or authorized the work, he has no way of knowing whether it is trustworthy. Furthermore, even where authors, publishers, and sponsors are indicated, he should investigate these individuals or groups. Pressure groups and others with special interests often create "foundations," "research institutes," and other front organizations with respectable names in order to issue publications designed to influence public opinion. The less respectable an organization, the greater need it has to conceal its true identity.

Failure to investigate one's sources thoroughly can lead to public embarassment, as the administrator of the Environmental Protection Agency learned in 1972. To support one of his arguments in a speech, he mentioned the findings of a "federally aided experiment" in California. Following the speech, when the E.P.A. was flooded with requests for more information about the study, the agency belatedly discovered that the administrator had misunderstood a conversation with a colleague and that no such study existed. (See Adapted Reading 12.9.)

Is the Source Reliable?

Having established who is responsible for the work, the speaker should next ask whether the source is reliable. Does it have a reputation for integrity? Does it aim at accurate reporting rather than sensationalism? Is it more interested in education than in propagandizing? Does it have a staff adequate in size and experience to undertake the type of study or investigation it purports to present? If a magazine or journal, are the articles signed? Do you know exactly who is responsible for the different parts of the publication? With the most reliable sources, the answers to all of the foregoing questions will be yes.

While it would be impossible to compile a list of all the sources considered reliable and futile to try to prepare one with which everyone would agree, some sources which are generally regarded as dependable can be suggested. Recognized encyclopedias such as the *Encyclopedia Americana*, the *Encyclopaedia Britannica*, and the *World Book Encyclopedia* have a reputation for reliability, as do other standard reference works such as the *World Almanac* and various yearbooks. Publications by government agencies such as the United States Census Bureau, the Library of Congress, the Department of Agriculture, the Department of Commerce, and others are usually dependable if the work consists of a presentation of purely factual information. On the other hand, one should regard with suspicion publications whose purpose seems to be to prove the success of some political program, to justify a committee's existence, or to demonstrate the competence of a bureau or agency. Reports of internal security committees, state sovereignty commissions, and other investigatory groups often fall into one of these categories.

In the field of newspapers, the *New York Times, Los Angeles Times, Louisville Courier-Journal, St. Louis Post-Dispatch, Washington Post,* and *Christian Science Monitor* have reputations for honesty and dependability. In surveys of publishers, these newspapers are consistently rated among the most reputable by their competitors (see Adapted Reading 12.4).

In evaluating sources, the speaker should be careful not to misjudge the reliability of one part or one article because of the nature of the rest of the publication in which it appears. The *Congressional Record,* for example, may seem to be a highly reputable source because it publishes the speeches and debates of Congress. However, since congressmen are allowed to insert anything they wish into the *Record,* a great deal of inaccurate material appears within its pages. Even the speeches may not be authentic since congressmen are permitted to revise them before publication. On the other hand, *Playboy* and *Esquire* magazines, which are better known for other diversions, often publish works of significance by very reputable writers.

Is the Source Unbiased?

A source may be said to be biased when it has a vested interest in the outcome of an issue. The source may sincerely believe it is acting objectively, but because it stands to gain or lose depending on the way the issue is resolved, it cannot be trusted to observe impartially. Thus, for example, a newspaper published by a labor union may strive for objectivity in discussing a proposed wage increase, but it is unlikely that it will be wholly unbiased. Furthermore, even if it were objective, the general public would probably question its impartiality.

As this example suggests, sources of evidence published by groups with special interests are likely to be biased. Such sources would include many publications issued by political parties, business firms, religious organizations, pressure groups, minorities, and others. In addition, some publications are designed to serve special segments of the community and so are not likely to publish anything offensive to them. *Fortune*, for example, is a magazine for and about big business and depends heavily on industry for advertising. For this reason, one might question the impartiality of *Fortune* on issues affecting business. On the other hand, some of the most reliable, objective evidence available concerning business trends might well be found within the pages of *Fortune*.

Among the biases a reader might expect to find in a few other publications are: *New Republic*, politically liberal; *Journal of the American Medical Association*, opposed to Medicare and federal interference in medical matters; *Broadcasting*, against stringent regulation of radio and television by the federal government; *Democratic Digest*, a publication of the Democratic Party; *Chicago Tribune*, politically conservative; *American Legion Magazine*, politically conservative, especially regarding defense and foreign affairs; *Monthly Review*, Marxist oriented; *The Worker*, pro-Communist; *Independent American*, pro-segregation; and *American Opinion*, published by the conservative John Birch Society.

Is the Source Honest?

While the publishers of a biased source may give a slanted analysis of a problem, they do so with a sincere belief that they are telling the truth. Others, however, sometimes set out deliberately to mislead the public. Such sources can be said to be intellectually dishonest. A popular national magazine once placed on its cover what appeared to be a secret photograph of a famous, wealthy recluse who had not been seen in public for many years. The magazine made no mention of the fact that the photograph was a fake. While trivial, this is an example of intellectual dishonesty.

A more serious example occurred when a television station was found repeatedly to have shown films supposedly depicting current events, but which actually were old films taken from the files and relabeled. A film of a crowd in Bucharest, Rumania, was said to show Prague during the Soviet occupation of Czechoslovakia; pictures taken of student demonstrations on one campus were presented as depicting a disturbance at another school; and old films of fighting in Vietnam were relabeled and used to illustrate later battles.

The authors of published material sometimes deliberately falsify in order to promote a cause or to create a better public image for an organization or individual. Campaign biographies written to advance the prospects of a candidate often omit unpleasant details, gloss over some facts, and play up others. Political tracts written to win support for or against some piece of legislation frequently quote out of context, select materials only favorable to their point of view, and in other ways distort the facts.

Disclosures of deliberate deception by prominent government officials and military officers in the 1960s and early 1970s did much to undermine the confidence of the American public in the honesty and integrity of its leadership. Clearly, if there is any evidence of dishonesty on the part of the author or publisher, the speaker should place no confidence in the work.

Is the Source Recent?

The speaker should check the publication dates of his sources to determine whether he has the latest available information. Conditions change rapidly and out-of-date information may be highly unreliable in analyzing a current situation. If the publication is a second, third, or fourth printing or edition, he should also check to see whether material in the latest issue has been brought up to date.

Is the Source Corroborated by Other Sources?

If information available in one source is not corroborated by other sources, the speaker has good reason to regard it with suspicion. The fact that other sources fail to corroborate it does not actually disprove the reliability of the evidence; but if the material is at all significant, its unavailability in other sources where one might reasonably expect to find it certainly raises doubts about its validity.

Anything that has been reprinted from another source should be verified by checking the data in the original source to make sure that it has been fully and accurately reported.

TESTING THE EVIDENCE

Having determined the reliability of his sources, the speaker is now ready to test the evidence itself. While a speaker may employ any of the types of supporting material used in exposition, in argumentative speaking the principal forms of evidence are specific instances, statistics, comparisons, the testimony of authorities, and causal relationships.

The speaker should support his arguments with the best available evidence for two reasons: (1) to make sure that his own analysis and understanding of the subject are correct and (2) to provide his listeners with the most conclusive case possible, as the audience for an argumentative speech is far more critical than other audiences.

Testing Specific Instances

In arguing from specific instances, the speaker attempts to support his contention inductively by citing specific examples, illustrations, or instances to prove a more general conclusion. The following excerpt from a speech made by Representative Patsy Mink of Hawaii in 1971 illustrates argument by specific instances. In attempting to prove that many Americans harbor prejudicial feelings toward Orientals, Congresswoman Mink said:

> The indictment drawn up by the Army against Lieutenant Calley stated in six separate charges that he did at My Lai murder four "Oriental human beings" . . . "murder not less than thirty Oriental human beings" . . . murder three "Oriental human beings" . . . murder an unknown number of "Oriental human beings" not less than seventy . . . and so on numbering 102. Thus, the Army did not charge him with the murder of human beings as presumably would have been the case had Caucasians been involved, but instead charged the apparently lesser offense of killing mere "Oriental human beings."

In developing an argument by employing specific instances, the speaker should apply the following tests:

1. Are Enough Instances Presented? If the speaker's argument is to be convincing to his listeners, he must cite enough specific instances to justify the conclusion that he draws. For example, an audience will not accept the conclusion that college students are rude if the speaker mentions only two or three examples of student discourtesy. Likewise, citing four or five faculty members who are poorly prepared for their classes is not enough to warrant any broad generalization about the competence of the entire faculty. While no fixed number of instances necessary to prove a contention can be prescribed, because the number will depend on what argument the speaker hopes to prove, he should present enough to convince his audience. Journalist Wes Gallagher, in a speech designed to prove that the government had created a "credibility gap," listed example after example of misleading statements by government officials, until finally even the most skeptical listener must have been convinced that the government had been guilty of at least *some* false statements. His piece is reprinted in Adapted Reading 12.5.

Even when a large number of instances are cited, however, the speaker should be careful that he does not overstate his argument, that he is not too sweeping in his generalization. Arguments claiming to prove contentions covering *all*, *every*, or even *most* parts of the whole are difficult to support with specific instances. The speaker is probably wise to qualify his conclusion with terms such as *generally*, *usually*, *frequently*, and *commonly*; or he might contend that the specific instances demonstrate a *serious* problem, a *major* failure, or a *pattern* of error.

2. Are the Instances Fairly Chosen? If the speaker wishes to generalize about a group or class, it is necessary that his specific instances be representative and typical of the whole, rather than exceptions or the unusual. Anyone who reads a daily newspaper has come across examples of clergymen who have been involved in scandals, government employees who have given secret information to foreign agents, respected businessmen who have been guilty of bigamy, college presidents with phony degrees, and judges who have committed criminal acts. However, these instances are so unrepresentative that it is difficult to see how they could be used as a basis for any kind of generalization about the clergy, the government, business, educators, or the judiciary. Arguments based on specific instances are valid only when the instances are representative.

3. Are There Significant Exceptions to the Instances? At times, a speaker may be able to compose an argument based on specific instances that are both frequent and representative but which fail to prove his generalization because of significant exceptions. For example, the contention that a big-time intercollegiate athletic program lends prestige to a college or university might be supported by examples of outstanding schools that are well known for their athletic teams. Among his instances, the speaker could cite Notre Dame, Southern California, Ohio State, Texas, Michigan, Georgia Tech, U.C.L.A., Illinois, and many others, In spite of the adequacy of his instances, the speaker could not logically conclude that emphasis on athletics was *essential* to the prestige of an institution because too many exceptions exist. One need only look to Harvard, Yale, Columbia, and the other Ivy League schools, Johns Hopkins, M.I.T., and the University of Chicago, where athletics are not stressed, to see the fallacy in the speaker's argument. Whenever a speaker argues from specific instances, he must investigate carefully to determine whether exceptions exist which invalidate his conclusions.

4. Are the Instances True? Are they what they appear to be? In verifying the accuracy of his specific instances, the speaker should first determine that the instance actually exists or occurred. After he is satisfied that the instance is true, he should investigate whether it actually is an example of what it seems to be. For example, whether a newspaper photograph of a police officer striking a demonstrator is evidence of police brutality would depend on the circumstances of the confrontation. Or, whether a school whose students are all of one race constitutes an example of segregation would depend on why students of only one race are enrolled. Often a condition or action that appears to illustrate one thing will, upon closer scrutiny, turn out to illustrate something quite different.

5. Are the Instances Recent? Since out-of-date instances are of little value in proving anything about current conditions, the speaker should make certain that his specific instances are recent enough to be applicable to the problem he is discussing.

Just how recent the instances should be will depend on the speaker's subject. In some fields, data becomes outdated very quickly. A discovery, a new law, a change in management or ownership, a court decision, adoption of new policies, or the election of different officials may drastically alter a situation almost overnight. For example, not too long ago, poliomyelitis was a serious national health problem. But the discovery and use of polio vaccines virtually eliminated the disease within a few years. Many questionable practices of manufacturers and lenders were curbed as soon as recent "fairness in packaging" and "fairness in lending" legislation went into effect. And Supreme Court decisions affirming the "one-man–one-vote" doctrine quickly led to reapportionment of many state legislatures, thereby correcting serious inequalities in representation. In each of these instances, the nature of the problem changed completely within a short period of time. In other areas, change may be more gradual. But, in either case, the speaker should take care that his instances are sufficiently recent to accurately represent conditions as they currently are.

Testing Statistics

When used properly, statistics often are the most conclusive kind of evidence for proving one's contention. A statistical total showing exactly how many armed robberies occurred over a fixed period of time, for example, is a far more accurate index of the incidence of this crime than a series of specific instances of armed robberies. However, while statistics may be highly accurate and definitive, they often are difficult to interpret. Like a bikini bathing suit, what they reveal is suggestive; what they conceal is vital.

Statistics may be employed in various ways to support an argument or contention. One example is cited below:

> The reasons why our unemployment rates are high seem clear. Over the past ten years or so our labor force has been growing faster than new jobs have been created. This trend has been accelerating and will continue to accelerate for some years to come as our so-called "war babies" move into the labor market at a phenomenal rate. As an example, in the decade between 1950 and 1960 only $7\frac{1}{2}$ million young workers entered the labor market; in the current decade, in contrast, some 26 million new young workers will enter the labor force and only $4\frac{1}{2}$ million of these intend to go to college. President Kennedy has said that nearly 8 million of them will not even have finished school — they are the "dropouts" we hear so much about. Now to these facts we must obviously add the impact of technological change, or automation, depending upon which phrase you prefer. There is no question that automation is displacing workers. (John L. Snyder, Jr., "The Total Challenge of Automation," Speech to AFL-CIO convention, November 15, 1963)

To make certain that he uses statistics properly, the speaker should ask several questions:

1. Are Enough Statistics Presented? As with specific instances, the speaker should determine whether he has enough statistical data to warrant the conclusion he draws from them. Statistics measuring only a part of the whole may not be a fair index to the complete picture. For example, statistics showing a rise in the cost of clothing or of dairy products reveal little about the overall cost of living. Likewise, figures on the incidence of asthma in one

part of the country are virtually useless as an index to the incidence of this disorder nationally. The speaker should employ statistics that are comprehensive, that cover the entire population with which he is concerned.

2. Are the Statistics Representative? Surveys that are restricted to one segment of the whole, that pertain to one class or group, or that are obtained under unusual or artificial circumstances may not be typical and representative. The Kinsey Report, for example, was widely criticized because the population interviewed was largely of one social class. Surveys requiring the respondent to complete a questionnaire may be misleading because they exclude the illiterates in the population. A survey conducted by telephone is likely to be biased because it does not include the lowest income group — people who do not have telephones. Statistics obtained by interviewing people in one part of a city or one section of a state may not be representative of the whole city or state population. A survey of student opinion might be greatly affected by whether the surveyor conducted his interviews at the library or at the student center, by the ratio of upperclassmen to freshmen, and by whether the sample has a fair proportion of students from the various colleges, divisions, or departments. Realizing that such factors affect statistical tabulations, the speaker should try to discover how the compiler obtained his statistics in order to verify that they are representative.

Many people place little confidence in surveys based on a sample of the whole, such as the Nielsen television ratings and the Gallup and Harris polls. Statisticians, however, agree that such surveys can be highly reliable indices of the entire population if they are based on a representative sample and the sample is large enough. The most representative sample is one in which the interviewees are chosen entirely at random or, in other words, in which every person has an equal chance of being selected to be counted or interviewed. A completely random sample, however, is difficult to obtain in many instances and so several of the polls which purport to survey a representative sample — that is, a sample containing allegedly correct ratios of persons of different religions, politics, income, age, sex, marital status, occupation, and other characteristics — do not, in fact, do so. Much of the lack of confidence in the reliability of polls stems from a doubt that their samples are truly representative of the whole population. So, when using surveys compiled by such organizations, the speaker should seek to discover the polling methods employed in collecting the statistics.

3. Are There Significant Exceptions to the Statistics? Some statistics can be highly misleading. Averages often give a false impression. For example, the statement that the homes in the block where I live have an average value of $100,000 gives the impression of an affluent neighborhood, when, in truth, one family may live in a $400,000 mansion and the remaining three families consist of paupers residing in cardboard shacks. Averages often conceal exceptions, thereby tending to hide serious problems and gross inequities. Thus, the average income of retired persons, the average salary of teachers, or the average number of years of education completed by a group may hide the fact that substantial numbers of retired persons live on pittances, that many teachers are underpaid, or that widespread illiteracy exists.

4. Are the Statistics Recent? It is obvious that statistics that measure changing conditions such as the crime rate, gross national product, cost of living, wages and salaries, the incidence of disease, production costs, defense spending, and similar factors must be recent if they are to reflect accurately the situation as it exists at the time. How recent should the speaker's statistics be? The only answer to that question is that they should be the most recent possible. Sometimes the passage of only a few weeks or months can greatly alter the accuracy of a speaker's statistics. For example, on the basis of public opinion surveys, it was freely predicted that Thomas Dewey would be elected president in 1948. However, the last survey was taken nearly two months before the election and, as the results indicated, did not reflect changing public attitudes. A single event—a scientific discovery, an invention, a political announcement, the outbreak of war, the enactment of a law, an assassination—may sometimes have great repercussions almost overnight on public opinion, the economy, and political conditions. The speaker must recognize that the most recent statistic available is the most reliable and that even that may no longer be accurate.

5. Are the Units Properly Defined? Since statistics are based on counting, it is important that the speaker know exactly what the compiler has counted. He should determine how the compiler defined his units. For example, if the statistics concern the student body at Metropolitan University, he should know what the compiler means by *students*. Does *students* include graduate students as well as undergraduates? Does it embrace part-time students, students enrolled in short-term workshops, seminars, and institutes? Are extension and correspondence students included? Does it cover students in branches or departments of the university located in other places? Unless the speaker knows the answers to such questions, he does not really know what the statistics reveal.

6. Are the Statistics an Index to What They Claim to Measure? At times, it is difficult to determine exactly what a set of statistics measures. For example, is a capacity audience at a campus lecture an indicator of student interest in the speech? Or were most of them required to attend? Or was the audience composed mainly of faculty and townspeople?

Is a coach's or sportswriter's ranking of college athletic teams an indicator of which school has the best team? If so, why are highly ranked teams often defeated by lower-ranked or unranked teams?

Does a decline in the number of arrests for speeding show that the public is driving more carefully? Or is it a sign of less stringent law enforcement?

Is the size of a nation's army an index to its military strength? How can military strength be measured?

Is an increase in attendance at football games throughout the country an indicator of increased popularity of that game? Or does it merely reflect the increase in population? Could it indicate that more people can afford to attend sports events? Could it be related to the expansion of professional football to several new cities?

If a country has a high suicide rate, is the statistic an indicator of the tension of daily life in that nation, of the mental instability of the people, or of stricter and more accurate reporting of suicides than in other places? Could the suicide rate be related to the predominant religious belief of the country?

As the above questions suggest, interpreting statistics can be a tricky task. David Burnham, in Adapted Reading 12.6, indicates how even official crime statistics can be misleading. So, before a speaker asserts that his statistics prove something, he should make sure that he knows exactly what they measure.

7. Were the Statistics Collected at the Proper Time or over a Sufficient Period of Time? Often the time of year, the particular day, or even the hour when a statistic is obtained can affect the accuracy of the tabulation. For example, a count of the number of vehicles passing a particular intersection to determine whether a traffic signal is needed can be misleading if the survey is taken on Sunday, a holiday, early in the morning, or late in the evening. To be certain that his statistic is valid, the speaker should know just when the data was collected.

In determining trends, the speaker should be certain that the statistics cover a sufficiently long period of time to permit an accurate judgment. For example, surveys of economic trends such as the unemployment rate, gross national product, cost of living, and balance of payments or surveys of social trends such as crime and divorce rates are meaningless if they cover only a limited span of time, because temporary fluctuations or abberrations may have severely distorted the general direction or nature of the trend.

The success of many experiments, laws, and programs often cannot be accurately measured until a considerable period of time has passed. For example, the introduction of a new method of teaching in a school system probably can be evaluated only after it has been in effect for several years and large numbers of children have been taught under the plan. Legislation to curb inflation, laws to discourage drunken driving, public education campaigns, and similar measures may have little immediate effect, but, in the long run, they may prove effective. Or, in other instances, the measure may seem highly successful at the outset only to diminish in effectiveness with the passage of time. The introduction of compulsory breatholator tests in Great Britain, designed to reduce accidents caused by intoxicated drivers, showed dramatic results when first passed, but only time will tell their long-range effectiveness. In the same manner, the effects of the repeal of most laws against the sale of pornography in Denmark cannot be assessed until a substantial period of time has elapsed. Statistics purporting to measure the consequence of such programs, laws, and experiments cannot be regarded as valid if the period of time covered is brief.

8. Have the Statistics Been Accurately Collected and Classified? Even in national elections, where great care is taken to ensure accuracy, the original unofficial announcement of the vote always differs from the final official tabulation, indicating that some errors were made in the initial count. In elections where a recount of the votes is ordered, additional mistakes are usually discovered. If inaccuracies of this type can occur in a carefully supervised election, it is not difficult to imagine the likelihood of error in collecting and classifying data in less well organized polls.

The speaker who plans to use statistics should try to determine how the statistics were collected and tabulated. If questionnaires were used, he should learn to whom they were sent, of what they consisted, how they were worded, and what percentage of them were returned. If interviews were conducted, he should discover whether the interviewers were well qualified and trained to conduct the interviews impartially. If the statistics are based on the reports of several different bodies, groups, agencies, or collectors, he should ask whether each participating unit collected and tabulated its data in the same way.

The speaker should also be aware that some subjects do not lend themselves to accurate statistical tabulation. For example, no one really knows how many heroin addicts there are in the United States because heroin is unlawful in this country and addicts simply are not going to confess to using it. On many topics, all we have is estimates. For example, how many alcoholics are there in the United States? How many homosexuals? How many aliens enter the country illegally each year? How many illegal abortions are performed?

Until the speaker knows how the statistics were collected and is assured that they were reliably tabulated, he can place little confidence in their accuracy.

Testing Comparisons

Perhaps the least conclusive form of evidence is an argument based on comparison or analogy. In constructing an argument by analogy that will be both logical and convincing, the speaker's principal problem is in finding two entities, conditions, or sets of circumstances enough alike that he can argue that what is true of one will also be true of the other.

Although argument by comparison is difficult to establish, at times the speaker has virtually no other means of support. For example, if the speaker proposes to demonstrate the effects that allegedly will result from the adoption of some untried policy, he has no statistics, instances, or testimony available to him on how the proposed policy has functioned in the past. The best that he can do is to show how the policy has worked elsewhere and, by comparison, attempt to predict how it will operate in the specific circumstances with which he is concerned. For example, if a speaker wished to argue for the creation of ombudsmen in the United States, he would have to look to various European countries for evidence of the utility of these officials. The basic premise of his argument would be: If ombudsmen serve a useful function in Europe, an ombudsman would be useful in the United

States. However, unless the speaker can demonstrate that the United States and those European countries with ombudsmen are much alike, the argument falls apart.

Educator Clark Kerr resorted to argument by comparison in advocating creation of 67 urban-grant universities in a 1967 speech. Kerr began by contending that in their 100-year existence the 67 land-grant colleges had contributed enormously to American agriculture and technology by remodeling the traditional curriculum, aiding research on agriculture, establishing extension services to help the individual farmer, and creating a concern for rural problems. The speaker then introduced his own proposal and proceeded to support it by analogy, saying:

> Tonight, I should like to suggest that we need a new model to add to our existing models for universities in the United States. I have called this new model the urban-grant university. . . . I use the term *urban-grant* . . . to indicate a type of university which would have an aggressive approach to the problems of the city, where the city itself and its problems would become the animating focus, as agriculture once was and to some extent still is of the land-grand universities. . . .
>
> The suggestion that the Federal Government should help with the land and with the money to build these new campuses or to change existing campuses is altogether reasonable. When the land-grant movement began, over 50 percent of the people in the United States lived on the land; today, only 10 percent do. The reasons for an urban-grant university now are at least as compelling as were those for the land-grant university in 1862. . . .
>
> Today, great national problems have to do with the cities, with equality of opportunity, with the ending of poverty, with the quality of life, and I think that the Federal Government might logically respond to these problems by again aiding the proper activities of higher education. The urban-grant university might parallel the land-grant institution not only via city-oriented curricula and on-campus research studies but also by setting up experiment stations to work on the problems of the city as they once worked on the problems of the land, and by setting up intensified urban extension services like agricultural extension. As a counterpart to the county agent, I can visualize a school agent, for example — one who through the research at his university is informed about the best new techniques for language teaching and who can take this knowledge directly into the public schools in his particular city area. It is true that many urban problems are more complex than those of the land, but this very complexity makes the prospect of confronting them more important and more challenging.

Kerr's use of comparison effectively illustrates how the speaker at times has no other alternate means for developing his argument. Since the United

States had not tried a system of federally supported urban-grant universities, Kerr could not point to statistics, specific instances, or testimony of authorities to prove their worth. Instead, he was required to locate a similar program and to argue on the basis of its operation that a system of urban-grant institutions would be comparably successful.

In arguing from analogy, the speaker should apply the following tests:

1. Do the Two Entities Being Compared Actually Have Many Similarities? In argument by comparison, the speaker must have two entities that possess a large number of actual, not figurative, similarities. Because both football and warfare are characterized by two opposing forces engaged in a contest that each seeks to win, one might conclude that the two constitute a suitable comparison. However, the resemblances between the two are largely figurative, for the grim realities of death and destruction, the seriousness of the conflict, and the international repercussions dependent upon the outcome of a war are totally absent in a football game.

A comparison between the operation of a business firm and the administration of government also would be invalid because the two really have little in common; one is concerned primarily with making a profit, while the other seeks to govern the people.

Comparisons between two different eras or two different types of activity usually are ineffective because of the lack of similarities. Space exploration, for example, has almost nothing in common with earlier types of exploration. Conditions today are so unlike those of a hundred years ago that in most fields a meaningful analogy cannot be drawn.

In argument by comparison, the speaker should make certain that the two entities being compared possess enough actual similarities that the speaker can convincingly contend that what is true of one is likely also to be true of the other.

2. Are the Similarities Significant? The speaker also needs to ask himself whether the observable similarities are significant ones. Two entities may possess many likenesses, but the resemblances may be unimportant. For example, both a kindergarten class and a college seminar are concerned with education. In each the students attend for the purpose of learning. Both involve a teacher, students, assignments, study, and class discussion. Both meet regularly in classrooms with basically similar equipment and facilities. However, except perhaps for the basic goal, most of the resemblances are not significant and, in spite of their number, do not constitute the basis for a convincing argument by analogy. One certainly could not expect an audience to accept the argument that because the sand box proved popular in the kindergarten, the seminar too should have one, or that term papers should be required of the kindergarteners because they were valuable in the seminar.

In argument by comparison, then, a large number of similarities is not enough for the development of a satisfactory analogy. In addition, the likenesses must be significant ones.

3. Do Important Differences Occur? Having constructed an argument by comparison between two entities possessing a large number of significant similarities, the speaker should look for any important differences that may invalidate the argument.

For example, two colleges may have a great deal in common, but because one is state supported and the other private, a comparison may not be possible. An analogy involving the urban problems of two similar cities could be invalidated by a difference in the laws of the states in which they are located. A comparison between two periods of time could be invalidated because of the enactment or repeal of a law. For example, repeal of all laws forbidding the sale and use of marijuana would greatly alter the number of arrests for the illegal use of narcotics, thereby making it difficult to compare drug addiction before and after the laws were repealed.

Even though two entities may appear much alike in significant ways, the speaker must be alert to the possibility that a single important difference may prevent him from constructing a persuasive analogy between the two.

Testing Authorities

In argument by authority, the strength of the argument rests upon the reputation of the expert or witness cited by the speaker. The authority may be a convincing source because he is regarded as a man of learning and intelligence, because he has a reputation for honesty and integrity, or because he possesses specialized knowledge derived from personal observation or investigation. In arguing from authority, if the authority is not acceptable to the audience, they will attach no significance to what the speaker says.

An example of argument by authority is found in President Lyndon Johnson's speech to the National Legislative Conference in 1967 in which he outlined what became known as the San Antonio doctrine. Under attack for United States involvement in the war in Vietnam, Johnson undertook a refutation of his critics and a reaffirmation of the administration's policies by quoting authorities to support his position. After citing two resolutions overwhelmingly approved by the Senate, Johnson then quoted statements endorsing American involvement in Vietnam by former presidents Dwight Eisenhower and John F. Kennedy, the president of the Philippines, the foreign minister of Thailand, the president of Korea, and the prime ministers of Australia, Malaysia, New Zealand, and Singapore. Johnson demonstrates the use of authority in Adapted Reading 12.7.

In determining the effectiveness of an authority, the speaker should employ the following tests:

1. Is the Authority Known to the Audience? If the listeners are not familiar with the expert, they are not going to attach much weight to what he says. To make sure that the audience is acquainted with the authority, the speaker should name him specifically. Identifying the source as "a leading doctor," "a high government official," "the author of one of the best books on the subject," or "a prominent physicist" leaves the audience in doubt as to just who the expert is and how much confidence they should place in his testimony. For this reason, the speaker should always give the authority's name.

If, after naming the expert, it is likely that the listeners still do not know who he is, the speaker should briefly indicate the man's qualifications as an authority. He may do so with a short phrase such as, "who is at present an under-secretary in the State Department, was formerly the United States ambassador to Pakistan, and has written three books on American foreign policy in Asia," or "who is editor of the *St. Louis News-Courier* and won the Pulitzer Prize for his exposé of the influence of the Mafia in Missouri" or "who is head of the speech department at Midland State University and a former president of the Speech Association of America." Well-known public figures, of course, need not be identified in this manner.

2. Is the Authority Recognized as an Expert in His Field? Almost everyone has an opinion on something he has observed firsthand. Students have opinions on education; veterans regard themselves as knowledgeable about the armed forces and military matters; tourists consider themselves experts on places they have visited; and Monday-morning quarterbacks authoritatively replay the game they saw on Saturday. But none of these qualify as authorities simply on the basis of their observations or personal involvement.

Whenever possible, the speaker should select authorities whose knowledge of the subject is not restricted to limited observation, partial understanding, or fleeting involvement. The best authorities are those who speak from a broad background of study, experience, and observation. Thus, a speaker would probably rely on a well-qualified educator for information on teaching; on an experienced statesman for an analysis of international affairs; on a trained historian for knowledge of the past; and on a recognized theologian for an interpretation of religious concepts.

In discussing specific events or incidents, however, the eyewitness is a highly respectable authority regardless of his lack of expertise. The man who observed a traffic accident, for example, is much better able to discuss it than a traffic safety engineer who was not present, just as a witness to a crime is more of an expert on this particular act than a criminologist, judge, or law-enforcement officer.

3. Is the Authority's Subject One He Is Qualified to Discuss? Many experts in one field take an interest in and frequently speak out on other matters. For example, Dr. Benjamin Spock, who is regarded as an expert on child care, often discusses political affairs as well; evangelist Billy Graham frequently expresses opinions on political subjects; Marianne Moore, the poetess, occasionally discussed baseball, in which she was keenly interested; and Admiral Hyman Rickover, the atomic physicist, is an outspoken critic of current educational methods.

While it is commendable for these individuals to take an interest in subjects other than their own areas of competence, it would be a mistake to assume that because they are well informed in one field, they automatically qualify as experts on other unrelated matters. When developing an argument by authority, the speaker will construct a more persuasive case if his experts are known for their knowledge of the speaker's subject rather than for expertise in another subject.

4. Has the Authority Had Opportunity to Observe? No matter how eminent an expert may be, he can be regarded as an authority only on those conditions or events which he has had ample opportunity to observe and study. Statements based on limited observation, secondhand information, or hearsay reports cannot be regarded as authoritative. If, for example, a speaker wants evidence concerning socialized medicine in Britain, he should seek the views of the minister of health or prominent British physicians or health officials who have been closely associated with the program, rather than the opinion of an American medical man whose knowledge comes largely from reading and limited observation.

Even when an expert has had an opportunity to observe personally the conditions about which he speaks, he does not qualify as an authority unless the period of study or observation was an extended one. For example, government officials and politicians who spend a few days in a foreign country, at a battle front, or at the scene of some disaster probably depart with only a superficial understanding of what they have observed. Likewise, biographies, books, and reports which seek to capitalize on public curiosity following the sudden death of a prominent figure, a disaster, or a major news event often are of questionable reliability because of the haste with which they have been prepared.

5. Is the Authority Unbiased? As pointed out in the discussion of prejudiced sources, bias refers to the inability of one to judge objectively because of self-interest or some preconceived attitude. Since the opinions of biased authorities are of little value either in understanding a problem or in persuading an audience, the speaker should rely on the testimony of impartial experts.

6. Is the Authority Acceptable to the Audience? Some men who meet all of the requirements of authorities presented so far will nevertheless prove unacceptable to some audiences. Persons who have been involved in scandals, censured for unethical conduct, convicted of crimes, or are highly controversial usually will not be regarded as authorities even if their misconduct is in no way related to the subjects upon which they have expert knowledge. Thus, the senator who was censured for using campaign contributions for personal expenses, the State Department official who was convicted of perjury, the Supreme Court justice who resigned because of opposition to his outside activities, and the labor leader who was imprisoned for attempted bribery all remain knowledgeable in their fields, but, because their reputations have been damaged, most listeners are no longer willing to place any confidence in what they say.

Even persons who have committed no crime or breach of conduct may at times be unacceptable to an audience because of their associations with unpopular or controversial causes, such as the Ku Klux Klan, the Black Panthers, the John Birch Society, the Communist Party, the Students for a Democratic Society, the American Nazi Party, the Minutemen, or some other radical group.

The views of controversial figures of the types just described are not necessarily wrong; but so long as the public is unwilling to trust such men, the speaker will find their testimony of little value in influencing his listeners.

7. Is the Authority Correctly Quoted? In a famous libel suit brought against the publisher of a book critical of the House of Commons, British lawyer Thomas Erskine convincingly demonstrated that by quoting out of context one may construe another person's statements to prove almost anything. Inaccurate quotations are not always deliberate or malicious. Paraphrasing, the need to condense to meet space limits of newspapers and magazines, and honest errors in understanding what a speaker said are some reasons why the statements of authorities are sometimes inaccurately reported. In other instances, a person's remarks may be deliberately distorted for political or other reasons.

Whatever the explanation, it is important that a speaker verify the statements of the authorities he plans to cite, as Meg Greenfield illustrates in Adapted Reading 12.8. To check on the accuracy of a quotation, one should go to the original source. If this cannot be done, a statement may sometimes be verified by comparing two or more independent reports of it.

Testing Causal Arguments

Argument from causation, or cause-to-effect argument, is not so much another kind of supporting material as a different way of using evidence to construct one's arguments. In cause-to-effect reasoning, the speaker may employ specific instances, statistics, comparisons, and testimony, but he uses them to establish a relationship between an action and its consequences or between a condition and its causes. In causal argument, the speaker seeks to explain why or how something happened or will happen. In a speech about air pollution, for example, the speaker might attempt to clarify the problem by explaining its causes or discussing its effects. Or, in a speech on foreign trade, he might try to predict the consequences of lowering our tariffs.

In 1966, Robert S. McNamara, then secretary of defense, employed causal argument in an effort to prove that poverty was one of the major causes of violent conflict. After pointing out that the number of outbreaks of violence among the nations of the world had increased each year between 1958 and 1965, McNamara argued:

But what is most significant of all is that there is a direct and constant relationship between the incidence of violence and the economic status of the countries affected. The World Bank divides nations, on the basis of per capita income, into four categories: rich, middle-income, poor, and very poor. The rich nations are those with a per capita income of $750 a year or more. The current United States level is more than $2700. There are 27 of these rich nations. They possess 75 percent of the world's wealth, though roughly only 25 percent of the world's population. Since 1958, only one of these 27 nations has suffered a major internal upheaval on its own territory.

But observe what happens at the other end of the economic scale. Among the 38 very poor nations—those with a per capita income of under $100 a year—no less than 32 have suffered significant conflicts. Indeed, they have suffered an average of two major outbreaks of violence per country in the eight-year period. That is a great deal of conflict. What is worse, it has been, predominantly, conflict of a prolonged nature.

The trend holds predictably constant in the case of the two other categories: the poor, and the middle-income nations. Since 1958, 87 percent of the very poor nations, 69 percent of the poor nations, and 48 percent of the middle-income nations have suffered serious violence.

There can, then, be no question but that there is an irrefutable relationship between violence and economic backwardness. And the trend of such violence is up, not down.

Note that in trying to establish a causal relationship between poverty and conflict, Secretary McNamara used two other forms of support: statistics and comparison.

In a causal argument, the speaker should test the causal relationship with the following four questions:

1. Can a Causal Relationship Be Established? Just because two events occur one after another does not prove that the two are in any way related to each other. The rooster, for example, crows every morning and the sun rises shortly thereafter, but no one will contend that the sun would not rise if the rooster failed to crow. So, clearly, there is no causal relationship between the two.

On the other hand, take the example of John, who failed the final examination in his speech course. In trying to explain his failure, John relates that a severe storm occurred during the test and that the thunder and lightning so badly distracted him that he could not concentrate on the exam. Is it possible that a relationship could exist between a storm and poor performance? Although it is conceivable and one may conclude that a causal relationship *could* exist, it still has not been established that a causal relationship *did* exist.

2. Is the Suggested Cause Adequate to Produce the Effect? While a possible relationship between two phenomena can sometimes be established, one must look further to determine whether the alleged cause actually was important enough to produce the result attributed to it.

Continuing with the example of John's failure on his final examination, if the duration of the storm was only five minutes of the two hours he had to complete the test, it seems unlikely that the proposed cause (the storm) was adequate to produce the consequence (distraction leading to failure). On the other hand, if the storm raged violently for most of the two hours, then perhaps the cause was sufficient to account for the effect.

3. Does the Effect Result from One or Many Causes? In attempting to establish a cause-to-effect or effect-to-cause link between two phenomena, after demonstrating that the alleged cause could have produced the effect, one should not overlook the possibility that other causes may also have contributed to the consequence.

Thus, while admitting that the prolonged storm could have caused John to fail his examination, one might also discover that John had gone to a party the night before, that he had slept only a few hours, that he had not reviewed for the examination, that he had not read the daily assignments, that he had not attended classes regularly, and that his fiancée had broken their engagement just before the examination. Any or all of these are possible explanations for why he failed the test and all are probably just as plausible as the explanation that the storm distracted him.

When the speaker is aware of the existence of other plausible causes, he cannot logically claim that the alleged cause singly produced the effect. He might still argue, however, that the storm was one of the causes or, perhaps, even the most important cause.

4. Is There Evidence That the Alleged Cause Did Not or Could Not Have Produced the Effect? When attempting to determine which of several causes might have produced an effect, the speaker should investigate each alleged cause to see if evidence exists that would discredit one or more of the causes.

Continuing with the illustration of John's failure on his final examination, one might ask whether other students were distracted by the storm? Did any students complain of the distraction? Did the class do as well as usual on the examination? Was John in a position where the storm may have distracted him more than the other students? If no one else complained about the storm, the class performance was generally good, and John was in no way more exposed to the thunder and lightning than the others writing the examination, it seems unlikely that the storm was the cause of his failure. Still, it is possible that John is unusually nervous and finds thunderstorms particularly unnerving, so one might try to determine how John reacted to the storm. Should this lead to the discovery that John dozed off and slept through part of the storm, it would seem unlikely that the storm could be considered a possible cause of his failure.

The example used above to illustrate the four tests of causal argument demonstrates how difficult it may be to establish a causal relationship even when dealing with a relatively simple question. One can imagine then the difficulty of trying to determine causes and effects when analyzing such complex problems as crime, civil rights, poverty, the urban crisis, national security, student dissent, inflation, unemployment, birth control, taxation, and foreign aid. Yet, many speakers propound simplistic explanations of these highly intricate issues, as Gilbert Highet shows in Adapted Reading 12.10. Unemployment, they say, is caused by laziness; just kick the shirkers off the welfare rolls and the problem will be solved. Riots and demonstrations are caused by lack of respect for law and order; just call the cops to bash their skulls and the problem will go away. For other speakers, behind almost every problem is a COMMUNIST PLOT TO OVERTHROW AMERICA!!!! Such easy resolutions of difficult issues are detrimental to the democratic process, which depends on an informed and compassionate electorate in dealing with the problems which confront the country. The speaker has an ethical responsibility to scrutinize critically and exhaustively all possible causes and effects of every problem before recommending his analysis to the public.

SUMMARY

Because of the more critical attitude of the listeners, in argumentative speaking the speaker must be particularly careful in his selection of supporting material. He should understand the difference between factual evidence and theories, opinions, and beliefs. The speaker's supporting documentation should be drawn from reputable, recent, and reliable sources.

When the speaker argues from specific instances, he should make sure that he presents enough instances; that they are representative, recent, and true; and that they are not invalidated by significant exceptions. If developing an argument with statistics, the speaker should use statistics that are adequate in number, representative, recent, properly defined, accurately collected, not contradicted by important exceptions, and that truly measure the phenomenon they purport to investigate.

If comparisons are employed to prove a contention, the two entities being compared should have many important similarities and should not differ in any significant feature. Authorities, witnesses, and experts who are cited in support of an idea should be recognized experts familiar and acceptable to the audience; they should be regarded as unbiased and trustworthy by the listeners. The authority's testimony should be confined to those areas of his field of competence that he has had an opportunity to study or observe carefully. In arguments based on causal reasoning, the speaker should determine whether a causal relationship is possible, whether it is probable, whether more than one cause acted to produce the effect, and whether evidence exists to contradict the alleged relationship.

HOW NOT TO ARGUE
Lionel Ruby

Taking people as they are, and desiring to mold them to one's purpose, an emotional appeal may be more effective than a rational one. Unscrupulous demagoguery may get results. One might wish it were otherwise, but in the real world, as distinguished from an ideal society, such is often the case. But talk also has a moral aspect. There is a moral obligation to tell the truth. And there is also the element we call "honorable conduct. . . ."

Logic has its proper place, and so has emotion. A purely intellectual approach to life is as insufficient as a purely emotional one. The activities of life may be divided into two broad categories, the logical and the nonlogical. By *nonlogical* we do not mean *illogical,* but rather activities that have nothing to do with logic. There are times when we reason, and argue, and draw inference. But, for the most part, we are engaged in nonlogical activities, like eating and sleeping, or narrating the events of the day, and so on. Logic enters only when we give reasons for our beliefs.

When we give reasons for our beliefs, we are reasoning. Reasoning is either logical or illogical. Illogical reasoning is bad reasoning, but the *non*logical has nothing to do with reasoning. When we seek to prove that something is or is not the case, then we engage in argument, in which we say: This is true because that is true, or This is so because that is so. When the reasoning is adequate, we say it is logical; when not, illogical.

When we assert beliefs which may be questioned, then we have an obligation to be rational. This common human obligation may be stated in the form of a "law of rationality" or "law of argument," that *we ought to support our beliefs by adequate evidence.* When we say that we know that something is true, we ought to be able to justify our belief by adequate evidence. What is adequate evidence? This term is best defined by example, and we shall give examples as we go along, but we shall assume here that we agree pretty well as to the distinction between evidence that is good and sufficient, and that which is not. In the end there is only one court of final appeal in settling a problem concerning what is rational and what is not: the community of reasonable men. Fortunately, the human race has always agreed pretty well on which of its members are reasonable and which not.

Logic is not all, then, but we have a common obligation to be logical when logic is relevant. . . . And when we act on emotion without concerning ourselves with the facts, we are likely to rush into disaster. Usually, when a politician . . . substitutes emotional appeals for proof, propaganda for rational persuasion, when he inflames rather than informs, we shall find that he does so for one of two reasons. Either he has a contempt for the people, treating them as if they were children, incapable of understanding the issues, or he doesn't want them to know the truth.

From *The Art of Making Sense* (Philadelphia: Lippincott, 1954), 78–90. Reprinted by permission of the publisher, J. B. Lippincott Company.

We are not saying that emotional appeals are never appropriate. On the contrary. When the facts are not in question, and action is desired, then an emotional appeal is appropriate, even indispensable. In the critical days of 1940 Prime Minister Winston Churchill made his great "blood, sweat, and tears" speech to the British people. He inspired his people and spurred them to heroic efforts. Emotion is the best fuel for this kind of energy, and this kind of stimulus is needed even in the best of causes.

Let us pause for a moment to get our bearings. . . . We have not condemned emotional appeals under all circumstances but only when we substitute emotion for proof when proof is required. The latter form of behavior is the essence of what is meant by "How Not to Argue." Let us look at some further illustrations.

Some years ago, when Mr. David Lilienthal was nominated as chairman of the Atomic Energy Commission, Senator McKellar attacked his fitness for the job. The Senator considered Mr. Lilienthal a dangerous man, he said, because his parents were born in Hungary, a country "now dominated by the Communists" (1947). Since Mr. Lilienthal's parents came to this country about 50 years before Hungary was taken over by the Communists, the fact cited by the Senator was grotesquely irrelevant. But it was not cited as evidence. Its purpose was to stir the emotions. The Senator believed that the mere mention of "Communists" would so inflame his audience that they would completely forget about asking for evidence concerning Mr. Lilienthal's fitness for his post.

The appeal to emotion sometimes takes the special form called "the appeal to laughter." If one is unable to refute an opponent's arguments by evidence, it is always possible to make him the butt of a joke and thereby evade the necessity of presenting evidence. A notorious example of this sort of thing, which apparently misfired, occurred in a celebrated debate over the theory of evolution in 1860. Bishop Wilberforce scored when he asked Thomas Huxley, who was defending the Darwinian theory, whether it was through his grandfather or his grandmother that he claimed descent from a monkey? Huxley, who was in no mood to appreciate the Bishop's humor, retorted that he preferred descent from a monkey to descent from a man who used his great gifts and versatile intellect to distract the attention of his hearers from the real point at issue by eloquent digressions and skilled appeals to prejudice.

We have been discussing bad logical behavior on the part of speakers and writers who try to divert our attention from the need for evidence by working on our emotions. They fool us in this way. But we also fool ourselves. We rationalize; we engage in "wishful thinking"; we may accept unfounded beliefs because they satisfy us emotionally. For example, do we find ourselves saying, "I believe thus and so because it makes me feel good so to believe"? Or do we say, "I *must* believe as I do because I couldn't bear to think my belief false"? We deceive ourselves if we believe that our emotions guarantee truth. . . . For alas, wishes are fathers to thoughts that just aren't so. The fact that we want something very strongly apparently does not guarantee that it will come our way. . . . Our emotions, in other words, may interfere with our logic, and prevent us from seeing the truth. . . . It is our emotions that make us adopt a double standard of intellectual morality, one for ourselves, another for the other fellow. . . .

So much for one of the major ways in which we evade what we have called the "law of rationality" or the "law of argument." We should aim to support our beliefs by adequate evidence. The form of evasion we have been discussing is called the "appeal to emotion." There are of course many other ways in which the law of rationality is evaded. Logicians have catalogued many types of errors of reasoning, but it would be impossible to list every possible kind of error, for there are an infinite number of ways in which we can miss the target. . . .

We shall discuss one other major evasion of the law of rationality, the *argumentum ad hominem*. This term, from the Latin, means "an argument directed to the man." To the man, that is, as distinguished from the point at issue. For example, let us suppose that we disagree with what a speaker says. Now we may try to disprove what he says by presenting contrary evidence. But sometimes we don't bother to present the evidence. Instead, we simply attack the speaker, verbally, that is.

If we believe that a statement is false, we ought to attack the statement, not the man who utters it. A speaker, let us say, attacks the Taft-Hartley labor law. He argues that the law unfairly discriminates against labor, on the ground that it may cause a union to lose its bargaining rights. Now, if you disagree with the speaker, you should support the position that the law does not unfairly discriminate against labor. But suppose, instead, you say to the speaker, "By the way, you're a union man, aren't you?" The question implies that the speaker's views must be false, on the ground that his union membership makes him so biased and prejudiced that it would be a waste of time to take his remarks seriously — they simply must be false. . . .

The point is that a man's statements are logically independent of who the man is, or what he is, and that we do not disprove what he says by raising doubts concerning his parentage. Logically, a statement stands or falls on its own merits, regardless of who makes it. Truth and falsity are determined only by evidence. Personalities do not determine logical issues, and discussion should not degenerate into name-calling. . . . It is quite legitimate to show that a speaker is unworthy of trust, or that he is prejudiced, or biased, or that special interests have paid him to say what he is now saying, that he is insincere and so on. "What you are," we say, "speaks so loudly that we cannot hear what you are saying." The important thing, however, is that we should clearly distinguish between convicting a speaker of prejudice, on the one hand, and disproving what he has specifically said, on the other. . . .

The history of warfare shows that every new offensive weapon encourages the development of new defensive weapons. The same is true of arguments. The *ad hominem* is an attack, and this attack often calls forth a counterattack. Logicians call this counterattack, or defensive weapon, the *tu quoque*. Translated into less dignified language, this means "You're another." This counterattack is appropriate only when one has been unjustly and irrelevantly attacked with an *ad hominem*. Here is a simple example: In the days before the United States instituted the peacetime drafting of members of the armed forces, there were many debates as to the desirability of the draft. A man in his forties argued that the draft was desirable, since it would make the United States ready for any emergency in the dangerous world situation. A young man, instead of trying to prove that the draft law was unnecessary, used the *ad hominem* attack. He said to the speaker, "You favor the draft because you are past the draft age and won't have to serve." This *ad hominem* approach calls for an obvious *tu quoque.* The older man replied, "By the same token, the only reason you are against the draft is because you are afraid you will have to serve." But the real question should have been, "Is the draft in the best interests of our country?" This question does not depend on who says what. An attack against the speaker proves nothing concerning the merits of what is being discussed. . . .

We have seen that there is a fundamental law of rationality, or, as we have also called it, a *law of argument,* which tells us that we ought to justify our beliefs by adequate evidence. We evade this law when we ignore the requirement of presenting evidence, and instead make an appeal to emotion, or attack the speaker instead of what he has said. These evasions furnish no evidence, either for or against the point at issue. These evasions, then, are the fundamental things to avoid, when we concern ourselves with how not to argue.

ADAPTED READING 12.2
THE ILLUSION OF PROOF
Barnet Baskerville

In December of 1953 . . . I analyzed the techniques of one of the most pernicious communicators of falsehood in our century, the late Senator Joe McCarthy. I was impressed . . . with the elaborate paraphernalia by means of which McCarthy professed to "prove" his preposterous assertions. You will recall the bulging briefcase, the fistful of photostats, the "I-have-here-in-my-hand" which became his trademark. I tried to show that much of his so-called "documentation" was bogus, and that his alleged proof was often no proof at all. I suggested . . . that this technique of elaborate though phony documentation, this knack of creating the illusion of proof where there was no proof, represented a distinct refinement, a notable advancement in the art of demagogy because it was so cleverly designed to meet the demands of a public impressed by an apparatus of "raw, harsh facts," and on the alert against "glittering generalities."

That was nearly eight years ago. McCarthy is no longer with us. His song is ended, but the melody lingers on. In the ensuing years I have been struck by frequent examples on radio and television and from the public platform of what have seemed to me similar attempts to create the illusion of proof — to produce the shadow but not the substance — in order to mislead. I do not

From *Western Speech,* Fall 1961, pp. 236–241.

mean to suggest that McCarthy is responsible for this, or that he initiated a trend which will be followed by future demagogues. But I do feel that this technique is sufficiently prevalent and sufficiently dangerous to warrant more detailed exposure. . . . Like the techniques of the hidden persuaders, this too is a manipulation of human personality for private ends, though not by bypassing the rational processes, but by seeming to appeal directly to them.

The very fact that this technique should be so widely employed, that persuaders should feel it necessary to create the illusion of proof, is evidence that some progress has been made in public education. It shows that Americans have by now been pretty thoroughly alerted to and innoculated against the more flagrant persuasive devices. . . . However, many who have learned to demand proof are not yet sophisticated enough to know what proof is, to know that all facts, however raw and harsh, are not relevant facts, and that all specific examples are not cases in point. The persuaders, aware that a little learning is a dangerous thing, have been quick to exploit this weakness.

McCarthy, of course, was the champion pseudo-prover of them all, and an impressive dossier of examples can be compiled from the utterances of this one man. Everyone remembers how he "proved" that the State Department was shot full of card-carrying Communists by holding up an alleged list of 205 or 81 or 57 names—a list which he most certainly did not possess. Some will recall the day he "proved" that the *Daily Worker* urged its readers to vote for Adlai Stevenson by holding up a copy of the *Daily Worker* (which was later found to say no such thing). In 1954, in a speech delivered from coast to coast, McCarthy "proved" the entire Democratic Party guilty of 20 years of treason, with a bizarre miscellany which he presented as "20 deeds of betrayal." Anderson and May illustrated McCarthy's method of proof with the now-famous story of the rabbit-hunter. When someone showed incredulity at the hunter's assertion that his quarry had run up a tree, he replied indignantly, "That rabbit certainly did climb a tree. What's more, my dog had to run up the tree to catch him. And if you don't believe me, I'll show you the tree."

But let us leave Senator McCarthy and look elsewhere for illustrations of the technique under discussion.

In the 1952 presidential campaign, Senator Nixon, the vice-presidential candidate, was accused of accepting a fund of $18,000, not as a campaign contribution, but for operating expenses as Senator. The question of improper influence was raised, and some demanded that Nixon be dropped from the Republican ticket. But Senator Nixon, in a coast-to-coast radio and television address, replied to the charges against him, "proved" his innocence, and received an avalanche of letters and telegrams proclaiming him an asset rather than a liability to his party's ticket. We need not concern ourselves here with the matter of Mr. Nixon's guilt or innocence; the point is that this single speech was accepted by millions of Americans as *proof* that he had done no wrong. We are therefore justified in examining its probative force. What do we find?

We find that considerably less than one-third of the speech deals even obliquely with the charges which are presumably being proved false. Nixon granted that his act could be adjudged wrong (he insisted he was not concerned merely with legality, but with morality) if it could be shown that (1) the money was used for his personal benefit, (2) it had been a secret fund, (3) any of the contributors received special favors for their contributions. These points were dealt with hastily, largely on the level of assertion: the money had not gone into Nixon's pocket; it had not been a secret fund; and no intercession had ever been made in behalf of any of the contributors. A portion of the legal opinion of Gibson, Dunn, and Crutcher was read as corroborating point one, but it merely made the point that no federal or state law had been violated.

Again it is not my intention to criticize Mr. Nixon for failure to prove these assertions. I doubt that the matter of influence, for example, is even susceptible of proof—or disproof. But I do object to his elaborate attempt to create the *illusion* of proof. More than two-thirds of this dramatic speech (unquestionably the part which many listeners regarded as the most convincing proof) had nothing at all to do with the case. It consisted, among other things, of:

1. An alleged financial history beginning with his birth in 1913, and including an account of his war experiences, a pointed reference to his wife's cloth coat, and the story of the cocker spaniel presented to his children.
2. Reference to an alleged Stevenson fund, and an invitation to both Stevenson and Sparkman to submit complete financial statements ("if they don't it will be an admission that they have something to hide").
3. A reminder of Nixon's part in the Hiss trial.
4. An extended indictment of the Truman-Acheson administration, which lost 600 million people to the Communists, caused the Korean war, coddled Communists at home, and created the mess in Washington.
5. An attack on Governor Stevenson as a man who "isn't fit to be President of the United States."
6. A letter from the wife of a U.S. Marine in Korea.
7. Lavish praise for General Eisenhower.

It was this array of evidence—of facts, figures, and testimony regarding mortgages, salary, dogs, and coats—this mélange of praise and blame, of attack and defense, which was accepted by millions as indisputable proof. And proof of what? Not proof that he was an unusually talented young man who had risen far and fast, but proof that he was innocent, that he stood vindicated of the specific charges made against him. "Complete vindication," said Senator Mundt, "against one of the most vicious smears in American history."

There is a sequel to this story, not irrelevant to our study of the illusion of proof, though this item might more accurately be described as the *self-delusion* of proof. Throughout the early stages of the Nixon affair, General Eisenhower had displayed considerable hesitance, so much so that Nixon was reported to have been furious with him. The General neither condemned nor supported his young running mate; he waited. He was deeply moved by Nixon's television speech; it showed, he thought, great courage. But he still withheld judgment pending further evidence. When, however, the mail began to show an overwhelming sentiment in favor of the vice-presidential candidate, Eisenhower became convinced that Nixon had indeed come clean as a hound's tooth. This is proof by popularity poll, the validity of the proposition being determined by the weight of the postman's mail bag.

This technique of making an ostentatious display of proof which I have been illustrating from political oratory cannot have escaped even the most casual observer of television commercials. "Here's proof," he is told, as objects A and B are sent bubbling through a maze of pipes, valves, elbows, joints, and tanks. Of what is this phenomenon taking place before his very eyes *proof*? Why, obviously, that Bufferin (B) reaches the human blood stream more rapidly than Aspirin (A). An eraser is drawn cleanly across a smudged blackboard, *proving* that Dial soap removes dirt film from human epidermis. A flying baseball is deflected by a pane of glass from crashing into the viewer's face, thus *proving* that Colgate with Gardol protects his teeth with an impervious, transparent film.

But it wasn't the advertisers who brought to television the most ponderous, pretentious, overwhelming machinery of proof; it was the quiz show producers. What skeptic could remain skeptical before those locked bank vaults, those armed bank guards, those dignified bank vice-presidents sent by the Guaranty Trust to protect those elaborately sealed envelopes? And those sound-proof isolation booths, where the agonizing contestant stood in antiseptic solitude struggling to dredge up the tiny esoteric fact that was to bring him fame and fortune. Surely, surely here was proof, if ever on earth proof was, of incorruptible honesty. But alas, as everyone now knows, it was all a hollow shell, a splendid, glittering *illusion* of proof. Someone had slipped past the seals, the vaults, the guards, the vice-presidents, and the sound-proof booths, and had corrupted the whole business at the center. . . . We have seen the candidates proving statistically that things were better under the Democrats, and under the Republicans. Even in the South, where old-style demagogy still flourishes, the new technique has appeared. I have in my possession a speech by a representative of the White Citizens' Councils which presents bushels of official statistics purporting to "prove" the same things about the Negro that a few years ago Senator Bilbo was merely *asserting* with characteristic vileness.

Thirty years ago William Allen White was explaining the success of demagogues by his "moronic underworld" theory. In every civilization, he maintained, "there is a moronic underworld which cannot be civilized. It can be taught to read and write, but not to think, and it lives upon the level of its emotions and prejudices." The intent of my remarks has been to suggest that segments of Mr. White's moronic underworld are beginning to learn to think, or at least to question. After having been flim-flammed, bilked, and sold to saturation, they are becoming increasingly skeptical and resistant to persuasion, both political and commercial. The existence of this skepticism has, according to Vance Packard, been one of the main reasons why the hidden persuaders have turned to subconscious appeals. And it also explains the antics of the "here's proof" boys.

We should welcome this skepticism, but we must also be aware of its dangers. Universal skepticism is as much to be avoided as universal credulity. A measure of belief is essential to communal existence. And there is danger, it seems to me, that continued exposure to the *illusion* of proof will bring about distrust of the genuine article. Viscount Morley once said that the first quality of an educated person is knowing what evidence is and when a thing is proved and when it is not proved. It is not a simple thing to know when a thing is proved and when it isn't; there are no quick, easy formulas for acquiring this faculty. But we have rules to guide us, tests to evaluate evidence and reasoning, the constituents of genuine proof. It is the responsibility of those of us who are familiar with these tests to use them ourselves and to aid others in their application. . . .

ADAPTED READING 12.3

THE TRICKS OF THE TRADE
Alfred McClung Lee and Elizabeth Briant Lee

Some of the devices now so subtly and effectively used by good and bad propagandists are as old as language. All have been used in one form or another by all of us in our daily dealings with each other. Propagandists have seized upon these methods we ordinarily use to convince each other, have analyzed and refined them, and have experimented with them until these homely devices of folk origin have been developed into tremendously powerful weapons for the swaying of popular opinions and actions.

The chief devices used in popular argument and by professional propagandists are:

Name calling — giving an idea a bad label — is used to make us reject and condemn the idea without examining the evidence.

Glittering generality — associating something with a "virtue word" — is used to make us accept and approve the thing without examining the evidence.

Card stacking involves the selection and use of facts or falsehoods, illustrations or distractions, and logical or illogical statements in order to give the best or the worst possible case for an idea, program, person, or product.

Transfer carries the authority, sanction, and prestige of something respected and revered over to something else in order to make the latter acceptable; or it carries authority, sanction, and disapproval to cause us to reject and disapprove something the propagandist would have us reject and disapprove.

Testimonial consists in having some respected or hated person say that a given idea or program or person is good or bad.

Plain folks is the method by which a speaker attempts to convince his

Abridged from Alfred McClung Lee and Elizabeth Briant Lee, *The Fine Art of Propaganda*, new ed. (New York: Octagon Books, 1972), pp. 22–24. Reprinted by permission of the authors, to whom a renewal of the copyright was granted in 1967.

audience that he and his ideas are good because they are "of the people," the "plain folks."

Band wagon has as its theme "Everybody — at least all of *us* — is doing it"; with it, the propagandist attempts to convince us that all members of a group to which we belong are accepting his program and that we must therefore follow our crowd and "jump on the band wagon."

Once we know that a speaker or writer is using one of these propaganda devices in an attempt to convince us of an idea, we can separate the device from the idea and see what the idea amounts to on its own merits.

ADAPTED READING 12.4

NEW YORK TIMES RATED NO. 1

The New York Times again has been rated the best newspaper in the country, according to a 1970 survey of newspaper publishers made public by Edward L. Bernays, public relations consultant here.

The Los Angeles Times, which was rated eighth in 1961, in the last of three similar polls, placed second this year. Eight of the top ten this year were on the 1961 list. The two additions are *The Miami Herald* and *The Wall Street Journal.*

Although *The New York Times* was listed first, the percentage of publishers who rated it among the top ten declined from 89 in 1961 to 61.

The 1970 survey, as in the previous three, requested the publishers to list the ten newspapers that had met the goals of "independent journalism, impartial news reporting and crusading for the public welfare, as set up in the credos of publishers Thomas Gibson of *The Rocky Mountain News* of Denver, Adolph S. Ochs of *The New York Times* and Joseph Pulitzer of *The New York World.*" The three publishers are now dead.

The 10 newspapers of 1970 in order of percentage as listed by the publishers follows:

New York Times	61
Los Angeles Times	51
Louisville Courier-Journal	42
St. Louis Post-Dispatch	38
Washington Post	38
Christian Science Monitor	30
Miami Herald	30
Milwaukee Journal	29
Chicago Tribune	23
Wall Street Journal	20

From *The New York Times*, April 28, 1970, p. 38.

The 1961 list and percentages were:

New York Times 89
St. Louis Post-Dispatch 62
Christian Science Monitor 52
Milwaukee Journal 45
Louisville Courier-Journal 42
New York Herald Tribune 39
Washington Post and Times Herald 37
Los Angeles Times 35
Chicago Tribune 34
Kansas City Star 32

ADAPTED READING 12.5

THE CREDIBILITY GAP:
ARGUMENT BY SPECIFIC INSTANCES
Wes Gallagher

In 1967, in a speech accepting the William Allen White Foundation Award, journalist Wes Gallagher employed argument by specific instances to show why the American people had become skeptical of government pronouncements.

This society doubts the credibility of almost everything and is immune — if I can pronounce it — to humbugability. And they have reasons for this attitude. In our time, the Vietnamese war has probably been the greatest contributor to the cynicism in this country. To cite a few examples of what they have heard:

"The war can only be won by the Vietnamese themselves and the United States will pull out more troops even if the war falters."

"Our responsibility is not to substitute ourselves for the Vietnamese but to train them to carry on the operation that they themselves are capable of."

Author — Secretary of Defense McNamara in 1963 and 1964. These are just a few of many such government statements made over five years of the war and proven wrong by events.

Within a week last fall, we had Secretary McNamara saying that the troop buildup in Vietnam would be slowed up and level off. Meanwhile, General Greene of the Marine Corps, in an off-the-record Tokyo press conference, said they would need 750,000 men in Vietnam. Senator Stennis set the figure needed at 600,000. Confusion multiplied!

The latest furor has been set off by the reporting of Harrison Salisbury of *The New York Times* and Bill Baggs of the *Miami News*. But the stage for Salisbury was set not by *The New York Times* but by the statements of United

From *Representative American Speeches, 1966–1967,* pp. 148–159.

States Government officials during two years of bombing in North Vietnam. . . . There was a concentrated effort on the part of every arm in government, including the Pentagon, to make it appear that the bombs fell only on military targets.

Questioned about the bombing accuracy in June of 1966, when the bombs were close to Hanoi and Haiphong, McNamara emphasized at a press conference that the pilots were carefully instructed to confine themselves to military targets. He said the pilots were told "not to destroy the Communist government of North Vietnam nor destroy or damage the people of North Vietnam."

A Pentagon spokesman said that the bombs fell "right on target."

McNamara added, "The pilots were especially briefed to avoid civilian areas. We have not hit Hanoi or Haiphong, we have hit oil storage facilities."

Senator Dirksen, a Republican who seems to echo the Administration, chimed in to say, "We are absolutely astounded at the real precision result."

On June 30, General Myers said that fuel dumps were hit by a "surgical type of treatment—this means holding civilian casualties to an absolute minimum and putting the bombs right on the money."

On the same day, Ambassador Goldberg said the bombings hit petroleum facilities "located away from the population center of Hanoi and Haiphong."

On July 1, Vice President Humphrey in Detroit said the raids were carried out "so as to avoid civilian casualties." July 2, an Administration spokesman said, "No more than one or two civilians—perhaps none—were killed in Wednesday's bombing of oil targets in Haiphong and Hanoi." The Administration spokesman said that this conclusion was based on aerial photographs of the raid. Just how such an exact count of civilian casualties could be deduced from photographs was not made clear, since the Administration first announced that 89 percent of the oil facilities were hit, then revised this a few days later to 40 percent to 60 percent. Then on July 17, Secretary Cyrus Vance said that 66 percent of the oil facilities had been destroyed.

These aerial photographs seem to be the most flexible in history—they provided any kind of an answer a speaker wanted.

At any rate, the Administration's own attempt to convey the impression that bombs fell only on military targets set the stage for Salisbury's articles. He pointed out the inevitable—that bombs fall today, just as they did in World War II, on most any place—on civilians and military installations alike, particularly if the bombings are heavy. Flying at 600 or 1000 miles an hour with only split seconds over a target—shot at by ground fire and rockets and possibly attacked by Migs—it is a wonder that the bombing is as accurate as it has been. As a matter of fact, the bombings probably were more accurate than the statements about them.

How much different the picture would have been these past two years if the Administration had said the bombs were directed toward military targets but "inevitably some of them fell outside the areas and probably caused civilian casualties." Such repeated statements would have been accurate, truthful, and believed.

ADAPTED READING 12.6

HOW SAFE IS YOUR CITY? STATISTICS CAN MISLEAD

David Burnham

In comparison with the 25 largest cities in the United States, New York City ranks twelfth in homicide, second in robbery, seventeenth in rape and twenty-third in larceny, according to the most recent reported crime statistics compiled by the Federal Bureau of Investigation.

But these comparative crime statistics, frequently cited by politicians, police chiefs and assorted civic groups to prove the relative strengths or weaknesses of law enforcement in a given city, are considered virtually useless for this purpose by many criminologists and policemen.

Although the Federal Bureau of Investigation for many years has compiled and publicized quarterly and annual reports containing the crime statistics submitted to it by police departments throughout the country, . . . the F.B.I. states that "individuals using these tabulations are cautioned against drawing conclusions by making direct comparisons between cities due to the existence of numerous factors which affect the amount and type of crime from place to place."

In a more complete warning printed in its annual report, the bureau lists a number of factors other than the effectiveness of the police, the toughness of the judges and the usefulness of the jails that affect crime in each city. These factors include the composition of a city's population particularly in reference to age and race, its climate, its architectural design and the attitude of its citizens toward crime and law enforcement.

One influence not mentioned by the F.B.I. is the deliberate manipulation of crime statistics by some police departments. Although the bureau attempts to detect and control such numbers games, many criminologists and policemen — and even experts inside the F.B.I. itself — acknowledge that some departments deliberately reduce the amount of reported crime in their cities.

Professor Lloyd Ohlin of the Harvard Law School, the former associate director of President Johnson's Crime Commission and a leading criminologist, said in an interview that "these statistics are influenced by so many different factors it really is impossible to determine what they mean."

Floyd Feeney, director of the Center on Administration of Criminal Justice at the University of California at Davis, said that although the F.B.I. comparative crime figures often were used by politicians, they prove nothing one way or the other about the prevention and control of crime in a given city.

The warnings about comparing reported crime statistics of various cities do not mean that the statistics from a given city over a limited period of time cannot be used by the police and the public to judge the performance of law enforcement or the impact of crime on different neighborhoods.

For example, if there is a sharp increase in robberies in one precinct over a six-month or one-year period, perhaps the department might transfer policemen there from a precinct where crime rates are stable.

The statistics so frequently misused by politicians and police chiefs include the four crimes against the person—homicide, rape, robbery and aggravated assault—and against property—burglary, larceny and auto theft. These crimes were selected in 1930 to provide an index, or level of criminality, for the United States and individual cities.

For each of these crimes, however, there are a number of different problems that are the basis for the warnings against making city-to-city comparisons. From conversations with police officials, criminologists and statistical experts, some of the problems in comparing these separate crimes include the following:

MURDER

Homicides, because they are bodies, are considered the most accurately reported of all crimes. But because there are so few homicides in comparison to all the index crimes—16,528 out of 7,557,405 for 1972—they are considered to have little impact on over-all trends in reported crime. Criminologists also point out that a substantial majority of homicides occur within the family, often in the privacy of a home, and thus are only marginally susceptible to influence by effective police work.

RAPE

Rape is considered by criminologists to be one of the least reliable of crime statistics. According to several studies of unreported crime, a large proportion of rapes are never reported to the police, partly because of the reluctance of women to talk to policemen about the crime and partly because of the often questioning attitude of policemen toward women who reported being raped.

ROBBERY

The crime of robbery, taking something of value by threat or use of force, includes some but not all purse snatches, stickups and bank holdups. Because robbery often involves violence, usually is committed by a stranger and is far more frequent an event than homicide, it is considered one of the key crimes included in the F.B.I.'s annual report.

But like all crimes but homicide, the number of robberies reported by the police can be influenced by narrow police judgments that are subject to manipulation. According to F.B.I. rules, for example, the question of whether a purse snatch is designated as a robbery or a larceny, for example, is decided by the policeman on the scene by whether the thief actually touched his victim while taking her purse.

In a city like Washington, for example, where the police have been under tremendous pressure from Congress and the Administration to "do something about crime," a number of police officials around the country believe that the individual classification judgments are being influenced by Chief Jerry Wilson's order to his commanders to reduce robberies or face removal from their commands. Given this pressure, many police administrators around the country feel that at least some district or precinct commanders are faking their statistics.

The number of times a city resident walks on a street or appears in other public places would appear to influence his chances of being mugged. Thus, if a large proportion of a city's population uses cars rather than public transportation or foot to go to work or go shopping, this might reduce the total number of opportunities for a mugger to attack a potential victim.

Although an almost endless number of factors are involved in how often a mugger attacks, an examination of the number of automobiles and trucks in relation to the populations shows that in cities where larger numbers of residents do not have cars—there are comparatively high rates of reported robberies.

AGGRAVATED ASSAULT

The rates of aggravated assault can also be heavily influenced by often unstated police department arrest policies, many policemen agree.

"This is the crime where there is least likely to be a kick if it's forgotten," said one senior police official. "No insurance is involved, no income tax, no missing hulk of a stolen car, no body."

The official said another factor leading to great variation in reported rates of assault is that the crime frequently involves a short fight between a wife and a husband or two friends in a bar who often are not interested in pressing charges once tempers cool.

"This crime, perhaps more than any other crime of violence, is subject to the widest latitude of precinct police or police department policy," the official concluded.

BURGLARY, LARCENY, AUTO THEFT

These three crimes against property account for about 85 percent of the F.B.I.'s seven index crimes and the relative frequency of their occurrence is believed to be subject to many influences other than the energy and effectiveness of law enforcement.

With 1,192.9 burglaries reported for every 100,000 residents during the first six months, Los Angeles burglars appeared to be almost twice as busy as those in New York, which only reported 707.7 such crimes for every 100,000 residents.

But a number of explanations, other than the relative energy of the burglars or effectiveness of police, may be responsible for the disparity between New York and Los Angeles. Perhaps New York's low rate of burglary should be attributed to building design—large numbers of highrise buildings that theoretically are less subject to break-ins than one-story ramblers.

Perhaps the variation can be attributed to New York's crime-hardened citizens who understand there is an arrest in only one out of every 10 reported burglaries and just do not bother to call the police. Or perhaps the explanation is that New York policemen are quicker to list a burglary under malicious mischief than their colleagues on the West Coast.

The variation in the larceny rates, which involve such crimes as shoplifting, pocket picking and some purse snatches, is even greater than is found in the burglary category. Phoenix, which ranks first in larceny, reports 2,484.5 such crimes for every 100,000 residents in the first six months of 1973. The big city with the lowest ranking was Philadelphia, which reported only 474.3 larcenies for every 100,000 residents.

Police Sergeant Edna Hurt, head of the police's crime analysis section in Phoenix, said in an interview that she believed her city's comparatively high rate of larceny was the result of a Phoenix Police Department policy decision to record and report every theft—no matter how small.

"We count everything here—even if it involves a garbage can or garden hose." Many law-enforcement officials are convinced that Philadelphia, which also has comparatively low rates of reported rapes, aggravated assaults and burglaries, has for many years systematically reduced its crime statistics in an effort to match its reputation as the City of Brotherly Love.

Some officials also wonder about New York's relatively low rate of reported larcenies, twenty-third out of the 25 largest cities.

"It may be true but I just can't believe that Milwaukee, Seattle and San Diego all have that many more thieves than New York," said one police sergeant.

A comparison of auto-theft rates of the standard metropolitan statistical areas around each of the 25 cities in relation to the auto and truck ownership rates in these cities, surprisingly indicated that the frequency of car theft does not appear to be related to the prevalence of cars.

More than 40 years ago, recalled Dr. Ohlin of Harvard, there was a Midwestern scientist named Robert Angell who attempted to devise a "morality index for America's cities, to rank them according to their relative goodness and badness. Angell couldn't make his morality index work then and the politicians can't make it work now."

ADAPTED READING 12.7
A PRESIDENT DEFENDS HIS POLICIES BY ARGUMENT FROM AUTHORITIES
Lyndon B. Johnson

Vietnam is . . . the scene of a powerful aggression that is spurred by an appetite for conquest. . . . Why should three Presidents and the elected representatives of our people have chosen to defend this Asian nation more than ten thousand miles from American shores? . . . That is the question which Dwight Eisenhower and John Kennedy and Lyndon Johnson had to answer in facing the issue in Vietnam.

That is the question that the Senate of the United States answered by a vote of 82 to 1 when it ratified and approved the SEATO treaty in 1955, and

From a speech before the National Legislative Conference, San Antonio, Texas, September 29, 1967.

to which the members of the United States Congress responded in a resolution that it passed in 1964 by a vote of 504 to 2, "The United States is, therefore, prepared as the President determines, to take all necessary steps, including the use of armed forces, to assist any member or protocol state of the Southeast Asia collective defense treaty requesting assistance in defense of its freedom. . . ."

For those who have borne the responsibility for decision during these past ten years, the stakes to us have seemed clear — and have seemed high.

President Dwight Eisenhower said in 1959: "Strategically, South Vietnam's capture by the Communists would bring their power several hundred miles into a hitherto free region. The remaining countries in Southeast Asia would be menaced by a great flanking movement. The freedom of 12 million people would be lost immediately, and that of 150 million in adjacent lands would be seriously endangered. The loss of South Vietnam would set in motion a crumbling process that could, as it progressed, have grave consequences for us and for freedom. . . ."

And President John F. Kennedy said in 1962: ". . . Withdrawal in the case of Vietnam and the case of Thailand might mean a collapse of the entire area." A year later, he reaffirmed that: "We are not going to withdraw from that effort. In my opinion, for us to withdraw from that effort would mean a collapse not only of South Vietnam, but Southeast Asia. So we are going to stay there."

This is not simply an American viewpoint, I would have you legislative leaders know. I am going to call the roll now of those who live in that part of the world — in the great arc of Asian and Pacific nations — and who bear the responsibility for leading their people, and the responsibility for the fate of their people.

The President of the Philippines has this to say: "Vietnam is the focus of attention now. . . . It may happen to Thailand or the Philippines, or anywhere, wherever there is misery, disease, ignorance. . . . For you to renounce your position of leadership in Asia is to allow the Red Chinese to gobble up all of Asia."

The Foreign Minister of Thailand said "[The American] decision will go down in history as the move that prevented the world from having to face another major conflagration."

The Prime Minister of Australia said: "We are there because while Communist aggression persists the whole of Southeast Asia is threatened."

President Park of Korea said: "For the first time in our history, we decided to dispatch our combat troops overseas . . . because in our belief any aggression against the Republic of Vietnam represented a direct and grave menace against the security and peace of free Asia, and therefore directly jeopardized the very security and freedom of our own people."

The Prime Minister of Malaysia warned his people that if the United States pulled out of South Vietnam, it would go to the Communists, and after that, it would only be a matter of time until they moved against neighboring states.

The Prime Minister of New Zealand said: "We can thank God that

America at least regards aggression in Asia with the same concern as it regards aggression in Europe—and is prepared to back up its concern with action."

The Prime Minister of Singapore said: "I feel the fate of Asia—South and Southeast Asia—will be decided in the next few years by what happens out in Vietnam."

ADAPTED READING 12.8

MISQUOTED QUOTE MAKES THE ROUNDS
Meg Greenfield

In choosing supporting materials, the speaker should always make certain that his evidence is accurate. Newspaper writer Meg Greenfield relates what can happen when the speaker fails to verify his information with the original source.

On May 3, 1966, the U.S. Commissioner of Education, Harold Howe II, gave a speech at Columbia University in which he said, "Building programs for the future should be planned so that new schools break up rather than continue segregation. The Office of Education will provide Federal planning funds for such efforts right now, and if I have my way about it, we will provide construction funds before long."

On August 2 of that year, the syndicated columnist, James Jackson Kilpatrick, cited—in a manner of speaking—Commissioner Howe's remark. Mr. Kilpatrick put the Commissioner's "if I have my way" into quotes, but he finished off the sentence with his own version of what the Commissioner in fact never said. Thus, Commissioner Howe as rendered by Mr. Kilpatrick in his column: "If I have my way," he said, "schools will be built for the primary purpose of social and economic integration."

Capitol Hill in its eagerness to get the goods on Commissioner Howe was insensitive to the finer points of quoting. It encircled the whole sentence with quotation marks, and the bogus statement was an immediate hit. ". . . Bureaucratic overlord of the Office of Education," Rep. Albert Watson of South Carolina inveighed, "is not really concerned with achieving the mere integration of faculty and pupils. In his own words, during an address at Columbia University, he stated his real intention; that is, and I quote: 'If I have my way, schools will be built for the primary purpose of social and economic integration.' Now, possibly I am just old-fashioned, but it seems to me that the primary purpose of any school is the education of our youth."

From time to time in the past couple of years, Commissioner Howe has entered into fruitless correspondences attempting to point out that he never ut-

From the *Washington Post*, October 13, 1968, p. B6. © The Washington Post.

tered the offending, impolitic words and that they do not represent either his intentions or his views. Even Mr. Kilpatrick has grudgingly conceded, "Howe never said this." But to no avail. For all the ghosts that haunt it and the "revisions" and "extensions" that distort it, the so-called *Congressional Record* is widely regarded as an authoritative source, so that the remark the Commissioner did not make has now found its way into print around the country—especially where the "guidelines" are at issue—and it will doubtless provide the lead sentence to the second paragraph of Commissioner Howe's obituary when that unhappy document comes to be written.

If there was ever any reason to believe that the apocryphal statement might fade into obscurity before the Commissioner did, it vanished with the campaign of 1968. For it was not until this year that the "quotation" hit the big time: it has become a staple of Richard Nixon's repertoire. In Washington, Anaheim, Milwaukee, and Detroit—to mention but a few of the towns it has played—the Howe remark has been invoked by Mr. Nixon by way, some might say, of avoiding an answer to the vexing question of guidelines.

Typically, the candidate when asked his view of the enforcement of desegregation rulings, declares that he is against segregation and proceeds to say that on the other hand he does not go along with the thinking of Commissioner Howe. Mr. Nixon alluded to the Commissioner's alleged statement no fewer than four times in a recent Detroit press conference. Here is the way it came out in Milwaukee: "On the other hand, I do not go with the Office of Education on the other side of the coin. In 1966, Mr. Howe, the Commissioner of Education, made this statement, and I quote him exactly. He said, 'The primary purpose of building schools in the United States should be for the purpose of promoting social and economic integration.' I don't agree with that. The primary purpose of building schools in the United States is education."

Should Mr. Nixon discover that he is using not only a strawman but a strawman's straw quote, he might be inclined to drop this set response to what is, after all, a rather important question. . . . However, no one who has followed the indestructible career of Commissioner Howe's Columbia University remark has reason to be very hopeful. And at this point it is almost safe to say that Mr. Nixon owes nearly as much to James Jackson Kilpatrick as he does to Senator Strom Thurmond. The pen, at least as wielded by Mr. Kilpatrick, would seem to be mightier than the word.

ADAPTED READING 12.9

NONRETURNABLE BOTTLES AND NONEXISTENT STUDIES

David Bird

The Federal Environmental Protection Agency, which has been citing a California "study" to back up its skepticism about requiring returnable cans and bottles to help solve the nation's waste and litter problems, has now conceded that such a study never existed.

The study was first mentioned publicly in October 1972 by William D. Ruckelshaus, administrator of the agency, in a news conference before making a dinner speech to the Aluminum Association here. The Aluminum Association and other industries that are involved in making one-way or nonreturnable cans and bottles have been strongly opposed to attempts to require returnable bottles.

Legislation to mandate returnable bottles, however, has won strong backing from environmentalists and municipal authorities who are concerned about the growing solid waste and litter problem posed by soft drink and beer bottles that are used just once and then thrown away.

But Mr. Ruckelshaus said that people were not returning bottles because it was too much trouble. Thus, he said, the returnable bottle, because it was much more durable and heavier, was adding more of a solid waste burden if it was thrown away after one use.

To back up his contention that returnable bottles may pose even more of a solid waste problem, Mr. Ruckelshaus cited what he termed a federally aided experiment that had shown that if the deposit on a bottle was raised high enough to encourage people to return it, counterfeiters would make the bottles just to collect the bounty. The test was in California, he said, and the deposit price was put at eleven cents. At that point, Mr. Ruckelshaus reported, counterfeiters found they could make the bottles cheaper than that, so they simply made the bottles to collect the deposit. The result, Mr. Ruckelshaus said, was even more bottles added to the solid waste glut.

Mr. Ruckelshaus's stand on returnable bottles stirred the concern of those people who have been pushing legislation to stem the tide of nonreturnable bottles. . . . There were inquiries to the E.P.A. for more details on the California study. At first inquirers were told that the agency was checking on the study. Finally, last week, . . . Samuel Hale, Jr., the E.P.A.'s deputy assistant administrator for solid waste management programs, conceded that the experiment had never existed.

"From all indications," Mr. Hale wrote, "it appears that erroneous information was received on this matter from somewhere within the agency." . . . Mr. Hale said that apparently Mr. Ruckelshaus had mistaken a conversation about the point at which counterfeiting might be possible for an actual test. Mr. Hale said that he knew of no evidence any place of counterfeiting. Jim

Barnes, a spokesman for Mr. Ruckelshaus, said yesterday: "Bill thought he had been told that such a study existed. He had apparently seized on some information and taken it way further than was true."

ADAPTED READING 12.10

THE TROUBLE WITH HALF-TRUTHS
Gilbert Highet

In high school and college just after World War I, we were all caught up in argument about the Cause of War, the Origin of Religion, the Meaning of Love, and so forth. These arguments usually ended with one of the glib generalizations which appeal to the young. The Cause of War, we were told, was "the power of monarchs" (like Wilhelm II and the Czar) or the sinister activity of "the munitions makers."

It was quite difficult to resist the pressure of these simple solutions. But at the same time I was studying history. And after long searching for the single cause of such great events as the fall of the Roman Empire, I realized that the search was absurd. To simplify history is to falsify it. No situation in which many strings of action are interwoven can be reduced to just one thread.

When at last I understood this, it gave me great relief: it cleared my thinking about a number of important problems in religion, in history, in politics, in personal life, and in art. It put me on guard against labels and slogans. It liberated me from the half-truths and over-simplifications of the propagandist, the doctrinaire, and the fanatic.

Realizing that complex events have complex causes has saved me from accepting dozens of those cure-all pills which are peddled by the ambitious and swallowed by the unwary. Anyone who says, "This 'ism' is the only disease of mankind, and this pill will cure it," is a quack. No one pill will cure all human ailments.

From *This Week* magazine.

ADDITIONAL READINGS

Baird, A. Craig, *Argumentation, Discussion and Debate* (New York: McGraw-Hill, 1950), chap. 8, "Evidence: Principles and Types" and chap. 9, "Evidence: Techniques and Tests."

Ehninger, Douglas and Wayne Brockriede, *Decision by Debate* (New York: Dodd, Mead, 1963), chap. 9, "Evidence"; chap. 10, "Substantive Proof"; chap. 11, "Authoritative and Motivational Proofs"; chap. 12, "Detecting Deficiencies of Proof."

Freeley, Austin, *Argumentation and Debate* (San Francisco: Wadsworth, 1961), chap. 5, "Evidence"; chap. 6, "The Tests of Evidence"; chap. 7, "Reasoning."

Gulley, Halbert E., *Discussion, Conference, and Group Process* (New York: Holt, Rinehart & Winston, 1968), 96–110.

Mudd, Charles and Malcolm Sillars, *Speech Content and Communication* (San Francisco: Chandler, 1969), chap. 6, "Supporting Material: Types and Uses."

Sattler, William and N. Edd Miller, *Discussion and Conference* (Englewood Cliffs, N.J.: Prentice-Hall, 1968), chap. 9, "Reasoning and Fallacies."

STUDY QUESTIONS

1. Why is effective supporting material particularly important in a speech to convince or to persuade?
2. What is a fact?
3. Are facts always true? Can facts always be proven?
4. How are facts determined? By whom?
5. Why is it important that a speaker be able to differentiate between facts and theories or opinions?
6. What six tests should a speaker apply to the sources of his evidence?
7. What is the difference between a biased source and a dishonest one?
8. What are the tests of argument by specific instances? Why is it important that the instances be representative?
9. What is the principal difficulty in constructing a valid argument using comparison? Why, in spite of this problem, is the speaker sometimes required to argue from comparison?
10. What is argument by authority? What is an authority?
11. What is a causal argument?
12. What tests should the speaker apply to test an argument based on statistics?

EXERCISES

1. From a newspaper, find five statements (complete sentences) that are facts. Also find five statements that clearly are opinions.
2. In a newspaper or magazine article, find an example of statistics being used to prove a point. Apply the tests of statistics and decide whether the statistics constitute conclusive proof.
3. Name someone who would be regarded as an authority by most students in your class in each of the following fields: newspaper publishing, medicine, professional football, college education, crime.
4. List three speech subjects where the speaker probably would employ causal argument to prove his central thought.
5. Test the following as authorities to support an argument in a persuasive speech. Be prepared to indicate why each one would or would not be satisfactory.
   a. A quotation by Sir Winston Churchill on American education.
   b. Testimony of a Big Ten football coach on qualities of leadership in college youth.
   c. Actor Bob Hope's opinion on pollution.
   d. The conclusions of a Peace Corps member who has just returned from two years work in Ecuador on needed political reform in Ecuador. On poverty in South America.
   e. The recommendations of an F.B.I. agent for handling student protests.
6. Test the following as evidence to support one's arguments in a speech to persuade. Be prepared to state why each would or would not be satisfactory.
   a. A comparison between German treatment of the Jews in the 1930s and the American treatment of Negroes today to prove the need for a solution to United States racial problems.
   b. Statistics showing that the major television networks devoted more time in their newscasts during the 1972 presidential campaign to Richard Nixon than to George McGovern as evidence of biased reporting and distortion of the news.
   c. An eye-witness account of how eight different passers-by failed to come to the assistance of a man being beaten by three assailants in a parking lot as evidence of the apathy and indifference of the American people to crime.
   d. Statistics showing that American Negroes enjoy a standard of living higher than that of Negroes in any other country in the world as evidence that the Negro is not discriminated against economically in this country.
   e. Several examples of violent crimes committed by juveniles resembling crimi-

nal acts depicted on television programs they had watched as evidence of the harmful effect of television upon youth.

7. Prepare a one-to two-minute talk in which you prove a single point. Members of the class will be asked to evaluate how conclusive you were in your proof.

8. Prepare a four- to five-minute speech to convince or persuade the class of an unpopular view. At least half of the class should be either opposed or neutral toward your proposition when you begin. Select a topic in which you believe strongly.

9. Prepare a four- to five-minute speech to persuade your listeners to do something within the next week that they otherwise would not do. At the end of the week, check to find out how many carried out the action urged. Report to the class the results of your survey and explain the reasons for your relative success or failure.

CHAPTER 13

PHYSICAL ATTRIBUTES OF DELIVERY

The nationally televised debates between John F. Kennedy and Richard M. Nixon in the 1960 election convincingly demonstrated the importance of the physical or visible elements of a speaker's delivery. Surveys conducted after the first debate showed that persons who had listened on radio felt that the two speakers were evenly matched, with Nixon perhaps somewhat more effective. Television viewers, however, gave Kennedy the victory by a considerable margin. The only difference in the two media — those watching television *saw* the speakers — clearly indicates that the physical attributes of delivery were decisive in the viewers' reactions.

On television, Kennedy projected an image of vigor, confidence, and maturity, which contrasted sharply with Nixon's tired, worn look. Theodore White describes Nixon's appearance as "tense, almost frightened, at times glowering and, occasionally, haggard-looking to the point of sickness." The difference in the response of radio listeners and television viewers emphasizes the importance of the two separate elements of delivery — the vocal or audible factors and the physical or visible characteristics. Vocally, Nixon was Kennedy's equal, but the visible elements of Kennedy's delivery were superior. Learning from this experience, Nixon subsequently took great pains to develop an effective visible presentation.

Chapters 13 and 14 deal with these two facets of delivery. This chapter discusses methods of delivery and the speaker's bodily action. The next chapter treats the speaker's vocal usage.

WHAT IS DELIVERY?

In improving one's speech, it is important that the speaker understand the difference between the delivery and the content of a speech.

Delivery refers to the actual presentation of the speech. It consists of both vocal and physical elements. Vocal elements include the speaker's voice quality, pitch, rate, volume, articulation, and pronunciation. The physical or bodily aspects of the speech include posture, movement, gesture, eye contact, and facial expression.

Perhaps the concept of delivery can be better understood by contrasting it with the content or subject matter of the speech. Speech content consists of *what* the speaker has to say, while delivery refers to *how* he says it. From a stenographic transcript of a speech a reader may learn *what* the speaker said. Such accounts frequently are published in newspapers, in the *Congressional Record,* and in collections of speeches. If they have not been subsequently edited or revised, these texts provide an accurate report of the content of the speech—the ideas, supporting materials, organization, and language. Stenographic and published versions, however accurate, do not provide a faithful reproduction of the complete speech, for they cannot transcribe the speaker's delivery. A written transcript does not record the speaker's voice quality, rate of speaking, inflection, changes in loudness, and other vocal characteristics of the address which may have added emphasis or provided effective contrast. A written transcript is further inadequate as an accurate report of the speech, for it cannot reproduce gestures, posture, facial expression, and other physical attributes of the speaker's address.

Those vocal and physical elements of a speech which are impossible to record in writing constitute the speaker's delivery. As already suggested, delivery is no less important than content in determining the effectiveness of a speech. The most eloquently worded, thoughtful text is likely to have little impact on an audience if it is inaudibly muttered by the speaker or presented in an awkward manner. Because he is primarily concerned with the response of his listeners rather than with the long-term judgment of literary critics, the speaker cannot afford to overlook the importance of effective delivery.

METHODS OF DELIVERY

One of the first questions asked by beginning speakers is how to prepare and deliver the speech. Some write out the speech in its entirety and then read it aloud to the audience. Others prepare a manuscript and attempt to memorize it. Still others develop an outline and deliver the speech from the outline or a set of notes. A few make no advance preparation and simply rely on the inspiration of the moment to see them through. Finally, some combine these approaches, memorizing portions of the speech, reading other parts, and extemporizing or speaking impromptu here and there. Even after deciding upon a method of delivery, many speakers do not know what steps to take in preparing to deliver the speech.

In choosing a method of presentation, the speaker should be aware that no single approach is better than another. One method may be appropriate to a particular speaking situation, but poorly suited to another. The choice of method will be dictated by the speaker's abilities, the nature of the situation, and the type and length of the speech.

A speaker has four methods of delivery from which to choose: manuscript, memory, extemporaneous, and impromptu. At times, he may combine these methods. Each has advantages and disadvantages.

Manuscript

The manuscript method of delivery consists of reading the speech from a complete prepared manuscript.

The advantages of this method are several. Perhaps the chief one is that it permits the speaker to determine in advance exactly what he wishes to say. He is able to select his words with care, to revise, to rework, and to polish so that the final version represents his most careful and considered effort. Another advantage to this method is that in presentation the speaker need not worry about forgetting part of his speech or becoming lost, for he has the complete text before him all of the time. Still another desirable feature is that, unlike the speaker using the extemporaneous method, the speaker who reads from a manuscript need never fumble for words or search for the precise language he wants.

This method is particularly useful in several speaking situations. If the speech is of great importance and the speaker wishes to make certain that he will not be misunderstood, a manuscript is almost essential. For example, the president of the United States in delivering a major address would not want to risk speaking extemporaneously, for in a pronouncement of such significance a careless or incorrect word or phrase might have national or international repercussions. A scientist reporting technical data and methodology would also wish to avoid confusion or misunderstanding by following a carefully prepared text. A manuscript is also useful if the speaker must adhere to rigidly enforced time limits. Radio and television rarely permit a speaker to exceed his scheduled time limit, nor do they appreciate the speaker who fails to utilize all of his time. Thus, if the speaker does not want his concluding remarks to be replaced by a commercial—as happened to Adlai Stevenson in Cincinnati in 1956—he may decide to speak from a carefully prepared and timed manuscript. Fortunately, most television stations now have teleprompters permitting the speaker to read his speech on the enlarged screen, eliminating the close following of the typewritten text and facilitating direct eye contact.

In spite of these values, the manuscript method has many drawbacks. First of all, many (perhaps most) speakers do not read well. Instead of appearing natural and spontaneous, they sound mechanical and leaden. They stumble over words, pause at awkward places, read too fast or too slow, and utilize monotonous pitch and loudness patterns. A second disadvantage is that many speakers find it difficult to maintain direct eye contact with their listeners when reading from a written text. A third weakness is that the use of a manuscript restricts movement. The speaker must either remain at the lectern or pick up the sheaf of papers, often obtrusively, and carry them with him if he wants to move about or is required to go to the blackboard or chart to illustrate a point. For many speakers, the use of a manuscript also seems to inhibit their gestures and to detract from the speaker's total involvement in the speech situation. Perhaps the most serious drawback, however, is that it makes audience adaptation difficult. With a manuscript, the speaker often finds it difficult to make on-the-spot adjustments to fit the mood and reactions of his listeners. If he inserts new or additional materials to create interest or to aid understanding, he may find it difficult to devise a smooth transition back to his text. If the remarks of a prior speaker or some unforeseen development suggests that portions of the speech should be altered or omitted, the speaker may find it difficult to make such changes in his text at the last minute.

Although the manuscript method poses problems for many speakers, one should not conclude that these difficulties cannot be overcome. With practice, a speaker using a manuscript can learn to read meaningfully and conversationally, to maintain direct eye contact, to move and gesture, and to appear communicative. He can also develop skill in last-minute adaptations and modification.

A speaker who plans to deliver his speech from a manuscript should keep in mind the following suggestions:

1. In writing the manuscript, he should remember that he is preparing a speech to be said aloud, not a discourse to be silently read. Each sentence should be read aloud to make sure that it can be easily and meaningfully said. The manuscript should contain direct references to the audience (i.e. *you, we, our, your*). The organization must be clear, obvious, and simple for a listening audience to grasp. Obvious literary phrases such as "the above" and "in the last paragraph" should be avoided.

2. The manuscript should be practiced aloud. Extensive oral practice will enable the speaker to catch and eliminate tongue twisters and overly involved or awkward sentences. It will also permit him to time the speech carefully. The importance of oral practice should be emphasized for two reasons. First, because most persons read silently at a much greater rate than they read aloud, if the speech is not practiced aloud the speaker probably will not have an accurate estimate of its length. Second, only by reading the speech aloud will the awkward, "unsayable" sentences and phrases be identified before actual presentation.

3. The speaker should give attention to his vocal usage, eye contact, facial expression, gestures, and movement while practicing. To avoid stumbling over words, becoming lost, and encountering other reading problems, the speaker needs to be very familiar with his manuscript. The speaker should be so well acquainted with his material that a glance at the first words of a sentence will be enough to remind him of the entire sentence. This familiarity can be acquired only through extensive rehearsal. In practicing the speech, the speaker should strive to achieve a natural and seemingly spontaneous manner of delivery. In order to judge his progress, he may at

times wish to observe himself in a mirror while he practices, to record and listen to the speech, and to deliver it to a friend or colleague.

4. The manuscript should be prepared so that it can be read easily. The speaker should use a typewritten manuscript, preferably outsized type, that has been triple spaced. The manuscript should be neat and free from spelling and punctuation errors. It should be typed on paper that can be handled easily. If the speech is to be broadcast or a public address system is to be used, it should be typed on a soft paper that will not create distracting noises when it is handled by the speaker. The pages should be carefully numbered. To facilitate his reading while turning the pages, the speaker may include the beginning words of the next page at the bottom of each sheet or the last words of the preceding page at the top of each sheet. Either arrangement permits him to look ahead and begin turning the page before he actually completes what is written on each page.

5. The speaker should not overrehearse. While extensive practice is desirable, the speaker should practice frequently for short periods of time, rather than once or twice for an extended period. Lengthy sessions are likely to produce carelessness, so that after the first 10 minutes the speaker may be reinforcing bad habits by continued rehearsal.

6. The speaker may wish to indicate in the manuscript the interpretation of key words or sentences. While practicing the speech, some speakers find it helpful to mark words and phrases that are to be emphasized, or where changes in rate and volume and similar vocal techniques are to occur. This is usually done with a colored pencil. The speaker employs whatever symbols and marks he chooses in order to indicate the desired interpretation. While such devices may prove helpful to some, for others they often are distracting and lead only to stilted and awkward vocal gymnastics. The inexperienced speaker probably is well advised to use this technique with caution.

Memory

The memory method of delivery consists of preparing a manuscript and then simply memorizing the entire speech.

The memorized speech has most of the advantages of the manuscript speech. It permits careful timing, precise choice of language, extensive polishing, and, if properly memorized, a smooth, effortless presentation.

The memory method is best suited to short addresses in which the speaker wishes to give the impression of sincerity and spontaneity while, at the same time, giving careful attention to the choice of words and composition of the speech. Speeches of presentation and acceptance of awards and honors, eulogies and commendations, speeches of welcome and farewell, and other short ceremonial and occasional addresses are often given from meomory.

The disadvantages of the memory method are several. The chief drawback is the time required to memorize the speech. If the speech is short, memorizing is not a serious problem. But for most people, memorization of a speech of 30 minutes or longer is an extremely time-consuming task. And for the speaker who must speak frequently—such as a candidate for political office or a classroom lecturer—the time involved is prohibitive.

A second shortcoming is that many people do not speak naturally and conversationally when reciting from memory. They tend to speak too rapidly, to develop inflection patterns, and to drone on in a singsong, monotonous manner.

A third weakness is the danger of a memory lapse. The speaker who has committed his entire talk to memory often finds it difficult to resume his speech if he momentarily forgets it.

Like the manuscript speech, the speech delivered from memory also hinders audience adaptation. If the speaker inserts new material at the last minute, he is likely to lose his train of thought and experience difficulty in resuming the memorized presentation. However, unlike the manuscript speech, the memorized address does facilitate direct eye contact and permit the speaker complete freedom of movement.

In preparing the speech to be delivered from memory, the speaker should keep in mind several of the recommendations for preparing a manuscript speech:

1. He should remember that the speech is to be presented orally and make certain that the language is conversational rather than written.

2. He should practice aloud.

3. In practicing, he should give attention to the vocal and physical aspects of delivery.

4. He should practice for several short rather than a few long periods of time.

In addition the speaker should:

1. Memorize the speech thoroughly. The speaker who commits his manuscript to memory at the last minute or who approaches the speaking situation with his speech poorly memorized is inviting difficulty. Unless he is confident that his speech is so well memorized that he cannot forget, he undoubtedly will be unduly apprehensive and nervous while speaking. Furthermore, if the speech is not thoroughly memorized, he will be required to devote his mind almost exclusively to remembering the text, thereby sacrificing attention to other vital aspects of delivery.

2. Concentrate on the sense or meaning of the speech. If the speaker is thinking about what he says as he presents the speech, not only is he much more likely to avoid memory lapses but he also will speak more convincingly and meaningfully.

3. If a memory lapse occurs, he should not panic. A pause while he reviews what he has said and tries to pick up the thread of his speech will not disturb the audience. He should not apologize for his lapse and, above all, he should not try to proceed until he has recalled what comes next.

Extemporaneous

The extemporaneous method of delivery consists of extensive advance study, careful organization of the speech, the preparation of an outline or notes, practice, and the presentation where the speaker relies only on an outline or set of notes. In preparing an extemporaneous address, some speakers like to write out the speech in its entirety, but when actually presenting the speech, they rely only on an outline or set of notes and make no effort to adhere strictly to the manuscript. Many speakers place their notes on small cards to which they refer when necessary, while others prefer to memorize the outline and use no notes at all.

For most speakers and most speaking situations, this method probably has more advantages and fewer disadvantages than the other types of delivery. Its chief advantage probably is its flexibility. It permits the speaker to make on-the-spot changes in response to the mood and reactions of the audience. It also encourages naturalness and spontaneity. Because his only guide is a sketchy outline or set of notes, he is almost inescapably forced into a conversational use of language.

An additional advantage is that, unlike the manuscript speech, eye contact is easily maintained and movement and gestures are in no way inhibited. Memory is no problem either because the speaker has his notes and he does not attempt to present the speech word-for-word as planned beforehand.

The extemporaneous method of speaking is well suited to most speech situations. Except for occasions in which an extremely precise statement of one's message is imperative, when a time limit is rigidly enforced, or when any reference to notes might suggest insincerity, the extemporaneous method is appropriate. Even when these conditions apply, a skillful speaker with careful preparation can employ the extemporaneous method effectively.

The principal handicap of speaking extemporaneously is that it may result in a pedestrian use of language. The speaker who lacks a good vocabulary and has little practice in speaking extemporaneously may mar his speech with awkward or incomplete sentences, vague and ambiguous language, nonfluencies, and vocalized pauses. Even the speaker skillful and experienced enough to avoid these weaknesses may be unable, when speaking extemporaneously, to summon the well-turned phrase or moving words required to transform a good speech into a truly eloquent address. However, experience and a familiarity with literature and great speaking can develop a facility with language which, accompanied by memorization of an occasional phrase or passage, will overcome even this shortcoming.

The speaker with little experience in speaking extemporaneously may encounter other difficulties. The lack of a manuscript or memorization of the speech may lead to a feeling of insecurity for the novice speaker. Some speakers who are not skilled in speaking extemporaneously also develop the habit of referring to their notes almost constantly—even though the notes are sparse and may contain no further information about the point he is discussing. However, with practice, both of these handicaps may be overcome.

The following suggestions should aid the speaker who is preparing to speak extemporaneously:

1. Prepare thoroughly. Since the speaker does not have a manuscript or memorized material to rely on, he will be required to develop his main ideas

as the speech progresses. If he has not decided exactly what he wishes to say about each point, he is likely to digress or to omit important supporting details. He may also encounter difficulty in finding the right word, example, or illustration to communicate clearly what he wishes to convey.

2. Keep the notes or outline simple and brief. Each speaker must determine, largely through trial and error, what kind of notes are most helpful to him in delivering the speech. Some speakers prefer to memorize the main headings of their outline and to rely on no written notes whatever during the speech. Some prepare a written outline, while others rely on a list of key words or phrases as reminders. The beginning speaker will want to experiment with each of these methods and various combinations of them to determine which is most helpful to him.

Whatever type of notes he plans to use, the speaker should keep them simple. A sentence outline is unnecessary. The notes should be sufficiently clear that a single glance will remind the speaker of what he wishes to say. The notes should be legible—preferably typewritten—so that the speaker does not waste time deciphering his own handwriting. The notes should be succinct. If the speaker is well prepared, he will not need extensive notes.

3. If notes are used, place them on small cards. While the extemporaneous speaker does not try to disguise the fact that he is relying on notes, the notes should be unobtrusive and should not interfere with his presentation of the speech. Notes placed on small cards (2″ × 4″ or 3″ × 5″) are more easily handled than those on larger cards or lighter paper. Furthermore, they can be casually picked up and carried by the speaker if he wishes to move away from the lectern. Also, because they can be held easily in one hand, they do not interfere with the speaker's gestures.

4. Practice the speech often and aloud. The fact that the speaker will be extemporizing from prepared notes does not lessen the need for extensive oral rehearsal. Although the speech will not be given twice in exactly the same way, practicing aloud will permit the speaker to become familiar with his notes or outline and will enable him to time the speech, to give attention to the vocal aspects of delivery, and to improve his bodily action. Most experienced speakers find it advisable to practice for several short periods of time rather than a few long ones.

Impromptu

The impromptu method of delivery consists of delivering the speech without any advance preparation. It is completely off the cuff.

The only advantage of this method is that it does guarantee spontaneity. The disadvantages are many and obvious. The method precludes careful consideration of subject, ideas, supporting materials, organization, style, or delivery. It permits no practice.

If the speaker has received any advance notice whatsoever—even a few minutes—he should avoid the impromptu method. Instead, in the time available he should attempt to select a topic, organize his ideas, and, if possible, jot down a few notes.

In spite of the many handicaps of the impromptu delivery, speakers are often required to employ this method. It is not uncommon for a person to be asked unexpectedly to give an opinion or to provide some information. He may decide, on the spur of the moment, to participate in a discussion or debate—in other words, to speak impromptu.

While he should avoid speaking impromptu under most circumstances, the experienced speaker may find the situation less formidable than one might expect. If he is well acquainted with the principles of effective speech and retains his composure, he can, even on the spur of the moment, compose and present a respectable speech.

Some specific suggestions that may assist the impromptu speaker are:

1. Don't panic. The speaker should remember that the audience will understand that he has had no time to prepare his remarks and that his listeners do not expect a Gettysburg Address.

2. Stick to the subject. Avoid digressions.

3. Be brief. Speaking without advance preparation, the speaker cannot hope to treat his subject exhaustively. Instead, he should concentrate on two or three aspects of the topic with which he is most familiar and which seem most important to him.

4. Keep in mind the principles of good organization. Although he has almost no time to plan his speech, at the very outset the speaker should attempt to formulate a simple organizational outline. He should formulate an introduction, body, and conclusion and he should attempt to determine the ideas he plans to develop before plunging into the talk.

Combining Methods of Delivery

Frequently a speaker will use more than one method of delivery within a speech. He may follow an outline or notes for portions of the speech. Responding to the reactions of his listeners, he may insert completely impromptu remarks. He may memorize his introduction, conclusion, or some other portion of the speech he wishes to present in a particular way. Or he may rely on a manuscript to develop one or more points of the speech. Political campaigners often are adept at combining several methods of delivery. They frequently deliver most of a speech extemporaneously because of the natural conversational quality of that method, but may interject impromptu material in response to the audience's reactions; they may recall from memory portions of the speech they have delivered several times before; and they may read from manuscript passages on which they do not want to be misunderstood or misquoted by their opponents. The speeches of John F. Kennedy in the 1960 presidential campaign, for example, revealed a remarkable combination of the various methods of delivery.

PRINCIPLES OF EFFECTIVE BODILY ACTION

The concept of delivery embraces both visible (or physical) and audible (or vocal) elements. The visible aspects of delivery include appearance, posture, movement, gestures, facial expression, and eye contact. The speaker who wishes to achieve his desired response cannot afford to neglect the physical aspects of delivery, for what the audience sees may influence them as much as what they hear.

At this point, it should be stressed that no single type or manner of delivery can be recommended for all. One need list only a few recent prominent speakers to illustrate the wide disparity in delivery among effective orators. The delivery of Martin Luther King, Jr., and Billy Graham might be described as dynamic and forceful; William F. Buckley and Eric Sevareid would probably be called suave and sophisticated; Eugene McCarthy might be described as calm and restrained; Hubert Humphrey and George Wallace could be labeled volatile and voluble; news commentator Walter Cronkite would be classified as conversational; while Sam Ervin's delivery might be characterized as folksy. Yet all of these speakers have demonstrated an ability to influence listeners. Since no particular manner of presentation is superior to another, the student speaker should avoid copying the delivery of someone else. Instead, he should strive to develop a manner of presentation suited to his own personality and temperament. Milton Viorst (Adapted Reading 13.3) relates how Everett Dirksen exploited many characteristics that others would regard as liabilities in order to create a peculiarly effective mode of delivery.

In developing good delivery, the beginning speaker should be aware that effective bodily activity is characterized by four qualities: (1) it is unobtrusive, (2) it reinforces the speaker's ideas, (3) it appears natural and spontaneous, and (4) it is appropriate to the audience and occasion.

Unobtrusiveness

A speaker's bodily action should never distract his listeners. At all times the speaker should remember that his goal is to obtain a specific response. If he is to achieve his purpose, the listener's attention must be focused on what he says. Anything that directs the audience's thought away from the speaker's ideas detracts from their comprehension and response to his remarks. Whenever the listeners start paying attention to the speaker's gestures, movements, appearance, or some other aspect of his physical delivery, they no longer are concentrating on the subject. Flamboyant dress, eccentric gestures, peculiar mannerisms, constant pacing, fidgeting with notes or adjusting clothing, and similar distractions are likely to call attention to themselves so that, instead of paying attention to what is being said, the auditors become engrossed in the speaker's physical activity.

Reinforces Ideas

Good bodily action should reinforce the speaker's ideas. It is not enough for the speaker to eliminate action that might distract his listeners: Good bodily activity should actually enhance or contribute to his communicativeness. If his subject is serious, the speaker's posture, gestures, and countenance should add to the impression of seriousness. When he relates an exciting experience, he should appear enthusiastic and stimulated; when he tells a humorous story, he should seem relaxed and at ease; and when he praises his auditors, his physical stance, expression, and appearance should reflect honesty and sincerity.

Naturalness

Effective bodily action appears natural and unplanned. Ideally, the speaker's physical activity will be spontaneous, arising from his desire to communicate, his enthusiasm for his topic, and his response to the mood of the audience and occasion. However, in actuality, this is often not the case. The speaker may be tired, depressed, self-conscious, listless, or uninspired, and consequently feels little inclination to gesture, move about, or react physically. Under such circumstances, he may find it necessary to simulate an interest in his topic, to force himself to incorporate appropriate gestures, movement, and facial expression, and to feign an enthusiasm and dynamism he does not feel. If the speaker resorts to simulated physical responses, he should try to avoid appearing artificial, forced, or rehearsed. It probably is better for the speaker to employ no gestures or movement than to engage in physical activity that calls attention to itself and distracts his audience. Often a speaker who begins by forcing himself to gesture and appear interested will find that as he progresses, his physical activity will begin to occur naturally and spontaneously.

> Much of delivery is the natural and unconscious bodily expression of the emotions.
>
> PHILODEMUS

Occasionally, speakers develop idiosyncratic mannerisms, unusual facial expressions, odd gestures, and awkward movements which, although entirely natural to them, appear strange or contrived to the listeners. Should this occur, the speaker will need to make a conscious effort to rid himself of the distracting habit or mannerism.

Appropriateness

As in all aspects of his speaking, the effective speaker is highly conscious of his audience and the occasion and will adapt the visible elements of his delivery to them. An audience of 10 people seated in relaxed, informal surroundings, for example, dictates a somewhat quiet, restrained delivery; 1000 people in a large auditorium may require more expansive gestures and greater emphasis on eye contact. The occasion, too, may suggest modifications in one's physical activity. A television speech, which is actually a talk to small groups of people sitting in their living rooms; an address to a political rally, where the audience expects to be aroused; a classroom lecture, where the listeners are accustomed to a dignified, decorous presentation;

and an after-dinner talk, where the audience has just finished a meal and is feeling somewhat lethargic, are all situations that place different demands on the speaker, and these should be reflected in his bodily action.

SPECIFIC ELEMENTS OF BODILY ACTION

Keeping in mind these four general principles — unobtrusiveness, the need to reinforce one's ideas, naturalness, and appropriateness — should aid the beginning speaker in achieving more effective bodily action. However, because student speakers often seem to be more troubled by this phase of speaking than any other, some specific aspects and techniques of bodily activity are discussed below in greater detail.

Appearance

A speaker's appearance undoubtedly contributes to his effectiveness. While a speaker can do little to alter the features with which he has been endowed by nature, he can at least present himself in the best possible light. Simply stated, the speaker should be groomed and dressed in a manner that is suitable to the audience and the occasion. His appearance should in no way distract the audience or detract from what he intends to say. The Christian Dior cocktail gown may be the height of fashion, the tartan plaid vest might be a hit at the racetrack, and the see-through blouse may be provocative, but all should probably be avoided in most speaking situations. Likewise, shorts, faded jeans, sneakers, and sweat shirts, while comfortable, would be inappropriate in most speaking situations. The speaker need only remember that every moment spent in admiration, awe, or shock because of the speaker's appearance is a moment when the listener is not giving his full attention to what is being said.

While the authors have no intention of dictating how anyone should dress, the speaker should be aware that extreme fashions in clothing and unusual grooming not only can distract, but may actually alienate some audiences and thereby increase the speaker's difficulty in obtaining his desired response.

For example, while it is everyone's right to sport a beard or mustache, to let his hair grow to his shoulders or shave it off entirely, to go barefoot, to wear beads, shorts, patched overalls, army fatigues, or any other item or apparel he may wish, the speaker should be conscious that such dress may offend some audiences. Right or wrong, some people do draw negative conclusions about speakers on the basis of their dress and grooming. In a similar manner, it is possible that a conservatively dressed and barbered speaker might find that his appearance is a handicap in influencing listeners with more radical tastes. The prejudice against speakers who dress unconventionally is not new. In the nineteenth century, British statesman Benjamin Disraeli was criticized for his flamboyant dress and hair style, as was Oscar Wilde during an American lecture tour. Fortunately, Americans today seem to be more tolerant than they were 10 years ago of differences in dress and grooming.

Every speaker must decide for himself how important it is to dress as he wishes, knowing the possible damage that his appearance may have on his chances of obtaining the response he desires from his audience. However, it would seem the better part of wisdom in most situations to accommodate, at least partially, one's dress and grooming to the audience's demands and expectations in order to achieve one's goal. Perhaps Samuel Butler's observation might serve as a rule of thumb: "The more unpopular an opinion is, the more necessary is it that the holder should be somewhat punctilious in his observance of conventionalities generally."

The Speaker's Approach and Departure

The speaker's manner of approaching the platform, podium, or stand is important, for at that time the audience forms its first impression of him. If he shuffles aimlessly, if he appears bored or indifferent, if he seems nervous and frightened, if he has difficulty locating his notes, or if he must spend considerable time assembling his materials before proceeding to the platform, he probably will make a poor initial impression. To make sure that the audience is ready to listen to him, the speaker should refrain from beginning his speech until he reaches the speaker's stand. He should not stop to greet friends, shake hands, or engage in other forms of distracting behavior on his way to the lectern. To make certain that he is ready to begin, upon arriving at the stand, the speaker should pause for a moment, survey his notes or materials, remind himself of his opening remarks and then, if the audience is quiet and prepared to listen, begin his speech.

Upon completing the speech, the speaker should pause briefly before leaving the platform. He should finish his remarks before starting to leave, so that the listeners will not have to try to catch his concluding words over the noise of his departure. If he used notes, books, visual aids, or other materials during his speech, he should not begin to gather up these items until he has completed the entire speech.

Speaking Position

The physical arrangement of the stage, platform, or dais at times dictates to the speaker where he must stand while he delivers his address. On other occasions, the speaker may have the opportunity to decide for himself exactly where he will stand. Given a choice, the speaker should select a position where he can be easily seen by all and where he, in return, can see his listeners without difficulty. Emily Kimbrough discusses this problem of delivery in Adapted Reading 13.4.

If the speaker wishes to establish the closest possible rapport with his audience and to speak to them on their level, he will avoid elevating himself in any way and will place no barriers between himself and the auditors. To an audience, the speaker who speaks from a stage, raised platform, or elevated dais seems psychologically above and removed from them. The speaker who stands behind a lectern, pulpit, desk, or table, likewise, places a barrier between himself and his listeners, which seems to set him apart from them. While there may be occasions in which the speaker actually wishes to create the feeling that he is above and apart from his audience, in most instances he will probably seek to establish the closest possible rapport and the greatest empathy with his listeners by speaking from a position on the same level as they, with few, if any, barriers between him and them.

Posture

While delivering the speech, the speaker's posture should be erect, but at ease. He should avoid an appearance of rigid or military bearing. At the same time, he should not look slovenly or ill at ease.

The question of where to place one's hands proves vexing to some speakers. The student may have read or been told of certain taboos: "Don't put your hands in your pockets," "Don't clasp your hands behind your back," or "Don't fold your hands in front of you." While these admonitions are generally worthy, they should not cause the speaker to become so preoccupied with the location of his hands that he loses sight of the main reason for speaking—to communicate ideas.

The speaker should be physically comfortable in front of his audience so that he can concentrate on what he has to say. If the speaker feels more natural with a hand in his pocket or clasped behind his back, then he should feel free to assume such a stance, at least temporarily. He should be aware, however, that such positions may inhibit natural, spontaneous gestures. He definitely should avoid distracting his listeners by rattling keys or coins in his pockets. As the speaker concentrates on what he is saying and as he gains experience in confronting audiences, he will probably find that he is capable of using his hands and arms freely to reinforce his ideas.

Occasionally, a speaker may find himself required to address his listeners from a sitting position; this might occur in a roundtable discussion or a television interview. Under such circumstances, he should maintain an alert and erect, but not stiff, posture.

Some speakers, especially in the classroom, like to deliver their talks seated on the edge of a desk. While this practice lends greater informality to the occasion, it probably should be discouraged in most instances, for the audience is better able to see the speaker if he stands and the speaker is more likely to achieve a dynamic, energetic presentation if he is not too relaxed.

Movement

In most situations, the speaker should feel free to move about the platform. This not only relaxes him, but such movement frequently can serve to achieve variety and rekindle flagging audience interest. The speaker may move toward the audience to emphasize an important point, he may take a few steps to either side of the lectern, or he may walk to a chart or map to illustrate a point.

In moving, the speaker should not let his activity interfere with communication. Constant pacing can distract and irritate an audience; noisy, plodding steps on an old or creaky platform can make it difficult for listeners to hear; abrupt or meaningless movement can startle an audience. Under certain circumstances, movement is virtually prohibited. If the speaker uses a public address system or the address is being broadcast, any movement away from the microphone may result in inaudibility or at least a sudden shift in volume. Furthermore, a speaker is sometimes restrained by the use of a pulpit, by the seating arrangement at a banquet speaker's table, or by the way a stage has been set up. In such situations, he should forsake any attempt to move about, as is pointed out in Adapted Reading 13.4.

Gestures

Gestures are normal and natural. Almost everyone gestures in conversation. Therefore, to convey the impression of naturalness and spontaneity, it is important that the speaker feel free to gesture while addressing an audience. The style of gestures used in public speaking has changed greatly in the last 50 years. Largely because of the conversational mode demanded by radio and television, the old arm-waving, flamboyant flourishes of the nineteenth century no longer seem appropriate in most speaking situations. Today, the gestures of the effective public speaker will be the more restrained, natural ones he uses in everyday conversation.

Some speakers at first feel self-conscious about gesturing. Each hand seems to weigh 50 pounds and the speaker has the feeling that if he so much as lifts a finger, every eye in the audience will be focused upon it. To overcome self-consciousness, the speaker may have to force himself to include a few gestures early in the speech. This is easily accomplished by deciding in advance upon two or three simple and obvious gestures. For example, the speaker might plan to raise two fingers when he says, "My second reason . . . ," or to use his hands to point to some object or to describe the size or shape of another object. By forcing himself to include a few simple gestures early in the speech, the speaker often relaxes, overcomes his self-consciousness, and later finds himself gesturing naturally and spontaneously. Ideally, the speaker will become so immersed in the speaking situation that all of his gestures will occur involuntarily.

The speaker should seek to achieve variety in his gestures. Some speakers develop one or two characteristic gestures which they employ repeatedly. If used too often, the audience may detect the repetitiousness and be distracted by it.

Use of Notes

Careful planning and preparation of his notes or manuscript can greatly assist the speaker in developing an effective delivery. While the speaker should not try to disguise the fact that he is using notes or a manuscript, he should use them as unobtrusively as possible. In order that they not attract undue attention, the notes should be both legible and easy to handle. Whether the speaker uses notes or a manuscript, he should be able to perceive at a glance what comes next. He should make certain that his copy is clear, large enough to be easily read, and arranged in proper order. For a manuscript speech, typewritten copy double- or triple-spaced on one side of each sheet is preferable to a longhand draft. During delivery, the manuscript should be placed on the lectern or speaker's stand. If he is to speak extemporaneously, the speaker probably will wish to type or write his outline or notes on small cards. As mentioned earlier, 2″ x 4″ or 3″ x 5″ cards are desirable because they are unobtrusive, easy to handle, and enable the speaker to gesture naturally and freely while holding them.

Use of the Speaker's Stand

The speaker's stand or lectern often is more of a handicap than a help to beginning speakers. While a lectern does have several legitimate uses — to hold a manuscript, visual aids, or reference works, for example — too many speech students use it as a crutch to lean upon or a wall to hide behind. It seems to invite lounging and to encourage poor posture. Speakers often grasp it tightly and, as a result, fail to gesture once during an entire speech. Others release the lectern only to employ gestures that are completely hidden by it from the view of the audience. Speakers who might normally — and to good effect — move about on the platform stand rooted behind it and, if they are absolutely forced to move away from it to use a blackboard or a visual aid, promptly scurry back to it as if it were home base. Short speakers remain almost completely hidden behind it, and lanky speakers will stoop to it, straining to see their notes. Speakers fondle it, cradle it, embrace it, play with it, lean on it, entwine their legs around it, and do almost everything else but leave it alone. Some speakers become so dependent upon it that if they are confronted with a speaking situation in which a lectern is not available, they are unable to go on.

If a speaker has a legitimate need for a lectern to hold the manuscript, charts, diagrams, or publications from which he plans to read, he should by all means use it for these purposes — and for these purposes only. But if a speaker has no real need for a speaker's stand, he would probably be well advised to learn to speak without one. If he has learned to speak without a lectern, he will be prepared to speak regardless of its presence or absence and will probably avoid all of the pitfalls that a speaker's stand seems to create.

Eye Contact

"Look me in the eye and say that" is an expression used to determine whether another person is telling the truth; the dishonest speaker is stereotyped as "shifty-eyed." While many speakers who are shifty-eyed, unable to look the other person in the eye, are undoubtedly honest and sincere, most listeners place greater confidence in a speaker who looks at them directly and steadily. Direct eye contact is also important because it enables a speaker to observe his listeners and gauge his remarks to their response.

To achieve and maintain good eye contact, the speaker should look directly at his audience — not over the tops of their heads, not out the window, not at the ceiling, nor to the floor. The speaker who stares out a window or at a corner of the room is likely to so arouse the curiosity of his listeners that they may turn around to discover what has caught the speaker's interest. Occasionally, a listener may even partially rise from his chair in order to get a better view of what is going on in that corner. Obviously, such behavior interferes with effective communication. Because any part of the audience that is steadily ignored will feel less involved than others in the speech, the speaker should also avoid directing his eye contact to any single segment of the audience throughout his speech. The speaker's goal, although physically impossible to achieve, should be to look at all of the audience all of the time.

> No phrase can convey the idea of surprise so vividly as opening the eyes and raising the eyebrows. A shrug of the shoulders would lose much by translation into words.
>
> HERBERT SPENCER

Facial Expression

Another important attribute of bodily action is the speaker's facial expression. If he is to be effective, the speaker's countenance should be consistent with his remarks and his facial expression should reinforce those ideas and emotions he seeks to convey. To smirk or grin while relating the grim details of a fatal automobile accident, to remain calm and impassive when describing the winning play in a thrilling football game, or to frown wearily while describing an enjoyable vacation trip is almost certain to diminish the audience's appreciation of what the speaker is saying. If his facial expression is not consistent with the feelings or information he is trying to convey, the audience quite naturally will suspect that the speaker is insincere.

A common fault of many beginning speakers is their almost complete impassivity in delivering the speech. From beginning to end, the speaker's facial expression betrays not the tiniest glimmer of any kind of emotion or feeling: He never smiles; he never frowns; he never appears excited; he never shows concern. The entire speech is delivered with stoical perseverance as if the assignment were the most boring type of drudgery. Such behavior may result from nervous tension, selection of a poor topic, or simply disinterest on the part of the speaker. Whatever the explanation, speeches delivered in this manner are never successful. To overcome a monotonous presentation, the speaker must learn to control his nervousness. He must develop a strong desire to communicate, he must select a subject in which he is deeply interested, and he must attempt to become so personally involved in his speech that he actually feels the emotions and attitudes he is trying to convey. If he accomplishes all of these, the chances are good that his facial expressions will reflect and reinforce the moods and feelings of his speech.

VISUAL AIDS

Another aspect of delivery the speaker should consider is how he might use visual aids in his speech. Available to him is a variety of different types of visual aids including charts, graphs, maps, drawings, paintings, blackboard sketches, models, photographs, slides, and motion pictures.

Visual aids are often extremely helpful to the speaker in communicating his ideas to the audience. In fact, at times, they are almost essential to an effective presentation. For example, the speaker who relies on words alone may experience considerable difficulty in describing the operation of a machine, the geographical location of an unfamiliar place, or a statistical trend; yet, in each instance, the information could be presented clearly and efficiently by using a model, map, or graph.

While visual aids often make it easier for an audience to grasp an idea, the speaker should not assume that they are always of assistance. In deciding whether to employ visual aids, the speaker should ask three questions: Do I need a visual aid? Can I effectively display it to this audience? Will the aids assist me in developing my subject without dominating or detracting from the speech? Each of these questions is important. In determining whether he needs a visual aid, the speaker should recognize that visual aids contribute very little to the development of some topics. If the speaker does not truly need a visual aid to clarify his ideas, he should not employ one. Second, he must consider whether the circumstances under which his speech will be given permit the effective utilization of visual aids. For example, he may have so many in his audience that visual aids large enough to be seen by all are not available; the site may not have electrical outlets for a motion-picture or slide projector; an operator may not be available; or it may be impossible to darken the room. Such considerations must be weighed by the speaker in determining whether to employ a visual aid. Finally, the speaker must make certain that the visual aid will not prove so fascinating that the audience will forget to pay attention to the speaker.

Preparation of Visual Aids

Assuming that he has decided he needs a visual aid, that he can effectively display it, and that it will not detract from his speech, the speaker is now ready to begin its preparation. An effective visual aid is accurate, legible, clear, and simple.

1. Accuracy. A visual aid that is not accurate serves no useful purpose, for it merely misleads the auditor. The careful speaker will make certain that his data is current; that his sketch, chart, or diagram contains no errors; that his map is up-to-date; that his model operates properly; that parts of the aid are properly identified; and that names and labels are spelled correctly.

2. Legibility. The speaker who displays a visual aid that cannot be easily seen and readily understood contributes little to the effectiveness of his communication. It is important that the speaker's visual aid can be *easily* seen and read; for if the listener must strain to see a small or illegible visual aid, he will quickly tire of the effort. To ensure easy viewing and comprehension by his audience, the speaker should make certain that the visual aid is large enough, that all labels are of good size, and that the lettering is clear and can be read easily.

3. Clarity. In addition to making sure that his visual aid is large enough, the speaker should strive for clarity in the preparation of charts, graphs, maps, and other aids. Clarity can be achieved through the use of bold and strong lines, shading, and contrasting colors. Adequate space between the various parts, consistency in the size and type of print used for labels, and neatness also contribute to a clear and effective visual aid.

4. Simplicity. Many beginning speakers make the mistake of assuming that visual aids must be sufficiently detailed to be completely self-explanatory, forgetting that the speaker has the opportunity — indeed, the obligation — to explain his visual materials and show how they are related to his speech. A good visual aid is simple. It includes only those details that are pertinent and necessary to an understanding of what the aid is intended to show. To include information which the speaker does not intend to discuss will only clutter the aid and may confuse the listener. Thus, a map designed to show the distribution of population in the United States need not include highways, rivers, mountain ranges, and similar irrelevant details.

To facilitate ready comprehension, the speaker should simplify his visual aids by rounding off numbers; by relegating incidental information to "miscellaneous" categories; and by omitting unimportant parts, statistics, or details. His aim in simplifying the visual aid, of course, is not to distort the facts through omission of information, but to direct the audience's attention to the most pertinent and important aspects of his subject. A good speaker will make certain that his audience understands that he is using the visual aid ethically and honestly.

Speakers should also take care that they do not complicate their visual aids through the use of too many labels. Since the speaker has the opportunity to explain his visual aid, it may not be necessary to label all of its parts.

Use of Visual Aids

Just as important as the speaker's careful preparation of the visual aid is his use of it during the speech. In planning the speech, the speaker should decide when he wants to introduce the visual aid, where he will place it, how he will use it, and how he will handle his notes or manuscript while referring to it.

If introduced at the wrong time, a visual aid can seriously interfere with the speaker's development of his topic. If a speaker displays his visual aid before beginning his speech, he may find that the audience is directing its attention to the aid rather than to his opening remarks. If he distributes visual aids — maps, outlines, charts, or photographs — to his listeners before he starts, the audience is likely to spend the first several minutes studying the visual aid rather than paying attention to the speaker. If a single visual aid is circulated among the audience, the speaker's difficulties are even greater, for at any given moment during the speech some member of the audience is examining or passing the visual aid rather than listening to the speaker.

To prevent such interference, the speaker should decide exactly when he wants the audience to see the visual aid. If it is to be displayed at the speaker's stand, he may wish to keep it out of sight until the exact moment when he wishes to have it shown. If he cannot place it on a convenient table or some other place within his reach but out of the audience's vision, he may wish to cover it with a blank sheet of paper until the time comes to refer to it. If materials are to be passed out, the speaker should determine exactly when he wishes to place them in the listeners' hands and arrange to have them distributed quickly and efficiently at the proper moment.

Having planned when he will introduce the visual aid, the speaker should then determine where he will place it. If he neglects this consideration, when the time comes to introduce his aid the speaker may discover that he has no place to display it. Well in advance of delivery, the speaker should investigate the availability of easels, flannel boards, blackboards, screens, projectors, electric outlets, and any other equipment necessary for the display of his visual material. If unavailable, the speaker may need to provide such items himself or he may be required to devise another method for presenting his visual material.

Even if all of the necessary equipment is available, the speaker still must determine, for example, whether to hold the visual aid or place it on an easel. He must give consideration to exactly where he wishes to place the easel or screen so that the audience can see it, who will operate the projector, when and how the room will be darkened, and similar related items.

After deciding when and where the visual aid is to be displayed, the speaker should next plan how he will use it. The speaker will destroy the effectiveness of his visual aid if he forgetfully blocks the audience's view by standing directly in front of it, if he loses contact with the audience by turning his back to his listeners in order to see it himself, or if he has no pointer and repeatedly obstructs the audience's view as he points to various parts of it.

Finally, the speaker should anticipate any problems that may arise because of the visual aid. For example, if colored slides are to be shown, the room will have to be darkened, thereby depriving the speaker of needed light to see his notes or manuscript. If a model or object is employed, the speaker may be required to move away from the lectern or use both hands, which will also take him from his notes. If he must hold the visual aid, he will find it difficult to handle a set of notecards or a manuscript. To solve such problems, the speaker may be required to memorize parts of the outline or text. For the speaker who plans to hold his visual aid, the solution may be to place his notes on the reverse side of the aid.

SUMMARY

Speech delivery refers to *how* the speech is presented as opposed to *what* is presented (content). Delivery consists of the speaker's vocal usage and physical activity.

Four methods of speech presentation are manuscript, memory, extemporaneous, and impromptu. Each has advantages and disadvantages. The method the speaker chooses for a particular speech will depend on the nature of the speech, the audience, and the occasion. Probably the most widely used is the extemporaneous method in which the speaker carefully prepares his talk and then delivers it from a few notes or a brief outline.

What the audience sees, as well as what it hears, is important in determining their response to a speech. Among the physical factors of delivery that may influence the listeners' reception of a speech are the speaker's appearance, his manner of approaching and departing from the podium, his posture, movement, gestures, handling of notes, use of the lectern, eye contact, and facial expression.

The speaker's physical characteristics should never distract the listener. Good bodily action reinforces the speaker's ideas, appears natural and spontaneous, and is appropriate to the audience and the occasion.

Speakers who use visual aids such as charts, maps, diagrams, models, and slides should give careful attention to their preparation and display. Visual aids should always be accurate, legible, clear, and simple. They should not dominate the speech or detract from any portion of it but should supplement the speaker's oral presentation at the appropriate time in the speech.

THE WAY WE SPEAK "BODY LANGUAGE"

Flora Davis

A number of the country's top-flight psychiatrists have taken their patients on a trip to Philadelphia in recent years for a visit to a research lab at the Eastern Pennsylvania Psychiatric Institute. There, psychiatrist and patient hold a therapy session while movie cameras purr in the background. What the filmmakers are primarily interested in is nonverbal communication: shifts of posture and muscle tone, gestures, eye movements, and the like. They are looking for recurring patterns, the constellations of body movement which they see as a kind of subliminal language that can be translated by the trained interpreter.

For example, in one particular film the psychiatrist was seeing a family — mother, father, daughter, grandmother — together for the first time. Again and again during the interview, the mother turned flirtatiously to the therapist. She would extend her legs and delicately cross her ankles. Resting one hand on her hip, she would lean forward and talk with great animation for perhaps 20 or 30 seconds. Then, quite suddenly, she would subside, sink back in her chair, pull in her legs, drop her hands to her sides. The withdrawal was so complete that she looked almost autistic.

So much one can see with the naked eye. But when the film is run through slow motion, a whole constellation of movement suddenly becomes clear. Each time the mother set out to charm the psychiatrist, her husband would begin to jiggle one foot nervously. At this, both daughter and grandmother — who were sitting on either side of the mother — would cross their knees so that their shoe tips almost met and their legs boxed her in. It was after this that she subsided. The sequence occurred 11 times in just 30 minutes of the film.

It is hardly a surprise, then, to learn that the mother's flirtatiousness was a family problem. Experts in kinesics — the study of communication through body motion — cite this fragment of nonverbal drama as a neatly documented example of the way people sometimes use body language to keep others who may be misbehaving in line. Kinesicists believe that all families have similar systems, though they are almost never conscious of having them.

Dr. Albert E. Sheflen has demonstrated that people in a group often mirror each other's posture. In a large gathering, as many as half a dozen may sit or stand with limbs arranged in an identical — or mirror-imaged way — and if one member of the set then shifts his body, the others quickly do the same. Where two different postures have been adopted by a gathering, those who share a posture usually turn out to share a viewpoint as well. When three people are together, most often one will arrange himself so that his upper body is congruent with one companion and his lower body with the other — making himself into a kind of human link between the two.

From *New York Times Magazine*, May 31, 1970, pp. 8–9. © 1970 by The New York Times Company. Reprinted by permission.

Some gestures have a conscious, understood meaning. The hitchhiker's thumbing is an example that comes easily to mind. Every culture has its own repertoire of these, and they vary from culture to culture. Catching sight of a pretty girl, an Italian will signal his appreciation by pulling one of his ear lobes, an Arab will stroke his beard, but the Englishman will assume an overly casual stance and elaborately look away.

It is often a mistake to interpret such gestures in isolation. The individual's facial expression or stance — or what he is saying — can give a gesture an ironic twist; as everyone knows, an army private, when he salutes, can convey everything from blind obedience to complete contempt, depending upon the speed and duration of the gesture and what he does with the rest of his body.

I talked to four pioneers in the field of body language — Birdwhistell, Scheflen, Goffman and Dr. Adam Kendon. Significantly, none of the four refer to it as nonverbal communication. Kendon prefers the term "visible behavior"; Scheflen and Birdwhistell, who refuse to segregate words from gestures, define their field simply as "communication." Goffman speaks of his specialty as "face-to-face interaction"; he is interested in how the unwritten body codes help people to get along with each other in public.

Sustained, systematic kinesics research really began with the publication of Ray Birdwhistell's book, *Introduction to Kinesics*, in 1952. Birdwhistell is an anthropologist born and educated in the Midwest. His interest in body language dates back to a field study he did of the Kutenai Indians of western Canada in 1946. While he was living among the Kutenai, he noticed that they looked quite different when speaking English from the way they looked when speaking Kutenai: their gestures, their facial expressions changed. It seems that some people are bilingual in body language as well as in spoken langauge!

Dr. Birdwhistell started out with a search for universal gestures, that is, for body language common to all cultures. He now states flatly:

"There are no universal gestures. As far as we know, there is no single facial expression, stance, or body position which conveys the same meaning in all societies."

This is a controversial statement, hotly disputed by others in the field, including psychologists such as Dr. Ekman, who has done cross-cultural research. In one study, armed with photographs of happy faces, sad faces, angry faces, surprised, disgusted and fearful faces, Ekman asked people in half-a-dozen different parts of the world to name the emotions portrayed in each one. And he concluded that the people in all the places selected, even those in isolated, primitive cultures, associated each photo with the same emotion. If people all over the world smile when they are happy, and recognize a happy face, is not the smile, then, a universal expression of emotion — part of our biological heritage (as no less an authority than Darwin said it was)?

Birdwhistell concedes that all humans smile — even blind babies do — for we all have the same face muscles. However, he contends that the *meaning* of the smile is not universal. Even in the United States he has found that there are "high-smile" areas, such as the South, where people do a lot of smiling, and "low-smile" areas, such as western New York State, where they do not (this is not a sign that Southerners are happier). In the South someone who does not often smile may be asked if he is angry, but in the Great Lakes region someone who does smile a lot may be asked what is so funny. It is culture, according to Birdwhistell, that supplies the meaning of the smile, and it cannot be said to be a simple pleasure reflex.

The meaning is always in the context, never in any particular, isolated body motion. One case in point is Birdwhistell's and Scheflen's assertion that a woman who tightly crosses her arms or legs is relatively inaccessible to any approach. Whether this is correct, both affirm, depends upon such circumstances as what other people are around, what else she does with her body, and so on.

Kinesic stress is one way people reduce verbal ambiguities. As everyone knows, an eyebrow lift often accompanies a question. However, it is also a way to stress a word in the speech stream. There are other ways to signal a question, too, such as an upward tilt of the head or hand, and one can as easily stress something with a nod of the foot or a blink of the eyelids.

Small movements of the head, eyes, hands, fingers or even the shoulders that accompany specific pronouns, verbs or phrases Birdwhistell describes as "markers." With the pronouns "I," "me," "we" and "us" as well as words such as "this" and "how," a hand "marker" would be a motion toward the speaker's body, while the shoulders would be squeezed, or hunched, in the direction of an imaginary vertical line through the center of the body. With future-tense verbs the marker motion is forward; with the past tense, it is backward. All this seems so logical to Americans that it is a surprise to learn that other peoples, for example some American-Indian cultures, sometimes find these markers confusing or even insulting when combined with their language. Dr. Birdwhistell explained his concept of "gender signals." In every culture he has studied people can distinguish feminine body behaviors from masculine ones. What is defined as masculine or feminine, furthermore, varies from one culture to the next.

"We think of male Arabs as effeminate and seductive because of the way they close their eyelids — very slowly — in contrast to the speed with which American males do it. We find the way Latin males cross their legs feminine in contrast to the broken-four spread typical of American males."

When sending gender signals, American women hold their thighs close together, according to Birdwhistell's studies. They walk with upper arms against their bodies and tilt their pelvises forward slightly. In contrast, American men sending gender signals stand with thighs somewhat apart. They hold their arms away from their bodies and swing them as they walk, and they carry their pelvises rolled slightly back.

Birdwhistell denies that these varying walking styles can be attributed to anatomical differences. Otherwise, he argues, they would be the same in all cultures — which they are not.

Inevitably, when Birdwhistell explains gender signals, people leap to the conclusion that what they signal is sexual attraction. Though this is sometimes true, very often it is not. Though gender emphasis may lead to a sexual relationship sometimes, at other times it is actually a way of preventing one from developing. A woman can protect herself from getting involved by sending inappropriate gender signals. "She sends them so strongly that they exclude all incoming messages. They're an insistence, not a response. That's the difference between a sexy woman and a sexual woman."

The belle of the coctail party, the siren in the low-cut dress who is surrounded by men, is—according to Birdwhistell—surrounded primarily by the men who do not like women or simply do not want to get involved. For them, she is the safest woman in the room to be around, just because she is not in any real sense responsive. Men simply do not turn her on—they cannot, because her volume is already on "high." The sexual woman, on the other hand, may stand on the sidelines looking pretty uninteresting until a man comes along. Then she will respond to him in dozens of subtle, nonverbal ways, perhaps by sending gender signals, perhaps with "courting behavior."

Relegated in the Birdwhistell scheme of things to a category called "parakinesics" are all kinds of fascinating things that he feels are definitely part of the communication system. They include stance and posture; the way skin varies from pale to flushed, dry to oily, flaccid to rigid. Then there are general categories such as beauty and ugliness, gracefulness and awkwardness.

How can being ugly be communicative? Birdwhistell refuses to see ugliness as an inborn characteristic. To begin with, he says, attractiveness may be a very transitory quality, which comes and goes like sunshine on a cloudy day. Everyone recognizes that people sometimes become quite beautiful when they fall in love, or ugly in moments of hate and anger. And on a more long-term basis, looks are one way in which society sorts people out, and being attractive is not necessarily good for a person if it means that too much is expected of him. Some people feel safer being part of the minority group of the unattractive. The point is that culture presents us with certain definitions, and we behave accordingly. If culture says that fat is ugly, then the fat person is saying something with his obesity about how he wants to be treated.

Scheflen's current project centers on a ghetto neighborhood and involves televising families in their own homes with a camera mounted high on a living room or kitchen wall. The camera is simply left in place for six to ten weeks and family members, self-conscious at first, after about a week seem to forget that it is there. The video signal is recorded in a nearby apartment and researchers work with the tapes of it.

He is not primarily concerned with the personalities of the people whose daily lives he studies. What he is mainly interested in is territoriality; he studies body behavior by which an individual indicates that he is—or is not—on his own "turf."

A colleague of Scheflen's, Dr. William Stewart, has a hunch that in poor black families, people look directly at each other less often than people do in middle-class white families. This is a small difference, but it may account for the fact that blacks meeting whites sometimes feel stared at, while whites feel that blacks are avoiding their eyes.

Scheflen has done a lot of research on courting behavior. Everyone knows that when two people are attracted to each other, they show it in subtle ways. Some of the symptoms are well known; others are not. Scheflen has reported that readiness to court is visible first of all as heightened muscle tone. The individual holds himself, or herself, erect; legs have tighter tone and even the face changes—sagging, jowliness and pouches under the eyes all decrease. Eyes seem brighter and skin may become either flushed or pale. And often the person preens. Feminine preening is easy to recognize. Some of the male preening gestures—hair-grooming, tie-preening, sock-preening—usually go unrecognized.

Courting couples, of course, exchange long looks. They cock their heads and roll their pelvises. A woman may cross her legs, slightly exposing one thigh, place a hand on her hip, or protrude her breasts. She may slowly stroke her own thigh or wrist or present a palm. Anglo-Saxon women ordinarily show their palms hardly at all, says Scheflen, but in courting they palm all over the place, even smoking or covering a cough with palm out.

"From that," says Scheflen, "you could perhaps derive a cheap rule: whenever a woman shows you her palm, she's courting you, whether she knows it or not." But in fact, he went on, people show palms in all sorts of relationships. "Showing the palm is an invitation to an encounter, and not necessarily sexual at all. It doesn't even mean one person necessarily likes the other, it just means they're coming together in some way, perhaps only on business. The whole thing is the context, again."

Scheflen has also discovered a phenomenon he calls quasi-courting, which can occur in practically any situation and need not signal sexual attraction at all. In the American middle class, quasi-courting may happen between parent and child, doctor and patient, at business meetings and at cocktail parties, even between people of the same sex. It is courting with a difference, with subtle qualifiers added that indicate that it is not to be taken seriously. A couple may momentarily seem to be courting, but closer observation will show that their bodies are turned slightly aside from each other, or their voices are a shade too loud for an intimate twosome. One or both may keep glancing about the room, or one person may extend an arm as if to include a third party, or drape the arm across his lap as a kind of barrier. Whatever the signal, it changes the whole significance of the behavior.

These days, while Dr. Scheflen concentrates on his televised families, other members of his research team are involved in their own projects. For example, Dr. Adam Kendon's current project, with Dr. Andrew Ferber as a collaborator, is a study of how humans greet one another.

"There are films of chimpanzee greetings," he says, "where you see two chimps approach each other. They shake hands, they embrace, they slap each other on the back. I can show you human greetings that look very similar."

Dr. Kendon's greetings film, made at a backyard birthday party, shows a whole series of people crossing the yard to the host, who greets them with open arms.

"Watch now," Dr. Kendon told me, running through a particular sequence with the hand crank. "You'll see that the host moves forward with his neck extended and lifts his arms out and away from his body. Now look at the guest. His trunk is erect, his neck is not extended, and when he puts his arms up for the embrace, they are on the inside, with the host's arms outside. There are several other greetings in the film where you see the same things. These are just some observations we've made lately, but we wonder whether this is a particular greeting posture that you will see in males being greeted on their own territory, a sort of dominant-greeter's posture."

Kendon hopes eventually to do a "typology" of greetings, describing those that take place at the edges of territories and in public places, between close acquaintances and strangers, formal greetings and informal. Then, since animals greet, too, it should be possible to do a comparative analysis—to spot similarities and differences between human and other primate greetings, for example.

The kinesicists are all given to quoting Erving Goffman. He has described what constitutes proper involvement in a conversation, as opposed to underinvolvement or overinvolvement, and how people accord each other "civil inattention" in public places. By this he means, for example, that a person passing a stranger in the street does not, under the rules, make gestures that indicate too much interest in the other; if he does, his behavior is likely to be interpreted as nosy or threatening.

Reading about Goffman's rules of public order, one gets a sense of just how vulnerable human beings really are. We simply assume that when we are out in public no one will attack us or block our way to suddenly start up a conversation; we depend on each other to behave properly. In recent years, though, the free and easy use of public and semipublic places has become subject to question. Goffman has written that everything an individual does in the presence of others is made up of tacit threats and promises: indications that he knows his place and will stay in it, that he knows it but will not stay in it, or that he does not and may not.

Young radicals attack the rules—and signify their refusal to know their place—when they occupy a building, seize the microphone at a public meeting or address a dean by his first name. Goffman cites the story of what happened when, during the student demonstrations at Columbia two years ago, Mark Rudd was invited to discuss the issues with some faculty members in a professor's apartment. After coffee was brought in on a silver service, Rudd took off his boots and socks, complaining that his feet were sweating.

This kind of pantomime is not hard to understand—it was an obvious attempt to shock others—but will you and I some day be able to read more obscure motives in a person's body behavior? Certainly some of us will try, though probably with marginal accuracy, since body language is subtle and complex. Most of the time, people simply use the motions prescribed by their culture as suitable in the context—which is actually the best way to conceal their true feelings. More important, we may learn to depend more on our intuitions, realizing that they are often based on actual body signals from other people which we perceive on a subliminal level.

As to the future uses of the field, someday language specialists will probably be taught the kinesics of a foreign language along with its grammar and vocabulary. Kinesics should prove a handy tool for the study of child development. And research on intercultural differences could clear up some of the small but alienating misunderstandings between men of different body languages.

But the study of human communication is still in its infancy and it is hard to get a really clear idea of what it might grow up to be. One thing seems certain, though: men will no longer be able to assume that when two people meet, all that is communicated is the words they speak. As Dr. Birdwhistell told me:

"Years ago I started with the question: How do body motions flesh out words? Now I ask instead: When is it appropriate to use words? They're very appropriate to teach or to talk on the telephone, but you and I are communicating on several levels now and on only one or two of them have words any relevance whatsoever. These days I put it another way: Man is a multisensorial being. Occasionally, he verbalizes."

ADAPTED READING 13.2

THE MANY FACES OF L.B.J.
Theodore H. White

Lyndon Johnson's personal campaign was more than efficient; it was entrancing. To travel with him was to climb one of the rare heights of American political and dramatic art. It was like watching a great performer, at the height of his power, moving through a repertory and range that could not be topped—and yet seeing him top them again and again.

Not for years had a campaigner—not even Mr. Harry Truman in 1948—brought so finished a style of country oratory to a national audience. . . . One had been tempted, even before the campaign began, to make a catalogue of all the Lyndon Johnsons there were. . . .

There was of course to start with, Lyndon Johnson as "Mr. President"—the solemn, grave man on television, talking of nuclear bombs, world peace, the public good, who spoke with ponderous gravity, licking his lips with pointed tongue between polished strophes written by speech writers, occasionally overstressing his "the's" and "and's."

There was occasionally the "Kindly Lyndon"—the man who at Kennedy's Inaugural had leaped from his seat to shade with his hat the sunstruck pages from which aging poet Robert Frost tried to read but could not for the glare. . . .

And then there was the "Imperial Lyndon"—as at the Convention in Atlantic City, lounging in his box in the gallery, one long leg crossed over the other, leaning back in the reclining position of a Caesar Augustus at the Roman games. . . .

But it was outdoors, on the road, . . . that he was most attractive. Raw and natural, casting away prepared text, reaching out for the hearts of the entire nation as he had reached out for hearts in his native land, translating the highest policy of the Western world into the simple speech of the old Texas Tenth Congressional District, the President of the United States could present a whole new series of *personae:* "Fair-Shares Johnson," "Preacher Johnson," "Old Doc Johnson," "Sheriff Johnson," "Uncle Lyndon," "Lonely-Acres Johnson," and several others.

"Fair-Shares Johnson," for example, arrived to open the Oklahoma State Fair in September, late in the afternoon, after a hard day's campaigning in Texas and Arkansas. When the helicopter deposited him on the fair grounds, a handsome roan horse was standing nearby. Nothing would do, then, but the President must mount the roan and, waving his cream-colored Stetson hat, urge the horse to a canter; arriving at the speakers' stand with a whoop. He announced that he had come "to talk to happy people. I came here to talk about what is right. I didn't come here to talk about what's wrong. . . . I'm proud of America and proud of Oklahoma." . . . Then after a few prepared passages, warming up as his audience warmed to him, he began to act out his "Fair-Shares" routine, identifying himself by gesture, drawl, and voice with each of the partners in the American system he loved to describe. . . .

"Preacher Johnson" was equally fetching. "Preacher Johnson" talked very slowly, even more slowly than "Mr. President Johnson" on TV — but with real quality, leaning one elbow on the rostrum, turning to face now the platform, now the audience, reasoning gently, urging people to be good, occasionally talking about the spirit of John F. Kennedy "up there in Heaven watching us." Sometimes "Preacher Johnson" could hush a huge auditorium and uplift his hearers, as in his oration at the Salt Lake City Mormon Tabernacle. But more often he offered just a plain, folksy, Sunday sermon. . . .

"Lonely-Acres Johnson" usually closed a speech by trying to make them understand the "awesome burden" of the Presidency. . . . Generally, "Lonely-Acres Johnson" made his appearance at dusk or nightfall when the President's voice would send the folks off to home and bed to think about what they could do for their country in the voting. But as for him, he had to go back to those lonely acres in Washington, and those iron gates would close behind him and he would be left alone with that awesome responsibility in the corridors where Lincoln and Wilson and Roosevelt and Kennedy had paced before him.

There was Lyndon Johnson the practical politician, too, fighting for every last vote as if he were still running in a primary. . . .

The most impressive of all Lyndon Johnsons was, however, "Sheriff Johnson." This was a drawling, easy, country-style, no-nonsense candidate. He knew he was President and he wanted you to know it, but he was doing it easily and simply as he told you who was boss. . . .

Every leader has his style — Goldwater and Johnson, Nixon and Eisenhower, Kennedy and Stevenson and Roosevelt; all were different and in retrospect one remembers them by the quality of their wit or eloquence or wrath or dignity or straight talk. What Johnson was discovering was that he could be President and be himself too. Folks were folks, and the same country-style campaigning that ran down South would also work in the North.

THE DELIVERY OF EVERETT M. DIRKSEN: THE SPEAKER EXPLOITS HIS LIABILITIES
Milton Viorst

Over the years Dirksen has learned to exploit those characteristics which others would treat as liabilities. At seventy, there is nothing boyish left about him. He has none of the dash of the teen-age thespian, none of the tone of the high-school athlete, none of the innocence of the young scholar. The hanging jowls give him, in repose, the expression of a faithful Basset hound. When he is in action, this excess of flesh becomes the raw material for setting expressions that can be alternately—or even in combination—quizzical, amused, bewildered, astounded, displeased, bored, excited. Dirksen is adroit at shifting the eyebrows over the bright blue eyes or twisting a corner of his copious mouth, as either may suit his purpose. He somehow makes use even of his body which, though six feet or more in height, is soft and round, with loose-hanging arms and legs that magnify its rotundity. Dirksen stands with it at an angle which conveys attention, walks with it in a roll that announces concern, sinks into a chair with it like a sack of potatoes as if to say, "All right, boys, there's the ice. Fill up."

But Dirksen's real triumph is his hair. Though an ignoble grey in color and shaggily thin in texture, it takes on a genuine dignity from the patrician head which is its pedestal. Dirksen's hair is his most evocative stage prop. From the center it grows in undulating curlicues and complex labyrinths to both sides of the head, until it finally takes flight over the ears, like little Cupid wings. Its look is one of fastidious neglect. In contrast to its delicacy are the big, rough, bony, farm-boy hands which Dirksen regularly runs through it as a gesture of distraction. Dirksen's hair, a defiant challenge to contemporary Senate manners, transports its wearer to another age, when Senators were supposed to be flamboyant, to say nothing of eccentric. The hair is to Dirksen what the corncob pipe is to MacArthur, the beard to Castro, the derby to Chaplin.

Dirksen's horn-rimmed glasses are another prop; so is the diamond ring that he wears, usually askew, on his little finger. His clothes became a prop only a few years ago, when, having lost on doctor's orders some fifty pounds, he found how useful to his purpose ill-fitting suits could be.

Dirksen, naturally, is resourceful enough to turn to his histrionic ends whatever new opportunities thrust themselves upon him. When he broke his thigh last spring, he had the choice of playing the crochety cripple or the gay convalescent. He didn't hesitate to choose the latter. In recent months, Dirksen has performed happily as the wounded Achilles, with confident laugh and stiff upper lip. Rolling merrily on his wheelchair through the corridors of the Capitol, he acknowledges the cheers of the crowd with a modest wave of the hand or a discreet tip of the cane.

From "Honk, Honk the Marigold," Reprinted by permission of Esquire Magazine. © 1966 by Esquire, Inc.

But whatever the props that Dirksen manipulates, they are all but a foil for the Dirksen voice. Ah, the voice! Surely the great Webster could not boast an instrument of such beauty and virtuosity. It can be a solo flute or a symphony orchestra, a call to love or to battle, a weapon to flay or to beguile, but always to fascinate, to captivate, to mesmerize. Its rhythm — slow and deliberate, like a Beethoven second movement — is under the perfect control of its conductor. His timing is as hypnotic as a metronome, his pauses refresh, his phrasing is precise, his nuances tap the widest range of emotions. The natural habitat of the Dirksen voice is the lower depths of the octave but if called upon it can sound any note. Its natural volume is modest but not because it cannot swell, if commanded, to a Wagnerian pitch. Rarely, however, does it need to. The master breathes like a diva and the voice throbs, pulsates, vibrates from deep within his caverns to cover vast audiences, to penetrate huge auditoriums.

"Shortly after Jack Kennedy was nominated," Dirksen relates, "and while he was preparing for the hustings, he came over to me and said, 'You know, Ev, there's one thing that bothers me. I'm afraid I'm going to lose my voice.' I said to him, 'Jack' — he was a fellow Senator and I could talk familiarly with him — 'Jack,' I said, 'you will lose your voice. You constantly talk off your cords. You must talk out of your diaphragm. If I were you, I'd pick up the best voice teacher in town. Three or four lessons and you'll be taught to let your voice come out of your belly.' And, by golly, that's what Jack did and he never had any trouble after that."

If there is anything that has saved Dirksen, with all his style, from being a plain old windbag, it is a certain perspective on himself. In an atmosphere inhospitable to Midwestern Republicanism, Dirksen's unique capacity to satirize himself comprises an essential part of the heroic image. Dirksen would be a stylistic failure if his entertainment depended on the gag, the clever repartee, a stab of ridicule, the exquisite thrust of wit. Dirksen, in fact, is not witty with words. His phrases are rather banal. His metaphors are familiar and often cliches. His stories are clean and wholesome and he has never been known to tell an off-color joke. Dirksen's humor is endearing because its subject matter is inherently fascinating. The fun that Dirksen makes is of an old-fashioned politician, a claghorn, a caricature, a prototype of the Senator as it has come down through American folklore. The fun he makes is of Dirksen. He is one of the rare souls who sees himself as others see him — which enables him, with his own gentle mockery, to beat others to the critical punch.

Satire dominates Dirksen's oratory. His typical speech begins with what its maker refers to as a "felicitous introduction." It is liberally laced with erudite quotations, most of them astonishingly accurate, from such authorities as Lincoln and Jefferson, Shakespeare and St. Paul, Wordsworth and Burke. It contains long, didactic sentences ("President Monroe said that Congress was really the seat or center of the government, meaning of course that virtually all the powers of government, whether for the Judicial Branch or for the Executive Branch, stem from the action by the Congress"), rendered palatable only by the seductive delivery. It is marked by such pretensions as "essay" for "try," "abode" for "home" and "discommode" for "inconvenience." It is illustrated at regular intervals by pithy stories, usually humorous and loving expositions of human foibles. Most of all, it is characterized by a confidence that permits its maker to say whatever comes to his mind without fear of making himself ridiculous. It is characterized by total poise. . . .

It is no coincidence that the smile is not one of Everett Dirksen's stage props. He abjures the device, dear to a Nixon, of exposing his teeth. He is sparing in reacting to his own humor, as John Kennedy used to do. Dirksen plays his satire straight, lugubriously, like the deadpan Chaplin. His solemnity affirms that, while funny, he is far from frivolous. Dirksen is a serious man whose humor is meant to purvey his personal brand of truth. He conveys the Calvinist dogma that man's fate is in God's hands and that government ought not interfere with it. But at the same time, he reflects a gentleness which softens his somber outlook on life and on the world. . . .

The Dirksen style, then, is a beautiful machine. It is complex, to be sure, but its pieces fit harmoniously with one another. The theatrics are linked to the ambition, the self-satire to the theatrics, the gentleness to the self-satire, the ambition to the gentleness. It is a curious combination to spell P-O-W-E-R, but its range is enormous.

ADAPTED READING 13.4

A LECTURER'S PROBLEMS
OF DELIVERY

Emily Kimbrough

Saint Nicholas magazine once published a poem which I can still repeat. I had no reason then to question its sentiments. Now, however, some thirty years later, which is a very gentle approximation, I have a low opinion of its smug young hero. The poem began:

> Once there was a little boy whose name was Robert Reece.
> And every Friday afternoon he had to speak a piece.

On the occasion which this poem records, Robert forgot his piece of that particular Friday afternoon. With an aplomb which at the time of my learning the poem, I considered magnificent, and now look upon as sickening, he substituted lines from the poems of preceding Fridays, and was very pleased with himself. The poem ends:

> You see it doesn't matter, Robert thought, what words I say,
> So long as I declaim with oratorical display.

After three seasons of lecture touring, I think I am qualified to assert that

From *It Gives Me Great Pleasure* (New York: Harper & Row, 1948), pp. 165–176. Copyright 1948 by Emily Kimbrough. Reprinted by permission of Harper & Row, Publishers, Inc.

either Robert's oratorical display was certainly very handsome indeed, or Robert was a young squirt who did not know what he was talking about. I should like to tell that young man about an oratorical display of mine at DePauw University last season, which I would match against any of his, and I wish he could know what response I collected.

DePauw University is at Greencastle, Indiana. I have known about it always, but last winter was my first visit there. Like that Reece boy's, my piece (at DePauw) was on a Friday too; Friday morning, however, January sixteenth, at ten o'clock. . . . I did not meet Dr. and Mrs. Wildman until Friday morning, although I arrived in Greencastle Thursday morning. . . .

As we left Mason Hall I asked if we had far to go. The weather was just as cold as I remembered from the day before. I learned for the first time, that I was speaking in a church—the Gobin memorial church—Dr. Wildman said, about a block away, and added that it was their only auditorium, but that they hoped some day to have another. I told him apprehensively that I was not sure that he knew that my lecture was not in any sense a church subject. Did he know that I was going to talk about Hollywood and motion pictures? He assured me that he did know. He had selected the subject himself. I need not be concerned, nor must I be put off by the incidental of speaking from the pulpit. It did put me off, however. I began to have misgivings about my being in Greencastle, Indiana, at all, in spite of my fondness up to this moment, for the people I had met there.

In the vestry, Dr. Wildman turned me over to a member of the English department, who was to introduce me. She told me that not only was I to speak from the pulpit, but I must speak into a microphone there, because the acoustics from that particular spot in the church were very faulty. I told her that I would be delighted to speak from any other spot. That was the only place, she said, from which I could be seen in the gallery. I protested that, born in the Middle West, I had a carrying voice, but she was firm. I dislike very much to use a microphone and told her so, but she repeated that there was no getting out of it.

She made the introduction from the chancel steps while I sat in a high-backed chair behind her. At the conclusion of the introduction, she waved me to the pulpit. I had never stood actually in a pulpit before, and somehow to be there made me more nervous than I have been on any platform. It must have been my nervousness which made me forget the microphone. It may, of course, have been an inner obstinacy on my part. At any rate, I opened without it, and with the most curious effect I have ever experienced. My first few words rolled back to me from corners of the gallery, some time after I had spoken them, and was well into the next sentence. The result was a jumble of sound which certainly no one could have understood. It brought me around immediately, however, to remembering the microphone. And I could not find it. I looked over the pulpit, peered around it, tilted my head back to see if it could be dangling above me. It was not.

It was at this moment that the memory of Robert Reece came back to me. I had not thought of the boy for years, but the whole story came before me with dazzling clarity, and brought me inspiration. If Robert had accomplished triumph by oratorical display, in spite of confusion of words, I would give an oratorical display DePauw would long remember.

Ordinarily I do not make gestures, I think. At least what I did that morning felt very unfamiliar. I skipped a little, I pranced, I wreathed my arms around my head, stretched them toward the audience, flung them out from my shoulders as if I were doing setting up exercises, and I was contemplating one above my head, the other out from the shoulder, when I caught sight of the microphone. I am not surprised that I had not seen it before. I would not have thought of looking inside the pulpit, but it was imbedded there, beneath the hood, at a level with the flat surface of the desk top. Evidently it had been planned for the reading of the lesson or sermon.

In my relief at finding it, I discontinued my oratorical display abruptly. I put my face toward the little disc, and discovered that the regular occupant of the pulpit for whom the microphone must have been installed, was of proportions very unlike mine. The only way I could come within speaking distance of it was to lean well over the surface of the desk, and bend my knees. When I did this I disappeared immediately and completely from the sight of the audience. The position itself was difficult and uncomfortable to maintain. To ease the discomfort in my knees, I tried coming out around the side of the pulpit, being careful to accompany each sally with strong gestures. I came out, too, because I felt an urgent necessity to re-establish communication with my audience, in order to see how we were getting on together. I am accustomed, when I speak, to watch the audience carefully. If I see—and it is very easy to see—that its temper is being tried by too long an exposition, I hurry to an anecdote. I have felt, too, an obligation to be visible. If I am engaged to appear before an audience, it has seemed to me that I ought to appear. But when I appeared skittishly around the pulpit at DePauw, interpreting the jumble of my words by sprightly pantomime, I had the uneasy impression that my audience was not happy to have me there. Accordingly, after perhaps three sorties, I retired behind the pulpit to stay, bent my knees, and maintained the position for the remaining fifty minutes of my allotted hour.

The speech finished, I came out for the last time from behind the pulpit to make my bow to the audience, and discovered that after fifty minutes of bending, I was unable to straighten my knees. The very effort to straighten them so intensified the cramp in my muscles, that I gave a sudden leer from excruciating pain. From the moment of my arrival in the town, I had loved the people there. Now I wanted only to get away from them all as quickly as possible. My exit, however, was not quick. Bent and cramped, I shuffled slowly off the stage. With the purpose of distracting attention from my posture, I accompanied my departure by a final flight of pantomime in as many gestures of farewell as I could conjure up during my passage.

I did not return for a second bow. I was in no position for it, but as I sat in the ante room, rubbing my knees, a woman approached me.

"I wanted to tell you, Miss Kimbrough," she said with certain emphasis, "that we enjoyed *what we heard* this morning very much."

ADDITIONAL READINGS

Anderson, Martin, E. Ray Nichols, Jr. and Herbert Booth, *The Speaker and His Audience* (New York: Harper & Row, 1974), chap. 13, "Communicating Through Physical Behavior."

Bowers, John Waite, "The Influence of Delivery on Attitudes Toward Concepts and Speakers," *Speech Monographs*, 32 (June 1965), 154–158.

Brigance, W. Norwood, *Speech: Its Techniques and Disciplines in a Free Society* (New York: Appleton, 1961), chap. 16, "Being Seen."

Bryant, Donald and Karl Wallace, *Fundamentals of Public Speaking* (New York: Appleton 1969), chap. 8, "Visual Materials."

Dickens, Milton, *Speech: Dynamic Communication* (New York: Harcourt Brace Jovanovich, 1963), chap. 9, "Visual Communication."

Hall, Edward, *The Silent Language* (New York: Fawcett, 1959).

Wittick, Walter and Charles Schuller, *Audio-Visual Materials: Their Nature and Use* (New York: Harper & Row, 1957).

STUDY QUESTIONS

1. How does the content of a speech differ from its delivery? Which is more important to effective communication?
2. Cite a speech that *you* might be required to give where you would want to use a manuscript; a memorized speech; the extemporaneous method.
3. How do the physical attributes of delivery differ from the vocal attributes? Which, in your opinion, are more important?
4. How much movement should the speaker permit himself when giving a speech? Under what circumstances could movement detract from a speech? Cite a speaker whose movement impaired his effectiveness.
5. Would you recommend that most speakers emulate the delivery of Everett Dirksen as described in Adapted Reading 13.3? Why or why not?
6. Of what value are gestures while speaking? Can a speech have too many gestures? Can a speech without gestures be effective? As effective as with gestures?
7. Why do you think television announcers always look straight at the screen? What relevance does this practice have to effective public speaking?
8. When should a speaker employ visual aids? How might a visual aid detract from a speech?

EXERCISES

1. Attend in person (not via radio or television) a speech, sermon, lecture, or debate and note the physical aspects of the speaker's delivery. Prepare a three- to four-minute oral report analyzing the strong and weak points of his bodily action. Present the report in class.
2. Observe the actions of someone you might describe as a character type. Present a two-minute pantomime of the behavior of this person, working out as much specific action or "business" as possible. In your pantomime give careful attention to the subject's age, size, physical characteristics, personality, and mannerisms.
3. Prepare a three- to four-minute informative speech in which you demonstrate some physical activity (for example, artificial respiration, driving signals, bowling, a golf stroke, fly casting, archery, a dance step, etc.)
4. Prepare a four-minute speech in which you employ at least two different kinds of visual aids. Give careful attention to their preparation and presentation.
5. In a two-minute oral report, demonstrate two or three physical characteristics of delivery you find particularly distracting or annoying when used by speakers.

VOCAL ATTRIBUTES OF DELIVERY

The way a speaker uses his voice may make the difference between a lackluster performance and an effective address. During one presidential campaign, Franklin D. Roosevelt evoked a roar of approval from the crowd simply because of the enthusiastic way he announced, "I've had a wonderful day in New England." His opponent, Wendell Willkie, on the other hand, strained his voice so badly that he was barely able to speak for much of the campaign. A problem John F. Kennedy had to overcome early in his bid for the presidential nomination was that he spoke so rapidly that his listeners often had difficulty following him. James Powell discusses this in Adapted Reading 14.4. Other speakers—Al Smith, Lyndon Johnson, and George Wallace—found their regional accents a handicap in speaking to some audiences. The manner and vocal characteristics of Senator Everett Dirksen proved distracting to many. And a prize-winning novelist once almost completely lost the interest of her audience because of her near inaudibility. These are a few examples of prominent speakers whose vocal attributes, at least at times, greatly influenced their effectiveness. Anyone who has listened to many speeches probably can recall similar examples among less well-known speakers.

The vocal elements of delivery are the audible symbols of the speech, or what the auditor hears. The listener does not hear ideas, supporting materials, organization, or language; he hears sounds. These sounds are uttered

Words were given us to communicate our ideas by; and there must be something inconceivably absurd in uttering them in such a manner as that either people cannot understand them or will not desire to understand them.

LORD CHESTERFIELD

with a particular voice quality, pitch, rate, volume, articulation, and pronunciation which reveal to the auditor the speaker's ideas, supporting materials, organization, and language. If the vocal presentation of the speech is marred by too rapid a rate, inadequate volume, distracting voice quality, confusing pitch inflection, sloppy articulation, mispronunciation, or some other fault, the listener may be unable to grasp the speaker's message. For this reason the speaker should give careful attention to the vocal attributes of delivery.

A speaker's vocal delivery is effective if it aids in the realization of six main goals:

1. The speaker's vocal attributes should contribute to the audience's easy understanding of what he is saying. His volume should be loud enough and his rate slow enough to enable the listeners to hear without difficulty. Words should be clearly articulated and properly pronounced so that they are readily recognizable.

2. The vocal characteristics of delivery should create interest in the speaker's message. Monotony in pitch, lack of emphasis, repetitious or patterned presentation, or too slow a rate may lead to a dull and uninspiring presentation. The speaker should maintain sufficient variety to create a high level of interest in his remarks.

3. The speaker's vocal usage should reinforce his ideas. His manner of speaking should contribute to the mood he seeks to create — serious, lighthearted, exciting, somber, or inspiring.

4. The speaker should seem natural and spontaneous. Harold Brack suggests in Adapted Reading 14.1 that a completely natural and conversational presentation might bore an audience. Nevertheless, whether speaking to one person or a group, the speaker's voice usage should *sound* natural and spontaneous, not artificial, stilted, or rehearsed.

5. The speaker's voice usage should be suited to the number of hearers, the medium, and to the occasion. An address by radio or television, for example, differs significantly from a speech to a live audience. Although the number of auditors for a broadcast talk could number in the millions, the speaker must keep in mind that he is really talking to many small groups of three or four persons seated in their homes and not to a multitude. Conscious of this difference, the speaker will modify his volume, rate, emphasis, and voice quality accordingly, states G. B. Shaw in Adapted Reading 14.2.

6. The speaker's vocal presentation should not distract the listener. It should be free of anything that might call attention to itself, such as errors in pronunciation, excessive vocalized pauses, awkward phrasing, voice breaks, lisping, abrupt changes in volume, and similar characteristics.

With these general goals in mind, let us now examine several specific aspects of voice usage.

VOLUME

Volume is the loudness or softness of the speaker's voice. The process of making a vocal sound begins with the exhalation of air from the lungs. The speaker's volume is determined by the amount of air supporting the sound production. If the speaker releases a greater quantity of air, the sound will be strong and loud; if he limits the amount of air released from the lungs, it will be soft and quiet.

Among beginning speakers, the most common difficulties are insufficient volume and lack of flexibility. Both of these weaknesses can impair the effectiveness of the speaker's communication. The speaker who cannot be heard because of inadequate volume is simply wasting his and his listeners' time. Communication is a two-way process; if the other party cannot hear what the speaker says, no communication can take place.

The speaker who talks with little or no variation in loudness is not likely to be successful. In addition to being monotonous, he gives the impression that everything he says is of equal importance. He may even confuse the listener by his monotony and lack of emphasis.

Other problems of volume that handicap some speakers include speaking too loudly, improper emphasis, and loudness patterns (such as beginning each sentence strongly and fading away at the end).

The following suggestions are intended to aid the speaker in achieving effective volume control in his speaking:

1. Maintain an adequate supply of air to achieve proper volume. To do this, learn to breathe deeply and to control exhalation. Adequate breath support usually can be maintained through either abdominal or thoracic breathing. However, the speaker whose breathing is shallow will find that he is almost constantly short of breath when speaking.

2. Adapt volume to the size and acoustics of the room and to the number of listeners. Communication will not occur if the listener cannot hear or if he tires of trying to hear and stops listening. The speaker should also take care that he does not speak too loudly. Few things are more irritating than a speaker who shouts at a few people in a small room as if he were addressing a multitude at Madison Square Garden.

3. Adjust loudness to overcome distracting noises. The hum of an air conditioner, the sound of traffic outside, or simply the shuffling of feet by members of an audience can make it difficult for the listener to hear, either momentarily or for a prolonged period of time. The speaker needs to be alert to such competing sounds and, when necessary, increase his volume to cope with them.

4. Maintain an interesting and flexible variation in volume. The speaker should stress important words, phrases, and sentences by varying his volume. At times, he will wish to stress something by saying it with additional volume. Other times, he may achieve emphasis and contrast by speaking more softly. Not only should he avoid using the same monotonous volume throughout, but he should also avoid repetitious patterns of loudness. Some speakers habitually begin each sentence with considerable volume and then gradually "run down," fading away at the end. Occasionally speakers develop other volume patterns which they repeat throughout the speech. Regardless of the nature of the pattern, such habits result in a dull, singsong type of delivery and should be avoided.

5. Discover and try to eliminate the causes of persistent problems with loudness. Failure to achieve proper volume and emphasis is not always the

result of poor breathing or failure to recognize the demands of the situation. The causes may be deeper. The speaker who habitually speaks too loudly or too softly may be suffering from a hearing problem which makes it difficult for him to judge accurately the required level of volume. In this instance, he should see an audiologist. A speaker may be speaking in a pitch range that strains his voice and precludes greater volume. Correction of this difficulty demands the assistance of a trained speech correctionist. The speaker's problem may not be related at all to sound production. It may simply be a problem of shyness or insecurity. Whatever the reason, if problems of loudness persist, the speaker should consult his instructor in an effort to discover the causes of the difficulty.

PITCH

Pitch refers to the highness or lowness of the speaker's voice and the changes in highness or lowness (inflections). Pitch originates with the vibration of the vocal folds. As the speaker exhales air, it passes up the throat (pharynx) to the vocal folds. The vocal folds are located in the larynx just behind the cricoid cartilage, commonly known as the Adam's apple. Stretched behind this cartilage are what can best be described as two "blobs" of muscle. The term "blobs" is used here because the appearance of the vocal folds almost defies description. However, it is important to realize that, contrary to the implication of the term vocal "cords," the vocal folds are not two sharp or taut bands.

As the air from the lungs reaches the vocal folds, the speaker must tense them if he wishes to produce a sound. (Not every exhalation of breath produces a sound.) As the air passes over the tensed folds of muscle, they vibrate and sound is formed. The degree of tension of the vocal folds as they vibrate determines the speaker's pitch: the greater the tension, the higher the pitch; the more relaxed the vocal folds, the lower the pitch.

The most common pitch problems among beginning speakers are use of a pitch range that strains the voice, use of a pitch level inconsistent with the audience's expectations of the speaker, inflexibility in pitch, and lack of variation in inflection. To achieve effective pitch usage, the speaker should:

1. Discover and speak in the pitch range best suited to his voice. Everyone has an *optimum pitch level*, or a range of tones best suited to the individual's voice. The person who habitually speaks in a pitch range considerably above or below his optimum pitch level is likely to find that he is unable to achieve the volume necessary to be easily heard; that his voice tires quickly, making it difficult to speak for an extended period of time; or that his voice becomes hoarse, raspy, or husky. Although they are not always related, a speaker's pitch usage may affect his voice quality. A hoarse or husky voice often is a sign that the speaker is straining his voice by using an improper pitch level.

The cause of a speaker's use of a pitch level unsuited to his vocal apparatus may be physical or psychological. Although it is not common, some speakers habitually employ a pitch level that is too high because of a protracted illness during puberty. At an age when most youths' voices are changing, the speaker may have been subjected to bronchitis, laryngitis, or some other disability that interfered with normal voice change. Following the illness, the speaker simply continues to use his childhood pitch.

Illness, however, is less likely to be a cause than is some psychological factor. Most speech characteristics are learned, usually through imitation of some admired person. Consciously or subconsciously, during childhood and adolescence the speaker models his speech after those he most respects — his parents, a teacher, a star athlete, an actress, or a prominent public figure. Because his model's pitch level may be wholly unsuitable to his own vocal mechanism, the individual at times develops a habitual pitch level which produces severe strain.

Feelings of insecurity may lead to improper pitch usage. The speaker who fears the responsibilities of adulthood may be reluctant to cut the apron strings. To maintain the parent–child relationship, he may deliberately seek to retain the speech of his childhood. Parents at times even encourage this. The result is that the individual often speaks with a high-pitched "little girl" or "little boy" voice.

To determine his optimum pitch level, the speaker should sing from the lowest pitch he can produce to the highest pitch he can reach using his falsetto voice. He should determine the number of full-step tones in the entire range of his voice, divide by three, and then count up from his lowest pitch one-third of the total range. This is his optimum pitch. The speaker, of course, should not use only that tone; but most of his normal speaking should center around four or five pitches above and below this note.

2. Speak in a pitch range that does not distract the listeners. Although rare, occasionally a speaker will find that speaking at his optimum pitch level, while comfortable and natural for him, disturbs his auditors. The big, rugged looking man whose optimum pitch level happens to be unusually high may sound effeminate to his listeners who expect a deeper, more masculine voice; the small, demure lass whose optimum pitch level is much lower than that of most women may be equally distracting. If the incongruity between the speaker's pitch level and the audience's expectations is too great, the speaker may wish to make some adjustment. Since habitual use of a pitch above or below one's optimum level is dangerous, the speaker should seek the assistance of a qualified speech correctionist in solving this problem.

3. Avoid monotony in pitch. Few speakers are more boring than the one who speaks at the same pitch throughout a speech. The monotone speaker is often the victim of his own disinterest. He simply doesn't care enough about his subject to make it interesting. At other times, monotony in pitch is caused by overdependence on a manuscript by a speaker who cannot read well or on memorization by a speaker who cannot recite effectively. Another cause may be that the speaker habitually speaks in a monotone because of poor pitch perception (tone deafness) or a hearing impairment.

To overcome these handicaps the speaker should choose a topic in which he is interested and which he is eager to discuss with his listeners. To determine whether he is speaking with enough variation in pitch, the speaker should record and listen to his speech from time to time as he practices it. If his pitch is habitually monotonous, the speaker should embark on a program to develop variety and flexibility. Imitation of a trained speaker who employs wide variations in pitch—such as a radio or television announcer reading a commercial—may help. He should not, of course, try to develop a style identical to that of his model, but he should attempt to "loosen up" his voice and extend the range of his pitch. The speaker may also achieve greater flexibility by repeating a single sentence aloud with varying patterns of rising and falling inflections. For example, he might speak the following sentence in several different ways by following the arrows indicating rising and falling inflections:

The broad, ↗ flat meadow was covered with daisies.
The broad, flat ↗ meadow was covered with daisies.
The broad, flat meadow ↗ was covered with daisies.
The broad, flat meadow was covered ↗ with daisies.
The broad, flat meadow was covered with daisies. ↗
The broad ↘ , flat meadow was covered with daisies.
The broad, flat ↘ meadow was covered with daisies.
The broad, flat meadow ↘ was covered with daisies.
The broad, flat meadow was covered ↘ with daisies.
The broad, flat meadow was covered with daisies. ↘
The broad ↗ , flat meadow was covered ↘ with daisies.
The broad ↘ , flat meadow ↗ was covered ↘ with daisies.

Any simple sentence and any combination of variations in pitch can be used in the above exercise. The important factor is the speaker's ability to achieve variety in pitch by saying the sentence in different ways.

If after several attempts a speaker is still unable to perform the above exercise, it may be that he is handicapped by a hearing impairment or tone deafness. To discover whether these are possible causes of his difficulty he should consult an audiologist.

4. Avoid distracting pitch patterns. The speaker who varies his pitch but does so in approximately the same manner throughout the speech is almost as boring as the speaker who never alters his pitch. Repetitious inflections, or pitch patterns, are detrimental to effective communication because most of the time the particular pitch pattern employed by the speaker is inconsistent with what he is saying. English is a complex language, capable of conveying an almost infinite number of ideas, depending on how it is used. To impose an unvarying pitch pattern on one's utterances is to eliminate one of the principal means of indicating precisely what one wishes to say, for without meaningful inflection a whole range of nuances, shadings, and interpretations is lost.

To deliver an entire speech in one pitch pattern would be about as interesting as an opera in which every line was sung to the same tune. Yet, regrettably, some speakers do precisely this. The group most commonly guilty of this is the clergy. So many preachers are addicted to the use of repetitious pitch patterns that the terms "ministerial monotone" and "preacher's pattern" are familiar to almost everyone.

VOICE QUALITY

Voice quality—or timbre—is the distinctive characteristic of one voice which distinguishes it from all other voices. Although it may be influenced by pitch and volume, voice quality consists of more than these factors. For example, when a person answers the telephone, in spite of the low fidelity of that instrument, he often immediately recognizes the voice he hears. What is familiar to the listener is not the speaker's pitch, volume, rate, articulation, or pronunciation, for thousands of other people say "hello" with an almost identical pitch, volume, rate, articulation, and pronunciation. The distinguishing feature is the speaker's voice quality. Each person's voice quality is unique, so much so in fact that "voice prints" are being studied by legal authorities as a possible complement to fingerprints for identifying individuals. Thomas Coon discusses this in Adapted Reading 14.3.

The quality of a speaker's voice is the result of the resonance of the sound formed in the vocal folds. The sound produced in the larynx by the vibration of the vocal cords is not the same sound the listener hears, for following its production it travels through the upper larynx, mouth, and nose. As it passes through these cavities, it is resonated—altered and modified—before finally being emitted. The size, shape, and texture of the resonating cavities determine the sound the listener eventually hears.

One can perhaps better understand what voice quality is and how it is determined by a comparison to quality or timbre in musical instruments. If one were to ask three musicians—a clarinetist, a trumpeter, and a violinist—to play individually to a blindfolded audience at exactly the same pitch with the same volume for the same period of time, most of the listeners could, without difficulty, identify the various instruments. The distinguishing characteristic is obviously not pitch, duration, or loudness, but the quality or timbre of the instrument. To carry the analogy a step further, the principal reason for the difference in the sound of the three instruments is the size, shape, and texture of the resonating cavities: In the clarinet it is a long wooden tube; in the trumpet, a circular brass tube; and in the violin, an unusually shaped wooden box. A modification of the size and shape of the resonating cavity (for example, the substitution of a viola for a violin or a French horn for a trumpet) would result in a change in the quality of the sound.

In much the same manner that the size, shape, and texture of the resonating cavities determine the timbre of a musical instrument, the size, shape, and texture of the mouth, nose, and larynx alter and modify the quality of the sound produced by the vocal cords. At this point, however, it should be pointed out that not all of the sounds used in speech are produced by vocalization and resonation. All vowels are produced by vocalization and resonation. Many speech sounds, however, are made without the use of the vocal folds. These include *t, p, k, f, s, sh, th, w,* and *wh*. The *t, p,* and *k* sounds are formed by building up a slight pressure of air and then "exploding" it. The *f, s, sh, th, w,* and *wh* sounds are produced by blowing breath over the tongue, teeth, and lips in various ways. If the vocal cords are vibrated while producing these sounds, with only slight modifications in the set of the mouth, tongue, teeth, and lips, *t* becomes *d, p* becomes *b, k* becomes *g, f* becomes *v, s* becomes *z, sh* becomes *z* (as in *azure*) and the silent *th* (as in *think*) becomes the voiced *th* (as in *those*). Voice quality is not influenced by the voiceless sounds. Only those sounds produced by vibration of the vocal cords contribute to the speaker's voice quality.

While good vocal quality can be defined as a voice that is pleasant and easy to listen to, this definition is too vague to be very helpful. Good voice quality can probably best be defined by telling what it is *not:* It is a voice whose quality is *not* harsh, husky, hoarse, breathy, shrill, strident, or nasal.

The causes of poor voice quality are many. A permanent huskiness or hoarseness may be the result of a prolonged cold or laryngitis. Inadequate breath support may lead to a whispering or breathy quality. Enlarged adenoids may contribute to nasality. Prolonged use of an unsuitable pitch level may lead to harshness.

But, as in the case of pitch, the most common cause of poor voice quality is imitation, either conscious or subconscious. Some young people deliberately try to develop speaking voices similar to those of admired adults. Unfortunately, the effort may strain the young person's voice and result in an unpleasant voice quality. Others, although totally unaware of it themselves, model their speech after parents or teachers whose voices are unpleasant. Thus, a son may develop a harsh, strident voice similar to that of his father, or a daughter may speak with a nasal quality like that of her mother's voice.

With beginning speakers, voice quality is most often marred by huskiness or hoarseness among males, breathiness (usually associated with "little-girl" voices) among females, and nasality in both sexes.

For someone with an unusually unpleasant voice, the process of improving voice quality requires considerable time and effort, for the individual must first rid himself of a manner of speaking that he has used for many years, and then adopt and practice a new voice quality until it becomes natural and habitual. Because the causes, diagnoses, and treatments of poor voice quality are so varied, the person with a serious voice impairment should work with a trained speech correctionist.

For others whose voice impairment is less severe, the following suggestions are made:

1. The speaker should learn to hear his voice as others hear it. An almost universal reaction of persons hearing a recording of their voices for the first time is, "That's not me. There must be something wrong with the recorder." But, of course, nothing is wrong with the recorder and the recording, as classmates or friends will verify; the sound is a faithful reproduction of the individual's speech. The speaker's initial reaction reveals that he does not hear himself as others hear him. This is in part because some of the sound is carried from the voice box to his ears through the cheek and

neck bones. But it is also because most people have become so accustomed to hearing their own voices that they really do not listen to themselves carefully or analytically.

Quite clearly, the first step in learning to hear one's voice as others hear it is for the speaker to record and listen to his speech frequently. The second step is to develop an awareness at all times of how one sounds.

2. To avoid strain, one should speak at a comfortable pitch level. For a discussion of how to determine optimum pitch level, see page 365.

3. The speaker should maintain adequate breath support.

4. He should remain relaxed while speaking.

5. If strain or hoarseness occurs regularly, the speaker should consult a speech correctionist.

RATE

A speaker's rate is the speed at which he talks. It consists of the duration of the individual sounds and syllables, pauses, fluency, and rhythm. A speaker's rate is determined primarily by the speed with which he manipulates his tongue, teeth, and lips to formulate various sounds, syllables, and words. It is more, however, than mere physical rapidity, for the speaker's rate also depends on his verbal facility and thought processes. If he loses his train of thought or cannot find the word he wants, he obviously will be forced to pause before continuing.

A desirable rate of speaking is one that is neither too fast to permit the hearer to grasp what the speaker says nor too slow to hold the listeners' interest; it is varied and flexible; and it is free from awkward hesitancies, pauses, and nonfluencies.

Among beginning speakers the most common problems of rate are speaking too rapidly, lack of variety, and vocalized pauses. The following suggestions are designed to assist the speaker in achieving a good rate of speaking:

1. Know what you are talking about. The speaker who is uncertain of what he is talking about is going to encounter difficulty in presenting his ideas fluently. If he knows what he wants to say, problems of memory and locating the right word are reduced and fluency is improved.

2. Practice aloud and often. Only by actually saying a speech aloud in practice can the speaker locate awkward sentences that are difficult to deliver orally, tongue-twisting phrases, and constructions that mar the rhythm and flow of the speech. By practicing aloud, the speaker is also forced to deal with nonfluencies and vocalized pauses. With extensive oral practice the speaker can develop a familiarity with his material that will permit him to deliver each sentence smoothly and meaningfully.

3. Make sure that the rate is neither too fast nor too slow. To check on his rate, the speaker should record and listen to himself during the preparation stages or ask a friend to listen to him. If he normally is nervous and tense while speaking, the speaker should commence at a deliberately slow pace. Because many speakers have a tendency to accelerate their rate as they progress, a slow start will discourage too rapid a rate.

4. Vary the rate. Speaking at the same speed detracts from the effectiveness of the speaker in communicating his message to his listeners. In addition to boring the listener, the speaker whose rate is monotonous deprives himself of an effective means of achieving variety, emphasis, and interest. By delivering an important sentence at a slower rate, the speaker can give added force to that remark. By accelerating his speed, he can create a sense of urgency or feeling of excitement. Through the use of pauses, he can achieve variety and emphasis.

5. Avoid excessive vocalized pauses. Many speakers seem to feel that every second must be filled with some kind of sound. So, instead of pausing naturally, they fill each pause with "uh," "er," "uhum," "you know," or some similar vocalization. Almost everyone employs the vocalized pause occasionally, but when a speaker fills almost every pause with a vocalization, the habit can be highly irritating to his listeners.

ARTICULATION

Articulation is the process of forming sounds, syllables, and words. Articulation differs from pronunciation in that articulation is primarily a matter of skill and habit, while pronunciation is a matter of knowledge. For example, the person who says stastistics instead of statistics, jist instead of just, or git instead of get probably is guilty of poor articulation, since he undoubtedly knows that these words are not pronounced *stastistics, jist,* and *git,* but through carelessness or habit he nevertheless continues to say them incorrectly. On the other hand, the person who pronounces the s in *Illinois* or says *revelant* for *relevant* probably does so because of lack of knowledge. He could say *Illinoi* or *relevant,* but he does not know that he should. For this reason, these mistakes would be classed as pronunciation errors.

Good articulation is clear and correct without being overly precise or pedantic. It is clear in the sense that each sound is distinct and each word is easily recognized. It is correct in that words are free from addition, omission, substitution, and transposition of sounds. In improving his articulation, the speaker needs to be familiar with these four common errors:

Addition of Sounds. This mistake occurs when the speaker adds to the word a sound that should not be included. An example would be *ath-a-lete* for *ath-lete.* Many persons commit this mistake because they find that it is difficult to make an *l* sound immediately after the *th* sound; when they add an *a* between the *th* and the *l,* the word is much easier for them to pronounce.

Omission of Sounds. This error consists of omitting from a word a sound that should be included (i.e., *doin* for *doing, goverment* for *government*).

Substitution of Sounds. This fault is the result of the speaker's substituting in a word an incorrect sound for the correct one (i.e., *git* for *get, jist* for *just,* and *undoubtebly* for *undoubtedly*).

Transposition of Sounds. This mistake occurs when the speaker inverts the order in which two sounds are uttered, saying the second sound first (i.e., *hunderd* for *hundred* and *modren* for *modern*).

The above examples would be classified as articulation errors rather than mistakes in pronunciation because in each instance if given a choice between the two ways of saying the word (*jist* or *just*, *goverment* or *government*, etc.) the speaker would be able to identify the correct pronunciation. Nevertheless, through carelessness or habit, he might continue to say the word incorrectly.

Additional examples of these common errors in articulation are found in the accompanying table.

The causes of poor articulation are many. It may result from such physiological factors as a cleft palate, a sluggish or overly large tongue, a malocclusion of the teeth, the spacing of the teeth, cerebral palsy, or other physical impairments. However, most articulation errors, rather than being caused by some physiological factor, are learned. If the child's model speaks carelessly and indistinctly or omits, distorts, or slurs certain sounds, the speaker is likely to develop the same articulation problems. Another cause of poor articulation is sheer carelessness or laziness. While he may have been surrounded by persons whose articulation was clear and correct, the speaker may have developed slovenly and indistinct speech because no one took the trouble to help him improve his articulation.

The speaker who is unable to make a particular sound probably needs the assistance of a speech correctionist, as does the speaker whose articulation is poor because of some physiological defect. However, those whose articulation is characterized by additions, omissions, and substitutions of sounds or by general carelessness or imprecision can do much to improve their speech by following these suggestions:

1. Develop a perceptive ear. Many speakers whose articulation is indistinct or incorrect simply are poor listeners. They don't listen carefully to their own speech or to the speech of others. Consequently, not only are they often unaware of what sounds a word should contain, but even if they are familiar with the proper articulation of a word, they may fail to recognize their own faulty articulation of it. The first step in improving articulation is to become aware of the different sounds each word contains.

2. Isolate articulation errors. Having become highly conscious and critical of his own and others' articulation, the speaker next must systematically seek to detect the specific articulatory problems that mar his speech. He will look for words and combinations of sounds that often cause him trouble; he will look for evidence of general carelessness and indistinctness.

3. Seek to break bad habits of articulation. Having determined the specific nature of his articulation difficulty, the speaker must be constantly alert to his problem. He must develop the habit of listening critically to his own speech in everyday conversation in order to detect and eliminate his articulation errors.

4. Seek to substitute new habits of good articulation. In addition to being conscious of his mistakes, the speaker should practice correcting the

COMMON ARTICULATION ERRORS

	WORD	MISARTICULATION
Additions	idea	idear
	athlete, athletic	ath-a-lete, ath-a-letic
	statistics	stastistics
Omissions	film	fim
	help	hep
	self	sef
	government	goverment, govement
	doing, coming	doin, comin
	going, nothing	goin, nothin
	seeing, morning	seein, mornin
	Europe	Eurpe
Substitutions	any, many	inny, minny
	undoubtedly	undoubtebly
	just	jist
	want	wont
	get	git
	gone	goan
	can't	cain't
	Massachusetts	Massatusetts
	Baptist	Babdist
	escape	excape
	ask, asked	ax, axed
Transposition	hundred	hunderd
	children	childern
	modern	modren

errors and make a deliberate effort to incorporate the new, correct articulation into his daily speech.

In practice, the speaker may find it necessary to drill extensively on the particular sounds or words that give him difficulty. However, his effort to improve cannot stop there; he must also attempt to incorporate these sounds and words correctly into his conversation and public speaking.

PRONUNCIATION

Pronunciation, as indicated earlier, is knowing how a word should be said. It includes a knowledge of which sounds in the word are voiced and which remain silent, how each sound is pronounced, what syllables are accented, and which regional variations in pronunciation are acceptable. Unlike an articulation error, which occurs because of carelessness or inability to say the word properly, a mistake in pronunciation is the result of a lack of knowledge of the accepted way of saying the word. Occasionally, however, a speaker may know the correct pronunciation, but, through habit, will continue to mispronounce the word.

Speakers who mispronounce words usually do so because the word is new and unfamiliar, because it resembles another word with which they are familiar, or because they have frequently heard it mispronounced by others. For example, a speaker who has come across the word *predacious* many times in his reading might be well acquainted with its meaning; yet, because he has never heard it spoken, he may pronounce the word incorrectly. Another speaker may mispronounce the word *relevant* as *revelant* because it resembles *revelry* or *reverent*. Or, a speaker who has regularly heard *Italian* pronounced *Eye-talian* may adopt this incorrect pronunciation.

In seeking the correct pronunciation of a word, the speaker's first recourse should be to an up-to-date standard dictionary. If he is totally unfamiliar with the word, the dictionary will provide him with a guide to which sounds are silent, how the vowels should be pronounced, and what syllables should be stressed. The dictionary, however, usually will not reveal accepted regional variations. Most dictionaries indicate only acceptable general American pronunciation. Even those dictionaries that include some approved regional variations may be of little help, for speakers in different regions of the country often pronounce the same sound in different ways. For example, many Southern speakers tend to prolong or diphthongize several of the vowel sounds. Thus, a Southern speaker consulting the dictionary to determine the correct pronunciation of a word such as *fate* would see that it is pronounced *fāt* with a long *a* as in *ape*. But because he normally prolongs the *a* in *ape* as if it were *ayup*, he will probably pronounce *fate* in the same manner: *fayut*. A midwesterner, on the other hand, would pronounce it *fāt*. So, unless the speaker is well acquainted with the phonetic symbols used to indicate the correct pronunciation of the words, the dictionary is not an entirely satisfactory guide to pronunciation.

A better source of information is a pronouncing dictionary such as John S. Kenyon and Thomas A. Knott's *A Pronouncing Dictionary of American English*. This volume, which includes no definitions, provides a comprehensive guide to acceptable regional variations in pronunciation. An unavoidable prerequisite to the use of this excellent work, however, is a knowledge of the phonetic alphabet because all pronunciations are noted phonetically.

In view of the shortcomings of both the standard dictionaries and Kenyon and Knott's pronouncing dictionary, most speakers will require an additional guide to correct pronunciation. The authors suggest two criteria for this additional guide. These are:

1. For most words, the speaker should accept the pronunciation of the educated people of the region in which he lives.
2. The names of persons and places should be pronounced as they are pronounced by the possessors of the name or the inhabitants of the place.

The first criterion is recommended because, unlike some nations, the United States has no official dialect or pronunciation. Instead, the country has three major dialects that are spoken in different regions and several variations within each of these three major dialects. The most common dialect is

COMMON ERRORS IN PRONUNCIATION

WORD	MISPRONUNCIATION	ACCEPTED PRONUNCIA- TION
often	off-ten	off-en
genuine	gen-you-wine	gen-you-win
gesture	guest-ure	jest-ure
direct	dye-rect	dir-rect
event	ee-vent	ee-vent
police	po-lice	po-lice
insurance	in-sur-ance	in-sur-ance
theatre	thee-ate-r	thee-a-ter
err	air	er
relevant	revelant	relevant
illegal	ee-legal	ill-legal
iron	arn	eye-urn
homage	hommage, hom-age	omm-age
subtle	sub-tul	suttle
aria	air-i-a	are-i-a
program	pro-grum	pro-gram
clique	click	cleek
cooperation	corporation	co-oper-a-tion
mayonnaise	my-on-aise	may-on-aise

the General American or midwestern, which is spoken by the majority of Americans. The Southern dialect is generally spoken in the states that comprised the Confederacy, with the exception of western Texas. The New England dialect is spoken by people residing in the six New England states and northeastern New York. The speech of people living in areas along boundaries of the major dialect regions, as might be expected, usually displays characteristics of the dialects of both regions. Within each region, variations in dialect are found also. For example, while both are regarded as Southern, the speech of Virginia differs considerably from that of Mississippi. Differences also occur in large cities, where the influence of immigrant groups may have altered the dialect. Ethnic groups speaking a language other than English have also modified the dialect of some areas. For instance, the French in southern Louisiana, the Germans in Wisconsin, and the Mexican–Americans in the Southwest have contributed to variations in those areas. Another major dialect variation found in many parts of the country is that of the black.

Since the United States has no officially correct or approved dialect, most speakers should seek to develop pronunciation habits consistent with the speech of the educated people in the region where they live.

In determining the pronunciation of names of people and places, however, the speaker should accept the pronunciation of those who possess the name or inhabit the place. Thus, the town of Monroe in Louisiana is pronounced *Mon'-roe* while Monroe, Michigan, is pronounced *Mon-roe'* because these are the pronunciations used by residents of the two communi-

COMMON ERRORS IN THE PRONUNCIATION
OF NAMES OF PERSONS AND PLACES

NAME	MISPRONUNCIATION	ACCEPTED PRONUNCIATION
Illinois	Ill-i-noise	Ill-i-noy
Detroit	Dee-troit	De-troit
United States	U-nited States	U-ni-ted States
Des Moines	De Moins, Des Moins	De Moin
Pierre (South Dakota)	Pi-air'	Peer
Iowa	Ioway	Iowuh
Italian	Eye-talian	It-talian
New Orleans	New Or-leens	New Or-lee-uns
Syracuse	Sarah-cuse	Seer-acuse
Biloxi	Bi-lock-si	Bi-uck-si
Louisiana	Lou-easy-anna, Lou-zee-anna	Lou-is-ee-anna
Richard Wagner	Wag-ner	Vahg-ner
Mozart	Mose-art	Moats-art

ties. For the same reason, Arkansas is pronounced *Arkansaw* rather than *Arkansas;* the capital of South Dakota, Pierre, is pronounced *Peer* rather than *Pi-air'*, and Detroit is correctly pronounced with the accent on the second rather than the first syllable. Eric Sevareid discusses this in Adapted Reading 14.5. The pronunciation of family names is determined in the same fashion.

SUMMARY

The audible or vocal elements of delivery include the speaker's volume, pitch, voice quality, rate, articulation, and pronunciation. The speaker's volume should be flexible, adapted to the speech situation, and neither too loud nor too soft. His pitch should be pleasant, varied, and suited to his vocal mechanism. The speaker should strive to develop a voice quality that is easy to listen to and free from distracting characteristics. A good speaker will vary his rate from time to time, speaking neither too rapidly nor too slowly.

Articulation refers to the speaker's skill or facility in saying a word correctly, while pronunciation is a matter of knowing how the word should be said. Good articulation is clear, distinct, and free from omissions, additions, distortions, or transpositions of sounds. The speaker's guide in pronunciation for most words should be the pronunciation of educated people in the region in which he lives. However, proper names of persons and places are correctly pronounced as the possessors of the name or inhabitants of the place pronounce them.

ADAPTED READING 14.1

IS EFFECTIVE PUBLIC SPEAKING "CONVERSATIONAL"?

Harold A. Brack

During the past two decades, authors of speech textbooks have been referring students to various characteristics of common conversation as guides to effective public speaking. To be sure, authors have spoken of "conversation as the basis for effective speech" or used such terms as "animated conversation." Their intention *has not* been to imply that the audible and visible efforts employed to communicate in the average conversation are adequate to communicate in the public speaking situation. In most instances, these authors have underscored the significant differences between public speech and colloquial conversation.

Students who have acquired the concept that effective public speaking is conversational more often than not have forgotten the qualifying terms. Consequently, when these students turn to the delivery of public speeches, they lapse into the vocal and bodily action habits of their normal conversational speech. . . .

When a teacher is working in the context of a theological school in which students are extremely apprehensive about any effort in delivery that might tend to direct attention to themselves rather than to "the word of God" or to an "act of worship," the difficulty becomes compounded. Students are far more frightened of accusations that their delivery is "too dramatic," "too forceful," or "too emotional" than they are of accusations that they are using their "vestry voice" or that they have a "ministerial tone." As a result, the teacher finds himself struggling against bland, inaudible, monotonous delivery frequently defended on the grounds that the student is striving for a conversational style that will not call attention to itself.

Such teaching experience causes me to raise the question as to whether the comparison of public speaking with conversation is so misleading, for the student, that the comparison should no longer be employed. . . . I see only one exception to be noted. In teaching a course in religious broadcasting, I find the comparison with conversation quite helpful. Here "conversational" is descriptive for both the speaker and the listener. "Conversational" describes those delivery characteristics which are pleasing to the listener and also the effort and skill which the radio speaker may employ in such aspects of his delivery as rate, force, and melody.

When the speaker steps to the rostrum in the classroom, onto the public speaking platform, or into the pulpit, "conversational" may still describe the way the audience would like the speaker to sound and appear but the adjective does not describe the effort or skill which the speaker must employ in order to seem to be conversational. Not even as I criticize my discussion groups do I find the term "conversational" adequate to characterize the

From *The Speech Teacher*, 14:4 (November 1965), pp. 276–277. Reprinted by permission of the author, Harold A. Brack, The Theological School, Drew University.

delivery effort and skill needed to be clear, distinct, and interesting in a group of eight or nine discussants and certainly not for the panel discussion where the group is participating in a discussion in the presence of an audience.

Although it is dangerous to generalize about delivery for television, even in the interview or panel show a minimum amount of "liveliness" and even of showmanship is required. A minimum amount of "liveliness" or showmanship demands more than the normal amount of speech effort employed in everyday conversation. Therefore, if we move from a radio to a television presentation, I find it necessary to move away from the conversation comparison.

Consequently, I find the student's concept of effective speech as being conversational an inhibitory one which results in inadequate voice production, limited vocal variety, restrained bodily action, and slovenly posture. One of my colleagues recently complained, "You've got to help that student. When he offers the pastoral prayer, he sounds like he's just chatting with God. . . ."

Since our normal conversation admittedly *does not* suggest the delivery skills and effort required for adequate communication in the public speaking situation and since students tend to assume that the concept that "good public speaking is conversational" implies that it *does,* let us ask seriously if we should abandon the favorable comparison of conversation with effective public speaking. . . .

ADAPTED READING 14.2

TRUTH BY RADIO
George Bernard Shaw

I love to speak to everybody, and I never could do that until this wonderful invention of the radio and the microphone enabled me to do it. I know very well that my friend Mr. [H. G.] Wells has told us that when you buy a wireless set you never use it after the first two days, and that here I am, talking to absolute vacancy under the impression that I am talking to millions. But I do not believe that. I always believe and feel that I really am talking to millions.

The politicians have not yet found out the microphone. They still imagine that they are addressing political meetings, and they do not understand that the microphone is a terrible tell-tale and a ruthless detective. If you speak insincerely on the platform to a political meeting, especially at election time, the more insincere you are the more they cheer you and the more they are delighted. But if you try that on the microphone, it gives you away instantly. The sober citizen at his fireside hears nothing but a senseless ranting by a speaker whose pretended earnestness is the result of the extra pint of champagne which has loosened his tongue and fuddled away his conscience and commonsense.

If there is anything wrong with you, remember that the microphone will

From a special talk filmed for the motion picture "B.B.C., the Voice of Britain," 1939, and published in *Platform and Pulpit,* Dan H. Laurence (ed.), (New York: Hill and Wang, 1961), pp. 273–274.

make the worst of it. If you nerve yourself to face it by taking, say, half a glass of whiskey, the microphone will convince all the listeners that you are shockingly drunk. I can tell by listening what the speaker has had for dinner.

The microphone tells you other things as well: for instance, where you were born. It brings out and exaggerates your native accent mercilessly. Tones in your voice that the naked ear cannot hear become audible through the microphone, betraying thoughts and feelings that you think you are concealing from every living listener. The preacher who is a hypocrite is unmasked as completely as the Cabinet Minister who is a bunk merchant. When this becomes known, it will raise the moral level of public life. It will raise the character of public speaking. It will even raise the character of our existing platform politicians, who will broadcast, not as spellbinders, but as repentant humbugs. Speeches made through the microphone to millions of listeners will take on a necessary sincerity hitherto unknown. If the speakers are insincere or pretentious for a moment, they will be found out and despised. And it is not very pleasant to be found out. I will go so far as to say that, when all parliamentary orators have to use the microphone, most of the governments in power at present will vanish into private life with badly damaged reputations.

I do not think this side of the microphone has ever been pointed out before. It is curious: it puts you into the confessional box. It makes you a perfectly different man. When I go away from the microphone and begin to speak to my friends, I tell them all sorts of things that I do not believe, because I think it will please them. But at the microphone, I know that those of you who have good ears will catch me out every time that I attempt to gammon you. Moral: never listen to great statesmen or great churchmen except through your wireless set.

ADAPTED READING 14.3

VOICEPRINT IDENTIFICATION GOES TO WORK

Thomas F. Coon

On April 11th of this year, a dramatic new identification device was introduced at a criminal trial in White Plains, Westchester County, New York. Dr. Lawrence G. Kersta, the father of voiceprints, was permitted to testify in a criminal case in which the defendant, a New Rochelle policeman, was charged with warning a gambler by telephone that his operation was about to be raided. Police had a legal wiretap on the phone and recorded the voices of the participants in the conversation. Wiretapping by law enforcement agencies in New York state through the medium of a court order is permissible.

With the need for identifying the voice of the person issuing the warning, Dr. Kersta was afforded his first opportunity to use his voiceprint system in a criminal trial. Judge Robert E. Dempsey permitted the testimony of Dr. Kersta,

From *Police* magazine, vol. 11, no. 1 (September–October 1966), pp. 67–69. Reprinted by permission of the author, Thomas F. Coon, and Charles C Thomas, Publishers, Springfield, Ill.

despite the vigorous opposition by the attorney for the defense. . . . Though Dr. Kersta had been previously called upon to help the police in several cities in connection with voice identification, this is the first time voiceprints were used as trial evidence. . . .

The doctor has also been consulted by the United States Air Force, the Civil Aeronautics Board, the Federal Aviation Agency, and other Federal agencies which perform in the "classified area." He has done work in the field of bomb threats on airplanes. He was also the instrument through which a suspect was absolved in connection with a series of death threats to a Connecticut state official in 1963. A suspect was picked up and the wife of the state official was sure he was the man who was doing the calling. The suspect indignantly denied it. The police asked for Dr. Kersta's aid and he compared the voice of the suspect against the voice of the person who had made the telephone calls. The caller's voice had been taped and recorded. Dr. Kersta stated the suspect was definitely not the guilty party. A couple of weeks later, the police questioned five other suspects and one confessed.

Voiceprints will undoubtedly also contribute immeasurably to the field of medicine. Doctors can match sounds made by ailing patients with previously recorded sounds which have been established as sounds made by a person with such ailments as heart or respiratory disease. Here, the doctor will have an excellent refinement in the use of the stethoscope, for sounds inaudible to the doctor will be picked up and recorded in a voiceprint. . . .

There are unlimited future uses for the doctor's technique. He has commented, "you could make a lock that would open only to the sound of your voice or the police could keep voiceprint files of people convicted of making obscene telephone calls." This latter "plague" has defied the best efforts of the police and telephone companies to date. It is an area where a tool of identification is much needed and desired.

Voiceprints represent a revolutionary step forward in the field of criminal identification. Lawyers and practitioners in the area of law enforcement look forward to the day when voiceprint identification will be as positive a means of identification as are fingerprints. . . .

From the doctor's research came the voiceprint — a pictorial representation of sound patterns. Dr. Kersta has described it as a method for transcribing a person's voice from a recording through an electronic machine called a spectrograph onto paper to get his sound pattern. The pattern looks very much like a child's drawing of irregular vertical lines and horizontal bands of varying widths. The pattern taken from a recording by the known individual is compared against the pattern of an unknown individual — such as a suspect in a bomb threat or obscene telephone call. A skilled man in the field, such as Dr. Kersta, can make a determination as to whether the two persons, as reflected in the patterns, are identical.

In laboratory tests conducted with high school girls, their matching results were 99.75 percent successful. In a broad area of testing encompassing 50,000 voiceprint identifications, assistants of Dr. Kersta achieved 97 percent accuracy. Of the identifications he had made himself, Dr. Kersta stated, "to my knowledge, I have not made any mistakes."

Voice pattern uniqueness is predicated upon the improbability that two speakers will have vocal cavities, dimensions, and articulator use patterns identical enough to confound voiceprint identification methods. The accuracy of voiceprint identification is based on the combination of the physical characteristics unique to each individual's voice cavities (the throat, mouth, nose, and sinuses) and the manner of manipulating the articulators (the lips, teeth, tongue, soft palate, and jaw muscles). In this regard, Dr. Kersta has said, "each man's voice is unique because learning to speak is a randomly learned process, in which an infant first tries thousands of combinations of his vocal equipment, finally coming up with one that is his alone. . . ." Of particular interest to the law enforcement agency which contemplates utilizing Dr. Kersta's method, is that it is not confounded by attempts to disguise the voice, nor does drunkenness have an effect upon it. Skilled mimics could not confuse the accuracy of voiceprint identification. The epitome of the extreme — a person talking with marbles in his mouth, was correctly probed by the system.

In that courtroom in White Plains, New York, on April 11, 1966, Dr. Kersta had the lights dimmed as he stepped forward to project pictures of six voiceprints on a screen, one of which was taken from a recording by the suspect and another of which was taken from the tapped phone to the gambling operation. Dr. Kersta gave his testimony. However, the jury disagreed on a verdict but he will be back to testify at the next trial. He will indeed be around testifying in many cases in the future, for men in law enforcement feel confident his system will become an integral part of standard procedure in future law enforcement identification.

ADAPTED READING 14.4

JOHN F. KENNEDY'S DELIVERY SKILLS DURING THE 1960 CAMPAIGN

James G. Powell

In retrospect, the urbanity of President Kennedy seemed as much a part of his total platform performance as the epigrammatic phrase and the flash of wit. Although he succeeded in achieving that urbanity as a public speaker, his success was not achieved without struggle, for John F. Kennedy began his 1960 campaign with a taut and tense voice, rapid and rushed delivery, and uncertain of the proper manner and posture of a man seeking the presidency.

In the early weeks of the campaign Kennedy had not learned to project his voice properly, and an ominous hoarseness crept into his voice from the sustained speaking that Marquis Childs believed would have put a strain on the vocal cords and lungs of a carnival barker. Even though Kennedy had been taking lessons in diaphragmatic breathing from a voice coach prior to Labor Day, continued shallow breathing abused his throat early in the cam-

From *Western Speech*, 32 (Winter 1968), pp. 59–68.

paign. Between speeches he would frequently rest his voice and communicate by writing notes. The misuse of the larynx (straining his throat muscles to try to control his projection through the use of the muscles of his neck) during the Senator's acceptance speech at the Democratic Convention was bothersome to many who listened.

Despite his high pitch, rapid rate, and poor rhythm, Kennedy was capable of a rich, resonant voice; yet with his habitual pitch higher than his optimum pitch, more often than not he was flat, nasal, and harsh. Further, he had a lateral lisp similar to that of Roosevelt; for example, "s" and "z" sounds came out "sh" and "zh." Words such as "percent," "question," "cause," and "us" became "pesshent," "queshion," "cawzh," and "ush." Additionally, Kennedy dropped the endings of many of his words or substituted other endings. Words such as "vigor," "more," "world," "just," "aware," and "Cuba" were pronounced as "viga," "moah," "wirl," "jes," "awaya," and "Cubar." A flat nasal "last" and "Castro" became "lasht" and Cahshtro."

Although Kennedy's voice and pronunciation drew negative comments from some analysts, his rate of speaking met with mixed reactions. With his head tilted back, the Senator rattled off lines at a ferocious pace; the *New York Times* noted that he had been clocked at 240 words per minute, approximately 100 words a minute faster than normal speaking rates. The result was a high, passionate ring which became hypnotically sing-song as he sped along. His timing, too, was deplorable in the early stages of his campaign; he did not try for applause and scarcely acknowledged it. On the other hand, Professor Hitchcock of the State University of Iowa was not at all concerned about Kennedy's pace. If anything, the rate of speed was in the Senator's favor. Hitchcock reported that he never daydreamed during a Kennedy speech, for the Senator kept "popping" ideas at him with energy and enthusiasm.

Kennedy's real delivery problem during much of the campaign (above and beyond the early voice factor) was not speed, but a lack of pause and emphasis. This failure to pause immediately, to give his audience an opportunity to react, smothered his own audience response. The belated pause, then, was ineffective, as if it were a sudden recognition on his part that he had scored a point. A second failing was Kennedy's inability (or refusal) to highlight his important points with emphasis.

But as the campaign progressed there were to be some notable improvements in delivery; he was to become less strident and was to control his speaking rate. Under the tutelage of voice coaches, he mastered the art of projecting his voice and eliminated some of its shrill, grating qualities.

If Kennedy's use of his voice was ineffectual, his appearance on the speaking platform was largely in his favor. He exhibited an infectious energy: he acted and talked vigorously; so much so that during the televised speeches of October 31 and November 4, 1960, Kennedy's characteristic jabbing of the lectern with his index finger came over the microphone as a heavy "thump-thump." But on other occasions he was less confident, especially when he was waiting his turn to speak on the stump. He often fidgeted with his coat buttons, smoothed his hair or swung his right foot restlessly. A gesture of extreme agitation was a desperate fingering of his necktie. There were moments, too, when Kennedy nervously shifted his weight—clearly noticeable in the televised Philadelphia speech of October 31, 1960.

Two gestures became characteristic of the Senator's style: the frequent "chop" was a short downward right jab with finger extended; whereas the rarer "swoop" resulted in bringing the right hand from behind, arcing it over in a flat trajectory, and pointing his finger at the platform in front of him. The chop was used for underlining points; the swoop was reserved for major emphasis.

It is clear that Kennedy's gestures, platform vigor, and thrust-out jaw projected a confidence that served to complement his theme of urgency— "Let's get this country moving!"

ADAPTED READING 14.5

LAMENT FOR THE LISTENER
Eric Sevareid

President Truman often complains about the burdens of his office, and what is good enough for a President should be good enough for a broadcaster. So— take the matter of pronunciation. We got on to Stromboli fairly quickly, but sometimes, as in the case of Hiroshima, listeners won't let you do right by the dictionary, and accuse you of being too high-toned for your britches.

But a broadcaster's real misery concerns the listener's home town. For example, it's plainly Versailles in France, but just as plainly Versayles in Kentucky. That Illinois town is Willamette but that Oregon river is Willam'ette.

Prague rhymes with frog in Europe, but it rhymes with plague in Oklahoma. Vienna is good enough for Europeans, but Vyenna suits Georgia. Madrid is in Spain, but Mad'rid is in Iowa; Peru is in South America, but Peeroo is in Illinois. How the French town of Calais' got to be the town of Ca'lace in Maine, we'll never understand, nor why Rheims, in France, rhymes with Screams in New York. Every third Frenchman is named Pi-erre, but the one and only capital of South Dakota is named Peer. There are more than a dozen Berlins in America, but most of them are called Ber'lin. Newark couldn't be anything else, in New Jersey, but it can be in Delaware, where it's New-Ark. Around New Smyrna, Florida, they are insulted unless you call it New Summerna. Montevide'o is in Uruguay, but Montevid'eo is in Minnesota; Bogo'ta is in New Jersey, but they call it Bogota' in Colombia. And the "g" in Elgin is soft in Illinois and hard in Texas.

You see what we go through in this business, ably guided as we are by Columbia's speech expert, Mr. Greet, whose first name is Cable or , perhaps, Cabell. It's still a hazardous way to make a living.

This is Eric Sevareid—or Sevareed—in Washington.

From *In One Ear* (New York: Knopf, 1952), pp. 257–258. Copyright 1952 by Eric Sevareid. Reprinted by permission of The Harold Matson Company, Inc.

YOU KNOWING
Dick West

She went, you know, to the bank yesterday and filled out, you know, a counter check and gave it, you know, to the cashier, who told her she was, you know, five dollars overdrawn.

I wish I could say the above sentence is, you know, an exaggeration, but it isn't. It is absolutely the way most people you know talk nowadays.

Verbal communications, which were, you know, never too good at best, have been beset by a horrendous outbreak of, you know, "you knowing."

In the average conversation, "you know" is arbitrarily interjected after every fifth word.

No, I don't know. And it is tedious to be constantly told that I do.

"You knowing" is by no means limited to persons who are, you know, inarticulate. You hear a steady stream of it on television talk shows from performers and other professional types who supposedly are facile with words.

I don't want to sound, you know, condescending about this, because I occasionally lapse into the same wearisome pattern.

But at least I am conscious of the defect and am, you know, desirous of overcoming it. Most chronic "you knowers" don't seem aware of their impediment.

What causes this? Why have Americans, almost overnight, begun inserting this, you know, extraneous element into their vocalization?

The best explanation I have is that "you knowing" is a form of "mental stuttering." Instead of tripping over one's tongue, one trips over one's brain.

People have always had a tendency to speak faster than they think. It is only recently, however, that the human tongue has become consistently quicker than the mind.

"You knowing" appears to have replaced hemming and hawing as the fetter that retards the tongue long enough for the brain to catch up.

As to whether "you know" is an improvement over "er" or "ah" is a matter of individual preference. Psychologically, however, "you knowing" is better attuned to the times in which we live.

People are bewildered by the modern age and need frequent reassurance. The introduction of "you know" in their speech reflects their hope that somebody somewhere knows what is going on.

Once we feel secure again, we will revert to the old-fashioned sputter, splutter, stammer and pregnant pause.

From the Baton Rouge *State-Times*, March 15, 1972. Reprinted by permission of United Press International.

ADDITIONAL READINGS

Canfield, William H., "A Phonetic Approach to Voice and Speech Improvement," *Speech Teacher*, 13 (January 1964), 42–46.

Dickens, Milton, *Speech: Dynamic Communication* (New York: Harcourt Brace Jovanovich, 1963), chap. 10, "Vocal Communication."

Gray, Giles and C. M. Wise, *The Bases of Speech* (New York: Harper & Row, 1959), chap. 3, "The Physiological Bases of Speech."

Hanley, Theodore and Wayne Thurman, *Developing Vocal Skills* (New York: Holt, Rinehart & Winston, 1970).

Rahskopf, Horace G., *Basic Speech Improvement* (New York: Harper & Row, 1965), chap. 14, "Audible Communication: Voice Production"; chap. 15, "Audible Communication: Vocal Expression"; and chap. 16, "Audible Communication: Articulation and Pronunciation."

Rizzo, Raymond, *The Voice as an Instrument* (New York: Odyssey, 1969).

STUDY QUESTIONS

1. What is meant by the audible or vocal elements of delivery?
2. What are some possible causes of persistent volume problems?
3. What is pitch? What is a speaker's optimum pitch level?
4. What is an inflection? What are pitch patterns?
5. How does a speaker's voice quality differ from his pitch? How may they be related?
6. What is the difference between an articulation error and a pronunciation error?
7. What standard of pronunciation should a speaker adopt for most words?
8. What should guide the speaker in his pronunciation of the names of persons and places?

EXERCISES

1. Prepare a three- to four-minute oral report in which you evaluate the vocal attributes of some speaker you have heard in person in the last two weeks. Possible subjects might be a classroom lecturer, a clergyman, a guest speaker, a political candidate, or a student speaker (other than a member of your speech class). Evaluate the speaker's voice quality, pitch, rate, loudness, articulation, and pronunciation, pointing out both good and bad qualities. You need not identify the speaker by name. Present your report in class.
2. Listen to several radio or television commercials delivered by announcers of your sex. Try to ignore what the announcer is saying and concentrate on his pitch usage. Attempt to imitate the speaker's use of pitch. Then compare his range and variation with your own voice.
3. Select a short passage from a speech, editorial, article, or column in which the speaker or author is attempting to persuade. Read the passage aloud first as if you believed deeply in what you are saying; second, as if you were bored by the passage; and, third, in a manner suggesting that you are skeptical of what you are reading.
4. From a speech you have already delivered or from one on which you are working, select a short passage of eight or ten sentences. Speak these extemporaneously and record your speaking. Play back the recording and listen carefully to your pitch variation, rate, and emphasis. Then:
   a. Speak and record the passage again, attempting to achieve greater variety of pitch. Don't worry about using exactly the same words. Then play back and compare the two versions. Repeat this several times and attempt to achieve a different pitch usage in each recording. Finally, play back each version and try to decide which sounds best.
   b. Perform the same exercise listed above only vary the rate of speaking for different sentences and phrases. Experiment with pauses, with speaking faster at times, and with slowing down at other times. Again, replay the several versions and select the best.

c. Perform the same exercise a third time, now varying emphasis and volume. Again seek to determine which version you think sounds best.

5. To train yourself to be more acutely aware of articulation and pronunciation, during the next week jot down every articulation or pronunciation error (or doubtful usage) that you hear in classroom lectures, student speeches, class discussions, and conversations. At the end of the week, check to see how many—if any—of these mistakes you are likely to make.

6. Determine your optimum pitch. Then record your voice, speaking impromptu for about one minute on some subject with which you are familiar. As you play the recording, hum your optimum pitch tone and attempt to determine whether you normally speak at this level.

CHAPTER 15

THE NATURE OF LANGUAGE

"Communication by means of language is man's distinctive activity," states Stuart Chase. Language is the most important element in any culture, not only for day-to-day communication, but for preserving the community from generation to generation, he continues; for, although individuals die, the culture that flows through them and that they help to create is all but immortal. Without words the flow would cease and the culture wither away.

Without language, speech could not exist. Although man might still communicate through the use of signs and gestures, lacking a system of words recognizable to others he would be incapable of speech. It is therefore obvious that effective use of language is not only important, but essential to good oral communication.

WORDS AS SYMBOLS

Because speech requires language, speakers should understand words. Words are symbols. Language is a system of symbols designed or intended to convey meaning or ideas. When used by persons who know what the symbols stand for, communication occurs.

The symbols employed in the act of communicating are both audible and visible. The most common audible symbols are the sounds of human speech which, when put together in a certain manner, convey messages to hearers acquainted with the language being spoken. The most common visible symbols of communication are written or printed words, which consist of marks of various kinds and shapes (letters) that are arranged to convey a message to someone familiar with the language.

Man has many forms of symbolic communication. One is gesture. By the way he signals, the hitchhiker clearly asks passing motorists, "Will you give me a lift?" The referee at a football game, the patrolman directing traffic, the conductor of a symphony, and the automobile driver signaling a turn, all relay specific information through a system of visible gestures. Other physical movements that convey meaning are the raised arms of surrender, the stiff-armed salute of the Nazis, the clenched fist of black power, removal of the hat as a sign of respect, turning one's thumbs down, the sign of the cross, and Churchill's two-fingered "V" for victory.

Abstract marks are another means of symbolic communication. Many of these identify groups, as do the Christian cross, the swastika, the hammer and sickle, the Star of David, the Republican elephant, the Democratic donkey, the interlocked rings of the Olympic Games, the striped barber pole, the maple leaf of Canada, the lone star of Texas, and the *fleur de lis* of the House of Bourbon. Some convey messages, such as the arrow indicating a turn in the highway or the skull and crossbones warning of poison.

> Perhaps of all the creations of man language is the most astonishing.
> LYTTON STRACHEY

Even colors may be used as symbols to communicate messages. The red, green, and amber of traffic signals, the yellow line down the middle of a highway, the black armband of mourning, the red flag of communism, the black flag of anarchy, and a school's colors are examples.

One more type of symbolic communication would include the torch of liberty, the scales of justice, the dove of peace, Uncle Sam, John Bull, and France's Marianne.

Recognizing that words are but another set of symbols for conveying ideas is essential to understanding language. As symbols, words have no connection or relationship to anything—except in the mind. Words are not things, but they make people think of things. James McCrimmon explains:

> The letters b-o-o-k make you think of this thing you are reading or of a similar thing. But any other combination of letters could perform the same function, provided people had agreed on that combination. Because of this general agreement, the same object is known by different names in different languages. Thus, what we call a book in English is also referred to as *Buch* (German), *bock* (Dutch), *bok* (Swedish), *bog* (Danish), *livre* (French), *libro* (Spanish), and so on. No one of these names is the "real" name for book. No one is better than the others. In so far as they point to the thing which we choose to call a book, they are all satisfactory names.

McCrimmon might have gone on to point out that we could even devise an entirely new set of letters or sounds — *pxkwobby* or *zuzu* — to refer to a book and, so long as they were understood by others to designate what we commonly call a book, they would be entirely satisfactory.

MISCONCEPTIONS ABOUT LANGUAGE

Effective use of language in communication is sometimes impaired because of misconceptions about the nature of words. Six common misunderstandings about language are the misconceptions of (1) singularity, (2) permanency, (3) authority, (4) mystical power, (5) morality, and (6) superiority.

The Singularity Misconception

A widespread misunderstanding about language is the belief that every word has only one meaning. This may be called the misconception of singularity because it implies that a single, correct definition exists for every word. In fact, however, many words have more than one meaning. For example, the 2,000 words most frequently used in oral discourse by educated people have 14,000 dictionary definitions. Besides all the words with more than one dictionary meaning, many others with only one definition in the dictionary are capable of expressing different ideas and shades of meaning depending upon how they are used.

> "When I use a word," Humpty Dumpty said, in a rather scornful tone, "it means just what I choose it to mean — neither more nor less."
> "The question is," said Alice, "whether you can make words mean so many different things."
> "The question is," said Humpty Dumpty, "which is to be master — that's all."
>
> LEWIS CARROLL
> *Through the Looking Glass*

The statement, "All men are created equal," illustrates how words may possess more than one meaning. In this sentence, the word *equal* may be used to mean that all men are born with identical traits, characteristics, and capacities; or, more likely, *equal* may mean that no man is inherently superior or inferior to another by reason of his race, religion, class, or nationality and that all men, therefore, are entitled to just and equitable treatment. Obviously, failure to understand how the word *equal* is used in this statement could lead to misunderstanding. In the same sentence, the word *men* is also susceptible to more than one interpretation. It could designate all members of the human race or, by another definition, it might refer only to the male species.

Other examples of how the meaning of a sentence is altered depending on the definition of a particular word include the following:

He was a *poor* student. (Academically weak? Financially hard up?)
Mr. Jones was a *religious* worker. (Diligent? Church worker?)
The man was *unemployed* at the time. (Idle? Out of a job?)
Mary bought some new *glasses.* (Spectacles? Tumblers?)
Father has *retired.* (Gone to bed? No longer working?)
She has a new *secretary.* (Desk? Stenographer?)

Sometimes the meaning of a word is clear when written but unclear when spoken. Look at these two examples.

It was a *democratic* meeting. (Democratic? democratic?)
The graduating class sat in *tiers.* (tiers? tears?)

The italicized words in the above illustrations are ambiguous. Each word has at least two different definitions, and if the listener is unaware of which meaning the speaker intends he probably will have difficulty in understanding the sentence.

In addition to the problems caused by ambiguous words, communication can be impaired by vague language. Vague words have no clear-cut meaning and even though the listener thinks he understands how the speaker is using the word, the speaker and the listener may have two very different concepts of what the word means. Some words of this type are *patriotic, un-American, liberal, conservative, socialistic, radical, constitutional rights, freedom, free enterprise, artistic, obscene.* For example, two people may both use the word *obscene* to mean pornography without being able to agree on whether a particular book, film, or painting is obscene. Another example is found in the way people react to protest demonstrations. Some citizens regard such protests as *un-American* or *disloyal,* while others define them as being in the best interests of the country. Both parties may use the word *un-American,* but clearly disagree as to what constitutes an *un-American* action.

Liberal and *conservative* are words with no clear-cut meaning. Tom Smith may be damned as a flaming liberal by the local Ultra-Conservative League and castigated as a die-hard conservative by the Ultra-Liberal Association. Or James Jones may be liberal in his politics, conservative in his spending, radical in his dress, and reactionary in his views on education.

Advertisements frequently contain words which, if one stops to think about them, actually have no clear-cut, specific meaning. For example, what is meant by the word *quality* in the claim that, "All aspirins are not alike. . . . For *quality,* Bayer is superior." Or what is meant by "*living* color" (the opposite of *dead* color?), "the *ketchupy* ketchup," "*un-cola,*" or "Sparko cleans your oven 33% *better*" (better than what?).

The meaning of a word may also differ from group to group and from area to area. For example, in the United States some people call the midday meal *lunch* or *luncheon* and the evening meal *dinner,* while others refer to the noon meal as *dinner* and the evening meal as *supper.* Thus, when invited to dinner, one should make certain which meal is intended.

Southern Americans often use the word *evening* to refer to any time after noon, while in the rest of the country it generally means after 6 P.M. Also in the South, *camp* may be used to describe what others would call a *cabin* or *lodge*.

One must be careful about differing meanings of words from one country to another. For example, a comparison of *unemployment* statistics in the United States and Britain, even if based on reputable government records, could be highly misleading because of the different ways the two governments define *unemployment*. To be regarded as unemployed in Britain, one must fit a set of criteria quite different from those which the United States government uses in determining whether a person is to be classified officially as *unemployed*.

Other British terms that could be confusing to an American include the following:

British Word	American Equivalent
public schools	private schools
rates	taxes
ground floor	first floor
first floor	second floor
lift	elevator
the underground	the subway
lorry	truck
assistant	sales clerk
flyover	overpass
chemist	pharmacist
chips	French fries
potato crisps	potato chips

Differences in customs, institutions, laws, and social mores between nations can cause words to have different meanings in different societies. Thus a *high school diploma* or a *college degree* may not reflect the same educational attainment in two different countries; *petit larceny* in one country might be classified as *grand larceny* in another; and an act considered criminal by one nation might be perfectly legal in another.

Some words in one language have no equivalent or counterpart in another. For example, Greek has no word for *blue*. English words for color distinguish color spectrally by the hue. The Greek words have to do almost entirely with depth and brightness, with the result that no single Greek word means *blue*, although it is possible to find a word that sometimes refers to the color we call *blue*. Because many words mean different things in other cultures, one must take care to understand exactly how a word is being used and what it means to the user.

Even within a culture, persons from different groups often find it difficult to communicate because of their experiential backgrounds. A civilian in unbombed America can never understand war in the same way that it is known to a returned serviceman who has seen combat duty. In a like manner, employer and employee, male and female, black and white, farmer and banker, all may be at at a loss to understand how the other is using words. Anthropologist Margaret Mead believes that the "generation gap" between youths and adults results from the fact that the young will never experience what their parents have experienced and that adults can never experience what the younger generation has experienced. She observes:

> In most discussions of the generation gap, the alienation of the young is emphasized, while the alienation of their elders may be wholly overlooked. What the commentators forget is that true communication is a dialogue and that both parties to the dialogue lack a vocabulary. . . . Once the fact of a deep, new, unprecedented worldwide generation gap is firmly established, in the minds of both the young and the old, communication can be established again. But as long as any adult thinks that he, like his parents and teachers of old, can become introspective, invoke his own youth to understand the youth before him, then he is lost. But this is what most elders are still doing.

It should be apparent that to regard words as having a single, correct meaning is a misconception. Words may have more than one meaning, no clear-cut meaning, or somewhat different meanings depending upon who is using the word and how it is being used.

The Permanency Misconception

Related to the misconception that words have only one meaning is the belief that, once defined, the meaning of a word remains unalterably the same. The idea that words do not change in their meanings is the misconception of permanency.

Contrary to the objections of purists, language is constantly changing: Some words drop out of use; other words acquire different meanings or are used in new ways; and new words are regularly introduced into our vocabularies.

Etymology, the study of the origins and derivations of words, reveals how greatly language has changed over the years. The word *surgeon*, for example, once meant anyone who worked with his hands and was properly applied to craftsmen and laborers. Today, however, it is used to denote a medical practitioner who performs operations. *Doctor* at one time referred to any learned or scholarly person. But today, even though persons holding doctoral degrees in academic fields are properly addressed as *doctor*, when one hears a statement such as "I have an appointment with my doctor tomorrow," one almost invariably concludes that the person is going to see a doctor of medicine.

Through wide usage, many words acquire meanings other than their original ones. When the United States was founded, it was regarded as a *republic*, not a *democracy*. In fact, the founding fathers probably would have objected to having the government described as a *democracy*. However, repeated use of the terms *democracy* and *democratic* in reference to the kind of government in this country has led to the acceptability of these words as accurate descriptions of the American system of government. In a similar manner, the word *flammable* has come to mean *inflammable* and *gas* to mean *gasoline*.

Other words drop out of the language because they are seldom used. *Canst, hast, shant, 'tis,* and *whilst,* for example, fall strangely upon our ears because we rarely hear them. Still other words fall into disuse because they are seldom needed any longer: *talkies, rumble seat, roadster, running board, ice box, antimacassar, washboard.* Some words are heard less often because they have been replaced by others. *Spectacles* today are generally called *glasses;* the *parlor* has become the *living room; dungarees* are called *jeans; saloons* have been replaced by *bars, taverns,* and *cocktail lounges;* the *verandah* has become the *porch; courting* has become *dating* or *going steady;* and *hillbilly* music has become *country, western,* or *folk music.*

Words are also constantly being replaced by others because they have fallen into disrepute. For example, some people feel that there is an odium attached to the term *insane asylum* and prefer to call such institutions *mental hospitals. Old people* or the *aged* similarly are called instead *elderly* or *senior citizens. Retarded* or *mentally retarded* are the words substituted for *feeble-minded; janitors* are *custodians;* and *garbage collectors* become *sanitation workers.* (For a more detailed discussion of this aspect of language, see Adapted Reading 15.3.)

To replace words that are dying out or no longer used, language is constantly being replenished and enlarged by the introduction of new words. Many of these new words are needed to describe new discoveries, processes, or conditions. In the following list, most of the words were nonexistent or, at best, little known no more than 25 years ago: *stereophonic, genocide, smog, astronaut, television, homogenized, psychotherapy, technicolor, fallout, antibiotic, supermarket, discotheque, rock-and-roll, hippie, disc jockey, cold war, beatnik, penicillin, dacron, miniskirt, scuba diving, pop art, jet set, transistor, black power, WASPs, urban renewal, brain-washing, cook-out, McCarthyism, sit-in, high rise.* The above list could be extended by the inclusion of the myriad of slang words and jargon terms that come and go. For a discussion of this see Adapted Reading 15.2.

The speed at which language changes is illustrated by the glossary of new words and expressions prepared by the United States Air Force for returning prisoners of war following the cease-fire in Vietnam. The brochure listed 85 new words or phrases which had come into popular usage in only about 10 years time, including *acid, Afro hair style, blow your cool, bread* (money), *cop out, dude, ego trip, happening, Ms, rap, rip off, split, up tight, vibes,* and *zap.*

Clearly, language is constantly changing as words fall into disuse, as they acquire different meanings, and as new words and phrases are added. To insist that a word has only one meaning—its original definition—is unrealistic. Indeed, if language is to serve man efficiently in his communications efforts, it must constantly evolve to meet the changing circumstances of the times.

The Authoritative Misconception

Do you prefer the *super-giant* box to the *large* size, the *new, improved* product to its *regular* predecessor, and the *bargain economy* item to its standard-priced counterpart? Would you rather live in *Leafy Glen Estates* than in *Briar Patch Hollow,* or on *Magnolia Plantation* rather than on the *Jones farm?* Would you rather have a *gown* from a *haute couture house* than a *frock* from *Molly's Dress Shop?* Does *continental cuisine* seem more inviting than *eats?* Does *Windsor Preparatory Academy* sound like a better school than *Public High School Number 34?* Are you interested in *antiques,* but not *used furniture?* Do you find *Aunt Beulah's pipin' hot fluffy wheat cakes with rich creamy dairy-fresh butter and honest-to-goodness homemade Vermont maple syrup* more appetizing than *flapjacks with butter and syrup?* Are you tempted by *discount* and *wholesale* sales in contrast to *retail* prices? If so, you may be suffering from the delusion that words guarantee quality, value, or worth.

Unaware that words are simply arbitrary symbols, some people tend to accept them at face value. If a package is labeled *super-giant* sized, they faithfully assume that it is bigger than other packages even though, in fact, there may be no difference between the two. If a product is described as *new* or *improved,* they unthinkingly believe that it must be better. The labels *discount* and *wholesale* are no guarantee of lower prices, but some persons assume that they are. *First class* accommodations may not differ in any way from those described as *tourist class* — in fact, exactly the same seat may be designated *first class* on some flights and *tourist* on other flights.

Nevertheless, many people believe that because a word says something is so, it must be so. One shrewd college football coach exploited this tendency by renaming his first, second, and third platoons the *Go team, White team,* and the *Chinese Bandits.* The strategem was highly successful, particularly with the third team. No longer regarded as bench-warmers and inspired by the fearless, marauding implications of their name, the Chinese Bandits became a highly effective platoon and the darlings of the fans. (How much this tactic contributed to the squad's success is debatable; however, it might be noted that the team was undefeated that season.)

Another illustration of this phenomenon is found in the ranking of various college sports teams by panels of "experts" for the Associated Press and United Press International. Great prestige is attached by most fans to the title of *national champion,* which these groups award to the top-ranking team at the end of the season. Coaches of the second and third place teams complain loudly and local sports writers berate the panels for their failure to recognize that Popcorn College was really better than Notre Dame. One politician, irate that his state university's football team was ranked only second in the final polls, went so far as to introduce in the state legislature a bill to declare the local team *national champion.*

What coaches, scribes, and fans alike forget is that the title *national champion* is no guarantee that the chosen team in fact was the best in the country. If, indeed, the *national champions* were better than all others, how could one account for the defeats these squads frequently suffer in post-season bowl games and tournaments? One *national championship* basketball team recently lost a post-season tournament game by 30 points! In other words, as in the examples cited earlier, simply calling a team *national champion* is no guarantee of the calibre of the product.

Another example of the authoritative misconception is provided by a student who gave a speech on graphoanalysis. On his written critique of the speech, the instructor jotted down the question, "Do you really believe it is possible to analyze a person's character and personality through his handwriting?" At the next class meeting, the student informed her teacher that she really did believe in graphoanalysis because the book from which she took her information stated that it was "based on fact."

The same type of thinking is also sometimes found in politics. Aware of the public's susceptibility to high-sounding titles, special interest groups often seek names that inspire confidence. Thus, groups may decide to call themselves the League of Christian Mothers, the Patriotic Sons of Democracy, the Better Government Party, the Society for Good Literature, or the Guardians of Decency (GOD). These must be good groups, as their names imply, for who is opposed to Christian mothers, patriotism, democracy, better government, or decency? But, of course, the name is no assurance that the organization truly represents a worthy cause. In reality, the goals of groups might be highly questionable or even subversive.

The authoritative misconception can easily lead to a type of fallacious reasoning that is known as *begging the question*. Examples of this are: "They must be the best, for they are the national champions"; "He should know, he has a Ph.D. in the field"; "Of course he's impartial, he's the judge, isn't he?" "How can you say it's no good, when it says on the bottle that it has been scientifically tested?" and "It should be a good place to eat; they advertise 'home cooking.'"

In summary, a want-ad appearing in a London newspaper effectively illustrates the dangers of the misconception of authority regarding language. It stated forthrightly: "We buy junk—We sell antiques."

The Mystical Power Misconception

"Open Sesame," says the genie, and the door magically swings open. "Abracadabra," mutters the witch, and the spell takes effect. While these examples are obviously the ingredients of a child's fairy tale, some adults suffer from the delusion that words possess a similar kind of mystical power that can alter their fortunes for good or ill.

This misconception is basically a form of superstition. The individual who makes a statement about his good luck (such as, "Fortunately, I have never had an automobile accident" or "No one in our family has ever had an attack of appendicitis") and then quickly adds, "I'd better knock on wood," illustrates the superstitious nature of this misconception. Obviously, his words can have no effect on his driving habits or his family's health — nor can his knocking on wood — but the speaker irrationally fears that they might and so seeks to "protect" himself with some ritualistic action.

Baseball players and sports announcers have long observed the taboo against mentioning the fact that a pitcher is throwing a no-hit game for fear that the words *no hit* or *no hitter* will spoil the pitcher's success. Thus, it is sometimes possible to listen to a broadcast of a baseball game without ever being told that it is a no-hitter until someone gets a hit or the game ends.

The constant chatter of players rolling dice — "shooting craps" — as they implore the dice to bring them good luck is another example of this misconception.

To ward off bad luck, some people say *bread and butter* or *salt and pepper* if they happen to pass on opposite sides of a tree, pole, or post when walking with someone else.

While these superstitious beliefs about the power of words are probably harmless, they represent another misunderstanding about the nature of language.

The Morality Misconception

Probably the most widely accepted misconception about language is the belief that words possess moral qualities — that there are "good" and "bad" words, "nice" and "dirty" words, and "acceptable" and "objectionable" words. If one keeps in mind the fact that words are nothing more than symbols, it is difficult to justify society's classification of language into these categories; for how can a group of marks, lines, circles, and other figures on a sheet of paper or a series of different sounds be either "good" or "bad"? Is an E-shaped mark good or bad? Is *A* nice or dirty? Is *T* in good or bad taste? If these symbols individually are neither good nor bad, do they acquire desirable or undesirable qualities when used in combination? Is *EAT* good or bad? Are *TEA*, *ATE*, and *ETA* acceptable or improper? When spoken aloud do these symbols, either singly or in combination, become good or bad? Obviously not. They are simply sounds.

Yet most people, ignoring the fact that words are only symbols, do regard some words as inherently bad, unacceptable, or improper, while others are considered good, nice, or acceptable. In fact, however, many words are taboo in polite society, are banned in public broadcasts, and are likely to shock the reader or hearer if used in print or motion pictures. So widespread is the belief that some words are bad that a speaker should avoid their use in most situations, for the consternation and ill will they may cause can only impair his chances of success. In spite of this warning, both speakers and hearers should be aware that words are simply symbols that are inherently neither good nor bad.

Words whose use society frowns upon can be divided into two classes: (1) disreputable language, words that are considered obscene or profane, and (2) derogatory language, words having an unpleasant or degrading connotation.

Disreputable Language. In spite of the great furor and indignation which their occasional use arouses, the number of English words that are regarded as disreputable is small and probably diminishing. Disreputable language consists primarily of words that are considered to be obscene or profane.

Almost without exception, obscene words refer to bodily functions or organs generally regarded as intimate. They are, almost without exception, short, which has led to their being called "four-letter" words. Profanity consists of the use of language considered blasphemous or irreverant.

The concepts of obscenity and profanity are both products of one's culture. What is regarded as vulgar or blasphemous in one culture may be considered harmless in another. Thus, *bloody* is objectionable to the British, but not to Americans. Although most American families would consider it blasphemous to name a son *Jesus*, the Spanish do it constantly. An illustration of how cultures differ in what they regard as obscene is afforded by a New Delhi audience's reaction to a foreign movie. Although showing even a kiss is prohibited in Indian films, virtually no censorship is exercised over foreign films. Viewing one of the more erotic European films in recent years, the Indian audience watched a heap of writhing nakedness with placid indifference. However, later, when the heroine tore up a letter, dropped it in the bathroom stool, and then, changing her mind, plunged her hand into the water to retrieve the pieces, the audience at once exploded with a gasp of horror and dismay.

As a culture changes, so do its concepts of obscenity and blasphemy. Victorian society, for example, regarded any reference to a person's legs as vulgar. People of that era moved about on *limbs,* which were expected to be fully covered. The show of an ankle by a lady was considered indiscreet. In their propriety, Victorians even went so far as to cover the legs of tables and benches with frilly, lace skirts. In those august times, no one became *pregnant,* although of course ladies occasionally found themselves *in a family way.* While these evasions may sound ridiculous now, it should be remembered that, not too long ago, use of the word *sex* was forbidden among respectable people. Unquestionably, some words considered obscene or profane today will become acceptable to future generations.

Of the two types of disreputable language, obscenity is probably objectionable to more people. While the English language probably does not suffer because society is reluctant to tolerate "four-letter" words, the repercussions that greet their use seem disproportionate to the seriousness of the offense. They not only produce widespread controversy, but can lead to the banning of films and books, the arrest of speakers, federal prosecution for violation of the mails, and prolonged law suits. Local and state governments often enact legislation regulating their use; religious groups render judgment on works in which these words appear; committees of citizens attempt to prohibit the circulation of publications containing such words; and libraries must decide how to cope with them. While obscene words constitute only an infinitesimal part of our language, the concern they provoke warrants caution in the speaker's usage of them.

An understanding of obscene language requires that a distinction be made between the *ideas* being represented and the *words* used to represent them. Many subjects are unpleasant or repulsive to contemplate, but could not be considered obscene: for example, murder, blackmail, war, cancer, and drug addiction. Any revulsion experienced when such topics are discussed is the result of the nature of the subject itself, rather than the language used. Even such subjects as sex, veneral disease, and perversion can be discussed in public without offending most people if the speaker's language is discreet. However, if, when discussing these topics, the speaker employs certain words generally regarded as vulgar, many persons will be distressed.

For example, the following statements all convey the same information in different ways: "They spent the night together"; "They slept together"; "She became his mistress"; "She gave herself to him"; "They made love"; "They spent the night in sin"; "They began an affair." These statements contain enough information to enable every reader to understand what is being described. While some may regard the *act* as immoral, probably no one would be offended by the *language*. If one were to become more specific, the following descriptions might be added: "They had intercourse"; "They engaged in sexual intercourse"; or "They had sex." None of the last three statements should offend the reader any more than the earlier ones because they all convey essentially the same information. If the example were to be carried one step further, however, and a common "four-letter" word was used, some readers probably would be upset. Why, it may be asked, since the same idea is conveyed? Clearly, it is the *language*, not the *information*, that produces such a response.

Why are people offended by the use of certain symbols when they find the same information inoffensive when conveyed by other symbols? The answer is that most persons have been so thoroughly conditioned from childhood to regard some words as vulgar or obscene that they automatically react to them with disgust or shock. The danger of this belief that some words are inherently immoral is that it is likely to confuse one's moral judgments and values. Armed with the misconception that certain words are inherently evil, well-intentioned would-be censors and guardians of decency too often focus their attention almost solely on communications employing "four-letter" words and neglect the possibly damaging effects of works glorifying violence, war, hypocrisy, prejudice, and corruption.

The second form of disreputable language, profanity, consists of words and phrases that are offensive on religious rather than moral grounds. Oaths, curses, and epithets that invoke the Deity are usually regarded as blasphemous or sacrilegious, regardless of whether the speaker gives thought to the meaning of the words or simply uses them out of habit. The Judeo-Christian objection to profanity stems from the Biblical injunction, "Thou shall not take the name of the Lord, thy God, in vain." Most oaths and curses regarded as profane unquestionably violate this commandment, and it is understandable that persons of deep religious conviction should find them repugnant. Still others of lesser faith may also consider them objectionable, regarding them as improper.

Regardless of the reason why profanity is considered distasteful, the reader once again should differentiate between the speaker's intent and the symbols used to express his thought. The words *God, Jesus Christ, hell*, and *damn* are not objectionable in most contexts. It is only when they are used to express certain ideas that they are deemed profane. So, clearly, profanity is largely a matter of intent.

What, then, is a reasonable attitude toward circumlocutions used to avoid outright profanity? One circumlocution found in written material is achieved by the omission of letters, for example, *G-d d--n, J---s Ch---t, g- to h--l*. All that has been done here is to substitute different symbols (dashes) for more readily recognizable symbols (letters). However, since the reader clearly comprehends the messages conveyed by the symbols, it is difficult to see how this circumvention is in any way less profane than the same words without the substitution of dashes for letters.

Conversely, some people become distressed when they see *Xmas* in print, regarding this as sacrilegious. Forgetting that letters and words are simply symbols, they regard the substitution of *X* for the letters C-h-r-i-s-t as a vulgarization. In this instance, their indignation is misguided. So long as readers recognize that *Xmas* means the same thing as *Christmas*—and not *Exmass* or *Thanksgiving*—there is nothing objectionable about using a different symbol to convey the same idea. Indeed, in other languages a totally different set of symbols is used to represent *Christmas*.

Somewhat more difficult to analyze are expressions that closely resemble profanity and are obvious derivations from profane language. Several of these milder expletives are *gosh, gosh darn, my gosh, gol darn, darn it, dang it, oh heck, gee, jeez, jeepers, cripes, for cripes sake*, and *the heck with it*. Although these expressions probably originated as circumlocutions to avoid outright profanity, most people probably do not consider them blasphemous and are not disturbed by their use.

Undesirable Language. "What's in a name?" asked Shakespeare. "That which we call a rose, by any other name would smell as sweet." But to some people, a rose by another name would not smell as sweet. Just as certain words are regarded as disreputable, other words are considered derogatory, demeaning, indelicate, or degrading. In discussing this phenomenon, we are not talking about words that are used with the intention of degrading or demeaning, such as *nigger, kike, coward, traitor, bigot, stupid, slob, liar*, and so forth. Instead, we are concerned about words that the ordinary person uses with no thought of being offensive or insulting but which others may regard as derogatory. For example, some people frown on the use of the word *slum*, preferring to call such neighborhoods *depressed areas*. Similarly, some people consider *sanitation worker* more acceptable than *garbage collector*. Additional examples include the following:

Undesirable Term	Preferred Term
ignorant, uneducated	culturally deprived
insane, crazy	mentally disturbed

janitor	custodian, maintenance engineer
leprosy	Hanson's disease
hillbilly music	country, western music
politician	legislator, statesman
funeral parlor	mortuary
insane asylum	mental hospital, rest home
crippled	physically handicapped
false teeth	dentures
wigs, toupees	hair pieces
hairdresser	beautician, cosmetologist
normal school, teachers college	college, university
state college	state university
charity	welfare
Civil War	War Between the States
mentally disturbed children	exceptional children
fat	stout, overweight
sweat	perspiration
old maid, spinster	unmarried, single
constipation	irregularity
Mrs., Miss	Ms

Since both derogatory words and their preferred substitutes are merely symbols, it is a mistake to assume that one set of words is inherently bad or degrading, while the other is good or uplifting. Regardless of whether he is called a *garbage collector* or a *sanitation worker,* he is still the man who picks up the garbage. Furthermore, there is a danger that the substitution of more complimentary terms for commonly used words may tend to disguise the true nature of important problems. For example, slum neighborhoods constitute a serious national problem. Calling these sections *depressed areas* in no way changes conditions in the slums and may actually disguise the seriousness of the problem. Other euphemisms are mentioned in Adapted Readings 15.3 and 15.4.

The Superiority Misconception

Most children in the United States are educated in schools in which they are taught to read and speak in what is known as *standard* language dialect, with standard pronunciations and standard grammatical and syntactical constructions. Many teachers and others have long considered persons who speak something other than the accepted dialect as *substandard* in their language development. For instance, the child who says, "I have 10 cent" ("I have 10 cents"), or "They gone" ("They are gone"), or "They be gone" ("They have gone"), or "Don't nobody care" ("nobody cares") is considered by some to be deficient in language development and, consequently, intellectually inferior. This attitude reflects the superiority misconception.

Researchers concerned with dialect differences do not agree that persons who speak in other than the accepted dialect are necessarily inferior; they argue instead that rather than being *substandard* in speech, they are *nonstandard* or different. *Nonstandard* means that although the child does not use the standard dialect, he may very well have a systematic language pattern that enables him to communicate effectively in his environment (for example, among Negroes, Chicanos, or American Indians). They contend that the youngster who says "I have 10 cent" is as aware of the plural nature of the number "10" as is the child who uses "cents," but that he finds it unnecessary in his language environment to pluralize the object.

These conclusions are the result of studies of *nonstandard* dialects within the broad social spectrum of economically disadvantaged populations and within the narrower scope of American blacks and Mexican Americans. Educational psychologists generally take the position that the child reared in the ghetto or in an economically disadvantaged area is deficient in learning because his speech is *substandard*; they reason from this that he is deprived of verbal stimulation, idea conceptualization, and proper sentence formations. Generally, their position is that, being culturally deficient, such youngsters lack the ability to reason logically and to communicate effectively. On the basis of research findings, however, most linguists take the position that these children are capable both of reasoning logically and communicating satisfactorily, but that they do so within their own language structure or within that of their primary social group. Studies have demonstrated, for instance, that black ghetto children enjoy a *nonstandard* language structure that provides verbalization as rich as that experienced by children reared in standard-dialect-speaking homes.

The assumption that nonstandard speech is in some way *sub*standard may impair the educational development of children who do not speak a standard dialect. The myth can be harmful if the teacher's or adult's expectation becomes a self-fulfilling prophecy. In other words, one who labors under the superiority misconception runs the risk of classifying the child who speaks a *nonstandard* dialect as inferior and then, in turn, convincing the youngster that he *is* inferior by criticizing his language development and thought processes. Once convinced that he is inferior, the child may lose interest in learning and he may become bored or a troublemaker, reinforcing the adult's misconception of the child's intellectual and social inferiority. The superiority misconception is perhaps the most troubling of the six misconceptions discussed here.

TYPES OF LANGUAGE

Language can be classified in several ways. Three categories to be discussed are (1) concrete and abstract language, (2) emotive and neutral words, and (3) informative, directive, and expressive language.

Concrete—Abstract Language

One way of classifying language is according to how specific it is. Words that are very specific are referred to as *concrete*. Tangible objects—persons, places, and things—usually are considered concrete. The following words are quite specific and so would be considered concrete: *aspirin, Time maga-*

A b s t r a c t	Mankind	A man	An American man	A man from Ohio	A man from Akron, Ohio	A policeman from Akron, Ohio	Sgt. John Q. Smith of Akron, Ohio	C o n c r e t e

Figure 8

zine, eighty-nine, *Golden Gate Bridge*, *a lemon*, *Rembrandt's "Night Watch,"* and *my wrist watch.* Less specific terms—intangible or theoretical ideas, conditions, and relationships—are called *abstract.* Some abstract words would be *medicine, communications, many, transportation, food, art,* and *time.*

Actually, it is more accurate to say that some words are more concrete than others than to classify language as being *either* concrete *or* abstract. In other words, there are degrees of concreteness and abstraction. One might illustrate this by placing several words on a continuum ranging from the highly abstract to the very concrete, as shown in Figure 8. At no place on the continuum can one draw a line and say all of the words on one side are abstract and all of the words on the other side are concrete. Instead it is a matter of some words being more or less concrete than others.

Emotive—Neutral Language

Language can also be classified according to how much emotion or feeling it arouses in the listener. Words that stimulate emotional responses are called *emotive* or *connotative;* words that evoke little or no emotional reaction are referred to as *neutral* or *denotative.*

Emotive or connotative language may affect the listener either favorably or unfavorably. It can arouse warm, pleasant feelings such as love, friendship, goodwill, forgiveness, nostalgia, gratification, pride, and generosity. Or it can create unpleasant, irritating emotions such as hatred, fear, selfishness, anger, shame, and insecurity.

A speaker's choice of words for conveying an idea can greatly influence the hearer's emotional response. Note the differences in the following passages, each embodying essentially the same thought:

He delivered a strongly worded attack.
He delivered a vicious tirade.

It was an unpleasant scene.
It was a disgusting spectacle.

He proposed major reforms.
He demanded radical changes.

Jones, president of the antiwar organization . . .
Jones, who claims to be the leader of the so-called "peace" group . . .

Smith, who is regarded as a successful businessman . . .
Smith, known to be a shrewd dealer (or slick operator) . . .

The troops made a strategic withdrawal . . .
The troops were driven back . . .

His resolute, determined opposition to . . .
His pig-headed, stubborn attitude toward . . .

Because human beings differ, not all persons will respond with the same reaction or intensity of feeling to a particular word or phrase. Differences in culture and experience shape each person's emotional responses to words. The individual who has never experienced poverty will not react to the word *hunger* in the same way as someone who has gone to bed on an empty stomach night after night. The word *tyranny* has unpleasant connotations for almost everybody, but for the person who has been imprisoned or tortured in a totalitarian state the word will have a different meaning than it does for the individual who, no matter how humanitarian, has never undergone these experiences. *Charity* is a word that suggests generosity and benevolence to the giver, but to someone who must rely on it for his existence, *charity* surely has a different meaning. Members of minority groups have special reactions to some words. (See Adapted Readings 15.6 and 15.7.)

Recognizing that cultural and experiential factors determine the way the hearer responds to a speaker's message, radical organizer Saul Alinsky urges speakers to gain an understanding of the background, values, and aspirations of his listeners. He says:

> Communication with others takes place when they understand what you're trying to get across to them. If they don't understand, then you are not communicating, regardless of words, pictures, or anything else. People only understand things in terms of their experience, which means that you must get within their experience.

The emotive content of a word depends, of course, on how it is used and what meaning it has in its particular context. To describe a balloon as *yellow* probably produces no emotional response; to call a man *yellow* would undoubtedly evoke some emotion. In the same way, when *plot* is used in reference to a story, it is largely neutral, but a *plot* to overthrow the government would be regarded as sinister. *Foul* balls leave us unmoved, but not *foul* play.

Some words that probably have no emotional overtones for most people might conceivably produce a profound reaction in others. For example, a person who had been permanently paralyzed as a result of a fall from a roof might regard the term *roof* with horror. Most people would not share this feeling. Undoubtedly it was this kind of association that prompted one businessman whose employees had been on strike for some time to protest against naming the university's new student center the Student *Union*.

Informative, Expressive, and Directive Language

A third method for classifying language is according to its use. Depending on the speaker's purpose, language may be described as informative, expressive, or directive.

Informative language seeks to enhance the listener's knowledge or understanding of something. Its sole purpose is to enlighten rather than to influence the auditor's beliefs or actions. Several examples of informative language follow:

> In the beginning of broadcasting, anyone with a transmitter could go on the air.
> I saw Mrs. Hagen at the grocery store this morning.
> Six inches of snow fell in New York City yesterday.
> Enrollment last semester was 11,642.
> The United Givers campaign begins on November 1.

Expressive language consists of statements made by a speaker to indicate his feelings. It seeks neither to inform nor to persuade the listener. Examples of expressive language are:

> Ouch!
> What a beautiful day.
> I'm worn out.
> I wish I were taller.
> This is delicious.

Directive language, unlike informative or expressive language, seeks to influence the auditor's beliefs or behavior. Some directive statements are:

> Will you please close the door!
> Save money by shopping at O'Neil's!
> If you believe in fiscal responsibility, vote against amendment nine!
> Aw c'mon, Jane, please!
> Don't miss the movie at the Paramount!

DIFFERENCES BETWEEN ORAL AND WRITTEN LANGUAGE

Charles James Fox, the great British debater, once said that "if a speech reads well it is not a good speech." While this probably is not entirely true, it does suggest that speech and writing are not the same. Differences between oral communication and written composition require the speaker to give special attention to the language he uses.

> It should be observed that each kind of rhetoric has its own appropriate style.
> That of written prose is not the same as that of spoken oratory.
>
> ARISTOTLE

One of the principal differences between oral and written communication is that in deciphering the written message, the reader usually has many visual aids to help him comprehend the communicator's message. One need only examine a few pages of this book to see that reading is made easier by the use of headings; different sizes and kinds of type; dividing the material into paragraphs; periods, question marks, and exclamation points that divide the paragraphs into sentences; commas, colons, semicolons, parentheses, and dashes within sentences to show relationships, subordination, and qualification. None of these visual clues are available to help the listener understand a speech. He must rely entirely upon the speaker's use of inflections, pauses, emphases, and changes of rate in order to grasp meaning.

Another important difference between the two kinds of communication is that the reader controls the pace at which he receives the message. He can pause, reread, alter his rate, stop to look up unfamiliar terms, and review earlier passages to make sure he understands the writer's ideas. Because the reader can set his own pace, writers can develop their material stylistically in a way that is considerably more complex, involved, and abstract than can the speaker. In a speaking situation the listener has no control over the rate at which the message is presented. He must grasp the speaker's meaning instantly. Because of this, the speaker must utilize language the listener can comprehend immediately.

A third difference between oral and written communication is found in the vocabularies the speaker and writer can safely employ. Most people have a considerably larger reading vocabulary than listening vocabulary; in other words, they recognize in print many words that they would not recognize when spoken. For this reason, good oral style is usually characterized by the use of more familiar words and shorter and simpler sentences than are found in written messages.

Because his audience is directly before him, the speaker also tends to be more direct, making extensive use of the personal pronouns *you, we, our, your,* and *us.* The printed word, however, because it is not aimed at any single, visible audience tends to be somewhat more formal, making less frequent use of the personal pronouns cited above.

The speaker also tends to be more colloquial and conversational than the writer. He will usually use the contractions *won't, don't, can't, couldn't, shouldn't, wouldn't, we'll, I'll,* and others rather than the more formal *will not, do not, cannot, could not, would not, we will,* and *I will.*

A final difference is in the syntax of oral and written communication. The writer, because his work must withstand careful scrutiny and study, usually is more exacting in his sentence structure, grammar, and syntax. The speaker, however, in his enthusiasm often violates the rules of good composition, leaving some sentences unfinished, starting other sentences anew, and inserting parenthetical digressions. Yet, frequently these errors in no way detract from the clarity of his message because of his use of inflection, pause, emphasis, rate, and gestures to supplement his verbal presentation.

SUMMARY

Language is the basis of man's communication with others. Although he also employs visible symbols, the speaker uses primarily audible symbols or spoken sounds. Understanding the nature of language is essential to its effective usage in oral communication. Six common misconceptions about language interfere with effective communication. The singularity misconception, or the belief that words have only one meaning, may lead to misunderstanding between the speaker and listener. The belief that the meanings of words never change can also cause a breakdown in communication. A third misconception is that words carry authority or in some way guarantee the worth or value of something. Some people even regard words as having mystical powers. Another misconception is that words can be inherently good or bad. A final misconception is the belief that the standard dialect speaker communicates more effectively and thinks more logically than the nonstandard speaker. The effective communicator is cognizant of these misconceptions and chooses his language accordingly, defining and clarifying where necessary, avoiding taboos, and making certain at all times that he and his listeners are using words in the same way.

Language may be studied in several ways. Words may be classified according to their degree of specificity or tangibility into concrete and abstract language. They may also be analyzed according to the emotional responses they arouse in listeners. Still a third approach is to analyze language according to its use, whether the words are informative, directive, or expressive.

Although both oral and written communication rely on words to convey their messages, language is used somewhat differently in speaking than in writing. The writer is assisted by many visual clues not available to the speaker in getting his ideas across to his audience. On the other hand, the speaker has the advantage of various vocal techniques to help clarify his meaning. The two methods of communication also differ significantly in vocabularies and syntax they use, and in the degree of control they have over the reception of the message. Because of these differences, the speaker's approach to style will differ from the writer's.

REGIONAL ENGLISH IS
FLOURISHING DESPITE TV

Israel Shenker

American English is the language of plain speaking, much of it plainly inimitable.

But a great deal of this libretto of life goes in one ear and out the other, leaving barest traces of fleeting story. Varying from region to region, percussively many expressions of American English die unrecollected and unmatched, but not unmourned.

There are now many scholars around the nation who ignore the common stock and commonplaces and immortalize the differences. At the University of Wisconsin, Professor Frederic G. Cassidy presides over a vast, comprehensive effort to give printed reality to the dream of a Dictionary of American Regional English (DARE).

"There's always a certain amount of regional expression disappearing," said Professor Cassidy, "and there's also a certain amount of creation, and I'd guess they compensate for each other. Radio and TV are affecting local usage, not ruining it. Just because Walter Cronkite speaks an average, educated English doesn't mean everybody will."

In search of the persisting variations in regional pronunciation and words, Professor Cassidy has sent fieldworkers (including himself) to 1002 communities (in all 50 states) bearing questionnaires with 1397 queries.

The communities were chosen as representative, urban and rural, with informants of various races and occupations. Ideal informants were those who still lived in their birthplace.

"What do you call a piece of land that's often wet, and has grass and weeds growing on it," DARE's fieldworkers asked informants. They garnered bot mucky (North Carolina), swag (Texas), and crawfishy (Alabama).

Nicknames for nearby settlements? Informants suggested such savory appellations as Cheesemaker's Town, Clay Bank, Happy Hill, Hell Ya Ride, Hot Kiss, Muttonburg, Old Lady, Scant City, Short Pint, Slab Town, and Snooze Junction. What was "across the tracks" to some was to others: Bean Row, Flatiron, Goat Hill, Greasy Corner, Happy Hill, Reilly's Quarter, Sweet Gum Bottom, and Tom Crow's Ridge.

A child born to unmarried parents was come-by-chance, orphan out of wedlock, Sunday child, sunshine child, and ketch colt.

Slanting or diagonal slipped in as slawnch-wise, antigodlin, kittycorner, skewgee, skywampus, slantndicular, and slonching.

There were also some fanciful slips. A Wisconsin woman spoke of crude cuts instead of crew cuts; a Tennessee man called a child who had taken his name a name-take; to one Alabamian, a whirlpool was a twirlpool, and in New York City people were forever bunking into each other.

What a difference a border makes! In Texas it gets hotter than the hinges of Hades, but in Arizona, hotter than the hubs.

Professor Cassidy wrote the Governor of every state a letter soliciting funds for the dictionary. He spiced each appeal with examples of the state's regionalisms.

For George C. Wallace of Alabama he listed bush whacking (to haul a boat along a stream by pulling on low branches) and goship (Saturday visit with fellow mountaineers). The Governor of Arizona was told that an Arizona nightingale is a burro, and the Governor of Arkansas that a waiter there is best man at a wedding.

Professor Cassidy informed the Governor of New Hampshire that a gripper is a very cold morning. Governor William T. Cahill of New Jersey learned that a gravy sermon is one that appeals to the emotions, and that a bucket of light is not moonshine but kerosene.

Governor Rockefeller of New York heard that a gin is an enclosure for livestock (Long Island), that clove is a deep gorge (Catskills), that water biscuits are flat pebbles (Canandaigua Lake), and that canawler is a canal boatman—half sailor and half landlubber (Erie Canal).

Colorado's Governor could feel at home with hootenkack—to talk someone into something he doesn't want to do. Connecticut's Governor Thomas J. Meskill heard that mercury is poison ivy, that a wag-on-the-wall clock is a pendulum clock without case, and that toloteet and tikiteet are other words for sofa.

He informed the Governor of Idaho that to sweethearten is to woo, to brush-whip is to rebuke mildly, and to be mouthalmighty is to boast.

Most of the Governors sent sympathetic replies.

A REGIONAL GLOSSARY OF AMERICAN ENGLISH

Here are some samples of the way people speak in different parts of the country as gathered by the compilers of the Dictionary of American Regional English.

Appearing-out clothes   best outfit (Minnesota)
Back-family   parents (Maine)
Bubbler   water fountain (Philadelphia)
Cork high and bottle deep   drunk (Georgia)
Foreparents   ancestors (Kentucky)
Dog-day singer   locust (Connecticut)
Hippins   diapers (South Carolina)
Hippo   malinger, as with hypochondria (Virginia)
Kettle cousin   sponger on relative at mealtime (Georgia)
Mize   act like a miser (Tennessee)
Mother   sediment of vinegar or cider (Pennsylvania)
Old maid   nonpopping popcorn (Wisconsin)
Play the promise box   make easy promises (Georgia)
Queen bee   henpecker (Kentucky)
Sliding pond   children's playground slide (New York City)

Smig mug, map, i.e., face (Arizona)
Sand on line stand in line (New York City)
Yankee cotton snow (Tennessee)

ADAPTED READING 15.2

SLANG WORDS BECOME PART OF OUR LANGUAGE

Pick up any new book or go to a movie and you'll know it instantly. We don't speak the same language our parents did. "Our language is changing fast," says Dr. H. Bosley Woolf, an authority on words. "I won't even predict what's in store for the '70s."

Woolf, who is managing editor of the Merriam-Webster dictionary, says words once considered too informal or colloquial for print are commonplace today. "There was a time when there were really two languages — one for formal writing and another one for speaking," he says. "But this is fast becoming a thing of the past."

In the late 1940s, people thought the word "jaywalk" was too informal, Woolf notes. "Now I can't think of any circumstances in which jaywalk would be inappropriate." Is "movies" a good word? Twenty years ago an editor might have substituted "motion pictures." Dictionaries as late as the 1950s labeled it slang. Even the term "moving picture" was considered colloquial for "motion picture," says Woolf.

And there are many other words that once were thought to be colloquial but which carry no label in today's dictionary because they now are part of the standard English vocabulary. For example, Woolf notes, the word "goof" has no label. There is no label for "shindig" or for the term "to level," meaning to be frank. And some new dictionaries contain many new words which clearly smack of today's generation: words such as hippie, acidhead, put-on, nitty-gritty, and trip.

Woolf points out that the context in which a word is used can be the most important factor, so a good rule of thumb might be: If the word communicates without calling attention to itself, if people use the word, then it works. And the fact that it does its job makes it a good word. "What we're really saying," Woolf explains, "is that informal English is standard English, so why not put it into the dictionary." And that, he says, includes slang.

"It's been a fairly consistent pattern for slang and nonstandard words to become a standard part of the language, although not all these words make the dictionary. Young people, Woolf says, are a prime source of slang. They devise whole sets of words or jargon to use among themselves, partly because outsiders will not fully understand.

Turning to a prime source of concern today — obscenity — Woolf points out that words such as "hell" and "damn" were considered strong 25 years

From the New Orleans *Times-Picayune*, March 8, 1970. Originated by the Associated Press.

ago. There are always people, he says, who want to maintain the status quo, to resist change. When Ibsen wrote "Ghosts" in the nineteenth century he caused a furor by alluding to syphillis, while never mentioning the word.

"In the '20s there was an elitist group that did all the professional writing," Woolf says. "They were all from the upper classes and educated in the Ivy League schools." Today, however, radio, television, newspapers, magazines, company house organs, and many other forms of writing have proliferated, and both writers and editors come from varied backgrounds and have varied educations. This has resulted in greater informality in the language used.

"I think language is a reflection of ideas," says Woolf. "Social mores are easing and informality is increasing all the way down the line. Language is no exception."

What's in store for tomorrow? "It's going to keep changing," Woolf says.

ADAPTED READING 15.3

THIS EUPHEMISTIC AGE
Ralph L. Woods

This fellow said to me, "I believe in calling a spade a spade. For instance, you take this payola. . . ."

Well, I took the payola—the word, that is—and I told him a true-blue spade-caller would not say "payola"; he'd probably designate by the correct term: "bribery" or "graft."

"You can't go around calling people grafters or bribers," protested the self-styled spade-caller.

"If that's what they truly are, you can't honestly call them anything else," I replied, terminating the colloquy. . . .

In the midst of the dangers, alarms and complexities of modern life it is easy to overlook this penchant for euphemisms—pastel words used to gloss over an ugly, unpleasant or unpopular fact, practice or situation, and with the softer term obscure or understate the truth.

These ever-so-polite fictions seem to have grown in popularity as our novelists increasingly employ the language of gutter and dive. Maybe it is a defensive reflex against the four-letter word subversion of conventional literature. But more probably it is a by-product of several other characteristics of our times—such as an unwillingness to face some of the grimmer realities of life and a desire to disguise sinfulness with verbal gentility or adventure, and thus eventually destroy the concept altogether. . . .

For example, people today rarely "commit adultery"; they have "affairs" or they are "intimate"—reassuring terms suggesting a measure of propriety or "spicy" romance. But it's still "adultery" in the Ten Commandments and in the law books. By the way, whatever happened to "companionate marriage," that deceptive neologism for fornication?

"Concubine" long ago was replaced by the clearer "kept woman" — but now we favor the softer and misleading "mistress," a word connoting respectability, position and authority. And since the "mistress" is living with a man not her husband, he is dashingly referred to as her "lover," since "keeper" does not have the same piquancy and touch of sophistication, and "adulterer" has a nasty sound.

Have you ever noticed that our really modern people never commit "sins"? No, merely "indiscretions" or "mistakes," which in turn some look upon as "symptoms." . . . "Prostitute" is a perfectly respectable word as far as usage is concerned, but these women are timidly called "erring sisters" or "fallen" or "wayward women" by the dainty; "ladies of the evening," "fille de joie," "demimondaine" or "courtesans" by the delicate or absurd; "call girls" by the press; "scarlet women" by old-time preachers; "chippies," "harpies," "tarts," "strumpets" and "tramps" by street-corner habitués; and in court the women call themselves "models." The Bible, a spade-calling book, without apology uses "whore" and "harlot." Contrary to polite opinions, these are perfectly decent words; it's the profession itself that is indecent, and euphemisms can't purify it. . . .

"Drunk" has for centuries been given so many euphemisms as to suggest a topic for a scholarly thesis — if there isn't one already. This may be because there are degrees of drunkenness and because many drunks are seldom convinced they are really potted — oops! drunk — as reported. It is also because in some circles it is highly improper to get drunk, and among others you are accounted a weakling if you can't guzzle to capacity without staggering or mumbling. And so today we commonly use "oiled," "plastered," "loaded," "squizzled," "crocked," "tipsy" and "tight." . . . But if you must be really correct always say, with the medical men, "intoxicated" — or "inebriated" is a nice sedate term. One is just as drunk under one term as another.

On the other hand, some currently employed euphemisms are highly commendable because they remove an unjust stigma from people in unfortunate conditions not of their own making. For example, people with physical impairments now are more kindly referred to as "handicapped"; those with mental difficulties are called "emotionally disturbed," and the use of the cruel "stupid" has been replaced by the more understanding "backward" or "retarded."

But then we go too far by calling vicious underage criminals by the sociologists' squishy term "juvenile delinquents," and unmitigated brats are said to be "insecure." Moreover, apparently we are trying to avoid or minimize an obligation to the poor and hungry by referring to them as "underprivileged." . . .

Perhaps most of us have a pet hate among the euphemisms. Mine is "The Man Upstairs," a cheap, music-hall, anthropomorphic term for the awesome word "God," which, by the way, some people mutter today as though it were a bad word.

"Die" is a word people have always desperately sought to avoid, as if thereby they would prevent death's coming to them. "Passed away" and "went to sleep" seem to be the favorite dodges today. "Gone west" was popular among World War I soldiers. One still hears "kicked the bucket" and "cashed in his chips" in robust circles. . . .

But we've topped our ancestors with "interment" instead of "burial" and "mortician" instead of "undertaker" or "embalmer."

However, you can't fool all of the people. I recall the story of a gambler who had died; as his cronies gathered at the bier to bid him farewell, one of them said, "Our friend here is not dead; he is only asleep." Immediately another raised his hand and called out: "I've got a C note that says he never wakes up."

Obviously spade-callers are as unpopular today as they were when Philip of Macedon said: "Those Macedonians are a rude and clownish people, that call a spade a spade." Maybe we have taken too much to heart the proverbial Scottish warning: "He that says what he likes will hear what he does not like."

ADAPTED READING 15.4

DEPARTMENT OF DELICACY

The following is from the report of a New York junior high school committee of teachers appointed by the principal and asked to find ways of saying things more tactfully on students' report cards.

Somewhat Harsh Expressions	Euphemisms
Awkward and clumsy	Appears to have difficulty with motor control and muscular coordination
Does all right if pushed	Accomplishes tasks when interest is frequently stimulated
Too free with fists	Resorts to physical means of winning his point or attracting attention
Could stand more baths; dirty; has bad odor	Needs guidance in development of good habits of hygiene
Lies	Shows difficulty in distinguishing between imaginary and factual material
Cheats	Needs help in learning to adhere to rules and standards of fair play
Steals	Needs help in learning to respect the property rights of others
Insolent	Needs guidance in learning to express himself respectfully

From *The New Yorker*, May 18, 1957, p. 126.

Lazy	Needs ample supervision in order to work well
Rude	Needs to develop a respectful attitude toward others
Dishonest	See either Lies or Steals, depending on what is meant
Selfish	Needs help in learning to enjoy sharing with others
Coarse	Needs assistance in developing social refinement
Noisy	Needs to develop quieter habits of communication
Has disgusting eating habits	Needs help in improving table manners
Is a bully	Has qualities of leadership but needs help in learning to use them democratically
Associates with "gangs"	Seems to feel secure only in group situations; needs to develop a sense of independence
Disliked by other children	Needs help in learning to form lasting friendships
Often late	Needs guidance in developing habits of punctuality
Is truant	Needs to develop sense of responsibility in regard to attendance

ADAPTED READING 15.5

WHAT'S IN A NAME? ASK YOUR COMPUTER

William K. Zinsser

"Why Exxon?" I kept asking myself this summer as I saw the familiar oval ESSO signs being taken down and replaced by rectangular signs that said EXXON. The ESSO trademark has been part of the American landscape for half a century, and part of our vocabulary. I still remember when I made the blinding discovery that it stood for the first two initials of Standard Oil—a moment almost as giddy as when I caught on to the Uneeda Biscuit. But what could EXXON be the first two initials of? The question nagged at me: "Why Exxon?" I could only think of one answer: "Because it's there."

But EXXON wasn't there, I learned, and never had been. On the contrary, the Standard Oil Company (New Jersey) spent over three years and millions of dollars looking for it and found it only last spring. So why didn't they just stick with ESSO and save the money?

The problem goes back to 1911, when a court decision broke the Standard Oil trust and forbade the company to use its ESSO trademark for its affiliates in 20 states, where, instead, it has since used ENCO, ENJAY and HUMBLE. How much better it would now be for the company to find one trademark that it could use all over the country and all over the world.

Linguistic experts were therefore summoned and put to work with a computer. The computer was given 10,000 combinations and told to produce a name that had only four or five letters and "no adverse connotations" in any language. Eventually it disgorged 234 names, which were reduced to six, the favorite being ENCO, which any vice-president could have disgorged after one martini. Alas, "enco" turned out to mean "stalled car" in Japanese, and, as the old Japanese adage goes, "Stalled car gathers no gas."

The search went on. One day the linguistic experts threw their studies of 100 languages into the hopper—a little basket attached to the computer for putting in input—and out came the wonderful news that no word with a double X exists in any language except Maltese. Remember the old Maltese first baseman, Jimmy Foxx?

EXXON thus seemed a sure bet to have no adverse connotations anywhere, except possibly in Malta, and it was duly selected a few months ago. Now all that remains is to spend $100 million changing the signs at the 25,000 gas stations of what will become the Exxon Corporation. In our town, in fact, the ESSO oval has already gone to the land of the Hupmobile, and the EXXON rectangle shares Main Street with GETTY, TEXACO and GULF.

How jealous those companies must be of a name so universally safe. As everybody knows, for instance, "getty" means "dirty carburetor" in Urdu and therefore has an image problem in Pakistan. Still, after analyzing 6,012 variants I don't think the firm is going to find anything better.

At first glance an ideal name might be formed simply by reversing the letters: YTTEG. Like EXXON, there's something a little different about it, and any town that had both an EXXON and an YTTEG station would be kind of special. But as luck would have it, "ytteg" means "outhouse" in Kazak, Uzbek and Azerbaijani ("yt"—"out," "teg"—"chamberpot"), so Getty might as well sit tight.

Actually it is better off than many of its competitors. "Texaco" is a common name for a pet parakeet in Honduras, Costa Rica and parts of Panama —which is ironic, because the "xac" combination doesn't exist in any language except Annamese and Manx—and "gulf," of course, means "hangover" in all the Slavonic languages except Lusatian.

I know these things because I was inspired by Standard Oil to make some computer trials of my own. I felt that the company's method of finding a lovely name like EXXON could be a solution to the always vexatious problem in America of naming our children, our animals and even our houses. (Frankly, I wouldn't mind a change here at "Belly Acres," and I know our neighbors are getting tired of "Dunrovin.")

First I instructed the computer to name our cat. I supplied 49 facts about its size, color, shape and habits and added that we did not foresee traveling with it to countries of the Finno-Ugric group. The computer made a print-out of 316 names that had no adverse connotations except in Magyar, from which it chose three: Irving, Howard and Kimberly-Sue. Then I did the same for our dog. The computer toyed with 2,118 combinations, asked one question ("What is the word for 'dandruff' in Basque?"), and submitted two names: Fair Winds and Harbor View.

But the best was still to come. I programmed the computer to give me a new name for our girl and our boy, and when it did I marveled, as the Standard Oil people must have when they got EXXON, that out of thousands of variables it found two names that were so exactly right: Fido and Spot.

ADAPTED READING 15.6

THE LANGUAGE OF WHITE RACISM

Haig Bosmajian

The attempts to eradicate racism in the United States have been focused notably on the blacks of America, not the whites. What is striking is that while we are inundated with TV programs portraying the plight of black Americans, and with panel discussions focusing on black Americans, we very seldom hear or see any extensive public discussion, literature, or programs directly related to the source of the racism, the white American.

White Americans, through the mass media and individually, must begin to focus their attention not on the condition of the victimized, but on the victimizer.

A step in that direction which most whites can take is to clean up their language to rid it of words and phrases which connote racism to the blacks. Whereas many blacks have demonstrated an increased sensitivity to language and an awareness of the impact of words and phrases upon both black and white listeners, the whites of this nation have demonstrated little sensitivity to the language of racial strife. "Whitey" has been for too long speaking and writing in terminology which, often being offensive to the blacks, creates hostility and suspicions and breaks down communication.

This concern for words and their implications in race relations was voiced by Martin Luther King who pointed out that "even semantics have conspired to make that which is black seem ugly and degrading." Writing in his last book before his death, *Where Do We Go From Here: Chaos or Community?*, King said: "In Roget's Thesaurus there are some 120 synonyms of *blackness* and at least 60 of them are offensive—such words as *blot*, *soot*, *grime*, *devil* and *foul*. There are some 134 synonyms for *whiteness*, and all are favorable, expressed in such words as *purity*, *cleanliness*, *chastity*, and *innocence*. A white lie is better than a black lie. The most degenerate member of the family is the *black sheep*, not the *white sheep*."

From *College English*, 31 (December 1969), 263–272.

In March 1962, *The Negro History Bulletin* published an article by Eldridge Cleaver, then imprisoned in San Quentin, who devoted several pages to a discussion of the black American's acceptance of a white society's standards for beauty and to an analysis of the negative connotations of the term *black* and the positive connotations of the term *white*. Cleaver tells black Americans that "what we must do is stop associating the Caucasian with these exalted connotations of the word *white* when we think or speak of him. At the same time, we must cease associating ourselves with the unsavory connotations of the word *black*."

Simon Podair, writing in a 1956 issue of *Phylon*, examines the connotations of such words as *blackmail, blacklist, black book, black sheep* and *blackball*. The assertion made by Podair that it has been white civilization which has attributed to the word *black* things undesirable and evil warrants brief examination. He is correct when he asserts that "language as a potent force in our society goes beyond being merely a communicative device. Language not only expresses ideas and concepts but it may actually shape them. Often the process is completely unconscious with the individual concerned unaware of the influence of the spoken or written expressions upon his thought processes. Language can thus become an instrument of both propaganda and indoctrination for a given idea." Further, Podair is correct in saying that "so powerful is the role of language in its imprint upon the human mind that even the minority group may begin to accept the very expressions that aid in its stereotyping."

Although King, Cleaver, Podair, and others who are concerned with the negative connotations of *black* in the white society are partially correct in their analysis, they have omitted in their discussions two points which, by their omission, effect an incomplete analysis. First, it is not quite accurate to say, as Podair has asserted, that the concepts of black as hostile, foreboding, wicked, and gloomy "cannot be considered accidental and undoubtedly would not exist in a society wherein whites were a minority. Historically, these concepts have evolved as a result of the need of the dominant group to maintain social and economic relationships on the basis of inequality if its hegemony was to survive." This is inaccurate because the terms *blackball, blacklist, black book,* and *blackmail* did not evolve as a result of the need of the dominant group to maintain social and economic relationships of any kind. The origins of these terms are to be found in the sixteenth and seventeenth centuries in England, where they were based mostly on the color of the book cover, the color of printing, or the color of the object from which the word got its meaning. For instance, the term *to blackball* came from the black ball which centuries ago was used as a vote against a person or thing. A *black-letter day* had its origin in the eighteenth century to designate an inauspicious day, as distinguished from a *red-letter day*, the reference being to the old custom of marking the saint's days in the calendar with red letters.

More important, the assertion that the negative connotations of *black* and the positive connotations of *white* could not exist in a society wherein whites were a minority is not accurate. Centuries ago, before black societies ever saw white men, *black* often had negative connotations and *white* positive in those societies. T. O. Beidelman has made quite clear in his article "Swazi Royal Ritual," which appeared in the October 1966 issue of *Africa,* that black societies in southeast Africa, while attributing to black positive qualities, can at the same time attribute to black negative qualities; the same applies to the color white.

What King, Cleaver, and Podair have failed to do in their discussions of the negative connotations of *black* and the positive connotations of *white* is to point out that in black societies *black* often connotes that which is hostile, foreboding, and gloomy and *white* has symbolized purity and divinity. Furthermore, in white societies, *white* has numerous negative connotations: white livered (cowardly), white flag (surrender), white elephant (useless), white plague (tuberculosis), whitewash (conceal), white feather (cowardice), etc. The ugliness and terror associated with the color white are portrayed by Melville in the chapter "The Whiteness of the Whale" in *Moby Dick.* At the beginning of the chapter, Melville says: "It was the whiteness of the whale that above all things appalled me."

What I am suggesting here is that the Negro writers, while legitimately concerned with the words and phrases which perpetuate racism in the United States, have, at least in their analysis of the term *black,* presented a partial analysis. This is not to say, however, that most of the analysis is not valid as far as it goes. Podair is entirely correct when he writes: "In modern American life language has become a fulcrum of prejudice as regards Negro-white relationships. Its effect has been equally potent upon the overt bigot as well as the confused member of the public who is struggling to overcome conscious or unconscious hostility towards minority groups. In the case of the Negro, language concepts have supported misconceptions and disoriented the thinking of many on the question of race and culture.

The Negroes' increased understanding and sensitivity to language as it is related to them demands that white Americans follow suit with a similar understanding and sensitivity which they have not yet adequately demonstrated. During the 1960s, at a time when black Americans have been attempting more than ever to communicate to whites through speeches, marches, sit-ins, demonstrations, through violence and nonviolence, the barriers of communication between blacks and whites seems to be almost as divisive as they have been in the past 100 years, no thanks to the whites. One has only to watch the TV panelists, blacks and whites, discussing the black American's protest and his aspirations, to see the facial expressions of the black panelists when a white on the panel speaks of "our colored boys in Vietnam." The black panelists knowingly smile at the racist phrasing and it is not difficult to understand the skepticism and suspicion which the blacks henceforth will maintain toward the white panelist who offends with "our colored boys in Vietnam." John Howard Griffin has pointed out something that applies not only to Southern whites, but to white Americans generally: "A great many of us Southern whites have grown up using an expression that Negroes can hardly bear to hear and yet tragically enough we use it because we believe it. It's an expression that we use when we say how much we love, what we patronizingly call 'our Negroes.' " The white American who talks of "our colored boys in Vietnam" offends the Negro triply; first, by referring to the black American men as "our" which is, as Griffin points out, patronizing; second, by using the nineteenth-century term "colored"; third, by referring to the black American men as "boys."

Most whites, if not all, know that "nigger" and "boy" are offensive to the Negro; in fact, such language could be classified as "fighting words." But the insensitive and offensive whites continue today to indulge in expressing their overt and covert prejudices by using these obviously derogatory terms.

Whites who would never think of referring to Negroes as "boy" or "nigger" do, however, reveal themselves through less obviously racist language. A day does not go by without one hearing, from people who should know better, about "the Negro problem," a phrase which carries with it the implication that the Negro is a problem. One is reminded of the Nazis talking about "the Jewish problem." There was no Jewish problem! Yet the phrase carried the implication that the Jews were a problem in Germany and hence being a problem invited a solution and the solution Hitler proposed and carried out was the "final solution." There are several indications that from here on out the black American is no longer going to accept the phrase "the Negro problem." As Lerone Bennett, Jr. said in the August 1965 issue of *Ebony*, "there is no Negro problem in America. The problem of race in America, insofar as that problem is related to packets of melanin in men's skins, is a white problem."

The racial brainwashing of whites in the United States leads them to utter such statements as "You don't sound like a Negro" or "Well, he didn't sound like a Negro to me." "There is an illusion in this land," said John Howard Griffin, "that unless you sound as though you are reading Uncle Remus you couldn't possibly have an authentic Negro dialect. But I don't know what we've been using for ears because you don't have to be in the Negro community five minutes before the truth strikes and the truth is that there are just as many speech patterns in the Negro community as there are in any other, particularly in areas of rigid segregation where your right shoulder may be touching the shoulder of a Negro PhD and your left shoulder the shoulder of the disadvantaged."

Psychiatrist Frantz Fanon points out that most whites "talk down" to the Negro, and this "talking down" is, in effect, telling the Negro, "You'd better keep your place." Fanon writes: "A white man addressing a Negro behaves exactly like an adult with a child and starts smirking, whispering, patronizing, cozening." The effect of the whites' manner of speaking to the Negro "makes him angry, because he himself is a pidgin-nigger-talker." "But I will be told," says Fanon, "there is no wish, no intention to anger him. I grant this; but it is just this absence of wish, this lack of interest, this indifference, this automatic manner of classifying him, imprisoning him, primitivizing him, decivilizing him, that makes him angry." If a doctor greets his Negro patient with "You not feel good, no?" or "G'morning pal. Where's it hurt? Huh? Lemme see—belly ache? Heart pain?" the doctor feels perfectly justified in speaking that way, writes Fanon, when in return the patient answers in the same fashion; the doctor can then say to himself, "You see? I wasn't kidding you. That's just the way they are." The whites, in effect, encourage the stereotype of the Negro; they perpetuate the stereotype through the manner in which they speak about and speak to Negroes.

Another facet of the racism of the whites' language is reflected in their habit of referring to talented and great writers, athletes, entertainers, and clergymen as "a great Negro singer" or "a great black poet" or "a great Negro ball player." What need is there for whites to designate the color or race of the person who has excelled? Paul Robeson and Marion Anderson are great and talented singers. James Baldwin and Leroi Jones are talented writers. Why must the whites qualify the greatness of these individuals with "black" or "colored" or "Negro"? This tendency to designate and identify a person as a Negro when the designation is not necessary carries over into newspaper and magazine reporting of crimes. If we were told, day in and day out, that "a *white* bank clerk embezzled" or "a *white* service station operator stole" or "a *white* unemployed laborer attacked," it would make a difference in the same sense that it makes a difference to identify the criminal suspect as "Negro" or "black."

If many Negroes find it hard to understand why whites have to designate a great writer or a great artist or a common criminal as "colored" or "Negro," so too do many Negroes find it difficult to understand why whites must designate a Negro woman as a "Negress." Offensive as "Negress" is to most blacks, many whites still insist on using the term. As Gordon Allport has written in *The Nature of Prejudice*, "Sex differentiations are objectionable since they seem doubly to emphasize ethnic differences: why speak of Jewess and not of Protestantess, or of Negress, and not of whitess?" Just as "Jewess" is offensive to the Jews, so too is "Negress" offensive to the Negroes.

The whites must make a serious conscious effort to discard the racist clichés of the past, the overt and covert language of racism. "Free, white, and 21" or "That's white of you" are phrases whites can no longer indulge in. Asking white Americans to change their language, to give up some of their clichés, is disturbing enough since the request implies a deficiency in the past use of that language; asking that they discard the language of racism is also disturbing because the people being asked to make the change, in effect, are being told that they have been the perpetrators and perpetuators of racism. Finally, and most important, calling the Negro "nigger" or "boy," or "speaking down" to the Negro, gives Whitey a linguistic power over the victimized black American, a power most whites are unwilling or afraid to give up. A person's language is an extension of himself and to attack his use of language is to attack him. The language of white racism and the racism of the whites are almost one and the same. Difficult and painful as it may be for whites to discard their racist terms, phrases, and clichés, it must be done before blacks and whites can discuss seriously the eradication of white racism.

NEGRO, BLACK,
OR AFRO-AMERICAN?

John A. Morsell

The revival of controversy over the "correct" name for persons of black African descent includes, as it has in the past, an effort to repudiate the term "Negro." Opponents of "Negro" demand its replacement by "black," or by such hyphenated variants as "Afro-American" or "African-American." In other years, the term "colored" found much favor.

The contemporary reformers are not content to argue in a context of personal preference or stylistic variety, modes which have largely prevailed heretofore. They insist that the psyche of the race is profoundly implicated, that "Negro" is a white man's term of opprobrium, and that those who continue to use it are guilty of betrayal or, at the least, of failure to identify with the masses of "black" people.

This was the burden of a young high school sophomore's letter to the late W. E. B. DuBois, answered by DuBois in *Crisis* magazine for March, 1928. The DuBois who had published "Souls of Black Folk" in 1903 and would publish "Black Reconstruction" in 1935 said: " 'Negro' is a fine word. Etymologically and phonetically, it is much better and more logical than 'African' or 'colored' or any of the various hyphenated circumlocutions. Of course, it is not historically accurate. No name was ever historically accurate . . . [but] 'Negro' is quite as accurate, quite as old, and quite as definite as the name of any great group of people."

In point of fact, there is simply no other word we can use if we wish to speak solely and exclusively of persons of black African descent. Black Africans, New Guineans, aboriginal Australians, East Indians (especially the *harijans*) and a host of diverse racial and ethnic strains are all properly called "blacks," and "black" therefore fails the tests of exclusivity and specificity.

"African-American" and "Afro-American" are equally deficient, since Ian Smith of Rhodesia is an African, as are President Nasser, the King of Morocco, and any of the thousands of whites who hold citizenship in Nigeria, Ghana, Kenya, and other black African states. Should any of these, or their descendants, become United States citizens, they, too, would be "African-Americans."

Only "Negro" possesses, by reason of years of wide and continued usage, a clear, specific, and exclusive denotation: a person of black African origin or descent. Proponents of other names may object that it is a white man's word; but so is "black" and so is "African-American." All these are "white men's words" by virtue of their being English. Moreover, it should be recalled that "blacks" was the white man's first designation for black Africans; historical circumstances brought into common English use the Spanish word for black, which is "Negro."

The intolerance with which the cause of this or that designation is pressed carries a special danger. We have already been told by some of the more extreme advocates of "black" that it is to be more than just an ethnic term; it is to be an elite designation, reserved for only those whom the extremists deem worthy, without regard to skin color or anything else.

Whether this absurdity gets very far or not, it is still a very likely prospect that, given *de rigeur* usage of "black," succeeding generations will indeed make darkness of skin an elite attribute which will irrevocably divide the Negro population. There could be no more ironic outcome of the generations of struggle against color prejudice than to find Negroes themselves split into rival camps on the basis of skin color.

This danger is great enough, it seems to me, to justify reasonable men in combatting any effort to restrict our usage to a single term, whatever it may be. Whites in particular should not, in an excess of fear lest they offend, cater to a movement of intolerance and divisiveness.

As DuBois observed to young Roland Barton forty years ago: "Suppose we arose tomorrow morning and lo! instead of being 'Negroes,' all the world called us 'Cheiropolidi'—do you really think this would make a vast and momentous difference to you and me? . . . Would you be any less ashamed of being descended from a black man, or would your schoolmates feel any less superior to you? The feeling of inferiority is in you, not in any name. The name merely evokes what is already there. Exorcise the hateful complex and no name can ever make you hang your head."

The truth has not been better stated since.

ADDITIONAL READINGS

Alexander, Hubert, *Language and Thinking* (New York: Van Nostrand Reinhold, 1967), part 1, "Symbols: Intellectual Coins" and part 2, "Process of Thinking."

Chase, Stuart, *Power of Words* (New York: Harcourt Brace Jovanovich, 1954).

DeCecco, John, *The Psychology of Language, Thought, and Instruction* (New York: Holt, Rinehart & Winston, 1967), especially chaps. 1–4 and 8.

Hayakawa, S. I., *Language in Thought and Action* (New York: Harcourt Brace Jovanovich, 1949), especially Book 1.

Hildum, Donald, (ed.), *Language and Thought* (New York: Van Nostrand Reinhold, 1967).

Jacobovits, Leon A. and Murray S. Miron (eds.), *Readings in the Psychology of Language* (Englewood Cliffs, N.J.: Prentice-Hall, 1967).

Vetter, Harold, *Language Behavior and Communication: An Introduction* (Itasca: F. E. Peacock, 1969).

Williams, Frederick, *Language and Poverty: Perspectives on a Theme* (Chicago: Markham, 1970).

STUDY QUESTIONS

1. What is the singularity misconception concerning language?
2. How does ambiguous language differ from vague language? Give an example of each.
3. What is meant by the permanency misconception of language? Why does it cause confusion?

4. What is the authority misconception? Give some examples of this misconception that you have observed.
5. How widely held is the morality misconception concerning language? Can a speaker afford to violate this misconception in a speech?
6. What are the differences between disreputable and derogatory language?
7. Are some words inherently bad, evil, or obscene? Defend your answer.
8. How does abstract language differ from concrete language?
9. What is the key to classifying words as either neutral or emotive? Can a word be both neutral and emotive?

EXERCISES
1. Define and give an example of each of the following kinds of language: (1) informative, (2) expressive, and (3) directive. Which kind do you think is used most frequently?
2. From a newspaper or magazine editorial, syndicated column, or speech, find a passage (at least 10 sentences long) containing an unusually large number of emotionally colored words. After copying the passage, underline all of the emotive words and then rewrite the passage replacing the emotive words with neutral ones.
3. List ten abstract words and for each word find a more concrete counterpart (for example: *fruit* and *a candied apple; journalism* and *The New York Times*).
4. From a book, magazine article, or speech, find a passage containing several abstract words. Rewrite the passage substituting more concrete words for the abstract terms.
5. Locate several advertisements that illustrate the authoritative misconception.
6. Locate a passage of approximately 150 words in a book or magazine. Rewrite the passage using an oral style. Read both versions aloud before the class.

CHAPTER

16

ACHIEVING GOOD ORAL STYLE

During the Crimean War in the late 1850s, John Bright made one of the most magnificent speeches in British Parliamentary history. He spoke in opposition to the war. "The Angel of Death has been abroad throughout the land," he said to a hushed House of Commons, "you may almost hear the beating of his wings." Afterward, when being congratulated, he said, "Ah, yes, but if I had said 'the flapping of his wings' they would have laughed." Bright's comment emphasizes the importance of selecting the right words to express one's ideas.

The speaker's use of language is known as his oral style. In developing an effective oral style, the speaker should strive to use language that is clear, correct, concrete, vivid, and appropriate. His language should be clear so that the listener understands him without difficulty. His choice of words and sentence structure should be correct so that he accurately expresses his ideas. He should strive to employ concrete language because it contributes to a precise communication of what he wishes to say and increases the audience's interest in his message. Through the use of vivid language, the speaker can make his ideas more colorful, more forceful, more readily understood, and more easily remembered. And, he should seek to use appropriate language so that he neither offends his listeners nor interferes with the communication of his ideas.

Style is the dress of thoughts.

PHILIP DORMER STANHOPE

ACHIEVING CLARITY

In any speech situation, if the speaker is to gain the response he wishes, the hearer must understand what he is saying. The basic test of a speaker's choice of words, according to Quintilian, is "not that language may be understood, but that it cannot be misunderstood."

A speaker's language may not be clear for various reasons, but three of the most common are: (1) His words may be totally unfamiliar to the listener; (2) they may have no clear-cut meaning; and (3) they may have more than one meaning. In each of these instances, the speaker must either define his terms or specify the precise meaning he is attaching to the word as he uses it. If the speaker employs technical jargon, highly abstract language, or completely unfamiliar terminology, he must indicate what these concepts mean if he expects to get his message across to his listeners.

Edgar Dale stresses in Adapted Reading 16.1 that speakers are often unclear because they do not appreciate the complexity of what they are communicating; they fail to consider how much or how little the other person knows about the subject; and they are sometimes unnecessarily detailed or technical in their explanations.

> "You should say what you mean," the March Hare went on.
> "I do," Alice hastily replied; "at least—at least I mean what I say—that's the same thing, you know."
> "Not the same thing a bit!" said the Hatter. "Why you might just as well say that 'I see what I eat' is the same as 'I eat what I see'!"
>
> LEWIS CARROLL
> *Alice's Adventures in Wonderland*

The speaker should be particularly careful to define vague and ambiguous words. If he uses terms such as *democratic*, *ethical*, *liberal*, or *romantic*, unless he indicates what he means by them, the listener may wholly misunderstand his message.

In defining terms, the speaker has many approaches from which to choose. Among the methods of definition are the following:

Definition by Synonym

A synonym is a word having the same or nearly the same meaning as another. Defining by synonym consists of stating another word or words that mean the same or approximately the same thing as the word being defined. In defining by synonym, the speaker should be sure that the synonym actually increases the listener's understanding of the concept. A synonym which is as vague or unfamiliar to the listener as the word being defined will only further confuse the listener. For example, to define a *god* as a *deity*; *virtuous* as *morally good*; or *legerdemain* as meaning *prestidigitation* may contribute little to the auditor's knowledge of what the speaker is talking about. For a synonymic definition to be meaningful, the synonym must be one which has a clear and specific meaning for the listener.

Another risk in defining by synonym is that there may be no word or words with exactly the same meaning as the term being defined. For example, it is difficult to find another word with precisely the same meaning as *house. Home* has an emotional connotation and implies that someone is living in the structure. *Cottage, bungalow, villa,* and *mansion* all suggest specific types of houses and so are not entirely satisfactory synonyms. Most other synonyms the reader can think of probably are not altogether suitable for the same or other reasons. So it may be that the speaker will find a definition by synonym difficult in clarifying the meaning of some words.

Definition by Example

Definition by example consists of giving an illustration—actual or hypothetical—of the concept or word to be defined. To show the usefulness of definitions by example, one might take the word *empathy,* which is difficult to explain and for which there is no exact synonym. Defining *empathy* as "projection of one's own feelings into the feelings of another" contributes little to an understanding of the concept. However, if the speaker were to offer some examples of empathy that his listeners had experienced, the meaning of the term might be clearer. He might, for example, ask the audience: "When you see someone bite into a lemon, do you pucker your lips and almost taste the sourness of the lemon?" "When someone scrapes his fingernail across a blackboard, do you feel chills up and down your spine?" "When you see a diver do a belly flop, do you gasp as he hits the water?" or "Have you ever ridden in an automobile with another driver and found yourself pressing a nonexistent brake on the floorboard to avoid a near collision?" All of these are examples of *empathy,* and if the listener has experienced any of them he will probably understand what the term means.

It is important to remember that if the definition is to be meaningful, the speaker's examples must be familiar ones. If the listener has no understanding of the example, his knowledge of the concept will remain incomplete.

Definition by Details

A common method of definition is for the speaker to provide additional information or details about a word so that the listener better understands its meaning.

In a speech on the environment, William D. Ruckelshaus used details to define the term *usufruct.* He said:

> Note that term "usufruct." Under an agreement of usufruct, a tenant may use the fruit of the orchard and the land, but he is bound to preserve the basic resources as they were received. He has the use of the land in his own time, but he must pass it on without damage.

Each of the following also illustrates how a term may be defined by giving details:

Jodhpurs are riding breeches made loose and full above the knees and close fitting below them.

Astigmatism is a structural defect of a lens or of the eyes that prevents light rays from an object from meeting in a single focal point, so that indistinct images are formed.

A *kiosk* is a small structure resembling a summerhouse or pavilion, which is open at one or more sides and often is used as a newsstand, bandstand, or covering for the entrance to a subway.

A *jingo* is a person who boasts of his patriotism and favors an aggressive, threatening, warlike foreign policy for his country.

A *trifle* is a popular English dessert consisting of spongecake soaked in wine and covered with fruit, macaroons, almonds, and custard or whipped cream.

Phrenology is a system by which an analysis of character and the development of a person's faculties can allegedly be made through study of the shape and protuberances of the skull.

Aphasia is the total or partial loss of the power to use or understand words, usually caused by brain disease or injury.

Definition by Comparison and Contrast

Sometimes a word can be most effectively defined by comparing or contrasting it with another item. This method is particularly useful in explaining technical concepts with which the audience has little familiarity. Muriel Beadle, in Adapted Reading 16.4, tells how her husband developed considerable skill in the use of analogy to clarify genetics principles for lay audiences. By comparing a concept in genetics to something familiar to his listeners—in one instance, he compared evolution by natural selection to the development of a prized recipe for angel food cake—Dr. Beadle was able to discuss highly technical, scientific material with audiences having little knowledge of his subject. The approach can be used effectively in other scientific and technological disciplines.

Educator Robert Hutchins, in a speech delivered at the University of Chicago in 1971, used contrast to define a *learning society*:

> There is a fundamental, though not always sharp and clear, distinction between a learning society and a society in training. Learning, as I am using the word, aims at understanding, which is good in itself, and hence at nothing beyond itself. Training is instrumental; it may not require or lead to any understanding at all; it aims at the performance of prescribed tasks by prescribed methods.

At times, comparison and contrast can be used to pinpoint the precise meaning of a word by showing how it both resembles and differs from a closely related idea. In this method, the speaker points out the similarities between the two concepts, but also emphasizes the distinguishing differences. Concepts such as *libel* and *slander*; *agnostic* and *atheist*; and *legal*, *ethical*, and *moral* probably can be better understood if compared and contrasted.

The following examples are designed to illustrate definition by comparison and contrast.

Libel and *slander*. *Libel* is a written or printed statement, sign, or picture, not made in the public interest, tending to expose a person to ridicule or contempt or to injure his reputation. *Slander* is the utterance or spreading of a false statement or statements harmful to another's character or reputation. Legally, *slander* is spoken, as distinguished from *libel*, which is written.

Agnostic and *atheist*. An *agnostic* is a person who thinks it is impossible to know whether there is a God or future life or anything beyond material phenomena. An *atheist*, on the other hand, is convinced that there definitely is no God or future life. An *atheist* rejects all religious belief and denies the existence of God, while an *agnostic* simply questions the existence of God because of the absence of material proof of His existence and because of his unwillingness to accept supernatural revelation. The *atheist* would say "There is no God," while the *agnostic* would say, "I don't know whether there is a God."

Legal, *ethical*, and *moral*. The term *legal* implies conformity with written, statute law. *Ethical*, on the other hand, means conforming to the standards or code of conduct of a given group or profession, while *moral* refers to conformity with generally accepted standards of rightness or goodness. For example, it is unethical for doctors and lawyers to advertise, but it is not illegal or immoral. Running a red light would be an illegal act, but it would not be unethical or immoral. Telling a lie under most circumstances would be neither unethical or illegal; however, it is generally considered immoral.

Other concepts that might lend themselves to definition by comparison and contrast include such words as *nationalism* and *patriotism*; *sympathy* and *empathy*; *apartheid* and *segregation*; *liberal*, *radical*, *conservative*, and *reactionary*; *tonal* and *atonal*; *articulation* and *pronunciation*; *illiteracy* and *ignorance*; *intelligence* and *knowledge*; *op art* and *pop art*; *romanticism* and *classicism*; *character* and *personality*; *dissent* and *disagreement*; and *inflation* and *deflation*.

Definition by Classification and Differentiation

Definition by classification and differentiation consists of placing a word within a class and then differentiating it from other concepts within that same classification by pointing out its dissimilar characteristics. For example, if one were to define *automobile* by this method, one would first place it in the general class of *vehicles*, and then show how it differs from other vehicles by listing such details as the following: It is four-wheeled, operates on land, runs on gasoline, is usually used for private transportation, etc. It is thereby distinguished from vehicles such as trains, bicycles, motorcycles, trucks, boats, and airplanes.

Definition by Historical Background

Some concepts can be clearly understood only by placing them in historical context and showing how they came into being. To do this, the speaker recounts the historical forces and circumstances that gave rise to the movement, attitude, or concept that he is defining. For example, the *romantic movement* or *romanticism* in music, art, and literature probably is completely understandable only if one knows something about the times and conditions that gave rise to it.

Other words that might require historical background in order to be fully understood are *populism, rationalism, muck-rakers, protestant, popular sovereignty, cold war, witch hunt, feudalism, Jacobin, lend-lease, commedia dell'arte, rotten borough, bimetallism, McCarthyism, speak-easy, spoils system, blue stocking,* and *blitzkrieg.*

Definition by Etymology

Etymology is the study of the origins and derivations of words. Occasionally, a term may be better understood if its origin — what it initially meant — and how its meaning has changed are known.

Some words that might be more easily recognized and remembered through definition by etymology are listed below as examples of this method.

Pyrotechnics is derived from the Greek *pyr* or *pyros* meaning a fire and the Greek *technic* meaning art. Combined, these words mean the art of making or using fireworks or a display of fireworks. From this, it has also come to mean a dazzling display of eloquence or wit.

The word *heterogeneous* is based on the Greek words *hetero,* meaning other or different, and *genes,* meaning race or kind. Thus, *heterogeneous* means composed of unrelated or unlike elements or parts; varied; miscellaneous; dissimilar; or differing in structure or quality.

Tergiversate is a word of Latin origin derived from *tergum,* which means back, and *versari,* which means to turn. In other words, to *tergiversate* is to turn one's back, to desert a cause or party, to become a renegade, to use evasions or subterfuge, and to equivocate.

The concept of *jurisprudence* is based on the Latin *jus* and *juris,* which mean right or law, and *prudentia,* which means a foreseeing, knowledge, or skill. When combined, they refer to the science or philosophy of law, a system of laws, or a part or division of law.

Polymorphous originated from the Greek *poly,* or many, and *morphe,* a form, and so means having, occurring in, or passing through several or various forms.

The word *orthodox* comes from the Greek *orthos,* which means correct, and *doxa,* which means opinion. Thus, *orthodox* refers to conforming to the usual beliefs or established doctrines; proper; correct; or conventional.

While an etymological definition often is helpful in understanding some words, this method is of little value and may even be misleading in explaining others. Because the meanings of words change, the original meaning of a term sometimes bears little relationship to its present meaning. For example, *surgeon* is derived from the Greek words *cheir* and *cheires,* meaning the hand, and *ergein*, which means to work, and referred to anyone who worked with his hands, such as artisans and craftsmen. Obviously, the meaning of the word has changed greatly since then, and today it refers to a doctor who treats disease or injury in a particular way. With a concept such as this, citing the origins of the word will add little to the audience's knowledge.

Definition by Operation, Action, or Purpose

Some concepts can be fully understood only if the listener knows about their operation, action, function, or purpose. To define such concepts, it often is necessary to explain how they work, what they are intended to accomplish, their causes and effects, and their uses. For example, it is almost impossible to understand *inflation* without knowing its causes and its effects on such factors as wages, salaries, prices, savings, and investments. *Radar* is another concept that is not readily understandable without knowing how it operates and its intended function. Similar terms that may necessitate explanation of their operation, action, or purpose in order to comprehend their meaning include:

ombudsman
polarization
natural selection
survival of the fittest
fermentation
distillation
jet propulsion
x-ray
crop rotation
free association
deficit spending
European Common Market
free trade zone
pogo stick
napalm
technocracy
T-formation
man-to-man defense
stereophonic sound
balance of payments
fluorescence
milk homogenization
rotary press
schizophrenia
policy of containment
balance of power
eggbeater
proportional representation

hydroplane
corkscrew
programmed learning
tutorial system
cartel
metronome
feudalism

Definition by Negation

At times, a speaker can clarify the meaning of a particular word by telling
what it is *not*. He may do this because (1) the word has more than one meaning and he wishes to make certain that the listener understands which meaning he attaches to the term; (2) the word is misunderstood by many people
and he wishes to eliminate any false conceptions the auditor may have; or (3)
he wishes to define the term in a new and different manner.

For example, when the concept *black power* first began to be used, the
phrase acquired a variety of meanings in the public mind. To some, *black
power* meant Negro superiority; to others, it meant Negro militancy; to still
others, it referred to Negro political and economic power; and to a few, it was
a synonym for black and white separatism. Because of this confusion over
the meaning of the term, most black-power spokesmen found it necessary to
clarify their usage of the term by indicating what it did not mean to them.

Similarly, a speaker using the term *freedom of speech* might take care
to point out that freedom of speech does not include the right to say anything
regardless of its consequences; that it does not give the speaker the right to
slander others, to use private facilities for a public speech, to demand free
radio or television time; and that it does not exempt the speaker from certain
restrictions designed to maintain law and order.

An example of definition by negation is the following excerpt from one
of the Godkin Lectures given by Adlai Stevenson at Harvard University in
1954:

> Diplomacy, for example, is not the art of asserting ever more emphat-
> ically that attitudes should not be what they clearly are. It is not the
> repudiation of actuality, but the recognition of actuality, and the use
> of actuality to advance our national interests.

Dr. Edward L. R. Elson also employed definition by negation in a sermon at the National Presbyterian Church in Washington, D.C., when he said:

> The Church, we must repeat over and over again, is not an institu-
> tion, much less a building. The Church has been institutionalized in
> order to promote the gospel of redeeming love and it has buildings
> in order to shelter its activities and provide centers from which its
> influence might radiate to the whole world.

Still another example of a speaker using negation to help clarify his meaning was author Alan Paton's statement in a lecture at Yale University in 1973:

> By liberalism, I don't mean the creed of any party or of any century. I mean a generosity of spirit, a tolerance of others, an attempt to comprehend otherness, a commitment to the rule of law, a high ideal of the worth and dignity of man, a repugnance for authoritarianism, and a love of freedom.

Other concepts that might profit from definition by negation include *patriotism*, *school spirit*, *ethical responsibility*, *separation of church and state*, *academic freedom*, *student rights*, *dissent*, *law and order*, *conservatism*, *free enterprise*, *God is dead*, and *disarmament*.

Visual Definition

Visual concepts are frequently difficult to define verbally. For example, a speaker trying to explain to an uninformed audience what the color *chrome yellow* looks like would probably struggle in vain if he were restricted to a verbal definition. However, the concept is immediately understood if the speaker shows his audience something chrome yellow. Colors that most listeners probably could not visualize without actually seeing them include *thalo green*, *sepia*, *cerise*, *magenta*, *burnt umber*, *cobalt blue*, *cadmium orange*, *yellow ochre*, and *French ultramarine blue*. The same is often true of definitions involving shapes, spatial relationships, textures, and concepts in the visual arts. For example, it is easier to draw a parallelogram on the blackboard by way of definition than it is to try to explain what a parallelogram looks like. Likewise, a map of Thailand showing the location of Bangkok would probably be more meaningful to most persons than verbal directions locating that city. In the same way, textures and various art concepts can be illustrated visually for the easy comprehension of the listener, whereas an oral explanation might be largely meaningless. Other concepts more easily explained by a visual representation include: *irridescent*, *homolaine projection*, *montage*, *hieroglyphics*, *impressionism*, *surrealism*, *pentimento*, and *optical illusion*.

Audible Definition

Just as some concepts are most easily explained by presenting them visually, other concepts are best understood if the listener can hear them. Many musical terms, concepts, and instruments are difficult to comprehend unless the speaker's explanation is accompanied by an audible illustration or example. For instance, one can imagine the problems a speaker would encounter in trying to discuss the sound of an unfamiliar musical instrument such as the *Flugelhorn*, *oboe*, *harmonium*, *lute*, *melodeon*, *harpsichord*, or *clavichord* without either playing a recording of its sound or playing a few notes on the instrument itself. Other musical concepts that almost necessitate audible demonstration if they are to be understood include *fanfare*, *syncopation*, *jazz*, *pizzicato*, *atonal*, *counterpoint*, and *leit motif*. Outside the realm of music, certain kinds of speech defects and deficiencies are more easily understood if they are accompanied by some audible imitation or illustration.

Combination of Methods

Usually, the most effective definitions are those that combine two or more of the methods just discussed. For example, a speaker might first list a few synonyms and then follow this with an example; or he might trace the origins of the word and then present details; or, after discussing the historical conditions giving rise to the concept, he might proceed to compare or contrast it with related concepts. The advantage to combining two or more methods of definition is that if one method does not completely clarify its meaning, perhaps another type of definition will clear up any uncertainty in the listener's mind.

ACHIEVING CORRECTNESS

A second characteristic of good oral style is correct use of language. Correctness implies not only that the speaker's language is grammatically correct, but that his words are the right words for expressing his ideas.

Correct language is important in speech for three reasons. The first and most important is that an incorrect choice of words may mislead or misinform. For example, the speaker who does not know the difference in meaning of *persecute* and *prosecute*, *rationalization* and *rational thinking*, or *integrate* and *assimilate*, and mistakenly uses one for the other, may convey a meaning quite different from what he intends.

Second, language that is incorrect, while not actually misleading the hearer, may succeed in confusing him. In other words, rather than being misinformed, he simply does not know what the speaker means.

Third, the speaker should aim for correctness in language if only to avoid distracting his audience. Errors in word choice and usage frequently call attention to themselves. Every time a listener detects a mistake in grammar, usage, or word choice, he shifts his attention, at least momentarily, from the speaker's subject to his language. If the speaker's errors are glaring or too numerous, respect for him may be diminished. The speaker who says, "You may think we're ignorant, but we ain't," or "Nobody will ever call us a bunch of heterosexuals," undoubtedly will suffer in the eyes of educated listeners.

A fairly common question asked by beginning speakers is whether it is correct to use slang. Some students argue that because slang words appear in dictionaries, they must be permissible. Whether or not the word appears in a dictionary is irrelevant, because inclusion in a dictionary simply indicates that the word is in common usage. Actually, the question of whether a speaker should employ slang is more one of appropriateness than of correctness. Slang is neither correct nor incorrect. It may be unfamiliar to some audiences, and it may be inappropriate for some topics or occasions. On the other hand, the president of the University of Minnesota, in addressing a convention of newspaper publishers recently, used the phrases, *scrounging for funds, testy speech,* and *tight against the barricades,* while the president of the First National City Bank of New York spoke to the International Chamber of Commerce about *rigged* conventions, *America-watchers,* and whether the country was *going to pot.*

Television commercials, lyrics of popular songs, and slogans of special interest groups that employ incorrect language are frequently repeated so often that the correct usages begin to sound strange. Most people have heard "Tell it like it is," "Winstons taste good like a cigarette should," and "very unique" so often that they no longer notice the incorrectness of the language. If few people are bothered by these mistakes, why shouldn't a speaker feel free to employ similar language? The main reason, as Russell Baker stresses in Adapted Reading 16.2, is that these usages usually are designed to circumvent thought rather than to provoke clear mental responses. The speaker whose code of ethics includes presenting lucid, logical arguments in support of his ideas will always find correct language preferable to incorrect usages.

> The difference between the right word and the almost right word is the difference between lightning and the lightning bug.
>
> MARK TWAIN

What are the principal causes of incorrect language usage? Grammatical mistakes are usually the result of an inadequate education in grammar, both in the home and at school. There probably is no other solution to this other than to study the rules of correct grammatical usage and to develop an ear for the language in order to detect such errors.

A person's language may also suffer from an inadequate vocabulary: The speaker simply cannot find the right word to convey his idea or to present the exact shade of meaning he has in mind. A speaker who repeatedly uses the same noun, verb, or adjective (for example, "It was a *very* enjoyable play. It was *very* well directed. The acting was *very* good. The last act was *very, very* funny," instead of "It was a *very* enjoyable play. It was *well* directed. The acting *exceptionally* good. The last act was *hilarious.*") usually is handicapped by an inadequate vocabulary. If the speaker finds that he frequently resorts to highly imprecise words such as "you know," "et cetera," "and so forth," "cute," and "great" in expressing himself, he should embark on a program of vocabulary development. Wide reading and a systematic study of language (learning a few new words every day) are the best cures for this deficiency.

A third and probably the most important reason why persons use words incorrectly is that they don't fully understand what they are talking about. If a person thoroughly understands his subject, he should have no trouble finding the right words to convey his ideas. On the other hand, if he is uncertain in his own mind concerning his subject, it is not surprising that he should experience difficulty in finding the right words to convey his ideas.

It would be impossible to provide in this text an exhaustive list of all of the kinds of language errors the speaker should avoid. However, a few commonly heard mistakes are listed below:

1. *like* and *as*
   Incorrect: Do like your mother says.
   Correct: Do as your mother says.
   Correct: She looks like her mother.
2. *only*
   Incorrect: I only have a quarter.
   Correct: I have only a quarter.
3. *even*
   Incorrect: He criticizes everyone; he even criticizes his mother.
   Correct: He criticizes everyone; he criticizes even his mother.
4. *lay* and *lie*
   Incorrect: I think I will lay down for a while.
   Correct: I think I will lie down for a while.
5. *is* and *are*
   Incorrect: None of them are going.
   Correct: None of them is going.
6. *enthused* and *enthusiastic*
   Incorrect: All of the critics were enthused about his performance.
   Correct: All of the critics were enthusiastic about his performance.
7. *regardless, irrespective,* and *irregardless*
   Incorrect: He decided to enter irregardless of his chances of winning.
                  (There is no such word as *irregardless*.)
   Correct: He decided to enter regardless of his chances of winning.
   Correct: He decided to enter irrespective of his chances of winning.
8. *further* and *farther*
   Incorrect: The church is further down the street.
   Correct: The church is farther down the street.
9. *less* and *fewer*
   Incorrect: Some schools play less basketball games than others.
   Correct: Some schools play fewer basketball games than others.
10. *most* and *best*
    Incorrect: He was the most educated man in the organization.
    Correct: He was the best educated man in the organization.
11. *between* and *among*
    Incorrect: Let's keep this secret strictly between the three of us.
    Correct: Let's keep this secret strictly among the three of us.
    Correct: Let's keep this secret strictly between the two of us.
12. *than* and *from*
    Incorrect: Conditions are no different now than when you were young.
    Correct: Conditions are no different now from when you were young.

13. *unique* and *unusual*

Incorrect: It is a very unique school.

Correct: It is a unique school.

Correct: It is a very unusual school.

14. *real* and *very*

Incorrect: It was a real entertaining show.

Correct: It was a very entertaining show.

15. *so* and *very*

Incorrect: It was so well planned.

Correct: It was very well planned.

Correct: It was so well planned that everyone found it easy to follow.

16. *hard* and *difficult*

Incorrect: He gave a hard examination.

Correct: He gave a difficult examination.

Correct: The seat was hard.

17. *orient*

Incorrect: The meeting was to orientate the new students.

Correct: The meeting was to orient the new students.

18. *crown*

Incorrect: She was coronated queen of homecoming.

Correct: She was crowned queen of homecoming.

19. *comment*

Incorrect: Her job was to commentate the style show.

Correct: Her job was to comment on the style show. (Or probably better: Her job was to serve as commentator for the style show.)

20. *infer* and *imply*

Incorrect: Your answers are insulting and infer that I am lying.

Correct: Your answers are insulting and imply that I am lying.

Correct: Your answers are insulting and I infer from them that you think I am lying.

These are but a few examples of words used incorrectly. The best guarantee against misusing language is a sound foundation in grammar, frequent use of the dictionary to learn the precise meanings of words, and an awareness of the way in which reputable speakers and writers use language to convey their ideas.

ACHIEVING CONCRETENESS

Words that refer to specific and usually tangible persons, places, and things are called concrete words, in contrast to abstract language which refers to general, often intangible concepts. From ancient times to the present, rhetoricians have urged speakers to employ concrete language because it reduces the likelihood of misunderstanding, is more quickly grasped by most auditors, and is usually more interesting than abstract language. Abstract words tend to evoke a different image or meaning in the mind of each listener. For example, when a speaker uses an abstract word such as *charity*, some members of his audience will think of large, philanthropic foundations; others will visualize a campaign such as the March of Dimes or American Cancer Society drives; a few will think of the charitable work carried on by churches and religious orders; still others will be reminded of small gifts to beggars, tramps, and the destitute.

> **It is a good thing to use few words and the best words, which are those which are simple and forcible.**
>
> JOHN BRIGHT

The speaker should strive to use concrete language because it is more readily grasped and understood by the listener than is abstract language. For example, even though this country has only one *national anthem*—and so the words are quite concrete—*The Star Spangled Banner* would probably be more immediately meaningful than the words *national anthem* to most people. Some additional terms that are fairly concrete, but could be replaced by even more specific words are:

Fairly Concrete	More Concrete
the chief executive	President Ford
the Democratic candidate	George McGovern
the state university	Ohio State University
the nation's largest city	New York
in the spring	May
the largest automobile manufacturer	General Motors
the state capital	Austin, Texas
the chief justice	Chief Justice Warren Burger

Another reason for preferring concrete terms to abstract words is that listeners usually find concrete language more vivid and interesting. *Rolls Royce*, for example, tells us more and is more interesting than *a big car*. *A six-year-old girl* is more interesting than *a child*. *Bad weather* is not nearly so specific or vivid as *a snowstorm*, *a blizzard*, *a hail storm*, *a tornado*, or *cold and windy*.

Still another reason for using concrete language is that some common expressions are so extremely general that they can mean almost anything and so should be avoided especially in the speaking situation. These include words and phrases such as *you know*, *things like that*, *cute*, *great*, *too much*, *far out*, *lots of*, *huge*, *stuff like that*, and *et cetera*.

Whether talking to one person or addressing a large audience, a speaker may use language that is clear, correct, and concrete, and still fail to attain a vivid, interesting oral style. To achieve vividness, the speaker should employ new, fresh, and colorful words to stimulate the imagination of the listener and to affect his feelings. Two kinds of language will help him achieve vividness: emotive words and figurative language. Emotive language, as discussed in Chapter 15, consists of words and phrases that arouse the feelings of the listeners. Thus, *home, mother, brother, hero, America, Old Glory, slaughtered,* and *war* are more emotive than *house, parent, sibling, soldier, this country, the flag, killed,* and *conflict*. Because emotive words tend to stimulate the hearer's feelings, they usually are more useful than neutral terms in arousing, inspiring, or persuading others.

Figurative language consists of words used in such a way that they are pleasing to the auditor's ear, stimulating to his imagination, and easily retained by his memory. Figurative language includes such devices as parallelism, repetition, alliteration, metaphor, simile, antithesis, quotations, and rhetorical questions. To illustrate the value of figurative language in enhancing the force of a speaker's statement, consider the following paraphrases of a few famous statements by recent prominent speakers:

"Instead of trying to find out what you can get from the government, you should try to figure out some things that you can do to help it," clearly is less memorable than John F. Kennedy's, "Ask not what your country can do for you; ask what you can do for your country."

"This is a fateful time," is surely less striking than Franklin D. Roosevelt's, "This generation has a rendezvous with destiny."

Had Adlai Stevenson in his acceptance of the Democratic presidential nomination in 1952 said, "When the convention is over, we have to face up to a lot of problems," his audience probably would not have been deeply impressed. What he actually said, however, struck many listeners as extremely eloquent: "When the tumult and the shouting die, when the bands are gone and the lights are dimmed, there is the stark reality of responsibility in an hour of history haunted with those gaunt, grim specters of strife, dissension, and materialism. . . ."

At times, a speaker can add color and interest to his remarks through the choice of a single word that is particularly striking or vivid. Notice how the italicized word in each of the following brief excerpts from recent speeches enhances the entire sentence or phrase:

Few things *rankle* in the human breast like a sense of injustice.
the great *travail* of race
an *agony* of the spirit
lurching from crisis to crisis
zestfully they informed us
mortared together by common sentiment
Our economic system is a *cornucopia* of goods and services piled high.

Shattered lies the myth of American omnipotence.
the Greek colonels who *strangled* freedom in democracy's home

To achieve a more vivid oral style, the speaker should keep in mind the following suggestions:

1. Avoid Triteness, Clichés, and Hackneyed Language
Triteness, clichés, and hackneyed language are phrases and expressions that have become commonplace by overuse and have lost any freshness, originality, or novelty. Such expressions may at one time have been colorful and unusual, but they have been worn out by constant usage. A few examples of trite language would include *pretty as a picture, but that is another story, too funny for words, my better half, it is a known fact, the good old days, the real thing, cool as a cucumber, white as a sheet, sharp as a tack, clear as a bell, down and out, to coin a phrase, smart as a whip, stranger than fiction, as the crow flies, better safe than sorry, a well-rounded education, without further ado, in conclusion let me say, slippery as an eel, a wooden nickel, the Southern way of life, so quiet you could hear a pin drop, the bitter end,* and others. If a speaker hopes to achieve an interesting and vivid style, he will shun overworked language and find new and more original ways of expressing his ideas.

2. Seek Variety in Language and Sentence Structure
While repetition at times can be an effective means for achieving emphasis and gaining attention, many speakers make the mistake of repeating the same word too frequently and of using the same type of sentences throughout much of their speeches. To overcome the monotony resulting from repetition of the same word, the speaker should use synonyms to achieve greater variety. For example, instead of repeating, "he *said*," "then he *said*," and "next he *said*," the speaker might use words such as *pointed out, commented, remarked, noted, mentioned, discussed, claimed, argued, explained, contended, asserted, charged, stated,* and *told.*

The speaker should also seek to achieve variety in the types and lengths of his sentences. For example, he would not want to use all simple sentences, but should vary them with compound, complex, and complex-compound sentences as well. He should not speak entirely in declarative sentences, but should insert imperative and interrogative statements from time to time. He should also avoid sentences that are approximately the same length, and instead try to heighten interest by using shorter or longer sentences at various points throughout the speech.

3. Use Repetition
While too much repetition can become monotonous, at times the speaker can effectively emphasize and stress important ideas through a graceful or forceful reiteration of key words, phrases, and even complete sentences. For example, Edward Brooke used the word *alike* three times in one sentence to

emphasize his point in a speech to the United States Senate when he said, "We do not want a world where all people look *alike*, talk *alike*, and, even worse, think *alike*."

In a speech at Washington University in St. Louis, Senator Frank Church used repetition as follows: "*Power* is the ubiquitous symbol and catchword: white *power*, black *power*, red *power*, student *power*, flower *power*." Later in the speech he employed repetition of a phrase to achieve emphasis:

> *For too long*, our people's problems have gone unattended here at home. *For too long*, our Presidents have been mesmerized by the quests of Caesar. *For too long*, our resources have been poured into distant lands, with which we have no former link or economic interest.

William D. Ruckelshaus, in a speech on the environment in 1972, said, "The concept of 'doing as *we please*' has always appealed to us Americans. We expect to live where *we please*, think as *we please*, drive where *we please*."

In his memorable speech at the 1963 Civil Rights March on Washington, Martin Luther King, Jr., employed repetition effectively to emphasize his point. He said:

> *One hundred years later*, the Negro still is not free. *One hundred years later*, the life of the Negro is still sadly crippled by the manacles of segregation and the chains of discrimination. *One hundred years later*, the Negro lives on a lonely island of poverty in the midst of a vast ocean of material prosperity.

At times, the repetition of a single word may serve to strengthen the speaker's statement. Note the repetition of *voices* by former President Richard M. Nixon in his First Inaugural Address:

> For its part government will listen. We will strive to listen in new ways—to the *voices* of quiet anguish, the *voices* that speak without words, the *voices* of the heart—to the injured *voices*, the anxious *voices*, the *voices* that have despaired of being heard.

In a similar manner, Congresswoman Bella Abzug employed repetition of a single word to achieve emphasis: "Women look at a nation run by a *male* executive branch, a *male* Congress, *male* governors and legislatures, a *male* Pentagon, and *male* corporations and banks."

A famous illustration of the repetition of a complete sentence is Charles James Fox's challenge to the House of Commons in his Westminster Scrutiny speech. Knowing that the House was aware of the government's unjust attempt to deprive him of his seat as the elected member for Westminster, Fox repeatedly defied the Speaker and the House by asserting at five different times early in the speech: "I have no reason to expect indulgence, nor do I know that I shall meet with bare justice in this House."

4. Use Parallelism

Parallelism or balanced construction is the arrangement of words, phrases, or sentences in a similar manner or in a pattern. Because the speaker frequently repeats words or phrases, parallel construction is often difficult to distinguish from repetition. Note the repetition of words in several of the following examples of parallelism.

> The choice was clear. We would stay the course. We shall stay the course. (Lyndon B. Johnson, Speech to the Tennessee State Legislature, March 15, 1967)

> Those who have been left out, we will try to bring in. Those left behind, we will help to catch up. (Richard M. Nixon, First Inaugural Address, January 20, 1969)

> The task is heavy, the toil is long, and the trials will be severe. (Winston S. Churchill, Speech to the House of Commons, February 22, 1944)

> I doubt that anyone would be able to label our age, although it might be called the age of frustrated expectations, the age of protest against almost everything, the age of unlimited possibilities and disappointing results. It is an age that can put men on the moon yet create an impossible traffic tangle in every metropolitan center. It is an age of unbelievable wealth and widespread poverty. It is an age of sensitivity to human dignity and human progress in which there is relatively little of either, despite the available resources. It is finally an age where the hopes, the expectations, and the promises of humanity have been more rhetorical than real. (Rev. Theodore M. Hesburgh, "Higher Education Begins the Seventies," Address to the faculty of the University of Notre Dame, October 5, 1970)

> There are two Americas. One is the America of Lincoln and Adlai Stevenson; the other is the America of Teddy Roosevelt and General MacArthur. One is generous and humane, the other narrowly egotistical; one is modest and self-critical, the other arrogant and self-righteous; one is sensible, the other romantic; one is good-humored, the other solemn; one is inquiring, the other pontificating; one is moderate and restrained, the other filled with passionate intensity. (J. William Fulbright, Brian McMahon Lecture, University of Connecticut, March 22, 1966)

> We have been told of success and seen defeat. We have been told of life and seen death. We have been told of tunnels of light and seen graves of darkness. We have been told of freedom and seen repression. (John V. Lindsay, Address at Harvard, Cambridge, Massachusetts, April 20, 1968)

Let us dare to have solitude: to face the eternal, to find others, to see ourselves. (Paul J. Tillich, Sermon to the Federated Theological Faculty, University of Chicago, January 6, 1957)

5. Use Antithesis

Antithesis is a type of parallel or balanced construction in which the parts contain opposing or contrasting ideas. Following are several examples of antithesis:

Let us never negotiate out of fear. But let us never fear to negotiate. (John F. Kennedy, Inaugural Address, 1961)

We believe it is better to discuss a question even without settling it than to settle a question without discussing it. (Adlai E. Stevenson, *What I Think*, 1954, p. xiii)

The test of our progress is not whether we add more to the abundance of those who have much; it is whether we provide enough for those who have too little. (Franklin D. Roosevelt, Second Inaugural Address, 1937)

Surely this is such a time, a time not of catastrophe but of choice, not of disaster but of decision, a time when the preferment of our aspirations over our fears becomes the duty of citizenship in civilization. (Adlai E. Stevenson, Address to the National Conference of Christians and Jews, November 11, 1957)

It's the duty of a newspaper to comfort the afflicted and afflict the comfortable. (Daniel J. Boorstin, Speech to the Associated Press Managing Editors' Association, Chicago, October 18, 1967)

Now this is not the end. It is not even the beginning of the end. But it is, perhaps, the end of the beginning. (Winston S. Churchill, Speech at Lord Mayor's Day Luncheon, London, November 10, 1942)

We cannot expect to make everyone our friend, but we can try to make no one our enemy. (Richard M. Nixon, First Inaugural Address, January 20, 1969)

Our destiny offers not the cup of despair, but the chalice of opportunity. (Richard M. Nixon, First Inaugural Address, January 20, 1969)

I am convinced that either one takes this job seriously—or one can be seriously taken. (Newton Minow, Address to National Broadcasters Association, May, 1961)

Men with large reputations on paper sometimes turn out to have paper reputations. (William J. McGill, "The Public Challenge and the Campus Response," Speech at the University of California, Berkeley, July 15, 1971)

6. Use Simile and Metaphor

Similes and metaphors are figures of speech that compare two essentially different or dissimilar things. In the simile, the comparison is actually stated through the use of words such as "like" or "as." The metaphor, on the other hand, omits "like" or "as" and merely implies the comparison.

The following are examples of the use of similes to make an idea more vivid:

> The world at our mid-century is, as someone has said, like a drum — strike it anywhere and it resounds everywhere. (Adlai E. Stevenson, Godkin Lectures, Harvard University, March, 1954)

> Our generation of political leaders and the campus leaders of student thought . . . move on different plains; they speak in different tongues. Their paths would never have collided, but passed each other by like ships in the night, except for the war. (Frank Church, "Foreign Policy and the Generation Gap," Thomas C. Hennings, Jr. Memorial Lecture, Washington University, St. Louis, Missouri, December 3, 1970)

> Reputations rise and fall, like stocks on Wall Street. (Arthur Schlesinger, Jr., "Roosevelt's Place in History," Speech at Hunter College, New York, January 30, 1972)

> We move students around like pawns on a chessboard through bits and pieces of academic time and campus space — from two-year college to four-year college, from college to graduate school, from technical center to liberal arts center. (William T. Birenbaum, "A Time for Reconstruction," Speech at Staten Island Community College, New York, September 30, 1969)

> For the most part, southern politicians have had a great deal in common with Lot's wife, preferring to look backward rather than forward. (Samuel R. Spencer, Jr., "A Call for New Missionaries," Commencement Address, Erskine College, Due West, South Carolina, May 23, 1971)

> No we are not satisfied, and we will not be satisfied until justice rolls down like waters and righteousness like a mighty stream. (Martin Luther King, Jr., "I Have a Dream," Address at the Civil Rights March on Washington, August, 1963)

> Unfortunately, people are individuals, and institutions deal in multitudes. There is never time to inspect each person, to grade him like a cut of beef, and stamp him prime, choice, or good. (Harold Howe II, Speech to the College Entrance Examination Board, Chicago, October 21, 1967)

> The overthrow, for a while, of British and United States sea-power in the Pacific was like the breaking of some mighty dam; the long-gathered, pent-up waters rushed down the peaceful valleys, carrying ruin and devastation forward on their foam, and spreading their in-

undations far and wide. (Winston S. Churchill, Broadcast, February 15, 1952)

The following are examples of metaphors used by speakers to add color and interest to their ideas:

If youth tells me that the Church is a religious chainstore, run by the Establishment, doling out packaged worship, packaged doctrine, packaged comfort, then I want to listen before I reply. (Dr. David H. C. Reid, Sermon to Madison Avenue Presbyterian Church, New York, April 9, 1967)

We are using a slingshot for a job that calls for nuclear weapons. We are applying band-aids in the curious expectation of stopping the growth of an advanced cancer. (Whitney Young, Jr., Speech to the Joint Center for Urban Studies of M.I.T. and Harvard University, February 20, 1967)

There are many ways in which we can build bridges toward nations who would cut themselves off from meaningful contact with us. . . . We have to know where it is we want to place this bridge; what sort of traffic we want to travel over it; and on what mutual foundations the whole structure can be designed. There are no one-cliff bridges. If you are going to span a chasm, you have to rest the structure on both cliffs. Now cliffs, generally speaking, are rather hazardous places. Some people are even afraid to look over the edge. But in a thermonuclear world, we cannot afford any political acrophobia. President Johnson has put the matter squarely. By building bridges to those who make themselves our adversaries we can help gradually to create a community of interest, a community of trust, and a community of effort. (Robert S. McNamara, Address to American Society of Newspaper Editors, May 18, 1966)

We are running an outer space civilization on a farm-based Constitution and with a national ideology more appropriate to nineteenth century Europe than to twentieth century America. (W. H. Ferry, Address to Southwest Regional Conference of California Junior Colleges, Santa Barbara, May 1, 1963)

With this faith we will be able to hew out of the mountains of despair a stone of hope. With this faith we will be able to transform the jangling discords of our nation into a beautiful symphony of brotherhood. (Martin Luther King, Jr., Address at the Civil Rights March on Washington, August, 1963)

7. Use Comparison

In addition to using the figurative metaphor and simile, a literal analogy or comparison at times will help the speaker to make his ideas more clear or vivid. Following are examples of the use of comparison:

In this continuing furor over the credibility gap, the reader associates the untrue statement of a public figure with the paper that publishes it. This is like getting mad at the local editor because the weatherman goofed. But it undoubtedly has a lot to do with public disbelief of journalism. (Wes Gallagher, Speech at the University of Kansas, Lawrence, February 10, 1967)

I'd like to go a step further and suggest that it is not inconceivable that our excellent plumber might also have the makings of an admirable philosopher. We have no accurate way of knowing that he would not. If we think he would not (and we probably do), it is most likely because he has no degree in philosophy. Which may be a bit like saying that Socrates wasn't a good teacher because he had no teaching credential — and suggest that we have forgotten that Spinoza earned his living as a lens grinder and that Tom Edison quit school at the age of nine. (Harold Howe II, Speech to the College Entrance Examination Board, Chicago, October 21, 1967)

This reporter has spent the last week trying to fish and think simultaneously and is obliged to report with some reluctance that both the fish and the ideas hauled up from the depths were pretty small, barely inside the legal limit, unsuitable for framing. So, after some contemplation, the contents of both catches were tossed back where they came from in the hope that they would survive and grow to more impressive proportions. (Eric Sevareid, *In One Ear* [New York: Knopf, 1952], p. 152)

8. Use Personification

Another figure of speech the speaker may use to achieve vividness is personification, or the endowment of ideas and objects with human traits, qualities, or attributes. Examples of personification are:

American higher education is currently suffering from an acute case of dyspepsia brought on by our inability to acknowledge our own digestive problems. (Edward D. Eddy, Speech to the American Council on Education, October 7, 1965)

There is a cancer here and the country is ready for surgery. (Robert S. McNamara, Speech to the American Society of Newspaper Editors, May 18, 1966)

The Cherokee nation was never dead; only asleep. Today it stirs and begins to waken. (W. W. Keeler, Inaugural Address of the Chief of the Cherokees, Tahlequah, Oklahoma, September 4, 1971)

Economic injustice has shown its ugly head in millions of American homes where five years ago it was unknown. (Shirley Chisholm, "Economic Injustice in America Today," Speech to the Newark College of Engineering, Newark, New Jersey, April 15, 1972)

It does not take overt censorship to cripple the free flow of ideas. (Frank Stanton, "An Address Before the International Radio and Television Society," New York, November 25, 1969)

If white South Africa is given a breathing space, she will go off to sleep again and not waken till death is knocking on the door. (Alan Paton, Lecture at Yale University, New Haven, Connecticut, *New York Times Magazine*, May 13, 1973, p. 24)

The spirit of dissent stalks our land. (Daniel J. Boorstin, Speech to the Associated Press Managing Editors' Association, Chicago, October 18, 1967)

9. Use Alliteration

Alliteration is a stylistic device in which the initial sounds in words or in stressed syllables within the words are repeated in a pleasing or memorable manner. Some illustrations of alliteration selected from recent speeches by prominent speakers follow:

reality not rhetoric
the professed purpose of protecting the peace
This is a day of dissent and divisiveness.
masculine mystique
in spite of deceit, demagoguery, and verbal violence
headless and hostile men
take a few facts and flail away
deluged daily
secret struggles and agonies
forms and formulae
design of democracy
unnoticed and unused
virtue over vice
as a counter to crumbling colonialism
lower level of life
a doctrine of rule or ruin
trifle with truth
our differences and our diversity
adversaries and allies
inevitable indiscretion
tragedy and travail
hallowed halls
this fell and ferocious war
We have within us a center of stillness surrounded by silence.
This requires patience and persistence.
the provincialism of our own privileges
without peer or precedent
maddening magnitude
political platitudes and promises

a sham and a shuck

mythology of murder

If this is freedom in its finest form, it is also freedom in its final hour.

10. Use Rhetorical Questions

Speakers can also create interest by introducing an idea in the form of a question. Rather than employing a direct statement or a declarative sentence, the speaker phrases his thought as a question which, of course, he does not expect the audience to answer. Some examples of rhetorical questions used by speakers are:

What is to come? Is this the year when women's political power will come of age? Or are we just going to make noise but no real progress? (Bella Abzug, "A New Kind of Southern Strategy," Address to the Southern Women's Conference on Education for Delegate Selection, Nashville, Tennessee, February 12, 1972)

A question poses itself. Why should anyone presume that newness, per se, is to be equated with worthiness? Why is that which is different automatically regarded as an improvement? (John A. Howard, "The Innovation Mirage," Convocation Address, Rockford College, Rockford, Illinois, September 9, 1970)

How have we come to this state of things? How has it come about that the greatest and richest of nations, a nation with a tradition of decency and humanity in its conduct both at home and abroad, a nation with the will and resources to contribute powerfully to peace and development in the world, is now caught up in a spiral of violence in a poor and backward Asian country, with results that are damaging our foreign relations all over the world and poisoning our political life at home? Is it entirely, as the Secretary of State seems to believe, because of the evil and malice of the "other side"? Or is there something wrong on our side as well, some failure of judgment, some weakness of character, some blind spot in our view of the world? (J. William Fulbright, Brian McMahon lecture, University of Connecticut, Storrs, March 22, 1966)

Consider the recent turn toward violence. Where will it lead? Where *can* it lead? (John W. Gardner, Address at the University of North Carolina, Chapel Hill, October 12, 1967)

Have we achieved the best medicine if we "cure" our patient only to find that he wishes we hadn't? (Seymour M. Farber, Speech at Conference on Biomedical Communication: Problems and Resources, New York City, April 4, 1966)

What does that mean? What does it take to be a certified teacher? (Harold Howe II, Speech to College Entrance Examination Board, Chicago, October 21, 1967)

And if either side yields to madness or miscalculation, can any number of arms save us? (George McGovern, Speech to the United States Senate, August 2, 1963)

Is all this conservative? Is all this liberal? Is it all progressive? It is, I say, all of these. (Walter Lippmann, Address to Women's National Press Club, January, 1962)

Who is man? Is he a rational animal? (Robert S. McNamara, Speech to American Society of Newspaper Editors, May 18, 1966)

So the question is this: Are the big corporations who pay the freight for radio and television programs wise to use that time exclusively for the sale of goods and services? Is it in their own interest and that of the stockholders to do so? (Edward R. Murrow, Speech to the Radio and Television News Directors Association, 1958)

11. Use Quotations

Another way in which a speaker may enhance his oral style is by the use of a quotation stating his idea in a particularly apt, graceful, or memorable manner. The quoted statement may be familiar or unfamiliar, folksy or lofty, direct or paraphrased. Unlike the introduction of a quotation by an expert or authority, the speaker's purpose here is not to *prove* a point but rather to illustrate or restate it in a pleasing, vivid, or forceful manner. Some examples of quotations used by recent speakers include the following:

With Job, the time has come for America to implore: "How long will ye vex my soul and break me in pieces with words?" (Frank Church, Thomas C. Hennings, Jr., Memorial Lecture, Washington University, St. Louis, December 3, 1970)

Lincoln was once trying a case in court. Following one of Lincoln's statements, the opposing attorney, with great indignation, snorted that he had never heard of such a thing. Lincoln replied, "Your honor, I cannot permit the distinguished counsel's ignorance, however great it may be, to take precedence over my knowledge, however limited it is." (John A. Howard, "The Innovation Mirage," Convocation Address, Rockford College, Rockford, Illinois, September 9, 1970)

The needs of blacks and whites are too strongly entwined to separate. As Whitney Young used to say, "We may have come here on different ships, but we're in the same boat now." (Vernon E. Jordan, Jr., "Blacks and the Nixon Administration: The Next Four Years," Address to the National Press Club, Washington, D.C., March 16, 1973)

As Thomas Jefferson, one of the moving forces of American independence, observed 150 years ago, "If a nation expects to be ignorant and free, it expects what never was and never will be!" (Robert F. Kennedy, Address to the Free University of Berlin, June 26, 1964)

Let us remember that often what we do may be less important than how we do it. "What one lives for may be uncertain," writes Lord Robert Cecil; "how one lives is not." (Dean Acheson, Address at Amherst College, December 9, 1964)

I remember the bitter lines of a great Anglo-American poet [W. H. Auden] who writes in an "Epitaph for an Unknown Soldier": "To save your world, you asked this man to die. Would this man, could he see you now, ask why?" It is our duty to the past, and it is our duty to the future, so to serve both our nations and the world as to be able to give a reply to that anguished question. (Dag Hammarskjold, Commencement Address, Stanford University, June 19, 1953)

The speaker who wishes to locate a vivid or apt quotation for use in his speech will find that most libraries own several collections of quotations. The best known probably is *Bartlett's Dictionary of Familiar Quotations*. Collections of quotations are also available in inexpensive paperback editions. Most of these works are arranged both by subject and author.

ACHIEVING APPROPRIATENESS

A fifth characteristic of good oral style is that it is appropriate to the speaker, his purpose and message, his listeners, and the occasion.

Not suprisingly, the public expects a speaker to use language that is consistent with his education, status, and profession. Thus, we expect formal language from our statesmen, decorum in word and action from members of the clergy, grammatical correctness and objectivity from university professors, precision and accuracy of word choice from scientists, informality of style from after-dinner speakers, and so on. For the president of the United States to speak in the jargon of hippies, for a clergyman to employ profanity or excessive slang, or for a sports announcer to describe a contest in the sterile language of science would surely distract and disturb most listeners. So a speaker's first responsibility in developing an appropriate oral style is to use the language the public expects of a person of his education and position.

Second, a speaker should use language that is appropriate to his purpose and message. If he wishes to inform, his language should be clear and objective. If he seeks to convince or persuade, he should probably use words that are more emotive, directive, and vivid than he would if only seeking to inform. The speaker whose object is to inspire will find that he needs figurative and colorful words that stimulate the feelings of his auditors and arouse desired respect and admiration. If a speaker, on the other hand, is merely engaging in social conversation or only wants to entertain his listeners, he can use a highly informal style, employing slang, colloquialisms, and even grammatically incorrect expressions freely.

The speaker's language should also be appropriate to the auditors. The speaker should be aware of the educational background, occupation, and special interests of his listeners in order to gauge his auditors' knowledge of his subject and its vocabulary. In talking with poorly educated listeners, the speaker will need to use simpler and less technical language than he would employ in talking to better educated persons. Psychologists, sports fans, housewives, musicians, automobile mechanics, and other groups all have specialized vocabularies of which he should be cognizant. Thus, such terms as *deuce, birdie, baste, carburetor,* and *contrapuntal* will be immediately recognized by those persons who are familiar with the fields in which these terms are used; but for others these words are meaningless. Children, obviously, have to be addressed in simpler language than adults. While the speaker should avoid using language which the hearers will not understand, he should also take care not to give the impression of "talking down" to his audience.

The speaker should also know something about the listeners' attitudes and beliefs. If he is trying to win over antagonistic or skeptical listeners, the speaker must be much more careful in his choice of language than he would be if his hearers already agreed with him. The language the speaker uses in talking to a highly religious individual or group probably will differ from what he might employ before less pious auditors. Whether the listeners are male or female, young or elderly, conservative or liberal, of similar or different background, race, or nationality, all might affect his choice of words.

Regardless of his listeners, the speaker's language should be in good taste. Words that refer to ethnic groups in a contemptuous or disparaging manner should be avoided. Such words not only irritate many members of these groups, but they may also alienate others who will regard such language as bigoted or intolerant. Thus the speaker will refrain from the use of terms such as: *kike, kraut, frog, spic, limey, wop, dago, Chink, Jap, Polack, yid, nigger, coon, spook, jigaboo, redneck, honky, whitey,* and *white trash.* Words disparaging other groups, such as *frat boys, jocks, cops, fuzz, pigs, head shrinkers, pill pushers, ambulance chasers, pencil pushers,* and *holy rollers* may also give offense to some. Since a capable speaker can get his message across without resorting to name-calling, he should also avoid such words as *fink, S.O.B., slob, commie, pinko, queer, pervert, hick, nut, kook, lush, goon, nigger lover, Uncle Tom, hop head, shylock,* and *quack.* In addition, making fun of personal handicaps such as stuttering, palsy, crossed eyes, deafness, blindness, a limp, or a foreign or regional accent will generally be considered in bad taste.

The speaker's oral style should also be adapted to the occasion. The number of listeners or participants, their reason for assembling, and the site of the speech may be important factors in determining the speaker's language. If the auditors have assembled for a special reason, such as a business meeting, to present an award, to honor an outstanding individual, to commemorate an event, or to pay their respects to the deceased, a somewhat formal choice of language is dictated. If, on the other hand, the occasion is purely social, greater informality of language would be permissible. In like manner, one's choice of language would probably differ for a large outdoor political rally from that which one would use in a small gathering in someone's home. The language the speaker uses in a church or synagogue will probably be more decorous and formal than the words he would use in other places.

In choosing the words in which he will clothe his ideas, the speaker should strive to develop an oral style that is appropriate to himself, to his purpose and ideas, to the listeners, and to the occasion.

IMPROVING ONE'S ORAL STYLE

Clear, correct, appropriate, and impressive language usage cannot be achieved overnight. One must develop standards of judgment and taste, a sensitivity to the meanings of words and their nuances, and skill in the selection and use of the right words at the proper time and occasion. The student of speech who is intent on improving his oral style needs to follow a systematic program of study and observation. Some suggestions for developing an awareness and knowledge of language follow:

Acquiring a Library of Language Reference Works. With the availability of inexpensive paperback editions of standard reference works, there is no excuse for a speaker not having a reputable, up-to-date dictionary, a thesaurus, and at least one collection of quotations in his own personal library. In addition, he will wish from time to time to acquire additional works dealing with semantics, style, rhetoric, and speech preparation.

Enlarging One's Vocabulary. Look up the meanings of unfamiliar words in a dictionary; consult a thesaurus to find synonyms and related words; and try to incorporate these words into your vocabulary by using them in writing, speaking, and everyday conversation.

Becoming Language Conscious. Listen critically and analytically to the language used by effective speakers and study the word choice and composition of reputable speakers and writers. Try to note differences in oral style among speakers of different personalities, on different occasions, and in treating different kinds of subjects.

Keeping a Notebook of Effective Language Usage. Record and file for future use words, phrases, quotations, figures of speech, slogans, puns, bits of humor, and other expressions that seem to be unusual, interesting, or particularly effective. In time, this collection should prove helpful in suggesting to the speaker stylistic devices he may wish to incorporate in his conversation and public speaking.

Revising One's Style. Certainly a speaker who plans to give a manuscript or memorized speech should rewrite and revise his speech as often as is necessary to achieve the most felicitous choice of words. However, even in preparing an extemporaneous speech, the speaker may at times find it helpful to write out the speech in its entirety and work on improving his style. Although he probably will not recall the precise language of the written version when he delivers the talk from his notes or outline, he may find that he remembers some of the terminology and phraseology on which he has worked.

Differentiating Between Oral and Written Style. Speak or read aloud your speech manuscripts. Often, the speaker will discover that what reads well on paper does not sound well when spoken aloud. He will then want to rewrite those passages in a more conversational, colloquial vein.

SUMMARY

Oral style refers to the language the speaker selects to express his ideas. Good oral style is clear, correct, concrete, vivid, and appropriate.

Clarity of language is achieved by using words that the listener understands and by defining unfamiliar terms. The speaker has a variety of methods of definition available to him, including definition by synonym; example; details; comparison and contrast; classification and differentiation; historical background; etymology; operation, action, or purpose; negation; and audible and visible examples. The best definitions often combine two or more of these methods.

Correctness of style refers to the use of language that is grammatically acceptable and properly chosen to express accurately the speaker's ideas. The speaker should also aim to use words that are concrete wherever possible because such language is more readily grasped by listeners and is usually more interesting than abstract language. To achieve vividness, the speaker should employ emotive and figurative language to stimulate the imagination and feelings of the hearer. He should avoid clichés and trite, hackneyed expressions. Variation in sentence structure and the use of such stylistic devices as repetition, parallelism, antithesis, simile, metaphor, comparison, contrast, personification, alliteration, and rhetorical questions are all helpful in achieving a vivid oral style. Appropriateness of language is concerned with the suitability of the speaker's words to himself, his purpose, his subject, the listener, and the occasion.

Improvement of one's oral style is a long-range process requiring the speaker to become language conscious through a constant and systematic program of vocabulary and stylistic development.

ADAPTED READING 16.1

CLEAR ONLY IF KNOWN
Edgar Dale

For years I have puzzled over the poor communication of simple directions, especially those given me when traveling by car. I ask such seemingly easy questions as: Where do I turn off Route 30 for the bypass around the business district? How do I get to the planetarium? Is this the way to the university? The individual whom I hail for directions either replies, "I'm a stranger here myself," or gives me in kindly fashion the directions I request. He finishes by saying pleasantly, "You can't miss it."

But about half the time you do miss it. You turn at High Street instead of Ohio Street. It was six blocks, not seven. Many persons tell you to turn right when they mean left. You carefully count the indicated five stoplights before the turn and discover that your guide meant that blinkers should be counted as stoplights. Some of the directions turn out to be inaccurate. Your guide himself didn't know how to get there.

Education is always a problem of getting our bearings, of developing orientation, of discovering in what direction to go and how to get there. An inquiry into the problem of giving and receiving directions may help us discover something important about the educational process itself. Why do people give directions poorly and sometimes follow excellent directions inadequately?

First of all, people who give directions do not always understand the complexity of what they are communicating. They think it a simple matter to get to the Hayden Planetarium because it is simple for them. When someone says, "You can't miss it," he really means, "I can't miss it." He is suffering from what has been called the COIK fallacy — Clear Only If Known. It's easy to get to the place you are inquiring about if you already know how to get there.

We all suffer from the COIK fallacy. For example, during a World Series game a recording was made of a conversation between a rabid baseball fan and an Englishman seeing a baseball game for the first time.

The Englishman asked, "What is a pitcher?"

"He's the man down there pitching the ball to the catcher."

"But," said the Englishman, "all of the players pitch the ball and all of them catch the ball. There aren't just two persons who pitch and catch."

Later the Englishman asked, "How many strikes do you get before you are out?"

The baseball fan said, "Three."

"But," replied the Englishman, "that man struck at the ball five times before he was out."

These directions about baseball, when given to the uninitiated, are clear only if known. They are, in short, COIK.

Try the experiment of handing a person a coat and asking him to explain how to put it on. He must assume that you have lived in the tropics,

From *The News Letter* (School of Education, Ohio State University, Columbus), April 1966.

have never seen a coat worn or put on, and that he is to tell you verbally how to do it. For example, he may say, "Pick it up by the collar." This you cannot do, since you do not know what a *collar* is. He may tell you to put your arm in the sleeve or to button up the coat. But you can't follow these directions because you have no previous experience with either a sleeve or a button. He knows the subject matter but he doesn't know how to teach it. He assumes that because it is clear to him it can easily be made clear to someone else.

The communication of teachers and pupils suffers from this COIK fallacy. An uninitiated person may think that the decimal system is easy to understand. It is — if you already know it. Some idea of the complexity of the decimal system can be gained by listening to an instructor explain the binary system — a system many children now learn in addition to the decimal system. It is not easy to understand with just one verbal explanation. But when you understand it, you wonder why it seemed so hard.

A teacher once presented a group of parents of first-grade children with material from a first-grade reader, which she had written out in shorthand. She then asked them to read it. It was a frustrating experience. But these parents no longer thought it was such a simple matter to learn how to read. Reading, of course, is easy if you already know how to do it.

Sometimes our directions are overcomplex and introduce unnecessary elements. They do not follow the law of parsimony. Any unnecessary element mentioned when giving directions may prove to be a distraction. Think of the directions given for solving problems in arithmetic or for making a piece of furniture or for operating a camera. Have all unrelated and unnecessary items been eliminated? Every unnecessary step or statement is likely to increase the difficulty of reading and understanding the directions. There is no need to elaborate the obvious. Aristotle once said: "Don't go into more detail than the situation requires."

In giving directions it is easy to overestimate the experience of our questioner. It is hard indeed for a Philadelphian to understand that anyone doesn't know where the City Hall is. Certainly if you go down Broad Street, you can't miss it. We know where it is; why doesn't our questioner? Some major highways are poorly marked. In transferring to Route 128 in Massachusetts from Route 1 you must choose between signs marked "North Shore" and "South Shore." In short, you must be from Boston to understand them.

It is easy to overestimate the historical experience of a student. The college instructor may forget that college seniors were babies when Franklin D. Roosevelt died. Children in the ninth grade are not familiar with John L. Lewis, Henry Kaiser, Quisling, Tojo. Events that the instructor has personally experienced have only been read or heard about by the student. The immediate knowledge of the instructor is mediated knowledge to the student.

Another frequent reason for failure in the communication of directions is that explanations are more technical than necessary. Thus a plumber once wrote to a research bureau pointing out that he had used hydrochloric acid to clean out sewer pipes and inquired whether there was any possible harm. The first written reply was as follows: "The efficacy of hydrochloric acid is indisputable, but the corrosive residue is incompatible with metallic permanence."

The plumber thanked them for this information approving his procedure. The dismayed research bureau wrote again, saying, "We cannot assume responsibility for the production of toxic and noxious residue with hydrochloric acid and suggest you use an alternative procedure." Once more the plumber thanked them for their approval. Finally, the bureau, worried about the New York sewers, called in a third scientist, who wrote: "Don't use hydrochloric acid. It eats hell out of the pipes."

We are surprised to discover that many college freshmen do not know such words as *accrue, acquiesce, enigma, epitome, harbinger, hierarchy, lucrative, pernicious, fallacious,* and *coerce.* The average college senior does not know such words as *ingenuous, indigenous, venal, venial, vitiate, adumbrate, interment, vapid, accoutrements, desultory.* These words aren't difficult — if you already know them.

Some words are not understood; others are misunderstood. For example, a woman said that the doctor told her that she had "very close veins." A patient was puzzled as to how she could take two pills three times a day. A parent objected to her boy being called a scurvy elephant. He was called a disturbing element. A little boy ended the Pledge of Allegiance calling for liver, tea, and just fish for all.

Another difficulty in communicating directions lies in the unwillingness of a person to say that he doesn't know. Someone drives up and asks you where Oxford Road is. You realize that Oxford Road is somewhere in the vicinity and feel a sense of guilt about not even knowing the streets in your own town. So you tend to give poor directions instead of admitting that you don't know.

Sometimes we use the wrong medium for communicating our directions. We make them entirely verbal, and the person is thus required to hold them in mind until he has followed out each step in the directions. Think, for example, how hard it is to remember Hanford 6-7249 long enough to dial it after looking it up.

A crudely drawn map will often make our directions clear. Some indication of distance would also help, although many people give wrong estimates of distances in terms of miles. A chart or a graph can often give us at a glance an idea that is communicated verbally only with great difficulty.

But we must not put too much of the blame for inadequate directions on those who give them. Sometimes, the persons who ask for help are also at fault. Communication, we must remember, is a two-way process.

Sometimes an individual doesn't understand directions but thinks he does. Only when he has lost his way does he realize that he wasn't careful enough to make sure that he really did understand. How often we let a speaker or instructor get by with such terms as "cognitive dissonance," "viable economy," "parameter," without asking the questions that might clear them up for us. Even apparently simple terms such as "needs," "individual instruction," or "interests" hide many confusions. Our desire to keep from appearing dumb, to be presumed "in the know," prevents us from understanding what has been said. Sometimes, too, the user of the term may not know what he is talking about.

We are often in too much of a hurry when we ask for directions. Like many tourists, we want to get to our destination quickly so that we can hurry back home. We don't bother to savor the trip or the scenery. So we impatiently rush off before our informant has really had time to catch his breath and make sure that we understand.

Similarly, we hurry through school and college subjects, getting a bird's-eye view of everything and a close-up of nothing. We aim to cover the ground when we should be uncovering it, probing for what is underneath the surface.

It is not easy to give directions for finding one's way around in a world whose values and directions are changing. Ancient landmarks have disappeared. What appears to be a lighthouse on the horizon turns out to be a mirage. But those who do have genuine expertness, those who possess tested, authoritative data, have an obligation to be clear in their explanations and in their presentation of ideas.

We must neither overestimate nor underestimate the knowledge of the inquiring traveler. We must avoid the COIK fallacy and realize that many of our communications are clear only if already known.

ADAPTED READING 16.2

IT'S HARD TO HEAR IN THIS LANGUAGE
Russell Baker

American is a very loud tongue. The last Lord Raglan classified languages into two broad groups, which he called "speaking languages" and "shouting languages." . . . As used in Britain and most of the Commonwealth, he observed, English was a "speaking language," but Americans, he went on, had created a new form of English that was a "shouting language," more akin in temper to the tongue of Naples than to the speech of London.

Two principal characteristics of a "shouting language" are disdain for understatement and a tendency to abandon grammar with the alibi that it impedes self-expression. Thus, a theatrical performance that is hailed in London as "really quite good" may become in Rome, "bellisimo." "Bellisimo" is a delightful word: one wants to shout it out. . . . It is almost impossible, on the other hand, to shout "really quite good." . . .

Disdaining understatement, the "shouting language" encourages an excessive use of superlatives. Thus, in America, the performance that was merely "really quite good" in London becomes simply and noisily, "Great!" In America, in fact, even the performance that was "dreadful" in London may very well become "Great!"

Any evening in Sardi's . . . there will be battalions of entertainers and actors shouting "Great!" at each other. This is the nature of Americans. In England, if an actor you know has given a run-of-the-mill performance, his ego is easily assuaged with, "You were really quite good." In America this

From *The New York Times*, January 23, 1969, p. 26. © 1969 by The New York Times Company. Reprinted by permission.

will be interpreted as a slur, and the actor will probably refuse to speak to you again.

"Tell it like it is" is a typical example of an American's tendency to play havoc with grammar in order to raise the noise level. The correct form—"tell it as it is"—cannot be shouted with any pleasure whatsoever. By maiming grammar, we turn the civilized suggestion into "Tell it like it is!" and have a battle cry. . . .

"Winston tastes good like a cigarette should" is fun to have shouted at you. "Winston tastes good as a cigarette should" on the other hand instantly alerts all the natural suspicions. "Who says so?" "How good should a cigarette taste anyhow?" "I've smoked them all my life and they've always tasted bad." And so on.

Slogans are designed to avert the precise mental responses apt to be provoked by precise statement. . . . The American has always been a voluminous creator of slogans. "Tippecanoe and Tyler too!" "Fifty-four forty or fight!" "Back to normalcy!" "I like Ike!" . . . "Two, four, six, eight, we don't want to integrate!" . . . "Black power!" "Law and order." . . .

Slogans as substitutes for thought are part of the habit of being American. The young radicals who want to overthrow everything on the ground that everything is crazy are just as dependent upon slogans as the old defenders who believe the radicals are crazy. . . . We are afflicted with a language that encourages our mouths to rob our ears.

ADAPTED READING 16.3
FIGURATIVELY SPEAKING
Edgar Dale

Nearly everyone has studied figurative language in a course in English. Unfortunately, the terms *simile, metaphor, metonymy, synecdoche, oxymoron, personification, hyperbole,* and *parables* and *myths* are often seen as quaint words or phrases in a dull textbook.

Language grows through lively metaphors. Figures of speech, especially those in slang, represent innovation and creativity in language development. They can provide the seasoning (a metaphor) for flat, tasteless writing, perk up commonplace expressions. They give a word extra work to do. G. K. Chesterton says, "All slang is metaphor and metaphor is poetry."

Figures of speech are easily understood. For example, this sentence isn't hard to dope out: "You're a dope if you use dope!" Many persons today, however, do not know "dope" as varnish, or as a sauce for ice cream. Metaphors move out of the language as well as in. If you see a *lousy* television show, you are sharing a metaphor which has been in use for over a hundred years. "Hayseed," "blockhead," "champing at the bit" are now dated metaphors. I used the term "snow job" in an Air Force manual written during

From *The News Letter* (School of Education, Ohio State University, Columbus), XXXVI, no. 2, November 1970.

World War II and wondered then whether it would survive. It did. And similes which once were fresh and inviting may turn into clichés through overuse. Some examples are: "easy as pie," "slow as molasses in January," "blind as a bat."

The word *metaphor* comes from *meta* meaning "across" and *phor* meaning "carry." When you metaphorize you carry a meaning across, transfer it, apply it in a fresh new way. Sometimes the comparison is stated using such words as *like, as, than,* and we label it a *simile,* the exact word for *like* in Latin. Sometimes the comparison is implied and we call it a metaphor.

Today we use metaphor as the general term and include under it similes and other figures of speech. Aristotle declared that the use of metaphor indicated an eye for resemblances. Indeed, poetry abounds in metaphor. The poet reflects on an object, such as a chambered nautilus, a daffodil, a lark, a tiger, a lamb, and draws conclusions, all of which involve stated or implied comparisons.

In *Romeo and Juliet* Mercutio describes his sword wound: " 'tis not so deep as a well, nor so wide as a church door." Homer said of Ulysses' manner of speaking: "His words fell soft, like snow upon the ground." Dickens spoke of a man as like a signpost, always pointing the way but never going there. A five-year-old describes a cattail as a hot dog with fur on it.

Mark Twain says in *Pudd'nhead Wilson's Calendar:* "Nothing so needs reforming as other people's habits." We say, "I can read him like a book." Lady Macbeth said to Macbeth: "Your face, my thane, is as a book where man may read strange matters." A little boy stands on the rocks at Pemaquid Point in Maine and watches the waves breaking against the rocky shore. "Look, Daddy," he says, "the water is mad." Here he likens the wild sea to an angry person. Walt Whitman uses a similar metaphor but adds to it when he says: "O madly the sea pushes upon the land, with love, with love."

Sometimes we create similes by simply adding *like* to a word, as lifelike, childlike, statesmanlike, godlike, ladylike, starlike, warlike, springlike, ghostlike. The Greek suffix *ine* also means like, and we use it frequently in metaphorizing animal words: aquiline, anserine (goose-like), asinine, bovine, canine, equine, feline, hircine (goat-like), hominine (man), piscine, porcine, vulpine.

We commonly metaphorize parts of the body, plants, and vegetables, fruits, animals. We make old words do new work. Edna St. Vincent Millay said: "O world, I cannot hold thee close enough!" Here she extends the idea of loving a person by putting one's arms around him, to that of embracing the whole world. *Embrace* is a metaphor deriving from the literal Latin meaning of "in the arm of," as in this sentence which can be read either literally or metaphorically: "Man embraces woman."

The head is a part of the body commonly used in metaphors—perhaps because it is the seat of the brain. The *World Book Dictionary* devotes three pages to the word *head* and its various combinations. Many of these "head" words are denigratory (hence, it is blackening). Such terms include blockhead, dunderhead, bonehead, cabbagehead, clunkhead, dumbhead, fathead, meathead, pinhead, swellhead. Egghead usually refers to an intellectual, often disapprovingly.

Other parts of the body are metaphorized in such terms as toothsome, lippy, loudmouth, jawbreaker (meaning a big word and also a marble-like hard candy), eye of the hurricane, taking it on the chin, bald truth, hair-raising, skull practice, at arm's length, put the finger on, knuckle down, thumb a ride, elbow your way in, footloose.

Animals figure prominently in metaphors: monkey on your back, lion-hearted, weasel out of, foxy, wolf down food, a social butterfly, catty, a bear hug, a whale of a good time, get skunked. Plants and vegetables produce many metaphors: clinging ivy, cauliflower ear, tomato, string bean, lettuce (folding money), corn, in clover, rhubarb. Many fruits are metaphorized: top banana, apple-cheeked, a peach, lemon, pear-shaped, raspberry.

Here are some examples of ways in which first grade children in the inner city of Columbus, Ohio, have metaphorically extended the meaning of certain words, as we discovered in interviews:

breeze   when the trees bow their heads
gray   in winter
honk   a pig
rain   when clouds get together
boat   it swims in the water
crosseyed   like when somebody's eyes are looking at their nose
a lot of   like 2500 bags of popcorn
popped   boing-g-g
tiptoe   you're at ballet school
white   white clouds. I like clean clouds.
barn   a garage for animals
bottle   a genie's in it
grass   it covers the bald spots.

Robert Frost called himself a synecdochist. Synecdoche is a figure of speech in which a part is used for a whole (and sometimes vice versa). Thus television becomes "the tube," a car becomes "wheels," the container names the thing contained. Frost wrote: "Something there is that doesn't love a wall . . ." and "Good fences make good neighbors." One of his best known quotations is: "Two roads diverged in a wood, and I — I took the one less traveled by. And that has made all the difference."

Sometimes we have metaphors which generalize a specific name, hence Don Juan, Solomon, Cassandra, Job, Samson, quixotic, machiavellian, malapropism. Or terms are created which are based on the name of the person closely associated with it — watt, ohm, ampere, fuchsia, pasteurize, poinsettia.

Metonymy is a figure of speech that consists of using the name of one thing for another that it suggests. Literally it means name changing. Thus "the cloth" means a clergyman, "court" means the judge and jury. The "pen" stands for writing, the "tongue" for speaking, the "eye" for seeing, the "ear" for hearing. A "sheepskin" stands for a college degree. Helen of Troy became "the face that launch'd a thousand ships."

A parable is a metaphor which presents a story or event to illustrate a point, thus making it comparable. Well-known Biblical parables include that of the Sower, the Lost Sheep, the Good Samaritan, a Certain Rich Young Man, the Prodigal Son, the Mustard Seed, and many others. Fables, too, are metaphors, giving us terms like sour grapes, crying wolf, dog in the manger, the hare and the tortoise, or killing the goose that laid the golden egg.

Shakespeare favored the oxymoron, another type of figure of speech. Oxymoron comes from two Greek words — *oxys* (sharp) plus *moros* (foolish). An oxymoron is a seeming self-contradiction, as "Parting is such *sweet sorrow*." Some other examples are priceless unessentials, gilt-edged insecurity, masterly inactivity, prudent failure, sophisticated irresponsibility, dynamic bore, silent applause, studied imprecision, fatiguing leisure, broadly ignorant, laborious indolence, precise misinformation, successful failure, trained incapacity, a hotbed of apathy, gentle strength. A famous current oxymoron is "benign neglect," originated by Daniel Moynihan, the presidential adviser.

The Greek myths have supplied us with many metaphors in which an action is characterized by using the name of the person originally performing the action, hence Herculean labors, Promethean daring. The Oedipus complex is named after the Greek king who unknowingly killed his father and married his mother. A long series of wanderings is called an odyssey, after Odysseus; endless labors are described as Sisyphean, after Sisyphus, who rolled a heavy stone up a hill in Hell only to have it roll down again when it neared the top. Procrustes tailored the length of victims to make them fit his bed, hence the term Procrustean to describe the way in which a learner is made to fit a curriculum.

Language is central in our lives. Unfortunately, in schools we keep asking: Is my language correct? when we should ask: Is my language effective, alive? We must look to our metaphors, study the images to which we give allegiance and devotion, realize the power of language. Ludwig Wittgenstein, the linguistic philosopher, declares: "Language is not only the vehicle of thought; it is also the driver."

ADAPTED READING 16.4

SAYING IT IN ENGLISH
Muriel Beadle

In the following passage, the wife of Nobel Laureate George W. Beadle relates how she came to write a book on genetics. Her explanation effectively stresses the importance and problems of communicating scientific information to the layman.

In 1953, I married a scientist. . . . George is a geneticist. Within the field of science, there has recently been an explosion of knowledge comparable in significance to Mendel's discoveries about inheritance in the nineteenth century. What has been learned is of great import to the whole of society. But all you have to do to scare my generation out of its wits is to say "deoxyribonucleic acid." . . . We leave it to the experts and hope for the best.

Unfortunately, the experts can't (or at least *shouldn't*) make decisions for all of us on the control of radioactive fallout or the right of people with inherited diseases to reproduce as freely as people without such diseases. Whether one race has an inherited superiority to another race is no longer a purely academic question, either.

In our kind of society, the formation of intelligent opinion about such matters isn't going to occur until ordinary citizens understand the new genetics much better than they do now. Which is why my husband so often used to make speeches on the subject to any group of nonscientists who were curious enough and concerned enough to try to understand it.

He developed great skill in the art of keeping people awake long enough to learn something of what's been happening in biology since they dissected a frog back in '48. For example, our Siamese cats often shared the platform with him. (Their pigmentation illustrates an important point about genetic control of body chemistry). . . . And he made much use of analogies drawn from everyday life.

It was one of these analogies, in fact, that got me into my recent difficulties.

As George told it, there was once a housewife who made such a good angel food cake that many people asked for her recipe. On one occasion when she wrote it out, however, she listed thirteen egg whites instead of the twelve egg whites she should have specified. The cook who followed that copy of the recipe got a cake so light and delicate that *her* recipe for angel food cake became the one that all the members of the Ladies' Guild requested. The twelve-egg cake thus became extinct and the thirteen-egg cake survived. The original cook's mistake when copying the recipe, George pointed out, was a mutation; and the subsequent replacement of the twelve-egg cake by the thirteen-egg cake was a perfect example of evolution by natural selection. . . .

On the evening that George first used the angel food cake analogy, I was full of praise. Riding home afterwards, I said, "That cake idea was

From *Saturday Review*, April 3, 1965, pp. 53–54.

great. . . . Say! I'll bet there would be a market for your lectures in written form. . . . Why don't you write one?"

Telling someone in academic life that he ought to write a book is like telling a pretty girl that she ought to be in the movies. They can't resist the idea. But in this case, I oversold it. George decided that I ought to do the writing!

ADDITIONAL READINGS

Anderson, Martin, Wesley Lewis and James Murray, *The Speaker and His Audience* (New York: Harper & Row, 1964), chap. 12, "Style in Speaking."

Baird, A. Craig and Franklin Knower, *Essentials of General Speech* (New York: McGraw-Hill, 1968), chap. 9, "Language."

Blankenship, Jane, "A Linguistic Analysis of Oral and Written Style," *Quarterly Journal of Speech*, 48 (December 1962), 419–422.

Dickens, Milton, *Speech: Dynamic Communication* (New York: Harcourt Brace Jovanovich, 1963), chap. 11, "Verbal Communication."

Mahaffey, Joseph H., "The Oral Mode," *Speech Teacher*, 15 (September 1956), 194–197.

Nilsen, Thomas, "The Use of Language," in Horace Rahskopf, *Basic Speech Improvement* (New York: Harper & Row, 1965), 318–336.

Ross, Raymond, *Speech Communication* (Englewood Cliffs, N.J.: Prentice-Hall, 1970), chap. 3, "Language: Meaning and Use."

Sebeok, Thomas, *Style in Language* (Cambridge: MIT Press, 1960).

Thomas, Gordon, "Oral Style and Intelligibility," *Speech Monographs*, 23 (March 1956), 46–54.

STUDY QUESTIONS

1. What kinds of language make it difficult for listeners to understand a speaker's ideas?
2. What are some of the problems that are encountered in defining with synonyms?
3. Explain definition by classification and differentiation.
4. How does definition by historical background differ from definition by etymology?
5. What is definition by negation? When is this method useful?
6. Cite three or four words where visual or audible definitions would be almost essential to the listeners' understanding.
7. Which method of definition do the authors recommend?
8. Why is correct language usage desirable in a speech?
9. Why should speakers strive whenever possible to use concrete rather than abstract language?
10. What is meant by triteness? What are clichés?
11. What six steps should a speaker follow to improve his oral style?

EXERCISES

1. Explain the meaning of a definition by details. List five words other than those discussed in the text that would lend themselves to effective definition by details.
2. Define and give an example (other than one in the text) of each of the following: (a) parallelism, (b) repetition, (c) antithesis, (d) simile, (e) metaphor, (f) personification, (g) alliteration, and (h) rhetorical question.
3. In 100 words or less, write your own definition of one of the following: (a) a well-rounded education, (b) a successful person, (c) the average man. Be as concrete as possible in your definition.
4. Prepare a three- to four-minute informative speech in which you define one of the terms listed below. Use at least two of the methods of definition discussed in this chapter:

1. aristocracy
2. justice
3. gauche
4. jazz
5. intuition
6. heresy
7. loyalty
8. impressionism
9. integrity
10. serendipity
11. cubism
12. ethnocentrism
13. gross national product
14. existentialism
15. agnosticism
16. rationalization
17. empathy
18. romanticism
19. humane
20. bel canto
21. socialism
22. automation
23. nationalism
24. intelligence

After you have delivered the speech, your instructor may call on some member of the class to explain what your concept means in order to test the effectiveness of your definition.

5. Locate five quotations you might use to achieve a more vivid style in discussing one of the following concepts:
   a. trust
   b. ignorance
   c. China
   d. gardens
   e. puzzles

6. Consult a thesaurus and list six synonyms for each of the following words:
   a. ostentation
   b. fluidity
   c. sedate
   d. perforator
   e. consanguinity

7. For your next speech, write out the speech in its entirety. Then revise the entire speech, seeking to improve your oral style. At the time of delivery, submit both your original and final drafts to your instructor.

INDEX